Words THAT MADE
AMERICAN HISTORY
❧ SINCE THE CIVIL WAR ☙

Selected Readings Edited by

RICHARD N. CURRENT   *The University of Wisconsin*

JOHN A. GARRATY   *Columbia University*

SECOND EDITION

Little, Brown and Company
BOSTON   TORONTO

FOURTH PRINTING

Published simultaneously in Canada
by Little, Brown & Company (Canada) Limited

PRINTED IN THE UNITED STATES OF AMERICA

Acknowledgments

Permission to quote from the following copyrighted works is gratefully acknowledged:

Upton Sinclair, from *The Jungle*. Reprinted by permission of the author. (*The Jungle* is published by Harper & Brothers in a hardbound edition, by Signet Books as a paperback.)

Herbert Croly, from *The Promise of American Life*. Copyright 1909 by The Macmillan Company and used with their permission.

Woodrow Wilson, from *The New Freedom*. Reprinted by permission of Edith Bolling Wilson.

Louis D. Brandeis, "The Money Trust." Reprinted by permission of the daughters of Louis D. Brandeis.

John Maynard Keynes, from *The Economic Consequences of The Peace*. Copyright 1920 by Harcourt, Brace & World, Inc.; renewed 1948 by Lydia Lopokova Keynes, and reprinted by permission of the publishers.

Bruce Barton, from *The Man Nobody Knows*. Copyright 1925 by The Bobbs-Merrill Company, Inc., R. 1952 by Bruce Barton; reprinted by permission of the publishers, The Bobbs-Merrill Company, Inc.

Herbert Hoover, from *American Individualism*. Reprinted with Mr. Hoover's permission.

H. L. Mencken, from *Notes on Democracy*. Reprinted by permission of Alfred A. Knopf, Inc. Copyright 1926 by Alfred A. Knopf, Inc.

John Steinbeck, from *The Grapes of Wrath*. Copyright 1939 by John Steinbeck. Reprinted by permission of The Viking Press, Inc.

Henry L. Stimson, from *Foreign Affairs* (October 1932). Copyright by the Council on Foreign Relations, Inc., New York, and reprinted with their permission.

Wendell Willkie, from *One World*. Reprinted by permission of Simon and Schuster, Inc. Copyright 1943 by Wendell L. Willkie.

Martin Luther King, from *Stride Toward Freedom*. Copyright 1958 by Harper & Brothers. Used by permission.

George F. Kennan, from *Foreign Affairs* (July 1947). Copyright by the Council on Foreign Relations, Inc., New York, and reprinted with their permission.

PREFACE

Our title, *Words That Made American History,* is not intended to suggest that American history has been made by words alone. We believe, however, that various speeches, pamphlets, books, and other writings have been quite literally epoch-making. Some have aroused people to immediate action. Some have rationalized and justified events after their occurrence. Others have exerted a lasting effect upon the thinking of the majority or of certain minorities. Still others, though not necessarily impelling people to thought or action, have reflected and recorded important aspects of the American character. Words that made American history in one or another of those senses form the substance of the present volume.

To include all such writings would require enough books to fill a good-sized library. Even to include only the most significant would take much more space than is available here. In preparing a book of readings of a size appropriate for college history courses, we have had to choose between two selection procedures. One was to be as inclusive as possible, to gather excerpts from a great many documents and then pare the excerpts down to fit within our space limits. The other possibility was to be more selective, to choose a relatively small number of items and present the whole, or at least an extensive part, of each one. We have adopted the second of these procedures. We think more is to be gained from a selection of well-rounded pieces than from a profusion of snippets, and we trust that most teachers and students will agree with us.

Our aim, then, is to present in fairly full detail a broadly representative collection of writings that have revealed or have influenced the thinking of Americans on important issues. We believe that supplementary readings of this kind, which stirred the minds and hearts of Americans in the past, will stir the interest of readers today and help bring history to life. Thus they will serve as a valuable supplement to the regular textbook.

In an introduction to each of the selections we have tried to supply essential information about the author and to place his work in its historical context, but we have deliberately avoided predigesting the author's words. We have tried not to give his message away in advance, and we have left the analysis and criticism of each item largely to the reader himself. We believe that this is pedagogically desirable. Among other possible exercises for the student, we suggest the making of *précis* that will capture the essence of the selection, and the providing of footnotes that will clarify obscure passages, identify allusions, criticize or evaluate positions, and the like.

R. N. C.

J. A. G.

CONTENTS

IV. INDUSTRIALISM AND OPPORTUNITY

V. PROGRESSIVE PROTEST

IX. CONTEMPORARY PROBLEMS, DOMESTIC AND FOREIGN

I. The Civil War and Reconstruction

Abraham Lincoln

THE PEOPLE'S CONTEST

1861, 1863, 1865   ABRAHAM LINCOLN (1809-1865) used to be pictured, at times, as an appealing but quaint and rather pathetic figure who for the most part merely presided, at a distance, over the stirring and fateful events of his presidency. Only in recent years has historical scholarship made it possible to do full justice to him as an actual leader. It is now clear that he was the dominant and decisive American of his day. To summarize, he used rare political skill not only to gain and hold office but also to unite the North and thus reunite the nation. A statesman as well as a politician, he led the way cautiously but surely toward the emancipation of the slaves as well as the preservation of the Union. As commander in chief of the Army and the Navy, he took responsibility for making and seeing to the execution of the strategic plans that at last brought victory. And he gave point and meaning to all the bloodshed by symbolizing and putting into deathless words the ideals which, alone, were worth fighting for.

It would take more space than is available here to present adequately the words of his that have helped Americans make up their minds. The following selections provide a sampling of his more significant statements on the causes and the meaning of the Civil War.

MESSAGE TO CONGRESS

(July 4, 1861)

HAVING been convened on an extraordinary occasion, as authorized by the Constitution, your attention is not called to any ordinary subject of legislation.

At the beginning of the present Presidential term, four months ago, the functions of the Federal Government were found to be generally suspended within the several States of South Carolina, Georgia, Alabama, Mississippi, Louisiana, and Florida, excepting only those of the Post Office Department.

Within these States, all the Forts, Arsenals, Dock-yards, Customhouses, and the like, including the movable and stationary property in, and about them, had been seized, and were held in open hostility to this Government, excepting only Forts Pickens, Taylor, and Jefferson, on, and near the Florida coast, and Fort Sumter, in Charleston harbor, South Carolina. The Forts thus seized had been put in improved condition; new ones had been

3

built and armed forces had been organized, and were organizing, all avowedly with the same hostile purpose.

The forts remaining in the possession of the Federal government, in, and near, these States, were either besieged or menaced by warlike preparations; and especially Fort Sumter was nearly surrounded by well-protected hostile batteries, with guns equal in quality to the best of its own, and outnumbering the latter as perhaps ten to one. A disproportionate share, of the Federal muskets and rifles, had somehow found their way into these States, and had been seized, to be used against the government. Accumulations of the public revenue, lying within them, had been seized for the same object. The Navy was scattered in distant seas; leaving but a very small part of it within the immediate reach of the government. Officers of the Federal Army and Navy, had resigned in great numbers; and, of those resigning, a large proportion had taken up arms against the government. Simultaneously, and in connection, with all this, the purpose to sever the Federal Union, was openly avowed. In accordance with this purpose, an ordinance had been adopted in each of these States, declaring the States, respectively, to be separated from the National Union. A formula for instituting a combined government of these states had been promulgated; and this illegal organization, in the character of confederate States was already invoking recognition, aid, and intervention, from Foreign Powers.

Finding this condition of things, and believing it to be an imperative duty upon the incoming Executive, to prevent, if possible, the consummation of such attempt to destroy the Federal Union, a choice of means to that end became indispensable. This choice was made; and was declared in the Inaugural address. The policy chosen looked to the exhaustion of all peaceful measures, before a resort to any stronger ones. It sought only to hold the public places and property, not already wrested from the Government, and to collect the revenue; relying for the rest, on time, discussion, and the ballot-box. It promised a continuance of the mails at government expense, to the very people who were resisting the government; and it gave repeated pledges against any disturbance to any of the people, or any of their rights. Of all that which a president might constitutionally, and justifiably, do in such a case, everything was foreborne, without which, it was believed possible to keep the government on foot.

On the 5th of March, (the present incumbent's first full day in office) a letter of Major Anderson, commanding at Fort Sumter, written on the 28th of February, and received at the War Department on the 4th of March, was, by that Department, placed in his hands. This letter expressed the professional opinion of the writer, that re-inforcements could not be thrown into that Fort within the time for his relief, rendered necessary by the limited supply of provisions, and with a view of holding possession of the same, with a force of less than twenty thousand good, and well-disciplined men. This opinion was concurred in by all the officers of his command; and their *memoranda* on the subject, were made enclosures of Major Anderson's letter. The whole was immediately laid before Lieutenant General Scott, who at once concurred with Major Anderson in opinion. On reflection, however, he took full time consulting with other officers, both of the Army and the Navy; and, at the end of four days, came reluctantly, but decidedly, to the same conclusion as before. He also stated at the same time that no such sufficient force was then at the control of the Government, or could be raised, and brought to the ground, within the time when the provisions in the Fort would be exhausted. In a purely military point of view, this reduced the duty of the administration, in the case, to the mere matter of getting the garrison safely out of the Fort.

It was believed, however, that to so abandon that position, under the circumstances, would be utterly ruinous; that the *necessity* under which it was to be done, would not be fully understood — that, by many, it would be construed as a part of a *voluntary* policy — that, at home, it would discourage the friends of the Union, embolden its adversaries, and go far to insure to the latter, a recognition abroad — that, in fact, it would be our national destruction consummated. This could not be allowed. Starvation was not yet upon the garrison; and ere it would be reached, *Fort Pickens* might be re-inforced. This last, would be a clear indication of *policy,* and would better enable the country to accept the evacuation of Fort Sumter, as a military *necessity.* An order was at once directed to be sent for that landing of the troops from the Steamship Brooklyn, into Fort Pickens. This order could not go by land, but must take the longer, and slower route by sea. The first return news from the order was received just one week before the fall of Fort Sumter. The news itself was, that the officer commanding the Sabine, to which vessel the troops had been transferred from the Brooklyn, acting upon some *quasi* armistice of the late administration, (and of the existence of which, the present administration, up to the time the order was despatched, had only too vague and uncertain rumors, to fix attention) had refused to land the troops. To now re-inforce Fort Pickens, before a crisis would be reached at Fort Sumter was impossible — rendered so by the near exhaustion of provisions in the latter-named Fort. In precaution against such a conjuncture, the government had, a few days before, commenced preparing an expedition, as well adapted as might be, to relieve Fort Sumter, which expedition was intended to be ultimately used, or not, according to circumstances. The strongest anticipated case, for using it, was now presented; and it was resolved to send it forward. As had been intended, in this contingency, it was also resolved to notify the Governor of South Carolina, that he might expect an attempt would be made to provision the Fort; and that, if the attempt should not be resisted, there would be no effort to throw in men, arms, or ammunition, without further notice, or in case of an attack upon the Fort. This notice was accordingly given; whereupon the Fort was attacked, and bombarded to its fall, without even awaiting the arrival of the provisioning expedition.

It is thus seen that the assault upon, and reduction of, Fort Sumter, was, in no sense, a matter of self defence on the part of the assailants. They well knew that the garrison in the Fort could, by no possibility, commit aggression upon them. They knew — they were expressly notified — that the giving of bread to the few brave and hungry men of the garrison, was all which would on that occasion be attempted, unless themselves, by resisting so much, should provoke more. They knew that this Government desired to keep the garrison in the Fort, not to assail them, but merely to maintain visible possession, and thus to preserve the Union from actual, and immediate dissolution — trusting, as hereinbefore stated, to time, discussion, and the ballot-box, for final adjustment; and they assailed, and reduced the Fort, for precisely the reverse object — to drive out the visible authority of the Federal Union, and thus force it to immediate dissolution.

That this was their object, the Executive well understood; and having said to them in the inaugural address, "You can have no conflict without being yourselves the aggressors," he took pains, not only to keep this declaration good, but also to keep the case so free from the power of ingenious sophistry, as that the world should not be able to misunderstand it. By the affair at Fort Sumter, with its surrounding circumstances, that point was reached. Then, and thereby, the assailants of the Government, began the conflict of arms, without a gun in sight, or in expectancy, to return their fire, save only the few in the Fort, sent to that harbor, years before, for their own protection, and still ready to give that protecion, in whatever was lawful. In this act, discarding all else, they have forced upon the country, the distinct issue: "Immediate dissolution, or blood."

And this issue embraces more than the fate of these United States. It presents to the whole family of man, the question, whether a constitutional republic, or a democracy — a government of the people, by the same people — can, or cannot, maintain its territorial integrity, against its own domestic foes. It presents the question, whether discontented individuals, too few in numbers to control administration, according to organic law, in any case, can always, upon the pretences made in this case, or on any other pretences, or arbitrarily, without any pretence, break up their Government, and thus practically put an end to free government upon the earth. It forces us to ask: "Is there, in all republics, this inherent, and fatal weakness?" "Must a government, of necessity, be too *strong* for the liberties of its people, or too *weak* to maintain its own existence?"

So viewing the issue, no choice was left but to call out the war power of the Government; and so to resist force, employed for its destruction, by force, for its preservation. . . .

It might seem, at first thought, to be of little difference whether the present movement at the South be called "secession" or "rebellion." The movers, however, well understand the difference. At the beginning, they knew they could never raise their treason to any respectable magnitude, by any name which implies *violation* of law. They knew their people possessed as much of moral sense, as much of devotion to law and order, and as much pride in, and reverence for, the history, and government, of their common country, as any other civilized, and patriotic people. They knew they could make no advancement directly in the teeth of these strong and noble sentiments. Accordingly they commenced by an insidious debauching of the public mind. They invented an ingenious sophism, which, if conceded, was followed by perfectly logical steps, through all the incidents, to the complete destruction of the Union. The sophism itself is, that any state of the Union may, *consistently* with the national Constitution, and therefore *lawfully,* and *peacefully,* withdraw from the Union, without the consent of the Union, or of any other state. The little disguise that the supposed right is to be exercised only for just cause, themselves to be the sole judge of its justice, is too thin to merit any notice.

With rebellion thus sugar-coated, they have been drugging the public mind of their section for more than thirty years; and, until at length, they have brought many good men to a willingness to take up arms against the government the day *after* some assemblage of men have enacted the farcical pretence of taking their State out of the Union, who could have been brought to no such thing the day *before*.

This sophism derives much — perhaps the whole — of its currency, from the assumption, that there is some omnipotent, and sacred supremacy, pertaining to a *State* — to each State of our Federal Union. Our States have neither more, nor less power, than that reserved to them, in the Union, by the Constitution — no one of them ever having been a State out of the Union. The original ones passed into the Union even before they cast off their British colonial dependence; and the new ones each came into the Union directly from a condition of dependence, excepting Texas. And even Texas, in its temporary independence, was never designated a State. The new ones only took the designation of States, on coming into the Union, while that name was first adopted for the old ones, in, and by, the

Declaration of Independence. Therein the "United Colonies" were declared to be "Free and Independent States"; but, even then, the object plainly was not to declare their independence of *one another,* or of the *Union;* but directly the contrary, as their mutual pledge, and their mutual action, before, at the time, and afterwards, abundantly show. The express plighting of faith, by each and all of the original thirteen, in the Articles of Confederation, two years later, that the Union shall be perpetual, is most conclusive. Having never been States, either in substance, or in name, *outside* of the Union, whence this magical omnipotence of "State rights," asserting a claim of power to lawfully destroy the Union itself? Much is said about the "sovereignty" of the states; but the word, even, is not in the national Constitution; nor, as is believed, in any of the State constitutions. What is a "sovereignty," in the political sense of the term? Would it be far wrong to define it "A political community, without a political superior"? Tested by this, no one of our States, except Texas, ever was a sovereignty. And even Texas gave up the character on coming into the Union; by which act, she acknowledged the Constitution of the United States, and the laws and treaties of the United States made in pursuance of the Constitution, to be, for her, the supreme law of the land. The States have their *status* IN the Union, and they have no other *legal status.* If they break from this, they can only do so against law, and by revolution. The Union, and not themselves separately, procured their independence, and their liberty. By conquest, or purchase, the Union gave each of them, whatever of independence, and liberty, it has. The Union is older than any of the States; and, in fact, it created them as States. Originally, some dependent colonies made the Union; and, in turn, the Union threw off their old dependence, for them, and made them States, such as they are. Not one of them ever had a State constitution, independent of the Union. Of course, it is not forgotten that all the new States framed their constitutions, before they entered the Union; nevertheless, dependent upon, and preparatory to, coming into the Union.

Unquestionably the States have the powers, and rights, reserved to them in, and by the National Constitution; but among these, surely, are not included all conceivable powers, however mischievous, or destructive; but, at most, such only, as were known in the world, at the time, as governmental powers; and certainly, a power to destroy the government itself, had never been known as a governmental — as a merely administrative power. This relative matter of National power, and State rights, as a principle, is no other than the principle of *generality,* and *locality.* Whatever concerns the whole, should be confided to the whole — to the general government; while, whatever concerns *only* the State, should be left exclusively, to the

State. This is all there is of original principle about it. Whether the National Constitution, in defining boundaries between the two, has applied the principle with exact accuracy, is not to be questioned. We are all bound by that defining without question.

What is now combatted, is the position that secession is *consistent* with the Constitution — is *lawful,* and *peaceful.* It is not contended that there is any express law for it; and nothing should ever be implied as law, which leads to unjust, or absurd consequences. The nation purchased, with money, the countries out of which several of these States were formed. Is it just that they shall go off without leave, and without refunding? The nation paid very large sums (in the aggregate, I believe, nearly a hundred millions) to relieve Florida of the aboriginal tribes. Is it just that she shall now be off without consent, or without making any return? The nation is now in debt for money applied to the benefit of these so-called seceding States, in common with the rest. Is it just, either that creditors shall go unpaid, or the remaining States pay the whole? A part of the present national debt was contracted to pay the old debts of Texas. Is it just that she shall leave, and pay no part of this herself?

Again, if one State may secede, so may another; and when all shall have seceded, none is left to pay the debts. Is this quite just to creditors? Did we notify them on this sage view of ours, when we borrowed their money? If we now recognize this doctrine, by allowing the seceders to go in peace, it is difficult to see what we can do, if others choose to go, or to extort terms upon which they will promise to remain.

The seceders insist that our Constitution admits of secession. They have assumed to make a National Constitution of their own, in which, of necessity, they have either *discarded,* or *retained,* the right of secession, as they insist, it exists in ours. If they have discarded it, they thereby admit that, on principle, it ought not to be in ours. If they have retained it, by their own construction of ours they show that to be consistent they must secede from one another, whenever they shall find it the easiest way of settling their debts, or effecting any other selfish, or unjust object. The principle itself is one of disintegration, and upon which no government can possibly endure.

If all the States, save one, should assert the power to *drive* that one out of the Union, it is presumed the whole class of seceder politicians would at once deny the power, and denounce the act as the greatest outrage upon State rights. But suppose that precisely the same act, instead of being called "driving the one out," should be called "the seceding of the others from that one," it would be exactly what the seceders claim to do; unless, indeed, they make the point, that the one, because it is a minority, may rightfully do, what the others, because they are a majority, may not rightfully do. These politicians are subtle, and profound, on the rights of minorities. They are not partial to that power which made the Constitution, and speaks from the preamble, calling itself "We, the People." . . .

This is essentially a People's contest. On the side of the Union, it is a struggle for maintaining in the world, that form, and substance of government, whose leading object is, to elevate the condition of men — to lift artificial weights from all shoulders — to clear the paths of laudable pursuit for all — to afford all, an unfettered start, and a fair chance, in the race of life. Yielding to partial, and temporary departures, from necessity, this is the leading object of the government for whose existence we contend. . . .

GETTYSBURG ADDRESS

(November 20, 1863)

Four score and seven years ago our fathers brought forth on this continent, a new nation, conceived in Liberty, and dedicated to the proposition that all men are created equal.

Now we are engaged in a great civil war, testing whether that nation, or any nation so conceived and so dedicated, can long endure. We are met on a great battle-field of that war. We have come here to dedicate a portion of that field, as a final resting place for those who here gave their lives that that nation might live. It is altogether fitting and proper that we should do this.

But, in a larger sense, we can not dedicate — we can not consecrate — we can not hallow — this ground. The brave men, living and dead, who struggled here, have consecrated it, far above our poor power to add or detract. The world will little note, nor long remember what we say here, but it can never forget what they did here. It is for us the living, rather, to be dedicated here to the unfinished work which they who fought here have thus far so nobly advanced. It is rather for us to be here dedicated to the great task remaining before us — that from these honored dead we take increased devotion to that cause for which they gave the last full measure of devotion — that we here highly resolve that these dead shall not have died in vain — that this nation, under God, shall have a new birth of freedom — and that government of the people, by the people, for the people, shall not perish from the earth.

SECOND INAUGURAL ADDRESS

(March 4, 1865)

AT THIS second appearing to take the oath of the presidential office, there is less occasion for an extended address than there was at the first. Then a statement, somewhat in detail, of a course to be pursued, seemed fitting and proper. Now, at the expiration of four years, during which public declarations have been constantly called forth on every point and phase of the great contest which still absorbs the attention, and engrosses the energies [*sic*] of the nation, little that is new could be presented. The progress of our arms, upon which all else chiefly depends, is as well known to the public as to myself; and it is, I trust, reasonably satisfactory and encouraging to all. With high hope for the future, no prediction in regard to it is ventured.

On the occasion corresponding to this four years ago, all thoughts were anxiously directed to an impending civil-war. All dreaded it — all sought to avert it. While the inaugural address was being delivered from this place, devoted altogether to *saving* the Union without war, insurgent agents were in the city seeking to *destroy* it without war — seeking to dissol[v]e the Union, and divide effects, by negotiation. Both parties deprecated war; but one of them would *make* war rather than let the nation survive; and the other would *accept* war rather than let it perish. And the war came.

One eighth of the whole population were colored slaves, not distributed generally over the Union, but localized in the Southern part of it. These slaves constituted a peculiar and powerful interest. All knew that this interest was, somehow, the cause of the war. To strengthen, perpetuate, and extend this interest was the object for which the insurgents would rend the Union, even by war; while the government claimed no right to do more than to restrict the territorial enlargement of it. Neither party expected for the war, the magnitude, or the duration, which it has already attained. Neither anticipated that the *cause* of the conflict might cease with, or even before, the conflict itself should cease. Each looked for an easier triumph, and a result less fundamental and astounding. Both read the same Bible, and pray to the same God; and each invokes His aid against the other. It may seem strange that any men should dare to ask a just God's assistance in wringing their bread from the sweat of other men's faces; but let us judge not that we be not judged. The prayers of both could not be answered; that of neither has been answered fully. The Almighty has His own purposes. "Woe unto the world because of offences! for it must needs be that offences come; but woe to that man by whom the offence cometh!" If we shall suppose that American Slavery is one of those offences which, in the providence of God, must needs come, but which, having continued through His appointed time, He now wills to remove, and that He gives to both North and South, this terrible war, as the woe due to those by whom the offence came, shall we discern therein any departure from those divine attributes which the believers in a Living God always ascribe to Him? Fondly do we hope—fervently do we pray—that this mighty scourge of war may speedily pass away. Yet, if God wills that it continue, until all the wealth piled by the bond-man's two hundred and fifty years of unrequited toil shall be sunk, and until every drop of blood drawn with the lash, shall be paid by another drawn with the sword, as was said three thousand years ago, so still it must be said "the judgments of the Lord, are true and righteous altogether."

With malice toward none; with charity for all; with firmness in the right, as God gives us to see the right, let us strive on to finish the work we are in; to bind up the nation's wounds; to care for him who shall have borne the battle, and for his widow, and his orphan—to do all which may achieve and cherish a just, and a lasting peace, among ourselves, and with all nations.

Alexander H. Stephens

THE WAR BETWEEN THE STATES

◈*1868, 1870*◈ As ABRAHAM LINCOLN (1809-1865) expressed the predominant Northern view before and during the Civil War, so Alexander H. Stephens (1812-1883), after the war was over, gave voice to the interpretation that came to prevail in the South. As a Whig from Georgia, Stephens once had been a congressional colleague and a close friend of Lincoln's. In 1860-1861 he at first opposed, then went along with, the secession of his state. Accepting office as Vice President of the Confederacy, he declared that the new government was built upon the "cornerstone" of slavery. During the war he disagreed with Jefferson Davis (1808-1889) when Davis took steps to increase the powers of the Confederate government as against the rights of the separate states. Stephens made himself the center of resistance to the Davis policies.

In 1865 he was imprisoned for several months in Fort Warren, in Boston harbor. In 1866 he was elected to the United States Senate but was excluded by the Republican majority, as were other senators and congressmen elected by the former Confederate states. In 1867, while Radical Reconstruction was getting under way, he began to write a work justifying the course of the South to secession and through the war. Like many Southerners, he now was much more wholeheartedly pro-Confederate than he ever had been.

The first volume of his work, significantly entitled *A Constitutional View of the Late War between the States,* was published in 1868, and the second volume in 1870. These volumes sold well and were read widely, especially in the South. Rationalizing the Lost Cause, Stephens played down the slavery question and played up the issue of state rights. He thus reflected and also helped to mold the opinions of his fellow Southerners. The conflict of 1861-1865, he argued, had been no "Civil War" but a "War between the States." Southerners adopted this designation and insisted upon it, though they had seldom if ever used it before 1868.

Stephens presented his case in the form of imaginary conversations, or "Colloquies," held at Liberty Hall, his Georgia plantation home. His guests (fictional characters, though based upon actual prototypes, he explained) were three Northerners: a War Democrat, a Conservative Republican, and a Radical Republican, "Judge Bynum," who appears in one of the selections reprinted below. Time and again, Stephens succeeds in demolishing the arguments of his visitors — at least to his own satisfaction.

COLLOQUY XII

MR. STEPHENS. . . . In what you consider, then, the weakness of our Government, according to my idea of its nature, I repeat, its chief strength, its great beauty, its complete symmetry, its ultimate harmony, and, indeed, its very perfection, mainly consist; certainly, so long as the objects aimed at in its formation are the objects aimed at in its administration. And, on this principle, on the full recognition of the absolute ultimate Sovereignty of the several States, I did consider it the best, and the strongest, and the grandest Government on earth! My whole heart and soul were devoted to the Constitution, and the Union under it, with this understanding of its nature, charter, objects, and functions!

When, therefore, the State of Georgia seceded, against my judgment, viewing the measure in the light of *policy,* only, and not of right (for the causes, as we have seen, and shall see more fully, hereafter, were more than ample to justify the act, as a matter of right), I felt it to be my duty to go with her, not only from a sense of the obligations of allegiance, but from other high considerations of patriotism of not much less weight and influence. These considerations pressed upon the mind the importance of maintaining *this principle,* which *lies at the foundation of all Federal systems;* and to which we were mainly indebted, in ours, for all the great achievements of the past. It was under this construction of the nature of our system, that all these achievements had been attained. This was the essential and vital principle of the system, to which I was so thoroughly devoted. It was that which secured all the advantages of Confederation, without the risk of Centralism and Absolutism; and on its preservation depended, not only the safety and welfare, and even existence, of my own State, but the safety, welfare, and ultimate existence of all the other States of the Union! The States were older than the Union! They made it! It was but their own creation! Their preservation was of infinitely more importance than its continuance! The Union might cease to exist, and yet the States continue to exist, as before! Not so with the Union, in case of the destruction or annihilation of the States! With their extinction, the Union necessarily becomes extinct also! They may survive it, and form another, more perfect, if the lapse of time and changes of events show it to be necessary, for the same objects had in view when it was formed; but it can never survive them! What may be called a Union may spring from the common ruins, but it would not be the Union of the Constitution! — the Union of States! By whatever name it might be called, whether Union, Nation, Kingdom, or any thing else, according to the taste of its dupes or its devotees, it would, in reality, be nothing but that deformed and hideous Monster which rises from the decomposing elements of dead States, the world over, and which is well known by the friends of Constitutional Liberty, everywhere, as the Demon of Centralism, Absolutism, Despotism! This is the necessary reality of that result, whether the Imperial Powers be seized and wielded by the hands of many, of few, or of one!

The question, therefore, with me, assumed a magnitude and importance far above the welfare and destiny of my own State, it embraced the welfare and ultimate destiny of all the States, North as well as South; nay, more, it embraced, in its range, the general interest of mankind, so far, at least, as the oppressed of all other lands and climes were looking to this country, not only for a present asylum against the evils of misrule in their own, but were anxiously and earnestly looking forward to the Federative principles here established, as "the World's best hope," in the great future, for the regeneration, the *renaisance,* of the Nations of the Earth! Such, in my judgment, were the scope and bearing of the question and the principles involved.

Had this foundation principle of the system then been generally acknowledged — had no military force been called out to prevent the exercise of this right of withdrawal on the part of the seceding States — had no war been waged against Georgia and the other States, for their assertion and maintenance of this right, had not this primary law of our entire system of Government been violated in the war so waged, I cannot permit myself to entertain the shadow of a doubt, that the whole controversy, between the States and Sections, would, at no distant day, have been satisfactorily and harmoniously adjusted, under the peaceful and beneficent operation of this very law itself. Just as all perturbations and irregularities are adjusted in the solar system, by the simple law of gravitation, from which alone it sprung in the beginning, and on which alone its continuance, with its wonderfully harmonious workings, depends!

A brief illustration will more clearly unfold this view. Had the right of withdrawal not been denied or resisted, those States, which had openly, confessedly, and avowedly disregarded their obligations, under the Compact, in the matter of the rendition of fugitives from service, and fugitives from justice, appealing, as they did, to "a higher Law" than the Constitution, would have reconsidered their acts, and renewed their covenants under the bonds of Union, and the Federal administration would have abandoned its policy of taking charge of subjects not within the limits of its delegated powers. The first aberrations in the system; that is the disregard of plighted faith, which had caused the second, that is the secession movement, would themselves have been rectified by that very movement! This rectification on the one side would have been attended by a corresponding rectification on the other. This would have been a *necessary* and *inevitable* result, whatever parties, under the influence of passion at the time, may have thought of the nature and permanency of the separation. That is, it would necessarily and inevitably have been the result, if the assumption on which the Union was founded be correct, namely, that it was for the best interest of all the States to be united upon the terms set forth in the Constitution — each State faithfully performing all its obligations, and the Federal Head confining its action strictly to the subjects with which it was charged. On this point, that the Union was best for all, my own convictions were strong and thorough for many reasons, that may be given hereafter. If this postulate was correct, then the ultimate result of this action and re-action in the operation of the system in bringing about a re-adjustment of the parts to their original places, would have been as *inevitable* as the continued harmonious re-adjustment of continual disturbances in the material world is being produced by like action and counter-action continually going on throughout its entire organization, and the whole resulting from the same all-pervading and all-controlling law, the same law continuing the organization which brought it at first into existence.

But if, on the contrary, the whole assumption on which the Union was formed was wrong, — if it were not for the true and best interests of all the States, constituted as they were, to be so united, — if it were true, as asserted by the controlling spirits of the derelict States, that the Constitution itself as to them, was but a "covenant with death and an agreement with Hell," — then, of course, the re-adjustment would not have taken place, and ought not to have taken place. But I did not believe that the masses of the people in these States entertained any such sentiments towards the work of their Fathers!

My opinion was, that it only required those masses to see, feel, and appreciate the great advantages of that Union to them; and to realize the fact that a Compact, broken by them, could not longer be binding upon others, as Mr. Webster had said, to cause them to compel their officials to comply with the terms of an engagement, which, upon the whole, was of so great importance to their best interests. My convictions were equally strong that, when this was done, the masses of the people at the South, influenced by like considerations, would have controlled all opposition to their cheerful and cordial return to their proper places.

There would have been no war, no bloodshed, no sacking of towns and cities, no desolation, no billions of treasure expended, on either side, and no million of lives sacrificed in the unnatural and fraticidal strife; there would have been none of the present troubles about restoration, or reconstruction; but, instead of these lamentable scenes, a new spectacle of wonder would have been presented for the guide and instruction of the astonished Nations of the earth, greater than that exhibited after the Nullification pacification, of the matchless workings of our American Institutions of Self-Government by the people!

You readily perceive, therefore, how thoroughly, looking to the grand results, my entire feelings, heart, and soul, with every energy of mind and body, became enlisted in the success of this cause, when force was invoked, when war was waged to put it down. It was the cause, not only of the seceding States, but the cause of all the States, and in this view it became, to a great extent, the cause of Constitutional Liberty everywhere. It was the cause of the Federative principle of Government, against the principle of Empire! The cause of the Grecian type of Civilization against the Asiatic! So, at least, I viewed it, with all the earnestness of the profoundest convictions.

The matter of Slavery, so-called, which was the proximate cause of these irregular movements on both sides, and which ended in the general collision of war, as we have seen, was of infinitely less importance to the Seceding States, than the recognition of this great principle. I say Slavery, so-called, because there was with us no such thing as Slavery in the full and proper sense of that word. No people ever lived more devoted to the principles of liberty, secured by free democratic institutions, than were the people of the South. None had ever given stronger proofs of this than they had done, from the day that Virginia moved in behalf of the assailed rights of Massachusetts, in 1774, to the firing of the first gun in Charleston Harbor, in 1861. What was called Slavery amongst us, was but a legal subordination of the African to the Caucasian race. This relation was so regulated by law as to promote, according to the intent and design of the system, the best interests of both races, the Black as well as the White, the Inferior, as well as the Superior. Both had rights secured, and both had duties imposed. It was a system of reciprocal service, and mutual bonds. But even the two thousand million dollars invested in the relation thus established, between private capital and the labor of this class of population, under the system, was but as the dust in the balance, compared with the vital attributes of the rights of Independence and Sovereignty on the part of the several States. For with these whatever changes and modifications, or improvements in this domestic institution, founded itself upon laws of nature, time, and experience, might have shown to be proper in the advancing progress of civilization, for the promotion of the great ends of society in all good Governments — that is the best interest of all classes, without wrong or injury to any — could, and would have been made by the superior race in these States, under the guidance of that reason, justice, philanthropy, and statemanship, which had ever marked their course, without the violent disruption of the entire social fabric, with all its attendant ills, and inconceivable wrongs, mischiefs, and sufferings; and especially without those terrible evils and consequences which must almost necessarily result from such disruptions and reorganizations as make a sudden and complete transfer of political power from the hands of the superior to the inferior race, in their present condition, intellectually and morally, in at least six States of the Union!

The system, as it existed, it is true, was not perfect. All admit this. No human systems are perfect. But great changes had been made in it, as this class of persons were gradually rising from their original barbarism, in their subordinate sphere, under the operation of the system, and from their contact, in this way, with the civilization of the superior race. Other changes would certainly have been made, even to the extinction of the system, if time, with its changes, and the progress of attainments on the part of those people had shown it to be proper — that is, best for both races. For if the system, as designed, was not really the best, or could not have been made the best for both races, or whenever it should have ceased to be so, it could and would have been thoroughly and radically changed, in due time, by the only proper and competent authority to act in the premises.

The erroneous dogma of the greatest good to the greatest number, was not the basis on which this Institution rested. Much less was it founded upon the dogma or principle of the sole interest or benefit of the white race to the exclusion of considerations embracing the interests and welfare of the other. It was erected upon no such idea as that *might,* barely, gives *right,* but it was organized and defended upon the immutable principles of justice to all, which is the foundation of all good Governments. This requires that society be so organized as to secure the greatest good possible, morally, intellectually, and politically, to all classes of persons within their jurisdictional control, without necessary wrong or detriment to any. This was the foundation principle on which this institution in these States was established and defended.

These questions are not now, however, before us. We are at present considering the workings of the Federal system, and not the wisdom or policy of the social systems of the several States, or the propriety of the *status* of their constituent elements respectively.

This whole question of Slavery, so-called, was but one relating to the proper *status* of the African as an element of a society composed of the Caucasian and African races, and the *status* which was best, not for the one race or the other, but best, upon the whole, for both.

Over these questions, the Federal Government had no rightful control whatever. They were expressly excluded, in the Compact of Union, from its jurisdiction or authority. Any such assumed control was a palpable violation of the Compact, which released all the parties to the Compact, affected by such action, from their obligations under the Compact. On this point there can be no shadow of doubt.

Waiving these questions, therefore, for the present, I repeat that this whole subject of Slavery, so-called, in any and every view of it, was, to the Seceding States, but a drop in the ocean compared with those other considerations involved in the issue. Hence, during the whole war, being thoroughly enlisted in it from these other and higher considerations, but being, at the same time, ever an earnest advocate for its speediest termination by an appeal from the arena of arms to the forum of reason, justice, and right, I was wedded to no idea as a basis of peace, but that of the recognition of the ultimate absolute Sovereignty of all the States as the essential basis of any permanent union between them, or any of them, consistent with the preservation of their ultimate existence and liberties. And I wanted, at no time, any recognition of Independence on the part of the Confederate States, but that of George III, of England. That is, the recognition of the Sovereignty and Independence of each, by name.

The Confederate States had made common cause for this great principle, as the original thirteen States had done in 1776. The recognition of this I regarded as essential to the future well-being, happiness, and prosperity of all the States, in existence and to be formed, as well as the countless millions of people who are hereafter to inhabit this half of the Western Hemisphere.

With this simple recognition I saw no formidable difficulty likely to arise in the future, from controversies between States or Sections. Whenever the passions of the day passed off, whatever Union or Unions were, or might be, really beneficial to all the States, would have resulted sooner or later, as inevitably as natural laws produce their natural effects. This they do in the moral and political world, if left to their proper and legitimate action, with as much certainty as they do in the material.

With this principle recognized, I looked upon it hereafter, and at no distant day, to become, by the natural law of political affinity — "mutual convenience and reciprocal advantage" — the great Continental Regulator of the Grand Federal Republic of "the United States of America," to whatever limits their boundaries might go, or to whatever extent their number might swell.

COLLOQUY XIII

MR. STEPHENS. We have now, gentlemen, gone through with the preliminary questions; we have taken that historical review, which was necessary and essential for a correct understanding of the nature and character of the Government of the United States, from a violation of the organic principles of which, as I stated in the outset, the war had its origin. We have seen from this review that ours is a Federal Government. In other words, we have seen that it is a Government formed by a Convention, a *Foedus,* or Compact between distinct, separate, and Sovereign States. We have seen that this Federal or Conventional Government, so formed possesses inherently no power whatever. All its powers are held by delegation only, and by delegation from separate States. These powers are all enumerated and all limited to specific objects in the Constitution. Even the highest Sovereign Power it is permitted to exercise — the war power, for instance — is held by it by delegation only. Sovereignty itself — the great source of all political power — under the system, still resides where it did before the Compact was entered into, that is, in the States severally, or with the people of the several States respectively. By the Compact, the Sovereign Powers to be exercised by the Federal Head were not surrendered by the States — were not alienated or parted with by them. They were delegated only. The States by voluntary engagements, agreed only to abstain from their exercise themselves, and to confer this exercise by delegation upon common agents under the Convention, for the better security of the great objects aimed at by the formation of the Compact, which was the regulation of their external and inter-State affairs. . . .

Out of the million and a half, and more, of men in the Northern States who voted against Mr. Lincoln, in 1860, perhaps not ten thousand could be said, with truth, to be in favor of the Institution, or would have lived in a State where it existed. It was a subject with which they were thoroughly convinced they had nothing to do, and could have nothing to do under the terms of the Union by which the States were confederated, except to carry out and faithfully perform all the obligations of the Constitutional Compact in regard to it. In opposing the "Liberty Party," so-called, they enlisted under no banner of Slavery of any sort, but only arrayed themselves against that organization, which had virtually hoisted the banner of Consolidation. The struggle or conflict, therefore, from its rise to its culmination, was between those who, in whatever State they lived, were for maintaining our Federal system as it was established, and those who were for a consolidation of power in the Central Head.

But the great fact now to be considered in this investigation, is, that this Anti-Constitutional Party, in 1860, came into power upon this question in the Executive branch of the Federal Government.

This is the state of things which produced so much excitement and apprehension in the popular mind of the Southern States at that time. This Anti-Slavery Party had not only succeeded in getting a majority of the Northern States to openly violate their Constitutional faith in the avowed breach of the Compact, as stated; but had succeeded in electing a President and Vice-President pledged to principles which were not only at war with the domestic Institutions of the States of the South, but which must inevitably, if carried out, ultimately lead to the absorption of all power in the Central Government, and end sooner or later in Absolutism or Despotism. These were the principles then brought into conflict, which, as stated, resulted in the conflict of arms.

The Seceding States feeling no longer bound by a Compact which had been so openly violated, and a majority of their people being deeply impressed with the conviction that the whole frame-work of the Constitution would be overthrown by this Party which would soon have control of the Executive Department of the Government, determined to withdraw from the Union, for the very reasons which had induced them to enter it in the beginning. Seven of these States, South Carolina, Georgia, Florida, Alabama, Mississippi, Louisiana, and Texas, did withdraw. Conventions of their people, regularly called by the proper authorities in each of these States respectively — Conventions representing the Sovereignty of the States similar in all respects to those which by Ordinances had ratified the Constitution of the United States — passed Ordinances resuming the Sovereign Powers therein delegated. These were the Secession Ordinances, which we may hereafter have occasion to look into. These Conventions also appointed Delegates, to meet in Montgomery, Alabama, on the 4th of February, 1861, with a view to form a new Confederation among themselves, upon the same essential basis of the Constitution of the United States.

It was not in opposition to the principles of that Government that they withdrew from it. They quit the Union to save the principles of the Constitution, and to perpetuate, on this Continent, the liberties which it was intended to secure and establish. Mr. Buchanan was then President of the United States. He held that the Federal Government had no power to coërce a Seceding State to remain in the Union, but, strangely enough, at the same time held, that no State could rightfully withdraw from the Union. Mr. Lincoln came into power on the 4th of March, 1861. He held that the Federal Government did possess the Constitutional Power to maintain the Union of States by force, and it was in the maintenance of these views, the war was inaugurated by him.

JUDGE BYNUM. Do you mean to say, Mr. Stephens, that the war was inaugurated by Mr. Lincoln?

MR. STEPHENS. Most assuredly I do.

JUDGE BYNUM. Why, how in the world, can you do that in the face of the well-known facts of the case? Did not General Beauregard in command of the Confederate forces, so-called, at Charleston, South Carolina, fire upon Fort Sumter in that Harbor? Did he not compel Major Anderson, the United States officer in command of that Fort, to capitulate and surrender? Was it not this outrage upon the American flag that caused such deep and universal excitement and indignation throughout the entire North? Was it not this that caused the great meetings in New York, Boston and every Northern city? Can you maintain in the face of these notorious facts, that the war was begun by Mr. Lincoln, or the Federal authorities? You rely mainly upon facts, as you say. Your whole argument professes to be based upon the facts of history. If there is any great fact that must go down to posterity forever, it is the fact that the

Insurgents, or Confederates, if you please, began this war. This is a fact, which, as you have said of other matters, "can never be erased or obliterated."

Mr. Stephens. Not quite so fast, Judge. My whole argument is based upon facts, and upon facts that can never be erased or obliterated. It is a fact that the *first gun* was fired by the Confederates. It is a fact that General Beauregard did, on the 12th of April, 1861, bombard Fort Sumter, before any blow had actually been struck by the Federal authorities. That is not disputed at all. That is a fact which I have no disposition to erase or obliterate in any way. That is a great truth which will live forever. But did the firing of the first gun, or the reduction of Fort Sumter inaugurate or begin the war? That is a question to be first solved, before we can be agreed upon the fact as to who *inaugurated* the war; and in solving this question, you must allow me to say that in personal or national conflicts, it is not he who strikes the first blow, or fires the first gun that inaugurates or begins the conflict. Hallam has well said that "the *aggressor* in a war (that is, he who begins it,) is not the *first* who *uses force,* but the first who renders force *necessary."*

Which side, according to this high authority, (that only announces the common sentiments of mankind,) was the *aggressor* in this instance? Which side was it that provoked and rendered the first blow necessary? The true answer to that question will settle the fact as to which side began the war.

I maintain that it was inaugurated and begun, though no blow had been struck, when the hostile fleet, styled the "Relief Squadron," with eleven ships, carrying two hundred and eighty-five guns and two thousand four hundred men, was sent out from New York and Norfolk, with orders from the authorities at Washington, to re-enforce Fort Sumter peaceably, if permitted — "but forcibly if they must."

The war was then and there inaugurated and begun by the authorities at Washington. General Beauregard did not open fire upon Fort Sumter until this fleet was, to his knowledge, very near the harbor of Charleston, and until he had inquired of Major Anderson, in command of the Fort, whether he would engage to take no part in the expected blow, then coming down upon him from the approaching fleet. Francis W. Pickens, Governor of South Carolina, and General Beauregard, had both been notified that the fleet was coming, and of its objects, by a messenger from the authorities at Washington. This notice, however, was not given until it was near its destination. When Major Anderson, therefore, would make no such promise, it became necessary for General Beauregard to strike the first blow, as he did; otherwise the forces under his command might have been exposed to two fires at the same time — one in front, and the other in the rear.

To understand this fully, let us see how matters stood in Charleston Harbor at the time.

The Confederate States, then seven in number, had, as stated, all passed Ordinances of Secession. All of them, in regularly constituted Conventions, had withdrawn all their Sovereign powers previously delegated to the United States. They had formed a new Confederation, with a regularly constituted Government, at Montgomery, Alabama, as they had a perfect right to do, if our past conclusions were correct, and these you have not been able to assail. This new Confederation had sent a commission to the authorities at Washington, as we shall see, to settle all matters amicably and peacefully. War was by no means the wish or desire of the authorities at Montgomery. Very few of the public men in the Seceding States even expected war. All of them, it is true, held themselves in readiness for it, if it should be forced upon them against their wishes and most earnest protestations.

This is abundantly and conclusively apparent from the speeches and addresses of their leading public men at the time. It is apparent from the resolutions of the State Legislatures, and the State Conventions, before, and in their acts of Secession. It is apparent and manifest from their acts in their new Confederation at Montgomery. It is apparent from the inaugural address of President Davis. It is apparent from the appointment of commissioners to settle all matters involved in the separation from their former Confederates honorably, peaceably, amicably, and justly. It is apparent and manifest from every act that truly indicates the objects and motives of men, or from which their real aims can be justly arrived at. Peace not only with the States from which they had separated, but peace with all the world, was the strong desire of the Confederate States.

It was under these circumstances, that the Confederate commissioners were given to understand, that Fort Sumter would be peacefully evacuated. An assurance to this effect was given, though in an informal manner, by Mr. Seward, the Secretary of State under Mr. Lincoln. This pledge was most strangely violated by sending the armed squadron, as stated, to reenforce and provision the Fort. The information that this fleet had put to sea with such orders, reached General Beauregard, when it was already near the offing, as I have stated. He immediately communicated the fact, by telegraph, to the authorities at Montgomery. In reply he received this order from the Secretary of War of the Confederate States Government:

"If you have no doubt of the authorized character of the agent who communicated to you the intention of the Washington Government to supply

Fort Sumter by force, you will at once demand its evacuation; and if this is refused, proceed in such manner as you may determine, to reduce it."

Accordingly, on the 11th of April, General Beauregard made a demand on Major Anderson, in command of the Fort, for its evacuation.

In reply Major Anderson stated:

"I have the honor to acknowledge the receipt of your communication demanding the evacuation of this Fort, and to say in reply thereto, that it is a demand with which I regret that my sense of honor and my obligation to my Government prevent my compliance."

To this he added, verbally, to the messenger: "I will await the first shot, and, if you do not batter us to pieces, we will be starved out in a few days."

This written reply, as well as the verbal remark, were forthwith sent by General Beauregard to the Secretary of War at Montgomery, who immediately returned the following response:

"Do not desire needlessly to bombard Fort Sumter. If Major Anderson will state the time at which, as indicated by himself, he will evacuate, and agree that, in the meantime, he will not use his guns against us, unless ours should be employed against Fort Sumter, you are authorized thus to avoid the effusion of blood. If this or its equivalent be refused, reduce the Fort, as your judgment decides most practicable."

This was communicated to Major Anderson. He refused to comply with the terms. He would not consent to any such arrangement.

Whereupon, General Beauregard opened fire on the Fort at 4.30, on the morning of the 12th of April. The fire was returned. The bombardment lasted for thirty-two hours, when Major Anderson agreed to capitulate. General Beauregard exhibited no less of the magnanimity of the true soldier in the terms of capitulation, than he had of high military skill and genius in forming his plans, and in their execution for the reduction of the Fort. The entire garrison numbering eighty in all, officers and men, was permitted to be marched out with their colors and music. They were permitted to salute their flag with fifty guns. All private as well as company property was also allowed to be taken by those to whom it belonged. These were the same terms that General Beauregard had offered on the 11th, before he opened fire. As Providence ordered it, not a life was lost in this most memorable and frightful combat. The firing on both sides, at some times, particularly at night, was represented by those who witnessed it, as both "grand and terrific."

This was the first blow. It is true, the first gun was fired on the Confederate side. That is fully admitted. But all the facts show that, if force was thus first used by them, it was so first used only, because it was rendered necessary in self-defence on the part of those thus using it, and so rendered necessary by the opposite side. This first use of force, therefore, under the circumstances, cannot, in fact, be properly and justly considered as the beginning of the war.

What has been stated, also, shows how earnestly the authorities at Montgomery, had in every possible way, consistent with honor and safety, endeavored to avoid a collision of forces. The whole question of the right or wrong, therefore, in striking this first blow, as well as the right or wrong of the war, depends upon the Constitutional points we have been discussing. If the Seceding States were right on these points, then their first blow was perfectly justifiable, even if it had not been given, as it was, to avert one then impending over them.

JUDGE BYNUM. Please allow me to interrupt you for a moment. The views you express seem to me not only novel, but altogether unsuited to the facts, even as you state them. Allow me to ask, if the Fort did not belong to the United States? Was it not the property of the United States? Were not the officers and men in it attached to the service of the United States? What right, therefore, had General Beauregard, or any body else, to attempt to prevent the United States Government from provisioning the garrison then holding it, and re-enforcing it, if they thought proper? Was it not the duty of Mr. Lincoln to do it, as well as his right?

MR. STEPHENS. Not if South Carolina had the Sovereign right to demand the possession of the Fort. Rights, whether civil, moral, or political, never conflict. If South Carolina had this Sovereign right to demand the possession of the place, which was within her jurisdiction, then Mr. Lincoln could have had no right to continue to hold it against this demand; nor was it his duty, in any sense, to attempt, even, to provision it by force, under the circumstances.

The Fort was within the jurisdiction of South Carolina. It was built specially for her protection, and belonged to her in part as well as to the other States jointly. On the 11th of January, Governor Pickens, in behalf of the Sovereign Rights of the State, demanded its possession of Major Anderson for the use of the State. On his refusal to deliver it up, the Governor immediately sent I. W. Hayne, the Attorney General of the State, to Washington, and made a like demand for its possession of Mr. Buchanan, the President, alleging that the possession of this Fort was necessary for the safety of the State for whose protection it had been erected. In this letter, Governor Pickens also stated, that a full valuation of the property would be accounted for, on settlement of the relations of South Carolina with the United States.

This whole question, relating to the right in this matter, and the side on which the right existed, depends, as I have said, upon the correctness of our conclusions on the points discussed. If South Carolina, after the resumption of her delegated powers, was a separate, Sovereign State (which is one of our established truths), then, of course, she had a perfect right to demand the possession of any landed property whatever, lying within the limits of her jurisdiction, if she deemed it of importance for her public use and benefit. This perfect right so to do, was subject to but one limitation, and that was the moral obligation to pay a fair and just compensation for the property so demanded for public use. There can be no question of the correctness of this principle. It is the foundation of the great right of Eminent domain, which ever accompanies Sovereignty. We have seen that this right of Eminent domain was never parted with by her, even under the Constitution. South Carolina, then, even before Secession, and while she held herself to be bound by the Constitution, had a perfect right to demand of the United States Government the possession of this identical property, on paying a just compensation for it, if she had deemed it essential for her public interests. This Fort never could have been erected on her soil without her consent, as we have seen. The title, therefore, of the United States to the land on which Fort Sumter was built, was in no essential respect different from the title of any other land-holder in the State. The tenure by which the United States claimed and held this property, differed in no essential respect from the tenure by which every other land-owner held similar property in the State; nor was this property of the United States, so purchased and held under grant from South Carolina, any less subject to the right of Eminent domain on the part of the State, than any other lands lying within her limits. If this was so even before Secession, (and no one can successfully assail the position,) then how much more clearly this right (by virtue of the principle of Eminent domain,) to demand the possession of this property for public use, for *her own protection,* appears after she had expressly resumed the exercise of all of her Sovereign powers? This right to demand the possession of this Fort, therefore, being unquestionably perfect in her as a Sovereign State after Secession, whether it was before or not, she had transferred to the Confederate States. Hence, their right to demand the evacuation of Fort Sumter, was perfect, viewed either morally, or politically.

The Confederate States had offered to come to a fair and just settlement with the United States, as to the value of this property, as well as all other public property belonging to all the States in common, at the time of their separation. This Fort, as well as all else that belonged to the United States, belonged in part to these seven Seceded States. They constituted seven of the United States, to which all this joint property belonged. All the Forts which lay within the limits of the Seceded States, had been turned over by these States, respectively, to the Confederacy, as we shall see. The Confederate States, therefore, through their authorities, had a right to demand, and take possession of all of these Forts, so lying within their limits, for their own public use, upon paying a just compensation for them to their former associates of the United States, who still adhered to that Union. These principles cannot be assailed. The offer so to pay whatever should be found to be due upon a general and just account, had been made. Mr. Lincoln, therefore, had no right under the circumstances, to hold any of these Forts by force, after the demand for the possession had been made; much less was it his duty either morally, or politically, when it was known that the attempt would inevitably lead to a war between the States. This is my answer to your property view.

Now, sir, I do stand upon facts, and these are the incontestable facts of this case, which will forever perpetuate the truth of my assertion, that upon the head of the Federal Government will forever rest the inauguration of this most terrible war which did ensue.

No part of its responsibility rests upon the Southern States. They were the aggressors in no instance. They were ever true to their plighted faith under the Constitution. No instance of a breach of its mutual covenants can be ever laid to their charge. The open and palpable breach was committed by a number of their Northern Confederates. No one can deny this. Those States at the North, which were untrue to their Constitutional engagements, claimed powers not delegated, and elected a Chief Magistrate pledged to carry out principles openly in defiance of the decision of the highest Judicial Tribunal known to the Constitution.

Their policy tended inevitably to a Centralized Despotism. It was under these circumstances that Secession was resorted to, as before stated; and, then, the war was begun and waged by the North to prevent the exercise of this Right. All that the Southern States did, was in defence, even in their firing the first gun. . . .

Carl Schurz

UNREPENTANT SOUTHERNERS

❧{ 1865 }❧ THE controversy over how to treat the defeated South after the Civil War was one of the angriest and most complex in all American history, one that in a sense has never been finally settled. President Andrew Johnson (1808-1875), upon whose shoulders the heavy burden of policy-making chiefly fell, was predisposed to carry out the policy that Lincoln had established of trying to restore self-rule to the region on easy terms and quickly. The radical faction in Congress, however, wished to adopt harsher measures that would punish "rebellion" and make sure that the recently freed Negroes were treated fairly by their former masters.

To obtain the latest information about conditions in the South, President Johnson sent a number of prominent Northerners into the area on inspection trips. Most of these men, including General Ulysses S. Grant (1822-1885) himself, reported that the South had accepted defeat in good spirit; they recommended that Johnson continue with the policy of quick reassimilation of the former Confederacy into the Union.

One sharp dissent was submitted, however. It was from the pen of Carl Schurz (1829-1906), a German-American soldier and politician closely allied with the radical faction in Congress. Schurz had criticized the President's policy and as a result Johnson had asked him to make a study of conditions in the South first hand. Schurz agreed to do so, and as the following excerpts from his report indicate, he came back feeling that a harsh reconstruction policy was necessary. This idea was most distasteful to Johnson. He received Schurz coolly and did not even ask for a formal report. Nevertheless, Schurz wrote out his findings, in the selection below, and at the behest of Congress they were published.

Because of the author's influence with such powerful Republican leaders as Charles Sumner (1811-1874) and Edward M. Stanton (1814-1869) (and because he said what these men wanted to hear), Schurz's report had a great contemporary influence. When the radical faction won control over Congress, views very much like Schurz's were in the ascendancy. Even General Grant was soon won over. It is ironic, therefore, that Schurz soon became disillusioned with the radical program, broke with his former friends, and joined the Liberal Republican faction. By the 1880's, after another trip through the area, he emerged as a defender of the South, even committing himself to a "let-alone policy" with regard to race relations.

REPORT ON THE CONDITION OF THE SOUTH

Sir: — When you did me the honor of selecting me for a mission to the States lately in rebellion, for the purpose of inquiring into the existing condition of things, of laying before you whatever information of importance I might gather, and of suggesting to you such measures as my observations would lead me to believe advisable, I accepted the trust with a profound sense of the responsibility connected with the performance of the task. The views I entertained at the time, I had communicated to you in frequent letters and conversations. I would not have accepted the mission, had I not felt that whatever preconceived opinions I might carry with me to the South, I should be ready to abandon or modify, as my perception of facts and circumstances might command their abandonment or modification. You informed me that your "policy of reconstruction" was merely experimental, and that you would change it if the experiment did not lead to satisfactory results. To aid you in forming your conclusions upon this point I understood to be the object of my mission, and this understanding was in perfect accordance with the written instructions I received through the Secretary of War.

These instructions confined my mission to the States of South Carolina, Georgia, Alabama, Mississippi, and the Department of the Gulf. I informed you, before leaving the North, that I could not well devote more than three months to the duties imposed upon me, and that space of time proved sufficient for me to visit all the States above enumerated, except Texas. I landed at Hilton Head, South Carolina, on July 15, visited Beaufort, Charleston, Orangeburg, and Columbia, returned to Charleston and Hilton Head; thence I went to Savannah, traversed the State of Georgia, visiting Augusta, Atlanta, Macon, Milledgeville and Columbus; went through Alabama, by way of Opelika, Montgomery, Selma and Demopolis and through Mississippi, by way of Meridian, Jackson and Vicksburg; then descended the Mississippi to New Orleans, touching at Natchez; from New Orleans I visited Mobile, Alabama, and the Teche country, in Louisiana, and then spent again some days at Natchez and Vicksburg, on my way to the North. These are the outlines of my journey.

Before laying the results of my observations before you, it is proper that I should state the *modus operandi* by which I obtained information and formed my conclusions. Wherever I went I sought interviews with persons who might be presumed to represent the opinions, or to have influence upon the conduct, of their neighbors; I had thus frequent meetings with individuals belonging to the different classes of society from the highest to the lowest; in the cities as well as on the roads and steamboats I had many opportunities to converse not only with inhabitants of the adjacent country, but with persons coming from districts which I was not able to visit; and finally I compared the impressions thus received with the experience of the military and civil officers of the government stationed in that country, as well as of other reliable Union men. . . .

RETURNING LOYALTY

It is a well-known fact that in the States south of Tennessee and North Carolina the number of white Unionists who during the war actively aided the Government, or at least openly professed their attachment to the cause of the Union, was very small. In none of those States were they strong enough to exercise any decisive influence upon the action of the people, not even in Louisiana, unless vigorously supported by the power of the General Government. But the white people at large being, under certain conditions, charged with taking the preliminaries of "reconstruction" into their hands, the success of the experiment depends upon the spirit and attitude of those who either attached themselves to the secession cause from the beginning, or, entertaining originally opposite views, at least followed its fortunes from the time that their States had declared their separation from the Union.

The first Southern men of this class with whom I came into contact immediately after my arrival in South Carolina expressed their sentiments almost literally in the following language: "We acknowledge ourselves beaten, and we are ready to submit to the results of the war. The war has practically decided that no State shall secede and that the slaves are emancipated. We cannot be expected at once to give up our principles and convictions of right, but we accept facts as they are, and desire to be reinstated as soon as possible in the enjoyment and exercise of our political rights." This declaration was repeated to me hundreds of times in every State I visited, with some variations of language, according to the different ways of thinking or the frankness or reserve of the different speakers. . . .

WHAT HAS BEEN ACCOMPLISHED

While the generosity and toleration shown by the Government to the people lately in rebellion have not met with a corresponding generosity shown by those people to the Government's friends, it has brought forth some results which, if properly developed, will become of value. It has facilitated the re-establishment of the forms of civil government, and led many of those who had been active in the rebellion to take part in the act of bringing back the States to their Constitutional relations; and if nothing else were necessary than the mere putting in operation of the mere machinery of government in point of form, and not also the acceptance of the results of the war and their development in point of spirit, these results, although as yet incomplete, might be called a satisfactory advance in the right direction. There is, at present, no danger of another insurrection against the authority of the United States on a large scale, and the people are willing to reconstruct their State governments, and to send their Senators and Representatives to Congress.

But as to the moral value of these results, we must not indulge in any delusions. There are two principal points to which I beg to call your attention. In the first place, the rapid return to power and influence of so many of those who but recently were engaged in a bitter war against the Union, has had one effect which was certainly not originally contemplated by the Government. Treason does, under existing circumstances, not appear odious in the South. The people are not impressed with any sense of its criminality. And, secondly, there is, as yet among the Southern people an *utter absence of national feeling*. I made it a business, while in the

South, to watch the symptoms of "returning loyalty" as they appeared not only in private conversation, but in the public press and in the speeches delivered and the resolutions passed at Union meetings. Hardly ever was there an expession of hearty attachment to the great republic, or an appeal to the impulses of patriotism; but whenever submission to the National authority was declared and advocated, it was almost uniformly placed upon two principal grounds: That, under present circumstances, the Southern people could "do no better"; and then that submission was the only means by which they could rid themselves of the Federal soldiers and obtain once more control of their own affairs. Some of the speakers may have been inspired by higher motives, but upon these two arguments they had principally to rely whenever they wanted to make an impression upon the popular mind. . . .

THE NEGRO QUESTION — FIRST ASPECTS

The principal cause of that want of national spirit which has existed in the South so long, and at last gave birth to the rebellion, was, that the Southern people cherished, cultivated, idolized their peculiar interests and institutions in preference to those which they had in common with the rest of the American people. Hence the importance of the negro question as an integral part of the question of union in general, and the question of reconstruction in particular.

When the war came to a close, the labor system of the South was already much disturbed. During the progress of military operations large numbers of slaves had left their masters and followed the columns of our armies; others had taken refuge in our camps; many thousands had enlisted in the service of the National Government. Extensive settlements of negroes had been formed along the seaboard and the banks of the Mississippi, under the supervision of army officers and treasury agents, and the Government was feeding the colored refugees, who could not be advantageously employed, in the so-called contraband camps. Many slaves had also been removed by their masters, as our armies penetrated the country, either to Texas or to the interior of Georgia and Alabama. Thus a considerable portion of the laboring force had been withdrawn from its former employments. But a majority of the slaves remained on the plantations to which they belonged, especially in those parts of the country which were not touched by the war, and where, consequently, the emancipation proclamation was not enforced by the military power. Although not ignorant of the stake they had in the result of the contest, the patient bondmen waited quietly for the development of things. But as soon as the struggle was finally decided, and our forces were scattered about in detachments to occupy the country, the so far unmoved masses began to stir. The report went among them that their liberation was no longer a mere contingency, but a fixed fact. Large numbers of colored people left the plantations; many flocked to our military posts and camps to obtain the certainty of their freedom, and others walked away merely for the purpose of leaving the places on which they had been held in slavery, and because they could now go with impunity. Still others, and their number was by no means inconsiderable, remained with their former masters and continued their work on the field, but under new and as yet unsettled conditions, and under the agitating influence of a feeling of restlessness. In some localities, however, where our troops had not yet penetrated and where no military post was within reach, planters endeavored and partially succeeded in maintaining between themselves and the negroes the relation of master and slave, partly by concealing from them the great changes that had taken place, and partly by terrorizing them into submission to their behests. But aside from these exceptions, the country found itself thrown into that confusion which is naturally inseparable from a change so great and so sudden. The white people were afraid of the negroes, and the negroes did not trust the white people; the military power of the National Government stood there, and was looked up to, as the protector of both.

Upon this power devolved the task to bring order into that chaos. But the order to be introduced was a new order, of which neither the late masters nor the late slaves had an adequate conception. All the elements of society being afloat, the difficulties were immense. The military officers and agents of the Freedmen's Bureau, to whom the negroes applied for advice and guidance, either procured them such employment as could be found, or persuaded them to return to their plantations and to continue in the cultivation of the crops, promising them that their liberty, rights, and interests should be protected. Upon the planters they urged the necessity of making fair and equitable contracts with the freedmen, admonishing them to treat their laborers as free men ought to be treated. These efforts met with such success as the difficulties surrounding the problem permitted to expect. Large numbers of negroes went back to the fields, according to the advice they had received, but considerable accumulations still remained in and around the towns and along the seaboard, where there was no adequate amount of profitable employment for them. The making and approving of contracts progressed as rapidly as the small number of officers engaged in that line of duty made it possible, but not rapidly in proportion to the vast amount of work to be accomplished. The business experience of many of the officers was but limited; here and there experiments were tried which had to be given up. In numerous cases contracts were made and then broken, either by the employers or the laborers, and the officers in charge were overwhelmed with complaints from both sides. While many planters wanted to have the laborers who had left them back on their plantations, others drove those that had remained away, and thus increased the number of the unemployed. Moreover, the great change had burst upon the country in the midst of the agricultural labor season when the crops that were in the ground required steady work to make them produce a satisfactory yield, and the interruption of labor, which could not but be very extensive, caused considerable damage. In one word, the efforts made could not prevent or remedy, in so short a time, the serious disorders which are always connected with a period of precipitous transition, and which, although natural, are exceedingly embarrassing to those who have to deal with them.

The solution of the social problem in the South, if left to the free action of the Southern people, will depend upon two things: (1) upon the ideas entertained by the whites, the "ruling class" of the problem, and the manner in which they act upon their ideas; and (2) upon the capacity and conduct of the colored people.

OPINIONS OF THE WHITES

That the result of the free labor experiment made under circumstances so extremely unfavorable should at once be a perfect success, no reasonable person would expect. Nevertheless, a large majority of the Southern men with whom I came into contact announced their opinions with so positive an assurance as to produce the impression that their minds were fully made up. In at least nineteen cases of twenty the reply I received to my inquiry about their views on the new system was uniformly this: "You cannot make the negro work without physical compulsion." I heard this hundreds of times, heard it wherever I went, heard it in nearly the same words from so many different persons, that at last I came to the conclusion that this is the prevailing sentiment among the Southern people. . . .

Here I will insert some remarks on the general treatment of the blacks as a class, from the whites as a class. It is not on the plantations and at the hands of the planters themselves that the negroes have to suffer the greatest hardships. Not only the former slaveholders, but the non-slaveholding whites, who, even previous to the war, seemed to be more ardent in their pro-slavery feelings than the planters themselves, are possessed by a singularly bitter and vindictive feeling against the colored race since the negro has ceased to be property. The pecuniary value which the individual negro formerly represented having disappeared, the maiming and killing of colored men seems to be looked upon by many as one of those venial offences which must be forgiven to the outraged feelings of a wronged and robbed people. Besides, the services rendered by the negro to the National cause during the war, which make him an object of special interest to the loyal people, make him an object of particular vindictiveness to those whose hearts were set upon the success of the rebellion. The number of murders and assaults perpetrated upon negroes is very great; we can form only an approximative estimate of what is going on in those parts of the South which are not closely garrisoned, and from which no regular reports are received, by what occurs under the very eyes of our military authorities. As to my personal experience, I will only mention that during my two days' sojourn at Atlanta one negro was stabbed with fatal effect on the street, and three were poisoned, one of whom died. While I was at Montgomery one negro was cut across the throat evidently with intent to kill, and another was shot, but both escaped with their lives. . . .

THE FREEDMAN

The first Southern men with whom I came into contact after my arrival at Charleston designated the general conduct of the emancipated slaves as surprisingly good. Some went even so far as to call it admirable. The connection in which they used these laudatory terms was this: A great many colored people while in slavery had undoubtedly suffered much hardship and submitted to great wrongs, partly inseparably connected with the condition of servitude, and partly aggravated by the individual wilfulness and cruelty of their masters and overseers. They were suddenly set free; and not only that: their masters, but a short time ago almost omnipotent on their domains, found themselves, after their defeat in the war, all at once face to face with their former slaves as a conquered and powerless class. Never was the temptation to indulge in acts of vengeance for wrongs suffered more strongly presented than to the colored people of the South; but no instance of such individual revenge was then on record, nor have I since heard of any case of violence that could be traced to such motives. The transition of the Southern negro from slavery to freedom was untarnished by any deeds of blood, and the apprehension so extensively entertained and so pathetically declaimed upon by many, that the sudden and general emancipation of the slaves would at once result in "all the horrors of St. Domingo," proved utterly groundless. This was the first impression I received after my arrival in the South, and I received it from the mouths of late slaveholders. Nor do I think the praise was unjustly bestowed. In this respect the emancipated slaves of the South can challenge comparison with any race long held in servitude and suddenly set free. As to the dangers of the future, I shall speak of them in another connection.

But at that point the unqualified praise stopped and the complaints began: the negroes would not work; they left their plantations and went wandering from place to place, stealing by the way; they preferred a life of idleness and vagrancy to that of honest and industrious labor; they either did not show any willingness to enter into contracts, or, if they did, showed a stronger disposition to break them than to keep them; they were becoming insubordinate and insolent to their former owners; they indulged in extravagant ideas about their rights and relied upon the Government to support them without work; in one word, they had no conception of the rights freedom gave, and of the obligations freedom imposed upon them. These complaints I heard repeated with endless variations wherever I went. Nor were they made without some show of reason. I will review them one after another.

Unwillingness to work. — That there are among the negroes a good many constitutionally lazy individuals is certainly true. The propensity to idleness seems to be rather strongly developed in the South generally, without being confined to any particular race. It is also true that the alacrity negroes put into their work depends in a majority of cases upon certain combinations of circumstances. It is asserted that the negroes have a prejudice against working in the cultivation of cotton, rice and sugar. Although this prejudice, probably arising from the fact that the cotton, rice and sugar fields remind the former slave of the worst experiences of his past life, exists to some extent, it has not made the freedman now on the plantations unwilling to cultivate such crops as the planters may have seen fit to raise. A few cases of refusal may have occurred. But there is another fact of which I have become satisfied in the course of my observations, and which is of great significance: while most of the old slaveholders complain of the laziness and instability of their negro laborers, the Northern men engaged in planting, with whom I have come into contact, almost uniformly speak of their negro laborers with satisfaction, and these Northern men almost exclusively devote themselves to the cultivation of cotton. . . .

Many freedmen — not single individuals, but whole "plantation gangs" — are working well; others do not. The difference in their efficiency coincides in a great measure with a certain difference in the conditions under which they live. The conclusion lies near, that if the conditions under which they work well become general, their efficiency as free laborers will become general also, aside from individual exceptions. Certain it is, that by far the larger portion of the work done in the South is done by freedmen.

Vagrancy. — Large numbers of colored people left the plantations as soon as they became aware that they could do so with impunity. That they could so leave their former masters was for them the first test of the reality of their freedom. A great many flocked to the military posts and towns to obtain from the "Yankees" reliable information as to their new rights. Others were afraid lest by staying on the plantations where they had been held as slaves they might again endanger their freedom. Still others went to the cities, thinking that there the sweets of liberty could best be enjoyed. In some places they crowded together in large numbers, causing serious inconvenience. But a great many, probably a very large majority, remained on the plantations and made contracts with their former masters. The military authorities, and especially the agents of the Freedmen's Bureau, succeeded by continued exertions in returning most of those who were adrift to the plantations, or in finding other employment for them. After the first rush was over the number of vagrants grew visibly less. It may be said that where the Freedmen's Bureau is best organized there is least vagrancy among the negroes. Here and there they show considerable restlessness, partly owing to local, partly to general causes. Among the former, bad treatment is probably the most prominent; among the latter, a feeling of distrust, uneasiness, anxiety about their future, which arises from their present unsettled condition. It is true, some are going from place to place because they are fond of it. The statistics of the Freedmen's Bureau show that the whole number of colored people supported by the Government since the close of the war was remarkably small and continually decreasing. This seems to show that the Southern negro, when thrown out of his accustomed employment, possesses considerable ability to support himself. It is possible, however, that in consequence of short crops, the destitution of the country and other disturbing influences, there may be more restlessness among the negroes next winter than there is at present. Where the results of this year's labor were very unsatisfactory, there will be a floating about of the population when the contracts of this year expire. It is to be expected, however, that the Freedmen's Bureau will be able to remedy evils of that kind. Other emancipatory movements, for instance the abolition of serfdom in Russia, have resulted in little or no vagrancy; but it must not be forgotten that the emancipated serfs were speedily endowed with the ownership of land, which gave them a permanent moral and material interest in the soil upon which they lived. A similar measure would do more to stop negro vagrancy in the South than the severest penal laws. . . .

Insolence and insubordination. — The new spirit which emancipation has awakened in the colored people has undoubtedly developed itself in some individuals, especially young men, to an offensive degree. Hence cases of insolence on the part of freedmen occur. But such occurrences are comparatively rare. On the whole, the conduct of the colored people is far more submissive than anybody had a right to expect. The acts of violence perpetrated by freedmen against white persons do not stand in any proportion to those committed by whites against negroes. Every such occurrence is sure to be noticed in the Southern papers, and we have heard of but very few.

When Southern people speak of the insolence of the negro, they generally mean something which persons who never lived under the system of slavery are not apt to appreciate. It is but very rarely what would be called insolence among equals. But, as an old planter said to me, "our people cannot realize yet that the negro is free." A negro is called insolent whenever his conduct varies in any manner from what a Southern man was accustomed to when slavery existed. . . .

Relations between the two races. — There are whites in the South who profess great kindness for the negro. Many of them are, no doubt, sincere in what they say. But as to the feelings of the masses, it is hardly necessary to add anything to what I have already stated. I have heard it asserted that the negroes also cherish feelings of hostility to the whites. Taking this as a general assertion, I am satisfied that it is incorrect. The negroes do not trust their late masters because they do not feel their freedom sufficiently assured. Many of them may harbor feelings of resentment towards those who now ill-treat and persecute them, but as they practiced no revenge after their emancipation for wrongs suffered while in slavery, so their present resentments are likely to cease as soon as the persecution ceases. If the persecution and the denial of their rights as freedmen continue, the resentments growing out of them will continue and spread. The negro is constitutionally docile and eminently good-natured. Instances of the most touching attachment of freedmen to their old masters and mistresses have come to my notice. To a white man whom they believe to be sincerely their friend they cling with greater affection than even to one of their own race. By some Northern speculators their confidence has been sadly abused. Nevertheless, the trust they place in persons coming from the North, or in any way connected with the Government, is most childlike and unbounded. There may be individual exceptions, but I am sure they are not numerous. Those who enjoy their confidence enjoy also their affection. Centuries of slavery have not been sufficient to make them the enemies of the white race. If in the future a feeling of mutual hostility should develop itself between the races, it will probably not be the fault of those who have shown such an inexhaustible patience under the most adverse and trying circumstances.

In some places that I visited I found apprehension entertained by whites of impending negro insurrections. Whenever our military commanders found it expedient to subject the statements made to that effect by whites to close investigation, they uniformly found them unwarranted by fact. In many instances there were just reasons for supposing that such apprehensions were industriously spread for the purpose of serving as an excuse for further persecution. . . . All classes of society are intensely dissatisfied with things as they are. General explosions may be prevented, but they are always imminent. This state of uncertainty impedes all successful working of the social forces; people, instead of devoting themselves with confidence and steadiness to solid pursuits, are apt to live from hand to mouth, or to indulge in fitful experiments; capital ventures out but with great timidity; the lawless elements of the community take advantage of the general confusion and dissatisfaction, and society drifts into anarchy. There is probably at the present moment no country in the civilized world which contains such an accumulation of anarchical elements as the South. The strife of the antagonistic tendencies here described is aggravated by the passions inflamed and the general impoverishment brought about by a long and exhaustive war, and the South will have to suffer the evils of anarchical disorder until means are found to effect a final settlement of the labor question in accordance with the logic of the great revolution.

THE TRUE PROBLEM — DIFFICULTIES AND REMEDIES

In seeking remedies for such disorders, we ought to keep in view, above all, the nature of the problem which is to be solved. As to what is commonly termed "reconstruction," it is not only the political machinery of the States and their constitutional relations to the General Government, but the whole organism of Southern society that must be reconstructed, or rather constructed anew, so as to bring it in harmony with the rest of American society. The difficulties of this task are not to be considered overcome when the people of the South take the oath of allegiance and elect governors and legislatures and members of Congress and militia captains. That this would be done had become certain as soon as the surrenders of the Southern armies had made further resistance impossible, and nothing in the world was left, even to the most uncompromising rebel, but to submit or to emigrate. It was also natural that they should avail themselves of every chance offered them to resume control of their home affairs and to regain their influence in the Union. But this can hardly be called the first step towards the solution of the true problem, and it is a fair question to ask, whether the hasty gratification of their desire to resume such control would not create new embarrassments.

The true nature of the difficulties of the situation is this: The General

Government of the republic has, by proclaiming the emancipation of the slaves, commenced a great social revolution in the South, but has, as yet, not completed it. Only the negative part of it is accomplished. The slaves are emancipated in point of form, but free labor has not yet been put in the place of slavery in point of fact. And now, in the midst of this critical period of transition, the power which originated the revolution is expected to turn over its whole future development to another power which from the beginning was hostile to it and has never yet entered into its spirit, leaving the class in whose favor it was made completely without power to protect itself and to take an influential part in that development. The history of the world will be searched in vain for a proceeding similar to this which did not lead either to a rapid and violent reaction, or to the most serious trouble and civil disorder. It cannot be said that the conduct of the Southern people since the close of the war has exhibited such extraordinary wisdom and self-abnegation as to make them an exception to the rule.

In my despatches from the South I repeatedly expressed the opinion that the people were not yet in a frame of mind to legislate calmly and understandingly upon the subject of free negro labor. And this I reported to be the opinion of some of our most prominent military commanders and other observing men. It is, indeed, difficult to imagine circumstances more unfavorable for the development of a calm and unprejudiced public opinion than those under which the Southern people are at present laboring. The war has not only defeated their political aspirations, but it has broken up their whole social organization. When the rebellion was put down, they found themselves not only conquered in a political and military sense, but economically ruined. The planters, who represented the wealth of the Southern country, are partly laboring under the severest embarrassments, partly reduced to absolute poverty. Many who are stripped of all available means, and have nothing but their land, cross their arms in gloomy despondency, incapable of rising in a manly resolution. Others, who still possess means, are at a loss how to use them, as their old way of doing things is, by the abolition of slavery, rendered impracticable, at least where the military arm of the government has enforced emancipation. Others are still trying to go on in the old way, and that old way is in fact the only one they understand, and in which they have any confidence. Only a minority is trying to adopt the new order of things. A large number of the plantations, probably a considerable majority of the more valuable estates, is under heavy mortgages, and the owners know that, unless they retrieve their fortunes in a comparatively short space of time, their property will pass out of their hands. Almost all are, to some extent, embarrassed. The nervous anxiety which such a state of things produces extends also to those classes of society which, although not composed of planters, were always in close business connection with the planting interest, and there was hardly a branch of commerce or industry in the South which was not directly or indirectly so connected. Besides, the Southern soldiers, when returning from the war, did not, like the Northern soldiers, find a prosperous community which merely waited for their arrival to give them remunerative employment. They found, many of them, their homesteads destroyed, their farms devastated, their families in distress; and those that were less unfortunate found, at all events, an impoverished and exhausted community which had but little to offer them. Thus a great many have been thrown upon the world to shift as best they can. They must do something honest or dishonest, and must do it soon, to make a living, and their prospects are, at present, not very bright. Thus that nervous anxiety to hastily repair broken fortunes, and to prevent still greater ruin and distress, embraces nearly all classes, and imprints upon all the movements of the social body a morbid character.

In which direction will these people be most apt to turn their eyes? Leaving the prejudice of race out of the question, from early youth they have been acquainted with but one system of labor, and with that one system they have been in the habit of identifying all their interests. They know of no way to help themselves but the one they are accustomed to. Another system of labor is presented to them, which, however, owing to circumstances which they do not appreciate, appears at first in an improvising light. To try it they consider an experiment which they cannot afford to make while their wants are urgent. They have not reasoned calmly enough to convince themselves that the trial must be made. It is, indeed, not wonderful that, under such circumstances, they should study, not how to introduce and develop free labor, but how to avoid its introduction, and how to return as much and as quickly as possible to something like the older order of things. Nor is it wonderful that such studies should find an expression in their attempts at legislation. But the circumstance that this tendency is natural does not render it less dangerous and objectionable. The practical question presents itself: Is the immediate restoration of the late rebel States to absolute self-control so necessary that it must be done even at the risk of endangering one of the great results of the war, and of bringing on in those States insurrection or anarchy, or would it not be better to postpone that restoration until such dangers are passed? If, as long as the change from slavery to free labor is known to the Southern people only by its destructive results, these people must be expected to throw obstacles in its way, would it not seem necessary that the movement of social "reconstruction" be kept in the right channel by the hand of the power which originated the change, until that change can have disclosed some of its beneficial effects?

It is certain that every success of free negro labor will augment the number of its friends, and disarm some of the prejudices and assumptions of its opponents. I am convinced one good harvest made by unadulterated free labor in the South would have a far better effect than all the oaths that have been taken, and all the ordinances that have as yet been passed by Southern conventions. But how can such a result be attained? The facts enumerated in this report, as well as the news we receive from the South from day to day, must make it evident to every unbiased observer that unadulterated free labor cannot be had at present, unless the National Government holds its protective and controlling hand over it. It appears, also, that the more efficient this protection of free labor against all disturbing and reactionary influences, the sooner may such a satisfactory result be looked for. One reason why the Southern people are so slow in accommodating themselves to the new order of things is, that they confidently expect soon to be permitted to regulate matters according to their own notions. Every concession made to them by the Government has been taken as an encouragement to persevere in this hope, and, unfortunately for them, this hope is nourished by influences from other parts of the country. Hence their anxiety to have their State governments restored *at once,* to have the troops withdrawn, and the Freedmen's Bureau abolished, although a good many discerning men know well that, in view of the lawless spirit still prevailing, it would be far better for them to have the general order of society firmly maintained by the Federal power until things have arrived at a final settlement. Had, from the beginning, the conviction been forced upon them that the adulteration of the new order of things by the admixture of elements belonging to the system of slavery would under no circumstances be permitted, a much larger number would have launched their energies into the new channel, and, seeing that they could do no "better," faithfully coöperated with the Government. It is hope which fixes them in their perverse notions. That hope nourished or fully gratified, they will persevere in the same direction. That hope destroyed, a great many will, by the force of necessity, at once accommodate themselves to the logic of the change. If, therefore, the National Government firmly and unequivocally announces its policy not to give up the control of the free-labor reform until it is finally accomplished, the progress of that reform will undoubtedly be far more rapid and far less difficult than it will be if the attitude of the Government is such as to permit contrary hopes to be indulged in. . . .

NEGRO SUFFRAGE

It would seem that the interference of the National authority in the home concerns of the Southern States would be rendered less necessary, and the whole problem of political and social reconstruction be much simplified, if, while the masses lately arrayed against the Government are permitted to vote, the large majority of those who were always loyal, and are naturally anxious to see the free-labor problem successfully solved, were not excluded from all influence upon legislation. In all questions concerning the Union, the National debt, and the future social organization of the South, the feelings of the colored man are naturally in sympathy with the views and aims of the National Government. While the Southern white fought against the Union, the negro did all he could to aid it; while the Southern white sees in the National Government his conqueror, the negro sees in it his protector; while the white owes to the National debt his defeat, the negro owes to it his deliverance; while the white considers himself robbed and ruined by the emancipation of the slaves, the negro finds in it the assurance of future prosperity and happiness. In all the important issues the negro would be led by natural impulse to forward the ends of the Government, and by making his influence, as part of the voting body, tell upon the legislation of the States, render the interference of the National authority less necessary.

As the most difficult of the pending questions are intimately connected with the status of the negro in Southern society, it is obvious that a correct solution can be more easily obtained if he has a voice in the matter. In the right to vote he would find the best permanent protection against oppressive class-legislation, as well as against individual persecution. The relations between the white and black races, even if improved by the gradual wearing off of the present animosities, are likely to remain long under the troubling influence of prejudice. It is a notorious fact that the rights of a man of some political power are far less exposed to violation than those of one who is, in matters of public interest, completely subject to the will of others. A voter is a man of influence; small as that influence may be in the single individual, it becomes larger when that individual belongs to a numerous class of voters who are ready to make common cause with him for the protection of his rights. Such an individual is an object of interest to the political parties that desire to have the benefit of his ballot. It is true, the bringing face to face at the ballot-box of the white and black races may here and there lead to an outbreak of feeling, and the first trials ought certainly to be made while the National power is still there to prevent or repress disturbances; but the practice once successfully inaugurated under the protection of that power, it would probably be more apt than anything else to obliterate old antagonisms, especially if the colored people — which is probable, as soon as their own rights are sufficiently secured — divide their votes between the different political parties.

The effect of the extension of the franchise to the colored people upon the development of free labor and upon the security of human rights in the South being the principal object in view, the objections raised on the ground of the ignorance of the freedmen become unimportant. Practical liberty is a good school, and, besides, if any qualification can be found, applicable to both races, which does not interfere with the attainment of the main object, such qualification would in that respect be unobjectionable. But it is idle to say that it will be time to speak of negro suffrage when the whole colored race will be educated, for the ballot may be necessary to him to secure his education. It is also idle to say that ignorance is the principal ground upon which Southern men object to negro suffrage, for if it were, that numerous class of colored people in Louisiana who are as highly educated, as intelligent and as wealthy as any corresponding class of whites, would have been enfranchised long ago.

It has been asserted that the negro would be but a voting machine in the hand of his employer. On this point opinions seem to differ. I have heard it said in the South that the freedmen are more likely to be influenced by their schoolmasters and preachers. But even if we suppose the employer to control to a certain extent the negro laborer's vote, two things are to be taken into consideration: (1) The class of employers, of landed proprietors, will in a few years be very different from what it was heretofore; in consequence of the general breaking up, a great many of the old slaveholders will be obliged to give up their lands and new men will step into their places; and (2) the employer will hardly control the vote of the negro laborer so far as to make him vote against his own liberty. The beneficial effect of an extension of suffrage does not always depend upon the intelligence with which the newly admitted voters exercise their right, but sometimes upon the circumstances in which they are placed; and the circumstances in which the freedmen of the South are placed are such that, when they vote only for their own liberty and rights, they vote for the rights of free labor, for the success of immediate important reform, for the prosperity of the country, and for the general interests of mankind. If, therefore, in order to control the colored vote, the employer, or whoever he may be, is first obliged to concede to the freedman the great point of his own rights as a man and a free laborer, the great social reform is completed, the most difficult problem is solved, and all other questions it will be comparatively easy to settle.

In discussing the matter of negro suffrage I deemed it my duty to confine myself strictly to the practical aspects of the subject. I have, therefore, not touched its moral merits nor discussed the question whether the National Government is competent to enlarge the elective franchise in the States lately in rebellion by its own act; I deem it proper, however, to offer a few remarks on the assertion frequently put forth, that the franchise is likely to be extended to the colored man by the voluntary action of the Southern whites themselves. My observation leads me to a contrary opinion. Aside from a very few enlightened men, I found but one class of people in favor of the enfranchisement of the blacks; it was the class of Unionists who found themselves politically ostracised and looked upon the enfranchisement of the loyal negroes as the salvation of the whole loyal element. But their numbers and influence are sadly insufficient to secure such a result. The masses are strongly opposed to colored suffrage; anybody that dares to advocate it is stigmatized as a dangerous fanatic; nor do I deem it probable that in the ordinary course of things prejudices will wear off to such an extent as to make it a popular measure. Outside of Louisiana only one gentleman who occupied a prominent political position in the South expressed to me an opinion favorable to it. He declared himself ready to vote for an amendment to the constitution of his State bestowing the right of suffrage upon all male citizens without distinction of color who could furnish evidence of their ability to read and write, without, however, disfranchising those who are now voters and are not able to fulfil that condition. This gentleman is now a member of one of the State conventions, but I presume he will not risk his political standing in the South by moving such an amendment in that body.

The only manner in which, in my opinion, the Southern people can be induced to grant to the freedman some measure of self-protecting power in the form of suffrage, is to make it a condition precedent to "readmission." . . .

Charles Sumner

JUSTICE FOR THE FORMER SLAVE

{1872} As a United States Senator, Charles Sumner (1811-1874) was almost unique in certain respects. For one thing, he was elected to the Senate with practically no previous experience in politics. For another, he was not the usual politician-type but was, instead, a "statesman doctrinaire" who took as his guide a set of inflexible moral principles rather than the shifting considerations of day-to-day expediency.

Sumner first won fame — or notoriety — with his 1856 "Crime against Kansas" speech, learnedly written and carefully rehearsed, in which he thoroughly damned slavery and the South. This philippic so enraged Southerners that one of them, Congressman Preston Brooks (1819-1857) of South Carolina, attacked Sumner with a cane and beat him almost senseless. Sumner thus became a martyr of the free-soil and antislavery cause.

His career touched upon most of the significant movements of his time. He was an advocate of international peace and of school and prison reform, one of the founders of the Republican Party, a leader of the Radical Republicans during and after the Civil War, and a promoter of the Liberal Republican campaign in 1872. As chairman of the Senate Committee on Foreign Relations, he made himself a powerful critic of American diplomacy during the Grant administration.

In opposing racial discrimination, Sumner was both consistent and persistent. As early as 1849 he challenged the legality of segregated schools in his home town, Boston. He maintained that both white and Negro children suffered from attending separate schools and that, no matter how good the facilities provided for Negroes, "the separate school is not an equivalent." Six years later the Massachusetts legislature, dominated by his friends, outlawed racial segregation in all the public schools of the Commonwealth. During the Civil War and after, he was the foremost Senate champion of emancipation for the slaves and then of political and legal rights for the freedmen.

In 1870 he brought in, as a supplement to the Civil Rights Act of 1866, a bill to prohibit the assignment of Negroes to separate facilities in public conveyances or public places, including schools. In 1871 he reintroduced his bill as an amendment to another bill for giving amnesty to leading ex-Confederates who had been deprived of political rights under the Fourteenth Amendment, and on January 15, 1872, he made a speech in favor of his amendment (most of this speech is included in the selection reprinted here). Not till 1875, after his death, did Congress finally pass his proposals, and even then they were not destined, for many years, to gain the popular and judicial support needed for their enforcement. But Sumner had been prophetic. A day was to come (in 1954) when the Supreme Court would adopt the very position he had held — that "separate but equal" is a contradiction in terms.

EQUAL RIGHTS

Mr. President, Slavery, in its foremost pretensions, reappears in the present debate. Again the barbarous tyranny stalks into this Chamber, denying to a whole race the Equal Rights promised by a just citizenship. Some have thought Slavery dead. This is a mistake. If not in body, at least in spirit, or as a ghost making the country hideous, the ancient criminal yet lingers among us, insisting upon the continued degradation of a race.

Property in man has ceased to exist. The human auction-block has departed. No human being can call himself master, with impious power to separate husband and wife, to sell child from parent, to shut out the opportunities of religion, to close the gates of knowledge, and to rob another of his labor and all its fruits. These guilty prerogatives are ended. To this extent the slave is free. No longer a chattel, he is a man, — justly entitled to all that is accorded by law to any other man.

Such is the irresistible logic of his emancipation. Ceasing to be a slave, he became a man, whose foremost right is Equality of Rights. And yet Slavery has been strong enough to postpone his entry into the great possession. Cruelly, he was not permitted to testify in court; most unjustly, he was not allowed to vote. More than four millions of people, whose only offence was a skin once the badge of Slavery, were shut out from the court-room, and also from the ballot-box, in open defiance of the great Declaration of our fathers, that all men are equal in rights, and that just government stands only on the consent of the governed. Such was the impudent behest of Slavery, prolonged after it was reported dead. At last these crying wrongs are overturned. The slave testifies; the slave votes. To this extent his equality is recognized.

Equality before the Law

But this is not enough. Much as it may seem, compared with the past, when all was denied, it is too little, because all is not yet recognized. The denial of any right is a wrong darkening the enjoyment of all the rest. Besides the right to testify and the right to vote, there are other rights without which Equality does not exist. The precise rule is Equality before the Law, nor more nor less; that is, that condition before the law in which all are alike, — being entitled, without discrimination, to the equal enjoyment of all institutions, privileges, advantages, and conveniences created or regulated by law, among which are the right to testify and the right to vote. But this plain requirement is not satisfied, logically or reasonably, by these two concessions, so that when they are recognized all others are trifles. The court-house and the ballot-box are not the only places for the rule. These two are not the only institutions for its operation. The rule is general; how, then, restrict it to two cases? It is, *All are equal before the law,* — not merely before the law in two cases, but before the law in all cases, without limitation or exception. Important as it is to testify and to vote, life is not all contained even in these possessions.

The new-made citizen is called to travel for business, for health, or for pleasure; but here his trials begin. His money, whether gold or paper, is the same as the white man's; but the doors of the public hotel, which from the earliest days of jurisprudence have always opened hospitably to the stranger, close against him, and the public conveyances, which the Common Law declares equally free to all alike, have no such freedom for him.

He longs, perhaps, for respite and relaxation at some place of public amusement, duly licensed by law; and here also the same adverse discrimination is made. With the anxieties of a parent, seeking the welfare of his child, he strives to bestow upon him the inestimable blessings of education, and takes him affectionately to the common school, created by law, and supported by the taxation to which he has contributed; but these doors slam rudely in the face of the child where is garnered up the parent's heart. "Suffer little children, and forbid them not, to come unto me": such were the words of the Divine Master. But among us little children are turned away and forbidden at the door of the common school, because of the skin. And the same insulting ostracism shows itself in other institutions of science and learning, also in the church, and in the last resting-place on earth. . . .

Equality in rights is not only the first of rights, it is an axiom of political truth. But an axiom, whether of science or philosophy, is universal, and without exception or limitation; and this is according to the very law of its nature. Therefore it is not stating an axiom to announce grandly that only white men are equal in rights; nor is it stating an axiom to announce with the same grandeur that all persons are equal in rights, but that colored persons have no rights except to testify and vote. Nor is it a self-evident truth, as declared; for no truth is self-evident which is not universal. The asserted limitation destroys the original Declaration, making it a ridiculous sham, instead of that sublime Magna Charta before which kings, nobles, and all inequalities of birth must disappear as ghosts of night at the dawn.

Real Issue of the War

All this has additional force, when it is known that this very axiom or self-evident truth declared by our fathers was the real issue of the war, and was so publicly announced by the leaders on both sides. Behind the embattled armies were ideas, and the idea on our side was Equality in Rights, which on the other side was denied. The Nation insisted that all men are created equal; the Rebellion insisted that all men are created unequal. Here the evidence is explicit.

The inequality of men was an original postulate of Mr. Calhoun, which found final expression in the open denunciation of the self-evident truth as "a self-evident lie." Echoing this denunciation, Jefferson Davis, on leaving the Senate, January 21, 1861, in that farewell speech which some among you heard, but which all may read in the "Globe," made the issue in these words: —

"It has been a belief that we are to be deprived in the Union of the rights which our fathers bequested to us, which has brought Mississippi into her present decision. *She has heard proclaimed the theory that all men are created free and equal, and this made the basis of an attack upon her social institutions; and the sacred Declaration of Independence has been invoked to maintain the position of the equality of the races."*

The issue thus made by the chief Rebel was promptly joined. Abraham Lincoln, the elected President, stopping at Independence Hall, February 22d, on his way to assume his duties at the National capital, in unpremeditated words thus interpreted the Declaration: —

"It was that which gave promise that in due time the weight should be lifted from the shoulders of all men, *and that all should have an equal chance.*"

Mark, if you please, the simplicity of this utterance. All are to have "an equal chance"; and this, he said, "is the sentiment embodied in the Declaration of Independence." Then, in reply to Jefferson Davis, he proceeded: —

"Now, my friends, can this country be saved upon that basis? If it can, I shall consider myself one of the happiest men in the world, if I can help to save it. If it cannot be saved upon that principle, it will be truly awful. But if this country cannot be saved without giving up that principle, I was about to say I would rather be assassinated on this spot than surrender it."

Giving these words still further solemnity, he added:

"I have said nothing but what I am willing to live by, and, if it be the pleasure of Almighty God, to die by."

And then, before raising the national banner over the historic Hall, he said: —

"It is on such an occasion as this that we can reason together, and reaffirm our devotion to the country and the principles of the Declaration of Independence."

Thus the gauntlet flung down by Jefferson Davis was taken up by Abraham Lincoln, who never forgot the issue.

The rejoinder was made by Alexander H. Stephens, Vice-President of the Rebellion, in a not-to-be forgotten speech at Savannah, March 21, 1861, when he did not hesitate to declare of the pretended Government, that —

"Its foundations are laid, its corner-stone rests, upon *the great truth that the Negro is not equal to the white man.*"

Then, glorying in this terrible shame, he added: —

"This, our new Government, is the first, in the history of the world, based upon this great physical, philosophical, and moral truth."

"This stone, which was rejected by the first builders, is become the chief stone of the corner."

To this unblushing avowal Abraham Lincoln replied in that marvelous, undying utterance at Gettysburg, — fit voice for the Republic, greater far than any victory:

"Fourscore and seven years ago our fathers brought forth on this continent a new Nation, *conceived in Liberty, and dedicated to the proposition that all men are created equal.*"

Thus, in precise conformity with the Declaration, was it announced that our Republic is dedicated to the Equal Rights of All; and then the prophet-President, soon to be a martyr, asked his countrymen to dedicate themselves to the great task remaining, highly resolving

"that this Nation, under God, shall have a new birth of Freedom; and that Government of the people, by the people, and for the people shall not perish from the earth."

The victory of the war is vain without the grander victory through which the Republic is dedicated to the axiomatic, self-evident truth declared by our fathers, and reasserted by Abraham Lincoln. With this mighty truth as a guiding principle, the National Constitution is elevated, and made more than ever a protection to the citizen.

All this is so plain that it is difficult to argue it. What is the Republic, if it fails in this loyalty? What is the National Government, coextensive with the Republic, if fellow-citizens, counted by the million, can be shut out from equal rights in travel, in recreation, in education, and in other things, all contributing to human necessities? Where is that great promise by which "the pursuit of happiness" is placed, with life and liberty, under the safeguard of axiomatic, self-evident truth? Where is justice, if this ban of color is not promptly removed? Where is humanity? Where is reason?

Two Excuses

The two excuses show how irrational and utterly groundless is this pretension. They are on a par with the pretension itself. One is, that the question is of society, and not of rights, which is clearly a misrepresentation; and the other is, that the separate arrangements provided for colored persons constitute a substitute for equality in the nature of an equivalent, — all of which is clearly a contrivance, if not a trick: as if there could be any equivalent for equality.

No Question of Society

Of the first excuse it is difficult to speak with patience. It is a simple misrepresentation, and wherever it shows itself must be treated as such. There is no colored person who does not resent the imputation that he is seeking to intrude himself socially anywhere. This is no question of society, no question of social life, no question of social equality, if anybody knows what this means. The object is simply Equality before the Law, a term which explains itself. Now, as the law does not presume to create or regulate social relations, these are in no respect affected by the pending measure. Each person, whether Senator or citizen, is always free to choose who shall be his friend, his associate, his guest. And does not the ancient proverb declare that "a man is known by the company he keeps"? But this assumes that he may choose for himself. His house is his "castle"; and this very designation, borrowed from the Common Law, shows his absolute independence within its walls; nor is there any difference, whether it be palace or hovel. But when he leaves his "castle" and goes abroad, this independence is at an end. He walks the streets, but always subject to the prevailing law of Equality; nor can he appropriate the sidewalk to his own exclusive use, driving into the gutter all whose skin is less white than his own. But nobody pretends that Equality in the highway, whether on pavement or sidewalk, is a question of society. And permit me to say that Equality in all institutions created or regulated by law is as little a question of society.

In the days of Slavery it was an oft-repeated charge, that Emancipation was a measure of social equality; and the same charge became a cry at the successive efforts for the right to testify and the right to vote. At each stage the cry was raised, and now it makes itself heard again, as you are called to assure this crowning safeguard.

Equality not Found in Equivalents

Then comes the other excuse, which finds Equality in separation. Separate hotels, separate conveyances, separate theatres, separate schools and institutions of learning and science, separate churches, and separate cemeteries, — these are the artificial substitutes. And this is the contrivance by which a transcendent right, involving a transcendent duty, is evaded: for Equality is not only a right, but a duty.

How vain to argue that there is no denial of Equal Rights when this separation is enforced! The substitute is invariably an inferior article. Does any Senator deny it? Therefore, it is not Equality; at best it is an equivalent only. But no equivalent is Equality. Separation imples one thing for a white person and another thing for a colored person; but Equality is where all have the same alike. There can be no substitute for Equality, — nothing but itself. Even if accommodations are the same, as notoriously they are not, there is no Equality. In the process of substitution the vital elixir exhales and escapes: it is lost, and cannot be recovered; for Equality is found only in Equality. "Nought but itself can be its parallel"; but Senators undertake to find parallels in other things. . . .

Assuming — what is most absurd to assume, and what is contradicted by all experience — that a substitute can be an equivalent, it is so in form only, and not in reality. Every such assumption is an indignity to the colored race, instinct with the spirit of Slavery; and this decides its character. It is Slavery in its last appearance. Are you ready to prolong the hateful tyranny? Religion and reason condemn Caste as impious and unchristian making republican institutions and equal laws impossible; but here is Caste not unlike that which separates the Sudra from the Brahmin. Pray, Sir, who constitutes the white man a Brahmin? Whence his lordly title? Down to a recent period in Europe the Jews were driven to herd by themselves, separate from the Christians; but this discarded barbarism is revived among us in the ban of color. There are millions of fellow-citizens guilty of no offence except the dusky livery of the sun appointed by the Heavenly Father, whom you treat as others have treated the Jews, as the Brahmin treats the Sudra. But, pray, Sir, do not pretend that this is the great equality promised by our fathers.

In arraigning this attempt at separation as a Caste, I say nothing new. For years I have denounced it as such; and here I followed good authorities, as well as reason. Alexander von Humboldt, speaking of the negroes of New Mexico when Slavery prevailed, called them a Caste. A recent political and juridical writer of France uses the same term to denote not only the discrimination in India, but that in our own country, — especially referring to the exclusion of colored children from the common schools as among "the humiliating and brutal distinctions" by which their Caste is characterized. The principle of separation on the ground of hereditary inferiority is the distinctive essence of Caste; but this is the outrage which flaunts in our country, crying out, "I am better than thou, because I am white. Get away!"

The Remedy

Thus do I reject the two excuses. But I do not leave the cause here. I go further, and show how consistent is the pending measure with acknowledged principles, illustrated by undoubted law.

The bill for Equal Rights is simply supplementary to the existing Civil

Rights Law, which is one of our great statutes of peace, and it stands on the same requirement of the National Constitution. If the Civil Rights Law is above question, as cannot be doubted, then also is this supplementary amendment; for it is only the complement of the other, and necessary to its completion. Without this amendment the original law is imperfect. It cannot be said, according to its title, that all persons are protected in their civil rights, so long as the outrages I expose continue to exist; nor is Slavery entirely dead.

Following reason and authority, the conclusion is easy. A Law Dictionary, of constant use as a repertory of established rules and principles, defines a "freeman" as "one in the possession of *the civil rights* enjoyed by the people generally." Happily, all are freemen now; but the colored people are still excluded from civil rights enjoyed by the people generally — and this, too, in the face of our new Bill of Rights intended for their especial protection.

By the Constitutional Amendment abolishing Slavery Congress is empowered "to enforce this article by appropriate legislation"; and in pursuance thereof the Civil Rights Law was enacted. That measure was justly accepted as "appropriate legislation." Without it Slavery would still exist in at least one of its most odious pretensions. By the Civil Rights Law colored persons were assured in the right to testify, which in most of the States was denied or abridged. So closely was this outrage connected with Slavery, that it was, indeed, part of this great wrong. Therefore its prohibition was "appropriate legislation" in the enforcement of the Constitutional Amendment. But the denial or abridgment of Equality on account of color is also part of Slavery. So long as it exists, Slavery is still present among us. Its prohibition is not only "appropriate," but necessary, to enforce the Constitional Amendment. Therefore it is strictly Constitutional, as if in the very text of the National Constitution.

The next Constitutional Amendment, known as the Fourteenth, contains two different provisions, which augment the power of Congress. The first furnishes the definition of "citizen," which down to this time had been left to construction only: —

"*All persons* born or naturalized in the United States, and subject to the jurisdiction thereof, are *citizens* of the United States, and of the States wherever they reside."

Here, you will remark, are no words of race or color. "*All* persons," and not "*all white* persons," born or naturalized in the United States, and subject to the jurisdiction thereof, are "citizens." Such is the definition supplied by this Amendment. This is followed by another provision in aid of the definition: —

"No State shall make or enforce any law which shall abridge the privileges or immunities of citizens of the United States; nor shall any State deprive any person of life, liberty, or property without due process of law, *nor deny to any person within its jurisdiction the equal protection of the laws.*"

And Congress is empowered to enforce this definition of Citizenship and this guaranty, by "appropriate legislation."

Here, then, are two Constitutional Amendments, each a fountain of power: the first, to enforce the Abolition of Slavery; and the second, to assure the privileges and immunities of citizens, and also the equal protection of the laws. If the Supplementary Civil Rights Bill, moved by me, is not within these accumulated powers, I am at a loss to know what is within those powers.

In considering these Constitutional provisions, I insist upon that interpretation which shall give them the most generous expansion, so that they shall be truly efficacious for human rights. Once Slavery was the animating principle in determining the meaning of the National Constitution: happily, it is so no longer. Another principle is now supreme, breathing into the whole the breath of a new life, and filling it in every part with one pervading, controlling sentiment, — being that great principle of Equality which triumphed at last on the battle-field, and, bearing the watchword of the Republic, now supplies the rule by which every word of the Constitution and all its parts must be interpreted, as much as if written in its text.

There is also an original provision of the National Constitution, not to be forgotten: —

"The citizens of each State shall be entitled to all privileges and immunities of citizens in the several States."

Once a sterile letter, this is now a fruitful safeguard, to be interpreted, like all else, so that human rights shall most prevail. The term "privileges and immunities" was at an early day authoritatively defined by Judge Washington, who announced that they embraced "protection by the Government, the enjoyment of life and liberty, with the right to acquire and possess property of every kind, and to *pursue and obtain happiness and safety,* . . . the right of a citizen of one State to pass through or to reside in any other State, for purposes of trade, agricultue, professional pursuits, or otherwise." But these "privileges and immunities" are protected by the present measure.

No doubt the Supplementary Law must operate, not only in National jurisdiction, but also in the States, precisely as the Civil Rights Law; otherwise it will be of little value. Its sphere must be coextensive with the Republic, making the rights of the citizen uniform everywhere. But this can be only by one uniform safeguard sustained by the Nation. Citizenship is universal, and the same everywhere. It cannot be more or less in one State than in another.

But legislation is not enough. An enlightened public opinion must be invoked. Nor will this be wanting. The country will rally in aid of the law, more especially since it is a measure of justice and humanity. The law is needed now as a help to public opinion. It is needed by the very people whose present conduct makes occasion for it. Prompted by the law, leaning on the law, they will recognize the equal rights of all; nor do I despair of a public opinion which shall stamp the denial of these rights as an outrage not unlike Slavery itself. Custom and patronage will then be sought in obeying the law. . . .

In the absence of the law people please too often by inhumanity, but with the law teaching the lesson of duty they will please by humanity. Thus will the law be an instrument of improvement, necessary in precise proportion to the existing prejudice. Because people still please by inhumanity, therefore must there be a counteracting force. . . .

Common Schools

The Common School . . . must open to all, or its designation is a misnomer and a mockery. It is not a school for whites, or a school for blacks, but a school for all, — in other words, a common school. . . . Its object is the education of the young; and it is sustained by taxation, to which all contribute. Not only does it hold itself out to the public by its name . . . but it assumes the place of parent to all children within its locality, bound always to exercise a parent's watchful care and tenderness, which can know no distinction of child.

It is easy to see that the separate school, founded on an odious discrimination, and sometimes offered as an equivalent for the common school, is an ill-disguised violation of the principle of Equality, while as a pretended equivalent it is an utter failure, and instead of a parent is only a churlish step-mother.

A slight illustration will show how it fails; and here I mention an incident occurring in Washington, but which must repeat itself often on a larger scale, wherever separation is attempted. Colored children, living near what is called the common school, are driven from its doors, and compelled to walk a considerable distance — often troublesome, and in certain conditions of the weather difficult — to attend the separate school. One of these children has suffered from this exposure, and I have myself witnessed the emotion of the parent. This could not have occurred, had the child been received at the common schools in the neighborhood. Now it is idle to assert that children compelled to this exceptional journey to and fro are in the enjoyment of Equal Rights. The superadded pedestrianism and its attendant discomfort furnish the measure of Inequality in one of its forms, increased by the weakness or ill-health of the child. What must be the feelings of a colored father or mother daily witnessing this sacrifice to the demon of Caste?

This is an illustration merely, but it shows precisely how impossible it is for a separate school to be the equivalent of the common school. And yet it only touches the evil, without exhibiting its proportions. The indignity offered to the colored child is worse than any compulsory exposure; and here not only the child suffers, but the race to which he belongs is degraded, and the whole community is hardened in wrong.

The separate school wants the first requisite of the common school, inasmuch as it is not equally open to all; and since this is inconsistent with the declared rule of republican institutions, such a school is not republican in character. Therefore it is not a preparation for the duties of life. The child is not trained in the way he should go; for he is trained under the ban of Inequality. How can he grow up to the stature of equal citizenship? He is pinched and dwarfed while the stigma of color is stamped upon him. This is plain oppression, which you, Sir, would feel keenly, were it directed against you or your child. Surely the race enslaved for generations has suffered enough without being doomed to this prolonged proscription. Will not the Republic, redeemed by most costly sacrifice, insist upon justice to the children of the land, making the common school the benign example of republican institutions, where merit is the only ground of favor?

Nor is separation without evil to the whites. The prejudice of color is nursed, when it should be stifled. The Pharisaism of race becomes an element of character, when, like all other Pharisaisms, it should be cast out. Better even than knowledge is a kindly nature and the sentiment of equality. Such should be the constant lesson, repeated by the lips and inscribed on the heart; but the school itself must practise the lesson. Children learn by example more than by precept. How precious the example which teaches that all are equal in rights! But this can be only where all commingle in the common school as in common citizenship. There is no separate ballot-box: there should be no separate school. It is not enough that all should be taught alike; they must all be taught together. They are not only to receive equal quantities of knowledge; all are to receive it in the same way. But they cannot be taught alike, unless all are taught together; nor can they receive equal quantities of knowledge in the same way, except at the common school.

The common school is important to all; but to the colored child it is a necessity. Excluded from the common school, he finds himself too frequently without any substitute. But even where a separate school is planted, it is inferior in character, buildings, furniture, books, teachers: all are second-rate. No matter what the temporary disposition, the separate school will not flourish as the common school. It is but an offshoot or sucker, without the strength of the parent stem. That the two must differ is seen at once; and that this difference is adverse to the colored child is equally apparent. For him there is no assurance of education except in the common school, where he will be under the safeguard of all. White parents will take care not only that the common school is not neglected, but that its teachers and means of instruction are the best possible; and the colored child will have the benefit of this watchfulness. This decisive consideration completes the irresistible argument for the common school as the equal parent of all without distinction of color.

If to him that hath is given, according to the way of the world, it is not doubted that to him that hath not there is a positive duty in proportion to the necessity. Unhappily, our colored fellow-citizens are in this condition. But just in proportion as they are weak, and not yet recovered from the degradation in which they have been plunged, does the Republic owe its completest support and protection. Already a component part of our political corporation, they must become part of the educational corporation also, with Equality as the supreme law. . . .

James S. Pike

SOUTH CAROLINA UNDER NEGRO GOVERNMENT

1873 As a condemnation of Radical Reconstruction, James S. Pike's *The Prostrate State: South Carolina under Negro Government* (1873) is a classic. The author, a Maine Republican and former abolitionist, appeared to be a most trustworthy witness because of his background. Contemporaries quoted and endorsed him as one "who, in view of his long and enthusiastic service in the anti-slavery cause, can hardly be accused of color-prejudice." Later historians cited him as a "Republican authority"; one of them praised his book as "the 'Uncle Tom's Cabin' of the redemption of the South." Certainly no other single work did so much to disillusion Northerners about Radical Reconstruction and prepare them for accepting the restoration of "white supremacy" in the South. Pike's description of rascality and misrule formed an image of the Negro-and-carpetbagger governments that still prevails in the popular mind.

Yet, as Robert F. Durden has recently shown, Pike (1811-1882) was by no means so disinterested as he seemed. Though indeed a veteran of the abolitionist crusade, he also was and always had been a Negrophobe. During the Civil War he had even proposed that the freed slaves be either deported or confined on a vast reservation, a "Negro pen," set aside for them within the conquered South. Moreover, when he made his reporting tour to South Carolina in 1873, he could hardly be described, without qualification, as a Republican. A friend of Horace Greeley (1811-1872), he had broken away from the regular party, denounced President U. S. Grant (1822-1885), and supported the Liberal Republican and Democratic candidate, Greeley, in the presidential campaign of 1872. After the failure of the Liberal Republican movement, Pike continued his attack on the Grant administration and its Negro and carpetbag following in the South. One way for him to discredit the Grant Republicans was to paint Radical Reconstruction in as bad a light as possible. His actual views, as he recorded them in the private journal of his travels, were far less severe than the strictures he published in a series of newspaper reports and then in his book.

The first four chapters of the book provide an adequate sampling of his published views.

THE PROSTRATE STATE

CHAPTER I

A Black Parliament. — Humiliation of the Whites. — Society Bottom-Side Up. — An Extraordinary Spectacle.

COLUMBIA, the capital of South Carolina, is charmingly situated in the heart of the upland country, near the geographical centre of the State. It has broad, open streets, regularly laid out, and fine, shady residences in and about the town. The opportunity for rides and drives can hardly be surpassed. There are good animals and good turnouts to be seen on the streets at all times; and now, in midwinter, the weather invites to such displays. It seems there was a little real winter here at Christmas and New Year's, when the whole country suffered such an excess of sudden cold. There was even skating and sleighing for a week. But now there is no frost, and the recollection of it is dispelled by the genial spring weather that prevails.

Yesterday, about 4 P.M., the assembled wisdom of the State, whose achievements are illustrated on that theatre, issued forth from the State-House. About three-quarters of the crowd belonged to the African race. They were of every hue, from the light octoroon to the deep black. They were such a looking body of men as might pour out of a market-house or a court-house at random in any Southern State. Every negro type and physiognomy was here to be seen, from the genteel serving-man to the rough-hewn customer from the rice or cotton field. Their dress was as varied as their countenances. There was the second-hand black frock-coat of infirm gentility, glossy and threadbare. There were the stove-pipe hat of many ironings and departed styles. There were also to be seen a total disregard of the proprieties of costume in the coarse and dirty garments of the field; the stub-jackets and slouch hats of soiling labor. In some instances, rough woolen comforters embraced the neck and hid the absence of linen. Heavy brogans, and short, torn trousers, it was impossible to hide. The dusky tide flowed out into the littered and barren grounds, and, issuing through the coarse wooden fence of the inclosure, melted away into the street beyond. These were the legislators of South Carolina.

In conspicuous base-relief over the door of exit, on the panels of the stately edifice, the marble visages of George McDuffie and Robert Y. Hayne overlooked the scene. Could they veritably witness it from their dread abode? What then? "I tremble," wrote Jefferson, when depicting the character of Southern slavery, "I tremble when I reflect that God is just." But did any of that old band of Southern Revolutionary patriots who wrestled in their souls with the curse of slavery ever contemplate such a descent into barbarism as this spectacle implied and typified? "My God, look at this!" was the unbidden ejaculation of a low-country planter, clad in homespun, as he leaned over the rail inside the House, gazing excitedly upon the body in session. "This is the first time I have been here. I thought I knew what we were doing when we consented to emancipation. I knew the negro, and I predicted much that has happened, but I never thought it would come to this. Let me go."

Here, then, is the outcome, the ripe, perfected fruit of the boasted civilization of the South, after two hundred years of experience. A white community, that had gradually risen from small beginnings, till it grew into wealth, culture, and refinement, and became accomplished in all the arts of civilization; that successfully asserted its resistance to a foreign tyranny by deeds of conspicuous valor, which achieved liberty and independence through the fire and tempest of civil war, and illustrated itself in the councils of the nation by orators and statesmen worthy of any age or nation — such a community is then reduced to this. It lies prostrate in the dust, ruled over by this strange conglomerate, gathered from the ranks of its own servile population. It is the spectacle of a society suddenly turned bottomside up. The wealth, the intelligence, the culture, the wisdom of the State, have broken through the crust of that social volcano on which they were contentedly reposing, and have sunk out of sight, consumed by the subterranean fires they had with such temerity braved and defied.

In the place of this old aristocratic society stands the rude form of the most ignorant democracy that mankind ever saw, invested with the functions of government. It is the dregs of the population habilitated in the robes of their intelligent predecessors, and asserting over them the rule of ignorance and corruption, through the inexorable machinery of a majority of numbers. It is barbarism overwhelming civilization by physical force. It is the slave rioting in the halls of his master, and putting that master under his feet. And, though it is done without malice and without vengeance, it is nevertheless none the less completely and absolutely done. Let us approach nearer and take a closer view. We will enter the House of Representatives. Here sit one hundred and twenty-four members. Of these, twenty-three are white men, representing the remains of the old civilization. These are good-looking, substantial citizens. They are men of weight and standing in the communities they represent. They are all from the hill country. The frosts of sixty and seventy winters whiten the heads of some among them. There they sit, grim and silent. They feel themselves to be but loose stones, thrown in to partially obstruct a current they are powerless to resist. They say little and do little as the days go by. They simply watch the rising tide, and mark the progressive steps of the inundation. They hold their places reluctantly. They feel themselves to be in some sort martyrs, bound stoically to suffer in behalf of that still great element in the State whose prostrate fortunes are becoming the sport of an unpitying Fate. Grouped in a corner of the commodious and well-furnished chamber, they stolidly survey the noisy riot that goes on in the great black Left and Centre, where the business and debates of the House are conducted, and where sit the strange and extraordinary guides of the fortunes of a once proud and haughty State. In this crucial trial of his pride, his manhood, his prejudices, his spirit, it must be said of the Southern Bourbon of the Legislature that he comports himself with a dignity, a reserve, and a decorum, that command admiration. He feels that the iron hand of Destiny is upon him. He is gloomy, disconsolate, hopeless. The gray heads of this generation openly profess that they look for no relief. They see no way of escape. The recovery of influence, of position, of control in the State, is felt by them to be impossible. They accept their position with a stoicism that promises no reward here or hereafter. They are the types of a conquered race. They staked all and lost all. Their lives remain, their property and their children do not. War, emancipation, and grinding taxation, have consumed them. Their struggle now is against complete confiscation. They endure, and wait for the night.

This dense negro crowd they confront do the debating, the squabbling, the law-making, and create all the clamor and disorder of the body. These twenty-three white men are but the observers, the enforced auditors of the dull and clumsy imitation of a deliberative body, whose appearance in their present capacity is at once a wonder and a shame to modern civilization.

Deducting the twenty-three members referred to, who comprise the entire strength of the opposition, we find one hundred and one remaining. Of this one hundred and one, ninety-four are colored, and seven are their white allies. Thus the blacks outnumber the whole body of whites in the House more than three to one. On the mere basis of numbers in the State the injustices of this disproportion is manifest, since the black population is relatively four to three of the whites. A just rectification of the disproportion, on the basis of population merely, would give fifty-four whites to seventy black members. And the line of race very nearly marks the line of hostile politics. As things stand, the body is almost literally a Black Parliament, and it is the only one on the face of the earth which is the representative of a white constituency and the professed exponent of an advanced type of modern civilization. But the reader will find almost any portraiture inadequate to give a vivid idea of the body, and enable him to comprehend the complete metamorphosis of the South Carolina Legislature, without observing its details. The Speaker is black, the Clerk is black, the door-keepers are black, the little pages are black, the chairman of the Ways and Means is black, and the chaplain is coal-black. At some of the desks sit colored men whose types it would be hard to find outside of Congo; whose costume, visages, attitudes, and expression, only befit the forecastle of a buccaneer. It must be remembered, also, that these men, with not more than half a dozen exceptions, have been themselves slaves, and that their ancestors were slaves for generations. Recollecting the report of the famous schooner Wanderer, fitted out by a Southern slave-holder twelve or fifteen years ago, in ostentatious defiance of the laws against the slave-trade, and whose owner and master boasted of having brought a cargo of slaves from Africa and safely landed them in South Carolina and Georgia, one thinks it must be true, and that some of these representatives are the very men then stolen from their African homes. If this be so, we will not now quarrel over their presence. It would be one of those extraordinary coincidences that would of itself almost seem to justify the belief of the direct interference of the hand of Providence in the affairs of men.

CHAPTER II

The Negro as a Legislator. — His Fluency in Debate. — Earnestness and Good-Humor his Characteristics. — The Future of the State.

ONE of the things that first strike a casual observer in this negro assembly is the fluency of debate, if the endless chatter that goes on there can be dignified with this term. The leading topics of discussion are all well understood by the members, as they are of a practical character, and appeal directly to the personal interests of every legislator, as well as to those of his constituents. When an appropriation bill is up to raise money to catch and punish the Ku-klux, they know exactly what it means. They feel it in their bones. So, too, with educational measures. The free school comes right home to them; then the business of arming and drilling the black militia. They are eager on this point. Sambo can talk on these topics and those of a kindred character, and their endless ramifications, day in and day out. There is no end to his gush and babble. The intellectual level is that of a bevy of fresh converts at a negro camp-meeting. Of course this kind of talk can be extended indefinitely. It is the doggerel of debate, and not beyond the reach of the lowest parts. Then the negro is imitative in the extreme. He can copy like a parrot or a monkey, and he is always ready for a trial of his skill. He believes he can do any thing, and never loses a chance to try, and is just as ready to be laughed at for his failure as applauded for his success. He is more vivacious than the white, and, being more volatile and good-natured, he is correspondingly more irrepressible. His misuse of language in his imitations is at times ludicrous beyond measure. He notoriously loves a joke or an anecdote, and will burst into a broad guffaw on the smallest provocation. He breaks out into an incoherent harangue on the floor just as easily, and being without practice, discipline, or experience, and wholly oblivious of Lindley Murray, or any other restraint on composition, he will go on repeating himself, dancing as it were to the music of his own voice, forever. He will speak half a dozen times on one question, and every time say the same things without knowing it. He answers completely to the description of a stupid speaker in Parliament, given by Lord Derby on one occasion. It was said of him that he did not know what he was going to say when he got up; he did not know what he was saying while he was speaking, and he did not know what he had said when he sat down.

But the old stagers admit that the colored brethren have a wonderful aptness at legislative proceedings. They are "quick as lightning" at detecting points of order, and they certainly make incessant and extraordinary use of their knowledge. No one is allowed to talk five minutes without interruption, and one interruption is the signal for another and another, until the original speaker is smothered under an avalanche of them. Forty questions of privilege will be raised in a day. At times, nothing goes on but alternating questions of order and of privilege. The inefficient colored friend who sits in the Speaker's chair cannot suppress this extraordinary element of the debate. Some of the blackest members exhibit a pertinacity of intrusion in raising these points of order and questions of privilege that few white men can equal. Their struggles to get the floor, their bellowings and physical contortions, baffle description. The Speaker's hammer plays a perpetual tattoo all to no purpose. The talking and the interruptions from all quarters go on with the utmost license. Every one esteems himself as good as his neighbor, and puts in his oar, apparently as often for love of riot and confusion as for any thing else. It is easy to imagine what are his ideas of propriety and dignity among a crowd of his own color, and these are illustrated without reserve. The Speaker orders a member whom he has discovered to be particularly unruly to take his seat. The member obeys, and with the same motion that he sits down, throws his feet on to his desk, hiding himself from the Speaker by the soles of his boots. In an instant he appears again on the floor. After a few experiences of this sort, the Speaker threatens, in a laugh, to call "the gemman" to order. This is considered a capital joke, and a guffaw follows. The laugh goes round, and then the peanuts are cracked and munched faster than ever; one hand being employed in fortifying the inner man with this nutriment of universal use, while the other enforces the views of the orator. This laughing propensity of the sable crowd is a great cause of disorder. They laugh as hens cackle — one begins and all follow.

But underneath all this shocking burlesque upon legislative proceedings, we must not forget that there is something very real to this uncouth and untutored multitude. It is not all sham, nor all burlesque. They have a genuine interest and a genuine earnestness in the business of the assembly which we are bound to recognize and respect, unless we would be accounted shallow critics. They have an earnest purpose, born of a conviction that their position and condition are not fully assured, which lends a sort of dignity to their proceedings. The barbarous, animated jargon in which they so often indulge is on occasion seen to be so transparently sincere and weighty in their own minds that sympathy supplants disgust. The whole thing is a wonderful novelty to them as well as to observers. Seven years ago these men were raising corn and cotton under the whip of the overseer. To-day they are raising points of order and questions of privilege. They find they can raise one as well as the other. They prefer the latter. It is easier, and better paid. Then, it is the evidence of an accomplished result.

It means escape and defense from old oppressors. It means liberty. It means the destruction of prison-walls only too real to them. It is the sunshine of their lives. It is their day of jubilee. It is their long-promised vision of the Lord God Almighty.

Shall we, then, be too critical over the spectacle? Perhaps we might more wisely wonder that they can do so well in so short a time. The barbarians overran Rome. The dark ages followed. But then the day finally broke, and civilization followed. The days were long and weary; but they came to an end at last. Now we have the printing-press, the railroad, the telegraph; and these denote an utter revolution in the affairs of mankind. Years may now accomplish what it formerly took ages to achieve. Under the new lights and influences shall not the black man speedily emerge? Who knows? We may fear, but we may hope. Nothing in our day is impossible. Take the contested supposition that South Carolina is to be Africanized. We have a Federal Union of great and growing States. It is incontestably white at the centre. We know it to possess vital powers. It is well abreast of all modern progress in ideas and improvements. Its influence is all-pervading. How can a State of the Union escape it? South Carolina alone, if left to herself, might fall into midnight darkness. Can she do it while she remains an integral part of the nation?

But will South Carolina be Africanized? That depends. Let us hear the judgment of an intelligent foreigner who has long lived in the South, and who was here when the war began. He does not believe it. White people from abroad are drifting in, bad as things are. Under freedom the blacks do not multiply as in slavery. The pickaninnies die off from want of care. Some blacks are coming in from North Carolina and Virginia, but others are going off farther South. The white young men who were growing into manhood did not seem inclined to leave their homes and migrate to foreign parts. There was an exodus after the war, but it has stopped, and many have come back. The old slave-holders still hold their lands. The negroes were poor and unable to buy, even if the land-owners would sell. This was a powerful impediment to the development of the negro into a controlling force in the State. His whole power was in his numbers. The present disproportion of four blacks to three whites in the State he believed was already decreasing. The whites seemed likely to more than hold their own, while the blacks would fall off. Cumulative voting would encourage the growth and add to the political power of the whites in the Legislature, where they were at present over-slaughed.

Then the manufacturing industry was growing in magnitude and vitality. This spread various new employments over the State, and every one became a centre to invite white immigration. This influence was already felt. Trade was increased in the towns, and this meant increase of white population. High taxes were a detriment and a drag. But the trader put them on to his goods, and the manufacturer on to his products, and made the consumer pay.

But this important question cannot be dismissed in a paragraph. It requires further treatment. It involves the fortunes of the State far too deeply, and the duties of the white people and the interests of the property holder, are too intimately connected with a just decision of it, to excuse a hasty or shallow judgment. We must defer its further consideration to another occasion. It is the question which is all in all to South Carolina.

CHAPTER III

Villainies of the State Government. — The Present Government no Improvement on the Last. — The Treasury Drained by the Thieves. — Venality of the Press.

THE corruption of the State government of South Carolina is a topic that has grown threadbare in the handling. The last administration stole right hand and left with a recklessness and audacity without parallel. The robbers under it embraced all grades of people. The thieves had to combine to aid one another. It took a combination of the principal authorities to get at the Treasury, and they had to share the plunder alike. All the smaller fry had their proportions, the legislators and lobbymen included. The principal men of the Scott administration are living in Columbia, and nobody undertakes to call them to account. They do not attempt even to conceal their plunder. If everybody was not implicated in the robberies of the Treasury, some way would be found to bring them to light. All that people know is, that the State bonded debt has been increased from five to fifteen millions, and that, besides this, there are all sorts of current obligations to pay afloat, issued by State officers who had authority to bind the Treasury. They are all tinctured with fraud, and some of them are such scandalous swindles that the courts have been able temporarily to stop their payment.

The whole of the late administration, which terminated its existence in November, 1872, was a morass of rottenness, and the present administration was born of the corruptions of that; but for the exhaustion of the State, there is no good reason to believe it would steal less than its predecessor. There seems to be no hope, therefore, that the villainies of the past will be speedily uncovered. The present Governor was Speaker of the last House, and he is credited with having issued during his term in office over $400,000 of pay "certificates" which are still unredeemed and for which there is no appropriation, but which must be saddled on the tax-payers sooner or later. The Blue Ridge Railroad scrip is another scandal embracing several millions of pure stealings. The case is briefly this: Some years ago a charter was obtained for a railroad across the southern end of the Blue Ridge from South Carolina into Kentucky. It was a difficult work, and the State promised it aid on certain conditions. The road was never made, and these conditions were never fulfilled, but since the restoration the State obligations were authorized to be issued. But this was not the worst of it. The sum authorized was $1,800,000. It turns out that on the strength of this authority over $5,000,000 of the scrip has been issued. It was rendered available to the holders by being made receivable for taxes, and in this way has got spread abroad. The whole scheme has been for the moment frustrated by a decision of the courts that the entire transaction is fraudulent and void from the start. With $5,000,000 of this stuff afloat, which the Legislature can legalize if the members are paid enough, what hope is there that the State will escape liability for the emission?

These are sample items of the corruptions of the late government outside of the increase of the bonded debt. The iniquity laps over into this administration, for the old Speaker has been chosen Governor, and the present Legislature has chosen Patterson Senator.

Yet the last canvass was carried on under the sting of the charges of corruption against the Scott administration, and it was hoped that the present would be an improvement upon that. The election of Patterson soon after the assembling of the Legislature, and the manner in which he was chosen, gave a sudden dash to those hopes. Then it has been found that some of the most unscrupulous white and black robbers who have, as members or lobbyists, long plied their nefarious trade at the capital still disfigure and disgrace the present Assembly. So tainted is the atmosphere with corruption, so universally implicated is everybody about the government, of such a character are the ornaments of society at the capital, that there is no such thing as an influential local opinion to be brought against the scamps. They plunder, and glory in it. They steal, and defy you to prove it. The legalization of fraudulent scrip is regarded simply as a smart operation. The purchase of a senatorship is considered only a profitable trade. Those who make the most out of the operation are the best fellows. "How did you get your money?" was asked of a prominent legislator and lobbyist. "I stole it," was the prompt reply. The same man pursues his trade today, openly and unabashed. A leading member of the last administration was told he had the credit of having robbed the State of his large fortune. "Let them prove it," was his only answer. Meanwhile, both of them openly revel in their riches under the very shadow of the lean and hungry Treasury whence their ill-gotten gains were filched. As has been already said, it is believed that the lank impoverishment of the Treasury and the total abasement and destruction of the State credit alone prevent the continuance of robbery on the old scale. As it is, taxation is not in the least diminished, and nearly two millions per annum are raised for State expenses where $400,000 formerly sufficed. This affords succulent pasturage for a large crowd. For it must be remembered that not a dollar of it goes for interest on the State debt. The barter and sale of the offices in which the finances of the State are manipulated, which are divided among the numerous small counties under a system offering unusual facilities for the business, go on with as much activity as ever. The new Governor has the reputation of spending $30,000 or $40,000 a year on a salary of $3,500, but his financial operations are taken as a matter of course, and only referred to with a slight shrug of the shoulders.

Not only are the residences of the white thieves who have stolen their half a million or more apiece, pointed out in Columbia, but here and there a comfortable abode of some sable ally, whose sole business is politics. But while the colored brother has had to be content hitherto with smaller sums than the white, which of itself would account for want of relative show, he is also more prodigal in his expenditures. Still his savings are not to be despised. Sambo takes naturally to stealing, for he is used to it. It was his notorious weakness in slavery, and in his unregenerate state he is far less culpable than the white. The only way he ever had to possess himself of any thing, was to steal it from somebody else. The white man is really the responsible party for his thefts. He may well turn and say to his former master, "The villainy you teach, I will execute." The narration I have given sufficiently shows how things have gone and are going in this State, but its effect would be much heightened if there were time and room for details. Here is one: The total amount of the stationery bill of the House for the twenty years preceding 1861 averaged $400 per annum. Last year it was $16,000. But the meanness of these legislative robberies is not less significant of the character of the legislation than their magnitude. Last year the Treasury was in great straits on one or two occasions for money to anticipate the taxes. Some of the banks came to its aid and advanced about $60,000. They were this year compelled to go before the Committee of Claims to get reimbursed. The shameless rascals refused to pay the claim unless they were allowed to bag some 15 or 20 per cent. of it for their share! Another class of men who are allowed to rob the State freely, comprises those who control the printing-offices. The influence of a free press is well understood in South Carolina. It was understood and dreaded under the old *régime,* and was muzzled accordingly. Nearly all the newspapers in the State are now subsidized. The State government employs and pays them *ad libitum*. One installment of $75,000 lately went to about twenty-five papers in sums ranging from $1,000 to $7,000 apiece, a list of which was published by order of a vote of the Legislature a short time ago. Down here these small weekly sheets can be pretty nearly kept going on these subsidies. Of course, none of the deviltry of the State government is likely to be exposed through them. The whole amount of the printing bills of the State last year, it is computed (for every thing here has to be in part guesswork), aggregated the immense sum of $600,000.

CHAPTER IV

The Pure Blacks the Ruling Power. — *Rivalries of Blacks and Yellows.*
— Carpet-Bag Rule wellnigh over. — *The State Governed*
by its own Citizens.

It is something more than a question of mere curiosity, "Who rules this Legislature?" It is, to an overwhelming extent, as we have already seen, composed of colored men. They are of every hue, running from coal-black through all the intermediate shades, out to what seems pure white. There appears to be scarcely any limit to the variety of shades of the colored population of the State, and their representatives in the Legislature are hardly less various. There is really no way of knowing whether any given individual in South Carolina has black blood in his veins, except by tracing his descent. The specimens of the whitened-out colored men in the Legislature demonstrate this. But who leads among this assembly of blacks and yellows? Is it the white men? By no means; Sambo has already outgrown that.

There is a strong disposition, among the old whites of the State, to say and believe that it is the white blood in the negro race which is managing affairs in the new *régime*. The pure blacks have been set so low in the scale, that it would show great want of penetration or great misrepresentation on the part of the old masters for them to admit the capacity of the black to conduct civic affairs, even as well as they are conducted here. Hence, all credit is apt to be denied them, and given to the element of white blood that courses in the veins of their lighter-colored brethren. Let us look about the Legislature and see how this is. The man who uniformly discharges his duties in the most unassuming manner and in the best taste, is the chaplain of the House. He is coal-black. In the dignities and proprieties of his office, in what he says, and, still better, in what he omits to say, he might be profitably studied as a model by the white political parsons who so often officiate in Congress. Take the chairman of the House Committee of Ways and Means. He is another full-black man. By his position, he has charge of the most important business of the House. He was selected for his solid qualities, and he seems always to conduct himself with discretion. Two of the best speakers in the House are quite black. Their abilities are about equal. Their moral qualities differ. One appears to be honest, and the other to be a rascal. They are both leaders rather than led. Go into the Senate. It is not too much to say that the leading man of the Republican party in that body is Beverly Nash, a man wholly black. He is apparently consulted more and appealed to more, in the business of the body, than any man in it. It is admitted by his white opposition colleagues that he has more native ability than half the white men in the Senate. There is the Senator from Georgetown. He boasts of being a negro, and of having no fear of the white man in any respect. He evidently has no love for him. He is truculent and audacious, and has as much force and ability as any of the lighter-colored members of his race about him. He appears to be also one of the leading "strikers," and is not led, except through his interests. To say the least, none of the lighter-colored members of the race command any more consideration, or possess any more marked influence or talent, than these and other specimen blacks who might be named. So that there seems to be no reason for the conclusion that it is the white element in the negro race that is enabling this body of former slaves to discharge the functions of legislators. The full blacks are just as much entitled to the credit of what is done as the mulattoes.

The future results of this are yet to be developed in affairs here. History indicates that there is nearly as great an antagonism, when disputes of race begin, between blacks and yellows as between blacks and whites. The germs of this antagonism already begin to show themselves here. The white blood often takes on airs when it is commingled as well as when it is unmingled. The negro begins, as he did in Hayti, by getting rid of the white man. After he is disposed of, the mulatto may be pursued with equal persistence. If South Carolina should be Africanized, the same tendency to make it a pure black government would, it is likely, manifest itself here as in Hayti. So far, however, the tendency has only been to get rid of white local leaders; and, as they have been hitherto mostly carpet-baggers, there should be nobody to complain. It is such a merit to drive them out, that nobody stops to ask or care who follows them and fills their places. Wherever those places have been filled by colored men, the change has been advantageous to the State. This is notably the case in the important office of State Treasurer, who is a colored man educated abroad by a rich father, who lived in Charleston. But, as the Treasury of South Carolina has been so thoroughly gutted by the thieves who have hitherto had possession of the State government, there is nothing left to steal. The note of any negro in the State is worth as much on the market as a South Carolina bond. It would puzzle even a Yankee carpet-bagger to make any thing out of the office of State Treasurer under such circumstances.

Three of these old carpet-bag leaders, now out of place, remain in Columbia; each, it is said, rolling in wealth. They, with a few remaining greedy legislative comrades, whom Sambo has not yet dismissed, together with the present Governor, constitute the chief ornaments of that privileged society. Speaking generally, then, we may say that the State government of South Carolina is no longer in the hands of the carpet-baggers. It is in the possession of her own people. The present State officers, legislative and executive, are all, or nearly all, South Carolinians. The Governor is a South Carolina white man, the Lieutenant-Governor, the President of the Senate, the Speaker of the House, the Treasurer, and other State officers, are all of the sable tint, and all are alike natives. South Carolina has, therefore, to all intents and purposes, the charge of her own affairs. The evils she suffers from the character of her rulers grow out of the nature of the constituency which chooses them.

That the State has been victimized, plundered, and robbed by audacious scoundrels from abroad is not to be denied. But at home she is mainly rescued from their clutches, and it is not they whom the people of the State will have much longer to contend with. Those who would reform South Carolina in the future, will have chiefly its native population only to deal with. The black man of the Legislature feels his oats, and considers that the time has already arrived when he can take care of himself. He is not going to throw away, however, his party relationships, or his party advantages. He will use these in the future as he is now using them, to advance his own purposes. He is familiar with the uses of the caucus and the league, and he feels strongly the advantages of combination and concentration, and he has learned the trick of using them as well as his white brethren. It is sometimes said that, in these caucuses and leagues, all legislative affairs are shaped, and that here the white man bears sway. The action of the Legislature does not bear out this view. There was a measure up for consideration the other day in the House, in which the negroes broke away and voted alone. It was a bill for a railroad very much needed, and to which there could be and was no honest objection. But some of the corrupt negro leaders thought the corporation could be forced to pay for the charter, and if the members opposed it they could get pay for their votes. Accordingly, the great body of the blacks combined, and the bill was refused a passage by a decisive majority, who chuckled over their achievement as they would have done if they had cornered a rabbit in a cotton-field. The opposition was so evidently corrupt and scandalous, that not a single white man on either side in the body would allow himself to be caught in opposing the measure, and not one white vote was given against it. This is one instance among many to show that Sambo is fast getting out of leading-strings, and is already his own leader in the Legislature.

Albion W. Tourgée
ROLE OF THE CARPETBAGGER

✧{ *1879* }✧ "CARPETBAGGER" was a contemptuous term that Democrats, Northern as well as Southern, applied to Northerners who went South after the Civil War and eventually concerned themselves, as Republicans, in Reconstruction politics. These men generally have been pictured as self-seeking adventurers who, in collaboration with the Negroes, grossly misgoverned the Southern states. Actually, many if not most of the so-called carpetbaggers do not fit the familiar stereotype. Many were men of high ideals.

Among such was Albion W. Tourgée (1838-1905). Born in Ohio and educated at the University of Rochester, he volunteered when the Civil War came, was repeatedly wounded, lost an eye, and spent several months in a Confederate prison. Shortly after the war's end, in search of health and economic opportunity, he settled with his wife in Greensboro, North Carolina. The $5,000 he had earned as a lawyer and had brought with him, he soon lost in unsuccessful business ventures. After the beginning of Radical Reconstruction, he took a prominent part in the writing of a new constitution for North Carolina, codified the laws of the state, and served for six years as a judge of the superior court. Most of the time he was threatened and harassed by the Ku Klux Klan and by hostile neighbors. He finally left the South in 1879, just before the publication, in New York, of his most important novel, the first noteworthy one ever written about Reconstruction.

This was *A Fool's Errand* (1879); the author was mentioned only as "one of the fools." The book was an odd mixture of melodramatics and preachment, presenting Tourgée's own experiences and conclusions in fictional form. Nevertheless it was an immediate success, and it eventually sold over 100,000 copies. (A play made from it, however, was hissed; it lasted only two weeks on the New York stage.) Tourgée's old acquaintance James A. Garfield (1831-1881) read *A Fool's Errand* with much interest and, after being elected President, wrote to the author: "But for the publication of your work I do not think my election would have been possible." Perhaps this was an overstatement; in any event, the novel had called forcefully to public attention the sad plight of the Republicans in the South, and this had been one of the leading issues in the presidential campaign.

The following chapter, telling of an interview between the carpetbagger Colonel Servosse and an old friend, after Servosse had lost his battle for Negro rights in the South, summarizes fairly well the thesis of *A Fool's Errand*.

WISDOM AND FOLLY MEET TOGETHER

IT WAS shortly after the rupture of his home-life and his departure from Warrington, that Servosse visited, by special invitation, Doctor Enos Martin, the ancient friend who had been at first his instructor, and afterward his revered and trusted counselor. In the years which had elapsed since the Fool had seen him, he had passed from a ripe manhood of surpassing vigor into that riper age which comes without weakness, but which, nevertheless, brings not a little of philosophic calm, — that true "sunset of life which gives mystical lore." It is in those calm years which come before the end, when ambition is dead, and aspiration ceases; when the restless clamor of busy life sweeps by unheeded as the turmoil of the crowded thoroughfare by the busy worker; when the judgment acts calmly, unbiased by hope or fear, — it is in these declining years that the best work of the best lives is usually done. The self which makes the balance waver is dead; but the heart, the intellect, the keen sympathy with that world which is fast slipping away, remain, and the ripened energies act without the wastefulness of passion. It was in this calm brightness which precedes the twilight, that Enos Martin sat down to converse with the man, now rugged and mature, whom he had watched while he grew from youth into manhood, and from early manhood to its maturity. A score of years had passed since they had met. To the one, these years had been full of action. He had been in the current, had breasted its buffetings, and been carried away out of the course which he had marked out for himself on life's great chart, by its cross-currents and counter-eddies. He had a scar to show for every struggle. His heart had throbbed in harmony with the great world-pulse in every one of the grand purposes with which it had swelled during those years. The other had watched with keenest apprehension those movements which had veered and whirled about in their turbid currents the life of the other, himself but little moved, but ever seeking to draw what lessons of value he might from such observation, for the instruction and guidance of other young souls who were yet but skirting the shore of the great sea of life.

This constant and observant interest in the great social movements of the world which he overlooked from so serene a height had led him to note with peculiar care the relations of the nation to the recently subjugated portion of the South, and more especially the conditions of the blacks. In so doing, he had been led to consider especially that transition period which comes between Chattelism, or some form of individual subordination and dependence, and absolute individual autonomy. This is known by different names in different lands and ages, — villenage in England, serfdom in Russia. In regard to this, his inquiries had been most profound, and his interest in all those national questions had accordingly been of the liveliest character: hence his keen desire to see his old pupil, and to talk with one in whom he had confidence as an observer, in regard to the phenomena he had witnessed and the conclusions at which he had arrived, and to compare the same, not only with his own more remote observations, but also with the facts of history. They sat together for a long time in the library where the elder had gathered the intellectual wealth of the world and the ages, and renewed the personal knowledge of each other which a score of years had interrupted. The happenings of the tumultuous life, the growth of the quiet one, were both recounted; and then their conversation drifted to that topic which had engrossed so much of the thought of both, — that great world-current of which both lives were but unimportant incidents.

"And so," said the elder gravely, "you think, Colonel Servosse, that what has been termed Reconstruction is a magnificent failure?"

"Undoubtedly," was the reply, "so far as concerns the attainment of the result intended by its projectors, expected by the world, and to be looked for as a logical sequence of the war."

"I do not know that I fully understand your limitation," said Martin doubtfully.

"I mean," said the younger man, "that Reconstruction was a failure so far as it attempted to unify the nation, to make one people in fact of what had been one only in name before the convulsion of civil war. It was a failure, too, so far as it attempted to fix and secure the position and rights of the colored race. They were fixed, it is true, on paper, and security of a certain sort taken to prevent the abrogation of that formal declaration. No guaranty whatever was provided against their practical subversion, which was accomplished with an ease and impunity that amazed those who instituted the movement."

"You must at least admit that the dogma of 'State Rights' was settled by the war and by that system of summary and complete national control over the erring commonwealths which we call Reconstruction," said Martin.

"On the contrary," answered Servosse, "the doctrine of 'State Rights' is altogether unimpaired and untouched by what has occurred, except in one particular; to wit, *the right of peaceable secession*. The war settled that. The Nation asserted its rights to defend itself against disruption."

"Did it not also assert its right to re-create, to make over, to reconstruct?" asked the elder man.

"Not at all," was the reply. "Reconstruction was never asserted *as a right*, at least not formally and authoritatively. Some did so affirm; but they were accounted visionaries. The act of reconstruction was *excused* as a necessary sequence of the failure of attempted secession: it was never defended or promulgated as a *right of the nation,* even to *secure its own safety."*

"Why, then, do you qualify the declaration of failure?" asked Martin. "It seems to me to have been absolute and complete."

"Not at all," answered Servosse with some vehemence. "A great deal was gained by it. Suppose a child does wrong a hundred times, is reproved for it each time, and only at the last reproof expresses sorrow, and professes a desire to do better, and the very next day repeats the offense. The parent does not despair, nor count the repentance as nothing gained. On the contrary, a great step has been made: the wrong has been admitted, and is thereafter without excuse. Thenceforward, Nathan-like, the parent can point the offender to his own judgment on his own act. So Reconstruction was a great step in advance, in that it formulated a confession of error. It gave us a construction of 'we the people' in the preamble of our Federal Constitution which gave the lie to that which had formerly prevailed. It recognized and formulated the universality of manhood in governmental power, and, in one phase or another of its development, compelled the formal assent of all sections and parties."

"And is this all that has been gained by all these years of toil and struggle and blood?" asked the old man with a sigh.

"Is it not enough, my friend?" replied the Fool, with a reproachful tone. "Is not almost a century of falsehood and hypocrisy cheaply atoned by a decade of chastisement? The confession of error is the hardest part of repentance, whether in a man or in a nation. It is there the Devil always makes his strongest fight. After that, he has to come down out of the mountain, and fight in the valley. He is wounded, crippled, and easily put to rout."

"You do not regard the struggle between the North and the South as ended, then," said Martin.

"Ended?" ejaculated the Fool sharply. "It is just begun! I do not mean the physical tug of war between definitely defined sections. That is a mere incident of a great underlying struggle, — a conflict which is ever going on between two antagonistic ideas. It was like a stream with here and there an angry rapid, before the war; then, for a time, it was like a foaming cascade; and since then it has been the sullen, dark, but deep and quiet whirlpool, which lies below the fall, full of driftwood and shadows, and angry mutterings, and unseen currents, and hidden forces, whose farther course no one can foretell, only that it must go on.

> 'The deepest ice that ever froze
> Can only o'er the river close:

The living stream lies quick below,
And flows — and can not cease to flow!' "

"Do you mean to say that the old battle between freedom and slavery was not ended by the extinction of slavery?" asked the doctor in surprise.

"I suppose it would be," answered the Fool, with a hint of laughter in his tones, "if slavery *were* extinct. I do not mean to combat the old adage that 'it takes two to make a quarrel;' but that is just where our mistake — the mistake of the North, for the South has not made one in this matter — has been. We have *assumed* that slavery was dead, because we had a Proclamation of Emancipation, a Constitutional Amendment, and 'laws passed in pursuance thereof,' all reciting the fact that involuntary servitude, except for crime, should no more exist. Thereupon, we have thrown up our hats, and crowed lustily for what we had achieved, as we had a good right to do. The Antislavery Society met, and congratulated itself on the accomplishment of its mission, on having no more worlds to conquer, no more oppression to resist, and no more victims to succor. And thereupon, in the odor of its self-laudation, it dissolved its own existence, dying of good works, and simply for the want of more good works to be done. It was an end that smacks of the millennium; but, unfortunately, it was farcical in the extreme. I don't blame Garrison and Phillips and yourself, and all the others of the old guard of abolitionists. It was natural that you should at least wish to try on your laurels while alive."

"Really, Colonel," said the old doctor laughingly, "you must not think that was our motive."

"Not confessedly, nor consciously of course," said the Fool. "Real motives are rarely formulated. I don't wonder, though, that men who had been in what our modern slang denominates the 'racket' of the antislavery reform should be tired. I fully realize that a life-time of struggle takes away a man's relish for a fight. Old men never become missionaries. Being in a conflict of ideas, they may keep up the fight till the last minute and the last breath. Old men have made good martyrs ever since Polycarp's day; but they don't long for martyrdom, nor advertise for it. If it is just as convenient to avoid it, they prefer to do so; and in this case they certainly deserved a rest, and more honor and glory than they will ever get, alive or dead.

"It was our fault, — the then youngsters who had just come out of the furnace-fire in which the shackles were fused and melted away from the cramped and shriveled limbs. We ought to have seen and known that only the shell was gone. Slavery as a formal state of society was at an end: as a force, a power, a moral element, it was just as active as before. Its conscious evils were obliterated: its unconscious ones existed in the dwarfed and twisted natures which had been subjected for generations to its influences, — master and slave alike. As a form of society, it could be abolished by proclamation and enactment: as a moral entity, it is as indestructible as the souls on which it has left its mark."

"You think the 'irrepressible conflict' is yet confronting us, then?" said Martin.

"Undoubtedly. The North and the South are simply convenient names for two distinct, hostile, and irreconcilable ideas, — two civilizations they are sometimes called, especially at the South. At the North there is somewhat more of intellectual arrogance; and we are apt to speak of the one as civilization, and of the other as a species of barbarism. These two must always be in conflict until the one prevails, and the other falls. To uproot the one, and plant the other in its stead, is not the work of a moment or a day. That was our mistake. We tried to superimpose the civilization, the idea of the North, upon the South at a moment's warning. We presumed, that, by the suppression of rebellion, the Southern white man had become identical with the Caucasian of the North in thought and sentiment; and that the slave, by emancipation, had become a saint and a Solomon at once. So we tried to build up communities there which should be identical in thought, sentiment, growth, and development, with those of the North. It was A FOOL'S ERRAND."

"On which we all ran, eh?" laughed the doctor.

"Precisely," answered Servosse sententiously.

"I am not sure but you are right," said the elder. "It looks like it now, and every thing which has happened is certainly consistent with your view. But, leaving the past, what have you to say of the future?"

"Well," answered Servosse thoughtfully, "the battle must be fought out. If there is to remain one nation on the territory we now occupy, it must be either a nation unified in sentiment and civilization, or the one civilization must dominate and control the other. As it stands now, that of the South is the most intense, vigorous, and aggressive. The power of the recent slave has been absolutely neutralized. The power of the Southern whites has been increased by exactly two-fifths of the colored adults, who were not counted in representation before the war. Upon all questions touching the nation and its future they are practically a unit, and are daily growing more and more united as those who once stood with us succumb to age or the force of their surroundings."

"But will not that change with immigration? Will not the two sections gradually mix and modify?" asked the doctor anxiously.

"Immigration to the South will in the future, as in the past, be very scattering and trivial, hardly an element worth considering. There are many reasons for this. In the first place, the South does not welcome immigration. Not that it is absolutely hostile, nor intolerant beyond endurance, except upon political subjects; but it has been exclusive until it has lost the power of assimilation; and the immigrant never becomes part and parcel of the people with whom he dwells. His children may do so sometimes, but not always. The West takes a stranger by the hand, and in a day makes him feel at home, — that he is *of* the people with whom he dwells. The South may greet him as cordially as the Orient welcomes the Caucasian trader, but, like the Orient, still makes him feel that he is an 'outside barbarian.' Besides that, the South has no need for mere labor, and the material success of those who have gone there since the war has not been such as to induce many others to follow."

"But why do you think the South more likely to rule than the more populous and more enterprising North?"

"Because they are thoroughly united, and are instinctive, natural rulers. They are not troubled with scruples, nor do they waste their energies upon frivolous and immaterial issues. They are monarchical and kinglike in their characteristics. Each one thinks more of the South than of himself, and any thing which adds to her prestige or glory is dearer to him than any personal advantage. The North thinks the Southern people are especially angry because of the loss of slave-property: in truth, they are a thousand times more exasperated by the elevation of the freed negro to equal political power. The North is disunited: a part will adhere to the South for the sake of power; and, just as before the civil war, the South will again dominate and control the nation."

"And when will this end?" asked the elder man, with a sigh of weariness.

"When the North learns to consider facts, and not to sentimentalize; or when the South shall have worked out the problem of race-conflict in her own borders, by the expiration or explosion of a system of unauthorized and illegal serfdom. The lords of the soil are the lords of the labor still, and will so remain until the laborers have grown, through the lapse of generations, either intelligent or desperate."

"Ah! my young friend," said the old man, with a glow of pride in his countenance, "there you are coming upon my ground, and, I must say, striking at my fears for the future too. The state of the newly-enfranchised freedmen at the South is most anomalous and remarkable. I can not help regarding it with apprehension. There are but few cases in history of an enslaved race leaping at once from absolute chattelism to complete self-rule. Perhaps the case of the ancient Israelites affords the closest analogy. Yet in their case, under divine guidance, two things were found necessary: First, an exodus which took them out from among the race which had been their masters, away from the scenes and surroundings of slavery; and, second, the growth of a new generation who had never known the lash of the task-master, nor felt in their own persons the degradation of servitude. The flight from Egypt, the hardships of the wilderness, the forty years of death and growth away from and beyond the ken of the Egyptian, all were neces-sary to fit the children of Israel for self-government and the exercise of national power, even without the direct and immediate interposition of di-vine aid and the daily recurrence of miraculous signs and wonders. Can the African slave of America develop into the self-governing citizen, the co-ordinate of his white brother in power, with less of preparation?"

"The analogy of the Israelitish people is so striking, that it seems to recur to almost every mind," said Servosse. "It is a favorite one with the colored people themselves. The only important difference which I can see is the lack of a religious element, — the want of a prophet."

"That is the very thing!" said the old Doctor, with animation. "Do you know that I doubt very much whether there was any special religious ele-ment in the minds of the Jewish people at that time? They did not leave Egypt, nor venture into the wilderness, because of religious persecution, or attachment to their faith. Those were things which came afterwards, both in point of time and in the sequence of their growth and development. It was to the feeling of servitude, the idea of oppression, that the twin-found-ers of the Judaic empire, Moses and Aaron, appealed, in order to carry *their* religious idea into effect. The Israelites followed them, not because they were their religious leaders, but because they promised relief from Egyptian bondage. The instinct of the slave is to flee from the scene of servitude when his soul begins to expand with the aspirations of independ-ent manhood. That this spirit has not manifested itself before, in our case, I think a matter of surprise: that it will come hereafter, I fear is a cer-tainty. I can not see how a race can become prepared for absolute auton-omy, real freedom, except by the gradual process of serfdom or villenage, or by the scath and tribulation of the sojourn in the wilderness, or its equiv-alent of isolated self-support, by which individual self-reliance, and col-lective hardihood and daring, may be nourished and confirmed."

"They are likely to have their forty years," said Servosse, "and to leave more than one generation in the wilderness, before they regain the rights which were promised them, and which they for a little time enjoyed."

"Yes," said the elder, "there is another dangerous element. They have tasted liberty, full and complete; and the loss of that, even by indirection, will add to the natural antipathy of the freedman for the associations and surroundings of his servitude. I very greatly fear that this unrest is inseparable from the state of suddenly-acquired freedom; and that, animated by both these feelings, the race may attempt an exodus which will yet upset all our finely-spun theories, and test, at our very doors, the humanitarianisms of which we boast. What do you think of it, Colonel?"

"Honestly, Doctor, I can not tell you," answered Servosse. "That such a feeling exists is beyond question. There is something marvelous and mysterious in the history of the African race in America, too, which appeals most powerfully to the superstitious mysticism which prevails among them. Brought here against their will; forced to undergo the harsh tutelage of slavery in sight and sound of the ceaseless service our nation offers up to liberty; mastering in two hundred years of slavery the rudiments of civilization, the alphabet of religion, of law, of mechanic art, the secrets of husbandry, and the necessity and reward of labor; freed almost without exertion upon their part, and entirely without their independent and intelligent co-operation, — with all this of history before their eyes, it is not strange they should consider themselves the special pets of Providence, — a sort of chosen people. This chapter of miracles, as they account these wonderful happenings, is always present to the fervid fancies of the race; and, while it has hitherto inclined them to inaction, would be a powerful motive, should it once come, to act in concert with a conviction that their future must be laid in a region remote from the scene of their past. If they were of the same stock as the dominant race, there might be a chance for the line of separation to disappear with the lapse of time. Marked as they are by a different complexion, and one which has long been accounted menial and debased, there is no little of truth in the sad refrain of their universal story, 'Niggers never can have a white man's chance here.'"

"But what can be done for their elevation and relief, or to prevent the establishment of a mediaeval barbarism in our midst?" asked the doctor anxiously.

"Well, Doctor," said the Fool jocosely, "that question is for some one else to answer, and it must be answered in deeds, too, and not in words. I have given the years of my manhood to the consideration of these questions, and am accounted a fool in consequence. It seems to me that the cure for these evils is in a nutshell. The remedy, however, is one that must be applied from the outside. The sick man can not cure himself. The South will never purge itself of the evils which affect it. Its intellect, its pride, its wealth, in short, its power, is all arrayed against even the slow and tedious development which time and semi-barbarism would bring. Hour by hour, the chains will be riveted closer. Look at the history of slavery in our land! See how the law-makers, the courts, public sentiment, and all the power of the land, grew year by year more harsh and oppressive on the slave and

his congener, the 'free person of color,' in all the slave States! I see you remember it, old friend. In direct conflict with all the predictions of statesmen, the thumb-screws of oppression were given a new and sharper turn
with every passing year. The vestiges of liberty and right were shred away
by legislative enactment, and the loop-holes of mercy closed by judicial
construction, until only the black gulf of hopeless servitude remained."

"I see the prospect, and admit the truth of your prevision; but I do not
get your idea of a remedy," said the elder man doubtfully.

"Well, you see that the remedy is not from within," said the Fool. "The
minority knows its power, and the majority realizes its weakness so keenly
as to render that impossible. That which has made bulldozing possible
renders progress impossible. Then it seems to me that the question is already answered, — *It must be from without!*"

"But how?" queried the old man impatiently.

"How?" said the Fool. "I am amazed that you do not see; that the country will not see; or rather, that, seeing, they will let the ghost of a dogma,
which rivers of blood have been shed to lay, frighten them from adopting
the course which lies before us, broad and plain as the king's highway: *The
remedy for darkness is light, for ignorance, knowledge, for wrong, righteousness.*"

"True enough as an abstraction, my friend; but how shall it be reduced
to practice?" queried his listener.

"The Nation nourished and protected slavery. The fruitage of slavery
has been the ignorant freedman, the ignorant poor-white man, and the ar-
rogant master. The impotence of the freedman, the ignorance of the poor-
white, the arrogance of the late master, are all the result of national power
exercised in restraint of free thought, free labor, and free speech. Now, let
the Nation undo the evil it has permitted and encouraged. Let it educate
those whom it made ignorant, and protect those whom it made weak. It is
not a matter of favor to the black, but of safety to the Nation. Make the
spelling-book the scepter of national power. Let the Nation educate the
colored man and the poor-white man *because* the Nation held them in
bondage, and is responsible for their education; educate the voter *because*
the Nation can not afford that he should be ignorant. Do not try to shuffle
off the responsibility, nor cloak the danger. Honest ignorance in the masses
is more to be dreaded than malevolent intelligence in the few. It furnished
the rank and file of rebellion and the prejudice-blinded multitudes who
made the Policy of Repression effectual. Poor-Whites, Freedmen, Ku-Klux,
and Bulldozers are all alike the harvest of ignorance. The Nation can not
afford to grow such a crop."

"But how," asked the doctor, "shall these citizens of the States be educated by the Government without infringement of the rights of the States?"

"Ah, my good old friend!" said Servosse, rising, and placing a hand upon the other's shoulder, "I will leave you, now that you have brought out for me to worship that Juggernaut of American politics by which so many hecatombs have been crushed and mangled. This demon required a million lives before he would permit slavery to be abolished: perhaps as many more would induce him to let the fettered souls be unbound and made free."

"You are bitter, my son," said the old man, rising also, and looking into his companion's eyes with a glance of calm reproof. "Do not indulge that spirit. Be patient, and remember that you would have felt just as we of your native North now feel, but for the glare of slumbering revolution in which you have lived. The man who has been in the crater ought not to wonder at his calmness who has only seen the smoke. I have often thought that St. Paul would have been more forbearing with his Jewish brethren if he had always kept in mind the miracle required for his own conversion."

"Perhaps you are right, Doctor," said the Fool; "but ought not something also be allowed to the zeal of the poor old Jonah who disturbed the slumbers of Nineveh? At any rate, I leave your question for the Wise Men to answer. I will only say two words about it. The South — that *pseudo* South which has the power — does not wish this thing to be done to her people, and will oppose it with might and main. If done at all, it must be done by the North — by the Nation moved, instigated, and controlled by the North, I mean — in its own self-defense. It must be an act of sovereignty, an exercise of power. The Nation expected the liberated slave to be an ally of freedom. It was altogether right and proper that it should desire and expect this. But it made the fatal mistake of expecting the freedman to do successful battle on his part of the line without training or knowledge. This mistake must be remedied. As to the means, I feel sure that when the Nation has smarted enough for its folly, it will find a way to undo the evil, whether the State-Rights Moloch stand in the way, or not."

II. The Gilded Age

Mark Twain

THE GILDED AGE

❧{*1873*}❧ THE post-Civil War generation was at the same time one of the most vital and the most sordid in all American history. Freed of the sectional rivalries that had hampered the development of broadly national projects like the transcontinental railroads before 1865, the people devoted their energies to exploiting the tremendous agricultural and industrial potentialities of their vast land. Every index of production spurted forward. At the same time, the heavy losses in blood and treasure occasioned by the war had failed to produce the age of brotherhood and fellowship that idealists had expected. Appomattox brought the bitterness of Reconstruction, not a new era of good feelings. Millions were disillusioned and resolved thereafter to pursue their own selfish interests rather than broad social goals. The age was flagrantly materialistic, coarse, aggressive, and corrupt. It produced prodigious results, accumulating immense wealth and transforming the country into a complex industrial power, but at the cost of exploiting the national resources recklessly, and ruthlessly crushing all who stood in the path of "progress."

No one better understood the strengths and weaknesses of the times than the novelist Samuel L. Clemens, "Mark Twain" (1835-1910). Missouri born, Twain grew up on the banks of the great Mississippi. After experience as a river pilot, he migrated to the mining country of Nevada and California, where he became a reporter and short-story writer. His humorous account of "The Celebrated Jumping Frog of Calaveras County" (1865) attracted national attention and his description of a triumphant European tour, *The Innocents Abroad* (1869), established his literary reputation. Twain abhorred the immorality and corruption of the day, but was also prisoner of its love of wealth and worship of material success. His satirical novel *The Gilded Age* (1873), written in collaboration with Charles Dudley Warner (1829-1900), gave the era its name and remains today the best imaginative reconstruction of its spirit.

THE SAGA OF STONE'S LANDING

STONE'S LANDING BECOMES CITY OF NAPOLEON — ON PAPER

NOBODY dressed more like an engineer than Mr. Henry Brierly. The completeness of his appointments was the envy of the corps, and the gay fellow himself was the admiration of the camp servants, axmen, teamsters, and cooks. . . .

Harry shouldered his rod and went to the field, tramped over the prairie by day, and figured up results at night, with the utmost cheerfulness and industry, and plotted the line on the profile paper, without, however, the least idea of engineering, practical or theoretical. Perhaps there was not a great deal of scientific knowledge in the entire corps, nor was very much needed. They were making what is called a preliminary survey, and the chief object of a preliminary survey was to get up an excitement about the road, to interest every town in that part of the state in it, under the belief that the road would run through it, and to get the aid of every planter upon the prospect that a station would be on his land.

Mr. Jeff Thompson was the most popular engineer who could be found for his work. He did not bother himself much about details or practicabilities of location, but ran merrily along, sighting from the top of one divide to the top of another, and striking "plumb" every town-site and big plantation within twenty or thirty miles of his route. In his own language he "just went booming."

This course gave Henry an opportunity, as he said, to learn the practical details of engineering, and it gave Philip a chance to see the country, and to judge for himself what prospect of a fortune it offered. Both he and Harry got the "refusal" of more than one plantation as they went along, and wrote urgent letters to their Eastern correspondents, upon the beauty of the land and the certainty that it would quadruple in value as soon as the road was finally located. It seemed strange to them that capitalists did not flock out there and secure this land.

They had not been in the field over two weeks when Harry wrote to his friend, Colonel Sellers, that he'd better be on the move, for the line was certain to go to Stone's Landing. Any one who looked at the line on the map, as it was laid down from day to day, would have been uncertain which way it was going; but Jeff had declared that in his judgment the only practicable route from the point they then stood on was to follow the divide to Stone's Landing, and it was generally understood that that town would be the next one hit.

"We'll make it boys," said the chief, "if we have to go in a balloon."

And make it they did. In less than a week, this indomitable engineer had carried his moving caravan over slues and branches, across bottoms and along divides, and pitched his tents in the very heart of the city of Stone's Landing.

"Well, I'll be dashed," was heard the cheery voice of Mr. Thompson, as he stepped outside the tent door at sunrise next morning. "If this don't get me. I say, you Grayson, get out your sighting-iron and see if you can find old Sellers's town. Blame me if we wouldn't have run plumb by it if twilight had held on a little longer. Oh! Sterling, Brierly, get up and see the city. There's a steamboat just coming around the bend." And Jeff roared with laughter. "The mayor'll be round here to breakfast."

The fellows turned out of the tents, rubbing their eyes, and stared about them. They were camped on the second bench of the narrow bottom of a crooked, sluggish stream, that was some five rods wide in the present good stage of water. Before them were a dozen log cabins, with stick and mud chimneys, irregularly disposed on either side of a not very well defined road. . . .

About the chief cabin, which was the store and grocery of this mart of trade, the mud was more liquid than elsewhere, and the rude platform in front of it and the dry-goods boxes mounted thereon were places of refuge for all the loafers of the place. Down by the stream was a dilapidated building which served for a hemp warehouse, and a shaky wharf extended out from it into the water. In fact, a flatboat was there moored by it, its setting poles lying across the gunwales. Above the town the stream was crossed by a crazy wooden bridge, the supports of which leaned all ways in the soggy soil; the absence of a plank here and there in the flooring made the crossing of the bridge faster than a walk an offense not necessary to be prohibited by law.

"This, gentlemen," said Jeff, "is Columbus River, *alias* Goose Run. If it was widened, and deepened, and straightened, and made long enough, it would be one of the finest rivers in the Western country."

As the sun rose and sent his level beams along the stream, the thin stratum of mist, or malaria, rose also and dispersed, but the light was not able to enliven the dull water nor give any hint of its apparently fathomless depth. Venerable mudturtles crawled up and roosted upon the old logs in the stream, their backs glistening in the sun, the first inhabitants of the metropolis to begin the active business of the day. . . .

About ten o'clock a horse and wagon was descried making a slow approach to the camp over the prairie. As it drew near, the wagon was seen to contain a portly gentleman, who hitched impatiently forward on his seat, shook the reins and gently touched up his horse, in the vain attempt to communicate his own energy to that dull beast, and looked eagerly at the tents. When the conveyance at length drew up to Mr. Thompson's door, the gentleman descended with great deliberation, straightened himself up, rubbed his hands, and, beaming satisfaction from every part of his radiant frame, advanced to the group that was gathered to welcome him, and which had saluted him by name as soon as he came within hearing.

"Welcome to Napoleon, gentlemen, welcome. I am proud to see you here, Mr. Thompson. You are looking well, Mr. Sterling. This is the country, sir. Right glad to see you, Mr. Brierly. You got that basket of champagne? No? Those blasted river thieves! I'll never send anything more by 'em. The best brand, Roederer. The last I had in my cellar, from a lot sent me by Sir George Gore — took him out on a buffalo-hunt, when he visited our country. Is always sending me some trifle. You haven't looked about any yet, gentlemen? It's in the rough yet, in the rough. Those buildings will all have to come down. That's the place for the public square, court-house, hotels, churches, jail — all that sort of thing. About where we stand, the deepo. How does that strike your engineering eye, Mr. Thompson? Down yonder the business streets, running to the wharves. The University up there, on rising ground, sightly place, see the river for miles. That's Columbus River, only forty-nine miles to the Missouri. You see what it is, placid, steady, no current to interfere with navigation, wants widening in places and dredging, dredge out the harbor and raise a levee in front of the town; made by nature on purpose for a mart. Look at all this country, not another building within ten miles, no other navigable stream, lay of the land points right here; hemp, tobacco, corn, must come here. The railroad will do it, Napoleon won't know itself in a year." . . .

While the engineer corps went to the field, to run back a couple of miles and ascertain, approximately, if a road could ever get down to the Landing, and to sight ahead across the Run, and see if it could ever get out again, Colonel Sellers and Harry sat down and began to roughly map out the city of Napoleon on a large piece of drawing-paper.

"I've got the refusal of a mile square here," said the Colonel, "in our names, for a year, with a quarter interest reserved for the four owners."

They laid out the town liberally, not lacking room, leaving space for the railroad to come in, and for the river as it was to be when improved.

The engineers reported that the railroad could come in, by taking a little sweep and crossing the stream on a high bridge, but the grades would be steep. Colonel Sellers said he didn't care so much about the grades, if the road could only be made to reach the elevators on the river. The next day Mr. Thompson made a hasty survey of the stream for a mile or two, so that the Colonel and Harry were enabled to show on their map how nobly that would accommodate the city. Jeff took a little writing from the Colonel and Harry for a prospective share, but Philip declined to join in, saying that he had no money, and didn't want to make engagements he couldn't fulfil.

The next morning the camp moved on, followed till it was out of sight by the listless eyes of the group in front of the store, one of whom remarked that "he'd be doggoned if he ever expected to see *that* railroad any mo'."

Harry went with the Colonel to Hawkeye to complete their arrangements, a part of which was the preparation of a petition to Congress for the improvement of the navigation of Columbus River. . . .

DILWORTHY, THE GOLDEN-TONGUED STATESMAN

THE visit of Senator Abner Dilworthy was an event in Hawkeye. When a Senator, whose place is in Washington moving among the Great and guiding the destinies of the nation, condescends to mingle among the people and accept the hospitalities of such a place as Hawkeye, the honor is not considered a light one. All parties are flattered by it, and politics are forgotten in the presence of one so distinguished among his fellows.

Senator Dilworthy, who was from a neighboring state, had been a Unionist in the darkest days of his country, and had thriven by it, but was that any reason why Colonel Sellers, who had been a Confederate and had not thriven by it, should give him the cold shoulder?

The Senator was the guest of his old friend, General Boswell, but it almost appeared that he was indebted to Colonel Sellers for the unreserved hospitalities of the town. It was the large-hearted Colonel who, in a manner, gave him the freedom of the city.

"You are known here, sir," said the Colonel, "and Hawkeye is proud of you. You will find every door open, and a welcome at every hearthstone. I should insist upon your going to my house, if you were not claimed by your older friend, General Boswell. But you will mingle with our people, and you will see here developments that will surprise you."

The Colonel was so profuse in his hospitality that he must have made the impression upon himself that he had entertained the Senator at his own mansion during his stay; at any rate, he afterward always spoke of him as his guest, and not seldom referred to the Senator's relish of certain viands on his table. He did, in fact, press him to dine upon the morning of the day the Senator was going away. . . .

Of course one of the entertainments offered the Senator was a public reception, held in the courthouse, at which he made a speech to his fellow-citizens. Colonel Sellers was master of ceremonies. He escorted the band from the city hotel to General Boswell's; he marshaled the procession of Masons, of Odd Fellows, and of Firemen, the Good Templars, the Sons of Temperance, the Cadets of Temperance, the Daughters of Rebecca, the Sunday-school children, and citizens generally, which followed the Senator to the court-house; he bustled about the room long after every one else was seated, and loudly cried "Order!" in the dead silence which preceded the introduction of the Senator by General Boswell. The occasion was one to call out his finest powers of personal appearance, and one he long dwelt on with pleasure. . . .

Colonel Sellers did not, of course, lose the opportunity to impress upon so influential a person as the Senator the desirability of improving the navigation of Columbus River. He and Mr. Brierly took the Senator over to Napoleon and opened to him their plan. It was a plan that the Senator could understand without a great deal of explanation, for he seemed to be familiar with the like improvements elsewhere. When, however, they reached Stone's Landing the Senator looked about him and inquired:

"Is this Napoleon?"

"This is the nucelus, the nucleus," said the Colonel, unrolling his map. "Here is the deepo, the church, the City Hall, and so on."

"Ah, I see. How far from here is Columbus River? Does that stream empty — "

"That, why, that's Goose Run. Thar ain't no Columbus, thout'n it's over to Hawkeye," interrupted one of the citizens, who had come out to stare at the strangers. "A railroad come here last summer, but it hain't been here no mo'."

"Yes, sir," the Colonel hastened to explain, "in the old records Columbus River is called Goose Run. You see how it sweeps round the town — forty-nine miles to the Missouri; sloop navigation all the way, pretty much, drains this whole country; when it's improved steamboats will run right up here. It's got to be enlarged, deepened. You see by the map, Columbus River. This country must have water communication!"

"You'll want a considerable appropriation, Colonel Sellers."

"I should say a million; is that your figure, Mr. Brierly?"

"According to our surveys," said Harry, "a million would do it; a million spent on the river would make Napoleon worth two millions at least."

"I see," nodded the Senator. "But you'd better begin by asking only for two or three hundred thousand, the usual way. You can begin to sell town lots on that appropriation, you know."

The Senator, himself, to do him justice, was not very much interested in the country or the stream, but he favored the appropriation, and he gave the Colonel and Mr. Brierly to understand that he would endeavor to get it through. Harry, who thought he was shrewd and understood Washington, suggested an interest.

But he saw that the Senator was wounded by the suggestion.

"You will offend me by repeating such an observation," he said. "Whatever I do will be for the public interest. It will require a portion of the appropriation for necessary expenses, and I am sorry to say that there are members who will have to be seen. But you can reckon upon my humble services."

This aspect of the subject was not again alluded to. The Senator possessed himself of the facts, not from his observation of the ground, but from the lips of Colonel Sellers, and laid the appropriation scheme away among his other plans for benefiting the public.

It was on that visit also that the Senator made the acquaintance of Mr. Washington Hawkins, and was greatly taken with his innocence, his guileless manner, and perhaps with his ready adaptability to enter upon any plan proposed. . . .

The result of several conferences with Washington was that the Senator proposed that he should go to Washington with him and become his private secretary and the secretary of his committee; a proposal which was eagerly accepted. . . .

THE CITY OF WASHINGTON

. . . Washington Hawkins's new life was an unceasing delight to him. Senator Dilworthy lived sumptuously, and Washington's quarters were charming — gas; running water, hot and cold; bathroom, coal-fires, rich carpets, beautiful pictures on the walls; books on religion, temperance, public charities, and financial schemes; trim colored servants, dainty food — everything a body could wish for. And as for stationery, there was no end to it; the government furnished it; postage-stamps were not needed — the Senator's frank could convey a horse through the mails, if necessary.

And then he saw such dazzling company. Renowned generals and admirals, who had seemed but colossal myths when he was in the Far West, went in and out before him or sat at the Senator's table, solidified into palpable flesh and blood; famous statesmen crossed his path daily; that once rare and awe-inspiring being, a Congressman, was become a common spectacle — a spectacle so common, indeed, that he could contemplate it without excitement, even without embarrassment; foreign ministers were visible to the naked eye at happy intervals; he had looked upon the President himself, and lived. And more, this world of enchantment teemed with speculation — the whole atmosphere was thick with it — and that, indeed, was Washington Hawkins's native air; none other refreshed his lungs so gratefully. He had found paradise at last.

The more he saw of his chief the Senator, the more he honored him, and the more conspicuously the moral grandeur of his character appeared to stand out. . . .

Washington wrote Sellers officially, now and then. In one of his letters it appeared that whereas no member of the House committee favored the scheme at first, there was now needed but one more vote to compass a majority report. Closing sentence:

Providence seems to further our efforts.

(Signed) ABNER DILWORTHY, U. S. S.,

per WASHINGTON HAWKINS, P. S.

At the end of a week, Washington was able to send the happy news — officially, as usual — that the needed vote had been added and the bill favorably reported from the committee. Other letters recorded its perils in committee of the whole, and by and by its victory, by just the skin of its teeth, on third reading and final passage. Then came letters telling of Mr. Dilworthy's struggles with a stubborn majority in his own committee in the Senate; of how these gentlemen succumbed, one by one, till a majority was secured.

Then there was a hiatus. Washington watched every move on the board, and he was in a good position to do this, for he was clerk of this committee, and also one other. He received no salary as private secretary, but these two clerkships, procured by his benefactor, paid him an aggregate of twelve dollars a day, without counting the twenty per cent extra compensation which would, of course, be voted to him on the last night of the session.

He saw the bill go into committee of the whole and struggle for its life again, and finally worry through. In the fullness of time he noted its second reading, and by and by the day arrived when the grand ordeal came, and it was put upon its final passage. Washington listened with bated breath to the "Aye!" "No!" "No!" "Aye!" of the voters, for a few dread minutes, and then could bear the suspense no longer. He ran down from the gallery and hurried home to wait.

At the end of two or three hours the Senator arrived in the bosom of his family, and dinner was waiting. Washington sprang forward, with the eager question on his lips, and the Senator said:

"We may rejoice freely, now, my son — Providence has crowned our efforts with success."

WORK AT NAPOLEON (STONE'S LANDING)

WASHINGTON sent grand good news to Colonel Sellers that night. . . .

The great news lifted Sellers into the clouds. He went to work on the instant. He flew hither and thither making contracts, engaging men, and steeping his soul in the ecstasies of business. He was the happiest man in Missouri. . . .

Harry joined the Colonel at Stone's Landing, and that dead place sprang into sudden life. A swarm of men were hard at work, and the dull air was filled with the cheery music of labor. Harry had been constituted engineer-in-general, and he threw the full strength of his powers into his work. He moved among his hirelings like a king. Authority seemed to invest him with a new splendor. Colonel Sellers, as general superintendent of a great public enterprise, was all that a mere human being could be — and more. These two grandees went at their imposing "improvement" with the air of men who had been charged with the work of altering the foundations of the globe.

They turned their first attention to straightening the river just above the Landing, where it made a deep bend, and where the maps and plans showed that the process of straightening would not only shorten distance but increase the "fall." They started a cut-off canal across the peninsula formed by the bend, and such another tearing-up of the earth and slopping around in the mud as followed the order to the men had never been seen in that region before. There was such a panic among the turtles that at the end of six hours there was not one to be found within three miles of Stone's Landing. They took the young and the aged, the decrepit and the sick upon their backs and left for tide-water in disorderly procession, the tadpoles following and the bullfrogs bringing up the rear.

Saturday night came, but the men were obliged to wait, because the appropriation had not come. Harry said he had written to hurry up the money, and it would be along presently. So the work continued, on Monday. Stone's Landing was making quite a stir in the vicinity, by this time. Sellers threw a lot or two on the market, "as a feeler," and they sold well. He reclothed his family, laid in a good stock of provisions, and still had money left. He started a bank-account, in a small way — and mentioned the deposit casually to friends; and to strangers, too; to everybody, in fact; but not as a new thing — on the contrary, as a matter of life-long standing. He could not keep from buying trifles every day that were not wholly necessary, it was such a gaudy thing to get out his bank-book and draw a check, instead of using his old customary formula, "Charge it." Harry sold a lot or two, also — and had a dinner-party or two at Hawkeye and a general good time with the money. Both men held on pretty strenuously for the coming big prices, however.

At the end of a month things were looking bad. Harry had besieged the New York headquarters of the Columbus River Slackwater Navigation Company with demands, then commands, and finally appeals, but to no purpose; the appropriation did not come; the letters were not even answered. The workmen were clamorous, now. . . .

The second month closed with a riot. Sellers was absent at the time, and Harry began an active absence himself with the mob at his heels. But being on horseback, he had the advantage. He did not tarry in Hawkeye, but went on, thus missing several appointments with creditors.

He was far on his flight eastward, and well out of danger when the next morning dawned. He telegraphed the Colonel to go down and quiet the laborers — *he* was bound East for money — everything would be right in a week — tell the men so — tell them to rely on him and not be afraid. . . .

HOW APPROPRIATION BILLS ARE CARRIED

WHATEVER may have been the language of Harry's letter to the Colonel, the information it conveyed was condensed or expanded, one or the other, from the following episode of his visit to New York:

He called, with official importance in his mien, at No. — Wall Street, where a great gilt sign betokened the presence of the headquarters of the "Columbus River Slackwater Navigation Company." . . .

He found a stately dignitary occupying a very official chair behind a long green morocco-covered table, in a room sumptuously carpeted and furnished, and well garnished with pictures.

"Good morning, sir; take a seat — take a seat."

"Thank you, sir," said Harry, throwing as much chill into his manner as his ruffled dignity prompted.

"We perceive by your reports and the reports of the chief superintendent, that you have been making gratifying progress with the work. We are all very much pleased."

"Indeed? We did not discover it from your letters — which we have not received; nor by the treatment our drafts have met with — which were not honored; nor by the reception of any part of the appropriation, no part of it having come to hand."

"Why, my dear Mr. Brierly, there must be some mistake. I am sure we wrote you and also Mr. Sellers, recently — when my clerk comes he will show copies — letters informing you of the ten per cent assessment."

"Oh, certainly, we got *those* letters. But what we wanted was money to carry on the work — money to pay the men."

"Certainly, certainly — true enough — but we credited you both for a large part of your assessments — I am sure that was in our letters."

"Of course that was in — I remember that."

"Ah, very well, then. Now we begin to understand each other."

"Well, I don't see that we do. There's two months' wages due the men, and — "

"How? Haven't you paid the men?"

"Paid them! How are we going to pay them when you don't honor our drafts?"

"Why, my *dear* sir, I cannot see how you can find any fault with us. I am sure we have acted in a perfectly straightforward business way. Now let us look at the thing a moment. You subscribed for one hundred shares of the capital stock, at one thousand dollars a share, I believe?"

"Yes, sir, I did."

"And Mr. Sellers took a like amount?"

"Yes, sir."

"Very well. No concern can get along without money. We levied a ten per cent assessment. It was the original understanding that you and Mr. Sellers were to have the positions you now hold, with salaries of six hundred dollars a month each, while in active service. You were duly elected to these places, and you accepted them. Am I right?"

"Certainly."

"Very well. You were given your instructions and put to work. By your reports it appears that you have expended the sum of $9,640 upon the said work. Two months' salary to you two officers amounts altogether to $2,400 — about one-eighth of your ten per cent assessment, you see; which leaves you in debt to the company for the other seven-eighths of the assessment — *viz.*, something over $8,000 apiece. Now, instead of requiring you to forward this aggregate of $16,000 or $17,000 to New York, the company voted unanimously to let you pay it over to the contractors, laborers from time to time, and give you credit on the books for it. And they did it without a murmur, too, for they were pleased with the progress you had made, and were glad to pay you that little compliment — and a very neat one it was, too, I am sure. The work you did fell short of $10,000, a trifle. Let me see — $9,640 from $20,000 — salary $2,400 added — ah, yes, the balance due the company from yourself and Mr. Sellers is $7,960, which I will take the responsibility of allowing to stand for the present, unless you prefer to draw a check now, and thus — "

"Confound it, do you mean to say that instead of the company owing us $2,400, we owe the company $7,960?"

"Well, yes."

"And that we owe the men and the contractors nearly ten thousand dollars besides?"

"Owe them! Oh bless my soul, you can't mean that you have not paid these people?"

"But I *do* mean it!" . . .

"My dear Mr. Bryerson, this is dreadful — perfectly dreadful. It will be found out. It is bound to tarnish the good name of the company; our credit will be seriously, most seriously impaired. How could you be so thoughtless — the men ought to have been paid though it beggared us all!"

"They ought, ought they? Then why the devil — my name is not Bryerson, by the way — why the mischief didn't the compa — why what in the nation ever became of the appropriation? Where *is* that appropriation? — if a stockholder may make so bold as to ask."

"The appropriation? — that paltry two hundred thousand dollars, do you mean?"

"Of course — but I didn't know that two hundred thousand dollars was so very paltry. Though I grant, of course, that it is not a large sum, strictly speaking. But where is it?"

"My dear sir, you surprise me. You surely cannot have had a large acquaintance with this sort of thing. Otherwise you would not have expected much of a result from a mere *initial* appropriation like that. It was never intended for anything but a mere nest-egg for the future and *real* appropriations to cluster around."

"Indeed? Well, was it a myth, or was it a reality? Whatever become of it"

"Why the matter is simple enough. A Congressional appropriation costs money. Just reflect, for instance. A majority of the House committee, say $10,000 apiece — $40,000; a majority of the Senate committee, the same each — say $40,000; a little extra to one or two chairmen of one or two such committees, say $10,000 each — $20,000; and there's $100,000 of the money gone, to begin with. Then, seven male lobbyists, at $3,000 each — $21,000; one female lobbyist, $10,000; a high moral Congressman or Senator here and there — the high moral ones cost more, because they give tone to a measure — say ten of these at $3,000 each, is $30,000; then a lot of small-fry country members who won't vote for anything whatever without pay — say twenty at $500 apiece, is $10,000; a lot of dinners to members — say $10,000 altogether; lot of jimcracks for Congressmen's wives and children — those go a long way — you can't spend too much money in that line — well, those things cost in a lump, say $10,000 — along there somewhere; — and then comes your printed documents — your maps, your tinted engravings, your pamphlets, your illuminated show-cards, your advertisements in a hundred and fifty papers at ever so much a line — because you've *got* to keep the papers all right or you are gone up, you know. Oh, my dear sir, printing bills are destruction itself. Ours, so far amount to — let me see — 10; 52; 22; 13; — and then there's 11; 14; 33 — well, never mind the details, the total in clean numbers foots up $118,254.42 thus far!"

"What!"

"Oh, yes indeed. Printing's no bagatelle, I can tell you. And then there's your contributions, as a company, to Chicago fires and Boston fires, and orphan asylums and all that sort of thing — head the list, you see, with the company's full name and a thousand dollars set opposite — great card, sir — one of the finest advertisements in the world — the preachers mention it in the pulpit when it's a religious charity — one of the happiest advertisements in the world is your benevolent donation. Ours have amounted to sixteen thousand dollars and some cents up to this time."

"Good heavens!"

"Oh, yes. Perhaps the biggest thing we've done in the advertising line was to get an officer of the U. S. government, of perfectly Himalayan official altitude, to write up our little internal improvement for a religious paper of enormous circulation — I tell you, that makes our bonds go handsomely among the pious poor. . . . Very, very expensive thing, take it all around, is a big internal-improvement concern — but you see that yourself, Mr. Bryerson — you see that, yourself, sir. . . . Have you figured up the total of the disbursements I told you of?"

"No, I didn't think of that."

"Well, let's see:

Spent in Washington, say, ...	$191,000
Printing, advertising, etc., say, ...	118,000
Charity, say, ...	16,000
Total, ...	$325,000

"The money to do that with, comes from —

Appropriation, ...	$200,000
Ten per cent. assessment on capital of $1,000,000, ...	100,000
Total, ...	$300,000

"Which leaves us in debt some $50,000 at this moment. Salaries of home officers are still going on; also printing and advertising. Next month will show a state of things!"

"And then — burst up, I suppose?"

"By no means. Levy another assessment."

"Oh, I see. That's dismal."

"By no means."

"Why isn't it? What's the road out?"

"Another appropriation, don't you see?"

"Bother the appropriations. They cost more than they come to."

"Not the next one. We'll call for half a million — get it, and go for a million the very next month."

"Yes, but the cost of it!"

The president smiled, and patted his secret letters affectionately. He said:

"All these people are in the next Congress. We sha'n't have to pay them a cent. And what is more, they will work like beavers for us — perhaps it might be to their advantage."

Harry reflected profoundly awhile. Then he said:

"We send many missionaries to lift up the benighted races of other lands. How much cheaper and better it would be if those people could only come here and drink of our civilization at its fountainhead."

"I perfectly agree with you, Mr. Beverly. Must you go? Well, good morning. Look in, when you are passing; and whenever I can give you any information about our affairs and prospects, I shall be glad to do it."

Harry's letter was not a long one, but it contained at least the calamitous figures that came out in the above conversation. The Colonel found himself in a rather uncomfortable place — no $1,200 salary forthcoming; and himself held responsible for half of the $9,640 due the workmen, to say nothing of being in debt to the company to the extent of nearly $4,000. . . .

Spring blossomed, summer came, dragged its hot weeks by, and the Colonel's spirits rose, day by day, for the railroad was making good progress. But by and by something happened. Hawkeye had always declined to subscribe anything toward the railway, imagining that her large business would be a sufficient compulsory influence; but now Hawkeye was frightened; and before Colonel Sellers knew what he was about, Hawkeye, in a panic, had rushed to the front and subscribed such a sum that Napoleon's attractions suddenly sank into insignificance, and the railroad concluded to follow a comparatively straight course instead of going miles out of its way to build up a metropolis in the muddy desert of Stone's Landing.

The thunderbolt fell. After all the Colonel's deep planning; after all his brain-work and tongue-work in drawing public attention to his pet project and enlisting interest in it; after all his faithful hard toil with his hands, and running hither and thither on his busy feet; after all his high hopes and splendid prophecies, the fates had turned their backs on him at last, and all in a moment his air-castles crumbled to ruins about him. Hawkeye rose from her fright triumphant and rejoicing, and down went Stone's Landing! One by one, its meager parcel of inhabitants packed up and moved away, as the summer waned and fall approached. Town lots were no longer salable, traffic ceased, a deadly lethargy fell upon the place once more, the *Weekly Telegraph* faded into an early grave, the wary tadpole returned from exile, the bullfrog resumed his ancient song, the tranquil turtle sunned his back upon bank and log and drowsed his grateful life away as in the old sweet days of yore.

Henry Grady
SECTIONAL HARMONY

❧{*1886*}❧ NEITHER victories on the battlefields, nor laws passed in Congress, nor even constitutional amendments could "settle" the sectional conflicts which had caused the Civil War. In some ways there was more bitterness and resentment between North and South during the Reconstruction Era than during the hate-filled years between the passage of the Kansas-Nebraska Act and Appomattox. However, beneath the conflicts of Reconstruction, wounds were healing and new bonds were developing that would reunite the two regions in fact as they had already been reunited in law. Industrial development of the South and a moderate agricultural prosperity were important in this connection, and so was the gradual realization in the Southern states that the past was truly dead beyond recall. Perhaps most important of all, the passage of time dulled memories and brought forward new leaders. At any rate, by the 1880's the old issues no longer seemed completely real. As Paul H. Buck says in *The Road to Reunion,* "the South had buried its resentments and had entered a new era of good feeling."

But this development was so gradual as to escape the notice of many observers. That is why the remarkable speech, "The New South," of Henry W. Grady, delivered before the New England Society of New York City on December 21, 1886, was so influential. Other Southerners had said substantially what Grady then enunciated, but only when phrased in his ornate but heartfelt language did the full impact of the changes taking place in the South hit the nation as a whole. Grady's plea for sectional harmony struck deep and hard. Newspapers all over the country commented upon it, and so did all the influential magazines of the day. In the light of present sectional conflicts it would be foolish to say that his speech marked the end of all bad feeling between North and South, but it was an exceptionally significant milestone along the "road to reunion."

Grady (1850-1889), an editor of the influential Atlanta *Constitution,* was an ideal spokesman for reconciliation, a man typical of the New South. Born into a family of tradesmen, he had no ties with the old planter class. Being a newspaperman by profession, he had a wide circle of acquaintances North and South. Finally, his oratorical style, "like a cannon ball in full flight fringed with flowers," as one Northern lawyer put it, suited both the taste of his age and also the particular needs of his topic, which called for both plain talk and smooth.

THE NEW SOUTH

"THERE was a South of slavery and secession — that South is dead. There is a South of union and freedom — that South, thank God, is living, breathing, growing every hour." These words, delivered from the immortal lips of Benjamin H. Hill, at Tammany Hall, in 1866, true then and truer now, I shall make my text to-night.

Mr. President and gentlemen: let me express to you my appreciation of the kindness by which I am permitted to address you. I make this abrupt acknowledgment advisedly, for I feel that if, when I raise my provincial voice in this ancient and august presence, it could find courage for no more than the opening sentence, it would be well if in that sentence I had met in a rough sense my obligation as a guest, and had perished, so to speak, with courtesy on my lips and grace in my heart.

Permitted, through your kindness, to catch my second wind, let me say that I appreciate the significance of being the first Southerner to speak at this board, which bears the substance, if it surpasses the semblance, of original New England hospitality, and honors the sentiment that in turn honors you, but in which my personality is lost, and the compliment to my people made plain.

I bespeak the utmost stretch of your courtesy to-night. I am not troubled about those from whom I come. You remember the man whose wife sent him to a neighbor with a pitcher of milk, and who, tripping on the top step, fell with such casual interruptions as the landings afforded into the basement, and, while picking himself up, had the pleasure of hearing his wife call out, "John, did you break the pitcher?"

"No, I didn't," said John, "but I'll be dinged if I don't."

So, while those who call me from behind may inspire me with energy, if not with courage, I ask an indulgent hearing from you. I beg that you will bring your full faith in American fairness and frankness to judgment upon what I shall say. There was an old preacher once who told some boys of the Bible lesson he was going to read in the morning. The boys, finding the place, glued together the connecting pages. The next morning he read on the bottom of one page, "When Noah was one hundred and twenty years old he took unto himself a wife, who was" — then turning the page — "140 cubits long, 40 cubits wide, built of gopher wood, and covered with pitch inside and out." He was naturally puzzled at this. He read it again, verified it, and then said: "My friends, this is the first time I ever met this in the Bible, but I accept this as an evidence of the assertion that we are fearfully and wonderfully made." If I could get you to hold such faith to-night, I could proceed cheerfully to the task I otherwise approach with a sense of consecration.

Pardon me one word, Mr. President, spoken for the sole purpose of getting into the volumes that go out annually freighted with the rich eloquence of your speakers — the fact that the Cavalier as well as the Puri-

tan was on the continent in its early days, and that he was "up and able
to be about." I have read your books carefully, and I find no mention of
this fact, which seems to me an important one for preserving a sort of
historical equilibrium, if for nothing else.

Let me remind you that the Virginia Cavalier first challenged France
on the continent — that Cavalier John Smith gave New England its very
name, and was so pleased with the job that he has been handing his own
name around ever since; and that while Myles Standish was cutting off
men's ears for courting a girl without her parents' consent, and forbade
men to kiss their wives on Sunday, the Cavalier was courting everything
in sight, and that the Almighty had vouchsafed great increase to the
Cavalier colonies, the huts in the wilderness being as full as the nests in
the woods.

But having incorporated the Cavalier as a fact in your charming little
books, I shall let him work out his own salvation, as he has always done,
with engaging gallantry, and we will hold no controversy as to his merits. Why should we? Neither Puritan nor Cavalier long survived as such.
The virtues and good traditions of both happily still live for the inspiration of their sons and the saving of the old fashion. But both Puritan
and Cavalier were lost in the storm of the first Revolution, and the American citizen, supplanting both and stronger than either, took possession
of the Republic bought by their common blood and fashioned to wisdom,
and charged himself with teaching men government and establishing the
voice of the people as the voice of God.

My friends, Dr. Talmage has told you that the typical American has
yet to come. Let me tell you that he has already come. Great types, like
valuable plants, are slow to flower and fruit. But from the union of these
colonists, Puritans and Cavaliers, from the straightening of their purposes
and the crossing of their blood, slow perfecting through a century, came
he who stands as the first typical American, the first who comprehended
within himself all the strength and gentleness, all the majesty and grace,
of this Republic — Abraham Lincoln. He was the sum of Puritan and
Cavalier, for in his ardent nature were fused the virtues of both, and in
the depths of his great soul the faults of both were lost. He was greater
than Puritan, greater than Cavalier, in that he was American, and that
in his honest form were first gathered the vast and thrilling forces of his
ideal government, charging it with such tremendous meaning and elevating it above human suffering, that martyrdom, though infamously aimed,
came as a fitting crown to a life consecrated from the cradle to human
liberty. Let us, each cherishing the traditions and honoring his fathers,

build with reverent hands to the type of this simple but sublime life, in which all types are honored, and in our common glory as Americans there will be plenty and to spare for your forefathers and for mine.

Dr. Talmage has drawn for you, with a master's hand, the picture of your returning armies. He has told you how, in the pomp and circumstance of war, they came back to you, marching with proud and victorious tread, reading their glory in a nation's eyes! Will you bear with me while I tell you of another army that sought its home at the close of the late war? — an army that marched home in defeat and not in victory, in pathos and not in splendor, but in glory that equaled yours, and to hearts as loving as ever welcomed heroes home! Let me picture to you the footsore Confederate soldier, as, buttoning up in his faded gray jacket the parole which was to bear testimony to his children of his fidelity and faith, he turned his face southward from Appomattox in April, 1865. Think of him as, ragged, half-starved, heavy-hearted, enfeebled by want and wounds, having fought to exhaustion, he surrenders his gun, wrings the hands of his comrades in silence, and lifting his tear-stained and pallid face for the last time to the graves that dot old Virginia hills, pulls his gray cap over his brow and begins the slow and painful journey.

What does he find — let me ask you who went to your homes eager to find, in the welcome you had justly earned, full payment for four years' sacrifice — what does he find when, having followed the battle-stained cross against overwhelming odds, dreading death not half so much as surrender, he reaches the home he left so prosperous and beautiful? He finds his house in ruins, his farm devastated, his slaves free, his stock killed, his barns empty, his trade destroyed, his money worthless, his social system, feudal in its magnificence, swept away, his people without law or legal status, his comrades slain, and the burdens of others heavy on his shoulders. Crushed by defeat, his very traditions are gone; without money, credit, employment, material, or training; and besides all this, confronted with the gravest problem that ever met human intelligence — the establishment of a status for the vast body of his liberated slaves.

What does he do — this hero in gray with a heart of gold? Does he sit down in sullenness and despair? Not for a day. Surely God, who had stripped him of his prosperity, inspired him in his adversity. As ruin was never before so overwhelming, never was restoration swifter. The soldier stepped from the trenches into the furrow; horses that had charged federal guns marched before the plow, and fields that ran red with human blood in April were green with the harvest in June; women reared in luxury cut up their dresses and made breeches for their husbands, and, with a patience and heroism that fit women always as a garment, gave their hands to work. There was little bitterness in all this. Cheerfulness and frankness prevailed. "Bill Arp" struck the keynote when he said, "Well, I killed as many of them as they did of me, and now I'm going to work." So did the soldier returning home after defeat and roasting some corn on the roadside who made the remark to his comrades, "You may leave the South if you want to, but I'm going to Sandersville, kiss my wife, and raise a crop, and if the Yankees fool with me any more, I'll whip 'em again."

I want to say to General Sherman, who is considered an able man in our parts, though some people think he is a kind of careless man about fire, that from the ashes he left us in 1864 we have raised a brave and beautiful city; that somehow or other we have caught the sunshine in the bricks and mortar of our homes, and have builded therein not one ignoble prejudice or memory.

But what is the sum of our work? We have found out that in the summing up the free negro counts more than he did as a slave. We have planted the schoolhouse on the hilltop and made it free to white and black. We have sown towns and cities in the place of theories, and put business above politics. We have challenged your spinners in Massachusetts and your ironmakers in Pennsylvania. We have learned that the $400,000,000 annually received from our cotton crop will make us rich when the supplies that make it are home-raised. We have reduced the commercial rate of interest from 24 to 6 per cent, and are floating 4 per cent bonds. We have learned that one Northern immigrant is worth fifty foreigners, and have smoothed the path to Southward, wiped out the place where Mason and Dixon's line used to be, and hung out the latch-string to you and yours.

We have reached the point that marks perfect harmony in every household, when the husband confesses that the pies which his wife cooks are as good as those his mother used to bake; and we admit that the sun shines as brightly and the moon as softly as it did before the war. We have established thrift in city and country. We have fallen in love with work. We have restored comfort to homes from which culture and elegance never departed. We have let economy take root and spread among us as rank as the crab-grass which sprung from Sherman's cavalry camps, until we are ready to lay odds on the Georgia Yankee as he manufactures relics of the battlefield in a one-story shanty and squeezes pure olive oil out of his cotton seed, against any downeaster that ever swapped wooden nutmegs for flannel sausage in the valleys of Vermont. Above all, we know that we have achieved in these "piping times of peace" a fuller independence for the South than that which our fathers sought to win in the forum by their eloquence or compel in the field by their swords.

It is a rare privilege, sir, to have had part, however humble, in this work. Never was nobler duty confided to human hands than the uplifting and upbuilding of the prostrate and bleeding South — misguided, perhaps, but beautiful in her suffering, and honest, brave, and generous always. In the record of her social, industrial, and political illustration we await with confidence the verdict of the world.

But what of the negro? Have we solved the problem he presents or progressed in honor and equity toward solution? Let the record speak to the point. No section shows a more prosperous laboring population than the negroes of the South, none in fuller sympathy with the employing and land-owning class. He shares our school fund, has the fullest protection of our laws, and the friendship of our people. Self-interest, as well as honor, demand that he should have this. Our future, our very existence, depend upon our working out this problem in full and exact justice. We understand that when Lincoln signed the Emancipation Proclamation, your victory was assured, for he then committed you to the cause of human liberty, against which the arms of man cannot prevail — while those of our statesmen who trusted to make slavery the corner stone of the Confederacy doomed us to defeat as far as they could, committing us to a cause that reason could not defend or the sword maintain in sight of advancing civilization.

Had Mr. Toombs said, which he did not say, "that he would call the roll of his slaves at the foot of Bunker Hill," he would have been foolish, for he might have known that whenever slavery became entangled in war it must perish, and that the chattel in human flesh ended forever in New England when your fathers — not to be blamed for parting with what didn't pay — sold their slaves to our fathers — not to be praised for knowing a paying thing when they saw it. The relations of the Southern people with the negro are close and cordial. We remember with what fidelity for four years he guarded our defenseless women and children, whose husbands and fathers were fighting against his freedom. To his eternal credit be it said that whenever he struck a blow for his own liberty, he fought in open battle, and when at last he raised his black and humble hands that the shackles might be struck off, those hands were innocent of wrong against his helpless charges, and worthy to be taken in loving grasp by every man who honors loyalty and devotion. Ruffians have maltreated him, rascals have misled him, philanthropists established a bank for him, but the South, with the North, protests against injustice to this simple and sincere people.

To liberty and enfranchisement is as far as law can carry the negro.

The rest must be left to conscience and common sense. It must be left to those among whom his lot is cast, with whom he is indissolubly connected, and whose prosperity depends upon their possessing his intelligent sympathy and confidence. Faith has been kept with him, in spite of calumnious assertions to the contrary by those who assume to speak for us or by frank opponents. Faith will be kept with him in the future, if the South holds her reason and integrity.

But have we kept faith with you? In the fullest sense, yes. When Lee surrendered — I don't say when Johnston surrendered, because I understand he still alludes to the time when he met General Sherman last as the time when he determined to abandon any further prosecution of the struggle — when Lee surrendered, I say, and Johnston quit, the South became, and has since been, loyal to this Union. We fought hard enough to know that we were whipped, and in perfect frankness accept as final the arbitrament of the sword to which we had appealed. The South found her jewel in the toad's head of defeat. The shackles that had held her in narrow limitations fell forever when the shackles of the negro slave were broken. Under the old régime the negroes were slaves to the South; the South was a slave to the system. The old plantation, with its simple police regulations and feudal habit, was the only type possible under slavery. Thus was gathered in the hands of a splendid and chivalric oligarchy the substance that should have been diffused among the people, as the rich blood, under certain artificial conditions, is gathered at the heart, filling that with affluent rapture, but leaving the body chill and colorless.

The old South rested everything on slavery and agriculture, unconscious that these could neither give nor maintain healthy growth. The new South presents a perfect democracy, the oligarchs leading in the popular movement; a social system compact and closely knitted, less splendid on the surface, but stronger at the core; a hundred farms for every plantation, fifty homes for every palace; and a diversified industry that meets the complex needs of this complex age.

The new South is enamored of her new work. Her soul is stirred with the breath of a new life. The light of a grander day is falling fair on her face. She is thrilling with the consciousness of growing power and prosperity. As she stands upright, full-statured and equal among the people of the earth, breathing the keen air and looking out upon the expanded horizon, she understands that her emancipation came because, through the inscrutable wisdom of God, her honest purpose was crossed and her brave armies were beaten.

This is said in no spirit of time-serving or apology. The South has noth-

ing for which to apologize. She believes that the late struggle between
the States was war and not rebellion, revolution and not conspiracy, and
that her convictions were as honest as yours. I should be unjust to the
dauntless spirit of the South and to my own convictions if I did not make
this plain in this presence. The South has nothing to take back.

In my native town of Athens is a monument that crowns its central
hill — a plain, white shaft. Deep cut into its shining side is a name dear
to me above the names of men — that of a brave and simple man who
died in brave and simple faith. Not for all the glories of New England,
from Plymouth Rock all the way, would I exchange the heritage he left
me in his soldier's death. To the foot of that shaft I shall send my children's children to reverence him who ennobled their name with his heroic
blood. But, sir, speaking from the shadow of that memory which I honor
as I do nothing else on earth, I say that the cause in which he suffered
and for which he gave his life was adjudged by a higher and fuller wisdom than his or mine, and I am glad that the omniscient God held the
balance of battle in His Almighty hand, and that human slavery was
swept forever from American soil — that the American Union was saved
from the wreck of war.

This message, Mr. President, comes to you from consecrated ground.
Every foot of soil about the city in which I live is sacred as a battle ground
of the Republic. Every hill that invests it is hallowed to you by the blood
of your brothers who died for your victory, and doubly hallowed to us
by the blood of those who died hopeless, but undaunted, in defeat —
sacred soil to all of us, rich with memories that make us purer and
stronger and better, silent but stanch witnesses in its red desolation of the
matchless valor of American hearts and the deathless glory of American
arms, speaking an eloquent witness in its white peace and prosperity to
the indissoluble union of American States and the imperishable brotherhood of the American people.

Now, what answer has New England to this message? Will she permit the prejudice of war to remain in the hearts of the conquerors, when
it has died in the hearts of the conquered? Will she transmit this prejudice to the next generation, that in their hearts, which never felt the generous ardor of conflict, it may perpetuate itself? Will she withhold, save
in strained courtesy, the hand which straight from his soldier's heart
Grant offered to Lee at Appomattox? Will she make the vision of a restored and happy people, which gathered above the couch of your dying
captain, filling his heart with grace, touching his lips with praise, and
glorifying his path to the grave — will she make the vision, on which the

last sigh of his expiring soul breathed a benediction, a cheat and delusion?

If she does, the South, never abject in asking for comradeship, must accept with dignity its refusal; but if she does not refuse to accept in frankness and sincerity this message of good will and friendship, then will the prophecy of Webster, delivered in this very society forty years ago amid tremendous applause, be verified in its fullest sense, when he said: "Standing hand to hand and clasping hands, we should remain united as we have been for sixty years, citizens of the same country, members of the same government, united, all united now and united forever. There have been difficulties, contentions, and controversies, but I tell you that in my judgment, —

> Those opposed eyes,
> Which like the meteors of a troubled heaven,
> All of one nature, of one substance bred,
> Did lately meet in th' intestine shock,
> Shall now, in mutual well-beseeming ranks,
> March all one way.

William Bradley and John M. Harlan
SEGREGATION

✤{ *1883* }✤ ON MARCH 1, 1875, in a last effort to force white men to treat Negroes fairly, Congress passed the Civil Rights Act. This measure guaranteed "all persons within the jurisdiction of the United States" regardless of their "nativity, race, color, or persuasion religious or political," equal treatment in hotels, theaters, trains, and other places of public accommodation. The law met with a mixed reception. In many areas railroad cars and theaters, for example, were desegregated. In Louisville, Kentucky, where Negroes had earlier forced desegregation of street cars by staging "ride-ins" similar to modern restaurant "sit-ins," Macauley's Theater was integrated without incident; in Washington, Willard's Hotel served Negroes at its bar.

However, in many other parts of the nation, North as well as South, the Civil Rights Act was ignored. As a result, a number of Negroes went to court to enforce their rights. In New York City William R. Davis, Jr., refused admission to the Grand Opera House, brought suit against the doorkeeper of the theater, one Samuel D. Singleton. In similar actions a Kansas Negro sued a Topeka restaurateur; a Missourian a Jefferson City hotelkeeper; a Tennesseean a conductor on the Nashville, Chattanooga, and St. Louis Railroad. All these cases finally reached the Supreme Court, where they were lumped together and settled in a decision that set back the cause of Negro equality for more than half a century. As Professor Alan F. Westin has said, because of this decision and others that followed it, "the chalk line of Jim Crow was drawn across virtually every area of public contact in the South." In addition to the majority opinion of Justice William Bradley, the notable dissent of Justice John Marshall Harlan is also here included.

CIVIL RIGHTS CASES

Mr. S. F. Phillips, *Solicitor-Gen.,* for the United States:
Is the Act of 1875 constitutional?
This is understood to depend upon its conformity to the provisions of one or another of the constitutional Amendments.

Several weighty judgments upon each of the Amendments have been delivered by this court, and to these, as greatly facilitating the present investigation it will be proper to advert. . . .

Upon the whole, these cases decide, that:

1. The 13th Amendment forbids all sorts of involuntary personal servitude, except penal, as to all sorts of men, the word servitude taking some color from the historical fact that the United States was then engaged in dealing with African slavery, as well as from the signification of the 14th and 15th Amendments, which must be construed as advancing constitutional rights previously existing;

2. The 14th Amendment expresses prohibitions and, consequently, implies corresponding positive immunities, limiting state action only, including in such action, however, action by all state agencies, executive, legislative and judicial, of whatsoever degree;

3. The 14th Amendment warrants legislation by Congress punishing violations of the immunities thereby secured, when committed by agents of States in the discharge of ministerial functions. . . .

Granting, that by involuntary servitude as prohibited by the 13th Amendment, is intended some institution, *viz.*: custom, etc., of that sort, and primarily, mere scattered trespasses against liberty, committed by private persons; yet, considering what must be the social tendency in at least large parts of the country, it is "appropriate legislation" against such an institution to forbid any action by private persons which, in the light of our history, may reasonably be apprehended to tend, on account of its being incidental to *quasi* public occupations, to create an institution.

Therefore, the above Act of 1875, in prohibiting persons from violating the rights of other persons to the full and equal enjoyment of the accommodations of inns and public conveyances, for any reason turning merely upon the race or color of the latter, partakes of the specific character of certain contemporaneous, solemn and effective action by the United States to which it was a sequel, and is constitutional.

MR. JUSTICE BRADLEY delivered the opinion of the court:

These cases are all founded on the 1st and 2d sections of the Act of Congress, known as the Civil Rights Act, passed March 1, 1875, entitled "An Act to Protect all Citizens in their Civil and Legal Rights." 18 Stat. at L., 335. Two of the cases, those against Stanley and Nichols, are indictments for denying to persons of color the accommodations and privileges of an inn or hotel; two of them, those against Ryan and Singleton, are, one an information, the other an indictment, for denying to individuals the privileges and accommodations of a theater. . . .

It is obvious that the primary and important question in all the cases, is the constitutionality of the law; for if the law is unconstitutional, none of the prosecutions can stand. . . .

The essence of the law is, not to declare broadly that all persons shall be entitled to the full and equal enjoyment of the accommodations, advantages, facilities and privileges of inns, public conveyances and theaters; but that such enjoyment shall not be subject to any conditions applicable only to citizens of a particular race or color, or who had been in a previous condition of servitude. . . .

Has Congress constitutional power to make such a law? Of course, no one will contend that the power to pass it was contained in the Constitution before the adoption of the last three Amendments. The power is sought, first, in the 14th Amendment, and the views and arguments of distinguished Senators, advanced whilst the law was under consideration, claiming authority to pass it by virtue of that Amendment, are the principal arguments adduced in favor of the power. We have carefully considered those arguments, as was due to the eminent ability of those who put them forward, and have felt, in all its force, the weight of authority which always invests a law that Congress deems itself competent to pass. But the responsibility of an independent judgment is now thrown upon this court; and we are bound to exercise it according to the best lights we have.

The 1st section of the 14th Amendment, which is the one relied on, after declaring who shall be citizens of the United States, and of the several States, is prohibitory in its character, and prohibitory upon the States. It declares that "No State shall make or enforce any law which shall abridge the privileges or immunities of citizens of the United States; nor shall any State deprive any person of life, liberty or property without due process of law; nor deny to any person within its jurisdiction the equal protection of the laws." It is state action of a particular character that is prohibited. Individual invasion of individual rights is not the subject matter of the Amendment. . . .

It does not invest Congress with power to legislate upon subjects which are within the domain of state legislation; but to provide modes of relief against state legislation or state action, of the kind referred to. It does not authorize Congress to create a code of municipal law for the regulation of private rights; but to provide modes of redress against the operation of state laws, and the action of state officers executive or judicial, when these are subversive of the fundamental rights specified in the Amendment. . . .

. . . The power of Congress to adopt direct and primary, as distinguished from corrective, legislation on the subject in hand, is sought, in the second place, from the 13th Amendment, which abolishes slavery. This Amendment declares "That neither slavery nor involuntary servitude, except as a punishment for crime, whereof the party shall have been duly convicted, shall exist within the United States, or any place subject to their jurisdiction;" and it gives Congress power to enforce the Amendment by appropriate legislation.

This Amendment, as well as the 14th, is undoubtedly self-executing without any ancillary legislation, so far as its terms are applicable to any existing state of circumstances. By its own unaided force and effect, it abolished slavery and established universal freedom. Still, legislation may be necessary and proper to meet all the various cases and circumstances to be affected by it, and to prescribe proper modes of redress for its violation in letter or spirit. And such legislation may be primary and direct in its character; for the Amendment is not a mere prohibition of state laws establishing or upholding slavery, but an absolute declaration that slavery or involuntary servitude shall not exist in any part of the United States. . . .

The only question under the present head, therefore, is, whether the refusal to any persons of the accommodations of an inn or a public conveyance or a place of public amusement, by an individual and without any sanction or support from any state law or regulation, does inflict upon such persons any manner of servitude, or form of slavery, as those terms are understood in this country? . . . Can the act of a mere individual, the owner of the inn, the public conveyance or place of amusement, refusing the accommodation, be justly regarded as imposing any badge of slavery or servitude upon the applicant, or only as inflicting an ordinary civil injury, properly cognizable by the laws of the State, and presumably subject to redress by those laws until the contrary appears?

After giving to these questions all the consideration which their importance demands, we are forced to the conclusion that such an act of refusal has nothing to do with slavery or involuntary servitude, and that if it is violative of any right of the party, his redress is to be sought under the laws of the State; or if those laws are adverse to his rights and do not protect him, his remedy will be found in the corrective legislation which Congress has adopted, or may adopt, for counteracting the effect of state laws, or state action, prohibited by the 14th Amendment. It would be running the slavery argument into the ground, to make it apply to every act of discrimination which a person may see fit to make as to the guests he will entertain, or as to the people he will take into his coach or cab or car, or admit to his concert or theater, or deal with in other matters of intercourse or business. Innkeepers and public carriers, by the laws of all the States, so far as we are aware, are bound, to the extent of their facilities, to furnish proper accommodation to all unobjectionable persons who in good faith apply for them. If the laws themselves make any unjust discrimination, untenable to the prohibitions of the 14th Amendment, Congress has full power to afford a remedy, under that Amendment and in accordance with it.

When a man has emerged from slavery, and by the aid of beneficent legislation has shaken off the inseparable concomitants of that state, there must be some stage in the progress of his elevation when he takes the rank of a mere citizen, and ceases to be the special favorite of the laws, and when his rights, as a citizen or a man, are to be protected in the ordinary modes by which other men's rights are protected. . . .

On the whole we are of opinion, that no countenance of authority for the passage of the law in question can be found in either the 13th or 14th Amendment of the Constitution; and no other ground of authority for its passage being suggested, it must necessarily be declared void, at least so far as its operation in the several States is concerned. . . .

Mr. Justice Harlan dissenting:

The opinion in these cases proceeds, it seems to me, upon grounds entirely too narrow and artificial. I cannot resist the conclusion that the substance and spirit of the recent Amendments of the Constitution have been sacrificed by a subtle and ingenious verbal criticism. "It is not the words of the law but the internal sense of it that makes the law; the letter of the law is the body; the sense and reason of the law is the soul." Constitutional provisions, adopted in the interest of liberty, and for the purpose of securing, through national legislation, if need be, rights inhering in a state of freedom, and belonging to American citizenship, have been so construed as to defeat the ends the people desired to accomplish, which they attempted to accomplish, and which they supposed they had accomplished by changes in their fundamental law. By this I do not mean that the determination of these cases should have been materially controlled by considerations of mere expediency or policy. I mean only, in this form, to express an earnest conviction that the court has departed from the familiar rule requiring, in the interpretation of constitutional provisions, that full effect be given to the intent with which they were adopted. . . .

There seems to be no substantial difference between my brethren and myself as to the purpose of Congress; for, they say that the essence of the law is, not to declare broadly that all persons shall be entitled to the full and equal enjoyment of the accommodations, advantages, facilities and privileges of inns, public conveyances and theaters; but that such enjoyment shall not be subject to conditions applicable only to citizens of a particular race or color, or who had been in a previous condition of servitude. . . .

The 13th Amendment, it is conceded, did something more than to prohibit slavery as an *institution*, resting upon distinctions of race, and upheld by positive law. My brethren admit that it established and decreed universal *civil freedom* throughout the United States. But did the freedom thus established involve nothing more than exemption from actual slavery? Was nothing more intended than to forbid one man from owning another as property? Was it the purpose of the Nation simply to destroy the institution, and then remit the race, theretofore held in bondage, to the several States for such protection, in their civil rights, necessarily growing out of freedom, as those States, in their discretion, might choose to provide? . . .

That there are burdens and disabilities which constitute badges of slavery and servitude, and that the power to enforce by appropriate legislation the 13th Amendment may be exerted by legislation of a direct and primary character, for the eradication, not simply of the institution, but of its badges and incidents, are propositions which ought to be deemed indisputable. . . . Congress, therefore, under its express power to enforce that Amendment, by appropriate legislation, may enact laws to protect that people against the deprivation, *because of their race,* of any civil rights granted to other freemen in the same State; and such legislation may be of a direct and primary character, operating upon States, their officers and agents and, also upon, at least, such individuals and corporations as exercise public functions and wield power and authority under the State. . . .

My brethen say, that when a man has emerged from slavery, and by the aid of beneficent legislation has shaken off the inseparable concomitants of that state, there must be some stage in the progress of his elevation when he takes the rank of a mere citizen, and ceases to be the special favorite of the laws, and when his rights as a citizen, or a man, are to be protected in the ordinary modes by which other men's rights are protected. It is, I submit, scarcely just to say that the colored race has been the special favorite of the laws. The Statute of 1875, now adjudged to be unconstitutional, is for the benefit of citizens of every race and color. What the Nation, through Congress, has sought to accomplish in reference to that race is — what had already been done in every State of the Union for the white race — to secure and protect rights belonging to them as freemen and citizens; nothing more. It was not deemed enough "to help the feeble up, but to support him after." The one underlying purpose of congressional legislation has been to enable the black race to take the rank of mere citizens. The difficulty has been to compel a recognition of the legal right of the black race to take the rank of citizens, and to secure the enjoyment of privileges belonging, under the law, to them as a component part of the people for whose welfare and happiness government is ordained. At every step in this direction, the Nation has been confronted with class tyranny, which a contemporary English historian says is, of all tyrannies, the most intolerable, "For it is ubiquitous in its operation, and weighs, perhaps, most heavily on those whose obscurity or distance would withdraw them from the notice of a single despot." Today, it is the colored race which is denied, by corporations and individuals wielding public authority, rights fundamental in their freedom and citizenship. At some future time, it may be that some other race will fall under the ban of race discrimination. If the constitutional Amendments be enforced, according to the intent with which, as I conceive, they were adopted, there cannot be in this Republic, any class of human beings in practical subjection to another class, with power in the latter to dole out to the former just such privileges as they may choose to grant. The supreme law of the land has decreed that no authority shall be exercised in this country upon the basis of discrimination, in respect of civil rights, against freemen and citizens because of their race, color or previous condition of servitude. To that decree — for the due enforcement of which, by appropriate legislation, Congress has been invested with express power — every one must bow, whatever may have been, or whatever now are, his individual views as to the wisdom or policy, either of the recent changes in the fundamental law, or of the legislation which has been enacted to give them effect.

For the reasons stated I feel constrained to withhold my assent to the opinion of the court.

Robert G. Ingersoll
THE BLOODY SHIRT

⋙{*1880*}⋘ ONE OF THE most tragic aspects of the Gilded Age was the persistence of the hatreds generated by the Civil War. That the ill feeling should continue was understandable considering the great losses in men and money suffered by each side and the stubborn refusal of southerners to treat the former slaves as truly free men. However, sordid political motives also acted to prolong inter-sectional hostility.

The Republican party was essentially a minority party in the years after 1865. Only by excluding southerners could they continue to control national elections. Even in many parts of the North, the Democrats were able to elect substantial numbers of Congressmen and local officials. This situation encouraged the Republicans to label the Democrats as "the party of the Rebellion" and to remind the public of the injuries done by southerners (who were also Democrats) during the war. They hoped thereby to distract the voters from the consideration of current issues in which the Republicans often appeared in a poor light. After one frantic Republican Congressman illustrated an anti-southern speech by brandishing the blood-stained tunic of a Union soldier on the floor of the House of Representatives, this practice was commonly known as "waving the bloody shirt."

One of the most accomplished practitioners of this art was Robert G. Ingersoll (1833-99), an Illinois lawyer who had served as a cavalry colonel during the war. Ingersoll was an outspoken agnostic, but despite his unorthodox religious views, widely popular in his day as a lecturer and orator. Before the war he had been a Democrat, but after 1865 he became a radical Republican. Both his oratorical style and his political technique are illustrated in the following remarks, delivered in Lewiston, Maine during the 1880 presidential campaign, which pitted the Republican James A. Garfield against the Democrat Winfield Scott Hancock.

SPEECH AT LEWISTON, MAINE

LADIES AND GENTLEMEN: This is in my opinion the grandest and best country in the world. [A voice: "Bully for you," followed by cheers.] And when I speak of "Our country" I mean the North, East, and West. There are parts of this country that are not yet civilized. There are parts of this country in which the people do not believe in the great principle of self-government. In other words, they don't believe in being governed at all. [Laughter.] The question we must settle is, whether our Government shall be preserved or not. That is the question for us. And the North must decide it! The Republicans, Democrats, and Greenbackers of the North, when they understand it as I understand it, will all unite, and overwhelm the solidity of barbarism with the solidity of civilization.

[Applause.] I do not pretend that the Republican party is perfectly good, and I do not pretend that the Democratic party is perfectly bad. I admit that there are thousands of good Democrats, men whom I like. And I cheerfully admit, with a mixture of regret, that there are many Republicans whom I do not like. [Laughter.] But there are thousands of only bad Democrats, and there are thousands of only good Republicans.

Now I think this is a good country. If so, I am bound to do all I can to preserve it; I am bound to do all I can to make it better. Man is the providence of man. As long as I live (whatever party may be in power and have the handling of the offices) I mean to talk on the side of human liberty. [Cheers and applause.] . . .

I believe in a country where every man has an equal chance. That's the reason why I work for the Republican party. Now, if there's anything that's dear to an American citizen it's the right of free speech! [Loud applause.] The grand reason is that every human being has a right to the public ear. If a man cannot speak, others cannot hear. The right of free speech is the priceless gem of the human soul. [Applause.] And a man that don't allow another man the right of free speech is a barbarian. What is the use of free speech, if all the results of free speech are to be reversed by fraud. What's the use for the counsel on one side of a case to address a jury, if, before he commences, the jury has been bought? What's the use to try a man, if, after he's tried, he's taken out and hung by a mob? [Laughter.]

This is a Government of liberty regulated by law. This is a Government founded on reason. This is a Government where the people have honest thought on every subject. The man who has these privileges himself and is not willing to accord them to others is a barbarian. I believe it. So do you. [Applause.] I'm not going to say a word to exclude my Democratic hearers. They believe it as well as I do. [Laughter.] It makes no matter what they say with their mouths. Inside they'll swear to it! [Uncontrollable laughter.] When a man hears what he knows to be true, he feels it, no matter what he says. I'm not going to say a word that a Democrat will dispute. Is there a Democrat who denies the common right of free speech? He dare not say it! Is there a Democrat who denies the right to talk and breathe in one common air? He dare not say it. [Applause.]

Now, if that liberty is to be preserved, whom will you have preserve it? Honor bright, now! [Tremendous applause and laughter.] Will you appoint the South to keep that treasure? [Cries of "No."] Will you leave it to Alabama? Is there a Democrat here who doesn't know that a man stands no chance for the right of free speech in Alabama? I'm not going there! I'm not going to put myself into the hands of a State where there is no law. I'm going further off, and the longer the lever the more I can lift! Maine is a good place in which to begin. Let a Republican try it in Alabama and see how soon he'll get Ku-Kluxed. Let a Greenbacker try it, and see how soon he'll get mobbed for attempting to draw voters away from the Democratic party!

I'll admit there are thousands of good men in the democratic party, but those men are not in the ascendant. They don't hold the power. There are many honest men in the party, but their voice has been lost. I'd rather trust Maine with my right to free speech than Louisiana. I'd rather intrust Massachusetts than Louisiana. In order to preserve this right, the North must be kept in power. [Loud applause.] There is an aristocracy in the South based on a trade in human beings. They are men who believed that lashes were a legal tender for a human being. That is the kind of aristocracy there is in the South. I sometimes feel like finding fault with the North because she ain't proud enough. I want the time to come when a Northern man will be as proud because his father was an honest man, as a Southern man is proud because his father was a slaveholder. I want the time to come when we will be as proud of breaking the chains of the slave as they were of forging them. [Applause.]

In this country we have our sovereign, our King — one power. That is the legally expressed will of the majority of the people. That's our king. [Applause.] Every solitary voter has a certain amount of King! Any man that will throw an illegal vote; any man that will count votes illegally after they have been thrown, is a traitor to the great principles of our Government. He is a traitor to the only King we have. He deserves the punishment of a traitor, too. Now, who are you going to have count your votes and protect your ballot-box for you? [A voice, "Garfield."] And he'll do it, too. Are you going to have the South protect your ballot-box for you? In the South elections are a farce. It is there that Bulldozing holds the election, Dishonesty counts their votes, and Fraud declares the result! [Prolonged cheers and applause.] Now it is a fact, my friends, that *since the Rebellion* the South has killed more men, in a time of profound peace, than our country lost in the two wars with Great Britain! Are they the men you will have to protect your ballot-box? Do you want to leave it with the masked man who shoots fathers, mothers, and children? Oh, Mr. Honest Greenbacker and Democrat! 'Way down in your soul I know you say "No!" no matter what you say outside. [Immense applause.] . . .

Another thing. We want to trust the Government to the best people.

Now, the best State in the South is Georgia. In that State criminals are rented out to task-masters, like slaves, for $10 or $11 apiece. They have overseers. They have the power of life and death over those men. They can shoot them down. They violate the laws of decency. They chain men and women together. The death-rate in the prisons of the North is about 1 per cent. per annum. There's something that I like in the North. It's a monument to Northern charity and honesty. In one of those Georgia camps the death-rate was 30 per cent. In another 40 per cent. In one of them it reached 50 per cent. In another it run up to 10 per cent per month. [Sensation.] Those are the kind of people the Northern Democrats will get on their knees to please in power. Robert Allston, as good a man as ever breathed, brought their atrocities to light. He went back to Georgia, and was assassinated.

They're the kind of men honest Democrats want to support; that the Greenbackers want to tie to. [Laughter.] And Georgia is the best State in the South. Her bonds are worth the most. I ask whether they're the people to be trusted with this Government! The Southern Church has no respect for men's rights. Good Northern men and women have gone South and taken letters from Northern churches. In the House of God they have been refused the Sacramental bread. Recollect it! There's not anybody in the South who will admit that there ever was a Northern gentleman or lady. Why? They wont admit that labor is honorable. I like the North because it respects its industry. There's only one way to make them respect us, and that is to respect ourselves. There's only one way to overcome the South. That is to hold fast to our own principles. . . .

I want you to know that every man that thinks the State is greater than the Union, is a Democrat. Every man that declared slavery was a Democrat. Every man that signed an ordinance of secession was a Democrat. Every man that lowered our flag from the skies was a Democrat. Every man that bred bloodhounds was a Democrat. Every preacher that said that slavery was a divine institution was a Democrat. Recollect it! Every man that shot a Union soldier was a Democrat. Every wound borne by you Union soldiers is a souvenir of a Democrat. You got your crutches from Democrats. Every man that starved a Union soldier was a Democrat. Every man who shot the emaciated maniac who happened to totter across the dead line, with a hellish grin on his face, was a Democrat. Nice company you're in! The keepers of Andersonville and Libby, those two wings that will bear the Confederacy to eternal infamy, were all Democrats. There were lots of splendid Democrats. I mean the war Democrats. I never will bear hard feelings against a man who bared his breast in his country's defense. [Cheers.] The men who attempted to spread yellow fever in our Northern cities were all Democrats. The men who proposed to give our Northern cities to the flames were all Democrats! Just think of it! Think what company you're in! Recollect it! The men who wanted to assassinate Northern Governors were Democrats.

Now all I ask you to do is what you believe to be right. If you really think liberty of speech, the ballot box, the revenue are safer with the South than with the North, then vote the Democratic ticket early and often. If you believe it is better to trust the men who fought against the country than the men who fought to preserve it; if you have more confidence in Chalmers than in Blaine [grand cheers]; if you have more confidence in Hampton than your own men; if you have a greater trust in the solvency of Mississippi than in Massachusetts, then vote the Democratic ticket. [Applause.] But there's not a Democrat in Maine who believes it! [Robert Martin, Esq., "Not one."]

I've got a little while to talk about candidates. I haven't much against Hancock. The most I have against him is that he was a creature of Andy Johnson. I would as soon vote for Andy Johnson as vote for him. What are his opinions on finance? What are his opinions on state rights? I don't know nor anybody else. The Democrats now have both houses of Congress. If they get the Executive they'll have the whole; they'll annul the legislation of the war. They'll make Unionism disreputable. They'd make a Union soldier ashamed to own he lost a leg on the field of glory and make him say he lost it in a thrashing machine. [Laughter.] I don't want to see them have that pleasure. The Rebel possessions and claims don't amount to anything in dollars and cents. Liberty is cheap at any price. [Cheers.] I want my Government to be proud and free. Liberty is a thing wherein extravagance is economy. . . .

William G. Sumner

PUNY MAN AND COSMIC FORCES

❧{ 1894 }❧ THE MOST pervasive intellectual influence on the men of the Gilded Age was the concept of evolution, first developed by the English scientist, Charles Darwin, in *The Origin of Species* (1859). Although Darwin never intended to apply his theory to human institutions, his work had a great impact on religion, politics, economics, and practically every other branch of man's social life. Americans particularly were quick to discover parallels between his explanation of the biological evolution of species and their own experiences. The idea that life was an endless struggle in which only "the fittest" survived and that intense competition between individuals led to progress for the race seemed to reflect American conditions exactly. The constant battle of frontiersmen against their harsh environment and the American tradition of individualism were but the most obvious examples of the working of evolution in the United States, many Americans believed.

The philosopher who systematically applied Darwin's theory to society was another Englishman, Herbert Spencer, but Spencer's writings were ponderous and obscure. Although his American reputation was towering, those who absorbed "social Darwinism" directly from him were relatively few. *His* disciple, William Graham Sumner (1840-1910), was far more effective in reaching the public. Sumner had been trained for the ministry, but spent most of his life as a professor at Yale College. He was a brilliant lecturer and teacher, and a persuasive essayist. Although his intensely individualistic philosophy was profoundly conservative, he roused much resistance among businessmen because he carried his theories to logical extremes that businessmen preferred to avoid. His belief in *laissez faire*, for example, led him to oppose the protective tariffs that most industrialists demanded. The following essay brings out Sumner's basic ideas and illustrates the forceful style for which he was famous.

THE ABSURD EFFORT TO MAKE THE WORLD OVER

IT WILL not probably be denied that the burden of proof is on those who affirm that our social condition is utterly diseased and in need of radical regeneration. My task at present, therefore, is entirely negative and critical: to examine the allegations of fact and the doctrines which are put forward to prove the correctness of the diagnosis and to warrant the use of the remedies proposed.

The propositions put forward by social reformers nowadays are chiefly of two kinds. There are assertions in historical form, chiefly in regard to the comparison of existing with earlier social states, which are plainly based on defective historical knowledge, or at most on current stock historical dicta which are uncritical and incorrect. Writers very often assert that something never existed before because they do not know that it ever existed before, or that something is worse than ever before because they are not possessed of detailed information about what has existed before. The other class of propositions consists of dogmatic statements which, whether true or not, are unverifiable. This class of propositions is the pest and bane of current economic and social discussion. Upon a more or less superficial view of some phenomenon a suggestion arises which is embodied in a philosophical proposition and promulgated as a truth. From the form and nature of such propositions they can always be brought under the head of "ethics." This word at least gives them an air of elevated sentiment and purpose, which is the only warrant they possess. It is impossible to test or verify them by any investigation or logical process whatsoever. It is therefore very difficult for anyone who feels a high responsibility for historical statements, and who absolutely rejects any statement which is unverifiable, to find a common platform for discussion or to join issue satisfactorily in taking the negative.

When anyone asserts that the class of skilled and unskilled manual laborers of the United States is worse off now in respect to diet, clothing, lodgings, furniture, fuel, and lights; in respect to the age at which they can marry; the number of children they can provide for; the start in life which they can give to their children, and their chances of accumulating capital, than they ever have been at any former time, he makes a reckless assertion for which no facts have been offered in proof. Upon an appeal to facts, the contrary of this assertion would be clearly established. It suffices, therefore, to challenge those who are responsible for the assertion to make it good.

If it is said that the employed class are under much more stringent discipline than they were thirty years ago or earlier, it is true. It is not true that there has been any qualitative change in this respect within thirty years, but it is true that a movement which began at the first settlement of the country has been advancing with constant acceleration and has become a noticeable feature within our time. This movement is the advance in the industrial organization. The first settlement was made by agriculturists, and for a long time there was scarcely any organization. There were scattered farmers, each working for himself, and some small towns with only rudimentary commerce and handicrafts. As the country has filled up, the arts and professions have been differentiated and the industrial organization has been advancing. This fact and its significance has hardly been noticed at all; but the stage of the industrial organization existing at any time, and the rate of advance in its development, are the absolutely controlling social facts. Nine-tenths of the socialistic and semi-socialistic, and sentimental or ethical, suggestions by which we are overwhelmed come from failure to understand the phenomena of the industrial organization and its expansion. It controls us all because we are all in it. It creates the conditions of our existence, sets the limits of our social activity, regulates the bonds of our social relations, determines our conceptions of good and evil, suggests our life-philosophy, molds our inherited political institutions, and reforms the oldest and toughest customs, like marriage and property. I repeat that the turmoil of heterogeneous and antagonistic social whims and speculations in which we live is due to the failure to understand what the industrial organization is and its all-pervading control over human life, while the traditions of our school of philosophy lead us always to approach the industrial organization, not from the side of objective study, but from that of philosophical doctrine. Hence it is that we find that the method of measuring what we see happening by what are called ethical standards, and of proposing to attack the phenomena by methods thence deduced, is so popular.

The advance of a new country from the very simplest social coordination up to the highest organization is a most interesting and instructive chance to study the development of the organization. It has of course been attended all the way along by stricter subordination and higher discipline. All organization implies restriction of liberty. The gain of power is won by narrowing individual range. The methods of business in colonial days were loose and slack to an inconceivable degree. The movement of industry has been all the time toward promptitude, punctuality, and reliability. It has been attended all the way by lamentations about the good old times; about the decline of small industries; about the lost spirit of comradeship between employer and employee; about the narrowing of the interests of the workman; about his conversion into a machine or into a "ware," and about industrial war. These lamentations have all had reference to unquestionable phenomena attendant on advancing organization. In all occupations the same movement is discernible — in the learned professions, in schools, in trade, commerce, and transportation. It is to go on faster than ever, now that the continent is filled up by the first superficial layer of population over its whole extent and the intensification of industry has begun. The great inventions both make the intension of the organization possible and make it inevitable, with all its consequences, whatever they may be. I must expect to be told here, according to the current fashions of thinking, that we ought to control the development of the organization. The first instinct of the modern man is to get a law passed to forbid or prevent what, in his wisdom, he disapproves. A thing which is inevitable, however, is one which we cannot control. We have to make up our minds to it, adjust ourselves to it, and sit down to live with it. Its inevitableness may be disputed, in which case we must reexamine it; but if our analysis is correct, when we reach what is inevitable we reach the end, and our regulations must apply to ourselves, not to the social facts.

Now the intensification of the social organization is what gives us greater social power. It is to it that we owe our increased comfort and abundance. We are none of us ready to sacrifice this. On the contrary, we want more of it. We would not return to the colonial simplicity and the colonial exiguity if we could. If not, then we must pay the price. Our life is bounded on every side by conditions. We can have this if we will agree to submit to that. In the case of industrial power and product the great condition is combination of force under discipline and strict coordination. Hence the wild language about wage-slavery and capitalistic tyranny.

In any state of society no great achievements can be produced without great force. Formerly great force was attainable only by slavery aggregating the power of great numbers of men. Roman civilization was built on this. Ours has been built on steam. It is to be built on electricity. Then we are all forced into an organization around these natural forces and adapted to the methods of their application; and although we indulge in rhetoric about political liberty, nevertheless we find ourselves bound tight in a new set of conditions, which control the modes of our existence and determine the directions in which alone economic and social liberty can go.

If it is said that there are some persons in our time who have become rapidly and in a great degree rich, it is true; if it is said that large aggregations of wealth in the control of individuals is a social danger, it is not true.

The movement of the industrial organization which has just been described has brought out a great demand for men capable of managing great enterprises. Such have been called "captains of industry." The analogy with military leaders suggested by this name is not misleading. The great leaders in the development of the industrial organization need those talents of executive and administrative skill, power to command, courage, and fortitude, which were formerly called for in military affairs and scarcely anywhere else. The industrial army is also as dependent on its captains as a military body is on its generals. One of the worst features of the existing system is that the employees have a constant risk in their employer. If he is not competent to manage the business with success, they suffer with him. Capital also is dependent on the skill of the captain of industry for the certainty and magnitude of its profits. Under these circumstances there has been a great demand for men having the requisite ability for this function. As the organization has advanced, with more impersonal bonds of coherence and wider scope of operations, the value of this functionary has rapidly increased. The possession of the requisite ability is a natural monopoly. Consequently, all the conditions have concurred to give to those who possessed this monopoly excessive and constantly advancing rates of remuneration.

Another social function of the first importance in an intense organization is the solution of those crises in the operation of it which are called the conjuncture of the market. It is through the market that the lines of relation run which preserve the system in harmonious and rhythmical operation. The conjuncture is the momentary sharper misadjustment of supply and demand which indicates that a redistribution of productive effort is called for. The industrial organization needs to be insured against these conjunctures, which, if neglected, produce a crisis and catastrophe; and it needs that they shall be anticipated and guarded against as far as skill and foresight can do it. The rewards of this function for the bankers and capitalists who perform it are very great. The captains of industry and the capitalists who operate on the conjuncture, therefore, if they are successful, win, in these days, great fortunes in a short time. There are no earnings which are more legitimate or for which greater services are rendered to the whole industrial body. The popular notions about this matter really assume that all the wealth accumulated by these classes of persons would be here just the same if they had not existed. They are supposed to have appropriated it out of the common stock. This is so far from being true that, on the contrary, their own wealth would not be but for themselves; and besides that, millions more of wealth, many-fold greater than their own, scattered in the hands of thousands, would not exist but for them.

Within the last two years I have traveled from end to end of the German Empire several times on all kinds of trains. I reached the conviction, looking at the matter from the passenger's standpoint, that, if the Germans could find a Vanderbilt and put their railroads in his hands for twenty-five years, letting him reorganize the system and make twenty-five million dollars out of it for himself in that period, they would make an excellent bargain.

But it is repeated until it has become a commonplace which people are afraid to question, that there is some social danger in the possession of large amounts of wealth by individuals. I ask, Why? I heard a lecture two years ago by a man who holds perhaps the first chair of political economy in the world. He said, among other things, that there was great danger in our day from great accumulations; that this danger ought to be met by taxation, and he referred to the fortune of the Rothschilds and to the great fortunes made in America to prove his point. He omitted, however, to state in what the danger consisted or to specify what harm has ever been done by the Rothschild fortunes or by the great fortunes accumulated in America. It seemed to me that the assertions he was making, and the measures he was recommending, ex-cathedra, were very serious to be thrown out so recklessly. It is hardly to be expected that novelists, popular magazinists, amateur economists, and politicians will be more responsible. It would be easy, however, to show what good is done by accumulations of capital in a few hands — that is, under close and direct management, permitting prompt and accurate application; also to tell what harm is done by loose and unfounded denunciations of any social component or any social group. In the recent debates on the income tax the assumption that great accumulations of wealth are socially harmful and ought to be broken down by taxation was treated as an axiom, and we had direct proof how dangerous it is to fit out the average politician with such unverified and unverifiable dogmas as his warrant for his modes of handling the direful tool of taxation.

Great figures are set out as to the magnitude of certain fortunes and the proportionate amount of the national wealth held by a fraction of the population, and eloquent exclamation-points are set against them. If the figures were beyond criticism, what would they prove? Where is the rich man who is oppressing anybody? If there was one, the newspapers would ring with it. The facts about the accumulation of wealth do not constitute a plutocracy, as I will show below. Wealth, in itself considered, is only power, like steam, or electricity, or knowledge. The question of its good or ill turns on the question how it will be used. To prove any harm in aggregations of wealth it must be shown that great wealth is, as a rule, in the ordinary course of social affairs, put to a mischievous use. This cannot be shown beyond the very slightest degree, if at all.

Therefore, all the allegations of general mischief, social corruption, wrong, and evil in our society must be referred back to those who make them for particulars and specifications. As they are offered to us we cannot allow them to stand, because we discern in them faulty observation of facts, or incorrect interpretation of facts, or a construction of facts according to some philosophy, or misunderstanding of phenomena and their relations, or incorrect inferences, or crooked deductions.

Assuming, however, that the charges against the existing "capitalistic" — that is, industrial — order of things are established, it is proposed to remedy the ill by reconstructing the industrial system on the principles of democracy. Once more we must untangle the snarl of half ideas and muddled facts.

Democracy is, of course, a word to conjure with. We have a democratic-republican political system, and we like it so well that we are prone to take any new step which can be recommended as "democratic" or which will round out some "principle" of democracy to a fuller fulfillment. Everything connected with this domain of political thought is crusted over with false historical traditions, cheap philosophy, and undefined terms, but it is useless to try to criticize it. The whole drift of the world for five hundred years has been toward democracy. That drift, produced by great discoveries and inventions, and by the discovery of a new continent, has raised the middle class out of the servile class. In alliance with the crown they crushed the feudal classes. They made the crown absolute in order to do it. Then they turned against the crown and, with the aid of the handicraftsmen and peasants, conquered it. Now the next conflict which must inevitably come is that between the middle capitalist class and the proletariat, as the word has come to be used. If a certain construction is put on this conflict, it may be called that between democracy and plutocracy, for it seems that industrialism must be developed into plutocracy by the conflict itself. That is the conflict which stands before civilized society to-day. All the signs of the times indicate its commencement, and it is big with fate to mankind and to civilization.

Although we cannot criticise democracy profitably, it may be said of it, with reference to our present subject, that up to this time democracy never has done anything, either in politics, social affairs, or industry, to prove its power to bless mankind. If we confine our attention to the United States, there are three difficulties with regard to its alleged achievements, and they all have the most serious bearing on the proposed democratization of industry.

1. The time during which democracy has been tried in the United States is too short to warrant any inferences. A century or two is a very short time in the life of political institutions, and if the circumstances change rapidly during the period the experiment is vitiated.

2. The greatest question of all about American democracy is whether it is a cause or a consequence. It is popularly assumed to be a cause, and we ascribe to its beneficent action all the political vitality, all the easiness of social relations, all the industrial activity and enterprise which we experience and which we value and enjoy. I submit, however, that, on a more thorough examination of the matter, we shall find that democracy is a consequence. There are economic and sociological causes for our political vitality and vigor, for the ease and elasticity of our social relations, and for our industrial power and success. Those causes have also produced democracy, given it success, and have made its faults and errors innocuous. Indeed, in any true philosophy, it must be held that in the economic forces which control the material prosperity of a population lie the real causes of its political institutions, its social class-adjustments, its industrial prosperity, its moral code, and its world-philosophy. If democracy and the industrial system are both products of the economic conditions which exist, it is plainly absurd to set democracy to defeat those conditions in the control of industry. If, however, it is not true that democracy is a consequence, and I am well aware that very few people believe it, then we must go back to the view that democracy is a cause. That being so, it is difficult to see how democracy, which has had a clear field here in America, is not responsible for the ills which Mr. Bellamy and his comrades in opinion see

in our present social state, and it is difficult to see the grounds of asking us to intrust it also with industry. The first and chief proof of success of political measures and systems is that, under them, society advances in health and vigor and that industry develops without causing social disease. If this has not been the case in America, American democracy has not succeeded. Neither is it easy to see how the masses, if they have undertaken to rule, can escape the responsibilities of ruling, especially so far as the consequences affect themselves. If, then, they have brought all this distress upon themselves under the present system, what becomes of the argument for extending the system to a direct and complete control of industry?

3. It is by no means certain that democracy in the United States has not, up to this time, been living on a capital inherited from aristocracy and industrialism. We have no pure democracy. Our democracy is limited at every turn by institutions which were developed in England in connection with industrialism and aristocracy, and these institutions are of the essence of our system. While our people are passionately democratic in temper and will not tolerate a doctrine that one man is not as good as another, they have common sense enough to know that he is not; and it seems that they love and cling to the conservative institutions quite as strongly as they do to the democratic philosophy. They are, therefore, ruled by men who talk philosophy and govern by the institutions. Now it is open to Mr. Bellamy to say that the reason why democracy in America seems to be open to the charge made in the last paragraph, of responsibility for all the ill which he now finds in our society, is because it has been infected with industrialism (capitalism); but in that case he must widen the scope of his proposition and undertake to purify democracy before turning industry over to it. The socialists generally seem to think that they make their undertakings easier when they widen their scope, and make them easiest when they propose to remake everything; but in truth social tasks increase in difficulty in an enormous ratio as they are widened in scope.

The question, therefore, arises, if it is proposed to reorganize the social system on the principles of American democracy, whether the institutions of industrialism are to be retained. If so, all the virus of capitalism will be retained. It is forgotten, in many schemes of social reformation in which it is proposed to mix what we like with what we do not like, in order to extirpate the latter, that each must undergo a reaction from the other, and that what we like may be extirpated by what we do not like. We may find that instead of democratizing capitalism we have capitalized democracy — that is, have brought in plutocracy. Plutocracy is a political system in which the ruling force is wealth. The denunciation of capital which we hear from all the reformers is the most eloquent proof that the greatest power in the world to-day is capital. They know that it is, and confess it most when they deny it most strenuously. At present the power of capital is social and industrial, and only in a small degree political. So far as capital is political, it is on account of political abuses, such as tariffs and special legislation on the one hand and legislative strikes on the other. These conditions exist in the democracy to which it is proposed to transfer the industries. What does that mean except bringing all the power of capital once for all into the political arena and precipitating the conflict of democracy and plutocracy at once? Can anyone imagine that the masterfulness, the overbearing disposition, the greed of gain, and the ruthlessness in methods, which are the faults of the master of industry at his worst, would cease when he was a functionary of the State, which had relieved him of risk and endowed him with authority? Can anyone imagine that politicians would no longer be corruptly fond of money, intriguing, and crafty when they were charged, not only with patronage and government contracts, but also with factories, stores, ships, and railroads? Could we expect anything except that, when the politician and the master of industry were joined in one, we should have the vices of both unchecked by the restraints of either? In any socialistic state there will be one set of positions which will offer chances of wealth beyond the wildest dreams of avarice; *viz.,* on the governing committees. Then there will be rich men whose wealth will indeed be a menace to social interests, and instead of industrial peace there will be such war as no one has dreamed of yet: the war between the political ins and outs — that is, between those who are on the committee and those who want to get on it.

We must not drop the subject of democracy without one word more. The Greeks already had occasion to notice a most serious distinction between two principles of democracy which lie at its roots. Plutarch says that Solon got the archonship in part by promising equality, which some understood of esteem and dignity, others of measure and number. There is one democratic principle which means that each man should be esteemed for his merit and worth, for just what he is, without regard to birth, wealth, rank, or other adventitious circumstances. The other principle is that each one of us ought to be equal to all the others in what he gets and enjoys. The first principle is only partially realizable, but, so far as it goes, it is elevating and socially progressive and profitable. The second is not capable of an intelligible statement. The first is a principle of industrialization. It proceeds from and is intelligible only in a society built on the industrial virtues, free endeavor, security of property, and repression of the baser vices; that is, in a society whose industrial system is built on labor and exchange. The other is only a rule of division for robbers who have to divide plunder or monks who have to divide gifts. If, therefore, we want to democratize industry in the sense of the first principle, we need only perfect what we have now, especially on its political side. If we try to democratize it in the sense of the other principle, we corrupt politics at one stroke; we enter upon an industrial enterprise which will waste capital and bring us all to poverty, and we set loose greed and envy as ruling social passions.

If this poor old world is as bad as they say, one more reflection may check the zeal of the headlong reformer. It is at any rate a tough old world. It has taken its trend and curvature and all its twists and tangles from a long course of formation. All its wry and crooked gnarls and knobs are therefore stiff and stubborn. If we puny men by our arts can do anything at all to straighten them, it will only be by modifying the tendencies of some of the forces at work, so that, after a sufficient time, their action may be changed a little and slowly the lines of movement may be modified. This effort, however, can at most be only slight, and it will take a long time. In the meantime spontaneous forces will be at work, compared with which our efforts are like those of a man trying to deflect a river, and these forces will have changed the whole problem before our interferences have time to make themselves felt. The great stream of time and earthly things will sweep on just the same in spite of us. It bears with it now all the errors and follies of the past, the wreckage of all the philosophies, the fragments of all the civilizations, the wisdom of all the abandoned ethical systems, the debris of all the institutions, and the penalties of all the mistakes. It is only in imagination that we stand by and look at and criticize it and plan to change it. Everyone of us is a child of his age and cannot get out of it. He is in the stream and is swept along with it. All his sciences and philosophy come to him out of it. Therefore the tide will not be changed by us. It will swallow up both us and our experiments. It will absorb the efforts at change and take them into itself as new but trivial components, and the great movement of tradition and work will go on unchanged by our fads and schemes. The things which will change it are the great discoveries and inventions, the new reactions inside the social organism, and the changes in the earth itself on account of changes in the cosmical forces. These causes will make it just what, in fidelity to them, it ought to be. The men will be carried along with it and be made by it. The utmost they can do by their cleverness will be to note and record their course as they are carried along, which is what we do now, and is that which leads us to the vain fancy that we can make or guide the movement. That is why it is the greatest folly of which a man can be capable, to sit down with a slate and pencil to plan out a new social world.

III. Imperialism

Josiah Strong

OUR COUNTRY

⊰{*1885*}⊱   ONE OF the most curious and revealing examples of post-Civil War expansionism in the United States was the Reverend Josiah Strong's *Our Country,* published in 1885. Strong (1847-1916) possessed, in the words of Richard Hofstadter, an "uncanny capacity for assimilating the writings of Darwin and Spencer to the prejudices of rural Protestant America." He was Secretary of the Congregational Home Missionary Society and the book, designed to explain American social trends to a mission-minded audience, dealt with the role of the United States in the world, and with the "dangers" which, according to Strong, threatened to prevent the nation from achieving its destiny.

In his account, Strong displayed nearly all the prejudices and limitations of his age. He was against immigrants, Catholics, and Mormons. Socialism, liquor, and materialism were grave threats to the nation. Big cities bred vice, political corruption, and most of the other problems he described. But despite his narrowness, Strong was a man of considerable vision. He saw America as the dominant power of the future. He appreciated the importance of the rapidly developing West, he predicted the day when the United States would be the center of the English-speaking world, and he pointed out the economic advantages of the development of colonies in the underdeveloped areas of the world.

Our Country was conceived with a rather limited audience in mind. But Strong's appeal both to the pride and prejudice of the native-born majority, plus his genuine insights and his broad synthesis of American civilization, made the book an immediate best-seller. 175,000 copies were sold. It surely helped prepare the way for public acceptance of imperialism in the decade following its publication, for, as the following selection shows, despite the dangers threatening on every side, Strong was convinced that "Anglo-Saxon" America would triumph over its enemies and march forward to the glorious destiny that awaited it. Without disturbing the self-satisfied ethnocentricity of his readers, he made them conscious of the role that America would play in future world affairs and prepared them to accept that role with equanimity.

THE ANGLO-SAXON AND THE WORLD'S FUTURE

EVERY race which has deeply impressed itself on the human family has been the representative of some great idea — one or more — which has given direction to the nation's life and form to its civilization. Among the Egyptians this seminal idea was life, among the Persians it was light, among the Hebrews it was purity, among the Greeks it was beauty, among the Romans it was law. The Anglo-Saxon is the representative of

131

two great ideas, which are closely related. One of them is that of civil liberty. Nearly all of the civil liberty in the world is enjoyed by Anglo-Saxons: the English, the British colonists, and the people of the United States. To some, like the Swiss, it is permitted by the sufferance of their neighbors; others, like the French, have experimented with it; but, in modern times, the peoples whose love of liberty has won it, and whose genius for self-government has preserved it, have been Anglo-Saxons. The noblest races have always been lovers of liberty. That love ran strong in early German blood, and has profoundly influenced the institutions of all the branches of the great German family; but it was left for the Anglo-Saxon branch fully to recognize the right of the individual to himself and formally to declare it the foundation stone of government.

The other great idea of which the Anglo-Saxon is the exponent is that of a pure *spiritual* Christianity. It was no accident that the great reformation of the sixteenth century originated among a Teutonic, rather than a Latin people. It was the fire of liberty burning in the Saxon heart that flamed up against the absolutism of the Pope. Speaking roughly, the peoples of Europe which are Celtic are Catholic, and those which are Teutonic are Protestant; and where the Teutonic race was purest, there Protestantism spread with the greatest rapidity . . .

It is not necessary to argue to those for whom I write that the two great needs of mankind, that all men may be lifted up into the light of the highest Christian civilization, are, first, a pure, spiritual Christianity, and, second, civil liberty. Without controversy, these are the forces which, in the past, have contributed most to the elevation of the human race, and they must continue to be, in the future, the most efficient ministers to its progress. It follows, then, that the Anglo-Saxon, as the great representative of these two ideas, the depositary of these two greatest blessings, sustains peculiar relations to the world's future, is divinely commissioned to be, in a peculiar sense, his brother's keeper. Add to this the fact of his rapidly increasing strength in modern times, and we have well nigh a demonstration of his destiny. In 1700 this race numbered less than 6,000,000 souls. In 1800, Anglo-Saxons (I use the term somewhat broadly to include all English-speaking peoples) had increased to about 20,500,000, and in 1880 they numbered nearly 10,000,000, having multiplied almost five-fold in eighty years. At the end of the reign of Charles II, the English colonists in America numbered 200,000. During these two hundred years, our population has increased two hundred and fifty-fold. And the expansion of this race has been no less remarkable than its multiplication. In one century the United States has increased its territory ten-fold, while the enormous acquisition of foreign territory by Great Britian — and chiefly within the last hundred years — is wholly uparalleled in history. This mighty Anglo-Saxon race, though comprising only one-fifteenth part of mankind, now rules more than one-third of the earth's surface, and more than one-fourth of its people. And if this race, while growing from 6,000,000 to 100,000,000, thus gained possession of a third portion of the earth, is it to be supposed that when it numbers 1,000,000,000, it will lose the disposition, or lack the power to extend its sway?

This race is multiplying not only more rapidly than any other European race, but far more rapidly than *all* the races of continental Europe. . . . Does it not look as if God were not only preparing in our Anglo-Saxon civilization the die with which to stamp the peoples of the earth, but as if he were also massing behind that die the mighty power with which to press it? My confidence that this race is eventually to give its civilization to mankind is not based on mere numbers — China forbid! I look forward to what the world has never yet seen united in the same race; viz., the greatest numbers, *and* the highest civilization.

There can be no reasonable doubt that North America is to be the great home of the Anglo-Saxon, the principal seat of his power, the center of his life and influence. Not only does it constitute seven-elevenths of his possessions, but his empire is unsevered, while the remaining four-elevenths are fragmentary and scattered over the earth. Australia will have a great population; but its disadvantages, as compared with North America, are too manifest to need mention. Our continent has room and resources and climate, it lies in the pathway of the nations, it belongs to the zone of power, and already, among Anglo-Saxons, do we lead in population and wealth. Of England, Franklin once wrote: "That pretty island which, compared to America, is but a stepping-stone in a brook, scarce enough of it above water to keep one's shoes dry." England can hardly hope to maintain her relative importance among Anglo-Saxon peoples when her "pretty island" is the home of only one-twentieth part of that race. With the wider distribution of wealth, and increasing facilities of intercourse, intelligence and influence are less centralized, and peoples become more homogeneous; and the more nearly homogeneous peoples are, the more do *numbers tell.* America is to have the great preponderance of numbers and of wealth, and by the logic of events will follow the scepter of controlling influence. This will be but the consummation of movement as old as civilization — a result to which men have looked forward for centuries. . . .

. . . It surely needs no prophet's eye to see that the civilization of the United States is to be the civilization of America, and that the future of the continent is ours. In 1880, the United States was the home of more than one-half of the Anglo-Saxon race; and, if the computations already given are correct, a much larger proportion will be here a hundred years hence. It has been shown that we have room for at least a thousand millions. According to recent figures, there is in France a population of 180.88 to the square mile; in Germany, 216.62; in England and Wales, 428.67; in Belgium, 481.71; in the United States — not including Alaska — 16.88. If our population were as dense as that of France, we should have this side of Alaska, 537,000,000; if as dense as that of Germany, 643,000,000; if as dense as that of England and Wales 1,173,000,000; if as dense as that of Belgium, 1,430,000,000.

But we are to have not only the larger portion of the Anglo-Saxon race for generations to come, we may reasonably expect to develop the highest type of Anglo-Saxon civilization. If human progress follows a law of development, if

"Time's noblest offspring is the last,"

our civilization should be the noblest; for we are

"The heirs of all the ages in the foremost files of time,"

and not only do we occupy the latitude of power, but *our land is the last to be occupied in that latitude.* There is no other virgin soil in the North Temperate Zone. If the consummation of human progress is not to be looked for here, if there is yet to flower a higher civilization, where is the soil that is to produce it? Whipple says: "There has never been a great migration that did not result in a new form of national genius." Our national genius is Anglo-Saxon, but not English, its distinctive type is the result of a finer nervous organization, which is certainly being developed in this country. . . .

Mr. Darwin is not only disposed to see, in the superior vigor of our people, an illustration of his favorite theory of natural selection, but even intimates that the world's history thus far has been simply preparatory for our future, and tributary to it. He says: "There is apparently much truth in the belief that the wonderful progress of the United States, as well as the character of the people, are the results of natural selection; for the more energetic, restless, and courageous men from all parts of Europe have emigrated during the last ten or twelve generations to that great country, and have there succeeded best. Looking at the distant future, I do not think that the Rev. Mr. Zincke takes an exaggerated view when he says: 'All other series of events — as that which resulted in the culture of mind in Greece, and that which resulted in the Empire of Rome — only appear to have purpose and value when viewed in connection with, or rather as subsidiary to, the great stream of Anglo-Saxon emigration to the West.'"

There is abundant reason to believe that the Anglo-Saxon race is to be, is, indeed, already becoming, more effective here than in the mother country. The marked superiority of this race is due, in large measure, to its highly mixed origin. Says Rawlinson: "It is a general rule, now almost universally admitted by ethnologists, that the mixed races of mankind are superior to the pure ones"; and adds: "Even the Jews, who are so often cited as an example of a race at once pure and strong, may, with more reason, be adduced on the opposite side of the argument." The ancient Egyptians, the Greeks, and the Romans, were all mixed races. Among modern races, the most conspicuous example is afforded by the Anglo-Saxons. Mr. Green's studies show that Mr. Tennyson's poetic line,

"Saxon and Norman and Dane are we,"

must be supplemented with Celt and Gaul, Welshman and Irishman, Frisian and Flamand, French Huguenot and German Palatine. What took place a thousand years ago and more in England again transpires today in the United States. "History repeats itself"; but, as the wheels of history are the chariot wheels of the Almighty, there is, with every revolution, an onward movement toward the goal of his eternal purposes. There is here a new commingling of races; and, while the largest injections of foreign blood are substantially the same elements that constituted the original Anglo Saxon admixture, so that we may infer the general type will be preserved, there are strains of other bloods being added, which, if Mr. Emerson's remark is true, that "the best nations are those most widely related," may be expected to improve the stock, and aid it to a higher destiny. If the dangers of immigration, which have been pointed out, can be successfully met for the next few years, until it has passed its climax, it may be expected to add value to the amalgam which will constitute the new Anglo-Saxon race of the New World. Concerning our future, Herbert Spencer says: "One great result is, I think, tolerably clear. From biological truths it is to be inferred that the eventual mixture of the allied varieties of the Aryan race, forming the population, will produce a more powerful type of man than has hitherto existed, and a type of man more plastic, more adaptable, more capable of undergoing the modifications needful for complete social life. I think, whatever difficulties they may have to surmount, and whatever tribulations they may have to pass through, the Americans may reasonably look forward to a time when they will have produced a civilization grander than any the world has known."

It may be easily shown, and is of no small significance, that the two great ideas of which the Anglo-Saxon is the exponent are having a fuller development in the United States than in Great Britain. There the union of Church and State tends strongly to paralyze some of the members of the body of Christ. Here there is no such influence to destroy spiritual life and power. Here, also, has been evolved the form of government consistent with the largest possible civil liberty. Furthermore, it is significant that the marked characteristics of this race are being here emphasized most. Among the most striking features of the Anglo-Saxon is his money-making power — a power of increasing importance in the widening commerce of the world's future. We have seen, in a preceding chapter, that, although England is by far the richest nation of Europe, we have already outstripped her in the race after wealth, and we have only begun the development of our vast resources.

Again, another marked characteristic of the Anglo-Saxon is what may be called an instinct or genius for colonizing. His unequaled energy, his indomitable perseverance, and his personal independence, made him a pioneer. He excels all others in pushing his way into new countries. It was those in whom this tendency was strongest that came to America, and this inherited tendency has been further developed by the westward sweep of successive generations across the continent. So noticeable has this characteristic become that English visitors remark it. Charles Dickens once said that the typical American would hesitate to enter heaven unless assured that he could go further west.

Again, nothing more manifestly distinguishes the Anglo-Saxon than his intense and persistent energy; and he is developing in the United States an energy which, in eager activity and effectiveness, is peculiarly American. This is due partly to the fact that Americans are much better fed than Europeans, and partly to the undeveloped resources of a new country, but more largely to our climate, which acts as a constant stimulus. Ten years after the landing of the Pilgrims, the Rev. Francis Higginson, a good observer, wrote: "A sup of New England air is better than a whole flagon of English ale." Thus early had the stimulating effect of our climate been noted. Moreover, our social institutions are stimulating. In Europe the various ranks of society are, like the strata of the earth, fixed and fossilized. There can be no great change without a terrible upheaval, a social earthquake. Here society is like the waters of the sea, mobile; as General Garfield said, and so signally illustrated in his own experience, that which is at the bottom to-day may one day flash on the crest of the highest wave. Every one is free to become whatever he can make of himself; free to transform himself from a rail-splitter or a tanner or a canal-boy, into the nation's President. Our aristocracy, unlike that of Europe, is open to all comers. Wealth, position, influence, are prizes offered for energy; and every farmer's boy, every apprentice and clerk, every friendless and penniless immigrant, is free to enter the lists. Thus many causes co-operate to produce here the most forceful and tremendous energy in the world.

What is the significance of such facts? These tendencies infold the future; they are the mighty alphabet with which God writes his prophecies. May we not, by a careful laying together of the letters, spell out something of his meaning? It seems to me that God, with infinite wisdom and skill, is training the Anglo-Saxon race for an hour sure to come in the world's future. Heretofore there has always been in the history of the world a comparatively unoccupied land westward, into which the crowded countries of the East have poured their surplus populations. But the widening waves of migration, which millenniums ago rolled east and west from the valley of the Euphrates, meet today on our Pacific coast. There are no more new worlds. The unoccupied arable lands of the earth are limited, and will soon be taken. The time is coming when the pressure of population on the means of subsistence will be felt here as it is now felt in Europe and Asia. Then will the world enter upon a new stage of its history — *the final competition of races, for which the Anglo-Saxon is being schooled*. Long before the thousand millions are here, the mighty *centrifugal* tendency, inherent in this stock and strengthened in the United States, will assert itself. Then this race of unequaled energy, with all the majesty of numbers and the might of wealth behind it — the representative, let us hope, of the largest liberty, the purest Christianity, the highest civilization — having developed peculiarly aggressive traits calculated to impress its institutions upon mankind, will spread itself over the earth. If I read not amiss, this powerful race will move down upon Mexico, down upon Central and South America, out upon the islands of the sea, over upon Africa and beyond. And can any one doubt that the result of this competition of races will be the "survival of the fittest"? . . . "At the present day," says Mr. Darwin, "civilized nations are everywhere supplanting barbarous nations, excepting where the climate opposes a deadly barrier; and they succeed mainly, though not exclusively, through their arts, which are the products of the intellect." Thus the Finns were supplanted by the Aryan races in Europe and Asia, the Tartars by the Russians, and thus the aborigines of North America, Australia and New Zealand are now disappearing before the all-conquering Anglo-Saxons. It would seem as if these inferior tribes were only precursors of a superior race, voices in the wilderness crying: "Prepare ye the way of the Lord!" The savage is a hunter; by the incoming of civilization the game is driven away and disappears before the hunter becomes a herder or an agriculturist. The savage is ignorant of many diseases of civilization which, when he is exposed to them, attack him before he learns how to treat them. Civilization also has its vices, of which the uninitiated savage is innocent. He proves an apt learner of vice, but dull enough in the school of morals. Every civilization has its destructive and preservative elements. The Anglo-Saxon race would speedily decay but for the salt of Christianity. Bring savages into contact with our civilization, and its destructive forces become operative at once, while years are necessary to render effective the saving influences of Christian instruction. Moreover, the pioneer wave of our civilization carries with it more scum than salt. Where there is one missionary, there are hundreds of miners or traders or adventurers ready to debauch the native. Whether the extinction of inferior races before the advancing Anglo-Saxon seems to the reader sad or otherwise, it certainly appears probable. I know of nothing except climatic conditions to prevent this race from populating Africa as it has peopled North America. And those portions of Africa which are unfavorable to Anglo-Saxon life are less extensive than was once supposed. The Dutch Boers, after two centuries of life there, are as hardy as any race on earth. The Anglo-Saxon has established himself in climates totally diverse — Canada, South Africa and India — and, through several generations, has preserved his essential race characteristics. He is not, of course, superior to climatic influences; but, even in warm climates, he is likely to retain his aggressive vigor long enough to supplant races already enfeebled. Thus, in what Dr. Bushnell calls "the out-populating power of the Christian stock," may be found God's final and complete solution of the dark problem of heathenism among many inferior peoples.

Some of the stronger races, doubtless, may be able to preserve their integrity; but, in order to compete with the Anglo-Saxon, they will probably be forced to adopt his methods and instruments, his civilization and his religion. . . .

Is there room for reasonable doubt that this race, unless devitalized by alcohol and tobacco, is destined to dispossess many weaker races, assimilate others, and mold the remainder, until, in a very true and important sense, it has Anglo-Saxonized mankind? Already "the English language, saturated with Christian ideas, gathering up into itself the best thought of all the ages, is the great agent of Christian civilization throughout the world; at this moment affecting the destinies and molding the character of half the human race." Jacob Grimm, the German philologist, said of this language: "It seems chosen, like its people, to rule in future times in a still greater degree in all the corners of the earth." He predicted, indeed, that the language of Shakespeare would eventually become the language of mankind. Is not Tennyson's noble prophecy to find its fulfillment in Anglo-Saxondom's extending its dominion and influence —

"Till the war-drum throbs no longer, and the battle-flags are furl'd
In the Parliament of man, the Federation of the world."

In my own mind, there is no doubt that the Anglo-Saxon is to exercise
the commanding influence in the world's future; but the exact nature of
that influence is, as yet, undetermined. How far his civilization will be
materialistic and atheistic, and how long it will take thoroughly to Chris-
tianize and sweeten it, how rapidly he will hasten the coming of the
kingdom wherein dwelleth righteousness, or how many ages he may re-
tard it, is still uncertain; but *it is now being swiftly determined.* . . .

Alfred Thayer Mahan
SEA POWER AND IMPERIALISM

❦[*1890*]❦ OF ALL American historical writings, those of Alfred T. Mahan
had the greatest practical importance. The son of a West Point professor,
Mahan (1840-1914) chose a career in the navy, graduated from the Naval
Academy at Annapolis, served as a Union officer during the Civil War, and
eventually rose to the rank of rear admiral. In 1894 he was appointed lecturer
on history, strategy, and tactics and president of the Naval War College at
Newport, R.I. During the Spanish-American War he was a member of the
naval board of strategy.

Meanwhile he wrote numerous books and articles on the role of sea power in
history. Sea power, he argued, had been and continued to be decisive in the
national struggles of the modern world. As means to greatness for the United
States, he advocated the construction of a big navy, the building of an Isthmian
canal, the acquisition of overseas bases, the promotion of foreign trade and
investment, and the cultivation of friendship with Great Britain. His writings
were used by American proponents of navalism and expansion, among them
his friends Theodore Roosevelt and Henry Cabot Lodge. His arguments appealed also to big-navy men abroad; his books were placed, at the direction of
Kaiser William II, in the ships' libraries of the German Navy.

Mahan's views are well summarized in his essay "The United States Looking
Outward," originally published as a magazine article in 1890 and republished
in *The Interest of America in Sea Power* (1897).

THE UNITED STATES LOOKING OUTWARD

INDICATIONS are not wanting of an approaching change in the thoughts
and policy of Americans as to their relations with the world outside their
own borders. For the past quarter of a century, the predominant idea,
which has asserted itself successfully at the polls and shaped the course of

the government, has been to preserve the home market for the home industries. The employer and the workman alike have been taught to look at the various economical measures proposed from this point of view, to regard with hostility any step favoring the intrusion of the foreign producer upon their own domain, and rather to demand increasingly rigorous measures of exclusion than to acquiesce in any loosening of the chain that binds the consumer to them. The inevitable consequence has followed, as in all cases when the mind or the eye is exclusively fixed in one direction, that the danger of loss or the prospect of advantage in another quarter has been overlooked; and although the abounding resources of the country have maintained the exports at a high figure, this flattering result has been due more to the superabundant bounty of Nature than to the demand of other nations for our protected manufactures.

For nearly the lifetime of a generation, therefore, American industries have been thus protected, until the practice has assumed the force of a tradition, and is clothed in the mail of conservatism. In their mutual relations, these industries resemble the activities of a modern ironclad that has heavy armor, but inferior engines and guns; mighty for defence, weak for offence. Within, the home market is secured; but outside, beyond the broad seas, there are the markets of the world, that can be entered and controlled only by a vigorous contest, to which the habit of trusting to protection by statute does not conduce.

At bottom, however, the temperament of the American people is essentially alien to such a sluggish attitude. Independently of all bias for or against protection, it is safe to predict that, when the opportunities for gain abroad are understood, the course of American enterprise will cleave a channel by which to reach them. Viewed broadly, it is a most welcome as well as significant fact that a prominent and influential advocate of protection, a leader of the party committed to its support, a keen reader of the signs of the times and of the drift of opinion, has identified himself with a line of policy which looks to nothing less than such modifications of the tariff as may expand the commerce of the United States to all quarters of the globe. Men of all parties can unite on the words of Mr. Blaine, as reported in a recent speech: "It is not an ambitious destiny for so great a country as ours to manufacture only what we can consume, or produce only what we can eat." In face of this utterance of so shrewd and able a public man, even the extreme character of the recent tariff legislation seems but a sign of the coming change, and brings to mind that famous Continental System, of which our own is the analogue, to support which Napoleon added legion to legion and enterprise to enterprise, till the fabric of the Empire itself crashed beneath the weight.

The interesting and significant feature of this changing attitude is the turning of the eyes outward, instead of inward only, to seek the welfare of the country. To affirm the importance of distant markets, and the relation to them of our own immense powers of production, implies logically the recognition of the link that joins the products and the markets, — that is, the carrying trade; the three together constituting that chain of maritime power to which Great Britain owes her wealth and greatness. Further, is it too much to say that, as two of these links, the shipping and the markets, are exterior to our own borders, the acknowledgment of them carries with it a view of the relations of the United States to the world radically distinct from the simple idea of self-sufficingness? We shall not follow far this line of thought before there will dawn the realization of America's unique position, facing the older worlds of the East and West, her shores washed by the oceans which touch the one or the other, but which are common to her alone.

Coincident with these signs of change in our own policy there is a restlessness in the world at large which is deeply significant, if not ominous. It is beside our purpose to dwell upon the internal state of Europe, whence, if disturbances arise, the effect upon us may be but partial and indirect. But the great seaboard powers there do not stand on guard against their continental rivals only; they cherish also aspirations for commercial extension, for colonies, and for influence in distant regions, which may bring, and, even under our present contracted policy, already have brought them into collision with ourselves. The incident of the Samoa Islands, trivial apparently, was nevertheless eminently suggestive of European ambitions. America then roused from sleep as to interests closely concerning her future. At this moment internal troubles are imminent in the Sandwich Islands, where it should be our fixed determination to allow no foreign influence to equal our own. All over the world German commercial and colonial push is coming into collision with other nations: witness the affair of the Caroline Islands with Spain; the partition of New Guinea with England; the yet more recent negotiation between these two powers concerning their share in Africa, viewed with deep distrust and jealousy by France; the Samoa affair; the conflict between German control and American interests in the islands of the western Pacific; and the alleged progress of German influence in Central and South America. It is noteworthy that, while these various contentions are sustained with the aggressive military spirit characteristic of the German Empire, they are credibly said to arise from the national temper more than from the deliberate policy of the government, which in this matter does not lead, but follows, the feeling of the people, — a condition much more formidable.

There is no sound reason for believing that the world has passed into a period of assured peace outside the limits of Europe. Unsettled political conditions, such as exist in Haïti, Central America, and many of the Pacific islands, especially the Hawaiian group, when combined with great military or commercial importance as is the case with most of these positions, involve, now as always, dangerous germs of quarrel, against which it is prudent at least to be prepared. Undoubtedly, the general temper of nations is more averse from war than it was of old. If no less selfish and grasping than our predecessors, we feel more dislike to the discomforts and sufferings attendant upon a breach of peace; but to retain that highly valued repose and the undisturbed enjoyment of the returns of commerce, it is necessary to argue upon somewhat equal terms of strength with an adversary. It is the preparedness of the enemy, and not acquiescence in the existing state of things, that now holds back the armies of Europe.

On the other hand, neither the sanctions of international law nor the justice of a cause can be depended upon for a fair settlement of differences, when they come into conflict with a strong political necessity on the one side opposed to comparative weakness on the other. In our still-pending dispute over the seal-fishing of Bering Sea, whatever may be thought of the strength of our argument, in view of generally admitted principles of international law, it is beyond doubt that our contention is reasonable, just, and in the interest of the world at large. But in the attempt to enforce it we have come into collision not only with national susceptibilities as to the honor of the flag, which we ourselves very strongly share, but also with a state governed by a powerful necessity, and exceedingly strong where we are particularly weak and exposed. Not only has Great Britain a mighty navy and we a long defenceless seacoast, but it is a great commercial and political advantage to her that her larger colonies, and above all Canada, should feel that the power of the mother country is something which they need, and upon which they can count. The dispute is between the United States and Canada, not the United States and Great Britain; but it has been ably used by the latter to promote the solidarity of sympathy between herself and her colony. With the mother country alone an equitable arrangement, conducive to well-understood mutual interests, could be reached readily; but the purely local and peculiarly selfish wishes of Canadian fishermen dictate the policy of Great Britain, because Canada is the most important link uniting her to her colonies and maritime interests in the Pacific. In case of a European war, it is possible that the British navy will not be able to hold open the route through the Mediterranean to the East; but having a strong naval station at Halifax, and another at Esquimalt, on the Pacific, the two connected by the Canadian Pacific Railroad, England possesses an alternate line of communication far less exposed to maritime aggression than the former, or than the third route by the Cape of Good Hope, as well as two bases essential to the service of her commerce, or other naval operations, in the North Atlantic and the Pacific. Whatever arrangement of this question is finally reached, the fruit of Lord Salisbury's attitude scarcely can fail to be a strengthening of the sentiments of attachment to, and reliance upon, the mother country, not only in Canada, but in the other great colonies. These feelings of attachment and mutual dependence supply the living spirit, without which the nascent schemes for Imperial Federation are but dead mechanical contrivances; nor are they without influence upon such generally unsentimental considerations as those of buying and selling, and the course of trade.

This dispute, seemingly paltry yet really serious, sudden in its appearance and dependent for its issue upon other considerations than its own merits, may serve to convince us of many latent and yet unforeseen dangers to the peace of the western hemisphere, attendant upon the opening of a canal through the Central American Isthmus. In a general way, it is evident enough that this canal, by modifying the direction of trade routes, will induce a great increase of commercial activity and carrying trade throughout the Caribbean Sea; and that this now comparatively deserted nook of the ocean will become, like the Red Sea, a great thoroughfare of shipping, and will attract, as never before in our day, the interest and ambition of maritime nations. Every position in that sea will have enhanced commercial and military value, and the canal itself will become a strategic centre of the most vital importance. Like the Canadian Pacific Railroad, it will be a link between the two oceans; but, unlike it, the use, unless most carefully guarded by treaties, will belong wholly to the belligerent which controls the sea by its naval power. In case of war, the United States will unquestionably command the Canadian Railroad, despite the deterrent force of operations by the hostile navy upon our seaboard; but no less unquestionably will she be impotent, as against any of the great maritime powers, to control the Central American canal. Militarily speaking, and having reference to European complications only, the piercing of the Isthmus is nothing but a disaster to the United States, in the present state of her military and naval preparation. It is especially dangerous to the Pacific coast; but the increased exposure of one part of our seaboard reacts unfavorably upon the whole military situation.

Despite a certain great original superiority conferred by our geographical nearness and immense resources, — due, in other words, to our natural advantages, and not to our intelligent preparations, — the United States is woefully unready, not only in fact but in purpose, to assert in the Caribbean and Central America a weight of influence proportioned to the extent of her interests. We have not the navy, and, what is worse, we are not willing to have the navy, that will weigh seriously in any disputes with those nations whose interests will conflict there with our own. We have not, and we are not anxious to provide, the defence of the seaboard which will leave the navy free for its work at sea. We have not, but many other powers have, positions, either within or on the borders of the Caribbean, which not only possess great natural advantages for the control of that sea, but have received and are receiving that artificial strength of fortification and armament which will make them practically inexpugnable. On the contrary, we have not on the Gulf of Mexico even the beginning of a navy yard which could serve as the base of our operations. Let me not be misunderstood. I am not regretting that we have not the means to meet on terms of equality the great navies of the Old World. I recognize, what few at least say, that, despite its great surplus revenue, this country is poor in proportion to its length of seaboard and its exposed points. That which I deplore, and which is a sober, just, and reasonable cause of deep national concern, is that the nation neither has nor cares to have its sea frontier so defended, and its navy of such power, as shall suffice, with the advantages of our position, to weight seriously when inevitable discussions arise, — such as we have recently had about Samoa and Bering Sea, and which may at any moment come up about the Caribbean Sea or the canal. Is the United States, for instance, prepared to allow Germany to acquire the Dutch stronghold of Curaçao, fronting the Atlantic outlet of both the proposed canals of Panama and Nicaragua? Is she prepared to acquiesce in any foreign power purchasing from Haïti a naval station on the Windward Passage, through which pass our steamer routes to the Isthmus? Would she acquiesce in a foreign protectorate over the Sandwich Islands, that great central station of the Pacific, equidistant from San Francisco, Samoa, and the Marquesas, and an important post on our lines of communication with both Australia and China? Or will it be maintained that any one of these questions, supposing it to arise, is so exclusively one-sided, the arguments of policy and right so exclusively with us, that the other party will at once yield his eager wish, and gracefully withdraw? Was it so at Samoa? Is it so as regards Bering Sea? The motto seen on so many ancient cannon, *Ultima ratio regum*, is not without its message to republics.

It is perfectly reasonable and legitimate, in estimating our needs of military preparation, to take into account the remoteness of the chief naval and military nations from our shores, and the consequent difficulty of maintaining operations at such a distance. It is equally proper, in framing our policy, to consider the jealousies of the European family of states, and their consequent unwillingness to incur the enmity of a people so strong as ourselves; their dread of our revenge in the future, as well as their inability to detach more than a certain part of their forces to our shores without losing much of their own weight in the councils of Europe. In truth, a careful determination of the force that Great Britain or France could probably spare for operations against our coasts, if the latter were suitably defended, without weakening their European position or unduly exposing their colonies and commerce, is the starting-point from which to calculate the strength of our own navy. If the latter be superior to the force that thus can be sent against it, and the coast be so defended as to leave the navy free to strike where it will, we can maintain our rights; not merely the rights which international law concedes, and which the moral sense of nations now supports, but also those equally real rights which, though not conferred by law, depend upon a clear preponderance of interest, upon obviously necessary policy, upon self-preservation, either total or partial. Were we so situated now in respect of military strength, we could secure our perfectly just claim as to the seal fisheries; not by seizing foreign ships on the open sea, but by the evident fact that, our cities being protected from maritime attack, our position and superior population lay open the Canadian Pacific, as well as the frontier of the Dominion, to do with as we please. Diplomats do not flourish such disagreeable truths in each other's faces; they look for a *modus vivendi,* and find it.

While, therefore, the advantages of our own position in the western hemisphere, and the disadvantages under which the operations of a European state would labor, are undeniable and just elements in the calculations of the statesman, it is folly to look upon them as sufficient alone for our security. Much more needs to be cast into the scale that it may incline in favor of our strength. They are mere defensive factors, and partial at that. Though distant, our shores can be reached; being defenceless, they can detain but a short time a force sent against them. With a probability of three months' peace in Europe, no maritime power would fear to support its demands by a number of ships with which it would be loath indeed to part for a year.

Yet, were our sea frontier as strong as it now is weak, passive self-defence, whether in trade or war, would be but a poor policy, so long as this world continues to be one of struggle and vicissitude. All around us now is strife; "the struggle of life," "the race of life," are phrases so familiar that we do not feel their significance till we stop to think about them. Everywhere nation is arrayed against nation; our own no less than others. What is our protective system but an organized warfare? In carrying it on, it is true, we have only to use certain procedures which all states now concede to be a legal exercise of the national power, even though injurious to themselves. It is lawful, they say, to do what we will with our own. Are our people, however, so unaggressive that they are likely not to want their own way in matters where their interests turn on points of disputed right, or so little sensitive as to submit quietly to encroachment by others, in quarters where they long have considered their own influence should prevail?

Our self-imposed isolation in the matter of markets, and the decline of our shipping interest in the last thirty years, have coincided singularly with an actual remoteness of this continent from the life of the rest of the world. The writer has before him a map of the North and South Atlantic oceans, showing the direction of the principal trade routes and the proportion of tonnage passing over each; and it is curious to note what deserted regions, comparatively, are the Gulf of Mexico, the Caribbean Sea, and the adjoining countries and islands. A broad band stretches from our northern Atlantic coast to the English Channel; another as broad from the British Islands to the East, through the Mediterranean and Red Sea, overflowing the borders of the latter in order to express the volume of trade. Around either cape — Good Hope and Horn — pass strips of about one-fourth this width, joining near the equator, midway between Africa and South America. From the West Indies issues a thread, indicating the present commerce of Great Britain with a region which once, in the Napoleonic wars, embraced one-fourth of the whole trade of the Empire. The significance is unmistakable: Europe has now little mercantile interest in the Caribbean Sea.

When the Isthmus is pierced, this isolation will pass away, and with it the indifference of foreign nations. From wheresoever they come and whithersoever they afterward go, all ships that use the canal will pass through the Caribbean. Whatever the effect produced upon the prosperity of the adjacent continent and islands by the thousand wants attendant upon maritime activity, around such a focus of trade will centre large commercial and political interests. To protect and develop its own, each nation will seek points of support and means of influence in a quarter where the United States always has been jealously sensitive to the intrusion of European powers. The precise value of the Monroe Doctrine is understood very loosely by most Americans, but the effect of the familiar phrase has been to develop a national sensitiveness, which is a more frequent cause of war than material interests; and over disputes caused by such feelings there will preside none of the calming influence due to the moral authority of international law, with its recognized principles, for the points in dispute will be of policy, of interest, not of conceded right. Already France and Great Britain are giving to ports held by them a degree of artificial strength uncalled for by their present importance. They look to the near future. Among the islands and on the mainland there are many positions of great importance, held now by weak or unstable states. Is the United States willing to see them sold to a powerful rival? But what right will she invoke against the transfer? She can allege but one, — that of her reasonable policy supported by her might.

Whether they will or no, Americans must now begin to look outward. The growing production of the country demands it. An increasing volume of public sentiment demands it. The position of the United States, between the two Old Worlds and the two great oceans, makes the same claim, which will soon be strengthened by the creation of the new link joining the Atlantic and Pacific. The tendency will be maintained and increased by the growth of the European colonies in the Pacific, by the advancing civilization of Japan, and by the rapid peopling of our Pacific States with men who have all the aggressive spirit of the advanced line of national progress. Nowhere does a vigorous foreign policy find more favor than among the people west of the Rocky Mountains.

It has been said that, in our present state of unpreparedness, a trans-isthmian canal will be a military disaster to the United States, and especially to the Pacific coast. When the canal is finished, the Atlantic seaboard will be neither more nor less exposed than it now is; it will merely share with the country at large the increased danger of foreign complications with inadequate means to meet them. The danger of the Pacific coast will be greater by so much as the way between it and Europe is shortened through a passage which the stronger maritime power can control. The danger will lie not merely in the greater facility for despatching a hostile squadron from Europe, but also in the fact that a more powerful fleet than formerly can be maintained on that coast by a European power, because it can be called home so much more promptly in case of need. The greatest weakness of the Pacific ports, however, if wisely met by our government, will go far to insure our naval superiority there. The two chief centres, San Francisco and Puget Sound, owing to the width and the great depth of the entrances, cannot be effectively protected by torpedoes; and consequently, as fleets can always pass batteries through an unobstructed channel, they cannot obtain perfect security by means of fortifications only. Valuable as such works will be to them, they must be further garrisoned by coast-defence ships, whose part in repelling an enemy will be co-ordinated with that of the batteries. The sphere of action of such ships should not be permitted to extend far beyond the port to which they are allotted, and of whose defence they form an essential part; but within that sweep they will always be a powerful reinforcement to the sea-going navy, when the strategic conditions of a war cause hostilities to centre around their port. By sacrificing power to go long distances, the coast-defence ship gains proportionate weight of armor and guns; that is, of defensive and offensive strength. It therefore adds an element of unique value to the fleet with which it for a time acts. No foreign states, except Great Britain, have ports so near our Pacific coast as to bring it within the radius of action of their coast-defense ships; and it is very doubtful whether even Great Britain will put such ships at Vancouver Island, the chief value of which will be lost to her when the Canadian Pacific is severed, — a blow always in the power of this country. It is upon our Atlantic seaboard that the mistress of Halifax, of Bermuda, and of Jamaica will now defend Vancouver and the Canadian Pacific. In the present state of our seaboard defence she can do so absolutely. What is all Canada compared with our exposed great cities? Even were the coast fortified, she still could do so, if our navy be no stronger than is designed as yet. What harm can we do Canada proportionate to the injury we should suffer by the interruption of our coasting trade, and by a blockade of Boston, New York, the Delaware, and the Chesapeake? Such a blockade Great Britain certainly could make technically efficient, under the somewhat loose definitions of international law. Neutrals would accept it as such.

The military needs of the Pacific States, as well as their supreme importance to the whole country, are yet a matter of the future, but of a future so near that provision should begin immediately. To weigh their importance, consider what influence in the Pacific would be attributed to a nation comprising only the States of Washington, Oregon, and California, when filled with such men as now people them and still are pouring in, and which controlled such maritime centres as San Francisco, Puget Sound, and the Columbia River. Can it be counted less because they are bound by the ties of blood and close political union to the great communities of the East? But such influence, to work without jar and friction, requires underlying military readiness, like the proverbial iron hand under the velvet glove. To provide this, three things are needful: First, protection of the chief harbors, by fortifications and coast-defence ships, which gives defensive strength, provides security to the community within, and supplies the bases necessary to all military operations. Secondly, naval force, the arm of offensive power, which alone enables a country to extend its influence outward. Thirdly, it should be an inviolable resolution of our national policy, that no foreign state should henceforth acquire a coaling position within three thousand miles of San Francisco, — and a distance which includes the Hawaiian and Galapagos islands and the coast of Central America. For fuel is the life of modern naval war; it is the food of the ship; without it the modern monsters of the deep die of inanition. Around it, therefore, cluster some of the most important considerations of naval strategy. In the Caribbean and in the Atlantic we are confronted with many a foreign coal depot, bidding us stand to our arms, even as Carthage bade Rome; but let us not acquiesce in an addition to our dangers, a further diversion of our strength, by being forestalled in the North Pacific.

In conclusion, while Great Britain is undoubtedly the most formidable of our possible enemies, both by her great navy and by the strong positions she holds near our coasts, it must be added that a cordial understanding with that country is one of the first of our external interests. Both nations doubtless, and properly, seek their own advantage; but both, also, are controlled by a sense of law and justice, drawn from the same sources, and deep-rooted in their instincts. Whatever temporary aberration may occur, a return to mutual standards of right will certainly follow. Formal alliance between the two is out of the question, but a cordial recognition of the similarity of character and ideas will give birth to sympathy, which in turn will facilitate a co-operation beneficial to both; for if sentimentality is weak, sentiment is strong.

Albert J. Beveridge

THE PHILIPPINES

◄{*1900*}► THE Spanish-American War transformed the issue of imperialism. In the first place it brought a string of island possessions under the American flag—Puerto Rico, Guam, the Philippines. The future isthmian canal demanded by Mahan and other imperialists thereupon became an urgent necessity. But the war also brought economic imperialism to the fore. Men like Mahan had argued that colonies would stimulate trade, but businessmen in general had opposed overseas ventures, which they feared would unsettle the domestic economy and lead to higher taxes. After the defeat of Spain, however, a massive shift of business sentiment occurred and there was much talk of colonies as markets and as sources of raw materials for American industry.

The most attractive region from the point of view of the economic imperialists was the Philippine archipelago, both for itself and for the supposed entree it provided to "the markets of China." However, the Filipinos, ardently nationalistic, had expected the United States to withdraw from their lands after defeating the Spanish, as the nation had promised to do in Cuba. When it did not, they took up arms against their "liberators" and a bloody guerrilla war ensued. This provoked a great debate in the United States between those who wished to hold the Islands and those who felt that the United States had no business imposing its will on any people who did not wish to be part of the American empire.

One of the key figures in this debate was Albert J. Beveridge of Indiana (1862-1927). A man of fierce enthusiasms and immense industry, Beveridge had been elected to the Senate in 1899, when only 36. He fastened upon the issue of imperialism as a means of making his reputation. Before taking his Senate seat he set out on a tour of the Philippines, determined to make himself an expert on the region. While in the Islands he talked to hundreds of persons, visited the battlefronts, and explored remote areas, cramming his notebook with facts and opinions. Then, when Congress met, he seized the first opportunity to make an elaborate speech on the subject, despite the fact that tradition required that freshmen senators ordinarily remain silent for a year before addressing their colleagues. Such was the interest in his views that the galleries were packed, when, on January 9, 1900, he rose to speak in defense of the proposition: *"Resolved . . . that the Philippines Islands are territory belonging to the United States; that it is the intention of the United States to retain them as such and to establish and maintain such governmental control throughout the archipelago as the situation may demand."*

SPEECH IN THE SENATE, 1900

MR. BEVERIDGE: Mr. President, I address the Senate at this time because Senators and Members of the House on both sides have asked that I give to Congress and the country my observations in the Philippines and the far East, and the conclusions which those observations compel; and because of hurtful resolutions introduced and utterances made in the Senate, every word of which will cost and is costing the lives of American soldiers.

Mr. President, the times call for candor. The Philippines are ours forever, "territory belonging to the United States," as the Constitution calls them. And just beyond the Philippines are China's illimitable markets. We will not retreat from either. We will not repudiate our duty in the archipelago. We will not abandon our opportunity in the Orient. We will not renounce our part in the mission of our race, trustee, under God, of the civilization of the world. And we will move forward to our work, not howling out regrets like slaves whipped to their burdens, but with gratitude for a task worthy of our strength, and thanksgiving to Almighty God that He has marked us as His chosen people, henceforth to lead in the regeneration of the world.

This island empire is the last land left in all the oceans. If it should prove a mistake to abandon it, the blunder once made would be irretrievable. If it proves a mistake to hold it, the error can be corrected when we will. Every other progressive nation stands ready to relieve us.

But to hold it will be no mistake. Our largest trade henceforth must

be with Asia. The Pacific is our ocean. More and more Europe will manufacture the most it needs, secure from its colonies the most it consumes.
Where shall we turn for consumers of our surplus? Geography answers
the question. China is our natural customer. She is nearer to us than to
England, Germany, or Russia, the commercial powers of the present and
the future. They have moved nearer to China by securing permanent bases
on her borders. The Philippines give us a base at the door of all the
East. . . .

But if they did not command China, India, the Orient, the whole Pacific
for purposes of offense, defense, and trade, the Philippines are so valuable
in themselves that we should hold them. I have cruised more than 2,000
miles through the archipelago, every moment a surprise at its loveliness
and wealth. I have ridden hundreds of miles on the islands, every foot of
the way a revelation of vegetable and mineral riches.

No land in America surpasses in fertility the plains and valleys of Luzon.
Rice and coffee, sugar and cocoanuts, hemp and tobacco, and many products of the temperate as well as the tropic zone grow in various sections
of the archipelago. I have seen hundreds of bushels of Indian corn lying
in a road fringed with banana trees. The forests of Negros, Mindanao,
Mindoro, Paluan, and parts of Luzon are invaluable and intact. The wood
of the Philippines can supply the furniture of the world for a century to
come. At Cebu the best informed man in the island told me that 40 miles
of Cebu's mountain chain are practically mountains of coal. Pablo Majia,
one of the most reliable men on the islands, confirmed the statement. Some
declare that the coal is only lignite; but ship captains who have used it
told me that it is better steamer fuel than the best coal of Japan.

I have a nugget of pure gold picked up in its present form on the banks
of a Philippine creek. I have gold dust washed out by crude processes of
careless natives from the sands of a Philippine stream. Both indicate great
deposits at the source from which they come. In one of the islands great
deposits of copper exist untouched. The mineral wealth of this empire of
the ocean will one day surprise the world. I base this statement partly on
personal observation, but chiefly on the testimony of foreign merchants in
the Philippines, who have practically investigated the subject, and upon
the unanimous opinion of natives and priests. And the mineral wealth is
but a small fraction of the agricultural wealth of these islands.

And the wood, hemp, copra, and other products of the Philippines supply what we need and can not ourselves produce. And the markets they
will themselves afford will be immense. Spain's export and import trade,
with the islands undeveloped, was $11,534,731 annually. Our trade with
the islands developed will be $125,000,000 annually, for who believes that

we can not do ten times as well as Spain? Consider their imperial dimensions. Luzon is larger and richer than New York, Pennsylvania, Illinois, or Ohio. Mindanao is larger and richer than all New England, exclusive of Maine. Manila, as a port of call and exchange, will, in the time of men now living, far surpass Liverpool. Behold the exhaustless markets they command. It is as if a half dozen of our States were set down between Oceania and the Orient, and those States themselves undeveloped and unspoiled of their primitive wealth and resources. . . .

It will be hard for Americans who have not studied them to understand the people. They are a barbarous race, modified by three centuries of contact with a decadent race. The Filipino is the South Sea Malay, put through a process of three hundred years of superstition in religion, dishonesty in dealing, disorder in habits of industry, and cruelty, caprice, and corruption in government. It is barely possible that 1,000 men in all the archipelago are capable of self-government in the Anglo-Saxon sense.

My own belief is that there are not 100 men among them who comprehend what Anglo-Saxon self-government even means, and there are over 5,000,000 people to be governed. . . . Aguinaldo is a clever, popular leader, able, brave, resourceful, cunning, ambitious, unscrupulous, and masterful. He is full of decision, initiative, and authority, and had the confidence of the masses. He is a natural dictator. His ideas of government are absolute orders, implicit obedience, or immediate death. He understands the character of his countrymen. He is a Malay Sylla; not a Filipino Washington.

These conclusions were forced upon me by observing the people in all walks of life in the different islands, and by conversations with foreign merchants, priests, mestizos, pure Filipinos, and every variety of mind, character, and opinion from San Fernando, in Luzon, on down through the entire archipelago to the interior of Sulu. . . .

Senators, it would be better to abandon this combined garden and Gibraltar of the Pacific, and count our blood and treasure already spent a profitable loss, than to apply any academic arrangement of self-government to these children. They are not capable of self-government. How could they be? They are not of a self-governing race. They are Orientals, Malays, instructed by Spaniards in the latter's worst estate.

They know nothing of practical government except as they have witnessed the weak, corrupt, cruel, and capricious rule of Spain. What magic will anyone employ to dissolve in their minds and characters those impressions of governors and governed which three centuries of misrule has created? What alchemy will change the oriental quality of their blood and set the self-governing currents of the American pouring through their Malay veins? How shall they, in the twinkling of an eye, be exalted to the heights of self-governing peoples which required a thousand years for us to reach, Anglo-Saxon though we are?

Let men beware how they employ the term "self-government." It is a sacred term. It is the watchword at the door of the inner temple of liberty, for liberty does not always mean self-government. Self-government is a method of liberty — the highest, simple, best — and it is acquired only after centuries of study and struggle and experiment and instruction and all the elements of the progress of man. Self-government is no base and common thing, to be bestowed on the merely audacious. It is the degree which crowns the graduate of liberty, not the name of liberty's infant class, who have not yet mastered the alphabet of freedom. Savage blood, oriental blood, Malay blood, Spanish example — are these the elements of self-government?

We must act on the situation as it exists, not as we would wish it. I have talked with hundreds of these people, getting their views as to the practical workings of self-government. The great majority simply do not understand any participation in any government whatever. The most enlightened among them declare that self-government will succeed because the employers of labor will compel their employees to vote as their employer wills and that this will insure intelligent voting. I was assured that we could depend upon good men always being in office because the officials who constitute the government will nominate their successors, choose those among the people who will do the voting, and determine how and where elections will be held.

The most ardent advocate of self-government that I met was anxious that I should know that such a government would be tranquil because, as he said, if anyone criticised it, the government would shoot the offender. A few of them have a sort of verbal understanding of the democratic theory, but the above are the examples of the ideas of the practical workings of self-government entertained by the aristocracy, the rich planters and traders, and heavy employers of labor, the men who would run the government.

Example for decades will be necessary to instruct them in American ideas and methods of administration. Example, example; always example —this alone will teach them. As a race, their general ability is not excellent. Educators, both men and women, to whom I have talked in Cebu and Luzon, were unanimous in the opinion that in all solid and useful education they are, as a people, dull and stupid. In showy things, like carving and painting or embroidery or music, they have apparent aptitude, but even this is superficial and never thorough. They have facility of speech, too.

The three best educators on the island at different times made to me the same comparison, that the common people in their stupidity are like their caribou bulls. They are not even good agriculturists. Their waste of cane is inexcusable. Their destruction of hemp fiber is childish. They are incurably indolent. They have no continuity or thoroughness of industry. They will quit work without notice and amuse themselves until the money they have earned is spent. They are like children playing at men's work.

No one need fear their competition with our labor. No reward could beguile, no force compel, these children of indolence to leave their trifling lives for the fierce and fervid industry of high-wrought America. The very reverse is the fact. One great problem is the necessary labor to develop these islands — to build the roads, open the mines, clear the wilderness, drain the swamps, dredge the harbors. The natives will not supply it. A lingering prejudice against the Chinese may prevent us from letting them supply it. Ultimately, when the real truth of the climate and human conditions is known, it is barely possible that our labor will go there. Even now young men with the right moral fiber and a little capital can make fortunes there as planters.

But the natives will not come here. Let all men dismiss that fear. . . .

The Declaration of Independence does not forbid us to do our part in the regeneration of the world. If it did, the Declaration would be wrong, just as the Articles of Confederation, drafted by the very same men who signed the Declaration, was found to be wrong. The Declaration has no application to the present situation. It was written by self-governing men for self-governing men.

It was written by men who, for a century and a half, had been experimenting in self-government on this continent, and whose ancestors for hundreds of years before had been gradually developing toward that high and holy estate. The Declaration applies only to people capable of self-government. How dare any man prostitute this expression of the very elect of self-governing peoples to a race of Malay children of barbarism, schooled in Spanish methods and ideas? And you, who say the Declaration applies to all men, how dare you deny its application to the American Indian? And if you deny it to the Indian at home, how dare you grant it to the Malay abroad?

The Declaration does not contemplate that all government must have the consent of the governed. It announces that man's "inalienable rights are life, liberty, and the pursuit of happiness; that to secure these rights governments are established among men deriving their just powers from the consent of the governed; that when any form of government becomes destructive of those rights, it is the right of the people to alter or abolish it." "Life, liberty, and the pursuit of happiness" are the important things; "consent of the governed" is one of the means to those ends. . . .

Self-government, when that will best secure these ends, as in the case of people capable of self-government; other appropriate forms when people are not capable of self-government. And so the authors of the Declaration themselves governed the Indian without his consent; the inhabitants of Louisiana without their consent; and ever since the sons of the makers of the Declaration have been governing not by theory, but by practice, after the fashion of our governing race, now by one form, now by another, but always for the purpose of securing the great eternal ends of life, liberty, and the pursuit of happiness, not in the savage, but in the civilized meaning of those terms — life according to orderly methods of civilized society; liberty regulated by law; pursuit of happiness limited by the pursuit of happiness by every other man.

If this is not the meaning of the Declaration, our Government itself denies the Declaration every time it receives the representative of any but a republican form of government, such as that of the Sultan, the Czar, or other absolute autocrats, whose governments, according to the opposition's interpretation of the Declaration, are spurious governments, because the people governed have not "consented" to them. . . .

Mr. President, this question is deeper than any question of party politics; deeper than any question of the isolated policy of our country even; deeper even than any question of constitutional power. It is elemental. It is racial. God has not been preparing the English-speaking and Teutonic peoples for a thousand years for nothing but vain and idle self-contemplation and self-admiration. No! He has made us the master organizers of the world to establish system where chaos reigns. He has given us the spirit of progress to overwhelm the forces of reaction throughout the earth. He has made us adepts in government that we may administer government among savage and senile peoples. Were it not for such a force as this the world would relapse into barbarism and night. And of all our race He has marked the American people as His chosen nation to finally lead in the regeneration of the world. This is the divine mission of America, and it holds for us all the profit, all the glory, all the happiness possible to man. We are trustees of the world's progress, guardians of its righteous peace. The judgment of the Master is upon us: "Ye have been faithful over a few things; I will make you ruler over many things."

What shall history say of us? Shall it say that we renounced that holy trust, left the savage to his base condition, the wilderness to the reign of waste, deserted duty, abandoned glory, forget our sordid profit even, because we feared our strength and read the charter of our powers with the doubter's eye and the quibbler's mind? Shall it say that, called by events to captain and command the proudest, ablest, purest race of history in history's noblest work, we declined that great commission? Our fathers would not have had it so. No! They founded no paralytic government, incapable of the simplest acts of administration. They planted no sluggard people, passive while the world's work calls them. They established no reactionary nation. They unfurled no retreating flag.

That flag has never paused in its onward march. Who dares halt it now — now, when history's largest events are carrying it forward; now, when we are at last one people, strong enough for any task, great enough for any glory destiny can bestow? How comes it that our first century closes with the process of consolidating the American people into a unit just accomplished, and quick upon the stroke of that great hour presses upon us our world opportunity, world duty, and world glory, which none but a people welded into an indivisible nation can achieve or perform?

Blind indeed is he who sees not the hand of God in events so vast, so harmonious, so benign. Reactionary indeed is the mind that perceives not that this vital people is the strongest of the saving forces of the world; that our place, therefore, is at the head of the constructing and redeeming nations of the earth; and that to stand aside while events march on is a surrender of our interests, a betrayal of our duty as blind as it is base. Craven indeed is the heart that fears to perform a work so golden and so noble; that dares not win a glory so immortal.

Do you tell me that it will cost us money? When did Americans ever measure duty by financial standards? Do you tell me of the tremendous toil required to overcome the vast difficulties of our task? What mighty work for the world, for humanity, even for ourselves, has ever been done with ease? Even our bread must we eat by the sweat of our faces. Why are we charged with power such as no people ever knew, if we are not to use it in a work such as no people ever wrought? Who will dispute the divine meaning of the fable of the talents?

Do you remind me of the precious blood that must be shed, the lives that must be given, the broken hearts of loved ones for their slain? And this is indeed a heavier price than all combined. And yet as a nation every historic duty we have done, every achievement we have accomplished, has been by the sacrifice of our noblest sons. Every holy memory that glorifies the flag is of those heroes who have died that its onward march might not be stayed. It is the nation's dearest lives yielded for the flag that makes it dear to us; it is the nation's most precious blood poured out for it that makes it precious to us. That flag is woven of heroism and grief, of the bravery of men and women's tears, of righteousness and battle, of sacrifice and anguish, of triumph and of glory. It is these which make our flag a holy thing. Who would tear from that sacred banner the glorious legends of a single battle where it has waved on land or sea? What son of a soldier of the flag whose father fell beneath it on any field would surrender that proud record for the heraldry of a king? In the cause of civilization, in the service of the Republic anywhere on earth, Americans consider wounds the noblest decorations man can win, and count the giving of their lives a glad and precious duty.

Pray God that spirit never fails. Pray God the time may never come when Mammon and the love of ease shall so debase our blood that we will fear to shed it for the flag and its imperial destiny. Pray God the time may never come when American heroism is but a legend like the story of the Cid, American faith in our mission and our might a dream dissolved, and the glory of our mighty race departed.

And that time will never come. We will renew our youth at the fountain of new and glorious deeds. We will exalt our reverence for the flag by carrying it to a noble future as well as by remembering its ineffable past. Its immortality will not pass, because everywhere and always we will acknowledge and discharge the solemn responsibilities our sacred flag, in its deepest meaning, puts upon us. And so, Senators, with reverent hearts, where dwells the fear of God, the American people move forward to the future of their hope and the doing of His work....

Mark Twain

THE CASE AGAINST IMPERIALISM

⊰{ *1901* }⊱   THE arguments of men like Beveridge unquestionably converted a majority of the American people to the idea of colonial expansion. Supposed economic advantages were important in this respect, but the appeal of purely emotional arguments was probably much greater. Suddenly conscious of their strength as a nation, the people were fascinated by the idea of empire, of the United States taking its place among the great powers of the world.

On the other hand, a vocal minority looked upon imperialism and especially upon the use of force to subjugate the Philippines, as a violation of the finest American traditions, a denial of the values so powerfully expressed in the Declaration of Independence. Some of these anti-imperialists were narrow isolationists, but others were men of the broadest interests—intellectuals, writers, old-fashioned statesmen, labor leaders, and businessmen. The steelmaster Andrew Carnegie and Samuel Gompers of the American Federation of Labor opposed keeping the Philippines. So did Grover Cleveland, former Speaker of the House of Representatives Thomas B. Reed, the philosopher William James, and many others. No one attacked imperialism more sharply than Mark Twain.

By 1900 Twain was world-famous as a humorist and widely regarded as one of the great literary geniuses of the day. But his original buoyant optimism had turned to the blackest, most sardonic pressimism; he was becoming a bitter critic of American society. No aspect of the times aroused his ire more than the new imperialism. The following selection is taken from an essay he published in the *North American Review* in 1901.

TO THE PERSON SITTING IN DARKNESS

SHALL WE? That is, shall we go on conferring our Civilization upon the peoples that sit in darkness, or shall we give those poor things a rest? Shall we bang right ahead in our old-time, loud, pious way, and commit the new century to the game; or shall we sober up and sit down and think it over first? Would it not be prudent to get our Civilization tools together, and see how much stock is left on hand in the way of Glass Beads and Theology, and Maxim Guns and Hymn Books, and Trade Gin and Torches of Progress and Enlightenment (patent adjustable ones, good to fire villages with, upon occasion), and balance the books, and arrive at the profit and loss, so that we may intelligently decide whether to continue the business or sell out the property and start a new Civilization Scheme on the proceeds?

Extending the Blessings of Civilization to our Brother who Sits in Darkness has been a good trade and has paid well, on the whole; and there is money in it yet, if carefully worked — but not enough, in my judgment, to make any considerable risk advisable. The People that Sit in Darkness are getting to be too scarce — too scarce and too shy. And such darkness as is now left is really of but an indifferent quality, and not dark enough for the game. The most of those People that Sit in Darkness have been furnished with more light than was good for them or profitable for us. We have been injudicious.

The Blessings-of-Civilization Trust, wisely and cautiously administered, is a Daisy. There is more money in it, more territory, more sovereignty, and other kinds of emolument, than there is in any other game that is played. But Christendom has been playing it badly of late years, and must certainly suffer by it, in my opinion. She has been so eager to get every stake that appeared on the green cloth, that the People who Sit in Darkness have noticed it — they have noticed it, and have begun to show alarm. They have become suspicious of the Blessings of Civilization. More— they have begun to examine them. This is not well. The Blessings of Civilization are all right, and a good commercial property; there could not be a better, in a dim light. In the right kind of a light, and at a proper distance, with the goods a little out of focus, they furnish this desirable exhibit to the Gentlemen who Sit in Darkness:

Love,	Law and Order,
Justice,	Liberty,
Gentleness,	Equality,
Christianity,	Honorable Dealing,
Protection to the Weak,	Mercy,
Temperance,	Education,

—and so on.

There. Is it good? Sir, it is pie. It will bring into camp any idiot that sits in darkness anywhere. But not if we adulterate it. It is proper to be emphatic upon that point. This brand is strictly for Export — apparently. *Apparently.* Privately and confidentially, it is nothing of the kind. Privately and confidentially, it is merely an outside cover, gay and pretty and attractive, displaying the special patterns of our Civilization which we reserve for Home Consumption, while *inside* the bale is the Actual Thing that the Customer Sitting in Darkness buys with his blood and tears and land and liberty. That Actual Thing is, indeed, Civilization, but it is only for Export. Is there a difference between the two brands? In some of the details, yes.

We all know that the Business is being ruined. The reason is not far to seek. It is because our Mr. McKinley, and Mr. Chamberlain, and the Kaiser, and the Tsar and the French have been exporting the Actual Thing *with the outside cover left off.* This is bad for the Game. It shows that these new players of it are not sufficiently acquainted with it. . . .

Our Master of the Game plays it badly — plays it as Mr. Chamberlain was playing it in South Africa. It was a mistake to do that; also, it was one which was quite unlooked for in a Master who was playing it so well in Cuba. In Cuba, he was playing the usual and regular *American* game, and it was winning, for there is no way to beat it. The Master, contemplating Cuba, said: "Here is an oppressed and friendless little nation which is willing to fight to be free; we go partners, and put up the strength of seventy million sympathizers and the resources of the United States: play!" Nothing but Europe combined could call that hand: and Europe cannot combine on anything. There, in Cuba, he was following our great traditions in a way which made us very proud of him, and proud of the deep dissatisfaction which his play was provoking in continental Europe. Moved by a high inspiration, he threw out those stirring words which proclaimed that forcible annexation would be "criminal aggression"; and in that utterance fired another "shot heard round the world." The memory of that fine saying will be outlived by the remembrance of no act of his but one — that he forgot it within the twelvemonth, and its honorable gospel along with it.

For, presently, came the Philippine temptation. It was strong; it was too strong, and he made that bad mistake: he played the European game, the Chamberlain game. It was a pity; it was a great pity, that error; that one grievous error, that irrevocable error. For it was the very place and time to play the American game again. And at no cost. Rich winnings to be gathered in, too; rich and permanent; indestructible; a fortune transmissible forever to the children of the flag. Not land, not money, not dominion — no, something worth many times more than that dross: our share, the spectacle of a nation of long harassed and persecuted slaves set free through our influence; our posterity's share, the golden memory of that fair deed. The game was in our hands. If it had been played according to the American rules, Dewey would have sailed away from Manila as soon as he had destroyed the Spanish fleet — after putting up a sign on shore guaranteeing foreign property and life against damage by the Filipinos, and warning the Powers that interference with the emancipated patriots would be regarded as an act unfriendly to the United States. The Powers cannot combine, in even a bad cause, and the sign would not have been molested.

Dewey could have gone about his affairs elsewhere, and left the competent Filipino army to starve out the little Spanish garrison and send it home, and the Filipino citizens to set up the form of government they might prefer, and deal with the friars and their doubtful acquisitions according to Filipino ideas of fairness and justice—ideas which have since been tested and found to be of as high an order as any that prevail in Europe or America.

But we . . . lost the chance to add another Cuba and another honorable deed to our good record. . . .

Now, my plan is: . . . let us audaciously present the whole of the facts, shirking none. . . . This daring truthfulness will astonish and dazzle the Person Sitting in Darkness, and he will take the Explanation down before his mental vision has had time to get back into focus. Let us say to him:

"Our case is simple. On the 1st of May, Dewey destroyed the Spanish fleet. This left the Archipelago in the hands of its proper and rightful owners, the Filipino nation. Their army numbered 30,000 men, and they were competent to whip out or starve out the little Spanish garrison; then the people could set up a government of their own devising. Our traditions required that Dewey should now set up his warning sign, and go away. But the Master of the Game happened to think of another plan —

the European plan. He acted upon it. This was, to send out an army —
ostensibly to help the native patriots put the finishing touch upon their
long and plucky struggle for independence, but really to take their land
away from them and keep it. That is, in the interest of Progress and
Civilization. The plan developed, stage by stage, and quite satisfactorily.
We entered into a military alliance with the trusting Filipinos, and they
hemmed in Manila on the land side, and by their valuable help the place,
with its garrison of 8,000 or 10,000 Spaniards, was captured — a thing
which we could not have accomplished unaided at that time. We got their
help by — by ingenuity. We knew they were fighting for their independence, and that they had been at it for two years. We knew they supposed
that we also were fighting in their worthy cause — just as we had helped
the Cubans fight for Cuban independence — and we allowed them to go
on thinking so. *Until Manila was ours and we could get along without
them.* Then we showed our hand. Of course, they were surprised — that
was natural; surprised and disappointed; disappointed and grieved. To
them it looked un-American; uncharacteristic; foreign to our established
traditions. And this was natural, too; for we were only playing the American Game in public — in private it was the European. It was neatly done,
very neatly, and it bewildered them. They could not understand it; for we
had been so friendly — so affectionate, even — with those simple-minded
patriots! We, our own selves, had brought back out of exile their leader,
their hero, their hope, their Washington — Aguinaldo; brought him in a
warship, in high honor, under the sacred shelter and hospitality of the
flag; brought him back and restored him to his people, and got their moving and eloquent gratitude for it. Yes, we had been so friendly to them,
and had heartened them up in so many ways! We had lent them guns
and ammunition; advised with them; exchanged pleasant courtesies with
them; placed our sick and wounded in their kindly care; intrusted our
Spanish prisoners to their humane and honest hands; fought shoulder to
shoulder with them against "the common enemy" (our own phrase);
praised their courage, praised their gallantry, praised their mercifulness,
praised their fine and honorable conduct; borrowed their trenches, borrowed strong positions which they had previously captured from the
Spaniards; petted them, lied to them — officially proclaiming that our land
and naval forces came to give them their freedom and displace the bad
Spanish Government — fooled them, used them until we needed them no
longer; then derided the sucked orange and threw it away. We kept the
positions which we had beguiled them of; by and by, we moved a force
forward and overlapped patriot ground — a clever thought, for we needed
trouble, and this would produce it. A Filipino soldier, crossing the ground,

where no one had a right to forbid him, was shot by our sentry. The badgered patriots resented this with arms, without waiting to know whether Aguinaldo, who was absent, would approve or not. Aguinaldo did not approve; but that availed nothing. What we wanted, in the interest of Progress and Civilization, was the Archipelago, unencumbered by patriots struggling for independence; and War was what we needed. We clinched our opportunity. . . .

At this point in our frank statement of fact to the Person Sitting in Darkness, we should throw in a little trade taffy about the Blessings of Civilization — for a change, and for the refreshment of his spirit — then go on with our tale:

"We and the patriots having captured Manila, Spain's ownership of the Archipelago and her sovereignty over it were at an end — obliterated — annihilated — not a rag or shred of either remaining behind. It was then that we conceived the divinely humorous idea of *buying* both of these specters from Spain! [It is quite safe to confess this to the Person Sitting in Darkness, since neither he nor any other sane person will believe it.] In buying those ghosts for twenty millions, we also contracted to take care of the friars and their accumulations. I think we also agreed to propagate leprosy and smallpox, but as to this there is doubt. But it is not important; persons afflicted with the friars do not mind other diseases.

"With our Treaty ratified, Manila subdued, and our Ghosts secured, we had no further use for Aguinaldo and the owners of the Archipelago. We forced a war, and we have been hunting America's guest and ally through the woods and swamps ever since."

At this point in the tale, it will be well to boast a little of our war work and our heroisms in the field, so as to make our performance look as fine as England's in South Africa; but I believe it will not be best to emphasize this too much. We must be cautious. . . .

Having now laid all the historical facts before the Person Sitting in Darkness, we should bring him to again, and explain them to him. We should say to him:

"They look doubtful, but in reality they are not. There have been lies; yes, but they were told in a good cause. We have been treacherous; but that was only in order that real good might come out of apparent evil. True, we have crushed a deceived and confiding people; we have turned against the weak and the friendless who trusted us; we have stamped out a just and intelligent and well-ordered republic; we have stabbed an ally in the back and slapped the face of a guest; we have bought a Shadow from an enemy that hadn't it to sell; we have robbed a trusting friend of his land and his liberty; we have invited our clean young men to shoulder a discredited musket and do bandits' work under a flag which bandits have been accustomed to fear, not to follow; we have debauched America's honor and blackened her face before the world; but each detail was for the best. We know this. The Head of every State and Sovereignty in Christendom and 90 per cent of every legislative body in Christendom, including our Congress and our fifty state legislatures, are members not only of the church, but also of the Blessings-of-Civilization Trust. This world-girdling accumulation of trained morals, high principles, and justice cannot do an unright thing, an unfair thing, an ungenerous thing, an unclean thing. It knows what it is about. Give yourself no uneasiness; it is all right."

Now then, that will convince the Person. You will see. It will restore the Business. Also, it will elect the Master of the Game to the vacant place in the Trinity of our national gods; and there on their high thrones the Three will sit, age after age, in the people's sight, each bearing the Emblem of his service: Washington, the Sword of the Liberator; Lincoln, the Slave's Broken Chains; the Master, the Chains Repaired.

It will give the Business a splendid new start. You will see.

Everything is prosperous, now; everything is just as we should wish it. We have got the Archipelago, and we shall never give it up. Also, we have every reason to hope that we shall have an opportunity before very long to slip out of our congressional contract with Cuba and give her something better in the place of it. It is a rich country, and many of us are already beginning to see that the contract was a sentimental mistake. But now — right now — is the best time to do some profitable rehabilitating work — work that will set us up and make us comfortable, and discourage gossip. We cannot conceal from ourselves that, privately, we are a little troubled about our uniform. It is one of our prides; it is acquainted with honor; it is familiar with great deeds and noble; we love it, we revere it; and so this errand it is on makes us uneasy. And our flag — another pride of ours, our chiefest! We have worshiped it so; and when we have seen it in far lands — glimpsing it unexpectedly in that strange sky, waving its welcome and benediction to us — we have caught our breaths, and uncovered our heads, and couldn't speak, for a moment, for the thought of what it was to us and the great ideals it stood for. Indeed, we *must* do something about these things; it is easily managed. We can have a special one — our states do it: we can have just our usual flag, with the white stripes painted black and the stars replaced by the skull and crossbones. . . .

By help of these suggested amendments, Progress and Civilization in that country can have a boom, and it will take in the Persons who are Sitting in Darkness, and we can resume Business at the old stand.

IV. Industrialism and Opportunity

Henry George
THE SINGLE TAX

◄§ *1879* §► Born in Philadelphia, Henry George (1839-1897) left school and went to sea at the age of fourteen. Eventually he landed in San Francisco, prospected for gold, clerked in a store, worked as a typesetter, and rose to be the editor of a newspaper. Throughout his early years he had to struggle for a livelihood; he knew what it meant to be poor. As a California newspaperman he became well acquainted with the fact that much of the state's natural resources were falling into the hands of a comparatively few men, especially Leland Stanford (1824-1893) and the other entrepreneurs of the Central Pacific Railroad. In 1869, at the age of thirty, he made a business trip to New York City. There he was shocked by the glaring contrast between extremes of wealth and poverty, side by side. He was moved to undertake a study of economics, which he soon concluded was, in its existing form, little more than a rationalization for things as they were. His interest in economic and social questions was intensified by the widespread suffering that accompanied the depression following the Panic of 1873.

Out of this background emerged his great book, which was privately printed in 1879 and commercially published in 1880. Its full title was *Progress and Poverty: An Inquiry into the Cause of Industrial Depressions and of Increase of Want with Increase of Wealth: The Remedy.* George looked upon his book as a contribution toward a wholly new science of economics. It was indeed a highly original as well as a powerfully written work. Once it had been published, he began to be in considerable demand as a newspaper and magazine writer and a platform lecturer. He spoke in many parts of the United States and also in England and Ireland. On the strength of his fame he ran, in 1886, as a reform candidate for mayor of New York. He polled more votes than one of his two opponents, Theodore Roosevelt (1858-1919), but fewer than the other, Abram Hewitt (1822-1903), who was elected.

For the rest of his life George devoted most of his time to organizing and leading the movement for a "single tax." He won thousands of followers, who were known as "single-taxers" and there is still an organization (the Robert Schalkenbach Foundation in New York) which propagates his views.

PROGRESS AND POVERTY

THE PROBLEM

The present century has been marked by a prodigious increase in wealth-producing power. The utilization of steam and electricity, the introduction of improved processes and labor-saving machinery, the greater sub-

167

division and grander scale of production, the wonderful facilitation of exchanges, have multiplied enormously the effectiveness of labor.

At the beginning of this marvelous era it was natural to expect, and it was expected, that labor-saving inventions would lighten the toil and improve the condition of the laborer; that the enormous increase in the power of producing wealth would make real poverty a thing of the past. Could a man of the last century — a Franklin or a Priestley — have seen, in a vision of the future, the steamship taking the place of the sailing vessel, the railroad train of the wagon, the reaping machine of the scythe, the threshing machine of the flail; could he have heard the throb of the engines that in obedience to human will, and for the satisfaction of human desire, exert a power greater than that of all the men and all the beasts of burden of the earth combined; could he have seen the forest tree transformed into finished lumber — into doors, sashes, blinds, boxes or barrels, with hardly the touch of a human hand; the great workshops where boots and shoes are turned out by the case with less labor than the old-fashioned cobbler could have put on a sole; the factories where, under the eye of a girl, cotton becomes cloth faster than hundreds of stalwart weavers could have turned it out with their handlooms; could he have seen steam hammers shaping mammoth shafts and mighty anchors, and delicate machinery making tiny watches; the diamond drill cutting through the heart of the rocks, and coal oil sparing the whale; could he have realized the enormous saving of labor resulting from improved facilities of exchange and communication — sheep killed in Australia eaten fresh in England, and the order given by the London banker in the afternoon executed in San Francisco in the morning of the same day; could he have conceived of the hundred thousand improvements which these only suggest, what would he have inferred as to the social condition of mankind?

It would not have seemed like an inference; further than the vision went it would have seemed as though he saw; and his heart would have leaped and his nerves would have thrilled, as one who from a height beholds just ahead of the thirst-stricken caravan the living gleam of rustling woods and the glint of laughing waters. Plainly, in the sight of the imagination, he would have beheld these new forces elevating society from its very foundations, lifting the very poorest above the possibility of want, exempting the very lowest from anxiety for the material needs of life; he would have seen these slaves of the lamp of knowledge taking on themselves the traditional curse, these muscles of iron and sinews of steel making the poorest laborer's life a holiday, in which every high quality and noble impulse could have scope to grow.

And out of these bounteous material conditions he would have seen arising, as necessary sequences, moral conditions realizing the golden age of which mankind has always dreamed. Youth no longer stunted and starved; age no longer harried by avarice; the child at play with the tiger; the man with the muck-rake drinking in the glory of the stars. Foul things fled, fierce things tame; discord turned to harmony! For how could there be greed where all had enough? How could the vice, the crime, the ignorance, the brutality, that spring from poverty and the fear of poverty, exist where poverty had vanished? Who should crouch where all were freemen; who oppress where all were peers?

More or less vague or clear, these have been the hopes, these the dreams born of the improvements which give this wonderful century its preëminence. They have sunk so deeply into the popular mind as radically to change the currents of thought, to recast creeds and displace the most fundamental conceptions. The haunting visions of higher possibilities have not merely gathered splendor and vividness, but their direction has changed — instead of seeing behind the faint tinges of an expiring sunset, all the glory of the daybreak has decked the skies before.

It is true that disappointment has followed disappointment, and that discovery upon discovery, and invention after invention, have neither lessened the toil of those who most need respite, nor brought plenty to the poor. But there have been so many things to which it seemed this failure could be laid, that up to our time the new faith has hardly weakened. We have better appreciated the difficulties to be overcome, but not the less trusted that the tendency of the times was to overcome them.

Now, however, we are coming into collision with facts which there can be no mistaking. From all parts of the civilized world come complaints of industrial depression; of labor condemned to involuntary idleness; of capital massed and wasting; of pecuniary distress among business men; of want and suffering and anxiety among the working classes. All the dull, deadening pain, all the keen, maddening anguish, that to great masses of men are involved in the words "hard times," afflict the world to-day. This state of things, common to communities differing so widely in situation, in political institutions, in fiscal and financial systems, in density of population and in social organization, can hardly be accounted for by local causes. There is distress where large standing armies are maintained, but there is also distress where the standing armies are nominal; there is distress where protective tariffs stupidly and wastefully hamper trade, but there is also distress where trade is nearly free; there is distress where autocratic government yet prevails, but there is also distress where political power is wholly in the hands of the people; in countries where paper is money, and in countries where gold and silver are the only currency. Evidently, beneath all such things as these, we must infer a common cause.

That there is a common cause, and that it is either what we call material progress or something closely connected with material progress, becomes more than an inference when it is noted that the phenomena we class together and speak of as industrial depression are but intensifications of phenomena which always accompany material progress, and which show themselves more clearly and strongly as material progress goes on. Where the conditions to which material progress everywhere tends are most fully realized — that is to say, where population is densest, wealth greatest, and the machinery of production and exchange most highly developed — we find the deepest poverty, the sharpest struggle for existence, and the most of enforced idleness.

It is to the newer countries — that is, to the countries where material progress is yet in its earlier stages — that laborers emigrate in search of higher wages, and capital flows in search of higher interest. It is in the older countries — that is to say, the countries where material progress has reached later stages — that widespread destitution is found in the midst of the greatest abundance. Go into one of the new communities where Anglo-Saxon vigor is just beginning the race of progress; where the machinery of production and exchange is yet rude and inefficient; where the increment of wealth is not yet great enough to enable any class to live in ease and luxury; where the best house is but a cabin of logs or a cloth and paper shanty, and the richest man is forced to daily work — and though you will find an absence of wealth and all its concomitants, you will find no beggars. There is no luxury, but there is no destitution. No one makes an easy living, nor a very good living; but every one *can* make a living, and no one able and willing to work is oppressed by the fear of want.

But just as such a community realizes the conditions which all civilized communities are striving for, and advances in the scale of material progress — just as closer settlement and a more intimate connection with the rest of the world, and greater utilization of labor-saving machinery, make possible greater economies in production and exchange, and wealth in consequence increases, not merely in the aggregate, but in proportion to population — so does poverty take a darker aspect. Some get an infinitely better and easier living, but others find it hard to get a living at all. The "tramp" comes with the locomotive, and almshouses and prisons are as surely the marks of "material progress" as are costly dwellings, rich warehouses, and magnificent churches. Upon streets lighted with gas and patrolled by uniformed policemen, beggars wait for the passer-by, and in the shadow of college, and library, and museum, are gathering the more hideous Huns and fiercer Vandals of whom Macaulay prophesied.

This fact — the great fact that poverty and all its concomitants show themselves in communities just as they develop into the conditions toward which material progress tends — proves that the social difficulties existing wherever a certain stage of progress has been reached, do not arise from local circumstances, but are, in some way or another, engendered by progress itself.

And, unpleasant as it may be to admit it, it is at last becoming evident that the enormous increase in productive power which has marked the present century and is still going on with accelerating ratio, has no tendency to extirpate poverty or to lighten the burdens of those compelled to toil. It simply widens the gulf between Dives and Lazarus, and makes the struggle for existence more intense. The march of invention has clothed mankind with powers of which a century ago the boldest imagination could not have dreamed. But in factories where labor-saving machinery has reached its most wonderful development, little children are at work; wherever the new forces are anything like fully utilized, large classes are maintained by charity or live on the verge of recourse to it; amid the greatest accumulations of wealth, men die of starvation, and puny infants suckle dry breasts; while everywhere the greed of gain, the worship of wealth, shows the force of the fear of want. The promised land flies before us like the mirage. The fruits of the tree of knowledge turn as we grasp them to apples of Sodom that crumble at the touch.

It is true that wealth has been greatly increased, and that the average of comfort, leisure, and refinement has been raised; but these gains are not general. In them the lowest class do not share.[1] I do not mean that the condition of the lowest class has nowhere nor in anything been improved; but that there is nowhere any improvement which can be credited to increase productive power. I mean that the tendency of what we call material progress is in nowise to improve the condition of the lowest class in the essentials of healthy, happy human life. Nay, more, that it is still further to depress the condition of the lowest class. The new forces, elevating in their nature though they be, do not act upon the social fabric from underneath, as was for a long time hoped and believed, but strike

---

[1] It is true that the poorest may now in certain ways enjoy what the richest a century ago could not have commanded, but this does not show improvement of condition so long as the ability to obtain the necessaries of life is not increased. The beggar in a great city may enjoy many things from which the backwoods farmer is debarred, but that does not prove the condition of the city beggar better than that of the independent farmer.

it at a point intermediate between top and bottom. It is as though an immense wedge were being forced, not underneath society, but through society. Those who are above the point of separation are elevated, but those
who are below are crushed down.

This depressing effect is not generally realized, for it is not apparent
where there has long existed a class just able to live. Where the lowest
class barely lives, as has been the case for a long time in many parts of
Europe, it is impossible for it to get any lower, for the next lowest step
is out of existence, and no tendency to further depression can readily show
itself. But in the progress of new settlements to the conditions of older
communities it may clearly be seen that material progress does not merely
fail to relieve poverty—it actually produces it. In the United States it is
clear that squalor and misery, and the vices and crimes that spring from
them, everywhere increase as the village grows to the city, and the march
of development brings the advantages of the improved methods of production and exchange. It is in the older and richer sections of the Union
that pauperism and distress among the working classes are becoming most
painfully apparent. If there is less deep poverty in San Francisco than in
New York, is it not because San Francisco is yet behind New York in
all that both cities are striving for? When San Francisco reaches the point
where New York now is, who can doubt that there will also be ragged
and barefooted children on her streets?

This association of poverty with progress is the great enigma of our
times. It is the central fact from which spring industrial, social, and political difficulties that perplex the world, and with which statesmanship
and philanthropy and education grapple in vain. From it come the clouds
that overhang the future of the most progressive and self-reliant nations.
It is the riddle which the Sphinx of Fate puts to our civilization, and
which not to answer is to be destroyed. So long as all the increased wealth
which modern progress brings goes but to build up great fortunes, to increase luxury and make sharper the contrast between the House of Have
and the House of Want, progress is not real and cannot be permanent.
The reaction must come. The tower leans from its foundations, and every
new story but hastens the final catastrophe. To educate men who must be
condemned to poverty, is but to make them restive; to base on a state of
most glaring social inequality political institutions under which men are
theoretically equal, is to stand a pyramid on its apex.

All-important as this question is, pressing itself from every quarter painfully upon attention, it has not yet received a solution which accounts for
all the facts and points to any clear and simple remedy. This is shown
by the widely varying attempts to account for the prevailing depression.

They exhibit not merely a divergence between vulgar notions and scientific theories, but also show that the concurrence which should exist between those who avow the same general theories breaks up upon practical questions into an anarchy of opinion. Upon high economic authority we have been told that the prevailing depression is due to over-consumption; upon equally high authority, that it is due to over-production; while the wastes of war, the extension of railroads, the attempts of workmen to keep up wages, the demonetization of silver, the issues of paper money, the increase of labor-saving machinery, the opening of shorter avenues to trade, etc., are separately pointed out as the cause, by writers of reputation.

And while professors thus disagree, the ideas that there is a necessary conflict between capital and labor, that machinery is an evil, that competition must be restrained and interest abolished, that wealth may be created by the issue of money, that it is the duty of government to furnish capital or to furnish work, are rapidly making way among the great body of the people, who keenly feel a hurt and are sharply conscious of a wrong. Such ideas, which bring great masses of men, the repositories of ultimate political power, under the leadership of charlatans and demagogues, are fraught with danger; but they cannot be successfully combated until political economy shall give some answer to the great question which shall be consistent with all her teachings, and which shall commend itself to the perceptions of the great masses of men.

It must be within the province of political economy to give such an answer. For political economy is not a set of dogmas. It is the explanation of a certain set of facts. It is the science which, in the sequence of certain phenomena, seeks to trace mutual relations and to identify cause and effect, just as the physical sciences seek to do in other sets of phenomena. It lays its foundations upon firm ground. The premises from which it makes its deductions are truths which have the highest sanction; axioms which we all recognize; upon which we safely base the reasoning and actions of everyday life, and which may be reduced to the metaphysical expression of the physical law that motion seeks the line of least resistance — viz., that men seek to gratify their desires with the least exertion. Proceeding from a basis thus assured, its processes, which consist simply in identification and separation, have the same certainty. In this sense it is as exact a science as geometry, which, from similar truths relative to space, obtains its conclusions by similar means, and its conclusions when valid should be as self-apparent. And although in the domain of political economy we cannot test our theories by artificially produced combinations or conditions, as may be done in some of the other sciences, yet we can apply tests no less conclusive, by comparing societies in which different conditions exist, or by, in imagination, separating, combining, adding or eliminating forces or factors of known direction.

I propose in the following pages to attempt to solve by the methods of political economy the great problem I have outlined. I propose to seek the law which associates poverty with progress, and increases want with advancing wealth; and I believe that in the explanation of this paradox we shall find the explanation of those recurring seasons of industrial and commercial paralysis which, viewed independently of their relations to more general phenomena, seem so inexplicable. Properly commenced and carefully pursued, such an investigation must yield a conclusion that will stand every test, and as truth, will correlate with all other truth. For in the sequence of phenomena there is no accident. Every effect has a cause, and every fact implies a preceding fact.

That political economy, as at present taught, does not explain the persistence of poverty amid advancing wealth in a manner which accords with the deep-seated perceptions of men; that the unquestionable truths which it does teach are unrelated and disjointed; that it has failed to make the progress in popular thought that truth, even when unpleasant, must make; that, on the contrary, after a century of cultivation, during which it has engrossed the attention of some of the most subtle and powerful intellects, it should be spurned by the statesman, scouted by the masses, and relegated in the opinion of many educated and thinking men to the rank of a pseudo-science in which nothing is fixed or can be fixed — must, it seems to me, be due not to any inability of the science when properly pursued, but to some false step in its premises, or overlooked factor in its estimates. And as such mistakes are generally concealed by the respect paid to authority, I propose in this inquiry to take nothing for granted, but to bring even accepted theories to the test of first principles, and should they not stand the test, freshly to interrogate facts in the endeavor to discover their law.

I propose to beg no question, to shrink from no conclusion, but to follow truth wherever it may lead. Upon us is the responsibility of seeking the law, for in the very heart of our civilization to-day women faint and little children moan. But what that law may prove to be is not our affair. If the conclusions that we reach run counter to our prejudices, let us not flinch; if they challenge institutions that have long been deemed wise and natural, let us not turn back.

HOW EQUAL RIGHTS TO THE LAND MAY BE ASSERTED AND SECURED

We have traced the want and suffering that everywhere prevail among the working classes, the recurring paroxysms of industrial depression, the scarcity of employment, the stagnation of capital, the tendency of wages to the starvation point, that exhibit themselves more and more strongly as material progress goes on, to the fact that the land on which and from which all must live is made the exclusive property of some.

We have seen that there is no possible remedy for these evils but the abolition of their cause; we have seen that private property in land has no warrant in justice, but stands condemned as the denial of natural right — a subversion of the law of nature that as social development goes on must condemn the masses of men to a slavery the hardest and most degrading.

We have weighed every objection, and seen that neither on the ground of equity or expediency is there anything to deter us from making land common property by confiscating rent.

But a question of method remains. How shall we do it?

We should satisfy the law of justice, we should meet all economic requirements, by at one stroke abolishing all private titles, declaring all land public property, and letting it out to the highest bidders in lots to suit, under such conditions as would sacredly guard the private right to improvements.

Thus we should secure, in a more complex state of society, the same equality of rights that in a ruder state were secured by equal partitions of the soil, and by giving the use of the land to whoever could procure the most from it, we should secure the greatest production.

Such a plan, instead of being a wild, impracticable vagary, has (with the exception that he suggests compensation to the present holders of land — undoubtedly a careless concession which he upon reflection would reconsider) been endorsed by no less eminent a thinker than Herbert Spencer, who ("Social Statics," Chap. IX, Sec. 8) says of it:

"Such a doctrine is consistent with the highest state of civilization; may be carried out without involving a community of goods, and need cause no very serious revolution in existing arrangements. The change required would simply be a change of landlords. Separate ownership would merge into the joint-stock ownership of the public. Instead of being in the possession of individuals, the country would be held by the great corporate body — society. Instead of leasing his acres from an isolated proprietor, the farmer would lease them from the nation. Instead of paying his rent to the agent of Sir John or his Grace, he would pay it to an agent or deputy agent of the community. Stewards would be public officials instead of private ones, and tenancy the only land tenure. A state of things so ordered would be in perfect harmony with the moral law. Under it all men would be equally landlords, all men would be alike free to become tenants. . . . Clearly, therefore, on such a system, the earth might be enclosed, occupied and cultivated, in entire subordination to the law of equal freedom."

But such a plan, though perfectly feasible, does not seem to me the best. Or rather I propose to accomplish the same thing in a simpler, easier, and quieter way, than that of formally confiscating all the land and formally letting it out to the highest bidders.

To do that would involve a needless shock to present customs and habits of thought — which is to be avoided.

To do that would involve a needless extension of governmental machinery — which is to be avoided.

It is an axiom of statesmanship, which the successful founders of tyranny have understood and acted upon — that great changes can best be brought about under old forms. We, who would free men, should heed the same truth. It is the natural method. When nature would make a higher type, she takes a lower one and develops it. This, also, is the law of social growth. Let us work by it. With the current we may glide fast and far. Against it, it is hard pulling and slow progress.

I do not propose either to purchase or to confiscate private property in land. The first would be unjust; the second, needless. Let the individuals who now hold it still retain, if they want to, possession of what they are pleased to call *their* land. Let them continue to call it *their* land. Let them buy and sell, and bequeath and devise it. We may safely leave them the shell, if we take the kernel. *It is not necessary to confiscate land; it is only necessary to confiscate rent.*

Nor to take rent for public uses is it necessary that the State should bother with the letting of lands, and assume the chance of the favoritism, collusion, and corruption this might involve. It is not necessary that any new machinery should be created. The machinery already exists. Instead of extending it, all we have to do is to simplify and reduce it. By leaving to land owners a percentage of rent which would probably be much less than the cost and loss involved in attempting to rent lands through State agency, and by making use of this existing machinery, we may, without jar or shock, assert the common right to land by taking rent for public uses.

We already take some rent in taxation. We have only to make some changes in our modes of taxation to take it all.

What I, therefore, propose, as the simple yet sovereign remedy, which will raise wages, increase the earnings of capital, extirpate pauperism, abolish poverty, give remunerative employment to whoever wishes it, afford free scope to human powers, lessen crime, elevate morals, and taste and intelligence, purify government and carry civilization to yet nobler heights, is — *to appropriate rent by taxation.*

In this way the State may become the universal landlord without calling herself so, and without assuming a single new function. In form, the ownership of land would remain just as now. No owner of land need be dispossessed, and no restriction need be placed upon the amount of land any one could hold. For, rent being taken by the State in taxes, land, no matter in whose name it stood, or in what parcels it was held, would be really common property, and every member of the community would participate in the advantages of its ownership.

Now, insomuch as the taxation of rent, or land values, must necessarily be increased just as we abolish other taxes, we may put the proposition into practical form by proposing—

To abolish all taxation save that upon land values.

As we have seen, the value of land is at the beginning of society nothing, but as society develops by the increase of population and the advance of the arts, it becomes greater and greater. In every civilized country, even the newest, the value of the land taken as a whole is sufficient to bear the entire expenses of government. In the better developed countries it is much more than sufficient. Hence it will not be enough merely to place all taxes upon the value of land. It will be necessary, where rent exceeds the present governmental revenues, commensurately to increase the amount demanded in taxation, and to continue this increase as society progresses and rent advances. But this is so natural and easy a matter, that it may be considered as involved, or at least understood, in the proposition to put all taxes on the value of land. That is the first step, upon which the practical struggle must be made. When the hare is once caught and killed, cooking him will follow as a matter of course. When the common right to land is so far appreciated that all taxes are abolished save those which fall upon rent, there is no danger of much more than is necessary to induce them to collect the public revenues being left to individual land holders.

Experience has taught me (for I have been for some years endeavoring to popularize this proposition) that wherever the idea of concentrating all taxation upon land values finds lodgment sufficient to induce consideration, it invariably makes way, but there are few of the classes most to be benefited by it, who at first, or even for a long time afterward, see its full significance and power. It is difficult for workingmen to get over the idea that here is a real antagonism between capital and labor. It is difficult for small farmers and homestead owners to get over the idea that to put all taxes on the value of land would be unduly to tax them. It is difficult for both classes to get over the idea that to exempt capital from taxation would be to make the rich richer, and the poor poorer. These ideas spring from confused thought. But behind ignorance and prejudice there is a powerful interest, which has hitherto dominated literature, education, and opinion. A great wrong always dies hard, and the great wrong which in every civilized country condemns the masses of men to poverty and want, will not die without a bitter struggle.

Edward Bellamy
A SOCIALIST UTOPIA

✠{1888}✠ By FAR the most popular of the attacks mounted against entrenched wealth and privilege in the post-Civil War years was that of Edward Bellamy (1850-1898). A reticent, bookish young man, son of a Baptist minister, Bellamy had engaged in newspaper work and written a number of interesting short stories when, in 1886, he began work on a novel describing a future society in which all production would be nationalized and every citizen would share equally in the fruits of the common labor. Two years later when this book, *Looking Backward,* appeared, it was an instant success. By 1890 over 200,000 copies had been sold and within another few years sales passed the million mark. Soon there were over 150 Nationalist Clubs in existence, dedicated to achieving the ideal system envisioned by Bellamy. During the nineties several dozen utopian novels were published, most no doubt inspired by the success of *Looking Backward.* None, however, approached the popularity of that book.

The following selection, covering the opening chapters of the book, contains the clever literary device which had so much to do with the success of *Looking Backward* and illustrates the nature of Bellamy's criticism of nineteenth-century American capitalism. The remainder of the novel, which is enlivened by a typical Victorian romance between the hero and Dr. Leete's daughter, explains elaborately the character of the egalitarian socialism of the year 2000. Throughout there are frequent asides devoted to illustrating the futility and unreasonableness of the "old" system. Some of these, of course, might as well be applied to our own society, now much closer to Dr. Leete's day in time than to his way of thinking. A number of the good Doctor's remarks would not sound unusual in the mouths of modern thinkers like John K. Galbraith or the late President Kennedy. "We might, indeed, have much larger incomes, individually, if we chose so to use the surplus of our product," Leete says at one point. "[B]ut we prefer to expend it upon public works and pleasures in which all share. . . ."

Bellamy wrote another novel, *Equality,* and contributed many articles to Nationalist journals. But his health declined rapidly and he died long before the modern concept of the welfare state attracted much support.

LOOKING BACKWARD

I

I FIRST saw the light in the city of Boston in the year 1857. "What!" you say "Eighteen fifty-seven? That is an odd slip. He means nineteen fifty-seven, of course." I beg your pardon, but there is no mistake. It was about four in the afternoon of December the 26th, one day after Christmas, in the year 1857, not 1957, that I first breathed the east wind of Boston, which, I assure the reader, was at that remote period marked by the same penetrating quality characterizing it in the present year of grace, 2000.

These statements seem so absurd on their face. especially when I add that I am a young man apparently of about thirty years of age, that no person can be blamed for refusing to read another word of what promises to be a mere imposition upon his credulity. Nevertheless I earnestly assure the reader that no imposition is intended, and will undertake, if he shall follow me a few pages, to entirely convince him of this. If I may, then, provisionally assume, with the pledge of justifying the assumption, that I know better than the reader when I was born, I will go on with my narrative. As every schoolboy knows, in the latter part of the nineteenth century the civilization of today, or anything like it, did not exist, although the elements which were to develop it were already in ferment. Nothing had, however, occurred to modify the immemorial division of society into the four classes, or nations, as they may be more fitly called, since the differences between them were far greater than those between any nations nowadays, of the rich and the poor, the educated and the ignorant. I myself was rich and also educated, and possessed, therefore, all the elements of happiness enjoyed by the most fortunate in that age. Living in luxury, and occupied only with the pursuit of the pleasures and refinements of life, I derived the means of my support from the labor of others, rendering no sort of service in return. My parents and grandparents had lived in the same way, and I expected that my descendants, if I had any, would enjoy a like easy existence.

But how could I live without service to the world? you ask. Why should the world have supported in utter idleness one who was able to render service? The answer is that my great-grandfather had accumulated a sum of money on which his descendants had ever since lived. The sum, you will naturally infer, must have been very large not to have been exhausted in supporting three generations of idleness. This, however, was not the fact. The sum had been originally by no means large. It was, in fact, much larger now that three generations had been supported upon it in idleness, than it was at first. This mystery of use without consumption, of warmth without combustion, seems like magic, but was merely an ingenious application of the art now happily lost but carried to great perfection by your ancestors, of shifting the burden of one's support on the shoulders of others. The man who had accomplished this, and it was the end all sought, was said to live on the income of his investments. To explain at this point how the ancient methods of industry made this possible would delay us too much. I shall only stop now to say that interest on investments was a species of tax in perpetuity upon the product of those engaged in industry which a person possessing or inheriting money was able to levy. It must not be supposed that an arrangement which seems so unnatural and preposterous according to modern notions was never criticized by your ancestors. It had been the effort of lawgivers and prophets from the earliest ages to abolish interest, or at least to limit it to the smallest possible rate. All these efforts had, however, failed, as they necessarily must so long as the ancient social organizations prevailed. At the time of which I write, the latter part of the nineteenth century, governments had generally given up trying to regulate the subject at all.

By way of attempting to give the reader some general impression of the way people lived together in those days, and especially of the relations of the rich and poor to one another, perhaps I cannot do better than to compare society as it then was to a prodigious coach which the masses of humanity were harnessed to and dragged toilsomely along a very hilly and sandy road. The driver was hunger, and permitted no lagging, though the pace was necessarily very slow. Despite the difficulty of drawing the coach at all along so hard a road, the top was covered with passengers who never got down, even at the steepest ascents. These seats on top were very breezy and comfortable. Well up out of the dust, their occupants could enjoy the scenery at their leisure, or critically discuss the merits of the straining team. Naturally such places were in great demand and the competition for them was keen, every one seeking as the first end in life to secure a seat on the coach for himself and to leave it to his child after him. By the rule of the coach a man could leave his seat to whom he wished, but on the other hand there were so many accidents by which it might at any time be wholly lost. For all that they were so easy, the seats were very insecure, and at every sudden jolt of the coach persons were slipping out of them and falling to the ground, where they were instantly compelled to take hold of the rope and help to drag the coach on which they had before ridden so pleasantly. It was naturally regarded as a terrible misfortune to lose one's seat, and the apprehension that this might happen to them or their friends was a constant cloud upon the happiness of those who rode.

But did they think only of themselves? you ask. Was not their very luxury rendered intolerable to them by comparison with the lot of their brothers and sisters in the harness, and the knowledge that their own weight added to their toil? Had they no compassion for fellow beings from whom fortune only distinguished them? Oh, yes, commiseration was frequently expressed by those who rode for those who had to pull the coach, especially when the vehicle came to a bad place in the road, as it was constantly doing, or to a particularly steep hill. At such times, the desperate straining of the team, their agonized leaping and plunging under the pitiless lashing of hunger, the many who fainted at the rope and were trampled in the mire, made a very distressing spectacle, which often called forth highly creditable displays of feeling on the top of the coach. At such times the passengers would call down encouragingly to the toilers of the rope, exhorting them to patience, and holding out hopes of possible compensation in another world for the hardness of their lot, while others contributed to buy salves and liniments for the crippled and injured. It was agreed that it was a great pity that the coach should be so hard to pull, and there was a sense of general relief when the specially bad piece of road was gotten over. This relief was not, indeed, wholly on account of the team, for there was always some danger at these bad places of a general overturn in which all would lose their seats.

It must in truth be admitted that the main effect of the spectacle of the misery of the toilers at the rope was to enhance the passengers' sense of the value of their seats upon the coach, and to cause them to hold on to them more desperately than before. If the passengers could only have felt assured that neither they nor their friends would ever fall from the top, it is probable that, beyond contributing to the funds for liniments and bandages, they would have troubled themselves extremely little about those who dragged the coach.

I am well aware that this will appear to the men and women of the twentieth century as incredible inhumanity, but there are two facts, both very curious, which partly explain it. In the first place, it was firmly and sincerely believed that there was no other way in which Society could get along, except when the many pulled at the rope and the few rode, and not only this, but that no very radical improvement even was possible, either in the harness, the coach, the roadway, or the distribution of the toil. It had always been as it was, and it always would be so. It was a pity, but it could not be helped, and philosophy forbade wasting compassion on what was beyond remedy.

The other fact is yet more curious, consisting in a singular hallucination which those on the top of the coach generally shared, that they were not exactly like their brothers and sisters who pulled at the rope, but of finer clay, in some way belonging to a higher order of beings who might justly expect to be drawn. This seems unaccountable, but, as I once rode on this very coach and shared that very hallucination, I ought to be believed. The strangest thing about the hallucination was that those who had but just climbed up from the ground, before they had outgrown the marks of the rope upon their hands, began to fall under its influence. As for those whose parents and grandparents before them had been so fortunate as to keep their seats on the top, the conviction they cherished of the essential difference between their sort of humanity and the common article was absolute. The effect of such a delusion in moderating fellow feeling for the sufferings of the mass of men into a distant and philosophical compassion is obvious. To it I refer as the only extenuation I can offer for the indifference which, at the period I write of, marked my own attitude toward the misery of my brothers.

In 1887 I came to my thirtieth year. Although still unmarried, I was engaged to wed Edith Bartlett. She, like myself, rode on the top of the coach. That is to say, not to encumber ourselves further with an illustration which has, I hope, served its purpose of giving the reader some general impression of how we lived then, her family was wealthy. In that age, when money alone commanded all that was agreeable and refined in life, it was enough for a woman to be rich, to have suitors, but Edith Bartlett was beautiful and graceful also.

My lady readers, I am aware, will protest at this. "Handsome she might have been," I hear them saying, "but graceful never, in the costumes which were the fashion at that period, when the head covering was a dizzy structure a foot tall, and the almost incredible extension of the skirt behind by means of artificial contrivances more thoroughly dehumanized the form than any former device of dressmakers. Fancy anyone graceful in such a costume!" The point is certainly well taken, and I can only reply that while the ladies of the twentieth century are lovely demonstrations of the effect of appropriate drapery in accenting feminine graces, my recollection of their great-grandmothers enables me to maintain that no deformity of costume can wholly disguise them.

Our marriage only waited on the completion of the house which I was building for our occupancy in one of the most desirable parts of the city, that is to say, a part chiefly inhabited by the rich. For it must be understood that the comparative desirability of different parts of Boston for residence depended then, not on natural features, but on the character of the neighboring population. Each class of nation lived by itself, in quarters of its own. A rich man living among the poor, an educated man among the uneducated, was like one living in isolation among a jealous and alien race. When the house had been begun, its completion by the winter of 1886 had been expected. The spring of the following year found it, however, yet incomplete, and my marriage still a thing of the future. The cause of a delay calculated to be particularly exasperating to an ardent lover was a series of strikes, that is to say, concerted refusals to work on the part of the bricklayers, masons, carpenters, painters, plumbers, and other trades concerned in house-building. What the specific causes of these strikes were I do not remember. Strikes had become so common at that period that people had ceased to inquire into their particular grounds. In one department of industry or another, they had been nearly incessant ever since the great business crisis of 1873. In fact, it had come to be the exceptional thing to see any class of laborers pursue their avocation steadily for more than a few months at a time.

The reader who observes the dates alluded to will of course recognize in these disturbances of industry the first and incoherent phase of the great movement which ended in the establishment of the modern industrial system with all its social consequences. This is all so plain in the retrospect that a child can understand it, but not being prophets, we of that day had no clear idea what was happening to us. What we did see was that industrially the country was in a very queer way. The relation between the workingman and the employer, between labor and capital, appeared in some unaccountable manner to have become dislocated. The working classes had quite suddenly and very generally become infected with a profound discontent with their condition, and an idea that it could be greatly bettered if they only knew how to go about it. On every side, with one accord, they preferred demands for higher pay, shorter hours, better dwellings, better educational advantages, and a share in the refinements and luxuries of life, demands which it was impossible to see the way to granting unless the world were to become a great deal richer than it then was. Though they knew something of what they wanted, they knew nothing of how to accomplish it, and the eager enthusiasm with which they thronged about anyone who seemed likely to give them any light on the subject lent sudden reputation to many would-be leaders, some of whom had little enough light to give. However chimerical the aspirations of the laboring classes might be deemed, the devotion with which they supported one another in the strikes, which were their chief weapon, and the sacrifices which they underwent to carry them out lent no doubt of their dead earnestness.

As to the final outcome of the labor troubles, which was the phrase by which the movement I have described was most commonly referred to, the opinions of the people of my class differed according to individual temperament. The sanguine argued very forcibly that it was in the very nature of things impossible that the new hopes of the workingmen could be satisfied, simply because the world had not the wherewithal to satisfy them. It was only because the masses worked very hard and lived on short commons that the race did not starve outright, and no considerable improvement in their condition was possible while the world, as a whole, remained so poor. It was not the capitalists whom the laboring men were contending with, these maintained, but the ironbound environment of humanity, and it was merely a question of the thickness of their skulls when they would discover the fact and make up their minds to endure what they could not cure.

The less sanguine admitted all this. Of course the workingmen's aspirations were impossible of fulfillment for natural reasons, but there were grounds to fear that they would not discover this fact until they had made a sad mess of society. They had the votes and the power to do so if they pleased, and their leaders meant they should. Some of these desponding observers went so far as to predict an impending social cataclysm. Humanity, they argued, having climbed to the top round of the ladder of civilization, was about to take a header into chaos, after which it would doubtless pick itself up, turn round, and begin to climb again. Repeated experiences of this sort in historic and prehistoric times possibly accounted for the puzzling bumps on the human cranium. Human history, like all great movements, was cyclical, and returned to the point of beginning. The idea of indefinite progress in a right line was a chimera of the imagination, with no analogue in nature. The parabola of a comet was perhaps a yet better illustration of the career of humanity. Tending upward and sunward from the aphelion of barbarism, the race attained the perihelion of civilization only to plunge downward once more to its nether goal in the regions of chaos.

This, of course, was an extreme opinion, but I remember serious men among my acquaintances who, in discussing the signs of the times, adopted a very similar tone. It was no doubt the common opinion of thoughtful men that society was approaching a critical period which might result in great changes. The labor troubles, their causes, course, and cure, took lead of all other topics in the public prints, and in serious conversation.

The nervous tension of the public mind could not have been more strikingly illustrated than it was by the alarm resulting from the talk of a small band of men who called themselves anarchists, and proposed to terrify the American people into adopting their ideas by threats of violence, as if a mighty nation which had but just put down a rebellion of half of its own numbers, in order to maintain its political system, were likely to adopt a new social system out of fear.

As one of the wealthy, with a large stake in the existing order of things, I naturally shared the apprehensions of my class. The particular grievance I had against the working classes at the time of which I write, on account of the effect of their strikes in postponing my wedded bliss, no doubt lent a special animosity to my feeling toward them. . . .

II

. . . The house in which I lived had been occupied by three generations of the family of which I was the only living representative in the direct line. It was a large, ancient wooden mansion, very elegant in an old-fashioned way within, but situated in a quarter that had long since become undesirable for residence, from its invasion by tenement houses and manufactories. It was not a house to which I could think of bringing a bride, much less so dainty a one as Edith Bartlett. I had advertised it for sale, and meanwhile merely used it for sleeping purposes, dining at my club. One servant, a faithful colored man by the name of Sawyer, lived with me and attended to my few wants. One feature of the house I expected to miss greatly when I should leave it, and this was the sleeping chamber which I had built under the foundations. I could not have slept in the city at all, with its never-ceasing nightly noises, if I had been obliged to use an upstairs chamber. But to this subterranean room no murmur from the upper world ever penetrated. When I had entered it and closed the door, I was surrounded by the silence of the tomb. In order to prevent the dampness of the subsoil from penetrating the chamber the walls had been laid in hydraulic cement and were very thick, and the floor was likewise protected. In order that the room might serve also as a vault, equally proof against violence and flames, for the storage of valuables, I had roofed it with stone slabs hermetically sealed, and the outer door was of iron with a thick coating of asbestos. A small pipe, communicating with a windmill on top of the house, insured the renewal of air.

It might seem that the tenant of such a chamber ought to be able to command slumber, but it was rare that I slept well, even there, two nights in succession. So accustomed was I to wakefulness that I minded little the loss of one night's rest. A second night, however, spent in my reading chair instead of my bed, tired me out, and I never allowed myself to go longer than that without slumber, from fear of nervous disorder.

From this statement it will be inferred that I had at my command some artificial means of inducing sleep in the last resort, and so in fact I had. If after two sleepless nights I found myself on the approach of the third without sensations of drowsiness, I called in Doctor Pillsbury.

He was a doctor by courtesy only, what was called in those days an "ir-regular" or "quack" doctor. He called himself a "Professor of Animal Magnetism." I had come across him in the course of some amateur investigations into the phenomena of animal magnetism. I don't think he knew anything about medicine, but he was certainly a remarkable mesmerist. It was for the purpose of being put to sleep by his manipulations that I used to send for him when I found a third night of sleeplessness impending. Let my nervous excitement or mental preoccupation be however great, Doctor Pillsbury never failed, after a short time, to leave me in a deep slumber, which continued till I was aroused by a reversal of the mesmerizing process. The process for awakening the sleeper was much simpler than that for putting him to sleep, and for convenience I had made Doctor Pillsbury teach Sawyer how to do it.

My faithful servant alone knew for what purpose Doctor Pillsbury visited me, or that he did so at all. Of course, when Edith became my wife I should have to tell her my secrets. I had not hitherto told her this, because there was unquestionably a slight risk in the mesmeric sleep, and I knew she would set her face against my practice. The risk, of course, was that it might become too profound and pass into a trance beyond the mesmerizer's power to break, ending in death. Repeated experiments had fully convinced me that the risk was next to nothing if reasonable precautions were exercised, and of this I hoped, though doubtingly, to convince Edith. I went directly home after leaving her, and at once sent Sawyer to fetch Doctor Pillsbury. Meanwhile I sought my subterranean sleeping chamber, and exchanging my costume for a comfortable dressing gown, sat down to read the letters by the evening mail which Sawyer had laid on my reading table.

One of them was from the builder of my new house, and confirmed what I had inferred from the newspaper item. The new strikes, he said, had postponed indefinitely the completion of the contract, as neither masters nor workmen would concede the point at issue without a long struggle. Caligula wished that the Roman people had but one neck that he might cut it off, and as I read this letter I am afraid that for a moment I was capable of wishing the same thing concerning the laboring classes of America. The return of Sawyer with the doctor interrupted my gloomy meditations.

It appeared that he had with difficulty been able to secure his services, as he was preparing to leave the city that very night. The doctor explained that since he had seen me last he had learned of a fine professional opening in a distant city, and decided to take prompt advantage of it. On my asking, in some panic, what I was to do for someone to put me to sleep, he gave me the names of several mesmerizers in Boston who, he averred, had quite as great powers as he.

Somewhat relieved on this point, I instructed Sawyer to rouse me at nine o'clock next morning, and, lying down on the bed in my dressing gown, assumed a comfortable attitude, and surrendered myself to the manipulations of the mesmerizer. Owing, perhaps, to my unusually nervous state, I was slower than common in losing consciousness, but at length a delicious drowsiness stole over me.

III and IV

"He is going to open his eyes, he had better see but one of us at first."

"Promise me, then, that you will not tell him."

The first voice was a man's, the second a woman's, and both spoke in whispers.

"I will see how he seems," replied the man.

"No, no, promise me," persisted the other.

"Let her have her way," whispered a third voice, also a woman.

"Well, well I promise, then," answered the man. "Quick, go! He is coming out of it."

There was a rustle of garments and I opened my eyes. A fine-looking man of perhaps sixty was bending over me, an expression of much benevolence mingled with great curiosity upon his features. He was an utter stranger. I raised myself on an elbow and looked around. The room was empty. I certainly had never been in it before, or one furnished like it. I looked back at my companion. He smiled.

"How do you feel?" he inquired.

"Where am I?" I demanded.

"You are in my house," was the reply.

"How came I here?"

"We will talk about that when you are stronger. Meanwhile, I beg you will feel no anxiety. You are among friends and in good hands. How do you feel?"

"A bit queerly," I replied, "but I am well, I suppose. Will you tell me how I came to be indebted to your hospitality? What has happened to me? How came I here? It was in my own house that I went to sleep."

"There will be time enough for explanations later," my unknown host replied, with a reassuring smile. "It will be better to avoid agitating talk until you are a little more yourself. Will you oblige me by taking a couple of swallows of this mixture? It will do you good. I am a physician."

I repelled the glass with my hand and sat up on the couch, although with an effort, for my head was strangely light.

"I insist upon knowing at once where I am and what you have been doing with me," I said.

"My dear sir," responded my companion, "let me beg that you will not agitate yourself. I would rather you did not insist upon explanations so soon, but if you do, I will try to satisfy you, provided you will first take this draught, which will strengthen you somewhat."

I thereupon drank what he offered me. Then he said, "It is not so simple a matter as you evidently suppose to tell you how you came here. You can tell me quite as much on that point as I can tell you. You have just been roused from a deep sleep, or, more properly, trance. So much I can tell you. You say you were in your own house when you fell into that sleep. May I ask you when that was?"

"When?" I replied. "When? Why, last evening, of course, at about ten o'clock. I left my man Sawyer orders to call me at nine o'clock. What has become of Sawyer?"

"I can't precisely tell you that," replied my companion, regarding me with a curious expression, "but I am sure that he is excusable for not being here. And now can you tell me a little more explicitly when it was that you fell into that sleep, the date, I mean?"

"Why, last night, of course. I said so, didn't I? That is, unless I have overslept an entire day. Great heavens! that cannot be possible, and yet I have an odd sensation of having slept a long time. It was Decoration Day that I went to sleep."

"Decoration Day?"

"Yes, Monday the 30th."

"Pardon me, the 30th of what?"

"Why, of this month, of course, unless I have slept into June, but that can't be."

"This month is September."

"September! You don't mean that I've slept since May! God in heaven! Why, it is incredible."

"We shall see," replied my companion. "You say that it was May 30th when you went to sleep?"

"Yes."

"May I ask of what year?"

I stared blankly at him, incapable of speech, for some moments.

"Of what year?" I feebly echoed at last.

"Yes, of what year, if you please? After you have told me that, I shall be able to tell you how long you have slept."

"It was the year 1887," I said.

My companion insisted that I should take another draught from the glass, and felt my pulse.

"My dear sir," he said, "your manner indicates that you are a man of culture, which I am aware was by no means the matter of course in your day it now is. No doubt, then, you have yourself made the observation that nothing in this world can be truly said to be more wonderful than anything else. The causes of all phenomena are equally adequate, and the results equally matter of course. That you should be startled by what I shall tell you is to be expected; but I am confident that you will not permit it to affect your equanimity unduly. Your appearance is that of a young man of barely thirty, and your bodily condition seems not greatly different from that of one just roused from a somewhat too long and profound sleep, and yet this is the tenth day of September in the year 2000, and you have slept exactly one hundred and thirteen years, three months, and eleven days." . . .

I had to admit that, if I were indeed the victim of a practical joke, its author had chosen an admirable agent for carrying out their imposition. The impressive and even eloquent manner of this man would have lent dignity to an argument that the moon was made of cheese. The smile with which I had regarded him as he advanced his trance hypothesis did not appear to confuse him in the slightest degree.

"Perhaps," I said, "you will go on and favor me with some particulars as to the circumstances under which you discovered this chamber of which you speak, and its contents. I enjoy good fiction."

"In this case," was the grave reply, "no fiction could be so strange as the truth. You must know that these many years I have been cherishing the idea of building a laboratory in the large garden beside this house, for the purpose of chemical experiments for which I have a taste. Last Thursday the excavation for the cellar was at last begun. It was completed by that night, and Friday the masons were to have come. Thursday night we had a tremendous deluge of rain, and Friday morning I found my cellar a frog pond and the walls quite washed down. My daughter, who had come out to view the disaster with me, called my attention to a corner of masonry laid bare by the crumbling away of one of the walls. I cleared a little earth from it, and, finding that it seemed part of a large mass, determined to investigate it. The workmen I sent for unearthed an oblong vault some eight feet below the surface, and set in the corner of what had evidently been the foundation walls of an ancient house. A layer of ashes and charcoal on the top of the vault showed that the house above had perished by fire. The vault itself was perfectly intact, the cement being as good as when first applied. It had a door, but this we could not force, and found entrance by removing one of the flagstones which formed the roof. The air which came up was stagnant but pure, dry and not cold. Descending with a lantern, I found myself in an apartment fitted up as a bedroom in the style of the nineteenth century. On the bed lay a young man. That he was dead and must have been dead a century was of course to be taken for granted; but the extraordinary state of preservation of the body struck me and the medical colleagues whom I had summoned with amazement. That the art of such embalming as this had ever been known we should not have believed, yet here seemed conclusive testimony that our immediate ancestors had possessed it. My medical colleagues, whose curiosity was highly excited, were at once for undertaking experiments to test the nature of the process employed, but I withheld them. My motive in so doing, at least the only motive I now need speak of, was the recollection of something I once had read about the extent to which your contemporaries had cultivated the subject of animal magnetism. It had occurred to me as just conceivable that you might be in a trance, and that the secret of your bodily integrity after so long a time was not the craft of an embalmer, but life. So extremely fanciful did this idea seem, even to me, that I did not risk the ridicule of my fellow physicians by mentioning it, but gave some other reason for postponing their experiments. No sooner, however, had they left me, than I set on foot a systematic attempt at resuscitation, of which you know the result." . . .

"I think you are going to be all right now," he said cheerily. "I should not have taken so abrupt a means to convince you of your position if your course, while perfectly excusable under the circumstances, had not rather obliged me to do so. I confess," he added, laughing, "I was a little apprehensive at one time that I should undergo what I believe you used to call a knockdown in the ninteenth century, if I did not act rather promptly. I remembered that the Bostonians of your day were famous pugilists, and thought best to lose no time. I take it you are now ready to acquit me of the charge of hoaxing you."

"If you had told me," I replied, profoundly awed, "that a thousand years instead of a hundred had elapsed since I last looked on this city, I should now believe you."

"Only a century has passed," he answered, "but many a millennium in the world's history has seen changes less extraordinary."

"And now," he added, extending his hand with an air of irresistible cordiality, "let me give you a hearty welcome to the Boston of the twentieth century and to this house. My name is Leete, Doctor Leete they call me."

"My name," I said as I shook his hand, "is Julian West."

"I am most happy in making your acquaintance, Mr. West," he responded. "Seeing that this house is built on the site of your own, I hope you will find it easy to make yourself at home in it."

After my refreshment Doctor Leete offered me a bath and a change of clothing, of which I gladly availed myself.

It did not appear that any very startling revolution in men's attire had been among the great changes my host had spoken of, for, barring a few details, my new habiliments did not puzzle me at all.

Physically, I was now myself again. But mentally, how it was with me, the reader will doubtless wonder. What were my intellectual sensations, he may wish to know, on finding myself so suddenly dropped as it were into a new world. In reply let me ask him to suppose himself suddenly, in the twinkling of an eye, transported from earth, say, to Paradise or Hades. What does he fancy would be his own experience? Would his thoughts return at once to the earth he had just left, or would he, after the first shock, well-nigh forget his former life for a while, albeit to be remembered later, in the interest excited by his new surroundings? All I can say is, that if his experience were at all like mine in the transition I am describing, the latter hypothesis would prove the correct one. The impressions of amazement and curiosity which my new surroundings produced occupied my mind, after the first shock, to the exclusion of all other thoughts. For the time the memory of my former life was, as it were, in abeyance.

No sooner did I find myself physically rehabilitated through the kind offices of my host, than I became eager to return to the housetop; and presently we were comfortably established there in easy chairs, with the city beneath and around us. After Doctor Leete had responded to numerous questions on my part, as to the ancient landmarks I missed and the new ones which had replaced them, he asked me what point of the contrast between the new and the old city struck me most forcibly.

"To speak of small things before great," I responded. "I really think that the complete absence of chimneys and their smoke is the detail that first impressed me."

"Ah!" ejaculated my companion with an air of much interest. "I had forgotten the chimneys, it is so long since they went out of use. It is nearly a century since the crude method of combustion on which you depended for heat became obsolete."

"In general," I said, "what impresses me most about the city is the material prosperity on the part of the people which its magnificence implies."

"I would give a great deal for just one glimpse of the Boston of your day," replied Doctor Leete. "No doubt, as you imply, the cities of that period were rather shabby affairs. If you had the taste to make them splendid, which I would not be so rude as to question, the general poverty resulting from your extraordinary industrial system would not have given you the means. Moreover, the excessive individualism which then prevailed was inconsistent with much public spirit. What little wealth you had seems almost wholly to have been lavished in private luxury. Nowadays, on the contrary, there is no destination of the surplus wealth so popular as the adornment of the city, which all enjoy in equal degree."

The sun had been setting as we returned to the housetop, and as we talked night descended upon the city.

"It is growing dark," said Doctor Leete. "Let us descend into the house. I want to introduce my wife and daughter to you." . . .

Doctor Leete, as well as the ladies, seemed greatly interested in my account of the circumstances under which I had gone to sleep in the underground chamber. All had suggestions to offer to account for my having been forgotten there, and the theory which we finally agreed on offers at least a plausible explanation, although whether it be in its details the true one, nobody, of course, will ever know. The layer of ashes found above the chamber indicated that the house had been burned down. Let it be supposed that the conflagration had taken place the night I fell asleep. It only remains to assume that Sawyer lost his life in the fire or by some accident connected with it, and the rest follows naturally enough. No one but he and Doctor Pillsbury either knew of the existence of the chamber or that I was in it, and Doctor Pillsbury, who had gone that night to New Orleans, had probably never heard of the fire at all. The conclusion of my friends, and of the public, must have been that I had perished in the flames. An excavation of the ruins, unless thorough, would not have disclosed the recess in the foundation walls connecting with my chamber. To be sure, if the site had been again built upon, at least immediately, such an excavation would have been necessary, but the troublous times and the undesirable character of the locality might well have prevented rebuilding. The size of the trees in the garden now occupying the site indicated, Doctor Leete said, that for more than half a century, at least, it had been open ground.

V

When, in the course of the evening the ladies retired, leaving Doctor Leete and myself alone, he sounded me as to my disposition for sleep, saying that if I felt like it my bed was ready for me; but if I was inclined to wakefulness nothing would please him better than to bear me company. "I am a late bird, myself," he said, "and, without suspicion of flattery, I may say that a companion more interesting than yourself could scarcely be imagined. It is decidedly not often that one has a chance to converse with a man of the nineteenth century."

Now I had been looking forward all the evening with some dread to the time when I should be alone, on retiring for the night. Surrounded by these most friendly strangers, stimulated and supported by their sympathetic interest, I had been able to keep my mental balance. Even then, however, in pauses of the conversation I had had glimpses, vivid as lightning flashes, of the horror of strangeness that was waiting to be faced when I could no longer command diversion. I knew I could not sleep that night, and as for lying awake and thinking, it argues no cowardice, I am sure, to confess that I was afraid of it. When, in reply to my host's question, I frankly told him this, he replied that it would be strange if I did not feel just so, but that I need have no anxiety about sleeping; whenever I wanted to go to bed, he would give me a dose which would insure me a sound night's sleep without fail. Next morning, no doubt, I would awake with the feeling of an old citizen.

"Before I acquire that," I replied, "I must know a little more about the sort of Boston I have come back to. You told me when we were upon the housetop that though a century only had elapsed since I fell asleep, it had been marked by greater changes in the conditions of humanity than many a previous millennium. With the city before me I could well believe that, but I am very curious to know what some of the changes have been. To make a beginning somewhere, for the subject is doubtless a large one, what solution, if any, have you found for the labor question? It was the Sphinx's riddle of the nineteenth century, and when I dropped out the Sphinx was threatening to devour society, because the answer was not forthcoming. It is well worth sleeping a hundred years to learn what the right answer was, if, indeed, you have found it yet."

"As no such thing as the labor question is known nowadays," replied Doctor Leete, "and there is no way in which it could arise, I suppose we may claim to have solved it. Society would indeed have fully deserved being devoured if it had failed to answer a riddle so entirely simple. In fact, to speak by the book, it was not necessary for society to solve the riddle at all. It may be said to have solved itself. The solution came as the result of a process of industrial evolution which could not have terminated otherwise. All that society had to do was to recognize and cooperate with that evolution, when its tendency had become unmistakable."

"I can only say," I answered, "that at the time I fell asleep no such evolution had been recognized."

"It was in 1887 that you fell into this sleep, I think you said."

"Yes, May 30, 1887."

My companion regarded me musingly for some moments. Then he observed, "And you tell me that even then there was no general recognition of the nature of the crisis which society was nearing? Of course, I fully credit your statement. The singular blindness of your contemporaries to the signs of the time is a phenomenon commented on by many of our historians, but few facts of history are more difficult for us to realize, so obvious and unmistakable as we look back seem the indications, which must also have come under your eyes, of the transformation about to come to pass. I should be intersted, Mr. West, if you would give me a little more definite idea of the view which you and men of your grade of intellect took of the state and prospects of society in 1887. You must, at least, have realized that the widespread industrial and social troubles, and the underlying dissatisfaction of all classes with the inequalities of society, and the general misery of mankind, were portents of great changes of some sort."

"We did, indeed, fully realize that," I replied. "We felt that society was dragging anchor and in danger of going adrift. Whither it would drift nobody could say, but all feared the rocks."

"Nevertheless," said Doctor Leete, "the set of the current was perfectly perceptible if you had but taken pains to observe it, and it was not toward the rocks, but toward a deeper channel."

"We had a popular proverb," I replied, "that 'hindsight is better than foresight,' the force of which I shall now, no doubt, appreciate more fully than ever. All I can say is, that the prospect was such when I went into that long sleep that I should not have been surprised had I looked down from your housetop today on a heap of charred and moss-grown ruins instead of this glorious city."

Doctor Leete had listened to me with close attention and nodded thoughtfully as I finished speaking. "What you have said," he observed, "will be regarded as a most valuable vindication of Storiot, whose account of your era has been generally thought exaggerated in its picture of the gloom and confusion of men's minds. That a period of transition like that should be full of excitement and agitation was indeed to be looked for; but seeing how plain was the tendency of the forces in operation, it was natural to believe that hope rather than fear would have been the prevailing temper of the popular mind."

"You have not yet told me what was the answer to the riddle which you found," I said. "I am impatient to know by what contradiction of natural sequence the peace and prosperity which you now seem to enjoy could have been the outcome of an era like my own."

"Excuse me," replied my host, "but do you smoke?" It was not till our cigars were lighted and drawing well that he resumed. "Since you are in the humor to talk rather than to sleep, as I certainly am, perhaps I cannot do better than to try to give you enough idea of our modern industrial system to dissipate at least the impression that there is any mystery about the process of its evolution. The Bostonians of your day had the reputation of being great askers of questions, and I am going to show my descent by asking you one to begin with. What should you name as the most prominent feature of the labor troubles of your day?"

"Why, the strikes, of course," I replied.

"Exactly. But what made the strikes so formidable?"

"The great labor organizations."

"And what was the motive of these great organizations?"

"The workmen claimed they had to organize to get their rights from the big corporations," I replied.

"That is just it," said Doctor Leete. "The organization of labor and the strikes were an effect, merely, of the concentration of capital in greater masses than had ever been known before. Before this concentration began, while as yet commerce and industry were conducted by innumerable petty concerns with small capital, instead of a small number of great concerns with vast capital, the individual workman was relatively important and independent in his relations to the employer. Moreover, when a little capital or a new idea was enough to start a man in business for himself, workingmen were constantly becoming employers and there was no hard and fast line between the two classes. Labor unions were needless then, and general strikes out of the question. But when the era of small concerns with small capital was succeeded by that of the great aggregations of capital, all this was changed. The individual laborer, who had been relatively important to the small employer, was reduced to insignificance and powerlessness over against the great corporation, while at the same time the way upward to the grade of employer was closed to him. Self-defense drove him to union with his fellows.

"The records of the period show that the outcry against the concentration of capital was furious. Men believed that it threatened society with a form of tyranny more abhorrent than it had ever endured. They believed that the great corporations were preparing for them the yoke of a baser servitude than had ever been imposed on the race, servitude not to men but to soulless machines incapable of any motive but insatiable greed. Looking back, we cannot wonder at their desperation, for certainly humanity was never confronted with a fate more sordid and hideous than would have been the era of corporate tyranny which they anticipated.

"Meanwhile, without being in the smallest degree checked by the clamor against it, the absorption of business by ever-larger monopolies continued. In the United States there was not, after the beginning of the last quarter of the century, any opportunity whatever for individual enterprise in any important field of industry, unless backed by a great capital. During the last decade of the century, such small businesses as still remained were fast-failing survivals of a past epoch, or mere parasites on the great corporations, or else existed in fields too small to attract the great capitalists. Small businesses, as far as they still remained, were reduced to the condition of rats and mice, living in holes and corners, and counting on evading notice for the enjoyment of existence. The railroads had gone on combining till a few great syndicates controlled every rail in the land. In manufactories, every important staple was controlled by a syndicate. These syndicates, pools, trusts, or whatever their name, fixed prices and crushed all competition except when combinations as vast as themselves arose. Then a struggle, resulting in a still greater consolidation, ensued. The great city bazaar crushed its country rivals with branch stores, and in the city itself absorbed its smaller rivals till the business of a whole quarter was concentrated under one roof, with a hundred former proprietors of shops serving as clerks. Having no business of his own to put his money in, the small capitalist, at the same time that he took service under the corporation, found no other investment for his money but its stocks and bonds, thus becoming doubly dependent upon it.

"The fact that the desperate popular opposition to the consolidation of business in a few powerful hands had no effect to check it proves that there must have been a strong economical reason for it. The small capitalists, with their innumerable petty concerns, had in fact yielded the field to the great aggregations of capital, because they belonged to a day of small things and were totally incompetent to the demands of an age of steam and telegraphs and the gigantic scale of its enterprises. To restore the former order of things, even if possible, would have involved returning to the day of stagecoaches. Oppressive and intolerable as was the regime of the great consolidations of capital, even its victims, while they cursed it, were forced to admit the prodigious increase of efficiency which had been imparted to the national industries, the vast economies effected by concentration of management and unity of organization, and to confess that since the new system had taken the place of the old the wealth of the world had increased at a rate before undreamed of. To be sure this vast increase had gone chiefly to make the rich richer, increasing the gap between them and the poor; but the fact remained that, as a means of producing wealth, capital had been proved efficient in proportion to its consolidation. The restoration of the old system with the subdivision of capital, if it were possible, might indeed bring back a greater equality of conditions, with more individual dignity and freedom, but it would be at the price of general poverty and the arrest of material progress.

"Was there, then, no way of commanding the services of the mighty wealth-producing principle of consolidated capital without bowing down to a plutocracy like that of Carthage? As soon as men began to ask themselves these questions, they found the answer ready for them. The movement toward the conduct of business by larger and larger aggregations of capital, the tendency toward monopolies, which had been so desperately and vainly resisted, was recognized at last, in its true significance, as a process which only needed to complete its logical evolution to open a golden future to humanity.

"Early in the last century the evolution was completed by the final consolidation of the entire capital of the nation. The industry and commerce of the country, ceasing to be conducted by a set of irresponsible corporations and syndicates of private persons at their caprice and for their profit, were entrusted to a single syndicate representing the people, to be conducted in the common interest for the common profit. The nation, that is to say, organized as the one great business corporation in which all other corporations were absorbed; it became the one capitalist in the place of all other capitalists, the sole employer, the final monopoly in which all previous and lesser monopolies were swallowed up, a monopoly in the profits and economies of which all citizens shared. The epoch of trusts had ended in The Great Trust. In a word, the people of the United States concluded to assume the conduct of their own business, just as one hundred-odd years before they had assumed the conduct of their own government, organizing now for industrial purposes on precisely the same grounds that they had then organized for political purposes. At last, strangely late in the world's history, the obvious fact was perceived that no business is so essentially the public business as the industry and commerce on which the people's livelihood depends, and that to entrust it to private persons to be managed for private profit is a folly similar in kind, though vastly greater in magnitude, to that of surrendering the functions of political government to kings and nobles to be conducted for their personal glorification."

"Such a stupendous change as you describe," said I, "did not, of course, take place without great bloodshed and terrible convulsions."

"On the contrary," replied Doctor Leete, "there was absolutely no violence. The change had been long foreseen. Public opinion had become fully ripe for it, and the whole mass of the people was behind it. There was no more possibility of opposing it by force than by argument. On the other hand the popular sentiment toward the great corporations and those identified with them had ceased to be one of bitterness, as they came to realize their necessity as a link, a transition phase, in the evolution of the true industrial system. The most violent foes of the great private monopolies were now forced to recognize how invaluable and indispensable had been their office in educating the people up to the point of assuming control of their own business. Fifty years before, the consolidation of the industries of the country under national control would have seemed a very daring experiment to the most sanguine. But by a series of object lessons, seen and studied by all men, the great corporations had taught the people an entirely new set of ideas on this subject. They had seen for many years syndicates handling revenues greater than those of states, and directing the labors of hundreds of thousands of men with an efficiency and economy unattainable in smaller operations. It had come to be recognized as an axiom that the larger the business the simpler the principles that can be applied to it; that, as the machine is truer than the hand, so the system, which in a great concern does the work of the master's eye in a small business, turns out more accurate results. Thus it came about that, thanks to the corporations themselves, when it was proposed that the nation should assume their functions, the suggestion implied nothing which seemed impracticable even to the timid. To be sure, it was a step beyond any yet taken, a broader generalization, but the very fact that the nation would be the sole corporation in the field would, it was seen, relieve the undertaking of many difficulties with which the partial monopolies had contended." . . .

David A. Wells
THE IMPACT OF INDUSTRIALIZATION

❧{1889}❧ THE remarkable economic expansion of the United States after the Civil War was accompanied by a general decline in prices. Severe depressions also punctuated the period, causing much distress. The industrial revolution was changing the country so rapidly that disruptions of the fabric of society inevitably resulted. But these conditions did not significantly check economic growth. Indeed, confusion and conflict marched hand and hand with progress, leaving men uncertain about the meaning, even about the direction of American life.

No observer achieved deeper insights into conditions at this time than David A. Wells (1828-98). Originally trained as a scientist, Wells won an international reputation as an economist with a pamphlet, *Our Burden and Our Strength* (1864), which argued that despite the strains placed on its economy by the Civil War, the North was actually growing richer and more powerful. Some 200,000 copies of this work were printed. After the war Wells served as Special Commissioner of the Revenue and wrote widely on economic subjects. He favored sound money but opposed high tariffs, believing that American industrial efficiency made protection unnecessary. Politically, he was a Democrat.

Although he misunderstood the significance of many of the changes taking place around him, Wells excelled every contemporary in his ability to observe and describe the complex alterations that industrialization was making in America. The breadth, clarity, and objectivity of his vision is even more apparent to modern readers than it was to the men of his own time. The following selection from his analysis of *Recent Economic Changes* (1889) provides an excellent example of his work.

RECENT ECONOMIC CHANGES

THE predominant feeling induced by a review and consideration of the numerous and complex economic changes and disturbances that have occurred since 1873 (as has been detailed in the foregoing chapters), is undoubtedly, in the case of very many persons, discouraging and pessimistic. The questions which naturally suggest themselves, and in fact are being continually asked, are: Is mankind being made happier or better by this increased knowledge and application of the forces of nature, and a consequent increased power of production and distribution? Or, on the contrary, is not the tendency of this new condition of things, as Dr. Siemens, of Berlin, has expressed it, "to the destruction of all of our ideals and to coarse sensualism; to aggravate injustice in the distribution of wealth; diminish to individual laborers the opportunities for independent work, and thereby bring them into a more dependent position; and, finally, is not the supremacy of birth and the sword about to be superseded by the still more oppressive reign of inherited or acquired property?"

What many think, but hesitate to say, finds forcible expression in the following extract from a letter addressed to the author by a large-hearted, sympathetic man, who is at the same time one of the best known of American journalists and leaders of public opinion. After referring to his great interest in the exhibit that has been made of the extraordinary economic disturbances since 1873 and their effect on persons, production, distribution, and prices, he says:

> But what a deplorable and quite awful picture you suggest of the future! The wheel of progress is to be run over the whole human race and smash us all, or nearly all, to a monstrous flatness! I get up from the reading of what you have written scared, and more satisfied than ever before that the true and wise course of every man is to get somewhere a piece of land, raise and make what he can for himself, and try thus to get out of the crushing process. It seems to me that what we call civilization is to degrade and incapacitate the mass of men and women; and how strange and incongruous a state it is! At the same time these masses of men are thrown out of their accustomed employments by the introduction or perfection of machinery — at that very time the number of women and children employed in factories rapidly increases; an unprecedented cheapness of all necessaries of life is coincident with an intensification of the bitter struggle for bread and shelter. It is a new form of slavery which, it seems to me, projects itself into view — universal slavery — not patriarchal, but mercantile. I get yearly more tired of what we call civilization. It seems to me a preposterous fraud. It does not give us leisure; it does not enable us to be clean except at a monstrous cost; it affects us with horrible diseases — like diphtheria and typhoid fever — poisoning our water and the air we breathe; it fosters the vicious classes — the politicians and the liquor-sellers — so that these grow continually more formidable; and it compels mankind to a strife for bread, which makes us all meaner than God intended us to be. Do you really think the 'game pays for the candle?'

From another, occupying high position as an economic thinker and writer, come also these questions:

> "What are the social and political results to follow the sweeping reconstruction of our material prices and our labor system? Are we not unconsciously, and from the sheer force of these new elements, drifting fast into a form of actual socialism — if not exactly such as the *doctrinaire* reformers preach, yet a form which in respect to material interests swallows up individualism in huge combinations? Does not the economizing of the new methods of production necessitate this tendency? And, if so, to what sort of social reconstruction is it likely to lead? Does it mean a future of industrial kings and industrial slaves? How far does the new situation harmonize with current aspirations of labor? Are these aspirations a reflex effect of the new conditions of industry?"

To form now any rational opinion concerning the present and future influences of the causes of the recent and existing economic disturbances, and to be able to return any intelligent answers to the questions and impressions which they have prompted or created, there is clearly but one practical, common-sense method to adopt, and that is to review and analyze the sociological sequences of these disturbances so far as they have been developed and determined. . . .

That many of the features of the situation are, when considered by themselves, disagreeable and even appalling, can not be denied. When one recalls, for example, through what seemingly weird power of genius, machinery has been summoned into existence — machinery which does not sleep, does not need rest, is not the recipient of wages; is most profitable when most unremittingly employed — and how no one agency has so stimulated its invention and use as the opposition of those whose toil it has supplemented or lightened — the first remedial idea of every employer whose labor is discontented being to devise and use a tool in place of a man; and how in the place of being a bond-slave it seems to be passing beyond control and assuming the mastery; when one recalls all these incidents of progress, the following story of Eastern magic might be almost regarded in the light of a purposely obscured old-time prophecy: A certain man, having great learning, obtained knowledge of an incantation whereby he could compel inanimate objects to work for him, commanded a stick to bring him water. The stick at once obeyed. But when water sufficient for the man's necessities had been brought, and there was threatened danger of an oversupply, he desired the stick to stop working. Having, however, omitted to learn the words for revoking the incantation, the stick refused to obey. Thereupon, the magician in anger caught up an axe, and, with a view to diminish or destroy the power of the stick to perform work, chopped it into several pieces; whereupon, each piece immediately began to bring as much water as one had formerly done; and in the end not only the magician but the whole world was deluged and destroyed.

The proposition that all transitions in the life of society, even those to a better stage, are inevitably accompanied by human suffering, is undoubtedly correct. It is impossible, as an old-time writer (Sir James Stewart, 1767) has remarked, to even sweep a room without raising a dust and occasioning temporary discomfort. But those who are inclined to take discouraging and pessimistic views of recent economic movements, seem not only to forget this, but also to content themselves with looking mainly at the bad results of such movements, in place of the good and bad together. So it is not difficult to understand how a person like the Russian novelist Tolstoi, a man of genius, but whose life and writings show him to be eccentric almost to the verge of insanity, should, after familiarizing himself with peasant-life in Russia, come to the conclusion that "the edifice of civil society, erected by the toil and energy of countless generations, is a crumbling ruin." But the trials and vicissitudes of life as Tolstoi finds them among the masses of Russia are the result of an original barbarism and savagery from which the composite races of that country have not yet been able to emancipate themselves; coupled with the existence of a typically despotic government, which throttles every movement for increased freedom in respect to both person and thought. But these are results for which the higher civilization of other countries is in no way responsible and can not at present help, but the indirect influence of which will, without doubt, in time powerfully affect and even entirely change. No one, furthermore, can familiarize himself with life as it exists in the slums and tenement-houses of all great cities in countries of the highest civilization; or in sterile Newfoundland, where all Nature is harsh and niggardly; or in sunny Mexico and the islands of the West Indies, where she is all bountiful and attractive, without finding much to sicken him with the aspects under which average humanity presents itself. But even here the evidence is absolutely conclusive that matters are not worse, but almost immeasurably better, than formerly; and that the possibilities for melioration, through what may be termed the general drift of affairs, is, beyond all comparison, greater than at any former period.

The first and signal result of the recent remarkable changes in the conditions of production and distribution, which in turn have been so conducive of industrial and societary disturbances, has been to greatly increase the abundance and reduce the price of most useful and desirable commodities. If some may say, "What of that, so long as distribution is impeded and has not been correspondingly perfected?" it may be answered, that production and distribution in virtue of a natural law are correlative or reciprocal. We produce to consume, and we consume to produce, and the one will not go on independently of the other; and although there may be, and actually is, and mainly through the influence of bad laws, more or less extensive maladjustment of these two great processes, the tendency is, and by methods to be hereafter pointed out, for the two to come into closer and closer harmony.

Next in order, it is important to recognize and keep clearly in view in reasoning upon this subject, what of good these same agencies, whose influence in respect to the future is now regarded by so many with alarm or suspicion, have already accomplished.

A hundred years ago the maintenance of the existing population of Great Britain, of the United States, and of all other highly-civilized countries, could not have been possible under the then imperfect and limited conditions of production and distribution. . . .

All the resources of the population of the United States, as they existed in 1840, would have been wholly inadequate to sow or harvest the present average annual corn or wheat crops of the country; and, even if these two results had been accomplished, the greater proportion of such a cereal product would have been of no value to the cultivator, and must have rotted on the ground for lack of any means of adequate distribution; the cost of the transportation of a ton of wheat, worth twenty-five dollars at a market, for a distance of a hundred and twenty miles over good roads, and with good teams and vehicles, entirely exhausting its initial value.

Fifty years ago corn (maize) was shelled in the United States by scraping the ears against the sharp edge of a frying-pan or shovel, or by using the cob of one ear to shell the corn from another. In this way about five bushels in ten hours could be shelled, and the laborer would have received about one fifth of the product. The six great corn States are Illinois, Indiana, Missouri, Iowa, Ohio, and Kansas. They produce more than one half the corn raised in the country. These States, by the census of 1880, had 2,056,770 persons engaged in agriculture, and it would have been necessary for this entire community to sit astride of shovels and frying-pans for one hundred and ten days out of three hundred and sixty-five to shell their corn-crop for the year 1880 by the old processes.

In 1790, before the grain-"cradle" was invented, an able-bodied farm-laborer in Great Britain could with a sickle reap only about a quarter of an acre of wheat in a day; at the present time a man with two horses can cut, rake, and bind in a day the wheat-product of twenty acres.

Forty years ago a deficient harvest in any one of the countries of Europe entailed a vast amount of suffering and starvation on their population. To-day the deficiency of any local crop of wheat is comparatively of little consequence, for the prices of cereals in every country readily accessible by railroad and steamships are now regulated, not by any local conditions, but by the combined production and consumption of the world; and the day of famines for the people of all such countries has passed forever. The extent to which all local advantages in respect to the supply and prices of food have been equalized in recent years through the railway service of the United States, is demonstrated by the fact that a full year's requirement of meat and bread for an adult person can now be moved from the points of their most abundant and cheapest production, a thousand miles, for a cost not in excess of the single day's wages of an average American mechanic or artisan. . . .

The existence of the present populations of Europe and the United States — nay, more, the continuance and progress of civilization itself — has therefore been made possible solely through the invention and use of the same labor-saving machinery which not a few are inclined to regard as likely to work permanent injury to the masses in the future. It is still easy to avoid all trouble arising out of the use of labor-saving machinery by going to the numerous countries — many of which are rich in the bounties of Nature — which do not possess it. But these are the very countries to which no person of average intelligence desires to go.

Restless and progressive humanity generally believes also that the continued betterment of the race is largely conditioned on the extension of free government based on popular representation and constitutional safeguards; and also on the successful continuation of the experiment under such conditions which was entered upon by the people of the United States just a hundred years ago. But the Government of the United States, under its existing Constitution, has been made possible only through the progress which man has made in recent years in his knowledge and control of the forces of nature. Without the perfected railroad and telegraph systems, the war for the maintenance of the Federal Union under the existing Constitution could not probably have been prosecuted to a successful conclusion; and even if no domestic strife had intervened, it is more than doubtful whether a federation of numerous States, sovereign in many particulars — floating down the stream of time like an elongated series of separate rafts, linked together — could have been indefinitely perpetuated, when the time necessary to overcome the distance between its extremities for the mere transmission of intelligence amounted to from twenty to thirty days. . . .

Finally, an absolute demonstration that the progress of mankind, in countries where the new economic conditions have been most influential in producing those disturbances and transitions in industry and society which to many seem fraught with disaster, has been for the better and not for the worse, is to be found in the marked prolongation of human life, or decline in the average death-rate, which has occurred within comparatively recent years in these same countries. Thus, the average annual death-rate in England and Wales, during the period from 1838 to 1875, was 22.3 per thousand. From 1876 to 1880, it was 20.08. But, for the six years from 1880 to 1887, the average has not exceeded 19.3; which means that about 500,000 persons in England and Wales were alive at the close of the year 1886 who would have been dead if the rate of mortality which prevailed between 1838 and 1875 had been maintained. . . . The average death-rate for the whole United States, for the census year 1880, was between 17 and 18 per thousand; which is believed to be a less mean rate than that of any European country except Sweden. . . .

On the other hand, there are certain sequences of the new conditions of civilization pertaining to individual and societary life which are less flattering and promising. In the same ratio as the facilities for the production and distribution of commodities have been expanded and quickened, the necessity of untiring attention to business, as a prerequisite for success, has been increased, and the intensity of competition stimulated. The forces of business life are no longer subject to the control of the man of business. Having subordinated the lightning to the demands of business, business must go at lightning speed. "The electric message is superseding the leisurely letter. There is now no quiet waiting for foreign correspondence. The cable announces a bargain struck on another continent, and the same day, before the goods have been even shipped, the cargo is sold and the transaction ended." If one trader keeps himself in instantaneous contact through the telegraph with markets and customers, all must do the same, or be left behind in the struggle for success. Thus dominated by new conditions, the merchant and financier of to-day has been rendered almost as much of a machine as the worker in the factories, whose every movement has been automatic, or subordinate to the physical forces acting through machinery; and one result of the continuous mental and nervous activity which modern high-tension methods of business have necessitated, coupled with the high living and the frequent use of alcoholic stimulants to which such activity leads, has been to increase (if not create) a class of diseases which may be regarded as diseases of civilization, and which have in turn entailed a rapidly increasing mortality. Thus, the statistics of the Health Departmnt of the city of New York show that, comparing 1870 and 1887, the death-rate from "Bright's disease" increased from 890 to 2,375 per annum, or nearly threefold; and in the case of "heart-disease," from about 700 to 2,020 per annum — an increase again of nearly threefold; and an increase in both cases in far greater ratio than any increase of the population of the city.* Besides the causes of death above enumerated, there is also a very serious mortality arising from what is commonly but vaguely denominated "nervous exhaustion," directly referable to the same influences under consideration. The accepted statistics for the European nations also show that the rate of suicide is increasing. . . . The statistics of divorce in the United States, recently collected by the order of the Federal Government, show an increase largely in excess of the percentage growth of population. Thus, the increase in the population from 1867 to

* The population of the city of New York was, in 1866, about 750,000; in 1870, 942,000; in 1880, 1,206,000; and in 1887, about 1,460,000.

1886 is estimated at about sixty per cent, while the number of divorces for the last year of the period exceeded that for the first year by 156.9 per cent. There has also been an increase in the proportion of divorces to the number of married couples. . . .

The steady drift of population, not only in the United States but in all countries in which railroads are numerous and the art of reading widely diffused, from the country to towns and cities, is undoubtedly one of the sequences of the recent changes in economic conditions, and, as suggestive of the impoverishment of rural sections, and discontent with agricultural pursuits, is popularly regarded as an unhealthy social phenomenon. . . .

Everywhere the aspirations of the rural classes are out of proportion to their intelligence and resources. The rise of wages has created a crowd of more or less factitious wants, which are difficult to meet and which keep alive a constant sense of privation. Education has created in the farming man an intellectual curiosity, which it is hard to satisfy, and which keeps him constantly in mind of his isolation, of the loneliness and dullness of his life. One effect of this state of things in France is the influx from Italy and Belgium of a very low grade of laborers, whom the farmers are only too glad to hire to prevent their fields lying waste, but who are anything but a wholesome addition to the French population. In fact, in every country, wherever we find the natives abandoning in disgust the cultivation of the soil, we find a lower grade of labor, a less civilized man, who asks for less and is content with less, taking their places. . . .

The causes of the almost universal discontent of labor, which has characterized the recent transitions in the world's methods of production and distribution, and which, intensified by such transitions, have been more productive of disturbances than at any former period (for, as previously shown, there are really no new factors concerned in the experiences under consideration), would seem to be mainly these:

1. *The displacement or supplanting of labor through more economical and effective methods of production and distribution.* . . .

Of the injury thus occasioned, and of the suffering attendant, no more pitiful and instructive example of recent date could be given than the following account, furnished to the United States Department of State, of the effect of the displacement of hand-loom weaving in the city of Chemnitz, Saxony, by the introduction and use of the power-loom:

In 1875 there were no less than 4,519 of the so-called *"master-weavers"* in Chemnitz, each of whom employed from one to ten journeymen at hand-loom weaving in his own house. The introduction of machinery, however, imposed conditions upon these weavers which they found the more difficult to meet the more the machinery was improved. The plainer goods were made on power-looms, and work in the factories was found to be more remunerative. Instead of giving work to others, they were gradually compelled to seek work for themselves. The independent "master" soon fell into ranks with the dependent factory-hand, but as he grew older and his eye-sight failed him he was replaced by younger and more active hands, and what once promised to become a well-to-do citizen in his old age now bids fair to become a burden upon the community. Those who had means of procuring the newer Jacquard contrivance, or even the improved "leaf" or "shaft-looms," managed to eke out a subsistence; but the prospects of the weavers who have learned to work only with the hand-looms are becoming more hopeless every day.

Now, while such cases of displacement of labor appeal most strongly to human sympathy, and pre-eminently constitute a field for individual or societary action for the purpose of relief, it should be at the same time remembered that the world, especially during the last century, has had a large experience in such matters, and that the following points may be regarded as established beyond the possibility of contradiction: 1. That such phases of human suffering are now, always have been, and undoubtedly always will be, the inevitable concomitants of the progress of civilization, or the transitions of the life of society to a higher and better stage. They seem to be in the nature of "growing-pains," or of penalty which Nature exacts at the outset, but for once only, whenever mankind subordinates her forces in greater degree to its own will and uses. 2. That it is not within the power of statute enactment to arrest such transitions, even when a large and immediate amount of human suffering can certainly be predicated as their consequent, except so far as it initiates and favors a return of society toward barbarism; for the whole progress in civilization consists in accomplishing greater or better results with the same or lesser effort, physical or mental. 3. All experience shows that, whatever disadvantage or detriment the introduction and use of new and improved instrumentalities or methods of production and distribution may temporarily entail on individuals or classes, the ultimate result is always an almost immeasurable degree of increased good to mankind in general. . . . There is little foundation for the belief largely entertained by the masses, and which has been inculcated by many sincere and humane persons, who have undertaken to counsel and direct them, that the amount of remunerative work to be done in the world is a fixed quantity, and that the fewer there are to do it the more each one will get; when the real truth is, that work as it were breeds work; that the amount to be done is not limited; that the more there is done the more there will be to do; and that the continued increasing material abundance which follows all new methods for effecting greater production and distribution is the true and permanent foundation for increasing general prosperity. . . .

Attention is next asked to the *second* (assumed) cause for the prevailing discontent of labor, namely:

Changes in the character or nature of employments consequent upon the introduction of new methods — machinery or processes — which it is claimed have tended to lower the grade of labor, impair the independence, and restrict the mental development of the laborer.

That such changes have been in the nature of evil, can not be questioned. . . . Happily, however, the number of industries, in which the division of labor and its subordination to machinery has been productive of such extreme results, is not very large; the manufacture of boots and shoes by modern machine methods, in which every finished shoe is said to represent sixty-two distinct mechanical employments or products, being prhaps the most notable. And yet even here there is not a little in way of compensating benefit to be credited to such a system. Thus, for example, it is stated that "the use of machinery has compelled employés to apply themselves more closely to their work; and, being paid by the piece, has enabled them to make better wages." When shoemaking was a handicraft, "the hours of labor were very irregular; the workmen, who decided their own hours of labor, working some days only a few hours, and then working far into the night for a few days to make up for lost time. It was once customary for shoemakers (in New England) to work on an average fifteen hours a day," now the hours of labor in the shoe-factories are not in excess of ten hours. It is also claimed that the introduction of the sewing-machine into the manufacture of boots and shoes has greatly increased the opportunities for the employment of women, at better rates of wages. . . .

The third cause which has especially operated in recent years to occasion discontent on the part of labor has been undoubtedly *the increase in intelligence or general information on the part of the masses in all civilized countries.*

The best definition, or rather statement, of the essential difference between a man and an animal, that has ever been given is, that a man has progressive wants, and an animal has not. Under the guidance of what is termed instinct, the animal wants the same habitat and quantity and quality of food as its progenitors, and nothing more. And the more nearly man approaches in condition to the animal, the more limited is the sphere of his wants, and the greater his contentment. A greater supply of blubber and skins to the Eskimo, more "pulque" to the native Mexican, to the West Indian negro a constant supply of yams and plantains without labor, and the ability to buy five salt herrings for the same price that he has now to give for three, would, in each case, temporarily fill the cup of individual happiness nearly to repletion. And, among civilized men, the contentment and also sluggishness of those neighborhoods in which the population come little in contact with the outer world and have little of diversity of employment open to them, are proverbial.

Now the wonderful material progress which has been made within the last quarter of a century has probably done more to overcome the inertia, and quicken the energy of the masses, than all that has been hitherto achieved in this direction in all preceding centuries. The railroad, the steamship, and the telegraph have broken down the barriers of space and time that formerly constituted almost insuperable obstacles in the way of frequent intercourse between people of different races, countries, and communities, and have made the civilized world, as it were, one great neighborhood. Every increased facility that is afforded for the dissemination of intelligence, or for personal movement, finds a marvelously quick response in an extended use. The written correspondence — letters and cards — exchanged through the world's postal service, more than doubled between the years 1873 and 1885, while in the United States the number of people annually transported on railroads alone exceeds every year many times the total population of the country, the annual number for the New England States being more than sixteen times greater than their population. Under these powerful but natural educating influences, there has been a great advance in the intelligence of the masses. They have come to know more of what others are doing; know better what they themselves are capable of doing; and their wants have correspondingly increased, not merely in respect to quantities of the things to which they have always been accustomed, but very many articles and services which within a comparatively recent period were regarded as luxuries, are now almost universally considered and demanded as necessaries. At the same time, the increased power of production and distribution, and the consequent reduction in the cost of most commodities and services, have also worked for the satisfaction of these wants in such a degree that a complete revolution has been effected during recent years in the every-day life of all classes of the people of the great industrial and commercial countries. Let any one compare the condition of even the abject poor of London, as described in recent publications, with the condition of English laborers as described by writers of acknowledged authority not more than forty years ago, and he can not resist the conclusion that the very outcasts of England are now better provided for than were multitudes of her common laboring-men at the period mentioned.

The widening of the sphere of one's surroundings, and a larger acquaintance with other men and pursuits, have long been recognized as not productive of content. Writing to his nephew more than one hundred years ago, Thomas Jefferson thus concisely expressed the results of his own observation: "Traveling," he says, "makes men wiser, but less happy. When men of sober age travel they gather knowledge, but they are, after all, subject to recollections mixed with regret; their affections are weakened by being extended over more objects, and they learn new habits which can not be gratified when they return home." Again, as the former few and simple requirements of the masses have become more varied and costly, the individual effort necessary for the satisfaction of the latter is not relatively less, even under the new conditions of production, than before, and in many instances is possibly greater. Hence, notwithstanding the large advance in recent years in the average rates of wages, and a greatly increased purchasing power of wages, there is no less complaint than ever of the cost of living. . . .

There is, therefore, unquestionably in these facts an explanation in no small part of what to many has seemed one of the greatest puzzles of the times — namely, that with undoubtedly greater and increasing abundance and cheapness of most desirable things, popular discontent with the existing economic condition of affairs does not seem to diminish, but rather to greatly increase. And out of such discontent, which is not based on anything akin to actual and unavoidable poverty, has originated a feeling that the new conditions of abundance should be further equalized by some other methods than intelligent individual effort, self-denial, and natural, progressive material and social development (the actuality of which is proved by all experience); and that the state could, if it would, make all men prosperous; and therefore should, in some way not yet clearly defined by anybody, arbitrarily intervene and effect it. And this feeling, so far as it assumes definiteness of idea and purpose, constitutes what is called "socialism." . . .

CONCLUSION

Finally, a comprehensive review of the economic changes of the last quarter of a century, and a careful balancing of what seems to have been good and what seems to have been evil in respect to results, would seem to warrant the following conclusions: That the immense material progress that these changes have entailed has been, for mankind in general, movement upward and not downward; for the better and not for the worse; and that the epoch of time under consideration will hereafter rank in history as one that has had no parallel, but which corresponds in importance with the periods that successively succeeded the Crusades, the invention of gunpowder, the emancipation of thought through the Reformation, and the invention of the steam-engine; when the whole plane of civilization and humanity rose to a higher level, each great movement being accompanied by social disturbances of great movement being accompanied by social disturbances of great magnitude and serious import, but which experience has proved were but temporary in their nature and infinitesimal in their influence for evil in comparison with the good that followed. And what the watchman standing on this higher eminence can now see is, that the time has come when the population of the world commands the means of a comfortable subsistence in a greater degree and with less of effort than ever before; and what he may reasonably expect to see at no very remote period is, the dawn of a day when human poverty will mean more distinctly than ever physical disability, mental incapacity, or unpardonable viciousness or laziness.

But, in order that this dawning may be hastened, it is of the first importance to recognize that civilized society in recent years, and under the new economic conditions which those years have evolved, has become a vastly more complicated machine than ever before — so complicated, in fact, that, in order to make it work smoothly, all possible obstructions need to be foreseen and removed from its mechanism. . . .

Andrew Carnegie
RESPONSIBILITIES OF THE RICH

<s 1889 >> THE popularity of works of protest like *Progress and Poverty* and *Looking Backward* indicates clearly the extent to which there was a deep public concern about the tremendous changes that were rocking the foundations of American society in the last decades of the nineteenth century. Thoughtful persons were deeply disturbed by the concentration of so much economic power in huge corporations and the resulting concentration of wealth and social influence in the hands of new multimillionaire business and financial tycoons. Masses of ordinary citizens, moved by a complex mixture of jealousy, fear, admiration, and awe, were confused and irritated when they thought about these new institutions and the men who ran them.

However, it would be wrong to assume that wealth and individual power were without defenders. The traditional American faith in freedom and individual enterprise of course played into the hands of those who wished to let well enough alone. The vogue of the British philosopher Herbert Spencer (1820-1903), who opposed even such minor interferences with the operation of "natural" forces as the public school system and the government-operated post office, reflects the continuing influence of this point of view. The relatively high standard of living in the United States and the continuing belief that America was the land of opportunity *par excellence* also encouraged people to look tolerantly on the power and wealth of the great leaders of business. When the Baptist preacher Russell Conwell (1843-1925) pointed out, in his oft-repeated address, *Acres of Diamonds,* that the accumulation of wealth was a Christian duty, he never lacked an appreciative audience.

But the most striking defense of the new order was that of Andrew Carnegie (1835-1919), himself one of the new economic potentates. His essay "Wealth," which appeared in the *North American Review* in 1889, took actually a compromise position. The millionaire's unquestioned right to accumulate a great fortune he argued, was balanced by his obligation to arrange for its disposition in socially useful ways. Although the *Review's* circulation was tiny, the message of this essay soon reached a gigantic audience. It was published in England, and in a short time magazines and newspapers all over the western world were discussing it. One may almost trace the history of modern philanthropy from this article.

THE GOSPEL OF WEALTH

THE PROBLEM OF THE ADMINISTRATION OF WEALTH

THE problem of our age is the proper administration of wealth, that the ties of brotherhood may still bind together the rich and poor in harmonious relationship. The conditions of human life have not only been changed, but revolutionized, within the past few hundred years. In former days there was little difference between the dwelling, dress, food, and environment of the chief and those of his retainers. The Indians are today where civilized man then was. When visiting the Sioux, I was led to the wigwam of the chief. It was like the others in external appearance, and even within the difference was trifling between it and those of the poorest of his braves. The contrast between the palace of the millionaire and the cottage of the laborer with us to-day measures the change which has come with civilization. This change, however, is not to be deplored, but welcomed as highly beneficial. It is well, nay, essential, for the progress of the race that the houses of some should be homes for all that is highest and best in literature and the arts, and for all the refinements of civilization, rather than that none should be so. Much better this great irregularity than universal squalor. Without wealth there can be no Maecenas. The "good old times" were not good old times. Neither master nor servant was as well situated then as to-day. A relapse to old conditions would be disastrous to both — not the least so to him who serves — and would sweep away civilization with it. But whether the change be for good or ill, it is upon us, beyond our power to alter, and, therefore, to be accepted and made the best of. It is a waste of time to criticize the inevitable.

It is easy to see how the change has come. One illustration will serve for almost every phase of the cause. In the manufacture of products we have the whole story. It applies to all combinations of human industry, as stimulated and enlarged by the inventions of this scientific age. Formerly, articles were manufactured at the domestic hearth, or in small shops which formed part of the household. The master and his apprentices worked side by side, the latter living with the master, and therefore subject to the same conditions. When these apprentices rose to be masters, there was little or no change in their mode of life, and they, in turn, educated succeeding apprentices in the same routine. There was, substantially, social equality, and even political equality, for those engaged in industrial pursuits had then little or no voice in the State.

The inevitable result of such a mode of manufacture was crude articles at high prices. To-day the world obtains commodities of excellent quality at prices which even the preceding generation would have deemed incredible. In the commercial world similar causes have produced similar results, and the race is benefited thereby. The poor enjoy what the rich could not before afford. What were the luxuries have become the necessaries of life. The laborer has now more comforts than the farmer had a few generations ago. The farmer has more luxuries than the landlord had, and is more richly clad and better housed. The landlord has books and pictures rarer and appointments more artistic than the king could then obtain.

The price we pay for this salutary change is, no doubt, great. We assemble thousands of operatives in the factory, and in the mine, of whom the employer can know little or nothing, and to whom he is little better than a myth. All intercourse between them is at an end. Rigid castes are formed, and, as usual, mutual ignorance breeds mutual distrust. Each caste is without sympathy with the other, and ready to credit anything disparaging in regard to it. Under the law of competition, the employer of thousands is forced into the strictest economies, among which the rates paid to labor figure prominently, and often there is friction between the employer and the employed, between capital and labor, between rich and poor. Human society loses homogeneity.

The price which society pays for the law of competition, like the price it pays for cheap comforts and luxuries, is also great; but the advantages of this law are also greater still than its cost — for it is to this law that we owe our wonderful material development, which brings improved conditions in its train. But, whether the law be benign or not, we must say of it, as we say of the change in the conditions of men to which we have referred: It is here; we cannot evade it; no substitutes for it have been found; and while the law may be sometimes hard for the individual, it is best for the race, because it insures the survival of the fittest in every department. We accept and welcome, therefore, as conditions to which we must accommodate ourselves, great inequality of environments; the concentration of business, industrial and commercial, in the hands of a few; and the law of competition between these, as being not only beneficial, but essential to the future progress of the race. Having accepted these, it follows that there must be great scope for the exercise of special ability in the merchant and in the manufacturer who has to conduct affairs upon a great scale. That this talent for organization and management is rare among men is proved by the fact that it invariably secures enormous rewards for its possessor, no matter where or under what laws or conditions. The experienced in affairs always rate the MAN whose services can be obtained as a partner as not only the first consideration, but such as render the question of his capital scarcely worth considering: for able men soon create capital; in the hands of those without the special talent required, capital soon takes wings. Such men become interested in firms or corporations using millions; and, estimating only simple interest to be made upon the capital invested, it is inevitable that their income must exceed their expenditure and that they must, therefore, accumulate wealth. Nor is there any middle ground which such men can occupy, because the great manufacturing or commercial concern which does not earn at least interest upon its capital soon becomes bankrupt. It must either go forward or fall behind; to stand still is impossible. It is a condition essential to its successful operation that it should be thus far profitable, and even that, in addition to interest on capital, it should make profit. It is a law, as certain as any of the others named, that men possessed of this peculiar talent for affairs, under the free play of economic forces must, of necessity, soon be in receipt of more revenue than can be juiciously expended upon themselves; and this law is as beneficial for the race as the others.

Objections to the foundations upon which society is based are not in order, because the condition of the race is better with these than it has been with any other which has been tried. Of the effect of any new substitutes proposed we cannot be sure. The Socialist or Anarchist who seeks to overturn present conditions is to be regarded as attacking the foundation upon which civilization itself rests, for civilization took its start from the day when the capable, industrious workman said to his incompetent and lazy fellow, "If thou dost not sow, thou shalt not reap," and thus ended primitive Communism by separating the drones from the bees. One who studies this subject will soon be brought face to face with the conclusion that upon the sacredness of property civilization itself depends — the right of the laborer to his hundred dollars in the savings-bank, and equally the legal right of the millionaire to his millions. Every man must be allowed "to sit under his own vine and fig-tree, with none to make afraid," if human society is to advance, or even to remain so far advanced as it is. To those who propose to substitute Communism for this intense Individualism, the answer therefore is: The race has tried that. All progress from that barbarous day to the present time has resulted from its displacement. Not evil, but good, has come to the race from the accumulation of wealth by those who have had the ability and energy to produce it. But even if we admit for a moment that it might be better for the race to discard its present foundation, Individualism, — that is a nobler ideal that man should labor, not for himself alone, but in and for a brotherhood of his fellows, and share with them all in common, realizing Swedenborg's idea of heaven, where, as he says, the angels derive their happiness, not from laboring for self, but for each other, — even admit all this, and a sufficient answer is, This is not evolution, but revolution. It necessitates the changing of human nature itself — a work of eons, even if it were good to change it, which we cannot know.

It is not practicable in our day or in our age. Even if desirable theoretically, it belongs to another and long-succeeding sociological stratum. Our duty is with what is practicable now — with the next step possible in our day and generation. It is criminal to waste our energies in endeavoring to uproot, when all we can profitably accomplish is to bend the universal tree of humanity a little in the direction most favorable to the production of good fruit under existing circumstances. We might as well urge the destruction of the highest existing type of man because he failed to reach our ideal as to favor the destruction of Individualism, Private Property, the Law of Accumulation of Wealth, and the Law of Competition; for these are the highest result of human experience, the soil in which society, so far, has produced the best fruit. Unequally or unjustly, perhaps, as these laws sometimes operate, and imperfect as they appear to the Idealist, they are, nevertheless, like the highest type of man, the best and most valuable of all that humanity has yet accomplished.

We start, then, with a condition of affairs under which the best interests of the race are promoted, but which inevitably gives wealth to the few. Thus far, accepting conditions as they exist, the situation can be surveyed and pronounced good. The question then arises, — and if the foregoing be correct, it is the only question with which we have to deal, — What is the proper mode of administering wealth after the laws upon which civilization is founded have thrown it into the hands of the few? And it is of this great question that I believe I offer the true solution. It will be understood that fortunes are here spoken of, not moderate sums saved by many years of effort, the returns from which are required for the comfortable maintenance and education of families. This is not wealth, but only competence, which it should be the aim of all to acquire, and which it is for the best interests of society should be acquired.

There are but three modes in which surplus wealth can be disposed of. It can be left to the families of the decedents; or it can be bequeathed for public purposes; or, finally, it can be administered by its possessors during their lives. Under the first and second modes most of the wealth of the world that has reached the few has hitherto been applied. Let us in turn consider each of these modes. The first is the most injudicious. In monarchical countries, the estates and the greatest portion of the wealth are left to the first son, that the vanity of the parent may be gratified by the thought that his name and title are to descend unimpaired to succeeding generations. The condition of this class in Europe to-day teaches the failure of such hopes or ambitions. The successors have become impoverished through their follies, or from the fall in the value of land. Even in Great Britain the strict law of entail has been found inadequate to maintain an hereditary class. Its soil is rapidly passing into the hands of the stranger. Under republican institutions the division of property among the children is much fairer; but the question which forces itself upon thoughtful men in all lands is, Why should men leave great fortunes to their children? If this is done from affection, is it not misguided affection? Observation teaches that, generally speaking, it is not well for the children that they should be so burdened. Neither is it well for the State. Beyond providing for the wife and daughters moderate sources of income, and very moderate allowances indeed, if any, for the sons, men may well hesitate; for it is no longer questionable that great sums bequeathed often work more for the injury than for the good of the recipients. Wise men will soon conclude that, for the best interests of the members of their families, and of the State, such bequests are an improper use of their means.

It is not suggested that men who have failed to educate their sons to earn a livelihood shall cast them adrift in poverty. If any man has seen fit to rear his sons with a view to their living idle lives, or, what is highly commendable, has instilled in them the sentiment that they are in a position to labor for public ends without reference to pecuniary considerations, then, of course, the duty of the parent is to see that such are provided for in moderation. There are instances of millionaires' sons unspoiled by wealth, who, being rich, still perform great services to the community. Such are the very salt of the earth, as valuable as, unfortunately, they are rare. It is not the exception, however, but the rule that men must regard; and, looking at the usual result of enormous sums conferred upon legatees, the thoughtful man must shortly say, "I would as soon leave to my son a curse as the almighty dollar," and admit to himself that it is not the welfare of the children, but family pride, which inspires these legacies.

As to the second mode, that of leaving wealth at death for public uses, it may be said that this is only a means for the disposal of wealth, provided a man is content to wait until he is dead before he becomes of much good in the world. Knowledge of the results of legacies bequeathed is not calculated to inspire the brightest hopes of much posthumous good being accomplished by them. The cases are not few in which the real object sought by the testator is not attained, nor are they few in which his real wishes are thwarted. In many cases the bequests are so used as to become only monuments of his folly. It is well to remember that it requires the exercise of not less ability than that which acquires it, to use wealth so as to be really beneficial to the community. Besides this, it may fairly be said that no man is to be extolled for doing what he cannot help doing, nor is he to be thanked by the community to which he only leaves wealth at death. Men who leave vast sums in this way may fairly be thought men who would not have left it at all had they been able to take it with them. The memories of such cannot be held in grateful remembrance, for there is no grace in their gifts. It is not to be wondered at that such bequests seem so generally to lack the blessing.

The growing disposition to tax more and more heavily large estates left at death is a cheering indication of the growth of a salutary change in public opinion. The State of Pennsylvania now takes — subject to some exceptions — one tenth of the property left by its citizens. The budget presented in the British Parliament the other day proposes to increase the death duties; and, most significant of all, the new tax is to be a graduated one. Of all forms of taxation this seems the wisest. Men who continue hoarding great sums all their lives, the proper use of which for public ends would work good to the community from which it chiefly came, should be made to feel that the community, in the form of the State, cannot thus be deprived of its proper share. By taxing estates heavily at death the State marks its condemnation of the selfish millionaire's unworthy life.

It is desirable that nations should go much further in this direction. Indeed, it is difficult to set bounds to the share of a rich man's estate which should go at his death to the public through the agency of the State, and by all means such taxes should be graduated, beginning at nothing upon moderate sums to dependents, and increasing rapidly as the amounts swell, until of the millionaire's hoard, as of Shylock's, at least

> The other half
> Comes to the privy coffer of the State.

This policy would work powerfully to induce the rich man to attend to the administration of wealth during his life, which is the end that society should always have in view, as being by far the most fruitful for the people. Nor need it be feared that this policy would sap the root of enterprise and render men less anxious to accumulate, for, to the class whose ambition it is to leave great fortunes and be talked about after their death, it will attract even more attention, and, indeed, be a somewhat nobler ambition, to have enormous sums paid over to the State from their fortunes.

There remains, then, only one mode of using great fortunes; but in this we have the true antidote for the temporary unequal distribution of wealth, the reconciliation of the rich and the poor — a reign of harmony, another ideal, differing, indeed, from that of the Communist in requiring only the further evolution of existing conditions, not the total overthrow of our civilization. It is founded upon the present most intense Individualism, and the race is prepared to put it in practice by degrees whenever it pleases. Under its sway we shall have an ideal State, in which the surplus wealth of the few will become, in the best sense, the property of the many, because administered for the common good; and this wealth, passing through the hands of the few, can be made a much more potent force for the elevation of our race than if distributed in small sums to the people themselves. Even the poorest can be made to see this, and to agree that great sums gathered by some of their fellow-citizens and spent for public purposes, from which the masses reap the principal benefit, are more valuable to them than if scattered among themselves in trifling amounts through the course of many years.

If we consider the results which flow from the Cooper Institute, for instance, to the best portion of the race in New York not possessed of means, and compare these with those which would have ensued for the good of the masses from an equal sum distributed by Mr. Cooper in his lifetime in the form of wages, which is the highest form of distribution, being for work done and not for charity, we can form some estimate of the possibilities for the improvement of the race which lie embedded in the present law of the accumulation of wealth. Much of this sum, if distributed in small quantities among the people, would have been wasted in the indulgence of appetite, some of it in excess, and it may be doubted whether even the part put to the best use, that of adding to the comforts of the home, would have yielded results for the race, as a race, at all comparable to those which are flowing and are to flow from the Cooper Institute from generation to generation. Let the advocate of violent or radical change ponder well this thought.

We might even go so far as to take another instance — that of Mr. Tilden's bequest of five millions of dollars for a free library in the city of New York; but in referring to this one cannot help saying involuntarily: How much better if Mr. Tilden had devoted the last years of his own life to the proper administration of this immense sum; in which case neither legal contest nor any other cause of delay could have interfered with his aims. But let us assume that Mr. Tilden's millions finally become the means of giving to this city a noble public library, where the treasures of the world contained in books will be open to all forever, without money and without price. Considering the good of that part of the race which congregates in and around Manhattan Island, would its permanent benefit have been better promoted had these millions been allowed to circulate in small sums through the hands of the masses? Even the most strenuous advocate of Communism must entertain a doubt upon this subject. Most of those who think will probably entertain no doubt whatever.

Poor and restricted are our opportunities in this life, narrow our horizon, our best work most imperfect; but rich men should be thankful for one inestimable boon. They have it in their power during their lives to busy themselves in organizing benefactions from which the masses of their fellows will derive lasting advantage, and thus dignify their own lives. The highest life is probably to be reached, not by such imitation of the life of Christ as Count Tolstoi gives us, but, while animated by Christ's spirit, by recognizing the changed conditions of this age, and adopting modes of expressing this spirit suitable to the changed conditions under which we live, still laboring for the good of our fellows, which was the essence of his life and teaching, but laboring in a different manner.

This, then, is held to be the duty of the man of wealth: To set an example of modest, unostentatious living, shunning display or extravagance; to provide moderately for the legitimate wants of those dependent upon him; and, after doing so, to consider all surplus revenues which come to him simply as trust funds, which he is called upon to administer, and strictly bound as a matter of duty to administer in the manner which, in his judgment, is best calculated to produce the most beneficial results for the community — the man of wealth thus becoming the mere trustee and agent for his poorer brethren, bringing to their service his superior wisdom, experience, and ability to administer, doing for them better than they would or could do for themselves.

We are met here with the difficulty of determining what are moderate sums to leave to members of the family; what is modest, unostentatious living; what is the test of extravagance. There must be different standards for different conditions. The answer is that it is as impossible to name exact amounts or actions as it is to define good manners, good taste, or the rule of propriety; but, nevertheless, these are verities, well known, although indefinable. Public sentiment is quick to know and to feel what offends these. So in the case of wealth. The rule in regard to good taste in the dress of men or women applies here. Whatever makes one conspicuous offends the canon. If any family be chiefly known for display, for extravagance in home, table, or equipage, for enormous sums ostentatiously spent in any form upon itself — if these be its chief distinctions, we have no difficulty in estimating its nature or culture. So likewise in regard to the use or abuse of its surplus wealth, or to generous, free-handed coöperation in good public uses, or to unabated efforts to accumulate and hoard to the last, or whether they administer or bequeath. The verdict rests with the best and most enlightened public sentiment. The community will surely judge, and its judgments will not often be wrong.

The best uses to which surplus wealth can be put have already been indicated. Those who would administer wisely must, indeed, be wise; for one of the serious obstacles to the improvement of our race is indiscriminate charity. It were better for mankind that the millions of the rich were thrown into the sea than so spent as to encourage the slothful, the drunken, the unworthy. Of every thousand dollars spent in so-called charity to-day, it is probable that nine hundred and fifty dollars is unwisely spent — so spent, indeed, as to produce the very evils which it hopes to mitigate or cure. A well-known writer of philosophic books admitted the other day that he had given a quarter of a dollar to a man who approached him as he was coming to visit the house of his friend. He knew nothing of the habits of this beggar, knew not the use that would be made of this money, although he had every reason to suspect that it would be spent improperly. This man professed to be a disciple of Herbert Spencer; yet the quarter-dollar given that night will probably work more injury than all the money will do good which its thoughtless donor will ever be able to give in true charity. He only gratified his own feelings, saved himself from annoyance — and this was probably one of the most selfish and very worst actions of his life, for in all respects he is most worthy.

In bestowing charity, the main consideration should be to help those who will help themselves; to provide part of the means by which those who desire to improve may do so; to give those who desire to rise the aids by which they may rise; to assist, but rarely or never to do all. Neither the individual nor the race is improved by almsgiving. Those worthy of assistance, except in rare cases, seldom require assistance. The really valuable men of the race never do, except in case of accident or sudden change. Every one has, of course, cases of individuals brought to his own knowledge where temporary assistance can do genuine good, and these he will not overlook. But the amount which can be wisely given by the individual for individuals is necessarily limited by his lack of knowledge of the circumstances connected with each. He is the only true reformer who is as careful and as anxious not to aid the unworthy as he is to aid the worthy, and, perhaps, even more so, for in almsgiving more injury is probably done by rewarding vice than by relieving virtue.

The rich man is thus almost restricted to following the examples of Peter Cooper, Enoch Pratt of Baltimore, Mr. Pratt of Brooklyn, Senator Stanford, and others, who know that the best means of benefiting the community is to place within its reach the ladders upon which the aspiring can rise — free libraries, parks, and means of recreation, by which men are helped in body and mind; works of art, certain to give pleasure and improve the public taste; and public institutions of various kinds, which will improve the general condition of the people; in this manner returning their surplus wealth to the mass of their fellows in the forms best calculated to do them lasting good.

Thus is the problem of rich and poor to be solved. The laws of accumulation will be left free, the laws of distribution free. Individualism will continue, but the millionaire will be but a trustee for the poor, intrusted for a season with a great part of the increased wealth of the community, but administering it for the community far better than it could or would have done for itself. The best minds will thus have reached a stage in the development of the race in which it is clearly seen that there is no mode of disposing of surplus wealth creditable to thoughtful and earnest men into whose hands it flows, save by using it year by year for the general good. This day already dawns. Men may die without incurring the pity of their fellows, still sharers in great business enterprises from which their capital cannot be or has not been withdrawn, and which is left chiefly at death for public uses; yet the day is not far distant when the man who dies leaving behind him millions of available wealth, which was free for him to administer during life, will pass away "unwept, unhonored, and unsung," no matter to what uses he leaves the dross which he cannot take with him. Of such as these the public verdict will then be: "The man who dies thus rich dies disgraced."

Such, in my opinion, is the true gospel concerning wealth, obedience to which is destined some day to solve the problem of the rich and the poor, and to bring "Peace on earth, among men good will."

Omaha Convention
THE POPULIST PROGRAM

⊰{1892}⊱ FOR American farmers, particularly those living in the South or in the Plains states west of the Mississippi, the early 1890's was a time of desperation. With the prices of staples like wheat and cotton falling to all-time lows and with the transportation and marketing facilities that they depended upon controlled by monopolistic corporations, many farmers found it impossible to operate at a profit. Since many were also burdened with heavy mortgage payments and other fixed costs, bankruptcy was a common occurrence. Such conditions led to the rise of the Alliance movement and then, in 1892, to the organization of the Populist party, for the farmers were convinced that both the Democratic and the Republican parties were controlled by heartless capitalists eager only to exploit the rural areas.

Much has been written by historians about the Populists. To some students populism has seemed a forerunner of the 20th-century liberal reform movements, to others an essentially reactionary effort of property-conscious citizens to overthrow the forces of modern industrial society that were usurping the dominant position in American society formerly held by agriculturalists. Were the Populists idealists trying to form a farmer-labor coalition against predatory capitalism, or were they merely selfish, embittered men resistant to all outside influence and paranoiacally suspicious of city life, immigrants, bankers, and anyone better off at the moment than themselves?

A completely satisfactory answer to this question will probably never be found. But it is instructive to study the first platform of the party, fashioned at the Populist convention at Omaha, Nebraska, in 1892. On this platform the party carried Kansas and elected a large number of local officials in other states. Its presidential candidate, James B. Weaver, polled over a million popular votes.

THE PLATFORM OF THE POPULIST PARTY

ASSEMBLED upon the 116th anniversary of the Declaration of Independence, the People's Party of America, in their first national convention, invoking upon their action the blessing of Almighty God, put forth in the name and on behalf of the people of this country, the following preamble and declaration of principles:

PREAMBLE

The conditions which surround us best justify our co-operation; we meet in the midst of a nation brought to the verge of moral, political, and material ruin. Corruption dominates the ballot-box, the Legislatures, the Congress, and touches even the ermine of the bench. The people are demoralized; most of the States have been compelled to isolate the voters at the polling places to prevent universal intimidation and bribery. The newspapers are largely subsidized or muzzled, public opinion silenced, business prostrated, homes covered with mortgages, labor impoverished, and the land concentrating in the hands of capitalists. The urban workmen are denied the right to organize for self-protection, imported pauperized labor beats down their wages, a hireling standing army, unrecognized by our laws, is established to shoot them down, and they are rapidly degenerating into European conditions. The fruits of the toil of millions are boldly stolen to build up colossal fortunes for a few, unprecedented in the history of mankind; and the possessors of these, in turn, despise the Republic and endanger liberty. From the same prolific womb of governmental injustice we breed the two great classes — tramps and millionaires.

The national power to create money is appropriated to enrich bondholders; a vast public debt payable in legal-tender currency has been funded into gold-bearing bonds, thereby adding millions to the burdens of the people.

Silver, which has been accepted as coin since the dawn of history, has been demonetized to add to the purchasing power of gold by decreasing the value of all forms of property as well as human labor, and the supply of currency is purposely abridged to fatten usurers, bankrupt enterprise, and enslave industry. A vast conspiracy against mankind has been organized on two continents, and it is rapidly taking possession of the world. If not met and overthrown at once it forebodes terrible social convulsions, the destruction of civilization, or the establishment of an absolute despotism.

We have witnessed for more than a quarter of a century the struggles of the two great political parties for power and plunder, while grievous wrongs have been inflicted upon the suffering people. We charge that the controlling influences dominating both these parties have permitted the existing dreadful conditions to develop without serious effort to prevent or restrain them. Neither do they now promise us any substantial reform. They have agreed together to ignore, in the coming campaign, every issue but one. They propose to drown the outcries of a plundered people with the uproar of a sham battle over the tariff, so that capitalists, corporations, national banks, rings, trusts, watered stock, the demonetization of silver and the oppressions of the usurers may all be lost sight of. They propose to sacrifice our homes, lives, and children on the altar of mammon; to destroy the multitude in order to secure corruption funds from the millionaires.

Assembled on the anniversary of the birthday of the nation, and filled with the spirit of the grand general and chief who established our independence, we seek to restore the government of the Republic to the hands of the "plain people," with which class it originated. We assert our purposes to be identical with the purposes of the National Constitution; to form a more perfect union and establish justice, insure domestic tranquillity, provide for the common defence, promote the general welfare, and secure the blessings of liberty for ourselves and our posterity.

We declare that this Republic can only endure as a free government while built upon the love of the people for each other and for the nation; that it cannot be pinned together by bayonets; that the Civil War is over, and that every passion and resentment which grew out of it must die with it, and that we must be in fact, as we are in name, one united brotherhood of free men.

Our country finds itself confronted by conditions for which there is no precedent in the history of the world; our annual agricultural productions amount to billions of dollars in value, which must, within a few weeks or months, be exchanged for billions of dollars' worth of commodities consumed in their production; the existing currency supply is wholly inadequate to make this exchange; the results are falling prices, the formation of combines and rings, the impoverishment of the producing class. We pledge ourselves that if given power we will labor to correct these evils by wise and reasonable legislation, in accordance with the terms of our platform.

We believe that the power of government — in other words, of the people — should be expanded (as in the case of the postal service) as rapidly and as far as the good sense of an intelligent people and the teachings of experience shall justify, to the end that oppression, injustice, and poverty shall eventually cease in the land.

While our sympathies as a party of reform are naturally upon the side of every proposition which will tend to make men intelligent, virtuous, and temperate, we nevertheless regard these questions, important as they are, as secondary to the great issues now pressing for solution, and upon which not only our individual prosperity but the very existence of free institutions depend; and we ask all men to first help us to determine whether we are to have a republic to administer before we differ as to the conditions upon which it is to be administered, believing that the forces of reform this day organized will never cease to move forward until every wrong is righted and equal rights and equal privileges securely established for all the men and women of this country.

PLATFORM

We declare, therefore —

First. — That the union of the labor forces of the United States this day consummated shall be permanent and perpetual; may its spirit enter into all hearts for the salvation of the Republic and the uplifting of mankind.

Second. — Wealth belongs to him who creates it, and every dollar taken from industry without an equivalent is robbery. "If any will not work, neither shall he eat." The interests of rural and civil labor are the same; their enemies are identical.

Third. — We believe that the time has come when the railroad corporations will either own the people or the people must own the railroads; and should the government enter upon the work of owning and managing all railroads, we should favor an amendment to the constitution by which all persons engaged in the government service shall be placed under a civil-service regulation of the most rigid character, so as to prevent the increase of the power of the national administration by the use of such additional government employes.

FINANCE. — We demand a national currency, safe, sound, and flexible issued by the general government only, a full legal tender for all debts, public and private, and that without the use of banking corporations; a just, equitable, and efficient means of distribution direct to the people, at a tax not to exceed 2 percent, per annum, to be provided as set forth in the sub-treasury plan of the Farmers' Alliance, or a better system; also by payments in discharge of its obligations for public improvements.

1. We demand free and unlimited coinage of silver and gold at the present legal ratio of 16 to 1.
2. We demand that the amount of circulating medium be speedily increased to not less than $50 per capita.
3. We demand a graduated income tax.
4. We believe that the money of the country should be kept as much as possible in the hands of the people, and hence we demand that all State and national revenues shall be limited to the necessary expenses of the government, economically and honestly administered.

5. We demand that postal savings banks be established by the government for the safe deposit of the earnings of the people and to facilitate exchange.

TRANSPORTATION. — Transportation being a means of exchange and a public necessity, the government should own and operate the railroads in the interest of the people. The telegraph and telephone, like the post-office system, being a necessity for the transmission of news, should be owned and operated by the government in the interest of the people.

LAND. — The land, including all the natural sources of wealth, is the heritage of the people, and should not be monopolized for speculative purposes, and alien ownership of land should be prohibited. All land now held by railroads and other corporations in excess of their actual needs, and all lands now owned by aliens should be reclaimed by the government and held for actual settlers only.

EXPRESSION OF SENTIMENTS

Your Committee on Platform and Resolutions beg leave unanimously to report the following:

Whereas, Other questions have been presented for our consideration, we hereby submit the following, not as a part of the Platform of the People's Party, but as resolutions expressive of the sentiment of this Convention.

1. RESOLVED, That we demand a free ballot and a fair count in all elections, and pledge ourselves to secure it to every legal voter without Federal intervention, through the adoption by the States of the unperverted Australian or secret ballot system.
2. RESOLVED, That the revenue derived from a graduated income tax should be applied to the reduction of the burden of taxation now levied upon the domestic industries of this country.
3. RESOLVED, That we pledge our support to fair and liberal pensions to ex-Union soldiers and sailors.
4. RESOLVED, That we condemn the fallacy of protecting American labor under the present system, which opens our ports to the pauper and criminal classes of the world and crowds out our wage-earners; and we denounce the present ineffective laws against contract labor, and demand the further restriction of undesirable emigration.
5. RESOLVED, That we cordially sympathize with the efforts of organized workingmen to shorten the hours of labor, and demand a rigid enforcement of the existing eight-hour law on Government work, and ask that a penalty clause be added to the said law.
6. RESOLVED, That we regard the maintenance of a large standing army

of mercenaries, known as the Pinkerton system, as a menace to our liberties, and we demand its abolition; and we condemn the recent invasion of the Territory of Wyoming by the hired assassins of plutocracy, assisted by Federal officers.

7. RESOLVED, That we commend to the favorable consideration of the people and the reform press the legislative system known as the initiative and referendum.

8. RESOLVED, That we favor a constitutional provision limiting the office of President and Vice-President to one term, and providing for the election of Senators of the United States by a direct vote of the people.

9. RESOLVED, That we oppose any subsidy or national aid to any private corporation for any purpose.

10. RESOLVED, That this convention sympathizes with the Knights of Labor and their righteous contest with the tyrannical combine of clothing manufacturers of Rochester, and declare it to be a duty of all who hate tyranny and oppression to refuse to purchase the goods made by the said manufacturers, or to patronize any merchants who sell such goods.

W. H. Harvey

THE COMMON MAN'S MONEY

⊰{1894}⊱ IN THE controversy between gold and silver advocates in the 1890's, the nearest thing to a bible for the silver men was the work of William Hope ("Coin") Harvey (1851-1936), an amateur economist of Chicago. His first tract, *Coin's Financial School* (1894), took the form of a series of imaginary lectures, in which Coin, like a schoolmaster, set forth the essential facts of the currency question, answered questions from "gold bugs" in his audience, and handily disposed of the case that was put up for gold as the nation's money. The book sold 400,000 copies in less than a year. It was followed by three other Harvey books, *The Tale of Two Nations, Coin's Financial School up to Date, and Coin's Handbook,* all of which developed a similar theme and sold almost as well as the first. The maligned gold men replied with heat. In an actual debate with Harvey, the University of Chicago economist J. Laurence Laughlin (1850-1933) denounced *Coin's Financial School* as "an avowed appeal to class prejudice," full of "unmistakable dishonesty, untruths, inaccuracies, and misleading arguments." Nevertheless, Hearvey's books kept on selling.

Encouraged by his literary success, Harvey founded an organization which he called "The Patriots of America" and through which he intended to rout the gold-minded bankers from their citadels of power. But he had no real organizing ability. The Populists and then the Democrats capitalized upon the sentiment his pamphleteering had helped to arouse. Finally, William Jennings

Bryan (1860-1925) captured the leadership of the silverites with his "Cross of Gold" speech at the Chicago convention of the Democratic party in 1896. Reprinted here is all of the first and most of the last chapter of *Coin's Financial School*.

COIN'S FINANCIAL SCHOOL

So MUCH uncertainty prevailing about the many facts connected with the monetary question, very few are able to intelligently understand the subject.

Hard times are with us; the country is distracted; very few things are marketable at a price above the cost of production; tens of thousands are out of employment; the jails, penitentiaries, workhouses and insane asylums are full; the gold reserve at Washington is sinking; the government is running at a loss with a deficit in every department; a huge debt hangs like an appalling cloud over the country; taxes have assumed the importance of a mortgage, and 50 per cent of the public revenues are likely to go delinquent; hungered and half-starved men are banding into armies and marching toward Washington; the cry of distress is heard on every hand; business is paralyzed; commerce is at a standstill; riots and strikes prevail throughout the land; schemes to remedy our ills when put into execution are smashed like box-cars in a railroad wreck, and Wall street looks in vain for an excuse to account for the failure of prosperity to return since the repeal of the silver purchase act.

It is a time for wisdom and sound sense to take the helm, and Coin, a young financier living in Chicago, acting upon such a suggestion, established a school of finance to instruct the youths of the nation, with a view to their having a clear understanding of what has been considered an abstruse subject; to lead them out of the labyrinth of falsehoods, heresies and isms that distract the country.

THE FIRST DAY

The school opened on the 7th day of May, 1894.

There was a good attendance, and the large hall selected in the Art Institute was comfortably filled. Sons of merchants and bankers, in fact all classes of business, were well represented. Journalists, however, predominated. Coin stepped on to the platform, looking the smooth little financier that he is, and said:

"I am pleased to see such a large attendance. It indicates a desire to learn and master a subject that has baffled your fathers. The reins of the government will soon be placed in your hands, and its future will be molded by your honesty and intelligence.

"I ask you to accept nothing from me that does not stand the analysis of reason; that you will freely ask questions and pass criticisms, and if there is any one present who believes that all who differ from *him* are lunatics and fools, he is requested to vacate his seat and leave the room."

The son of Editor Scott of the *Chicago Herald,* here arose and walked out. Coin paused a moment, and then continued: "My object will be to teach you the A, B, C of the questions about money that are now a matter of every-day conversation."

The Money Unit

"In money there must be a unit. In arithmetic, as you are aware, you are taught what a unit is. Thus, I make here on the blackboard the figure 1. That, in arithmetic, is a unit. All countings are sums or multiples of that unit. A unit, therefore, in mathematics, was a necessity as a basis to start from. In making money it was equally as necessary to establish a unit. The constitution gave the power to Congress to 'coin money and regulate the value thereof.' Congress adopted silver and gold as money. It then proceeded to fix the unit.

"That is, it then fixed what should constitute one dollar, the same thing that the mathematician did when he fixed one figure from which all others should be counted. Congress fixed the monetary unit to consist of 371¼ grains of pure silver, and provided for a certain amount of alloy (baser metals) to be mixed with it to give it greater hardness and durability. This was in 1792, in the days of Washington and Jefferson and our revolutionary forefathers, who had a hatred of England, and an intimate knowledge of her designs on this country.

"They had fought eight long years for their independence from British domination in this country, and when they had seen the last red-coat leave our shores, they settled down to establish a permanent government, and among the first things they did was to make 371¼ grains of silver the unit of values. That much silver was to constitute a dollar. And each dollar was a unit. They then provided for all other money to be counted from this unit of a silver dollar. Hence, dimes, quarters and half-dollars were exact fractional parts of the dollar so fixed.

"Gold was made money, but its value was counted from these silver units or dollars. The ratio between silver and gold was fixed at 15 to 1, and afterward at 16 to 1. So that in making gold coins their relative weight was regulated by this ratio.

"This continued to be the law up to 1873. During that long period, the unit of values was never changed and always contained 371¼ grains of pure silver. While that was the law it was impossible for any one to say that the silver in a silver dollar was only worth 47 cents, or any other number of cents less than 100 cents, or a dollar. For it was itself the unit of values. While that was the law it would have been as absurd to say that the silver in a silver dollar was only worth 47 cents, as it would be to say that this figure 1 which I have on the blackboard is only forty-seven one-hundredths of one.

"When the ratio was changed from 15 to 16 to 1 the silver dollar or unit was left the same size and the gold dollar was made smaller. The latter was changed from 24.7 grains to 23.2 grains pure gold, thus making it smaller. This occurred in 1834. The silver dollar still remained the unit and continued so until 1873.

"Both were legal tender in the payment of all debts, and the mints were open to the coinage of all that came. So that up to 1873, we were on what was known as a bimetallic basis, but what was in fact a silver basis, with gold as a companion metal enjoying the same privileges as silver, except that silver fixed the unit, and the value of gold was regulated by it. This was bimetallism.

"Our forefathers showed much wisdom in selecting silver, of the two metals, out of which to make the unit. Much depended on this decision. For the one selected to represent the unit would thereafter be unchangeable in value. That is, the metal in it could never be worth less than a dollar, for it would be the unit of value itself. The demand for silver in the arts or for money by other nations might make the quantity of silver in a silver dollar sell for more than a dollar, but it could never be worth less than a dollar. Less than itself.

"In considering which of these two metals they would thus favor by making it the unit, they were led to adopt silver because it was the most reliable. It was the most favored as money by the people. It was scattered among all the people. Men having a design to injure business by making money scarce, could not so easily get hold of all the silver and hide it away, as they could gold. This was the principal reason that led them to the conclusion to select silver, the more stable of the two metals, upon which to fix the unit. It was so much handled by the people and preferred by them, that it was called the people's money.

"Gold was considered the money of the rich. It was owned principally by that class of people, and the poor people seldom handled it, and the very poor people seldom ever saw any of it."

The First Interruption

Here young Medill, of the *Chicago Tribune,* held up his hand, which indicated that he had something to say or wished to ask a question. Coin paused and asked him what he wanted.

He arose in his seat and said that his father claimed that we had been on a gold basis ever since 1837, that prior to 1873 there never had been but eight million dollars of silver coined. Here young Wilson, of the *Farm, Field and Fireside,* said he wanted to ask, who owns the *Chicago Tribune?*

Coin tapped the little bell on the table to restore order, and ruled the last question out, as there was one already before the house by Mr. Medill.

"Prior to 1873," said Coin, "there were one hundred and five millions of silver coined by the United States and eight million of this was in silver dollars. When your father said that 'only eight million dollars in silver' had been coined, he meant to say that 'only eight million silver dollars had been coined.' He also neglected to say — that is — he forgot to state, that ninety-seven millions had been coined into dimes, quarters and halves.

"About one hundred millions of foreign silver had found its way into this country prior to 1860. It was principally Spanish, Mexican and Canadian coin. It had all been made legal tender in the United States by act of Congress. We needed more silver than we had, and Congress passed laws making all foreign silver coins legal tender in this country. I will read you one of these laws — they are scattered all through the statutes prior to 1873." Here Coin picked up a copy of the laws. . . .

The Crime of 1873

"We now come to the act of 1873," continued Coin. "On February 12, 1873, Congress passed an act purporting to be a revision of the coinage laws. The law covers 15 pages of our statutes. It repealed the *unit* clause in the law of 1792, and in its place substituted a law in the following language:

"That the gold coins of the United States shall be a one-dollar piece which at the standard weight of twenty-five and eight-tenths grains *shall be the unit of value.*

"It then deprived silver of its right to unrestricted free coinage, and destroyed it as legal tender money in the payment of debts, except to the amount of five dollars.

"At that time we were all using paper money. No one was handling silver and gold coins. It was when specie payments were about to be resumed that the country appeared to realize what had been done. The newspapers on the morning of February 13, 1873, and at no time in the vicinity of that period, had any account of the change. General Grant, who was President of the United States at that time, said afterwards, that he had no idea of it, and would not have signed the bill if he had known that it demonetized silver.

"In the language of Senator Daniel of Virginia, it seems to have gone through Congress 'like the silent tread of a cat.'

"An army of a half million of men invading our shores, the warships of the world bombarding our coasts, could not have made us surrender the money of the people and substitute in its place the money of the rich. A few words embraced in fifteen pages of statutes put through Congress in the rush of bills did it. The pen was mightier than the sword.

"But we are not here to deal with sentiment. We are here to learn facts. Plain, blunt facts.

"The law of 1873 made gold the *unit* of values. And that is the law to-day. When the silver was the unit of value, gold enjoyed *free coinage,* and was legal tender in the payment of all debts. Now things have changed. Gold is the unit and silver does not enjoy free coinage. It is refused at the mints. We might get along with gold as the *unit,* if silver enjoyed the same right gold did prior to 1873. But that right is now denied to silver. When silver was the unit, the unlimited demand for gold to coin into money, made the demand as great as the supply, and this held up the value of gold bullion."

Here Victor F. Lawson, Jr., of the Chicago *Evening News,* interrupted the little financier with the statement that his paper, the *News,* had stated time and again that silver had become so plentiful it had ceased to be a precious metal. And that this statement believed by him to be a fact had more to do with his prejudice to silver than anything else. And he would like to know if that was not a fact?

"There is no truth in the statement," replied Coin. "On page 21 of my Handbook you will find a table on this subject, compiled by Mulhall, the London statistician. It gives the quantity of gold and silver in the world both coined and uncoined at six periods — at the years 1600, 1700, 1800, 1848, 1880, and 1890. It shows that in 1600 there were 27 tons of silver to one ton of gold. In 1700, 34 tons of silver to one ton of gold. In 1800, 32 tons of silver to one ton of gold. In 1848, 31 tons of silver to one ton of gold. In 1880, 18 tons of silver to one ton of gold. In 1890, 18 tons of silver to one ton of gold.

"The United States is producing more silver than it ever did, or was until recently. But the balance of the world is producing much less. They are fixing the price on our silver and taking it away from us, at their price. The report of the Director of the Mint shows that since 1850 the world has produced less silver than gold, while during the first fifty years of the century the world produced 78 per cent more silver than gold. Instead of becoming more plentiful, it is less plentiful. So it is less, instead of more.

"Any one can get the official statistics by writing to the treasurer at Washington, and asking for his official book of statistics. Also write to the Director of the Mint and ask him for his report. If you get no answer write to your Congressman. These books are furnished free and you will get them.

"At the time the United States demonetized silver in February, 1873, silver as measured in gold was worth $1.02. The argument of depreciated silver could not then be made. Not one of the arguments that are now made against silver was then possible. They are all the bastard children of the crime of 1873.

"It was demonetized secretly, and since then a powerful money trust has used deception and misrepresentations that have led tens of thousands of honest minds astray."

William Henry Smith, Jr., of the Associated Press, wanted to know if the size of the gold dollar was ever changed more than the one time mentioned by Coin, viz., in 1834.

"Yes," said Coin. "In 1837 it was changed from 23.3 to 23.22. This change of 2/100ths was for convenience in calculation, but the change was made in the gold coin — never in the silver dollar (the *unit*) till 1873.

Adjourned. . . .

THE SIXTH DAY

The manner in which the little lecturer had handled his subject on the fifth day had greatly enhanced his popularity. What he had said, had been in the nature of a revelation to nearly all that heard it, and his grouping of facts had made a profound impression.

What created the most comment, was his statement as to the space in which all the gold and silver of the world could be placed. In all the hotel lobbies it was the subject of conversation. The bare statement that all the gold in the world could be put in a cube of 22 feet appeared ridiculous — absurd.

Few that had entertained the single gold standard view of the monetary question were willing to believe it. They argued that it was impossible; that the business of the world could not be transacted on such an insignificant amount of property for primary money. They said, "Wait till the morning papers come out; the *Tribune* would puncture it, the *Inter Ocean, Herald,* in fact, all of the papers would either admit it by their silence, contradict it or give the facts."

At the Grand Pacific Hotel the cashier was kept busy answering re- quests to see a twenty-dollar gold piece. They wanted to measure it — to get its diameter and thickness. As none was to be had, they had to con- tent themselves with measuring up silver dollars and figuring out how much space all the silver in the world would occupy. This resulted in confirming Coin's statement.

Mr. George Sengel, a prominent citizen of Fort Smith, Arkansas, while discussing the subject with a large party in the rotunda of the Palmer House, stood up in a chair and addressed the crowd, saying:

"Gentlemen, I have just been up in Coin's room and examined the gov- ernment reports as to the amount of gold and silver in the world, and have made the calculation myself as to the quantity of it, and I find that the statements made are true. All the gold and silver in the world obtain- able for money can be put in the office of this hotel, and all the gold can be put in this office and not materially interfere with the comfort of the guests of the house.

"I have been until to-day in favor of a single gold standard, but hard times, and this fact that all the gold in the world available for money can be put in a space of twenty-two feet each way, has knocked it out of me. Count on me and old Arkansas for bimetallism."

Mr. Sengel's speech was greeted with applause, and he was followed by others expressing similar views.

The morning papers gave full reports of the previous day's lecture. All editorially confirmed Coin's statement as to the quantity of gold and silver in the world, and the space it would occupy, except the *Herald* and *Tribune*; they were silent on the subject.

It was generally known that Coin would discuss independent action of the United States on the last day, and from the number that tried to gain admission, a hall many times as large could have been easily filled.

At the hour for opening the hall large crowds surrounded the entrance to the Art Institute, and the corridors were filled with people. In the large hall where the lectures were delivered the walls had been decorated with the American colors. This had been seen to by a committee of bimetallists; they had given special attention to the decorations around the platform, and though assuming many forms, each piece had been made from United States' flags. The scene presented was striking and patriotic.

When the doors were opened the hall was soon filled and thousands were turned away.

Coin was escorted by a committee of bimetallists in carriages from his hotel to the Art Institute, each carriage used by the committee being draped in the American colors. It was the first demonstration of the kind made in honor of the little financier of the people, since the lectures had begun.

The evidences of his popularity were now to be seen on every hand. Many, however, had reserved their judgment to hear from him on the United States taking independent action, and all were anxious to listen to what he would say on that subject.

His appearance upon the platform was the signal for an ovation. He had grown immensely popular in those last five days.

He laid his silk hat on the table, and at once stepped to the middle of the platform. He raised his eyes to the audience; slowly turned his head to the right and left, and looked into the sea of faces that confronted him.

Independent Free Coinage

"In the midst of plenty, we are in want," he began.

"Helpless children and the best womanhood and manhood of America appeal to us for release from a bondage that is destructive of life and liberty. All the nations of the Western Hemisphere turn to their great sister republic for assistance in the emancipation of the people of at least one-half the world.

"The Orient, with its teeming millions of people, and France, the cradle of science and liberty in Europe, look to the United States to lead in the struggle to roll back the accumulated disasters of the last twenty-one years. What shall our answer be? [Applause.]

"If it is claimed we must adopt for our money the metal England selects, and can have no independent choice in the matter, let us make the test and find out if it is true. It is not American to give up without trying. If it is true, let us attach England to the United States and blot her name out from among the nations of the earth. [Applause.]

"A war with England would be the most popular ever waged on the face of the earth. [Applause.] If it is true that she can dictate the money of the world, and thereby create world-wide misery, it would be the most just war ever waged by man. [Applause.]

"But fortunately this is not necessary. Those who would have you think that we must wait for England, either have not studied this subject, or have the same interest in continuing the present conditions as England. It is a vain hope to expect her voluntarily to consent. England is the creditor nation of the globe, and collects hundreds of millions of dollars in interest annually in gold from the rest of the world. We are paying her two hundred millions yearly in interest. She demands it in gold; the contracts call for it in gold. Do you expect her to voluntarily release any part of it? It has a purchasing power twice what a bimetallic currency would have. She knows it.

"The men that control the legislation of England are citizens of that country with fixed incomes. They are interest gatherers to the amount annually of over one thousand millions of dollars. The men over there holding bimetallic conventions, and passing resolutions, have not one-fifth the influence with the law-making power that the bimetallists in the United States have with our Congress and President. No; nothing is to be expected from England.

"Whenever property interests and humanity have come in conflict, England has ever been the enemy of human liberty. All reforms with those so unfortunate as to be in her power have been won with the sword. She yields only to force. [Applause.]

"The money lenders in the United States, who own substantially all of our money, have a selfish interest in maintaining the gold standard. They, too, will not yield. They believe that if the gold standard can survive for a few years longer, the people will get used to it — get used to their poverty — and quietly submit.

"To that end they organize international bimetallic committees and say, 'Wait on England, she will be forced to give us bimetallism.' Vain hope! Deception on this subject has been practiced long enough upon a patient and outraged people.

"With silver remonetized, and gold at a premium, not one-tenth the hardships could result that now afflict us. Why? First: it would double the value of all property. Second: only 4 per cent of the business of the people of this nation is carried on with foreign countries; and a part of this 4 per cent would be transactions with silver using nations; while 96 per cent of the business of our people is domestic transactions. Home business. Is it not better to legislate in the interest of 96 per cent of our business, than the remaining 4 per cent? . . .

"In the impending struggle for the mastery of the commerce of the world, the financial combat between England and the United States cannot be avoided if we are to retain our self-respect, and our people their freedom and prosperity. [Applause.]

"The gold standard will give England the commerce and wealth of the world. The bimetallic standard will make the United States the most prosperous nation on the globe. [Applause.]

"To avoid the struggle means a surrender to England. It means more —

it means a tomb raised to the memory of the republic. Delay is dangerous. At any moment an internecine war may break out among us. Wrongs and outrages will not be continuously endured. The people will strike at the laws that inflict them.

"To wait on England is puerile and unnecessary. Her interests are not our interests. 'But,' you ask me, 'how are we to do it?' It will work itself. We have been frightened at a shadow. We have been as much deceived in this respect as we have about other matters connected with this subject.

"Free coinage by the United States will at once establish a parity between the two metals. Any nation that is big enough to take all the silver in the world, and give back merchandise and products in payment for it, will at once establish the parity between it and gold. [Applause.] . . .

"When it is considered that we are giving two dollars worth of property now, in payment for one dollar in gold, you will realize that we are now paying 100 per cent premium on gold. [Applause.]

"And this applies not only to our foreign business, but to our home business.

"With silver remonetized, and a just and equitable standard of values, we can, if necessary, by act of Congress, reduce the number of grains in a gold dollar till it is of the same value as the silver dollar. [Applause.] We can legislate the premium out of gold. [Applause.] Who will say that this is not an effective remedy? I pause for a reply!"

Coin waited for a reply. No one answering him, he continued:

"Until an answer that will commend itself to an unbiased mind is given to this remedy, that guarantees a parity between the metals, write upon the character of every 'international bimetallist' the words 'gold monometallist.'"

Pausing for a moment, as if still waiting for his position to be attacked, he proceeded:

"Give the people back their favored primary money! Give us two arms with which to transact business! Silver the right arm and gold the left arm! Silver the money of the people, and gold the money of the rich.

"Stop this legalized robbery, that is transferring the property of the debtors to the possession of the creditors!

"Citizens! the integrity of the government has been violated. A Financial Trust has control of your money, and with it, is robbing you of your property. Vampires feed upon your commercial blood. The money in the banks is subject to the check of the money lenders. They expect you to quietly submit, and leave your fellow citizens at their mercy. Through the instrumentality of law they have committed a crime that overshadows all other crimes. And yet they appeal to law for their protection. If the starving workingman commits the crime of trespass, they appeal to the law they have contaminated, for his punishment. Drive these money-changers from your temples. Let them discover by your aspect, their masters — the people." [Applause.]

"The United States commands the situation, and can dictate bimetallism to the world at the ratio she is inclined to fix.

"Our foreign ministers sailing out of the New York harbor past the statue of 'Liberty Enlightening the World' should go with instructions to educate the nations of the earth upon the American Financial Policy. We should negative the self-interested influence of England, and speak for industrial prosperity.

"We are now the ally of England in the most cruel and unjust persecution against the weak and defenseless people of the world that was ever waged by tyrants since the dawn of history. [Applause.]

"Our people are losing each year hundreds of millions of dollars; incalculable suffering exists throughout the land; we have begun the work of cutting each other's throats; poor men crazed with hunger are daily shot down by the officers of the law; want, distress and anxiety pervades the entire Union.

"If we are to act let us act quickly.

"It has been truthfully said:

" 'It is at once the result and security of oppression that its victim soon becomes incapable of resistance. Submission to its first encroachments is followed by the fatal lethargy that destroys every noble ambition, and converts the people into cowardly poltroons and fawning sycophants, who hug their chains and lick the hand that smites them!'

"Oppression now seeks to enslave this fair land. Its name is greed. Surrounded by the comforts of life, it is unconscious of the condition of others. Despotism, whether in Russia marching its helpless victims to an eternal night of sorrow, or in Ireland where its humiliating influences are ever before the human eye, or elsewhere; it is the same.

"It is already with us. It has come in the same form that it has come everywhere — by regarding the interests of property as paramount to the interests of humanity. That influence extends from the highest to the lowest. The deputy sheriff regards the $4 a day he gets as more important to him than the life or cause of the workmen he shoots down.

"The Pullman Palace Car Company recently reduced the already low wages of its employees 33⅓ per cent. Unable to make a living, they laid down their tools. A few days later the company declared a quarterly dividend of 2 per cent on watered capital of $30,000,000. This quarterly dividend was $600,000.

"Had this company sent for the committee of the workmen and said, 'We were about to declare our regular quarterly dividend of 2 per cent; it amounts to $600,000; we have concluded to make it 1½ per cent; this will give us $475,000 for three months, or one quarter's profits, and we are going to use the other $125,000 to put back the wages of the men. There would have been no strike. The men would have hailed it as generosity, and the hearts of 4,000 workmen would have been made glad.

"It was not done. It was not to be thought of. These stockholders living in comfort with all their wants provided for, think more of their property interests than they do of humanity, and will see men starve or reduced to the condition of serfs rather than concede an equitable distribution of the profits of their business.

"This has occurred here in the city of your homes; in the World's Fair city; a city supposed to be as patriotic as any we have; if this is human nature here, what do you expect from the men in England who hold our bonds, notes and mortgages payable in gold.

"We are forced to take independent action. To hesitate is cowardly! Shall we wait while the cry of the helpless is heard on every hand? Shall we wait while our institutions are crumbling?" (Cries of "No — no — no!")

"This is a struggle for humanity. For our homes and firesides. For the purity and integrity of our government.

"That all the people of this country sufficiently intelligent to vote cannot understand that the reduction of our primary money to one half its former quantity reduces the value of property proportionately, is one of the inexplainable phenomena in human history.

"Those who do understand it should go among the people and awake them to the situation of peril, in which they are placed. Awake them as you would with startling cries at the coming of flood and fires.

"Arouse them as did Paul Revere as he rode through the streets shouting: 'The British are on our shores.' " . . .

Booker T. Washington

THE NEGRO'S PLACE

❧[*1895*]❧ "IT WAS an ex-slave who eventually framed the *modus vivendi* of race relations in the New South," the historian C. Vann Woodward has written. "Booker T. Washington was more than the leader of his race. He was also a leader of white opinion with a national following, and he propounded not merely an educational theory but a social philosophy."

After working his way as a janitor through Hampton Institute, Booker T. Washington (1856-1915) studied and taught for several years and then, in 1881, founded the Tuskegee Institute in Alabama. Here he stressed practical training rather than liberal education for Negroes. He assumed his position of national leadership, which he was to maintain until his death, with his speech at the opening of the Atlanta Cotton States and International Exposition in 1895. This was the first significant occasion on which a Negro addressed a mixed group of white and colored people in the South. By that time, most of the Negroes and their white friends were becoming disillusioned with the high hopes that had been born of emancipation and Reconstruction. Legal disfranchisement was beginning to be imposed, and the lines of segregation were being tightened. Washington did nothing to head off these trends. Instead, he proposed what came to be known as the "Atlanta Compromise," by which political rights and social privileges were to be sacrificed for economic opportunities. Full rights and privileges would, presumably, follow upon economic advance.

Ironically, this modest man, who foreswore social and political pretensions for his people, associated freely with Northern capitalists, advised Presidents on the disposal of Southern patronage, and influenced the distribution of Northern philanthropic funds. But his racial leadership did not go unchallenged. A growing minority of Negroes looked to W. E. B. Du Bois (1868-1964), a Massachusetts-born descendant of free Negroes, a man who repudiated the Tuskegee program, demanded "aggressive action" for full equality, and became the first Negro official in the National Association for the Advancement of Colored People.

In his autobiography, *Up from Slavery* (1901), Washington quoted his famous Atlanta Exposition address and told of its reception and its significance.

THE ATLANTA EXPOSITION ADDRESS

THE Atlanta Exposition, at which I had been asked to make an address as a representative of the Negro race, . . . was opened with a short address from Governor Bullock. After other interesting exercises, including an invocation from Bishop Nelson, of Georgia, a dedicatory ode by Albert Howell, Jr., and addresses by the President of the Exposition and Mrs. Joseph Thompson, the President of the Woman's Board, Governor

Bullock introduced me with the words, "We have with us to-day a representative of Negro enterprise and Negro civilization."

When I arose to speak, there was considerable cheering, especially from the coloured people. As I remember it now, the thing that was uppermost in my mind was the desire to say something that would cement the friendship of the races and bring about hearty coöperation between them. So far as my outward surroundings were concerned, the only thing that I recall distinctly now is that when I got up, I saw thousands of eyes looking intently into my face. The following is the address which I delivered: —

Mr. President and Gentlemen of the Board of Directors and Citizens:

One-third of the population of the South is of the Negro race. No enterprise seeking the material, civil, or moral welfare of this section can disregard this element of our population and reach the highest success. I but convey to you, Mr. President and Directors, the sentiment of the masses of my race when I say that in no way have the value and manhood of the American Negro been more fittingly and generously recognized than by the managers of this magnificent Exposition at every stage of its progress. It is a recognition that will do more to cement the friendship of the two races than any occurrence since the dawn of our freedom.

Not only this, but the opportunity here afforded will awaken among us a new era of industrial progress. Ignorant and inexperienced, it is not strange that in the first years of our new life we began at the top instead of at the bottom; that a seat in Congress or the state legislature was more sought than real estate or industrial skill; that the political convention or stump speaking had more attractions than starting a dairy farm or truck garden.

A ship lost at sea for many days suddenly sighted a friendly vessel. From the mast of the unfortunate vessel was seen a signal, "Water, water; we die of thirst!" The answer from the friendly vessel at once came back, "Cast down your bucket where you are." A second time the signal, "Water, water; send us water!" ran up from the distressed vessel, and was answered, "Cast down your bucket where you are." And a third and fourth signal for water was answered, "Cast down your bucket where you are." The captain of the distressed vessel, at last heeding the injunction, cast down his bucket, and it came up full of fresh, sparkling water from the mouth of the Amazon River. To those of my race who depend on bettering their condition in a foreign land or who underestimate the importance of cultivating friendly relations with the Southern white man, who is their next-door neighbour, I would say: "Cast down your bucket where you are" — cast it down in making friends, in every manly way, of the people of all races by whom we are surrounded.

Cast it down in agriculture, mechanics, in commerce, in domestic service, and in the professions. And in this connection it is well to bear in mind that whatever other sins the South may be called to bear, when it comes to business, pure and simple, it is in the South that the Negro is given a man's chance in the commercial world, and in nothing is this Exposition more eloquent than in emphasizing this chance. Our greatest danger is that in the great leap from slavery to freedom we may overlook the fact that the masses of us are to live by the productions of our hands, and fail to keep in mind that we shall prosper in proportion as we learn to dignify and glorify common labour and put brains and skill into the common occupations of life; shall prosper in proportion as we learn to draw the line between the superficial and the substantial, the ornamental gewgaws of life and the useful. No race can prosper till it learns that there is as much dignity in tilling a field as in writing a poem. It is at the bottom of life we must begin, and not at the top. Nor should we permit our grievances to overshadow our opportunities.

To those of the white race who look to the incoming of those of foreign birth and strange tongue and habits for the prosperity of the South, were I permitted I would repeat what I say to my own race, "Cast down your bucket where you are." Cast it down among the eight millions of Negroes whose habits you know, whose fidelity and love you have tested in days when to have proved treacherous meant the ruin of your firesides. Cast down your bucket among these people who have, without strikes and labour wars, tilled your fields, cleared your forests, builded your railroads and cities, and brought forth treasures from the bowels of the earth, and helped make possible this magnificent representation of the progress of the South. Casting down your bucket among my people, helping and encouraging them as you are doing on these grounds, and to education of head, hand, and heart, you will find that they will buy your surplus land, make blossom the waste places in your fields, and run your factories. While doing this, you can be sure in the future, as in the past, that you and your families will be surrounded by the most patient, faithful, law-abiding, and unresentful people that the world has seen. As we have proved our loyalty to you in the past, in nursing your children, watching by the sick-bed of your mothers and fathers, and often following them with tear-dimmed eyes to their graves, so in the future, in our humble way, we shall stand by you with a devotion that no foreigner can approach, ready to lay down our lives, if need be, in defence of yours, interlacing our industrial, commercial, civil, and religious life with yours in a way that shall make the interests of both races one. In all things that are purely social we can be as separate as the fingers, yet one as the hand in all things essential to mutual progress.

There is no defence or security for any of us except in the highest intelligence and development of all. If anywhere there are efforts tending to curtail the fullest growth of the Negro, let these efforts be turned into stimulating, encouraging, and making him the most useful and intelligent citizen. Effort or means so invested will pay a thousand per cent interest. These efforts will be twice blessed — "blessing him that gives and him that takes."

There is no escape through law of man or God from the inevitable: —

> The laws of changeless justice bind
> Oppressor with oppressed;
> And close as sin and suffering joined
> We march to fate abreast.

Nearly sixteen millions of hands will aid you in pulling the load upward, or they will pull against you the load downward. We shall constitute one-third and more of the ignorance and crime of the South, or one-third its intelligence and progress; we shall contribute one-third to the business and industrial prosperity of the South, or we shall prove a veritable body of death, stagnating, depressing, retarding every effort to advance the body politic.

Gentlemen of the Exposition, as we present to you our humble effort at an exhibition of our progress, you must not expect overmuch. Starting thirty years ago with ownership here and there in a few quilts and pumpkins and chickens (gathered from miscellaneous sources), remember the path that has led from these to the inventions and production of agricultural implements, buggies, steam-engines, newspapers, books, statuary, carving, paintings, the management of drug-stores and banks, has not been trodden without contact with thorns and thistles. While we take pride in what we exhibit as a result of our independent efforts, we do not for a moment forget that our part in this exhibition would fall far short of your expectations but for the constant help that has come to our educational life, not only from the Southern states, but especially from Northern philanthropists, who have made their gifts a constant stream of blessing and encouragement.

The wisest among my race understand that the agitation of questions of social equality is the extremest folly, and that progress in the enjoyment of all the privileges that will come to us must be the result of severe and constant struggle rather than of artificial forcing. No race that has anything to contribute to the markets of the world is long in any degree ostracized. It is important and right that all privileges of the law be ours, but it is vastly more important that we be prepared for the exercises of these privileges. The opportunity to earn a dollar in a factory just now is worth infinitely more than the opportunity to spend a dollar in an opera-house.

In conclusion, may I repeat that nothing in thirty years has given us more hope and encouragement, and drawn us so near to you of the white race, as this opportunity offered by the Exposition; and here bending, as it were, over the altar that represents the results of the struggles of your race and mine, both starting practically empty-handed three decades ago, I pledge that in your effort to work out the great and intricate problem which God has laid at the doors of the South, you shall have at all times the patient, sympathetic help of my race; only let this be constantly in mind, that, while from representations in these buildings of the product of field, of forest, of mine, of factory, letters, and art, much good will come, yet far above and beyond material benefits will be that higher good, that, let us pray God, will come, in a blotting out of sectional differences and racial animosities and suspicions, in a determination to administer absolute justice, in a willing obedience among all classes to the mandates of law. This, this, coupled with our material prosperity, will bring into our beloved South a new heaven and a new earth.

The first thing that I remember, after I had finished speaking, was that Governor Bullock rushed across the platform and took me by the hand, and that others did the same. I received so many and such hearty congratulations that I found it difficult to get out of the building. I did not appreciate to any degree, however, the impression which my address seemed to have made, until the next morning, when I went into the business part of the city. As soon as I was recognized, I was surprised to find myself pointed out and surrounded by a crowd of men who wished to shake hands with me. This was kept up on every street on to which I went, to an extent which embarrassed me so much that I went back to my boarding-place. The next morning I returned to Tuskegee. At the station in Atlanta, and at almost all of the stations at which the train stopped between that city and Tuskegee, I found a crowd of people anxious to shake hands with me.

The papers in all parts of the United States published the address in full, and for months afterward there were complimentary editorial references to it. Mr. Clark Howell, the editor of the Atlanta *Constitution,* telegraphed to a New York paper, among other words, the following, "I do not exaggerate when I say that Professor Booker T. Washington's address yesterday was one of the most notable speeches, both as to character and as to the warmth of its reception, ever delivered to a Southern audience. The address was a revelation. The whole speech is a platform upon which blacks and whites can stand with full justice to each other."

The Boston *Transcript* said editorially: "The speech of Booker T. Washington at the Atlanta Exposition, this week, seems to have dwarfed all the other proceedings and the Exposition itself. The sensation that it has caused in the press has never been equalled."

I very soon began receiving all kinds of propositions from lecture bureaus, and editors of magazines and papers, to take the lecture platform, and to write articles. One lecture bureau offered me fifty thousand dollars, or two hundred dollars a night and expenses, if I would place my services at its disposal for a given period. To all these communications I replied that my life-work was at Tuskegee; and that whenever I spoke it must be in the interests of the Tuskegee school and my race, and that I would enter into no arrangements that seemed to place a mere commercial value upon my services.

Some days after its delivery I sent a copy of my address to the President of the United States, the Hon. Grover Cleveland. I received from him the following autograph reply: —

GRAY GABLES, BUZZARD'S BAY, MASS.,
October 6, 1895

BOOKER T. WASHINGTON, ESQ:

MY DEAR SIR: I thank you for sending me a copy of your address delivered at the Atlanta Exposition.

I thank you with much enthusiasm for making the address. I have read it with intense interest, and I think the Exposition would be fully justified if it did not do more than furnish the opportunity for its delivery. Your words cannot fail to delight and encourage all who wish well for your race; and if our coloured fellow-citizens do not from your utterances gather new hope and form new determinations to gain every valuable advantage offered them by their citizenship, it will be strange indeed.

Yours very truly,

GROVER CLEVELAND

Later I met Mr. Cleveland, for the first time, when, as President, he visited the Atlanta Exposition. At the request of myself and others he consented to spend an hour in the Negro Building, for the purpose of inspecting the Negro exhibit and of giving the coloured people in attendance an opportunity to shake hands with him. As soon as I met Mr.

Cleveland I became impressed with his simplicity, greatness, and rugged honesty. I have met him many times since then, both at public functions and at his private residence in Princeton, and the more I see of him the more I admire him. When he visited the Negro Building in Atlanta he seemed to give himself up wholly, for that hour, to the coloured people. He seemed to be as careful to shake hands with some old coloured "auntie" clad partially in rags, and to take as much pleasure in doing so, as if he were greeting some millionnaire. Many of the coloured people took advantage of the occasion to get him to write his name in a book or on a slip of paper. He was as careful and patient in doing this as if he were putting his signature to some great state document.

Mr. Cleveland has not only shown his friendship for me in many personal ways, but has always consented to do anything I have asked of him for our school. This he has done, whether it was to make a personal donation or to use his influence in securing the donations of others. Judging from my personal acquaintance with Mr. Cleveland, I do not believe that he is conscious of possessing any colour prejudice. He is too great for that. In my contact with people I find that, as a rule, it is only the little, narrow people who live for themselves, who never read good books, who do not travel, who never open up their souls in a way to permit them to come into contact with other souls — with the great outside world. No man whose vision is bounded by colour can come into contact with what is highest and best in the world. In meeting men, in many places, I have found that the happiest people are those who do the most for others; the most miserable are those who do the least. I have also found that few things, if any, are capable of making one so blind and narrow as race prejudice. I often say to our students, in the course of my talks to them on Sunday evenings in the chapel, that the longer I live and the more experience I have of the world, the more I am convinced that, after all, the one thing that is most worth living for — and dying for, if need be — is the opportunity of making some one else more happy and more useful.

The coloured people and the coloured newspapers at first seemed to be greatly pleased with the character of my Atlanta address, as well as with its reception. But after the first burst of enthusiasm began to die away, and the coloured people began reading the speech in cold type, some of them seemed to feel that they had been hypnotized. They seemed to feel that I had been too liberal in my remarks toward the Southern whites, and that I had not spoken out strongly enough for what they termed the "rights" of the race. For a while there was a reaction, so far as a certain element of my own race was concerned, but later these reactionary ones seemed to have been won over to my way of believing and acting. . . .

I am often asked to express myself more freely than I do upon the political condition and the political future of my race. These recollections of my experience in Atlanta give me the opportunity to do so briefly. My own belief is, although I have never before said so in so many words, that the time will come when the Negro in the South will be accorded all the political rights which his ability, character, and material possessions entitle him to. I think, though, that the opportunity to freely exercise such political rights will not come in any large degree through outside or artificial forcing, but will be accorded to the Negro by the Southern white people themselves, and that they will protect him in the exercise of those rights. Just as soon as the South gets over the old feeling that it is being forced by "foreigners," or "aliens," to do something which it does not want to do, I believe that the change in the direction that I have indicated is going to begin. In fact, there are indications that it is already beginning in a slight degree.

Let me illustrate my meaning. Suppose that some months before the opening of the Atlanta Exposition there had been a general demand from the press and public platform outside the South that a Negro be given a place on the opening programme, and that a Negro be placed upon the board of jurors of award. Would any such recognition of the race have taken place? I do not think so. The Atlanta officials went as far as they did because they felt it to be a pleasure, as well as a duty, to reward what they considered merit in the Negro race. Say what we will, there is something in human nature which we cannot blot out, which makes one man, in the end, recognize and reward merit in another, regardless of colour or race.

I believe it is the duty of the Negro — as the greater part of the race is already doing — to deport himself modestly in regard to political claims, depending upon the slow but sure influences that proceed from the possession of property, intelligence, and high character for the full recognition of his political rights. I think that the according of the full exercise of political rights is going to be a matter of natural, slow growth, not an over-night, gourd-vine affair. I do not believe that the Negro should cease voting, for a man cannot learn the exercise of self-government by ceasing to vote, any more than a boy can learn to swim by keeping out of the water, but I do believe that in his voting he should more and more be influenced by those of intelligence and character who are his next-door neighbours.

I know coloured men who, through the encouragement, help, and advice of Southern white people, have accumulated thousands of dollars' worth of property, but who, at the same time, would never think of going to those same persons for advice concerning the casting of their ballots. This, it seems to me, is unwise and unreasonable, and should cease. In saying this I do not mean that the Negro should truckle, or not vote from principle, for the instant he ceases to vote from principle he loses the confidence and respect of the Southern white man even.

I do not believe that any state should make a law that permits an ignorant and poverty-stricken white man to vote, and prevents a black man in the same condition from voting. Such a law is not only unjust, but it will react, as all unjust laws do, in time; for the effect of such a law is to encourage the Negro to secure education and property, and at the same time it encourages the white man to remain in ignorance and poverty. I believe that in time, through the operation of intelligence and friendly race relations, all cheating at the ballot-box in the South will cease. It will become apparent that the white man who begins by cheating a Negro out of his ballot soon learns to cheat a white man out of his, and that the man who does this ends his career of dishonesty by the theft of property or by some equally serious crime. In my opinion, the time will come when the South will encourage all of its citizens to vote. It will see that it pays better, from every standpoint, to have healthy, vigorous life than to have that political stagnation which always results when one-half of the population has no share and no interest in the Government.

As a rule, I believe in universal, free suffrage, but I believe that in the South we are confronted with peculiar conditions that justify the protection of the ballot in many of the states, for a while at least, either by an educational test, a property test, or by both combined; but whatever tests are required, they should be made to apply with equal and exact justice to both races.

V. Progressive Protest

Lincoln Steffens

MUNICIPAL CORRUPTION

❧*1904*❧ THE STORY of that particular type of journalism which Theodore Roosevelt (1858-1919) called "muckraking" and which has been defined as "the exposing of evils and corruption for the real or ostensible purpose of promoting righteousness and social justice," can be told from two quite different points of view. Seen one way, it was the inevitable outgrowth of certain economic and social trends in American life, the result of the rise of industrial monopolies, the festering expansion of vast cities, the migration of millions of people previously inexperienced with democracy, and the dislocation of most aspects of life in a time of rapid change. The development of the cheap mass-circulation magazine provided, when muckraking is placed in this context, the catalyst in which these trends were precipitated and called to the attention of an indignant public.

From a different point of view, however, muckraking can be said to have developed haphazardly; those responsible for it did not foresee the results of their activities. S. S. McClure, an authentic genius of early-twentieth century journalism, wanted to sell copies of his magazine. To accomplish this end, Lincoln Steffens, who worked for McClure, hired a St. Louis reporter named Claude H. Wetmore to write an article about a crusading St. Louis attorney who was trying to break up a ring of corrupt politicians. The article, when written, seemed too tame so Steffens revised it. The author, alarmed by the changes, demanded that Steffens add his own name to the piece. Steffens agreed. Thus he became a great celebrity in reform journalism and *McClure's Magazine* the leading publication in its field. "The era of the muckrakers had begun."

For the response to "Tweed Days in St. Louis" when it appeared in October 1902 was tremendous. Steffens, "to make sure that the process was identical everywhere," rushed off to Minneapolis, Pittsburgh, Philadelphia, and other cities to study local corruption. The results appeared in *McClure's* (its circulation zoomed to half a million) and then, in 1904, in Steffens' remarkable book, *The Shame of The Cities.* Thus a major addition was made to the accumulating forces of protest and reform. "Tweed Days in St. Louis" and Steffens's later adventures, the significance of which he summarized in the preface to his book, helped to shape the frame of mind that we characterize as "progressive."

Steffens (1866-1936) went on to a long, interesting, and somewhat controversial career in journalism. His *Autobiography* (1931) is one of the finest in the English language.

THE SHAME OF THE CITIES

. . . WHEN I set out on my travels, an honest New Yorker told me honestly that I would find that the Irish, the Catholic Irish, were at the bottom of it all everywhere. The first city I went to was St. Louis, a German city. The next was Minneapolis, a Scandinavian city, with a leadership of New Englanders. Then came Pittsburg, Scotch Presbyterian, and that was what my New York friend was. "Ah, but they are all foreign populations," I heard. The next city was Philadelphia, the purest American community of all, and the most hopeless. And after that came Chicago and New York, both mongrel-bred, but the one a triumph of reform, the other the best example of good government that I had seen. The "foreign element" excuse is one of the hypocritical lies that save us from the clear sight of ourselves.

Another such conceit of our egotism is that which deplores our politics and lauds our business. This is the wail of the typical American citizen. Now, the typical American citizen is the business man. The typical business man is a bad citizen; he is busy. If he is a "big business man" and very busy, he does not neglect, he is busy with politics, oh, very busy and very businesslike. I found him buying boodlers in St. Louis, defending grafters in Minneapolis, originating corruption in Pittsburg, sharing with bosses in Philadelphia, deploring reform in Chicago, and beating good government with corruption funds in New York. He is a self-righteous fraud, this big business man. He is the chief source of corruption, and it were a boon if he would neglect politics. But he is not the business man that neglects politics; that worthy is the good citizen, the typical business man. He is too busy, he is the one that has no use and therefore no time for politics. When his neglect has permitted bad government to go so far that he can be stirred to action, he is unhappy, and he looks around for a cure that shall be quick, so that he may hurry back to the shop. Naturally, too, when he talks politics, he talks shop. His patent remedy is quack; it is business.

"Give us a business man," he says ("like me," he means). "Let him introduce business methods into politics and government; then I shall be left alone to attend to my business."

There is hardly an office from United States Senator down to Alderman in any part of the country to which the business man has not been elected; yet politics remains corrupt, government pretty bad, and the selfish citizen has to hold himself in readiness like the old volunteer firemen to rush forth at any hour, in any weather, to prevent the fire; and he goes out sometimes and he puts out the fire (after the damage is done) and he goes back to the shop sighing for the business man in politics. The business man has failed in politics as he has in citizenship. Why?

Because politics is business. That's what's the matter with it. That's what's the matter with everything, — art, literature, religion, journalism, law, medicine, — they're all business, and all — as you see them. Make politics a sport, as they do in England, or a profession, as they do in Germany, and we'll have — well, something else than we have now, — if we want it, which is another question. But don't try to reform politics with the banker, the lawyer, and the dry-goods merchant, for these are business men and there are two great hindrances to their achievement of reform: one is that they are different from, but no better than, the politicians; the other is that politics is not "their line." . . .

But there is hope, not alone despair, in the commercialism of our politics. If our political leaders are to be always a lot of political merchants, they will supply any demand we may create. All we have to do is to establish a steady demand for good government. The bosses have us split up into parties. To him parties are nothing but means to his corrupt ends. He "bolts" his party, but we must not; the bribe-giver changes his party, from one election to another, from one county to another, from one city to another, but the honest voter must not. Why? Because if the honest voter cared no more for his party than the politician and the grafter, then the honest vote would govern, and that would be bad — for graft. It is idiotic, this devotion to a machine that is used to take our sovereignty from us. If we would leave parties to the politicians, and would vote not for the party, not even for men, but for the city, and the State, and the nation, we should rule parties, and cities, and States, and nation. If we would vote in mass on the more promising ticket, or, if the two are equally bad, would throw out the party that is in, and wait till the next election and then throw out the other party that is in — then, I say, the commercial politican would feel a demand for good government and he would supply it. That process would take a generation or more to complete, for the politicians now really do not know what good government is. But it has taken as long to develop bad government, and the politicians know what that is. If it would not "go," they would offer something else, and, if the demand were steady, they, being so commercial, would "deliver the goods."

But do the people want good government? Tammany says they don't. Are the people honest? Are the people better than Tammany? Are they better than the merchant and the politician? Isn't our corrupt government, after all, representative?

President Roosevelt has been sneered at for going about the country preaching, as a cure for our American evils, good conduct in the individual, simple honesty, courage, and efficiency. "Platitudes!" the sophisticated say. Platitudes? If my observations have been true, the literal adoption of Mr. Roosevelt's reform scheme would result in a revolution, more radical and terrible to existing institutions, from the Congress to the Church, from the bank to the ward organization, than socialism or even than anarchy. Why, that would change all of us — not alone our neighbors, not alone the grafters, but you and me.

No, the contemned methods of our despised politics are the master methods of our braggart business, and the corruption that shocks us in public affairs we practice ourselves in our private concerns. There is no essential difference between the pull that gets your wife into society or for your book a favorable review, and that which gets a heeler into office, a thief out of jail, and a rich man's son on the board of directors of a corporation; none between the corruption of a labor union, a bank, and a political machine; none between a dummy director of a trust and the caucus-bound member of a legislature; none between a labor boss like Sam Parks, a boss of banks like John D. Rockefeller, a boss of railroads like J. P. Morgan, and a political boss like Matthew S. Quay. The boss is not a political, he is an American institution, the product of a freed people that have not the spirit to be free.

And it's all a moral weakness; a weakness right where we think we are strongest. Oh, we are good — on Sunday, and we are "fearfully patriotic" on the Fourth of July. But the bribe we pay to the janitor to prefer our interests to the landlord's, is the little brother of the bribe passed to the alderman to sell a city street, and the father of the air-brake stock assigned to the president of a railroad to have this life-saving invention adopted on his road. And as for graft, railroad passes, saloon and bawdy-house blackmail, and watered stock, all these belong to the same family. We are pathetically proud of our democratic institutions and our republican form of government, of our grand Constitution and our just laws. We are a free and sovereign people, we govern ourselves and the government is ours. But that is the point. We are responsible, not our leaders, since we follow them. We *let* them divert our loyalty from the United States to some "party"; we *let* them boss the party and turn our municipal democracies into autocracies and our republican nation into a plutocracy. We cheat our government and we let our leaders loot it, and we let them wheedle and bribe our sovereignty from us. . . .

. . . When I set out to describe the corrupt systems of certain typical cities, I meant to show simply how the people were deceived and betrayed. But in the very first study — St. Louis — the startling truth lay bare that corruption was not merely political; it was financial, commercial, social; the ramifications of boodle were so complex, various, and far-reaching, that one mind could hardly grasp them, and not even

Joseph W. Folk, the tireless prosecutor, could follow them all. This state of things was indicated in the first article which Claude H. Wetmore and I compiled together, but it was not shown plainly enough. Mr. Wetmore lived in St. Louis, and he had respect for names which meant little to me. But when I went next to Minneapolis alone, I could see more independently, without respect for persons, and there were traces of the same phenomenon. The first St. Louis article was called "Tweed Days in St. Louis," and though the "better citizen" received attention the Tweeds were the center of interest. In "The Shame of Minneapolis," the truth was put into the title; it was the Shame of Minneapolis; not of the Ames administration, not of the Tweeds, but of the city and its citizens. And yet Minneapolis was not nearly so bad as St. Louis; police graft is never so universal as boodle. It is more shocking, but it is so filthy that it cannot involve so large a part of society. So I returned to St. Louis, and I went over the whole ground again, with the people in mind, not alone the caught and convicted boodlers. And this time the true meaning of "Tweed Days in St. Louis" was made plain. The article was called "The Shamelessness of St. Louis," and that was the burden of the story. In Pittsburg also the people was the subject, and though the civic spirit there was better, the extent of the corruption throughout the social organization of the community was indicated. But it was not till I got to Philadelphia that the possibilities of popular corruption were worked out to the limit of humiliating confession. That was the place for such a study. There is nothing like it in the country, except possibly, in Cincinnati. Philadelphia certainly is not merely corrupt, but corrupted, and this was made clear. Philadelphia was charged up to — the American citizen.

It was impossible in the space of a magazine article to cover in any one city all the phases of municipal government, so I chose cities that typified most strikingly some particular phase or phases. Thus as St. Louis exemplified boodle; Minneapolis, police graft; Pittsburg, a political and industrial machine; and Philadelphia, general civic corruption; so Chicago was an illustration of reform, and New York of good government. All these things occur in most of these places. There are, and long have been, reformers in St. Louis, and there is to-day police graft there. Minneapolis has had boodling and council reform, and boodling is breaking out there again. Pittsburg has general corruption, and Philadelphia a very perfect political machine. Chicago has police graft and a low order of administrative and general corruption which permeates business, labor, and society generally. As for New York, the metropolis might exemplify almost anything that occurs anywhere in American cities, but no city has had for many years such a good administration as was that of Mayor Seth Low.

That which I have made each city stand for, is that which it had most highly developed. It would be absurd to seek for organized reform in St. Louis, for example, with Chicago next door; or for graft in Chicago with Minneapolis so near. After Minneapolis, a description of administrative corruption in Chicago would have seemed like a repetition. Perhaps it was not just to treat only the conspicuous element in each situation. But why should I be just? I was not judging; I arrogated to myself no such function. I was not writing about Chicago for Chicago, but for the other cities, so I picked out what light each had for the instruction of the others. But, if I was never complete, I never exaggerated. Every one of those articles was an understatement, especially where the conditions were bad, and the proof thereof is that while each article seemed to astonish other cities, it disappointed the city which was its subject. Thus my friends in Philadelphia, who knew what there was to know, and those especially who knew what I knew, expressed surprise that I reported so little. And one St. Louis newspaper said that "the facts were thrown at me and I fell down over them." There was truth in these flings. I cut twenty thousand words out of the Philadelphia article and then had not written half my facts. I know a man who is making a history of the corrupt construction of the Philadelphia City Hall, in three volumes, and he grieves because he lacks space. You can't put all the known incidents of the corruption of an American city into a book.

This is all very unscientific, but then, I am not a scientist. I am a journalist. I did not gather with indifference all the facts and arrange them patiently for permanent preservation and laboratory analysis. I did not want to preserve, I wanted to destroy the facts. My purpose was no more scientific than the spirit of my investigation and reports; it was, as I said above, to see if the shameful facts, spread out in all their shame, would not burn through our civic shamelessness and set fire to American pride. That was the journalism of it. I wanted to move and to convince. That is why I was not interested in all the facts, sought none that was new, and rejected half those that were old. I often was asked to expose something suspected. I couldn't; and why should I? Exposure of the unknown was not my purpose. The people: what they will put up with, how they are fooled, how cheaply they are bought, how dearly sold, how easily intimidated, and how led, for good or for evil — that was the inquiry, and so the significant facts were those only which everybody in each city knew, and of these, only those which everybody in every other town would recognize, from their common knowledge of such things, to be probable. But these, understated, were charged always to the guilty persons when individuals were to blame, and finally brought home to the people themselves, who, having the power, have also the responsibility, they and those they respect, and those that guide them. . . .

But of course the tangible results are few. The real triumph of the year's work was the complete demonstration it has given, in a thousand little ways, that our shamelessness is superficial, that beneath it lies a pride which, being real, may save us yet. And it is real. The grafters who said you may put the blame anywhere but on the people, where it belongs, and that Americans can be moved only by flattery, — they lied. They lied about themselves. They, too, are American citizens; they too, are of the people; and some of them also were reached by shame. The great truth I tried to make plain was that which Mr. Folk insists so constantly upon: that bribery is no ordinary felony, but treason, that the "corruption which breaks out here and there and now and then" is not an occasional offense, but a common practice, and that the effect of it is literally to change the form of our government from one that is representative of the people to an oligarchy, representative of special interests. Some politicians have seen that this is so, and it bothers them. I think I prize more highly than any other of my experiences the half-dozen times when grafting politicians I had "roasted," as they put it, called on me afterwards to say, in the words of one who spoke with a wonderful solemnity:

"You are right. I never thought of it that way, but it's right. I don't know whether you can do anything, but you're right, dead right. And I'm all wrong. We're all, all wrong. I don't see how we can stop it now; I don't see how I can change. I can't, I guess. No, I can't, not now. But, say, I may be able to help you, and I will if I can. You can have anything I've got."

So you see, they are not such bad fellows, these practical politicians. I wish I could tell more about them: how they have helped me; how candidly and unselfishly they have assisted me to facts and an understanding of the facts, which, as I warned them, as they knew well, were to be used against them. If I could — and I will some day — I should show that one of the surest hopes we have is the politician himself. Ask him for good politics; punish him when he gives bad, and reward him when he gives good; make politics pay. Now, he says, you don't know and you don't care, and that you must be flattered and fooled — and there, I say, he is wrong. I did not flatter anybody; I told the truth as near as I could get it, and instead of resentment there was encouragement.

After "The Shame of Minneapolis," and "The Shamelessness of St. Louis," not only did citizens of these cities approve, but citizens of other cities, individuals, groups, and organizations, sent in invitations, hundreds of them, "to come and show us up; we're worse than they are." We Americans may have failed. We may be mercenary and selfish. Democracy with us may be impossible and corruption inevitable, but these articles, if they have proved nothing else, have demonstrated beyond doubt that we can stand the truth; that there is pride in the character of American citizenship; and that this pride may be a power in the land. So this little volume, a record of shame and yet of self-respect, a disgraceful confession, yet a declaration of honor, is dedicated, in all good faith, to the accused — to all the citizens of all the cities in the United States.

TWEED DAYS IN ST. LOUIS

St. Louis, the fourth city in size in the United States, is making two announcements to the world: one that it is the worst-governed city in the land; the other that it wishes all men to come there (for the World's Fair) and see it. It isn't our worst-governed city; Philadelphia is that. But St. Louis is worth examining while we have it inside out.

There is a man at work there, one man, working all alone, but he is the Circuit (district or State) Attorney, and he is "doing his duty." That is what thousands of district attorneys and other public officials have promised to do and boasted of doing. This man has a literal sort of mind. He is a thin-lipped, firm-mouthed, dark little man, who never raises his voice, but goes ahead doing, with a smiling eye and a set jaw, the simple thing he said he would do. The politicians and reputable citizens who asked him to run urged him when he declined. When he said that if elected he would have to do his duty, they said, "Of course." So he ran, they supported him, and he was elected. Now some of these politicians are sentenced to the penitentiary, some are in Mexico. The Circuit Attorney, finding that his "duty" was to catch and convict criminals, and that the biggest criminals were some of these same politicians and leading citizens, went after them. It is magnificent, but the politicians declare it isn't politics.

The corruption of St. Louis came from the top. The best citizens — the merchants and big financiers — used to rule the town, and they ruled it well. They set out to outstrip Chicago. The commercial and industrial war between these two cities was at one time a picturesque and dramatic spectacle such as is witnessed only in our country. Business men were not mere merchants and the politicians were not mere grafters; the two kinds of citizens got together and wielded the power of banks, railroads, factories, the prestige of the city, and the spirit of its citizens to gain business and population. And it was a close race. Chicago, having the start, always led, but St. Louis had pluck, intelligence, and tremendous energy. It pressed Chicago hard. It excelled in a sense of civic beauty and good government; and there are those who think yet it might have won. But a change occurred. Public spirit became private spirit, public enterprise became private greed.

Along about 1890, public franchises and privileges were sought, not only for legitimate profit and common convenience, but for loot. Taking but slight and always selfish interest in the public councils, the big men misused politics. The riffraff, catching the smell of corruption, rushed into the Municipal Assembly, drove out the remaining respectable men, and sold the city — its streets, its wharves, its markets, and all that it had — to the now greedy business men and bribers. In other words, when the leading men began to devour their own city, the herd rushed into the trough and fed also.

So gradually has this occurred that these same citizens hardly realize it. Go to St. Louis and you will find the habit of civic pride in them; they still boast. The visitor is told of the wealth of the residents, of the financial strength of the banks, and of the growing importance of the industries, yet he sees poorly paved, refuse-burdened streets, and dusty or mud-covered alleys; he passes a ramshackle fire-trap crowded with the sick, and learns that it is the City Hospital; he enters the "Four Courts," and his nostrils are greeted by the odor of formaldehyde used as a disinfectant, and insect powder spread to destroy vermin; he calls at the new City Hall, and finds half the entrance boarded with pine planks to cover up the unfinished interior. Finally, he turns a tap in the hotel, to see liquid mud flow into wash-basin or bath-tub.

The St. Louis charter vests legislative power of great scope in a Municipal Assembly, which is composed of a council and a House of Delegates. Here is a description of the latter by one of Mr. Folk's grand juries:

"We have had before us many of those who have been, and most of those who are now, members of the House of Delegates. We found a number of these utterly illiterate and lacking in ordinary intelligence, unable to give a better reason for favoring or opposing a measure than a desire to act with the majority. In some, no trace of mentality or morality could be found; in others, a low order of training appeared, united with base cunning, groveling instincts, and sordid desires. Unqualified to respond to the ordinary requirements of life, they are utterly incapable of comprehending the significance of an ordinance, and are incapacitated, both by nature and training, to be the makers of laws. The choosing of such men to be legislators makes a travesty of justice, sets a premium on incompetency, and deliberately poisons the very source of the law."

These creatures were well organized. They had a "combine" — a legislative institution — which the grand jury described as follows:

"Our investigation, covering more or less fully a period of ten years, shows that, with few exceptions, no ordinance has been passed wherein valuable privileges or franchises are granted until those interested have paid the legislators the money demanded for action in the particular case. Combines in both branches of the Municipal Assembly are formed by members sufficient in number to control legislation. To one member of this combine is delegated the authority to act for the combine, and to receive and to distribute to each member the money agreed upon as the price of his vote in support of, or opposition to, a pending measure. So long has this practice existed that such members have come to regard the receipt of money for action on pending measures as a legitimate perquisite of a legislator."

One legislator consulted a lawyer with the intention of suing a firm to recover an unpaid balance on a fee for the grant of a switch-way. Such difficulties rarely occurred, however. In order to insure a regular and indisputable revenue, the combine of each house drew up a schedule of bribery prices for all possible sorts of grants, just such a list as a commercial traveler takes out on the road with him. There was a price for a grain elevator, a price for a short switch; side tracks were charged for by the linear foot, but at rates which varied according to the nature of the ground taken; a street improvement cost so much; wharf space was classified and precisely rated. As there was a scale for favorable legislation, so there was one for defeating bills. It made a difference in the price if there was opposition, and it made a difference whether the privilege asked was legitimate or not. But nothing was passed free of charge. Many of the legislators were saloon-keepers — it was in St. Louis that a practical joker nearly emptied the House of Delegates by tipping a boy to rush into a session and call out, "Mister, your saloon is on fire," — but even the saloon-keepers of a neighborhood had to pay to keep in their inconvenient locality a market which public interest would have moved.

From the Assembly, bribery spread into other departments. Men empowered to issue peddlers' licenses and permits to citizens who wished to erect awnings or use a portion of the sidewalk for storage purposes charged an amount in excess of the prices stipulated by law, and pocketed the difference. The city's money was loaned at interest, and the interest was converted into private bank accounts. . . .

The blackest years were 1898, 1899, and 1900. Foreign corporations came into the city to share in its despoliation, and home industries were driven out by blackmail. Franchises worth millions were granted without one cent of cash to the city, and with provision for only the smallest future payment; several companies which refused to pay blackmail had to leave; citizens were robbed more and more boldly; pay-rolls were padded with the names of non-existent persons; work on public improvements was neglected, while money for them went to the boodlers.

Some of the newspapers protested, disinterested citizens were alarmed, and the shrewder men gave warnings, but none dared make an effective stand. Behind the corruptionists were men of wealth and social standing, who, because of special privileges granted them, felt bound to support and defend the looters. Independent victims of the far-reaching conspiracy submitted in silence, through fear of injury to their business. Men whose integrity was never questioned, who held high positions of trust, who were church members and teachers of Bible classes, contributed to the support of the dynasty, — became blackmailers, in fact, — and their excuse was that others did the same, and that if they proved the exception it would work their ruin. The system became loose through license and plenty till it was as wild and weak as that of Tweed in New York.

Then the unexpected happened — an accident. There was no uprising of the people, but they were restive; and the Democratic party leaders, thinking to gain some independent votes, decided to raise the cry "reform" and put up a ticket of candidates different enough from the usual offerings of political parties to give color to their platform. These leaders were not in earnest. There was little difference between the two parties in the city; but the rascals that were in had been getting the greater share of the spoils, and the "outs" wanted more than was given to them. "Boodle" was not the issue, no exposures were made or threatened, and the bosses expected to control their men if elected. Simply as part of the game, the Democrats raised the slogan, "'reform" and "no more Ziegenheinism."

Mayor Ziegenhein, called "Uncle Henry," was a "'good fellow," "one of the boys," and though it was during his administration that the city grew ripe and went to rot, his opponents talked only of incompetence and neglect, and repeated such stories as that of his famous reply to some citizens who complained because certain street lights were put out: "You have the moon yet — ain't it?"

When somebody mentioned Joseph W. Folk for Circuit Attorney the leaders were ready to accept him. They didn't know much about him. He was a young man from Tennessee; had been President of the Jefferson Club, and arbitrated the railroad strike of 1898. But Folk did not want the place. He was a civil lawyer, had had no practice at the criminal bar, cared little about it, and a lucrative business as counsel for corporations was interesting him. He rejected the invitation. The committee called again and again, urging his duty to his party, and the city, etc.

"Very well," he said, at last, "I will accept the nomination, but if elected I will do my duty. There must be no attempt to influence my actions when I am called upon to punish lawbreakers."

The committeemen took such statements as the conventional platitudes of candidates. They nominated him, the Democratic ticket was elected, and Folk became Circuit Attorney for the Eighth Missouri District.

Three weeks after taking the oath of office his campaign pledges were put to the test. A number of arrests had been made in connection with the recent election, and charges of illegal registration were preferred against men of both parties. Mr. Folk took them up like routine cases of ordinary crime. Political bosses rushed to the rescue. Mr. Folk was reminded of his duty to his party, and told that he was expected to construe the law in such a manner that repeaters and other election criminals who had hoisted Democracy's flag and helped elect him might be either discharged or receive the minimum punishment. The nature of the young lawyer's reply can best be inferred from the words of that veteran political leader, Colonel Ed Butler who, after a visit to Mr. Folk, wrathfully exclaimed, "D—n Joe! he thinks he's the whole thing as Circuit Attorney."

The election cases were passed through the courts with astonishing rapidity; no more mercy was shown Democrats than Republicans, and before winter came a number of ward heelers and old-time party workers were behind the bars in Jefferson City. He next turned his attention to grafters and straw bondsmen with whom the courts were infested, and several of these leeches are in the penitentiary to-day. The business was broken up because of his activity. But Mr. Folk had made little more than the beginning.

One afternoon, late in January, 1903, a newspaper reporter, known as "Red" Galvin, called Mr. Folk's attention to a ten-line newspaper item to the effect that a large sum of money had been placed in a bank for the purpose of bribing certain Assemblymen to secure the passage of a street railroad ordinance. No names were mentioned, but Mr. Galvin surmised that the bill referred to was one introduced on behalf of the Suburban Railway Company. An hour later Mr. Folk sent the names of nearly one hundred persons to the sheriff, with instructions to subpoena them before the grand jury at once. The list include Councilmen, members of the House of Delegates, officers and directors of the Suburban Railway, bank presidents and cashiers. In three days the investigation was being pushed with vigor, but St. Louis was laughing at the "huge joke." Such things had been attempted before. The men who had been ordered to appear before the grand jury jested as they chatted in the anterooms, and newspaper accounts of these preliminary examinations were written in the spirit of burlesque.

It has developed since that Circuit Attorney Folk knew nothing, and was not able to learn much more during the first days; but he says he saw here and there puffs of smoke and he determined to find the fire. It was not an easy job. The first break into such a system is always difficult. Mr. Folk began with nothing but courage and a strong personal conviction. He caused peremptory summons to be issued, for the immediate attendance in the grand jury room of Charles H. Turner, president of the Suburban Railway, and Philip Stock, a representative of brewers' interests, who, he had reason to believe, was the legislative agent in this deal.

"Gentlemen," said Mr. Folk, "I have secured sufficient evidence to warrant the return of indictments against you for bribery, and I shall prosecute you to the full extent of the law and send you to the penitentiary unless you tell to this grand jury the complete history of the corruptionist methods employed by you to secure the passage of Ordinance No. 44. I shall give you three days to consider the matter. At the end of that time, if you have not returned here and given us the information demanded, warrants will be issued for your arrest."

They looked at the audacious young prosecutor and left the Four Courts building without uttering a word. He waited. Two days later, ex-Lieutenant Governor Charles P. Johnson, the veteran criminal lawyer, called, and said that his client, Mr. Stock, was in such poor health that he would be unable to appear before the grand jury.

"I am truly sorry that Mr. Stock is ill," replied Mr. Folk, "for his presence here is imperative, and if he fails to appear he will be arrested before sundown."

That evening a conference was held in Governor Johnson's office, and the next day this story was told in the grand jury room by Charles H. Turner, millionaire president of the Suburban Railway, and corroborated by Philip Stock, man-about-town and a good fellow: The Suburban, anxious to sell out a large profit to its only competitor, the St. Louis Transit Co., caused to be drafted the measure known as House Bill No. 44. So sweeping were its grants that Mr. Turner, who planned and executed the document, told the directors in his confidence that its enactment into law would enhance the value of the property from three to six million dollars. The bill introduced, Mr. Turner visited Colonel Butler, who had long been known as a legislative agent, and asked his price for securing the passage of the measure. "One hundred and forty-five thousand dollars will be my fee," was the reply. The railway president demurred. He would think the matter over, he said, and he hired a cheaper man, Mr. Stock. Stock conferred with the representative of the combine in the House of Delegates and reported that $75,000 would be necessary in this branch of the Assembly. Mr. Turner presented a note indorsed by two of the directors whom he could trust, and secured a loan from the German American Savings Bank.

Bribe funds in pocket, the legislative agent telephoned John Murrell, at that time a representative of the House combine, to meet him in the office of the Lincoln Trust Company. There the two rented a safe-deposit box. Mr. Stock placed in the drawer the roll of $75,000, and each subscribed to an agreement that the box should not be opened unless both were present. Of course the conditions spread upon the bank's daybook made no reference to the purpose for which this fund had been deposited, but an agreement entered into by Messrs. Stock and Murrell was to the effect that the $75,000 should be given Mr. Murrell as soon as the bill became an ordinance, and by him distributed to the members of the combine. Stock turned to the Council, and upon his report a further sum of $60,000 was secured. These bills were placed in a safe-deposit box of the Mississippi Valley Trust Co., and the man who held the key as representative of the Council combine was Charles H. Kratz.

All seemed well, but a few weeks after placing these funds in escrow, Mr. Stock reported to his employer that there was an unexpected hitch due to the action of Emil Meysenburg, who, as a member of the Council Committee on Railroads, was holding up the report on the bill. Mr. Stock said that Mr. Meysenburg held some worthless shares in a defunct corporation and wanted Mr. Stock to purchase this paper at its par value of $9,000. Mr. Turner gave Mr. Stock the money with which to buy the shares.

Thus the passage of House Bill 44 promised to cost the Suburban Railway Co. $144,000, only one thousand dollars less than that originally named by the political boss to whom Mr. Turner had first applied. The bill, however, passed both houses of the Assembly. The sworn servants of the city had done their work and held out their hands for the bribe money.

Then came a court mandate which prevented the Suburban Railway Co. from reaping the benefit of the vote-buying, and Charles H. Turner, angered at the check, issued orders that the money in safe-deposit boxes should not be touched. War was declared between bribe-givers and bribe-takers, and the latter resorted to tactics which they hoped would frighten the Suburban people into submission — such as making enough of the story public to cause rumors of impending prosecution. It was that first item which Mr. Folk saw and acted upon.

When Messrs. Turner and Stock unfolded in the grand jury room the details of their bribery plot, Circuit Attorney Folk found himself in possession of verbal evidence of a great crime; he needed as material exhibits the two large sums of money in safe-deposit vaults of two of the largest banking institutions of the West. Had this money been withdrawn? Could he get it if it was there? Lockboxes had always been considered sacred and beyond the power of the law to open. "I've always held," said Mr. Folk, "that the fact that a thing never had been done was no reason for thinking it couldn't be done." He decided in this case that the magnitude of the interests involved warranted unusual action, so he selected a committee of grand jurors and visited one of the banks. He told the president, a personal friend, the facts that had come into his possession, and asked permission to search for the fund.

"Impossible," was the reply. "Our rules deny anyone the right."

"Mr. ——," said Mr. Folk, "a crime has been committed, and you hold concealed the principal evidence thereto. In the name of the State of Missouri I demand that you cause the box to be opened. If you refuse, I shall cause a warrant to be issued, charging you as an accessory."

For a minute not a word was spoken by anyone in the room; then the banker said in almost inaudible tones:

"Give me a little time, gentlemen. I must consult with our legal adviser before taking such a step."

"We will wait ten minutes," said the Circuit Attorney. "By that time we must have access to the vault or a warrant will be applied for."

At the expiration of that time a solemn procession wended its way from the president's office to the vaults in the sub-cellar — the president, the cashier, and the corporation's lawyer, the grand jurors, and the Circuit Attorney. All bent eagerly forward as the key was inserted in the lock. The iron drawer yielded, and a roll of something wrapped in brown paper was brought to light. The Circuit Attorney removed the rubber bands, and national bank notes of large denomination spread out flat before them. The money was counted, and the sum was $75,000!

The boodle fund was returned to its repository, officers of the bank were told they would be held responsible for it until the courts could act. The investigators visited the other financial institution. They met with more resistance there. The threat to procure a warrant had no effect until

Mr. Folk left the building and set off in the direction of the Four Courts. Then a messenger called him back, and the second box was opened. In this was found $60,000. The chain of evidence was complete.

From that moment events moved rapidly. Charles Kratz and John K. Murrell, alleged representatives of Council and House combines, were arrested on bench warrants and placed under heavy bonds. Kratz was brought into court from a meeting at which plans were being formed for his election to the National Congress. Murrell was taken from his undertaking establishment. Emil Meysenburg, millionaire broker, was seated in his office when a sheriff's deputy entered and read a document that charged him with bribery. The summons reached Henry Nicolaus while he was seated at his desk, and the wealthy brewer was compelled to send for a bondsman to avoid passing a night in jail. The cable flashed the news to Cairo, Egypt, that Ellis Wainwright, many times a millionaire, proprietor of the St. Louis brewery that bears his name, had been indicted. Julius Lehmann, one of the members of the House of Delegates, who had joked while waiting in the grand jury's anteroom, had his laughter cut short by the hand of a deputy sheriff on his shoulder and the words, "You are charged with perjury." He was joined at the bar of the criminal court by Harry Faulkner, another jolly good fellow.

Consternation spread among the boodle gang. Some of the men took night trains for other States and foreign countries; the majority remained and counseled together. Within twenty-four hours after the first indictments were returned, a meeting of bribe-givers and bribe-takers was held in South St. Louis. The total wealth of those in attendance was $30,000,000, and their combined political influence sufficient to carry any municipal election under normal conditions.

This great power was aligned in opposition to one man, who still was alone. It was not until many indictments had been returned that a citizens' committee was formed to furnish funds, and even then most of the contributors concealed their identity. Mr. James L. Blair, the treasurer, testified in court that they were afraid to be known lest "it ruin their business."

At the meeting of corruptionists three courses were decided upon. Political leaders were to work on the Circuit Attorney by promise of future reward, or by threats. Detectives were to ferret out of the young lawyer's past anything that could be used against him. Witnesses would be sent out of town and provided with money to remain away until the adjournment of the grand jury.

Mr. Folk at once felt the pressure, and it was of a character to startle one. Statesmen, lawyers, merchants, clubmen, churchmen — in fact, men prominent in all walks of life — visited him at his office and at his home, and urged that he cease such activity against his fellow-townspeople. Political preferment was promised if he would yield; a political grave if he persisted. Threatening letters came, warning him of plots to murder, to disfigure, and to blackguard. Word came from Tennessee that detectives were investigating every act of his life. Mr. Folk told the politicians that he was not seeking political favors, and not looking forward to another office; the others he defied. Meantime he probed the deeper into the municipal sore. With his first successes for prestige and aided by the panic among the boodlers, he soon had them suspicious of one another, exchanging charges of betrayal, and ready to "squeal" or run at the slightest sign of danger. One member of the House of Delegates became so frightened while under the inquisitorial cross-fire that he was seized with a nervous chill; his false teeth fell to the floor, and the rattle so increased his alarm that he rushed from the room without stopping to pick up his teeth, and boarded the next train.

It was not long before Mr. Folk had dug up the intimate history of ten years of corruption, especially of the business of the North and South and the Central Traction franchise grants, the last-named being even more iniquitous than the Suburban.

Early in 1898 a "promoter" rented a bridal suite at the Planters' Hotel, and having stocked the rooms with wines, liquors, and cigars until they resembled a candidate's headquarters during a convention, sought introduction to members of the Assembly and to such political bosses as had influence with the city fathers. Two weeks after his arrival the Central Traction bill was introduced "by request" in the Council. The measure was a blanket franchise, granting rights of way which had not been given to old-established companies, and permitting the beneficiaries to parallel any track in the city. It passed both Houses despite the protests of every newspaper in the city, save one, and was vetoed by the mayor. The cost to the promoter was $145,000.

Preparations were made to pass the bill over the executive's veto. The bridal suite was restocked, larger sums of money were placed on deposit in the banks, and the services of three legislative agents were engaged. Evidence now in the possession of the St. Louis courts tells in detail the disposition of $250,000 of bribe money. Sworn statements prove that $75,000 was spent in the House of Delegates. The remainder of the $250,000 was distributed in the Council, whose members, though few in number, appraised their honor at a higher figure on account of their higher positions in the business and social world. Finally, but one vote was needed to complete the necessary two-thirds in the upper Chamber. To secure this a councilman of reputed integrity was paid $5,000 in consideration that he vote aye when the ordinance should come up for final passage. But the promoter did not dare risk all upon the vote of one man, and he made this novel proposition to another honored member, who accepted it:

"You will vote on roll call after Mr. ——. I will place $45,000 in the hands of your son, which amount will become yours, if you have to vote for the measure because of Mr. ——'s not keeping his promise. But if he stands out for it you can vote against it, and the money shall revert to me."

On the evening when the bill was read for final passage the City Hall was crowded with ward heelers and lesser politicians. These men had been engaged by the promoter, at five and ten dollars a head, to cheer on the boodling Assemblymen. The bill passed the House with a rush, and all crowded into the Council Chamber. While the roll was being called the silence was profound, for all knew that some men in the Chamber whose reputations had been free from blemish, were under promise and pay to part with honor that night. When the clerk was two-thirds down the list those who had kept count knew that but one vote was needed. One more name was called. The man addressed turned red, then white, and after a moment's hesitation he whispered "Aye"! The silence was so death-like that his vote was heard throughout the room, and those near enough heard also the sigh of relief that escaped from the member who could now vote "no" and save his reputation.

The Central Franchise bill was a law, passed over the mayor's veto. The promoter had expended nearly $300,000 in securing the legislation, but within a week he sold his rights of way to "Eastern capitalists" for $1,250,000. The United Railways Company was formed, and without owning an inch of steel rail, or a plank in a car, was able to compel every street railroad in St. Louis, with the exception of the Suburban, to part with stock and right of way and agree to a merger. Out of this grew the St. Louis Transit Company of to-day. . . .

Pitiful? Yes, but typical. Other cities are today in the same condition as St. Louis before Mr. Folk was invited in to see its rottenness. Chicago is cleaning itself up just now, so is Minneapolis, and Pittsburg recently had a bribery scandal; Boston is at peace, Cincinnati and St. Paul are satisfied, while Philadelphia is happy with the worst government in the world. As for the small towns and the villages, many of these are busy as bees at the loot.

St. Louis, indeed, in its disgrace, has a great advantage. It was exposed late; it has not been reformed and caught again and again, until its citizens are reconciled to corruption. But, best of all, the man who has turned St. Louis inside out, turned it, as it were, upside down, too. In all cities, the better classes — the business men — are the sources of corruption; but they are so rarely pursued and caught that we do not fully realize whence the trouble comes. Thus most cities blame the politicians and the ignorant and vicious poor.

Mr. Folk has shown St. Louis that its bankers, brokers, corporation officers, — its business men are the sources of evil, so that from the start it will know the municipal problem in its true light. With a tradition for public spirit, it may drop Butler and its runaway bankers, brokers, and brewers, and pushing aside the scruples of the hundreds of men down in blue book, and red book, and church register, who are lying hidden behind the statutes of limitations, the city may restore good government. Otherwise the exposures by Mr. Folk will result only in the perfection of the corrupt system. For the corrupt can learn a lesson when the good citizens cannot. The Tweed régime in New York taught Tammany to organize its boodle business; the police exposure taught it to improve its method of collecting blackmail. And both now are almost perfect and safe. The rascals of St. Louis will learn in like manner; they will concentrate the control of their bribery system, excluding from the profit-sharing the great mass of weak rascals, and carrying on the business as a business in the interest of a trustworthy few. District Attorney Jerome cannot catch the Tammany men, and Circuit Attorney Folk will not be able another time to break the St. Louis ring. This is St. Louis' one great chance.

But, for the rest of us, it does not matter about St. Louis any more than it matters about Colonel Butler *et al.* The point is, that what went on in St. Louis is going on in most of our cities, towns, and villages. The problem of municipal government in America has not been solved. The people may be tired of it, but they cannot give it up — not yet.

Theodore Roosevelt

PRESERVING HEMISPHERIC PEACE

1905 THE emergence of the United States as a world power with possessions and spheres of influence scattered across the Caribbean and the Pacific made it impossible to maintain a policy of isolation, however much sentiment and selfishness might make it attractive to do so. "Traditional" policies simply had to be reconsidered and modified, and it was fortunate for the country that at the critical period when this was happening an intelligent, far-sighted, and forceful man, Theodore Roosevelt, was President.

Roosevelt (1858-1919) was an imperialist and his policies were widely criticized by men who objected to the nation "owning" another country or holding subject peoples under its collective thumb. Our own generation has rejected his way of looking at under-developed areas. Yet no one has suggested how the United States could have played its destined role in the affairs of the early twentieth century without adopting an attitude somewhat like Roosevelt's. Far more important, Roosevelt understood the responsibilities of power, the wide implications of the new role America had begun to play in the world.

No one more effectively than Roosevelt persuaded the public to accept the new conditions. He always stressed the importance of military and naval preparedness as the best insurance against war, and he argued powerfully against meaningless international agreements that the country would not be willing to honor in a crisis. Particularly where Latin American affairs were concerned, he expanded the scope of action of the United States to meet changing conditions. These aspects of Roosevelt's approach to foreign affairs, and his forceful manner of expressing his views, so important in convincing the people that they were correct, are well brought out in his fifth annual message to Congress, which was delivered on December 5, 1905. It was in this message that his well-known "corollary" to the Monroe Doctrine was first spelled out.

MESSAGE TO CONGRESS

(December 5, 1905)

IT [is] . . . proper at this time to say something as to the general attitude of this Government toward peace. More and more war is coming to be looked upon as in itself a lamentable and evil thing. A wanton or useless war, or a war of mere aggression — in short, any war begun or carried on in a conscienceless spirit, is to be condemned as a peculiarly atrocious crime against all humanity. We can, however, do nothing of permanent value for peace unless we keep ever clearly in mind the ethical element which lies at the root of the problem. Our aim is righteousness. Peace is normally the hand-maiden of righteousness; but when peace and righteousness conflict then a great and upright people can never for a moment hesitate to follow the path which leads toward righteousness, even though that path also leads to war. There are persons who advocate peace at any price; there are others who, following a false analogy, think that because it is no longer necessary in civilized countries for individuals to protect their rights with a strong hand, it is therefore unnecessary for nations to be ready to defend their rights. These persons would do irreparable harm to any nation that adopted their principles, and even as it is they seriously hamper the cause which they advocate by tending to render it absurd in the eyes of sensible and patriotic men. There can be no worse foe of mankind in general, and of his own country in particular, than the demagogue of war, the man who in mere folly or to serve his own selfish ends continually rails at and abuses other nations, who seeks to excite his countrymen against foreigners on insufficient pretexts, who excites and inflames a perverse and aggressive national vanity, and who may on occasions wantonly bring on conflict between his nation and some other nation. But there are demagogues of peace just as there are demagogues of war, and in any such movement as this for The Hague conference it is essential not to be misled by one set of extremists any more than by the other. Whenever it is possible for a nation or an individual to work for real peace, assuredly it is failure of duty not so to strive, but if war is necessary and righteous then either the man or the nation shrinking from it forfeits all title to self-respect. We have scant sympathy with the sentimentalist who dreads oppression less then physical suffering, who would prefer a shameful peace to the pain and toil sometimes lamentably necessary in order to secure a righteous peace. As yet there is only a partial and imperfect analogy between international law and internal or municipal law, because there is no sanction of force for executing the former while there is in the case of the latter. The private citizen is protected in his rights by the law, because he can call upon the police, upon the sheriff's posse, upon the militia, or in certain extreme cases upon the army, to defend him. But there is no such sanction of force for international law. At present there could be no greater calamity than for the free peoples, the enlightened, independent, and peace-loving peoples, to disarm while yet leaving it open to any barbarism or despotism to remain armed. So long as the world is as unorganized as now the armies and navies of those peoples who on the whole stand for justice, offer not only the best, but the only possible, security for a just peace. For instance, if the United States alone, or in company only with the other nations that on the whole tend to act justly, disarmed, we might sometimes avoid bloodshed, but we would cease to be of weight in securing the peace of justice — the real peace for which the most law-abiding and high-minded men must at times be willing to fight. As the world is now, only that nation is equipped for peace that knows how to fight, and that will not shrink from fighting if ever the conditions become such that war is demanded in the name of the highest morality.

So much it is emphatically necessary to say in order both that the position of the United States may not be misunderstood, and that a genuine effort to bring nearer the day of the peace of justice among the nations may not be hampered by a folly which, in striving to achieve the impossible, would render it hopeless to attempt the achievement of the practical. But, while recognizing most clearly all above set forth, it remains our clear duty to strive in every practicable way to bring nearer the time when the sword shall not be the arbiter among nations. At present the practical thing to do is to try to minimize the number of cases in which it must be the arbiter, and to offer, at least to all civilized powers, some substitute for war which will be available in at least a considerable number of instances. Very much can be done through another Hague conference in this direction, and I most earnestly urge that this Nation do all in its power to try to further the movement and to make the result of the decisions of The Hague conference effective. I earnestly hope that the conference may be able to devise some way to make arbitration between nations the customary way of settling international disputes in all save a few classes of cases, which should themselves be as sharply defined and rigidly limited as the present governmental and social development of the world will permit. If possible, there should be a general arbitration treaty negotiated among all the nations represented at the conference. Neutral rights and property should be protected at sea as they are protected on land. There should be an international agreement to this purpose and a similar agreement defining contraband of war.

During the last century there has been a distinct diminution in the number of wars between the most civilized nations. International relations have become closer and the development of The Hague tribunal is not only a symptom of this growing closeness of relationship, but is a means by which the growth can be furthered. Our aim should be from time to time to take such steps as may be possible toward creating something like an organization of the civilized nations, because as the world becomes more highly organized the need for navies and armies will diminish. It is not possible to secure anything like an immediate disarmament, because it would first be necessary to settle what peoples are on the whole a menace to the rest of mankind, and to provide against the disarmament of the rest being turned into a movement which would really chiefly benefit these obnoxious peoples; but it may be possible to exercise some check upon the tendency to swell indefinitely the budgets for military expenditure. Of course such an effort could succeed only if it did not attempt to do too much; and if it were undertaken in a spirit of sanity as far removed as possible from a merely hysterical pseudo-philanthropy. It is worth while pointing out that since the end of the insurrection in the Philippines this Nation has shown its practical faith in the policy of disarmament by reducing its little army one-third. But disarmament can never be of prime importance; there is more need to get rid of the causes of war than of the implements of war.

I have dwelt much on the dangers to be avoided by steering clear of any mere foolish sentimentality because my wish for peace is so genuine and earnest; because I have a real and great desire that this second

Hague conference may mark a long stride forward in the direction of securing the peace of justice throughout the world. No object is better worthy the attention of enlightened statesmanship than the establishment of a surer method than now exists of securing justice as between nations, both for the protection of the little nations and for the prevention of war between the big nations. To this aim we should endeavor not only to avert bloodshed, but, above all, effectively to strengthen the forces of right. The Golden Rule should be, and as the world grows in morality it will be, the guiding rule of conduct among nations as among individuals; though the Golden Rule must not be construed, in fantastic manner, as forbidding the exercise of the police power. This mighty and free Republic should ever deal with all other States, great or small, on a basis of high honor, respecting their rights as jealously as it safeguards its own.

One of the most effective instruments for peace is the Monroe Doctrine as it has been and is being developed by this Nation and accepted by other nations. No other policy could have been as efficient in promoting peace in the Western Hemisphere and in giving to each nation thereon the chance to develop along its own lines. If we had refused to apply the doctrine to changing conditions it would now be completely outworn, would not meet any of the needs of the present day, and, indeed, would probably by this time have sunk into complete oblivion. It is useful at home, and is meeting with recognition abroad because we have adapted our application of it to meet the growing and changing needs of the hemisphere. When we announce a policy such as the Monroe Doctrine we thereby commit ourselves to the consequences of the policy, and those consequences from time to time alter. It is out of the question to claim a right and yet shirk the responsibility for its exercise. Not only we, but all American republics who are benefited by the existence of the doctrine, must recognize the obligations each nation is under as regards foreign peoples no less than its duty to insist upon its own rights.

That our rights and interests are deeply concerned in the maintnance of the doctrine is so clear as hardly to need argument. This is especially true in view of the construction of the Panama Canal. As a mere matter of self-defense we must exercise a close watch over the approaches to this canal; and this means that we must be thoroughly alive to our interests in the Caribbean Sea.

There are certain essential points which must never be forgotten as regards the Monroe Doctrine. In the first place we must as a Nation make it evident that we do not intend to treat it in any shape or way as an excuse for aggrandizement on our part at the expense of the republics to the south. We must recognize the fact that in some South American countries there has been much suspicion lest we should interpret the Monroe Doctrine as in some way inimical to their interests, and we must try to convince all the other nations of this continent once and for all that no just and orderly Government has anything to fear from us. There are certain republics to the south of us which have already reached such a point of stability, order, and prosperity that they themselves, though as yet hardly consciously, are among the guarantors of this doctrine. These republics we now meet not only on a basis of entire equality, but in a spirit of frank and respectful friendship, which we hope is mutual. If all of the republics to the south of us will only grow as those to which I allude have already grown, all need for us to be the especial champions of the doctrine will disappear, for no stable and growing American Republic wishes to see some great non-American military power acquire territory in its neighborhood. All that this country desires is that the other republics on this continent shall be happy and prosperous; and they cannot be happy and prosperous unless they maintain order within their boundaries and behave with a just regard for their obligations toward outsiders. It must be understood that under no circumstances will the United States use the Monroe Doctrine as a cloak for territorial aggression. We desire peace with all the world, but perhaps most of all with the other peoples of the American Continent. There are, of course, limits to the wrongs which any self-respecting nation can endure. It is always possible that wrong actions toward this Nation, or towards citizens of this Nation, in some State unable to keep order among its own people, unable to secure justice from outsiders, and unwilling to do justice to those outsiders who treat it well, may result in our having to take action to protect our rights; but such action will not be taken with a view to territorial aggression, and it will be taken at all only with extreme reluctance and when it has become evident that every other resource has been exhausted.

Moreover, we must make it evident that we do not intend to permit the Monroe Doctrine to be used by any nation on this Continent as a shield to protect it from the consequences of its own misdeeds against foreign nations. If a republic to the south of us commits a tort against a foreign nation, such as an outrage against a citizen of that nation, then the Monroe Doctrine does not force us to interfere to prevent punishment of the tort, save to see that the punishment does not assume the form of territorial occupation in any shape. The case is more difficult when it refers to a contractual obligation. Our own Government has always refused to enforce such contractual obligations on behalf of its citizens by an appeal to arms. It is much to be wished that all foreign governments would take the same view. But they do not; and in consequence we are liable at any time to be brought face to face with disagreeable alternatives. On the one hand, this country would certainly decline to go to war to prevent a foreign government from collecting a just debt; on the other hand, it is very inadvisable to permit any foreign power to take possession, even temporarily, of the custom houses of an American Republic in order to enforce the payment of its obligations; for such temporary occupation might turn into a permanent occupation. The only escape from these alternatives may at any time be that we must ourselves undertake to bring about some arrangement by which so much as possible of a just obligation shall be paid. It is far better that this country should put through such an arrangement, rather than allow any foreign country to undertake it. To do so insures the defaulting republic from having to pay a debt of an improper character under duress, while it also insures honest creditors of the republic from being passed by in the interest of dishonest or grasping creditors. Moreover, for the United States to take such a position offers the only possible way of insuring us against a clash with some foreign power. The position is, therefore, in the interest of peace as well as in the interest of justice. It is of benefit to our people; it is of benefit to foreign peoples; and most of all it is really of benefit to the people of the country concerned.

This brings me to what should be one of the fundamental objects of the Monroe Doctrine. We must ourselves in good faith try to help toward peace and order those of our sister republics which need such help. Just as there has been a gradual growth of the ethical element in the relations of one individual to another, so we are, even though slowly, more and more coming to recognize the duty of bearing one another's burdens, not only as among individuals, but also as among nations. . . .

We cannot consider the question of our foreign policy without at the same time treating of the army and the navy. We now have a very small army indeed, one well-nigh infinitesimal when compared with the army of any other large nation. Of course the army we do have should be as nearly perfect of its kind and for its size as is possible. I do not believe that any army in the world has a better average of enlisted men or a better type of junior officer; but the army should be trained to act effectively in a mass. Provision should be made by sufficient appropriations for manœuvres of a practical kind, so that the troops may learn how to take care of themselves under actual service conditions; every march, for instance, being made with the soldier loaded exactly as he would be in active campaign. . . . Promotion by mere seniority can never result in a thoroughly efficient corps of officers in the higher ranks unless there accompanies it a vigorous weeding-out process. Such a weeding-out process — that is, such a process of selection — is a chief feature of the four years' course of the young officer at West Point. There is no good reason why it should stop immediately upon his graduation. While at West Point he is dropped unless he comes up to a certain standard of excellence, and when he graduates he takes rank in the army according to his rank of graduation. The results are good at West Point; and there should be in the army itself something that will achieve the same end. After a certain age has been reached the average officer is unfit to do good work below a certain grade. Provision should be made for the promotion of exceptionally meritorious men over the heads of their comrades and for the retirement of all men who have reached a given age without getting beyond a given rank; this age of retirement of course changing from rank to rank. In both the army and the navy there should be some principle of selection, that is, of promotion for merit, and there should be a resolute effort to eliminate the aged officers of reputable character who possess no special efficiency. . . .

Our navy must, relatively to the navies of other nations, always be of greater size than our army. We have most wisely continued for a number of years to build up our navy, and it has now reached a fairly high standard of efficiency. This standard of efficiency must not only be maintained, but increased. It does not seem to be necessary, however, that the navy should — at least in the immediate future — be increased beyond the present number of units. What is now clearly necessary is to substitute efficient for inefficient units as the latter become worn out or as it becomes apparent that they are useless. Probably the result would be attained by adding a single battleship to our navy each year, the superseded or outworn vessels being laid up or broken up as they are thus replaced. The four single-turret monitors built immediately after the close of the Spanish War, for instance, are vessels which would be of but little use in the event of war. The money spent upon them could have been more usefully spent in other ways. Thus it would have been far better never to have built a single one of these monitors and to have put the money into an ample supply of reserve guns. Most of the smaller cruisers and gunboats, though they serve a useful purpose so far as they are needed for international police work, would not add to the strength of our navy in a conflict with a serious foe. There is urgent need of providing a large increase in the number of officers, and especially in the number of enlisted men.

Recent naval history has emphasized certain lessons which ought not to, but which do, need emphasis. Sea-going torpedo-boats or destroyers are indispensable, not only for making night attacks by surprise upon an enemy, but even in battle for finishing already crippled ships. Under exceptional circumstances submarine boats would doubtless be of use. Fast scouts are needed. The main strength of the navy, however, lies, and can only lie, in the great battleships, the heavily armored, heavily gunned vessels which decide the mastery of the seas. Heavy-armed cruisers also play a most useful part, and unarmed cruisers, if swift enough, are very useful as scouts. Between antagonists of approximately equal prowess the comparative perfection of the instruments of war will ordinarily determine the fight. But it is, of course, true that the man behind the gun, the man in the engine-room, and the man in the conning-tower, considered not only individually, but especially with regard to the way in which they work together, are even more important than the weapons with which they work. The most formidable battleship is, of course, helpless against even a light cruiser if the men aboard it are unable to hit anything with their guns, and thoroughly well-handled cruisers may count seriously in an engagement with much superior vessels, if the men aboard the latter are ineffective, whether from lack of training or from any other cause. . . . We need additional seamen; we need a large store of reserve guns; we need sufficient money for ample target practice, ample practice of every kind at sea. We should substitute for comparatively inefficient types — the old third-class battleship *Texas,* the single turreted monitors above mentioned, and, indeed, all the monitors and some of the old cruisers — efficient, modern seagoing vessels. Seagoing torpedo-boat destroyers should be substituted for some of the smaller torpedo-boats. During the present Congress there need be no additions to the aggregate number of units of the navy. Our navy, though very small relatively to the navies of other nations, is for the present sufficient in point of numbers for our needs, and while we must constantly strive to make its efficiency higher, there need be no additions to the total of ships now built and building, save in the way of substitution as above outlined. I recommend the report of the secretary of the navy to the careful consideration of the Congress, especially with a view to the legislation therein advocated. . . .

Upton Sinclair

POISONED MEAT AND POISONED LIVES

⇛{*1906*}⇚ No ONE reflects the crusading spirit of the Progressive Era better than Upton Sinclair. From the time of his graduation from the City College of New York in 1897 he was temperamentally committed to improving the world. A socialist, he was early convinced not only that capitalism was wrong but that all of its weaknesses could be quickly cured by drastic economic and political reforms. Quick to become indignant at evil and deceit, he resolved to try to "make it impossible for joy and tenderness and rapture and awe to be lashed at and spit upon and trampled and smashed into annihilation."

Sinclair was determined to be a great writer as well as a reformer. Early in his career he made a quiet study of the lives of Chicago stockyard workers. Dressed in old clothes and carrying a dinner pail, he spent seven weeks wandering through the meat packing plants observing all their gruesome horrors. Then he began to write a novel describing in vivid detail everything that he had seen. For months he worked away, living in a small shack he had built with his own hands near Princeton, New Jersey. He published parts of his story in a socialist weekly called *Appeal to Reason* (which is ironic, since his tale was so obviously aimed at men's emotions). He also wrote two muckraking articles on the slaughterhouses for *Collier's*. Finally, after much controversy and a change of publishers, *The Jungle* appeared in 1906. In Sinclair's own words, it "became a sensation overnight." For months it was a best seller; soon it was being translated into many languages. President Theodore Roosevelt ordered an investigation of the packers and within the year Congress had passed the Pure Food and Drug Act and a stiff meat-inspection act.

The Jungle thus accomplished the author's immediate objectives. It sold over 150,000 copies within a generation, and is still widely read. It made Sinclair famous. But like those other immensely popular reform tracts, *Progress and Poverty* and *Looking Backward,* it did not accomplish its ultimate goal of changing the basic structure of society. The thousands who read Sinclair's melodramatic, sentimental, and diffuse story of the Lithuanian worker, Jurgis Rudkus and his wife Ona Lukoszaite, were properly indignant about the evils it described, but they did not follow Jurgis along the path to socialism.

Upton Sinclair (1878-   ) is one of the most prolific and widely read novelists of the twentieth century. His *Dragon's Teeth* (1942) won a Pulitzer prize. He has also been frequently a Socialist candidate for political office, and in 1934, he was the unsuccessful Democratic candidate for Governor of California.

THE JUNGLE

A FULL hour before the party reached the city they had begun to note the perplexing changes in the atmosphere. It grew darker all the time, and upon the earth the grass seemed to grow less green. Every minute, as the train sped on, the colors of things became dingier; the fields were grown parched and yellow, the landscape hideous and bare. And along with the thickening smoke they began to notice another circumstance, a strange, pungent odor. They were not sure that it was unpleasant, this odor; some might have called it sickening, but their taste in odors was not developed, and they were only sure that it was curious. Now, sitting in the trolley car, they realized that they were on their way to the home of it — that they had travelled all the way from Lithuania to it. It was now no longer something far off and faint, that you caught in whiffs; you could literally taste it, as well as smell it — you could take hold of it, almost, and examine it at your leisure. They were divided in their opinions about it. It was an elemental odor, raw and crude; it was rich, almost rancid, sensual, and strong. There were some who drank it in as if it were an intoxicant; there were others who put their handkerchiefs to their faces. The new emigrants were still tasting it, lost in wonder, when suddenly the car came to a halt, and the door was flung open, and a voice shouted —"Stockyards!"

They were left standing upon the corner, staring; down a side street there were two rows of brick houses, and between them a vista: half a dozen chimneys, tall as the tallest of buildings, touching the very sky — and leaping from them half a dozen columns of smoke, thick, oily, and black as night. It might have come from the center of the world, this smoke, where the fires of the ages still smoulder. It came as if self-impelled, driving all before it, a perpetual explosion. It was inexhaustible; one stared, waiting to see it stop, but still the great streams rolled out. They spread in vast clouds overhead, writhing, curling; then, uniting in one giant river, they streamed away down the sky, stretching a black pall as far as the eye could reach.

Then the party became aware of another strange thing. This, too, like the odor, was a thing elemental; it was a sound, a sound made up of ten thousand little sounds. You scarcely noticed it at first — it sunk into your consciousness, a vague disturbance, a trouble. It was like the murmuring of the bees in the spring, the whisperings of the forest; it suggested endless activity, the rumblings of a world in motion. It was only by an effort that one could realize that it was made by animals, that it was the distant lowing of ten thousand cattle, the distant grunting of ten thousand swine.
. . .

There is over a square mile of space in the yards, and more than half of it is occupied by cattle pens; north and south as far as the eye can reach there stretches a sea of pens. And they were all filled — so many cattle no one had ever dreamed existed in the world. Red cattle, black, white, and yellow cattle; old cattle and young cattle; great bellowing bulls and little calves not an hour born; meek-eyed milch cows and fierce, long-horned Texas steers. The sound of them here was as of all the barn-yards of the universe; and as for counting them — it would have taken all day simply to count the pens. . . .

"And what will become of all these creatures?" cried Teta Elzbieta.

"By tonight," Jokubas answered, "they will all be killed and cut up; and over there on the other side of the packing houses are more railroad tracks, where the cars come to take them away."

There were two hundred and fifty miles of track within the yards, their guide went on to tell them. They brought about ten thousand head of cattle every day, and as many hogs, and half as many sheep — which meant some eight or ten million live creatures turned into food every year. One stood and watched, and little by little caught the drift of the tide, as it set in the direction of the packing houses. There were groups of cattle being driven to the chutes, which were roadways about fifteen feet wide, raised high above the pens. In these chutes the stream of ani-mals was continuous; it was quite uncanny to watch them, pressing on to their fate, all unsuspicious — a very river of death. Our friends were not poetical, and the sight suggested to them no metaphors of human des-tiny; they thought only of the wonderful efficiency of it all. The chutes into which the hogs went climbed high up — to the very top of the dis-tant buildings, and Jokubas explained that the hogs went up by the power of their own legs, and then their weight carried them back through all the processes necessary to make them into pork.

"They don't waste anything here," said the guide, and then he laughed and added a witticism, which he was pleased that his unsophisticated friends should take to be his own: "They use everything about the hog except the squeal." . . .

They climbed a long series of stairways outside of the building, to the top of its five or six stories. Here were the chute, with its river of hogs, all patiently toiling upward; there was a place for them to rest to cool off, and then through another passageway they went into a room from which there is no returning for hogs.

It was a long, narrow room, with a gallery along it for visitors. At the head there was a great iron wheel, about twenty feet in circumference, with rings here and there along its edge. Upon both sides of this wheel there was a narrow space, into which came the hogs at the end of their journey; in the midst of them stood a great burly Negro, bare-armed and bare-chested. He was resting for the moment, for the wheel had stopped while men were cleaning up. In a minute or two, however, it began slowly to revolve, and then the men upon each side of it sprang to work. They had chains which they fastened about the leg of the nearest hog, and the other end of the chain they hooked into one of the rings upon the wheel. So, as the wheel turned, a hog was suddenly jerked off his feet and borne aloft.

At the same instant the ear was assailed by a most terrifying shriek; the visitors started in alarm, the women turned pale and shrank back. The shriek was followed by another, louder and yet more agonizing — for once started upon that journey, the hog never came back; at the top of the wheel he was shunted off upon a trolley, and went sailing down the room. And meantime another was swung up, and then another, and another, until there was a double line of them, each dangling by a foot and kicking in frenzy — and squealing. The uproar was appalling, perilous to the eardrums; one feared there was too much sound for the room to hold — that the walls must give way or the ceiling crack. There were high squeals and low squeals, grunts, and wails of agony; there would come a momentary lull, and then a fresh outburst, louder than ever, surging up to a deafening climax. It was too much for some of the visitors — the men would look at each other, laughing nervously, and the women would stand with hands clenched, and the blood rushing to their faces, and the tears starting in their eyes.

Meantime, heedless of all these things, the men upon the floor were going about their work. Neither squeals of hogs nor tears of visitors made any difference to them; one by one they hooked up the hogs, and one by one with a swift stroke they slit their throats. There was a long line of hogs, with squeals and life-blood ebbing away together, until at last each started again, and vanished with a splash into a huge vat of boiling water.

It was all so very businesslike that one watched it fascinated. It was pork-making by machinery, pork-making by applied mathematics. And yet somehow the most matter-of-fact person could not help thinking of the hogs; they were so innocent, they came so very trustingly; and they were so very human in their protests — and so perfectly within their rights! They had done nothing to deserve it, and it was adding insult to injury, as the thing was done here, swinging them up in this cold-blooded, impersonal way, without a pretence at apology, without the homage of a tear. Now and then a visitor wept, to be sure; but this slaughtering machine ran on, visitors or no visitors. It was like some horrible crime committed in a dungeon, all unseen and unheeded, buried out of sight and of memory.

One could not stand and watch very long without becoming philosophical, without beginning to deal in symbols and similes, and to hear the hog-squeal of the universe. Was it permitted to believe that there was nowhere upon the earth, or above the earth, a heaven for hogs, where they were requited for all this suffering? Each one of these hogs was a separate creature. Some were white hogs, some were black; some were brown, some were spotted; some were old, some were young; some were long and lean, some were monstrous. And each of them had an individuality of his own, a will of his own, a hope and a heart's desire; each was full of self-confidence, of self-importance, and a sense of dignity. And trusting and strong in faith he had gone about his business, the while a black shadow hung over him and a horrid Fate waited in his pathway. Now suddenly it had swooped upon him, and had seized him by the leg. Relentless, remorseless, it was; all his protests, his screams, were nothing to it — it did its cruel will with him, as if his wishes, his feelings, had simply no existence at all; it cut his throat and watched him gasp out his life. And now was one to believe that there was nowhere a god of hogs, to whom this hog-personality was precious, to whom these hog-squeals and agonies had a meaning? Who would take this hog into his arms and comfort him, reward him for his work well done, and show him the meaning of his sacrifice? Perhaps some glimpse of all this was in the thoughts of our humble-minded Jurgis, as he turned to go on with the rest of the party, and muttered: "*Dieve* — but I'm glad I'm not a hog!"

The carcass hog was scooped out of the vat by machinery, and then it fell to the second floor, passing on the way through a wonderful machine with numerous scrapers, which adjusted themselves to the size and shape of the animal, and sent it out at the other end with nearly all of its bristles removed. It was then again strung up by machinery, and sent upon another trolley ride; this time passing between two lines of men, who sat upon a raised platform, each doing a certain single thing to the carcass as it came to him. One scraped the outside of a leg; another scraped the inside of the same leg. One with a swift stroke cut the throat; another with two swift strokes severed the head, which fell to the floor and vanished through a hole. Another made a slit down the body; a second opened the body wider; a third with a saw cut the breastbone; a fourth loosened the entrails; a fifth pulled them out — and they also slid through a hole in the floor. There were men to scrape each side and men to scrape the back; there were men to clean the carcass inside, to trim it and wash it. Looking down this room, one saw, creeping slowly, a line of dangling hogs a hundred yards in length; and for every yard there was a man, working as if a demon were after him. At the end of this hog's progress every inch of the carcass had been gone over several times, and then it was rolled into the chilling room, where it stayed for twenty-four hours, and where a stranger might lose himself in a forest of freezing hogs.

Before the carcass was admitted here, however, it had to pass a government inspector, who sat in the doorway and felt of the glands in the neck for tuberculosis. This government inspector did not have the manner of a man who was worked to death; he was apparently not haunted by a fear that the hog might get by him before he had finished his testing. If you were a sociable person, he was quite willing to enter into conversation with you, and to explain to you the deadly nature of the ptomaines which are found in tubercular pork; and while he was talking with you you could hardly be so ungrateful as to notice that a dozen carcasses were passing him untouched. This inspector wore an imposing silver badge, and he gave an atmosphere of authority to the scene, and, as it were, put the stamp of official approval upon the things which were done in Durham's.

Jurgis went down the line with the rest of the visitors, staring openmouthed, lost in wonder. He had dressed hogs himself in the forest of Lithuania; but he had never expected to live to see one hog dressed by several hundred men. It was like a wonderful poem to him, and he took it all in guilelessly — even to the conspicuous signs demanding immaculate cleanliness of the employees. Jurgis was vexed when the cynical Jokubas translated these signs with sarcastic comments, offering to take them to the secret rooms where the spoiled meats went to be doctored.

The party descended to the next floor, where the various waste materials were treated. Here came the entrails, to be scraped and washed clean for sausage casings; men and women worked here in the midst of a sickening stench, which caused the visitors to hasten by, gasping. To another room came all the scraps to be "tanked," which meant boiling and pumping off the grease to make soap and lard; below they took out the refuse, and this, too, was a region in which the visitors did not linger. In still other places men were engaged in cutting up the carcases that had been through the chilling rooms. First there were the "splitters," the most expert workmen in the plant, who earned as high as fifty cents an hour, and did not a thing all day except chop hogs down the middle. Then there were "cleaver men," great giants with muscles of iron; each had two men to attend him — to slide the half carcass in front of him on the table, and hold it while he chopped it, and then turn each piece so that he might chop it once more. His cleaver had a blade about two feet long, and he never made but one cut; he made it so neatly, too, that his implement did not smite through and dull itself — there was just enough force for a perfect cut, and no more. So through various yawning holes there slipped to the floor below — to one room hams, to another forequarters, to another sides of pork. One might go down to this floor and see the pickling rooms, where the hams were put into vats, and the great smoke rooms, with their airtight iron doors. In other rooms they prepared salt pork — there were whole cellars full of it, built up in great towers to the ceiling. In yet other rooms they were putting up meat in boxes and barrels, and wrapping hams and bacon in oiled paper, sealing and labeling and sewing them. From the doors of these rooms went men with loaded trucks, to the platform where freight cars were waiting to be filled; and one went out there and realized with a start that he had come at last to the ground floor of this enormous building. . . .

. . . No tiniest particle of organic matter was wasted in Durham's. Out of the horns of the cattle they made combs, buttons, hairpins, and imitation ivory; out of the shin bones and other big bones they cut knife and tooth brush handles, and mouthpieces for pipes; out of the hoofs they cut hairpins and buttons, before they made the rest into glue. From such things as feet, knuckles, hide clippings, and sinews came such strange and unlikely products as gelatin, isinglass, and phosphorus, bone black, shoe blacking, and bone oil. They had curled-hair works for the cattle tails, and a "wool pullery" for the sheep skins; they made pepsin from the stomachs of the pigs, and albumen from the blood, and violin strings from the ill-smelling entrails. When there was nothing else to be done with a thing, they first put it into a tank and got out of it all the tallow and grease, and then they made it into fertilizer. All these industries were gathered into buildings near by, connected by galleries and railroads with the main establishment, and it was estimated that they had handled nearly a quarter of a billion of animals since the founding of the plant by the elder Durham a generation and more ago. If you counted with it the other big plants — and they were now really all one — it was, so Jakubas informed them, the greatest aggregation of labor and capital ever gathered in one place. It employed thirty thousand men; it supported directly two hundred and fifty thousand people in its neighborhood, and indirectly it supported half a million. It sent its products to every country in the civilized world, and it furnished the food for no less than thirty million people! . . .

Now Antanas Rudkus was the meekest man that God ever put on earth, and so Jurgis found it a striking confirmation of what the men all said, that his father had been at work only two days before he came home as bitter as any of them, and cursing Durham's with all the power of his soul. For they had set him to cleaning out the traps; and the family sat round and listened in wonder while he told them what that meant. It seemed that he was working in the room where the men prepared the beef for canning, and the beef had lain in vats full of chemicals, and men with great forks speared it out and dumped it into trucks, to be taken to the cooking room. When they had speared out all they could reach, they emptied the vat on the floor, and then with shovels scraped off the balance and dumped it into the truck. This floor was filthy, yet they set Antanas with his mop slopping the "pickle" into a hole that connected with a sink, where it was caught and used over again forever; and if that was not enough, there was a trap in the pipe, where all the scraps of meat and odds and ends of refuse were caught, and every few days it was the old man's task to clean these out, and shovel their contents into one of the trucks with the rest of the meat!

This was the experience of Antanas; and then there came also Jonas and Marija with tales to tell. Marija was working for one of the independent packers, and was quite beside herself and outrageous with triumph over the sums of money she was making as a painter of cans. But one day she walked home with a pale-faced little woman who worked opposite to her, Jadvyga Marcinkus by name, and Jadvyga told her how she, Marija, had chanced to get her job. She had taken the place of an Irish woman who had been working in that factory ever since anyone could remember, for over fifteen years, so she declared. Mary Dennis was her name, and a long time ago she had been seduced, and had a little boy; he was a cripple, and an epileptic, but still he was all that she had in the world to love, and they had lived in a little room alone somewhere back of Halsted Street, where the Irish were. Mary had had consumption, and all day long you might hear her coughing as she worked; of late she had been going all to pieces, and when Marija came, the "forelady" had suddenly decided to turn her off. The forelady had to come up to a certain standard herself, and could not stop for sick people, Jadvyga explained. The fact that Mary had been there so long had not made any difference to her — it was doubtful if she even knew that, for both the forelady and the superintendent were new people, having only been there two or three years themselves. Jadvyga did not know what had become of the poor creature; she would have gone to see her, but had been sick herself. She had pains in her back all the time, Jadvyga explained, and feared that she had womb trouble. It was not fit work for a woman, handling fourteen-pound cans all day.

It was a striking circumstance that Jonas, too, had gotten his job by the misfortune of some other person. Jonas pushed a truck loaded with hams from the smoke rooms on to an elevator, and thence to the packing rooms. The trucks were all of iron, and heavy, and they put about threescore hams on each of them, a load of more than a quarter of a ton. On the uneven floor it was a task for a man to start one of these trucks, unless he was a giant; and when it was once started he naturally tried his best to keep it going. There was always the boss prowling about, and if there was a second's delay he would fall to cursing; Lithuanians and Slovaks and such, who could not understand what was said to them, the bosses were wont to kick about the place like so many dogs. Therefore these trucks went for the most part on the run; and the predecessor of Jonas had been jammed against the wall by one and crushed in a horrible and nameless manner.

All of these were sinister incidents; but they were trifles compared to what Jurgis saw with his own eyes before long. One curious thing he had noticed, the very first day, in his profession of shoveler of guts; which was the sharp trick of the floor bosses whenever there chanced to come a "slunk" calf. Any man who knows anything about butchering knows that the flesh of a cow that is about to calve, or has just calved, is not fit for food. A good many of these came every day to the packing houses — and, of course, if they had chosen, it would have been an easy matter for the packers to keep them till they were fit for food. But for the saving of time and fodder, it was the law that cows of that sort came along with the others, and whoever noticed it would tell the boss, and the boss would start up a conversation with the government inspector, and the two would stroll away. So, in a trice the carcass of the cow would be cleaned out, and the entrails would have vanished; it was Jurgis' task to slide them into the trap, calves and all, and on the floor below they took out these "slunk" calves, and butchered them for meat, and used even the skins of them.

One day a man slipped and hurt his leg; and that afternoon, when the last of the cattle had been disposed of, and the men were leaving, Jurgis was ordered to remain and do some special work which this injured man had usually done. It was late, almost dark, and the government inspectors had all gone, and there were only a dozen or two of men on the floor. That day they had killed about four thousand cattle, and these cattle had come in freight trains from far states, and some of them had got hurt. There were some with broken legs, and some with gored sides; there were some that had died, from what cause no one could say; and they were all to be disposed of, here in the darkness and silence. "Downers," the men called them; and the packing house had a special elevator upon which they were raised to the killing beds, where the gang proceeded to handle them, with an air of businesslike nonchalance which said plainer than any words that it was a matter of everyday routine. It took a couple of hours to get them out of the way, and in the end Jurgis saw them go into the chilling rooms with the rest of the meat, being carefully scattered here and there so that they could not be identified. When he came home that night he was in a very somber mood, having begun to see at last how those might be right who had laughed at him for his faith in America. . . .

. . . "Bubbly Creek" is an arm of the Chicago River, and forms the southern boundary of the yards; all the drainage of the square mile of packing houses empties into it, so that it is really a great open sewer a hundred or two feet wide. One long arm of it is blind, and the filth stays there forever and a day. The grease and chemicals that are poured into it undergo all sorts of strange transformations, which are the cause of its name; it is constantly in motion, as if huge fish were feeding in it, or great leviathans were disporting themselves in its depths. Bubbles of carbonic acid gas will rise to the surface and burst, and make rings two or three feet wide. Here and there the grease and filth have caked solid, and the creek looks like a bed of lava; chickens walk about on it, feeding, and many times an unwary stranger has started to stroll across, and vanished temporarily. The packers used to leave the creek that way, till every now and then the surface would catch on fire and burn furiously, and the fire department would have to come and put it out. Once, however, an ingenious stranger came and started to gather this filth in scows, to make lard out of; then the packers took the cue, and got out an injunction to stop him, and afterwards gathered it themselves. The banks of "Bubbly Creek" are plastered thick with hairs, and this also the packers gather and clean.

And there were things even stranger than this, according to the gossip of the men. The packers had secret mains, through which they stole billions of gallons of the city's water. The newspapers had been full of this scandal — once there had even been an investigation, and an actual uncovering of the pipes; but nobody had been punished, and the thing went right on. And then there was the condemned meat industry, with its endless horrors. The people of Chicago saw the government inspectors in Packingtown, and they all took that to mean that they were protected from diseased meat; they did not understand that these hundred and sixty-three inspectors had been appointed at the request of the packers, and that they were paid by the United States government to certify that all the diseased meat was kept in the state. They had no authority beyond that; for the inspection of meat to be sold in the city and state the whole force in Packingtown consisted of three henchmen of the local political machine! And shortly afterward one of these, a physician, made the discovery that the carcasses of steers which had been condemned as tubercular by the government inspectors, and which therefore contained ptomaines, which are deadly poisons, were left upon an open platform

and carted away to be sold in the city; and so he insisted that these carcasses be treated with an injection of kerosene — and was ordered to resign
the same week! So indignant were the packers that they went farther,
and compelled the mayor to abolish the whole bureau of inspection; so
that since then there has not been even a pretence of any interference with
the graft. There was said to be two thousand dollars a week hush money
from the tubercular steers alone, and as much again from the hogs which
had died of cholera on the trains, and which you might see any day being
loaded into box cars and hauled away to a place called Globe, in Indiana,
where they made a fancy grade of lard.

Jurgis heard of these things little by little, in the gossip of those who
were obliged to perpetrate them. It seemed as if every time you met a
person from a new department, you heard of new swindles and new
crimes. There was, for instance, a Lithuanian who was a cattle butcher
for the plant where Marija had worked, which killed meat for canning
only; and to hear this man describe the animals which came to his place
would have been worthwhile for a Dante or a Zola. It seemed that they
must have agencies all over the country, to hunt out old and crippled and
diseased cattle to be canned. There were cattle which had been fed on
"whiskey malt," the refuse of the breweries, and had become what the
men called "steerly" — which means covered with boils. It was a nasty job
killing these, for when you plunged your knife into them they would
burst and splash foul-smelling stuff into your face; and when a man's
sleeves were smeared with blood, and his hands steeped in it, how was he
ever to wipe his face, or to clear his eyes so that he could see? It was
stuff such as this that made the "embalmed beef" that had killed several
times as many United States soldiers as all the bullets of the Spaniards;
only the army beef, besides, was not fresh canned, it was old stuff that
had been lying for years in the cellars.

Then one Sunday evening, Jurgis sat puffing his pipe by the kitchen
stove, and talking with an old fellow whom Jonas had introduced, and
who worked in the canning-rooms at Durham's; and so Jurgis learned
a few things about the great and only Durham canned goods, which had
become a national institution. They were regular alchemists at Durham's; they advertised a mushroom-catsup, and the men who made it did
not know what a mushroom looked like. They advertised "potted chick-
en" — and it was like the boarding-house soup of the comic papers,
through which a chicken had walked with rubbers on. Perhaps they had
a secret process for making chickens chemically — who knows? said
Jurgis's friend; the things that went into the mixture were tripe, and the
fat of pork, and beef suet, and hearts of beef, and finally the waste ends

of veal, when they had any. They put these up in several grades, and sold them at several prices; but the contents of the cans all came out of the same hopper. And then there was "potted game" and "potted grouse," "potted ham," and "deviled ham" — de-vyled, as the men called it. "De-vyled" ham was made out of the waste ends of smoked beef that were too small to be sliced by the machines; and also tripe, dyed with chemicals so that it would not show white, and trimmings of hams and corned beef, and potatoes, skins and all, and finally the hard cartilaginous gullets of beef, after the tongues had been cut out. All this ingenious mixture was ground up and flavored with spices to make it taste like something. Anybody who could invent a new imitation had been sure of a fortune from old Durham, said Jurgis's informant, but it was hard to think of anything new in a place where so many sharp wits had been at work for so long; where men welcomed tuberculosis in the cattle they were feeding, because it made them fatten more quickly; and where they bought up all the old rancid butter left over in the grocery stores of a continent, and "oxidized" it by a forced-air process, to take away the odor, rechurned it with skim milk, and sold it in bricks in the cities! Up to a year or two ago it had been the custom to kill horses in the yards — ostensibly for fertilizer; but after long agitation the newspapers had been able to make the public realize that the horses were being canned. Now it was against the law to kill horses in Packingtown, and the law was really complied with — for the present, at any rate. Any day, however, one might see sharp-horned and shaggy-haired creatures running with the sheep — and yet what a job you would have to get the public to believe that a good part of what it buys for lamb and mutton is really goat's flesh!

There was another interesting set of statistics that a person might have gathered in Packingtown — those of the various afflictions of the workers. When Jurgis had first inspected the packing plants with Szedvilas, he had marveled while he listened to the tale of all the things that were made out of the carcasses of animals, and of all the lesser industries that were maintained there; now he found that each one of these lesser industries was a separate little inferno, in its way as horrible as the killing-beds, the source and fountain of them all. The workers in each of them had their own peculiar diseases. And the wandering visitor peering down through the damp and the steam, and as old Durham's architects had not built the killing room for the convenience of the hoisters, at every few feet they would have to stoop under a beam, say four feet above the one they ran on, which got them into the habit of stooping, so that in a few years they would be walking like chimpanzees. Worst of any, however, were the fertilizer men, and those who served in the cooking rooms. These people could not be shown to the visitor — for the odor of a fertilizer man would scare any ordinary visitor at a hundred yards, and as for the other men, who worked in tank rooms full of steam, and in some of which there were open vats near the level of the floor, their peculiar trouble was that they fell into the vats; and when they were fished out, there was never enough of them left to be worth exhibiting — sometimes they would be overlooked for days, till all but the bones of them had gone out to the world as Durham's Pure Leaf Lard! . . .

With one member trimming beef in a cannery, and another working in a sausage factory, the family had a first-hand knowledge of the great majority of Packingtown swindles. For it was the custom, as they found, whenever meat was so spoiled that it could not be used for anything else, either to can it or else to chop it up into sausage. With what had been told them by Jonas, who had worked in the pickle rooms, they could now study the whole of the spoiled-meat industry on the inside, and read a new and grim meaning into that old Packingtown jest — that they use everything of the pig except the squeal.

Jonas had told them how the meat that was taken out of pickle would often be found sour, and how they would rub it up with soda to take away the smell, and sell it to be eaten on free-lunch counters; also of all the miracles of chemistry which they performed, giving to any sort of meat, fresh or salted, whole or chopped, any color and any flavor and any odor they chose. In the pickling of hams they had an ingenious apparatus, by which they saved time and increased the capacity of the plant — a machine consisting of a hollow needle attached to a pump; by plunging this needle into the meat and working with his foot a man could fill a ham with pickle in a few seconds. And yet, in spite of this, there would be hams found spoiled, some of them with an odor so bad that a man could hardly bear to be in the room with them. To pump into these the packers had a second and much stronger pickle which destroyed the odor — a process known to the workers as "giving them thirty per cent." Also, after the hams had been smoked, there would be found some that had gone to the bad. Formerly these had been sold as "Number Three Grade," but later on some ingenious person had hit upon a new device, and now they would extract the bone, about which the bad part generally lay, and insert in the hole a white-hot iron. After this invention there was no longer Number One, Two, and Three Grade — there was only Number One Grade. The packers were always originating such schemes — they had what they called "boneless hams," which were all the odds and ends of pork stuffed into casings; and "California hams," which were the shoulders, with big knuckle joints, and nearly all the meat cut out; and fancy "skinned hams," which were made of the oldest hogs, whose skins were so heavy and coarse that no one would buy them — that is, until they had been cooked and chopped fine and labelled "head cheese"!

It was only when the whole ham was spoiled that it came into the department of Elzbieta. Cut up by the two-thousand-revolutions-a-minute flyers, and mixed with half a ton of other meat, no odor that ever was in a ham could make any difference. There was never the least attention paid to what was cut up for sausage; there would come all the way back from Europe old sausage that had been rejected, and that was mouldy and white — it would be dosed with borax and glycerine, and dumped into the hoppers, and made over again for home consumption. There would be meat that had tumbled out on the floor, in the dirt and sawdust, where the workers had tramped and spit uncounted billions of consumption germs. There would be meat stored in great piles in rooms; and the water from leaky roofs would drip over it, and thousands of rats would race about on it. It was too dark in these storage places to see well, but a man could run his hand over these piles of meat and sweep off handfuls of the dried dung of rats. These rats were nuisances, and the packers would put poisoned bread out for them, they would die, and then rats, bread, and meat would go into the hoppers together. This is no fairy story and no joke; the meat would be shovelled into carts, and the man who did the shoveling would not trouble to lift out a rat even when he saw one — there were things that went into the sausage in comparison with which a poisoned rat was a tidbit. There was no place for the men to wash their hands before they ate their dinner, and so they made a practice of washing them in the water that was to be ladled into the sausage. There were the butt-ends of smoked meat, and the scraps of corned beef, and all the odds and ends of the waste of the plants, that would be dumped into old barrels in the cellar and left there. Under the system of rigid economy which the packers enforced, there were some jobs that it only paid to do once in a long time, and among these was the cleaning out of the waste barrels. Every spring they did it; and in the barrels would be dirt and rust and old nails and stale water — and cart load after cart load of it would be taken up and dumped into the hoppers with fresh meat, and sent out to the public's breakfast. Some of it they would make into "smoked" sausage — but as the smoking took time, and was therefore expensive, they would call upon their chemistry department, and preserve it with borax and color it with gelatine to make it brown. All of their sausage came out of the same bowl, but when they came to wrap it they would stamp some of it "special," and for this they would charge two cents more a pound. . . .

Poor Jurgis was not very happy in his home life. Elzbieta was sick a good deal now, and the boys were wild and unruly, and very much the worse for their life upon the streets. But he stuck by the family nevertheless, for they reminded him of his old happiness; and when things went wrong he could solace himself with a plunge into the Socialist movement. Since his life had been caught up into the current of this great stream, things which had before been the whole of life to him came to seem of relatively slight importance; his interests were elsewhere, in the world of ideas. His outward life was commonplace and uninteresting; he was just a hotel porter, and expected to remain one while he lived; but meantime, in the realm of thought, his life was a perpetual adventure. There was so much to know — so many wonders to be discovered! Never in all his life did Jurgis forget the day before election, when there came a telephone message from a friend of Harry Adams, asking him to bring Jurgis to see him that night; and Jurgis went, and met one of the minds of the movement.

The invitation was from a man named Fisher, a Chicago millionaire who had given up his life to settlement work, and had a little home in the heart of the city's slums. He did not belong to the party, but he was in sympathy with it; and he said that he was to have as his guest that night the editor of a big Eastern magazine, who wrote against Socialism, but really did not know what it was. The millionaire suggested that Adams bring Jurgis along, and then start up the subject of "pure food," in which the editor was interested.

Young Fisher's home was a little two-story brick house, dingy and weather-beaten outside, but attractive within. The room that Jurgis saw was half lined with books, and upon the walls were many pictures, dimly visible in the soft, yellow light; it was a cold, rainy night, so a log fire was crackling in the open hearth. Seven or eight people were gathered about it when Adams and his friend arrived, and Jurgis saw to his dismay that three of them were ladies. He had never talked to people of this sort before, and he fell into an agony of embarrassment. He stood in the doorway clutching his hat tightly in his hands, and made a deep bow to each of the persons as he was introduced; then, when he was asked to have a seat, he took a chair in a dark corner, and sat down upon the edge of it, and wiped the perspiration off his forehead with his sleeve. He was terrified lest they should expect him to talk.

There was the host himself, a tall, athletic young man, clad in evening dress, as also was the editor, a dyspeptic-looking gentleman named Maynard. There was the former's frail young wife, and also an elderly lady, who taught kindergarten in the settlement, and a young college student, a beautiful girl with an intense and earnest face. She only spoke once or twice while Jurgis was there — the rest of the time she sat by the table in the center of the room, resting her chin in her hands and drinking in the conversation. There were two other men, whom young Fisher had introduced to Jurgis as Mr. Lucas and Mr. Schliemann; he heard them address Adams as "Comrade," and so he knew that they were Socialists. . . .

. . . Mr. Maynard, the editor, took occasion to remark, somewhat naïvely, that he had always understood that Socialists had a cut-and-dried program for the future of civilization; whereas here were two active members of the party, who, from what he could make out, were agreed about nothing at all. Would the two, for his enlightenment, try to ascertain just what they had in common, and why they belonged to the same party? This resulted, after much debating, in the formulating of two carefully worded propositions: First, that a Socialist believes in the common ownership and democratic management of the means of producing the necessities of life; and, second, that a socialist believes that the means by which this is to be brought about is the class-conscious political organization of the wage-earners. Thus far they were at one; but no farther. To Lucas, the religious zealot, the co-operative commonwealth was the New Jerusalem, the kingdom of Heaven, which is "within you." To the other, Socialism was simply a necessary step toward a far-distant goal, a step to be tolerated with impatience. Schliemann called himself a "philosophic anarchist"; and he explained that an anarchist was one who believed that the end of human existence was the free development of every personality, unrestricted by laws save those of its own being. Since the same kind of match would light every one's fire and the same-shaped loaf of bread would fill every one's stomach, it would be perfectly feasible to submit industry to the control of a majority vote. There was only one earth, and the quantity of material things was limited. Of intellectual and moral things, on the other hand, there was no limit, and one could have more without another's having less; hence "Communism in material production, anarchism in intellectual," was the formula of modern proletarian thought. As soon as the birth agony was over, and the wounds of society had been healed, there would be established a simple system whereby each man was credited with his labor and debited with his purchases; and after that the processes of production, exchange, and consumption would go on automatically, and without our being conscious of them, any more than a man is conscious of the beating of his heart. And then, explained Schliemann, society would break up into independent, self-governing communities of mutually congenial persons; examples of which at present were clubs, churches, and political parties. After the revolution, all the intellectual, artistic, and spiritual activities of men would be cared for by such "free associations"; romantic novelists would be supported by those who liked to read romantic novels, and impressionist painters would be supported by those who liked to look at impressionist pictures — and the same with preachers and scientists, editors and actors and musicians. If any one wanted to work or paint or pray, and could find no one to maintain him, he could support himself by working part of the time. That was the case at present, the only difference being that the competitive wage system compelled a man to work all the time to live, while, after the abolition of privilege and exploitation, anyone would be able to support himself by an hour's work a day. Also the artist's audience of the present was a small minority of people, all debased and vulgarized by the effort it had cost them to win in the commercial battle; of the intellectual and artistic activities which would result when the whole of mankind was set free from the nightmare of competition, we could at present form no conception whatever.

And then the editor wanted to know upon what ground Dr. Schliemann asserted that it might be possible for a society to exist upon an hour's toil by each of its members. "Just what," answered the other, "would be the productive capacity of society if the present resources of science were utilized, we have no means of ascertaining; but we may be sure it would exceed anything that would sound reasonable to minds inured to the ferocious barbarities of Capitalism. After the triumph of the international proletariat, war would of course be inconceivable; and who can figure the cost of war to humanity — not merely the value of the lives and the material that it destroys, not merely the cost of keeping millions of men in idleness, of arming and equipping them for battle and parade, but the drain upon the vital energies of society by the war-attitude and the war-terror, the brutality and ignorance, the drunkenness, prostitution, and crime it entails, the industrial impotence and the moral deadness? Do you think that it would be too much to say that two hours of the working time of every efficient member of a community goes to feed the red fiend of war?"

And then Schliemann went on to outline some of the wastes of competition: the losses of industrial warfare; the ceaseless worry and friction; the vices — such as drink, for instance, the use of which had nearly doubled in twenty years, as a consequence of the intensification of the economic struggle; the idle and unproductive members of the community, the frivolous rich and the pauperized poor; the law and the whole machinery of repression; the wastes of social ostentation, the milliners and tailors, the hairdressers, dancing masters, chefs and lackeys. "You understand," he said, "that in a society dominated by the fact of commercial competition, money is necessarily the test of prowess, and wastefulness the sole criterion of power. So we have, at the present moment, a society with, say, thirty per cent of the population occupied in producing useless articles, and one per cent occupied in destroying them. And this is not all; for the servants and panders of the parasites are also parasites, the milliners and the jewelers and the lackeys have also to be supported by the useful members of the community. And bear in mind also that this monstrous disease affects not merely the idlers and their menials, its poison penetrates the whole social body. Beneath the hundred thousand women of the élite are a million middle-class women, miserable because they are not of the élite, and trying to appear of it in public; and beneath them, in turn, are five million farmers' wives reading 'fashion papers' and trimming bonnets, and shopgirls and serving maids selling themselves into brothels for cheap jewelry and imitation sealskin robes. And then consider that, added to this competition in display, you have, like oil on the flames, a whole system of competition in selling! You have manufacturers contriving tens of thousands of catchpenny devices, storekeepers displaying them, and newspapers and magazines filled up with advertisements of them!"

"And don't forget the wastes of fraud," put in young Fisher.

"When one comes to the ultra-modern profession of advertising," responded Schliemann — "the science of persuading people to buy what they do not want, he is in the very center of the ghastly charnel-house of capitalist destructiveness, and he scarcely knows which of a dozen horrors to point out first. But consider the waste in time and energy incidental to making ten thousand varieties of a thing for purposes of ostentation and snobbishness, where one variety would do for use! Consider all the waste incidental to the manufacture of cheap qualities of goods, of goods made to sell and deceive the ignorant; consider the wastes of adulteration — the shoddy clothing, the cotton blankets, the unstable tenements, the ground-cork life-preservers, the adulterated milk, the aniline soda-water, the potato-flour sausages —"

"And consider the moral aspects of the thing," put in the ex-preacher.

"Precisely," said Schliemann; "the low knavery and the ferocious cruelty incidental to them, the plotting and the lying and the bribing, the blustering and bragging, the screaming egotism, the hurrying and worrying. Of course, imitation and adulteration are the essence of competition — they are but another form of the phrase 'to buy in the cheapest market and sell in the dearest.' A government official has stated that the nation suffers a loss of a billion and a quarter dollars a year through adulterated foods; which means, of course, not only materials wasted that might have been useful outside of the human stomach, but doctors and nurses for people who would otherwise have been well, and undertakers for the whole human race ten or twenty years before the proper time. Then again, consider the waste of time and energy required to sell these things in a dozen stores, where one would do. There are a million or two of business firms in the country, and five or ten times as many clerks; and consider the handling and rehandling, the accounting and reaccounting, the planning and worrying, the balancing of petty profit and loss. Consider the whole machinery of the civil law made necessary by these processes; the libraries of ponderous tomes, the courts and juries to interpret them, the lawyers studying to circumvent them, the pettifogging and chicanery, the hatreds and lies! Consider the wastes incidental to the blind and haphazard production of commodities — the factories closed, the workers idle, the goods spoiling in storage; consider the activities of the stock-manipulator, the paralyzing of whole industries, the over-stimulation of others, for speculative purposes; the assignments and bank failures, the crises and panics, the deserted towns and the starving populations! Consider the energies wasted in the seeking of markets, the sterile trades, such as drummer, solicitor, billposter, advertising agent. Consider the wastes incidental to the crowding into cities, made necessary by competition and by monopoly railroad rates; consider the slums, the bad air, the disease and the waste of vital energies; consider the office buildings, the waste of time and material in the piling of story upon story, and the burrowing underground! . . .

Dr. Schliemann paused for a moment. "That was a lecture," he said with a laugh, "and yet I am only begun!"

"What else is there?" asked Maynard.

"I have pointed out some of the negative wastes of competition," answered the other. "I have hardly mentioned the positive economies of co-operation. Allowing five to a family, there are fifteen million families in this country; and at least ten million of these live separately, the domestic drudge being either the wife or a wage slave. Now set aside the modern system of pneumatic house-cleaning, and the economies of co-operative cooking; and consider one single item, the washing of dishes. Surely it is moderate to say that the dish-washing for a family of five takes half an hour a day; with ten hours as a day's work, it takes, therefore, half a million able-bodied persons — mostly women — to do the dish-washing of the country. And note that this is most filthy and deadening and brutalizing work; that it is a cause of anemia, nervousness, ugliness,

and ill-temper; of prostitution, suicide, and insanity; of drunken husbands and degenerate children — for all of which things the community
has naturally to pay. And now consider that in each of my little free communities there would be a machine which would wash and dry the
dishes, and do it, not merely to the eye and the touch, but scientifically
—sterilizing them — and do it at a saving of all of the drudgery and
nine-tenths of the time! All of these things you may find in the books of
Mrs. Gilman; and then take Kropotkin's *Fields, Factories, and Work-
shops,* and read about the new science of agriculture, which has been
built up in the last ten years; by which, with made soils and intensive
culture, a gardener can raise ten or twelve crops in a season, and two
hundred tons of vegetables upon a single acre; by which the population
of the whole globe could be supported on the soil now cultivated in
the United States alone! It is impossible to apply such methods now, owing to the ignorance and poverty of our scattered farming population;
but imagine the problem of providing the food supply of our nation
once taken in hand systematically and rationally, by scientists! All the
poor and rocky land set apart for a national timber reserve, in which
our children play, and our young men hunt, and our poets dwell! The
most favorable climate and soil for each product selected; the exact requirements of the community known, and the acreage figured accordingly; the most improved machinery employed, under the direction of
expert agricultural chemists! I was brought up on a farm, and I know
the awful deadliness of farm work; and I like to picture it all as it will be
after the revolution. To picture the great potato-planting machine, drawn
by four horses, or an electric motor, ploughing the furrow, cutting and
dropping and covering the potatoes, and planting a score of acres a day!
To picture the great potato-digging machine, run by electricity, perhaps,
and moving across a thousand-acre field, scooping up earth and potatoes,
and dropping the latter into sacks! To see every other kind of vegetable
and fruit handled in the same way — apples and oranges picked by machinery, cows milked by electricity — things which are already done, as
you may know. To picture the harvest fields of the future, to which millions of happy men and women come for a summer holiday, brought
by special trains, the exactly needful number to each place! And to contrast all this with our present agonizing system of independent small
farming — a stunted, haggard, ignorant man, mated with a yellow, lean,
and sad-eyed drudge, and toiling from four o'clock in the morning until
nine at night, working the children as soon as they are able to walk,
scratching the soil with his primitive tools, and shut out from all knowledge and hope, from all the benefits of science and invention, and all

the joys of the spirit — held to a bare existence by competition in labor, and boasting of his freedom because he is too blind to see his chains!"

Dr. Schliemann paused a moment. "And then," he continued, "place beside this fact of an unlimited food supply, the newest discovery of physiologists, that most of the ills of the human system are due to over-feeding! And then again, it has been proven that meat is unnecessary as a food; and meat is obviously more difficult to produce than vegetable food, less pleasant to prepare and handle, and more likely to be unclean. But what of that, so long as it tickles the palate more strongly?"

"How would Socialism change that?" asked the girl-student, quickly. It was the first time she had spoken.

"So long as we have wage slavery," answered Schliemann, "it matters not in the least how debasing and repulsive a task may be, it is easy to find people to perform it. But just as soon as labor is set free, then the price of such work will begin to rise. So one by one the old, dingy, and unsanitary factories will come down — it will be cheaper to build new; and so the steamships will be provided with stoking-machinery, and so the dangerous trades will be made safe, or substitutes will be found for their products. In exactly the same way, as the citizens of our Industrial Republic become refined, year by year the cost of slaughterhouse products will increase; until eventually those who want to eat meat will have to do their own killing — and how long do you think the custom would survive then? — To go on to another item — one of the necessary accompaniments of capitalism in a democracy is political corruption; and one of the consequences of civic administration by ignorant and vicious politicians, is that preventable diseases kill off half of our population. And even if science were allowed to try, it could do little, because the majority of human beings are not yet human beings at all, but simply machines for the creating of wealth for others. They are penned up in filthy houses and left to rot and stew in misery, and the conditions of their life make them ill faster than all the doctors in the world could heal them; and so, of course, they remain as centers of contagion, poisoning the lives of all of us, and making happiness impossible for even the most selfish. For this reason I would seriously maintain that all the medical and surgical discoveries that science can make in the future will be of less importance than the application of the knowledge we already possess, when the disinherited of the earth have established their right to a human existence."

And here the Herr Doctor relapsed into silence again. Jurgis had noticed that the beautiful young girl who sat by the center table was listening with something of the same look that he himself had worn, the time when he had first discovered Socialism. Jurgis would have liked to talk to her, he felt sure that she would have understood him. Later on in the evening, when the group broke up, he heard Mrs. Fisher say to her, in a low voice, "I wonder if Mr. Maynard will still write the same things about Socialism"; to which she answered, "I don't know — but if he does we shall know that he is a knave!" . . .

Herbert Croly

A NEW REFORM PHILOSOPHY

1909 TRADITIONALLY, the debate between liberals and conservatives in America, at least as far back as the time of the Revolution, has centered around the question of how active a part the government should play in regulating the lives and activities of the people. Jefferson and Hamilton have become convenient symbols for identifying the clash of ideas of the two groups.

While liberals never denied *all* power over economic and social affairs to the government, in the Jeffersonian tradition they tended to argue that individuals could best manage their own affairs, that liberty was the supreme value in American society. Conservatives, while generally rejecting extreme forms of government regulation, placed their faith in a system of state sponsorship of economic development that followers of Jefferson found unduly restrictive and overly favorable to men of means and status in society. Without being anti-libertarian, when forced to choose, conservatives usually valued economic progress over economic opportunity.

However, the rapid industrial expansion and the ever-increasing intricacy of the economic system in the last half of the nineteenth century led to a monumental shift of position in both camps. Positive action by state and federal governments now seemed to liberals the only way to control the power of the new industrial giants. "Vested interests," on the other hand, now became the defenders of laissez faire and the old Jeffersonian maxim: "that government is best which governs least." Thus, in our own day, "the welfare state" is a liberal slogan, whereas formerly it would have appealed to those conservatives who worshipped Alexander Hamilton.

This shift was clearly noticeable in the closing decades of the nineteenth century. However, it was left to Herbert Croly (1869-1930) to point out in the strongest terms the nature of the change—to argue forcefully not simply for specific reforms but for the basic idea that positive government control over social and economic affairs was a desirable progressive goal and a logical development from democratic principles. Croly's *Promise of American Life,* published in 1909, was never a best-seller. But it was not aimed at a mass audience. Its direct influence, even upon progressive leaders like Theodore Roosevelt, has also been exaggerated. Nevertheless, it served a vital function (not unlike that of Paine's *Common Sense*) in showing Americans the full implications of the policies they had already come to adopt. "Jeffersonian" liberals read it with a sense of liberation and drew from it a new confidence, for it enabled them to advocate Hamiltonian policies without feeling that they were committing heresy.

THE PROMISE OF AMERICAN LIFE

ALL the conditions of American life have tended to encourage an easy, generous, and irresponsible optimism. As compared to Europeans, Americans have been very much favored by circumstances. Had it not been for the Atlantic Ocean and the virgin wilderness, the United States would never have been the Land of Promise. The European Powers have been obliged from the very conditions of their existence to be more circumspect and less confident of the future. They are always by way of fighting for their national security and integrity. With possible or actual enemies on their several frontiers, and with their land fully occupied by their own population, they need above all to be strong, to be cautious, to be united, and to be opportune in their policy and behavior. . . . The United States was divided from the mainland of Europe not by a channel but by an ocean. Its dimensions were continental rather than insular. We were for the most part freed from alien interference, and could, so far as we dared, experiment with political and social ideals. The land was unoccupied, and its settlement offered an unprecedented area and abundance of economic opportunity. After the Revolution the whole political and social organization was renewed, and made both more serviceable and more flexible. Under such happy circumstances the New World was assuredly destined to become to its inhabitants a Land of Promise, — a land in which men were offered a fairer chance and a better future than the best which the Old World could afford.

No more explicit expression has ever been given to the way in which the Land of Promise was first conceived by its children than in the "Letters of an American Farmer." This book was written by a French immigrant, Hector St. John de Crèvecoeur before the Revolution, and is informed by an intense consciousness of the difference between conditions in the Old and in the New World. "What, then, is an American, this new man?" asks the Pennsylvanian farmer. "He is either a European or the descendant of a European; hence the strange mixture of blood, which you will find in no other country. . . .

"He becomes an American by being received in the broad lap of our great *Alma Mater*. Here individuals of all nations are melted into a new race of men, whose labors and prosperity will one day cause great changes in the world. Here the rewards of his industry follow with equal steps the progress of his labor; this labor is founded on the basis of *self-interest*; can it want a stronger allurement? Wives and children, who before in vain demanded a morsel of bread, now fat and frolicsome, gladly help their father to clear those fields, whence exuberant crops are to arise to feed them all; without any part being claimed either by a despotic prince, a rich abbot, or a mighty lord. . . . The American is a new man, who acts upon new principles; he must therefore entertain new ideas and form new opinions. From involuntary idleness, servile dependence, penury, and useless labor, he has passed to toils of a very different nature rewarded by ample subsistence. This is an American."

Although the foregoing is one of the first, it is also one of the most explicit descriptions of the fundamental American; and it deserves to be analyzed with some care. According to the French convert the American is a man, or the descendant of a man, who has emigrated from Europe chiefly because he expects to be better able in the New World to enjoy the fruits of his own labor. The conception implies, consequently, an Old World, in which the ordinary man cannot become independent and prosperous, and, on the other hand, a New World in which economic opportunities are much more abundant and accessible. America has been peopled by Europeans primarily because they expected in that country to make more money more easily. To the European immigrant — that is, to the aliens who have been converted into Americans by the advantages of American life — the Promise of America has consisted largely in the opportunity which it offered of economic independence and prosperity. Whatever else the better future, of which Europeans anticipate the enjoyment in America, may contain, these converts will consider themselves cheated unless they are in a measure relieved of the curse of poverty.

This conception of American life and its Promise is as much alive today as it was in 1780. Its expression has no doubt been modified during four generations of democratic political independence, but the modification has consisted of an expansion and a development rather than of a transposition. The native American, like the alien immigrant, conceives the better future which awaits himself and other men in America as fundamentally a future in which economic prosperity will be still more abundant and still more accessible than it has yet been either here or abroad. No alteration or attenuation of this demand has been permitted. With all their professions of Christianity their national idea remains thoroughly worldly. They do not want either for themselves or for their descendants an indefinite future of poverty and deprivation in this world, redeemed by beatitude in the next. The Promise, which bulks so large in their patriotic outlook, is a promise of comfort and prosperity for an ever increasing majority of good Americans. At a later stage of their social development they may come to believe that they have ordered a larger supply of prosperity than the economic factory is capable of producing. Those who are already rich and comfortable, and who are keenly alive to the difficulty of distributing these benefits over a larger social area, may come to tolerate the idea that poverty and want are an essential part of the social order. But as yet this traditional European opinion has found few echoes in America, even among the comfortable and the rich. The general belief still is that Americans are not destined to renounce, but to enjoy.

Let it be immediately added, however, that this economic independence and prosperity has always been absolutely associated in the American mind with free political institutions. The "American Farmer" traced the good fortune of the European immigrant in America, not merely to the abundance of economic opportunity, but to the fact that a ruling class of abbots and lords had no prior claim to a large share of the products of the soil. . . .

Inevitably, however, this aspect of the American Promise has undergone certain important changes since the establishment of our national independence. When the colonists succeeded in emancipating themselves from political allegiance to Great Britain, they were confronted by the task of organizing a stable and efficient government without encroaching on the freedom, which was even at that time traditionally associated with American life. The task was by no means an easy one, and required for its performance the application of other political principles than that of freedom. The men who were responsible for this great work were not, perhaps, entirely candid in recognizing the profound modifications in their traditional ideas which their constructive political work had implied; but they were at all events fully aware of the great importance of their addition to the American idea. That idea, while not ceasing to be at bottom economic, became more than ever political and social in its meaning and contents. The Land of Freedom became in the course of time also the Land of Equality. The special American political system, the construction of which was predicted in the "Farmer's" assertion of the necessary novelty of American modes of thought and action, was made explicitly, if not uncompromisingly, democratic; and the success of this democratic political system was indissolubly associated in the American mind with the persistence of abundant and widely distributed economic prosperity. Our democratic institutions became in a sense the guarantee that prosperity would continue to be abundant and accessible. In case the majority of good Americans were not prosperous, there would be grave reasons for suspecting that our institutions were not doing their duty.

The more consciously democratic Americans became, however, the less they were satisfied with a conception of the Promised Land, which went no farther than a pervasive economic prosperity guaranteed by free institutions. The amelioration promised to aliens and to future Americans was to possess its moral and social aspects. The implication was, and still is, that by virtue of the more comfortable and less trammeled lives which Americans were enabled to lead, they would constitute a better society and would become in general a worthier set of men. The confidence which American institutions placed in the American citizen was considered equivalent to a greater faith in the excellence of human nature. In our favored land political liberty and economic opportunity were by a process of natural education inevitably making for individual and social amelioration. In Europe the people did not have a fair chance. Population increased more quickly than economic opportunities, and the opportunities which did exist were largely monopolized by privileged classes. Power was lodged in the hands of a few men, whose interest depended upon keeping the people in a condition of economic and political servitude; and in this way a divorce was created between individual interest and social stability and welfare. The interests of the privileged rulers demanded the perpetuation of unjust institutions. The interest of the people demanded a revolutionary upheaval. In the absence of such a revolution they had no sufficient inducement to seek their own material and moral improvement. The theory was proclaimed and accepted as a justification for this system of popular oppression that men were not to be trusted to take care of themselves — that they could be kept socially useful only by the severest measures of moral, religious, and political discipline. The theory of the American democracy and its practice was proclaimed to be the antithesis of this European theory and practice. The people were to be trusted rather than suspected and disciplined. They must be tied to their country by the strong bond of self-interest. Give them a fair chance, and the natural goodness of human nature would do the rest. Individual and public interest will, on the whole, coincide, provided no individuals are allowed to have special privileges. Thus the American system will be predestined to success by its own adequacy, and its success will constitute an enormous stride towards human amelioration. Just because our system is at bottom a thorough test of the ability of human nature to respond admirably to a fair chance, the issue of the experiment is bound to be of more than national importance. The American system stands for the highest hope of an excellent worldly life that mankind has yet ventured, — the hope that men can be improved without being fettered, that they can be saved without even vicariously being nailed to the cross.

Such are the claims advanced on behalf of the American system; and within certain limits this system has made good. Americans have been more than usually prosperous. They have been more than usually free. They have, on the whole, made their freedom and prosperity contribute to a higher level of individual and social excellence. Most assuredly the average Americanized American is neither a more intelligent, a wiser, nor a better man than the average European; but he is likely to be a more energetic and hopeful one. Out of a million well-established Americans, taken indiscriminately from all occupations and conditions, compared to a corresponding assortment of Europeans, a larger proportion of the former will be leading alert, active, and useful lives. Within a given social area there will be a smaller amount of social wreckage and a larger amount of wholesome and profitable achievement. The mass of the American people is, on the whole, more deeply stirred, more thoroughly awake, more assertive in their personal demands, and more confident of satisfying them. In a word, they are more alive, and they must be credited with the moral and social benefit attaching to a larger amount of vitality.

Furthermore, this greater individual vitality, although intimately connected with the superior agricultural and industrial opportunities of a new country, has not been due exclusively to such advantages. Undoubtedly the vast areas of cheap and fertile land which have been continuously available for settlement have contributed, not only to the abundance of American prosperity, but also to the formation of American character and institutions; and undoubtedly many of the economic and political evils which are now becoming offensively obtrusive are directly or indirectly derived from the gradual monopolization of certain important economic opportunities. Nevertheless, these opportunities could never have been converted so quickly into substantial benefits had it not been for our more democratic political and social forms. A privileged class does not secure itself in the enjoyment of its advantages merely by legal intrenchments. It depends quite as much upon disqualifying the "lower classes" from utilizing their opportunities by a species of social inhibition. The rail-splitter can be so easily encouraged to believe that rail-splitting is his vocation. The tragedy in the life of Mr. J. M. Barrie's "Admirable Crichton" was not due to any legal prohibition of his conversion in England, as on the tropic island, into a veritable chief, but that on English soil he did not in his own soul want any such elevation and distinction. His very loyalty to the forms and fabric of English life kept him fatuously content with the mean truckling and meaner domineering of his position of butler. On the other hand, the loyalty of an American to the American idea would tend to make him aggressive and self-confident. Our democratic prohibition of any but occasional social distinctions and our democratic dislike to any suggestion of authentic social inferiority have contributed as essentially to the fluid and elastic substance of American life as have its abundant and accessible economic opportunities. . . .

In the preceding section I have been seeking to render justice to the actual achievements of the American nation. A work of manifest individual and social value has been wrought; and this work, not only explains the expectant popular outlook towards the future, but it partially determines the character as distinguished from the continued fulfillment of the American national Promise. The better future, whatever else it may bring, must bring at any rate a continuation of the good things of the past. . . .

The fault in the vision of our national future possessed by the ordinary American does not consist in the expectation of some continuity of achievement. It consists rather in the expectation that the familiar benefits will continue to accumulate automatically. In his mind the ideal Promise is identified with the processes and conditions which hitherto have very much simplified its fulfillment, and he fails sufficiently to realize that the conditions and processes are one thing and the ideal Promise quite another. Moreover, these underlying social and economic conditions are themselves changing, in such wise that hereafter the ideal Promise, instead of being automatically fulfilled, may well be automatically stifled. For two generations and more the American people were, from the economic point of view, most happily situated. They were able, in a sense, to slide down hill into the valley of fulfillment. Economic conditions were such that, given a fair start, they could scarcely avoid reaching a desirable goal. But such is no longer the case. Economic conditions have been profoundly modified, and American political and social problems have been modified with them. The Promise of American life must depend less than it did upon the virgin wilderness and the Atlantic Ocean, for the virgin wilderness has disappeared, and the Atlantic Ocean has become merely a big channel. The same results can no longer be achieved by the same easy methods. Ugly obstacles have jumped into view, and ugly obstacles are peculiarly dangerous to a person who is sliding down hill. . . .

. . . A considerable proportion of the American people is beginning to exhibit economic and political, as well as personal, discontent. A generation ago the implication was that if a man remained poor and needy, his poverty was his own fault, because the American system was giving all its citizens a fair chance. Now, however, the discontented poor are beginning to charge their poverty to an unjust political and economic organization, and reforming agitators do not hesitate to support them in this contention. Manifestly a threatened obstacle has been raised against the anticipated realization of our national Promise. Unless the great majority of Americans not only have, but believe they have, a fair chance, the better American future will be dangerously compromised.

The conscious recognition of grave national abuses casts a deep shadow across the traditional American patriotic vision. The sincere and candid reformer can no longer consider the national Promise as destined to automatic fulfillment. The reformers themselves are, no doubt, far from believing that whatever peril there is cannot be successfully averted. They make a point of being as patriotically prophetic as the most "old-fashioned Democrat." They proclaim even more loudly their conviction of an indubitable and a beneficent national future. But they do not and cannot believe that this future will take care of itself. As reformers they are bound to assert that the national body requires for the time being a good deal of medical attendance, and many of them anticipate that even after the doctors have discontinued their daily visits the patient will still need the supervision of a sanitary specialist. He must be persuaded to behave so that he will not easily fall ill again, and so that his health will be permanently improved. Consequently, just in so far as reformers are reformers they are obliged to abandon the traditional American patriotic fatalism. The national Promise has been transformed into a closer equivalent of a national purpose, the fulfillment of which is a matter of conscious work.

The transformation of the old sense of a glorious national destiny into the sense of a serious national purpose will inevitably tend to make the popular realization of the Promise of American life both more explicit and more serious. As long as Americans believed they were able to fulfill a noble national Promise merely by virtue of maintaining intact a set of political institutions and by the vigorous individual pursuit of private ends, their allegiance to their national fulfillment remained more a matter of words than of deeds; but now that they are being aroused from their patriotic slumber, the effect is inevitably to disentangle the national idea and to give it more dignity. The redemption of the national Promise has become a cause for which the good American must fight, and the cause for which a man fights is a cause which he more than ever values. The American idea is no longer to be propagated merely by multiplying the children of the West and by granting ignorant aliens permission to vote. Like all sacred causes, it must be propagated by the Word and by that right arm of the Word, which is the Sword.

The more enlightened reformers are conscious of the additional dignity and value which the popularity of reform has bestowed upon the American idea, but they still fail to realize the deeper implications of their own programme. In abandoning the older conception of an automatic fulfillment of our national destiny, they have abandoned more of the traditional American point of view than they are aware. The traditional American optimistic fatalism was not of accidental origin, and it cannot be abandoned without involving in its fall some other important ingredients in the accepted American tradition. Not only was it dependent on economic conditions which prevailed until comparatively recent times, but it has been associated with certain erroneous but highly cherished political theories. It has been wrought into the fabric of our popular economic and political ideas to such an extent that its overthrow necessitates a partial revision of some of the most important articles in the traditional American creed.

The extent and the character of this revision may be inferred from a brief consideration of the effect upon the substance of our national Promise of an alteration in its proposed method of fulfillment. The substance of our national Promise has consisted, as we have seen, of an improving popular economic condition, guaranteed by democratic political institutions, and resulting in moral and social amelioration. These manifold benefits were to be obtained merely by liberating the enlightened self-interest of the American people. The beneficent result followed inevitably from the action of wholly selfish motives — provided, of course, the democratic political system of equal rights was maintained in its integrity. The fulfillment of the American Promise was considered inevitable because it was based upon a combination of self-interest and the natural goodness of human nature. On the other hand, if the fulfillment of our national Promise can no longer be considered inevitable, if it must be considered as equivalent to a conscious national purpose instead of an inexorable national destiny, the implication necessarily is that the trust reposed in individual self-interest has been in some measure betrayed. No preëstablished harmony can then exist between the free and abundant satisfaction of private needs and the accomplishment of a morally and socially desirable result. The Promise of American life is to be fulfilled — not merely by a maximum amount of economic freedom, but by a certain measure of discipline; not merely by the abundant satisfaction of individual desires, but by a large measure of individual subordination and self-denial. And this necessity of subordinating the satisfaction of individual desires to the fulfillment of a national purpose is attached particularly to the absorbing occupation of the American people, — the occupation, viz.: of accumulating wealth. The automatic fulfillment of the American national Promise is to be abandoned, if at all, precisely because the traditional American confidence in individual freedom has resulted in a morally and socially undesirable distribution of wealth. . . .

I am fully aware, as already intimated, that the forgoing interpretation of the Promise of American life will seem fantastic and obnoxious to the great majority of Americans, and I am far from claiming that any reasons as yet alleged afford a sufficient justification for such a radical transformation of the traditional national policy and democratic creed. All that can be claimed is that if a democratic ideal makes an express consideration of the social problem inevitable, it is of the first importance for Americans to realize this truth and to understand the reasons for it. Furthermore, the assumption is worth making, in case the traditional American system is breaking down, because a more highly socialized democracy is the only practical substitute on the part of convinced democrats for an excessively individualized democracy. Of course, it will be claimed that the traditional system is not breaking down, and again no absolute proof of the breakdown has been or can be alleged. Nevertheless, the serious nature of contemporary American political and economic symptoms at least pointedly suggests the existence of some radical disease, and when one assumes such to be the case, one cannot be accused of borrowing trouble. . . .

The Federal political organization has always tended to confuse to the American mind the relation between democracy and nationality. The nation as a legal body was, of course, created by the Constitution, which granted to the central government certain specific powers and responsibilities, and which almost to the same extent diminished the powers and the responsibilities of the separate states. Consequently, to the great majority of Americans, the process of increasing nationalization has a tendency to mean merely an increase in the functions of the central government. For the same reason the affirmation of a constructive relation between the national and the democratic principles is likely to be interpreted merely as an attempt on the grounds of an abstract theory to limit state government and to disparage states rights. Such an interpretation, however, would be essentially erroneous. It would be based upon the very idea against which I have been continually protesting — the idea that the American nation, instead of embodying a living formative political principle, is merely the political system created by the Federal Constitution; and it would end in the absurd conclusion that the only way in which the Promise of American democracy can be fulfilled would be by the abolition of American local political institutions.

The nationalizing of American political, economic, and social life means something more than Federal centralization and something very different therefrom. To nationalize a people has never meant merely to centralize their government. Little by little a thoroughly national political organization has come to mean in Europe an organization which combined effective authority with certain responsibilities to the people; but the national interest has been just as likely to demand de-centralization as it has to demand centralization. The Prussia of Frederick the Great, for instance, was over-centralized; and the restoration of the national vitality, at which the Prussian government aimed after the disasters of 1806, necessarily took the form of reinvigorating the local members of the national body. In this and many similar instances the national interest and welfare was the end, and a greater or smaller amount of centralized government merely the necessary machinery. The process of centralization is not, like the process of nationalization, an essentially formative and enlightening political transformation. When a people are being nationalized, their political, economic, and social organization or policy is being coördinated with their actual needs and their moral and political ideals. Governmental centralization is to be regarded as one of the many means which may or may not be taken in order to effect this purpose. Like every other special aspect of the national organization, it must be justified by its fruits. There is no presumption in its favor. Neither is there any general presumption against it. Whether a given function should or should not be exercised by the central government in a Federal system is from the point of view of political logic a matter of expediency — with the burden of proof resting on those who propose to alter any existing Constitutional arrangement.

It may be affirmed, consequently, without paradox, that among those branches of the American national organization which are greatly in need of nationalizing is the central government. Almost every member of the American political body has been at one time or another or in one way or another perverted to the service of special interests. The state governments and the municipal administrations have sinned more in this respect than the central government; but the central government itself has been a grave sinner. The Federal authorities are responsible for the prevailing policy in respect to military pensions, which is one of the most flagrant crimes ever perpetrated against the national interest. The Federal authorities, again, are responsible for the existing tariff schedules, which benefit a group of special interests at the expense of the national welfare. The Federal authorities, finally, are responsible for the Sherman Anti-Trust Law, whose existence on the statute books is a fatal bar to the treatment of the problem of corporate aggrandizement from the standpoint of genuinely national policy. These instances might be multiplied, but they suffice to show that the ideal of a constructive relation between the American national and democratic principles does not imply that any particular piece of legislation or policy is national because it is Federal. The Federal no less than the state governments has been the victim of special interests; and when a group of state or city officials effectively assert the public interest against the private interests, either of the machine or of the local corporations, they are acting just as palpably, if not just as comprehensively, for the national welfare, as if their work benefited the whole American people. The process of nationalization in its application to American political organization means that political power shall be distributed among the central, state, and municipal officials in such a manner that it can be efficiently and responsibly exerted in the interest of those affected by its action.

Be it added, however, in the same breath, that under existing conditions and simply as a matter of expediency, the national advance of the American democracy does demand an increasing amount of centralized action and responsibility. In what respect and for what purposes an increased Federal power and responsibility is desirable will be considered in a subsequent chapter. In this connection it is sufficient to insist that a more scrupulous attention to existing Federal responsibilities, and the increase of their number and scope, is the natural consequence of the increasing concentration of American industrial, political, and social life. American government demands more rather than less centralization merely and precisely because of the growing centralization of American activity. The state governments, either individually or by any practicable methods of coöperation, are not competent to deal effectively in the national interest and spirit with the grave problems created by the aggrandizement of corporate and individual wealth and the increasing classification of the American people. They have, no doubt, an essential part to play in the attempted solution of these problems; and there are certain aspects of the whole situation which the American nation, because of its Federal organization, can deal with much more effectually than can a rigidly centralized democracy like France. But the amount of responsibility in respect to fundamental national problems, which, in law almost as much as in practice, is left to the states, exceeds the responsibility which the state governments are capable of efficiently redeeming. They are attempting (or neglecting) a task which they cannot be expected to perform with any efficiency.

The fact that the states fail properly to perform certain essential functions such as maintaining order or administering justice, is no sufficient reason for depriving them thereof. Functions which should be bestowed upon the central government are not those which the states happen to perform badly. They are those which the states, even with the best will in the world, cannot be expected to perform satisfactorily; and among these functions the regulation of commerce, the organization of labor, and the increasing control over property in the public interest are assuredly to be included. The best friends of local government in this country are those who seek to have its activity confined within the limits of possible efficiency, because only in case its activity is so confined can the states continue to remain an essential part of a really efficient and well-coördinated national organization.

Proposals to increase the powers of the central government are, however, rarely treated on their merits. They are opposed by the majority of American politicians and newspapers as an unqualified evil. Any attempt to prove that the existing distribution of responsibility is necessarily fruitful of economic and political abuses, and that an increase of centralized power offers the only chance of eradicating these abuses is treated as irrelevent. It is not a question of the expediency of a specific proposal, because from the traditional point of view any change in the direction of increased centralization would be a violation of American democracy. Centralization is merely a necessary evil which has been carried as far as it should, and which cannot be carried any farther without undermining the foundations of the American system. Thus the familiar theory of many excellent American democrats is rather that of a contradictory than a constructive relation between the democratic and the national ideals. The process of nationalization is perverted by them into a matter merely of centralization, but the question of the fundamental relation between nationality and democracy is raised by their attitude, because the reasons they advance against increasingly centralized authority would, if they should continue to prevail, definitely and absolutely forbid a gradually improving coördination between American political organization and American national economic needs or moral and intellectual ideals. The conception of democracy out of which the supposed contradiction between the democratic and national ideals issues is the great enemy of the

American national advance, and is for that reason the great enemy of the real interests of democracy.

To be sure, any increase in centralized power and responsibility, expedient or inexpedient, is injurious to certain aspects of traditional American democracy. But the fault in that case lies with the democratic tradition; and the erroneous and misleading tradition must yield before the march of a constructive national democracy. . . .

Theodore Roosevelt
SOCIAL JUSTICE

❧*1910*❧ DESPITE Theodore Roosevelt's (1858-1919) reputation as a "trust-buster" (and it was well deserved, for it was his leadership that led to the revival of the moribund Sherman Anti-Trust Act), "T.R." was not opposed in principle to large corporations or even to monopolies of some kinds. Indeed, from quite early in his career he showed a continuing and growing interest in developing the power of the federal government to control the economic affairs of the nation. Although he made use of measures like the anti-trust law, he never had much real confidence in the ability of the economy to run itself under the benevolent supervision of a government that was no more than a policeman catching and punishing flagrant wrongdoers.

However, this essential commitment of Roosevelt was not entirely clear as late as 1909, when he finished his second term as President and headed to Africa to hunt lions. But upon his return in 1910, he found himself quickly caught up in the controversy within the party between the liberals and the Old Guard. Although he honestly tried to steer a middle course, events and the increasing conservative leanings of his successor, William Howard Taft (1857-1930) pushed him steadily toward the liberal side. And as he took an increasingly liberal position, he found himself arguing more and more forcibly for a strong federal government actively intervening in the economic and social affairs of the nation. It was in a speech to a group of Civil War veterans at Osawatomie, Kansas, on August 31, 1910, that he codified the new proposals he had come to advocate, and gave his philosophy the graphic title of "The New Nationalism."

The speech was a turning point both in Roosevelt's career and in the history of the nation. Many conservative Republicans were alarmed by some of Roosevelt's proposals and by the whole tone of his remarks. He in turn was driven eventually by their rejection of his position to form the Progressive party. The whole course of national politics was disrupted by this splitting of the Republican party into liberal and conservative branches.

THE NEW NATIONALISM

WE COME here to-day to commemorate one of the epoch-making events of the long struggle for the rights of man — the long struggle for the uplift of humanity. Our country — this great Republic — means nothing unless it means the triumph of a real democracy, the triumph of popular government, and, in the long run, of an economic system under which each man shall be guaranteed the opportunity to show the best that there is in him. That is why the history of America is now the central feature of the history of the world; for the world has set its face hopefully toward our democracy; and, O my fellow citizens, each one of you carries on your shoulders not only the burden of doing well for the sake of your own country, but the burden of doing well and of seeing that this nation does well for the sake of mankind.

There have been two great crises in our country's history: first, when it was formed, and then, again, when it was perpetuated; and, in the second of these great crises — in the time of stress and strain which culminated in the Civil War, on the outcome of which depended the justification of what had been done earlier, you men of the Grand Army, you men who fought through the Civil War, not only did you justify your generation, not only did you render life worth living for our generation, but you justified the wisdom of Washington and Washington's colleagues. If this Republic had been founded by them only to be split asunder into fragments when the strain came, then the judgment of the world would have been that Washington's work was not worth doing. . . .

I do not speak of this struggle of the past merely from the historic standpoint. Our interest is primarily in the application to-day of the lessons taught by the contest of half a century ago. It is of little use for us to pay lip-loyalty to the mighty men of the past unless we sincerely endeavor to apply to the problems of the present precisely the qualities which in other crises enabled the men of that day to meet those crises. It is half melancholy and half amusing to see the way in which well-meaning people gather to do honor to the men who, in company with John Brown, and under the lead of Abraham Lincoln, faced and solved the great problems of the nineteenth century, while, at the same time, these same good people nervously shrink from, or frantically denounce, those who are trying to meet the problems of the twentieth century in the spirit which was accountable for the successful solution of the problems of Lincoln's time.

Of that generation of men to whom we owe so much, the man to whom we owe most is, of course, Lincoln. Part of our debt to him is because he forecast our present struggle and saw the way out. He said:

"I hold that while man exists it is his duty to improve not only his own conditions, but to assist in ameliorating mankind."

And again:

"Labor is prior to, and independent of, capital. Capital is only the fruit of labor, and could never have existed if labor had not first existed. Labor is the superior of capital, and deserves much the higher consideration."

If that remark was original with me, I should be even more strongly denounced as a Communist agitator than I shall be anyhow. It is Lincoln's. I am only quoting it; and that is one side; that is the side the capitalist should hear. Now, let the working man hear his side.

"Capital has its rights, which are as worthy of protection as any other rights. . . . Nor should this lead to a war upon the owners of property. Property is the fruit of labor; . . . property is desirable; is a positive good in the world."

And then comes a thoroughly Lincolnlike sentence:

"Let not him who is houseless pull down the house of another, but let him work diligently and build one for himself, thus by example assuring that his own shall be safe from violence when built."

It seems to me that, in these words, Lincoln took substantially the attitude that we ought to take; he showed the proper sense of proportion in his relative estimates of capital and labor, of human rights and property rights. Above all, in this speech, as in many others, he taught a lesson in wise kindliness and charity; an indispensable lesson to us of to-day. But this wise kindliness and charity never weakened his arm or numbed his heart. We cannot afford weakly to blind ourselves to the actual conflict which faces us to-day. The issue is joined, and we must fight or fail.

In every wise struggle for human betterment one of the main objects, and often the only object, has been to achieve in large measure equality of opportunity. In the struggle for this great end, nations rise from barbarism to civilization, and through it people press forward from one stage of enlightenment to the next. One of the chief factors in progress is the destruction of special privilege. The essence of any struggle for healthy liberty has always been, and must always be, to take from some one man or class of men the right to enjoy power, or wealth, or position, or immunity, which has not been earned by service to his or their fellows. That is what you fought for in the Civil War, and that is what we strive for now.

At many stages in the advance of humanity, this conflict between the men who possess more than they have earned and the men who have earned more than they possess is the central condition of progress. In our day it appears as the struggle of freemen to gain and hold the right of self-government as against the special interests, who twist the methods of free government into machinery for defeating the popular will. At every stage, and under all circumstances, the essence of the struggle is to equalize opportunity, destroy privilege, and give to the life and citizenship of every individual the highest possible value both to himself and to the commonwealth. That is nothing new. All I ask in civil life is what you fought for in the Civil War. I ask that civil life be carried on according to the spirit in which the army was carried on. You never get perfect justice, but the effort in handling the army was to bring to the front the men who could do the job. Nobody grudged promotion to Grant, or Sherman, or Thomas, or Sheridan, because they earned it. The only complaint was when a man got promotion which he did not earn.

Practical equality of opportunity for all citizens, when we achieve it, will have two great results. First, every man will have a fair chance to make of himself all that in him lies; to reach the highest point to which his capacities, unassisted by special privilege of his own and unhampered by the special privilege of others, can carry him, and to get for himself and his family substantially what he has earned. Second, equality of opportunity means that the commonwealth will get from every citizen the highest service of which he is capable. No man who carries the burden of the special privileges of another can give to the commonwealth that service to which it is fairly entitled.

I stand for the square deal. But when I say that I am for the square deal, I mean not merely that I stand for fair play under the present rules of the game, but that I stand for having those rules changed so as to work for a more substantial equality of opportunity and of reward for equally good service. One word of warning, which, I think, is hardly necessary in Kansas. When I say I want a square deal for the poor man, I do not mean that I want a square deal for the man who remains poor because he has not got the energy to work for himself. If a man who has had a chance will not make good, then he has got to quit. And you men of the Grand Army, you want justice for the brave man who fought, and punishment for the coward who shirked his work. Is not that so?

Now, this means that our government, National and State, must be freed from the sinister influence or control of special interests. Exactly as the special interests of cotton and slavery threatened our political integrity before the Civil War, so now the great special business interests too often control and corrupt the men and methods of government for their own profit. We must drive the special interests out of politics. That is one of our tasks to-day. Every special interest is entitled to justice — full, fair, and complete — and, now, mind you, if there were any attempt by mob-violence to plunder and work harm to the special interest, whatever it may be, that I most dislike, and the wealthy man, whomsoever he may be, for whom I have the greatest contempt, I would fight for him, and you would if you were worth your salt. He should have justice. For every special interest is entitled to justice, but not one is entitled to a vote in Congress, to a voice on the bench, or to representation in any public office. The Constitution guarantees protection to property, and we must make that promise good. But it does not give the right of suffrage to any corporation.

The true friend of property, the true conservative, is he who insists that property shall be the servant and not the master of the commonwealth; who insists that the creature of man's making shall be the servant and not the master of the man who made it. The citizens of the United States must effectively control the mighty commercial forces which they have themselves called into being.

There can be no effective control of corporations while their political activity remains. To put an end to it will be neither a short nor an easy task, but it can be done.

We must have complete and effective publicity of corporate affairs, so that the people may know beyond peradventure whether the corporations obey the law and whether their management entitles them to the confidence of the public. It is necessary that laws should be passed to prohibit the use of corporate funds directly or indirectly for political purposes; it is still more necessary that such laws should be thoroughly enforced. Corporate expenditures for political purposes, and especially such expenditures by public-service corporations, have supplied one of the principal sources of corruption in our political affairs.

It has become entirely clear that we must have government supervision of the capitalization, not only of public-service corporations, including, particularly, railways, but of all corporations doing an interstate business. I do not wish to see the nation forced into the ownership of the railways if it can possibly be avoided, and the only alternative is thoroughgoing and effective regulation, which shall be based on a full knowledge of all the facts, including a physical valuation of property. This physical valuation is not needed, or, at least, is very rarely needed, for fixing rates; but it is needed as the basis of honest capitalization.

We have come to recognize that franchises should never be granted except for a limited time, and never without proper provision for compensation to the public. It is my personal belief that the same kind and degree of control and supervision which should be exercised over public-service corporations should be extended also to combinations which control necessaries of life, such as meat, oil, and coal, or which deal in them on an important scale. I have no doubt that the ordinary man who has control of them is much like ourselves. I have no doubt he would like to do well, but I want to have enough supervision to help him realize that desire to do well.

I believe that the officers, and, especially, the directors, of corporations should be held personally responsible when any corporation breaks the law.

Combinations in industry are the result of an imperative economic law which cannot be repealed by political legislation. The effort at prohibiting all combination has substantially failed. The way out lies, not in attempting to prevent such combinations, but in completely controlling them in the interest of the public welfare. For that purpose the Federal Bureau of Corporations is an agency of first importance. Its powers, and, therefore, its efficiency, as well as that of the Interstate Commerce Commission, should be largely increased. We have a right to expect from the Bureau of Corporations and from the Interstate Commerce Commission a very high grade of public service. We should be as sure of the proper conduct of the interstate railways and the proper management of interstate business as we are now sure of the conduct and management of the national banks, and we should have as effective supervision in one case as in the other. The Hepburn Act, and the amendment to the act in the shape in which it finally passed Congress at the last session, represent a long step in advance, and we must go yet further.

There is a wide-spread belief among our people that, under the methods of making tariffs which have hitherto obtained, the special interests are too influential. Probably this is true of both the big special interests and the little special interests. These methods have put a premium on selfishness, and, naturally, the selfish big interests have gotten more than their smaller, though equally selfish, brothers. The duty of Congress is to provide a method by which the interest of the whole people shall be all that receives consideration. To this end there must be an expert tariff commission, wholly removed from the possibility of political pressure or of improper business influence. Such a commission can find the real difference between cost of production, which is mainly the difference of labor cost here and abroad. As fast as its recommendations are made, I believe in revising one schedule at a time. A general revision of the tariff almost inevitably leads to log-rolling and the subordination of the general public interest to local and special interests.

The absence of effective State, and, especially, national, restraint upon unfair money-getting has tended to create a small class of enormously wealthy and economically powerful men, whose chief object is to hold and increase their power. The prime need is to change the conditions which enable these men to accumulate power which it is not for the general welfare that they should hold or exercise. We grudge no man a fortune which represents his own power and sagacity, when exercised with entire regard to the welfare of his fellows. Again, comrades over there, take the lesson from your own experience. Not only did you not grudge, but you gloried in the promotion of the great generals who gained their promotion by leading the army to victory. So it is with us. We grudge no man a fortune in civil life if it is honorably obtained and well used. It is not even enough that it should have been gained without doing damage to the community. We should permit it to be gained only so long as the gaining represents benefit to the community. This, I know, implies a policy of a far more active governmental interference with social and economic conditions in this country than we have yet had, but I think we have got to face the fact that such an increase in governmental control is now necessary.

No man should receive a dollar unless that dollar has been fairly earned. Every dollar received should represent a dollar's worth of service rendered — not gambling in stocks, but service rendered. The really big fortune, the swollen fortune, by the mere fact of its size acquires qualities which differentiate it in kind as well as in degree from what is possessed by men of relatively small means. Therefore, I believe in a graduated income tax on big fortunes, and in another tax which is far more easily collected and far more effective — a graduated inheritance tax on big fortunes, properly safeguarded against evasion and increasing rapidly in amount with the size of the estate. . . .

. . . Conservation means development as much as it does protection. I recognize the right and duty of this generation to develop and use the natural resources of our land; but I do not recognize the right to waste them, or to rob, by wasteful use, the generations that come after us. I ask nothing of the nation except that it so behave as each farmer here behaves with reference to his own children. That farmer is a poor creature who skins the land and leaves it worthless to his children. The farmer is a good farmer who, having enabled the land to support himself and to provide for the education of his children, leaves it to them a little better than he found it himself. I believe the same thing of a nation.

Moreover, I believe that the natural resources must be used for the benefit of all our people, and not monopolized for the benefit of the few, and here again is another case in which I am accused of taking a revolutionary attitude. People forget now that one hundred years ago there were public men of good character who advocated the nation selling its public lands in great quantities, so that the nation could get the most money out of it, and giving to the men who could cultivate it for their own uses. We took the proper democratic ground that the land should be granted in small sections to the men who were actually to till it and live on it. Now, with the water-power, with the forests, with the mines, we are brought face to face with the fact that there are many people who will go with us in conserving the resources only if they are to be allowed to exploit them for their benefit. That is one of the fundamental reasons why the special interests should be driven out of politics. Of all the questions which can come before this nation, short of the actual preservation of its existence in a great war, there is none which compares in importance with the great central task of leaving this land even a better land for our descendants than it is for us, and training them into a better race to inhabit the land and pass it on. Conservation is a great moral issue, for it involves the patriotic duty of insuring the safety and continuance of the nation. Let me add that the health and vitality of our people are at least as well worth conserving as their forests, waters, lands, and minerals, and in this great work the national government must bear a most important part.

I have spoken elsewhere also of the great task which lies before the farmers of the country to get for themselves and their wives and children not only the benefits of better farming, but also those of better business methods and better conditions of life on the farm. The burden of this great task will fall, as it should, mainly upon the great organizations of the farmers themselves. I am glad it will, for I believe they are all well able to handle it. In particular, there are strong reasons why the Departments of Agriculture of the various States, the United States Department of Agriculture, and the agricultural colleges and experiment stations should extend their work to cover all phases of farm life, instead of limiting themselves, as they have far too often limited themselves in the past, solely to the question of the production of crops. And now a special word to the farmer. I want to see him make the farm as fine a farm as it can be made; and let him remember to see that the improvement goes on indoors as well as out; let him remember that the farmer's wife should have her share of thought and attention just as much as the farmer himself.

Nothing is more true than that excess of every kind is followed by reaction; a fact which should be pondered by reformer and reactionary alike. We are face to face with new conceptions of the relations of property to human welfare, chiefly because certain advocates of the rights of property as against the rights of men have been pushing their claims too far. The man who wrongly holds that every human right is secondary to his profit must now give way to the advocate of human welfare, who rightly maintains that every man holds his property subject to the general right of the community to regulate its use to whatever degree the public welfare may require it.

But I think we may go still further. The right to regulate the use of wealth in the public interest is universally admitted. Let us admit also the right to regulate the terms and conditions of labor, which is the chief element of wealth, directly in the interest of the common good. The fundamental thing to do for every man is to give him a chance to reach a place in which he will make the greatest possible contribution to the public welfare. Understand what I say there. Give him a chance, not push him up if he will not be pushed. Help any man who stumbles; if he lies down, it is a poor job to try to carry him; but if he is a worthy man, try your best to see that he gets a chance to show the worth that is in him. No man can be a good citizen unless he has a wage more than sufficient to cover the bare cost of living, and hours of labor short enough so that after his day's work is done he will have time and energy to bear his share in the management of the community, to help in carrying the general load. We keep countless men from being good citizens by the conditions of life with which we surround them. We need comprehensive workmen's compensation acts, both State and national laws to regulate child labor and work for women, and, especially, we need in our common schools not merely education in book-learning, but also practical training for daily life and work. We need to enforce better sanitary conditions for our workers and to extend the use of safety appliances for our workers in industry and commerce, both within and between the States. Also, friends, in the interest of the working man himself we need to set our faces like flint against mob-violence just as against corporate greed; against violence and injustice and lawlessness by wage-workers just as much as against lawless cunning and greed and selfish arrogance of employers. If I could ask but one thing of my fellow countrymen, my request would be that, whenever they go in for reform, they remember the two sides, and that they always exact justice from one side as much as from the other. . . . The State must be made efficient for the work which concerns only the people of the State; and the nation for that which concerns all the people. There must remain no neutral ground to serve as a refuge for lawbreakers, and especially for lawbreakers of great wealth, who can hire the vulpine legal cunning which will teach them how to avoid both jurisdictions. It is misfortune when the national legislature fails to do its duty in providing a national remedy, so that the only national activity is the purely negative activity of the judiciary in forbidding the State to exercise power in the premises.

I do not ask for overcentralization; but I do ask that we work in a spirit of broad and far-reaching nationalism when we work for what concerns our people as a whole. We are all Americans. Our common interests are as broad as the continent. I speak to you here in Kansas exactly as I would speak in New York or Georgia, for the most vital problems are those which affect us all alike. The National Government belongs to the whole American people, and where the whole American people are interested, that interest can be guarded effectively only by the National Government. The betterment which we seek must be accomplished, I believe, mainly through the National Government.

The American people are right in demanding that New Nationalism, without which we cannot hope to deal with new problems. The New Nationalism puts the national need before sectional or personal advantage. It is impatient of the utter confusion that results from local legislatures attempting to treat national issues as local issues. It is still more impatient of the importance which springs from overdivision of governmental powers, the impotence which makes it possible for local selfishness or for legal cunning, hired by wealthy special interests, to bring national activities to a deadlock. This New Nationalism regards the executive power as the steward of the public welfare. It demands of the judiciary that it shall be interested primarily in human welfare rather than in property, just as it demands that the representative body shall represent all the people rather than any one class or section of the people.

I believe in shaping the ends of government to protect property as well as human welfare. Normally, and in the long run, the ends are the same; but whenever the alternative must be faced, I am for men and not for property, as you were in the Civil War. I am far from underestimating the importance of dividends; but I rank dividends below human character. Again, I do not have any sympathy with the reformer who says he does not care for dividends. Of course, economic welfare is necessary, for a man must pull his own weight and be able to support his family. I know well that the reformers must not bring upon the people economic ruin, or the reforms themselves will go down in the ruin. But we must be ready to face temporary disaster, whether or not brought on by those who will war against us to the knife. Those who oppose all reform will do well to remember that ruin in its worst form is inevitable if our national life brings us nothing better than swollen fortunes for the few and the triumph in both politics and business of a sordid and selfish materialism.

If our political institutions were perfect, they would absolutely prevent the political domination of money in any part of our affairs. We need to make our political representatives more quickly and sensitively responsive to the people whose servants they are. More direct action by the people in their own affairs under proper safeguards is vitally necessary. The direct primary is a step in this direction, if it is associated with a corrupt-practices act effective to prevent the advantage of the man willing recklessly and unscrupulously to spend money over his more honest competitor. It is particularly important that all moneys received or expended for campaign purposes should be publicly accounted for, not only after election, but before election as well. Political action must be made simpler, easier, and freer from confusion for every citizen. I believe that the prompt removal of unfaithful or incompetent public servants should be made easy and sure in whatever way experience shall show to be most expedient in any given class of cases.

One of the fundamental necessities in a representative government such as ours is to make certain that the men to whom the people delegate their power shall serve the people by whom they are elected, and not the special interests. I believe that every national officer, elected or appointed, should be forbidden to perform any service or receive any compensation, directly or indirectly, from interstate corporations; and a similar provision could not fail to be useful within the States.

The object of government is the welfare of the people. The material progress and prosperity of a nation are desirable chiefly so far as they lead to the moral and material welfare of all good citizens. Just in proportion as the average man and woman are honest, capable of sound judgment and high ideals, active in public affairs — but, first of all, sound in their home life, and the father and mother of healthy children whom they bring up well — just so far, and no farther, we may count our civilization a success. We must have — I believe we have already — a genuine and permanent moral awakening, without which no wisdom of legislation or administration really means anything; and, on the other hand, we must try to secure the social and economic legislation without which any improvement due to purely moral agitation is necessarily evanescent. . . . No matter how honest and decent we are in our private lives, if we do not have the right kind of law and the right kind of administration of the law, we cannot go forward as a nation. That is imperative; but it must be an addition to, and not a substitution for, the qualities that make us good citizens. In the last analysis, the most important elements in any man's career must be the sum of those qualities which, in the aggregate, we speak of as character. If he has not got it, then no law that the wit of man can devise, no administration of the law by the boldest and strongest executive, will avail to help him. We must have the right kind of character — character that makes a man, first of all, a good man in the home, a good father, a good husband — that makes a man a good neighbor. You must have that, and, then, in addition, you must have the kind of law and the kind of administration of the law which will give to those qualities in the private citizen the best possible chance for development. The prime problem of our nation is to get the right type of good citizenship, and, to get it, we must have progress, and our public men must be genuinely progressive.

Woodrow Wilson
BACK TO LIBERTY

❧*1913*❧ WHILE the logic of Herbert Croly's *Promise of American Life* was becoming almost daily more evident in the Progressive Era, millions of forward-looking Americans still hesitated to surrender the old, individualistic, self-reliant standards of an earlier and simpler time. These millions were ready enough to admit that society was plagued by evils and eager to see something done to correct this state of affairs. But they hoped that reform could be accomplished without abandoning traditional freedoms and without submitting to tight controls by a centralized bureaucracy. The "New Freedom" of Governor Woodrow Wilson of New Jersey perfectly suited the feelings of such people, and their support had much to do with his election to the Presidency in 1912.

In his eloquent campaign speeches, Wilson (1856-1924) hammered away at the theme that the times were out of joint and that the government must step in to put things straight. This was in line wih Croly's philosophy. But Wilson went on to argue that once the government had rooted out the evils the old laissez-faire, free-enterprise system could function again. Thus the "new" freedom would be established. The growth of giant corporations, for example, had destroyed the "old" freedom of individuals to operate small businesses profitably. But once strict anti-trust legislation had destroyed the giants, small businessmen would again be able to operate unfettered by government controls. As Croly himself described Wilson's philosophy, the New Freedom argued "that if the system of letting things alone was properly regulated and its abuses eliminated, a permanent peace would be restored to the . . . nation."

Immediately after Wilson's election, William Bayard Hale (1869-1924), a journalist who had written his official campaign biography, put together a compilation based on Wilson's speeches. This was published in 1913 as *The New Freedom*. The volume had a wide sale and a still wider influence, for it brought together in convenient form the ideas Wilson had developed piecemeal during the campaign. It is fair to say that it became the almanac and almost the Bible of the first Wilson administration.

THE NEW FREEDOM

THERE is one great basic fact which underlies all the questions that are discussed on the political platform at the present moment. That singular fact is that nothing is done in this country as it was done twenty years ago.

We are in the presence of a new organization of society. Our life has broken away from the past. The life of America is not the life that it was twenty years ago; it is not the life that it was ten years ago. We have changed our economic conditions, absolutely, from top to bottom; and, with our economic society, the organization of our life. The old political formulas do not fit the present problems; they read now like documents taken out of a forgotten age. The older cries sound as if they belonged to a past age which men have almost forgotten. Things which used to be put into the party platforms of ten years ago would sound antiquated if put into a platform now. We are facing the necessity of fitting a new social organization, as we did once fit the old organization, to the happiness and prosperity of the great body of citizens; for we are conscious that the new order of society has not been made to fit and provide the convenience or prosperity of the average man. The life of the nation has grown infinitely varied. It does not centre now upon questions of governmental structure or of the distribution of governmental powers. It centres upon questions of the very structure and operation of society itself, of which government is only the instrument. Our development has run so fast and so far along the lines sketched in the earlier day of constitutional definition, has so crossed and interlaced those lines, has piled upon them such novel structures of trust and combination, has elaborated within them a life so manifold, so full of forces which transcend the boundaries of the country itself and fill the eyes of the world, that a new nation seems to have been created which the old formulas do not fit or afford a vital interpretation of.

We have come upon a very different age from any that preceded us. We have come upon an age when we do not do business in the way in which we used to do business, — when we do not carry on any of the operations of manufacture, sale, transportation, or communication as men used to carry them on. There is a sense in which in our day the individual has been submerged. In most parts of our country men work, not for themselves, not as partners in the old way in which they used to work, but generally as employees, — in a higher or lower grade, — of great corporations. There was a time when corporations played a very minor part in our business affairs, but now they play the chief part, and most men are the servants of corporations.

You know what happens when you are the servant of a corporation. You have in no instance access to the men who are really determining the policy of the corporation. If the corporation is doing the things that it ought not to do, you really have no voice in the matter and must obey the orders, and you have oftentimes with deep mortification to co-operate in the doing of things which you know are against the public interest. Your individuality is swallowed up in the individuality and purpose of a great organization.

It is true that, while most men are thus submerged in the corporation, a few, a very few, are exalted to a power which as individuals they could never have wielded. Through the great organizations of which they are the heads, a few are enabled to play a part unprecedented by anything in history in the control of the business operations of the country and in the determination of the happiness of great numbers of people.

Yesterday, and ever since history began, men were related to one another as individuals. To be sure there were the family, the Church, and the State, institutions which associated men in certain wide circles of relationship. But in the ordinary concerns of life, in the ordinary work, in the daily round, men dealt freely and directly with one another. To-day, the everyday relationships of men are largely with great impersonal concerns, with organizations, not with other individual men.

Now this is nothing short of a new social age, a new era of human relationships, a new stage-setting for the drama of life.

In this new age we find, for instance, that our laws with regard to the relations of employer and employee are in many respects wholly antiquated and impossible. They were framed for another age, which nobody now living remembers, which is, indeed, so remote from our life that it would be difficult for many of us to understand it if it were described to us. The employer is now generally a corporation or a huge company of some kind; the employee is one of hundreds or of thousands brought together, not by individual masters whom they know and with whom they have personal relations, but by agents of one sort or another. Workingmen are marshaled in great numbers for the performance of a multitude of particular tasks under a common discipline. They generally use dangerous and powerful machinery, over whose repair and renewal they have no control. New rules must be devised with regard to their obligations and their rights, their obligations to their employers and their responsibilities to one another. Rules must be devised for their protection, for their compensation when injured, for their support when disabled.

There is something very new and very big and very complex about these new relations of capital and labor. A new economic society has sprung up, and we must effect a new set of adjustments. We must not pit power against weakness. The employer is generally, in our day, as I have said, not an individual, but a powerful group; and yet the workingman when dealing with his employer is still, under our existing law, an individual.

Why is it that we have a labor question at all? It is for the simple and very sufficient reason that the laboring man and the employer are not intimate associates now as they used to be in time past. Most of our laws were formed in the age when employer and employees knew each other, knew each other's characters, were associates with each other, dealt with each other as man with man. That is no longer the case. You not only do not come into personal contact with the men who have the supreme command in those corporations, but it would be out of the question for you to do it. Our modern corporations employ thousands, and in some instances hundreds of thousands, of men. The only persons whom you see or deal with are local superintendents or local representatives of a vast organization, which is not like anything that the workingmen of the time in which our laws were framed knew anything about. A little group of workingmen, seeing their employer every day, dealing with him in a personal way, is one thing, and the modern body of labor engaged as employees of the huge enterprises that spread all over the country, dealing with men of whom they can form no personal conception, is another thing. A very different thing. You never saw a corporation, any more than you ever saw a government. Many a workingman to-day never saw the body of men who are conducting the industry in which he is employed. And they never saw him. What they know about him is written in ledgers and books and letters, in the correspondence of the office, in the reports of the superintendents. He is a long way off from them.

So what we have to discuss is, not wrongs which individuals intentionally do, — I do not believe there are a great many of those, — but the wrongs of a system. I want to record my protest against any discussion of this matter which would seem to indicate that there are bodies of our fellow-citizens who are trying to grind us down and do us injustice. There are some men of that sort. I don't know how they sleep o' nights, but there are men of that kind. Thank God, they are not numerous. The truth is, we are all caught in a great economic system which is heartless. The modern corporation is not engaged in business as an individual. When we deal with it, we deal with an impersonal element, an immaterial piece of society. A modern corporation is a means of co-operation in the conduct of an enterprise which is so big that no one man can conduct it, and which the resources of no one man are sufficient to finance. A company is formed; that company puts out a prospectus; the promoters expect to raise a certain fund as capital stock. Well, how are they going to raise it? They are going to raise it from the public in general, some of whom will buy their stock. The moment that begins, there is formed — what? A joint stock corporation. Men begin to pool their earnings, little piles, big piles. A certain number of men are elected by the stockholders to be directors, and these directors elect a president. This president is the head of the undertaking, and the directors are its managers.

Now, do the workingmen employed by that stock corporation deal with that president and those directors? Not at all. Does the public deal with that president and that board of directors? It does not. Can anybody bring them to account? It is next to impossible to do so. If you undertake it you will find it a game of hide and seek, with the objects of your search taking refuge now behind the tree of their individual personality, now behind that of their corporate irresponsibility.

And do our laws take note of this curious state of things? Do they even attempt to distinguish between a man's act as a corporation director and as an individual? They do not. Our laws still deal with us on the basis of the old system. The law is still living in the dead past which we have left behind. This is evident, for instance, with regard to the matter of employers' liability for workingmen's injuries. Suppose that a superintendent wants a workman to use a certain piece of machinery which it is not safe for him to use, and that the workman is injured by that piece of machinery. Some of our courts have held that the superintendent is a fellow-servant, or, as the law states it, a fellow-employee, and that, therefore, the man cannot recover damages for his injury. The superintendent who probably engaged the man is not his employer. Who is his employer? And whose negligence could conceivably come in there? The board of directors did not tell the employee to use that piece of machinery; and the president of the corporation did not tell him to use that piece of machinery. And so forth. Don't you see by that theory that a man never can get redress for negligence on the part of the employer? When I hear judges reason upon the analogy of the relationships that used to exist between workmen and their employers a generation ago, I wonder if they have not opened their eyes to the modern world. You know, we have a right to expect that judges will have their eyes open, even though the law which they administer hasn't awakened.

Yet that is but a single small detail illustrative of the difficulties we are in because we have not adjusted the law to the facts of the new order.

Since I entered politics, I have chiefly had men's views confided to me privately. Some of the biggest men in the United States, in the field of commerce and manufacture, are afraid of somebody, are afraid of something. They know that there is a power somewhere so organized, so subtle, so watchful, so interlocked, so complete, so pervasive, that they had better not speak above their breath when they speak in condemnation of it.

They know that America is not a place of which it can be said, as it used to be, that a man may choose his own calling and pursue it just as far as his abilities enable him to pursue it; because to-day, if he enters certain fields there are organizations which will use means against him that will prevent his building up a business which they do not want to have built up; organizations that will see to it that the ground is cut from under him and the markets shut against him. For if he begins to sell to certain retail dealers, to any retail dealers, the monopoly will refuse to sell to those dealers, and those dealers, afraid, will not buy the new man's wares.

And this is the country which has lifted to the admiration of the world its ideals of absolutely free opportunity, where no man is supposed to be under any limitation except the limitations of his character and of his mind; where there is supposed to be no distinction of class, no distinction of blood, no distinction of social status, but where men win or lose on their merits.

I lay it very close to my own conscience as a public man whether we can any longer stand at our doors and welcome all newcomers upon those terms. American industry is not free, as once it was free; American enterprise is not free; the man with only a little capital is finding it harder to get into the field, more and more impossible to compete with the big fellow. Why? Because the laws of this country do not prevent the strong from crushing the weak. That is the reason, and because the strong have crushed the weak the strong dominate the industry and the economic life of this country. No man can deny that the lines of endeavor have more and more narrowed and stiffened; no man who knows anything about the development of industry in this country can have failed to observe that the larger kinds of credit are more and more difficult to obtain, unless you obtain them upon the terms of uniting your efforts with those who already control the industries of the country; and nobody can fail to observe that any man who tries to set himself up in competition with any process of manufacture which has been taken under the control of large combinations of capital will presently find himself either squeezed out or obliged to sell and allow himself to be absorbed.

There is a great deal that needs reconstruction in the United States. I should like to take a census of the business men, — I mean the rank and file of the business men, — as to whether they think that business conditions in this country, or rather whether the organization of business in this country, is satisfactory or not. I know what they would say if they dared. If they could vote secretly they would vote overwhelmingly that the present organization of business was meant for the big fellows and was not meant for the little fellows; that it was meant for those who are at the top and was meant to exclude those who are at the bottom; that it was meant to shut out beginners, to prevent new entries in the race, to prevent the building up of competitive enterprises that would interfere with the monopolies which the great trusts have built up.

What this country needs above everything else is a body of laws which will look after the men who are on the make rather than the men who are already made. Because the men who are already made are not going to live indefinitely, and they are not always kind enough to leave sons as able and as honest as they are.

The originative part of America, the part of America that makes new enterprises, the part into which the ambitious and gifted workingman makes his way up, the class that saves, that plans, that organizes, that presently spreads its enterprises until they have a national scope and character, — that middle class is being more and more squeezed out by the processes which we have been taught to call processes of prosperity. Its members are sharing prosperity, no doubt; but what alarms me is that they are not *originating* prosperity. No country can afford to have its prosperity originated by a small controlling class. The treasury of America does not lie in the brains of the small body of men now in control of the great enterprises that have been concentrated under the direction of a very small number of persons. The treasury of America lies in those ambitions, those energies, that cannot be restricted to a special favored class. It depends upon the inventions of unknown men, upon the originations of unknown men, upon the ambitions of unknown men. Every country is renewed out of the ranks of the unknown, not out of the ranks of those already famous and powerful and in control.

There has come over the land that un-American set of conditions which enables a small number of men who control the government to get favors from the government; by those favors to exclude their fellows from equal business opportunity; by those favors to extend a network of control that will presently dominate every industry in the country, and so make men forget the ancient time when America lay in every hamlet, when America was to be seen in every fair valley, when America displayed her great forces on the broad prairies, ran her fine fires of enterprise up over the mountainsides and down into the bowels of the earth, and eager men were everywhere captains of industry, not employees; not looking to a distant city to find out what they might do, but looking about among their neighbors, finding credit according to their character, not according to their connections, finding credit in proportion to what was known to be in them and behind them, not in proportion to the securities they held that were approved where they were not known. In order to start an enterprise now, you have to be authenticated, in a perfectly impersonal way, not according to yourself, but according to what you own that somebody else approves of your owning. You cannot begin such an enterprise as those that have made America until you are so authenticated, until you have succeeded in obtaining the good-will of large allied capitalists. Is that freedom? That is dependence, not freedom.

We used to think in the old-fashioned days when life was very simple that all that government had to do was to put on a policeman's uniform, and say, "Now don't anybody hurt anybody else." We used to say that the ideal of government was for every man to be left alone and not interfered with, except when he interfered with somebody else; and that best government was the government that did as little governing as possible. That was the idea that obtained in Jefferson's time. But we are coming now to realize that life is so complicated that we are not dealing with the old conditions, and that the law has to step in and create new conditions under which we may live, the conditions which will make it tolerable for us to live. . . .

. . . We are in a new world, struggling under old laws. As we go inspecting our lives to-day, surveying this new scene of centralized and complex society, we shall find many more things out of joint.

One of the most alarming phenomena of the time, — or rather it would be alarming if the nation had not awakened to it and shown its determination to control it, — one of the most significant signs of the new social era is the degree to which government has become associated with business. I speak, for the moment, of the control over the government exercised by Big Business. Behind the whole subject, of course, is the truth that, in the new order, government and business must be associated closely. But that association is at present of a nature absolutely intolerable; the precedence is wrong, the association is upside down. Our government has been for the past few years under the control of heads of great allied corporations with special interests. It has not controlled these interests and assigned them a proper place in the whole system of business; it has submitted itself to their control. As a result, there have grown up vicious systems and schemes of governmental favoritism (the most obvious being the extravagant tariff), far-reaching in effect upon the whole fabric of life, touching to his injury every inhabitant of the land, laying unfair and impossible handicaps upon competitors, imposing taxes in every direction, stifling everywhere the free spirit of American enterprise.

Now this has come about naturally; as we go on we shall see how very naturally. It is no use denouncing anybody, or anything, except human nature. Nevertheless, it is an intolerable thing that the government of the republic should have got so far out of the hands of the people; should have been captured by interests which are special and not general. In the train of this capture follow the troops of scandals, wrongs, indecencies, with which our politics swarm.

There are cities in America of whose government we are ashamed. There are cities everywhere, in every part of the land, in which we feel that, not the interests of the public, but the interests of special privileges, of selfish men, are served; where contracts take precedence over public interest. Not only in big cities is this the case. Have you not noticed the growth of socialistic sentiment in the smaller towns? Not many months ago I stopped at a little town in Nebraska, and while my train lingered I met on the platform a very engaging young fellow dressed in overalls who introduced himself to me as the mayor of the town, and added that he was a Socialist. I said, "What does that mean? Does that mean that this town is socialistic?" "No, sir," he said; "I have not deceived myself; the vote by which I was elected was about 20 per cent socialistic and 80 per cent protest." It was protest against the treachery to the people of those who led both the other parties of that town.

All over the Union people are coming to feel that they have no control over the course of affairs. I live in one of the greatest States in the union, which was at one time in slavery. Until two years ago we had witnessed with increasing concern the growth in New Jersey of a spirit of almost cynical despair. Men said: "We vote; we are offered the platform we want; we elect the men who stand on that platform, and we get absolutely nothing." So they began to ask: "What is the use of voting? We know that the machines of both parties are subsidized by the same persons, and therefore it is useless to turn in either direction."

This is not confined to some of the state governments and those of some of the towns and cities. We know that something intervenes between the people of the United States and the control of their own affairs at

Washington. It is not the people who have been ruling there of late.

Why are we in the presence, why are we at the threshold, of a revolution? Because we are profoundly disturbed by the influences which we see reigning in the determination of our public life and our public policy. There was a time when America was blithe with self-confidence. She boasted that she, and she alone, knew the processes of popular government; but now she sees her sky overcast; she sees that there are at work forces which she did not dream of in her hopeful youth.

Don't you know that some man with eloquent tongue, without conscience, who did not care for the nation, could put this whole country into a flame? Don't you know that this country from one end to the other believes that something is wrong? What an opportunity it would be for some man without conscience to spring up and say: "This is the way. Follow me!" — and lead in paths of destruction!

The old order changeth — changeth under our very eyes, not quietly and equably, but swiftly and with the noise and heat and tumult of reconstruction.

I suppose that all struggle for law has been conscious, that very little of it has been blind or merely instinctive. It is the fashion to say, as if with superior knowledge of affairs and of human weakness, that every age has been an age of transition, and that no age is more full of change than another; yet in very few ages of the world can the struggle for change have been so widespread, so deliberate, or upon so great a scale as in this in which we are taking part.

The transition we are witnessing is no equable transition of growth and normal alteration; no silent, unconscious unfolding of one age into another, its natural heir and successor. Society is looking itself over, in our day, from top to bottom; is making fresh and critical analysis of its very elements; is questioning its oldest practices as freely as its newest, scrutinizing every arrangement and motive of its life; and it stands ready to attempt nothing less than a radical reconstruction, which only frank and honest counsels and the forces of generous co-operation can hold back from becoming a revolution. We are in a temper to reconstruct economic society, as we were once in a temper to reconstruct political society, and political society may itself undergo a radical modification in the process. I doubt if any age was ever more conscious of its task or more unanimously desirous of radical and extended changes in its economic and political practice.

We stand in the presence of a revolution, — not a bloody revolution; America is not given to the spilling of blood, — but a silent revolution, whereby America will insist upon recovering in practice those ideals which she has always professed, upon securing a government devoted to the general interest and not to special interests.

We are upon the eve of a great reconstruction. It calls for creative statesmanship as no age has done since that great age in which we set up the government under which we live, that government which was the admiration of the world until it suffered wrongs to grow up under it which have made many of our own compatriots question the freedom of our institutions and preach revolution against them. I do not fear revolution. I have unshaken faith in the power of America to keep its self-possession. Revolution will come in peaceful guise, as it came when we put aside the crude government of the Confederation and created the great Federal Union which governs individuals, not States, and which has been these hundred and thirty years our vehicle of progress. Some radical changes we must make in our law and practice. Some reconstructions we must push forward, which a new age and new circumstances impose upon us. But we can do it all in calm and sober fashion, like statesmen and patriots.

I do not speak of these things in apprehension, because all is open and above-board. This is not a day in which great forces rally in secret. The whole stupendous program must be publicly planned and canvassed. Good temper, the wisdom that comes of sober counsel, the energy of thoughtful and unselfish men, the habit of co-operation and of compromise which has been bred in us by long years of free government, in which reason rather than passion has been made to prevail by the sheer virtue of candid and universal debate, will enable us to win through to still another great age without violence.

Louis D. Brandeis

THE MONEY TRUST

❧*1913*❧ THE growing concern in early twentieth-century America about the ever-increasing concentration of wealth and economic power reached a climax in the election of 1912 with a sweeping victory for the forces of protest and reform. Three candidates split the liberal vote, Wilson, Roosevelt, and the Socialist Eugene V. Debs (1855-1926), yet the single champion of conservatism, President Taft (1857-1930), was overwhelmingly defeated. This result, of course, did not automatically solve the problem of concentration, nor did it end the argument over how the problem was to be attacked. Increasingly it was becoming apparent that the ultimate stronghold of monopoly was Wall Street; that financial concentration of power was the key to concentration in steel, railroads, and every other field.

Much light was thrown upon the so-called "money trust" by the investigations of the Pujo Committee of the House of Representatives in 1913, which showed how a handful of bankers dominated the affairs of most of the big corporations. This information, in turn, stimulated a brilliant Boston lawyer named Louis D. Brandeis (1856-1941) to make further investigations on his own. These he published during late 1913 and early 1914 as a series of articles in *Harper's Weekly*. Later they appeared in book form as *Other People's Money*.

Brandeis' attacks on the "money trust" were widely read, but their influence was even greater than this alone would indicate. Many important leaders and opinion makers were profoundly impressed by his argument. Woodrow Wilson (1856-1924), for example, already much influenced by Brandeis, read these articles carefully, scoring the margins of his copies of *Harper's Weekly* with his comments. That powerful foe of Wall Street and the trusts, Senator Robert La Follette (1855-1925), considered Brandeis' analysis of "epoch-making" importance. And if the concentration of financial power was not then broken up, the nation's thinking was at least prepared for change. When the New Deal financial reforms of the 1930's were achieved, everyone recognized that 20 years earlier Brandeis, then a Supreme Court justice, had seen both the nature of the problem and the best way of handling it.

OUR FINANCIAL OLIGARCHY

THE dominant element in our financial oligarchy is the investment banker. Associated banks, trust companies and life insurance companies are his tools. Controlled railroads, public service and industrial corporations are his subjects. Though properly but middlemen, these bankers bestride as masters America's business world, so that practically no large enterprise can be undertaken successfully without their participation or approval. These bankers are, of course, able men possessed of large fortunes; but the most potent factor in their control of business is not the possession of extraordinary ability or huge wealth. The key to their power is Combination — concentration intensive and comprehensive — advancing on three distinct lines:

First: There is the obvious consolidation of banks and trust companies; the less obvious affiliations, — through stockholdings, voting trusts and interlocking directorates, — of banking institutions which are not legally connected; and the joint transactions, gentlemen's agreements, and "banking ethics" which eliminate competition among the investment bankers.

Second: There is the consolidation of railroads into huge systems, the large combinations of public service corporations and the formation of industrial trusts, which, by making businesses so "big" that local, independent banking concerns cannot alone supply the necessary funds, has created dependence upon the associated New York bankers.

But combination, however intensive, along these lines only, could not have produced the Money Trust — another and more potent factor of combination was added.

Third: Investment bankers, like J. P. Morgan & Co., dealers in bonds, stocks and notes, encroached upon the functions of the three other classes of corporations with which their business brought them into contact. They became the directing power in railroads, public service and industrial companies through which our great business operations are conducted — the makers of bonds and stocks. They became the directing power in the life insurance companies, and other corporate reservoirs or the people's savings — the buyers of bonds and stocks. They became the directing power also in banks and trust companies — the depositaries of the quick capital of the country — the life blood of business, with which they and others carried on their operations. Thus four distinct functions, each essential to business, and each exercised, originally, by a distinct set of men, became united in the investment banker. It is to this union of business functions that the existence of the Money Trust is mainly due.

The development of our financial oligarchy followed, in this respect, lines with which the history of political despotism has familiarized us: — usurpation, proceeding by gradual encroachment rather than by violent acts; subtle and often long-concealed concentration of distinct functions, which are beneficent when separately administered, and dangerous only when combined in the same persons. It was by processes such as these that Caesar Augustus became master of Rome. The makers of our own Constitution had in mind like dangers to our political liberty when they provided so carefully for the separation of governmental powers.

The original function of the investment banker was that of dealer in bonds, stocks and notes; buying mainly at wholesale from corporations, municipalities, states and governments which need money, and selling to those seeking investments. The banker performs, in this respect, the function of a merchant; and the function is a very useful one. Large business enterprises are conducted generally by corporations. The permanent capital of corporations is represented by bonds and stocks. The bonds and stocks of the more important corporations are owned, in large part, by small investors, who do not participate in the management of the company. Corporations require the aid of a banker-middleman, for they lack generally the reputation and clientele essential to selling their own bonds and stocks direct to the investor. Investors in corporate securities, also, require the services of a banker-middleman. The number of securities upon the market is very large. Only a part of these securities is listed on the New York Stock Exchange; but its listings alone comprise about sixteen hundred different issues aggregating about $26,500,000,000, and each year new listings are made averaging about two hundred and thirty-three to an amount of $1,500,00,000. For a small investor to make an intelligent selection from these many corporate securities — indeed, to pass an intelligent judgment upon a single one — is ordinarily impossible. He lacks the ability, the facilities, the training and the time essential to a proper investigation. Unless his purchase is to be little better than a gamble, he needs the advice of an expert, who, combining special knowledge with judgment, has the facilities and incentive to make a thorough investigation. This dependence, both of corporations and investors, upon the banker has grown in recent years, since women and others who do not participate in the management, have become the owners of so large a part of the stocks and bonds of our great corporations. Over half of the stockholders of the American Sugar Refining Company and nearly half of the stockholders of the Pennsylvania Railroad and of the New York, New Haven & Hartford Railroad are women. . . .

But this enlargement of their legitimate field of operations did not satisfy investment bankers. They were not content merely to deal in securities. They desired to manufacture them also; and became promoters, or allied themselves with promoters. Thus it was the J. P. Morgan & Company formed the Steel Trust, the Harvester Trust and the Shipping Trust. And, adding the duties of undertaker to those of midwife, the investment bankers became in times of corporate disaster, members of the security-holders' "Protective Committees"; then they participated as "Reorganization Managers" in the reincarnation of the unsuccessful corporations and ultimately became directors. It was in this way that the Morgan associates acquired their hold upon the Southern Railway, the Northern Pacific, the Reading, the Erie, the Père Marquette, the Chicago and Great Western, and the Cincinnati, Hamilton & Dayton. Often they insured the continuance of that control by the device of the voting trust; but even where no voting trust was created, a secure hold was acquired upon reorganization. It was in this way also that Kuhn, Loeb & Co. became potent in the Union Pacific and the Baltimore & Ohio.

But the banker's participation in the management of the corporations was not limited to cases of promotion or reorganization. An urgent or extensive need of new money was considered a sufficient reason for the banker's entering a board of directors. And often without even such excuse the investment banker has secured a place upon the Board of Directors, through his powerful influence or the control of his customers' proxies. Such seems to have been the fatal entrance of Mr. Morgan into the management of the then prosperous New York, New Haven & Hartford Railroad, in 1892. And when once a banker has entered the Board, — whatever may have been the occasion, — his grip proves tenacious and his influence usually supreme, for he controls the supply of new money.

The investment banker is naturally on the lookout for good bargains in bonds and stocks. Like other merchants, he wants to buy his merchandise cheap. But when he becomes director of a corporation he occupies a position which prevents the transaction by which he acquires its corporate securities from being properly called a bargain. Can there be real bargaining where the same man is on both sides of a trade? The investment banker, through his controlling influence on the Board of Directors, decides that the corporation shall issue and sell the securities, decides the price at which it shall sell them, and decides that it shall sell the securities to himself. The fact that there are other directors besides the banker on the Board does not, in practice, prevent this being the result. The banker, who holds the purse-strings, becomes usually the dominant spirit. Through voting-trusteeships, exclusive financial agencies, membership on executive or finance committees, or by mere directorships, J. P. Morgan & Co., and their associates, hold such financial power in at least thirty-two transportation systems, public utility corporations and industrial companies — companies with an aggregate capitalization of $17,273,000,000. Mainly for corporations so controlled, J. P. Morgan & Co. procured the public marketing in ten years of security issues aggregating $1,950,000,000. This huge sum does not include any issues marketed privately, nor any issues, however marketed, of intra-state corporations. Kuhn, Loeb & Co. and a few other investment bankers exercise similar control over many other corporations.

Such control of railroads, public service and industrial corporations assures to the investment bankers an ample supply of securities at attractive prices; and merchandise well bought is half sold. But these bond and stock merchants are not disposed to take even a slight risk as to their ability to market their goods. They saw that if they could control the security-buyers, as well as the security-makers, investment banking would, indeed, be "a happy hunting ground"; and they have made it so.

The numerous small investors cannot, in the strict sense, be controlled; but their dependence upon the banker insures their being duly influenced. A large part, however, of all bonds issued and of many stocks are bought by the prominent corporate investors; and most prominent among these are the life insurance companies, the trust companies, and the banks. The purchase of a security by these institutions not only relieves the banker of the merchandise, but recommends it strongly to the small investor, who believes that these institutions are wisely managed. These controlled corporate investors are not only large customers, but may be particularly accommodating ones. Individual investors are moody. They buy only when they want to do so. They are sometimes inconveniently reluctant. Corporate investors, if controlled, may be made to buy when the bankers need a market. It was natural that the investment bankers proceeded to get control of the great life insurance companies, as well as of the trust companies and the banks.

The field thus occupied is uncommonly rich. The life insurance companies are our leading institutions for savings. Their huge surplus and reserves, augmented daily, are always clamoring for investment. No panic or money shortage stops the inflow of new money from the perennial stream of premiums on existing policies and interest on existing investments. The three great companies — the New York Life, the Mutual of New York, and the Equitable — would have over $55,000,000 of *new* money to invest annually, even if they did not issue a single new policy. . . .

It was natural that the investment bankers should seek to control these never-failing reservoirs of capital. George W. Perkins was Vice-President of the New York Life, the largest of the companies. While remaining such he was made a partner in J. P. Morgan & Co., and in the four years preceding the Armstrong investigation, his firm sold the New York Life $38,804,918.51 in securities. The New York is a mutual company, supposed to be controlled by its policy-holders. But "the so-called control of life insurance companies by policy-holders through mutualization is a farce" and "its only result is to keep in office a self-constituted, self-perpetuating management."

The Equitable Life Assurance Society is a stock company and is controlled by $100,000 of stock. The dividend on this stock is limited by law to seven per cent; but in 1910 Mr. Morgan paid about $3,000,000 for $51,000, par value of this stock, or $5,882.35 a share. The dividend return on the stock investment is less than one-eighth of one per cent; but the assets controlled amount now to over $500,000,000. And certain of these assets had an especial value for investment bankers; — namely, the large holdings of stock in banks and trust companies. . . .

The banks and trust companies are depositaries, in the main, not of the people's savings, but of the business man's quick capital. Yet, since the investment banker acquired control of banks and trust companies, these institutions also have become, like the life companies, large purchasers of bonds and stocks. Many of our national banks have invested in this manner a large part of all their resources, including capital, surplus and deposits. The bond investments of some banks exceed by far the aggregate of their capital and surplus, and nearly equal their loanable deposits.

The goose that lays golden eggs has been considered a most valuable possession. But even more profitable is the privilege of taking the golden eggs laid by somebody else's goose. The investment bankers and their associates now enjoy that privilege. They control the people through the people's own money. If the bankers' power were commensurate only with their wealth, they would have relatively little influence on American business. Vast fortunes like those of the Astors are no doubt regrettable. They are inconsistent with democracy. They are unsocial. And they seem peculiarly unjust when they represent largely unearned increment. But the wealth of the Astors does not endanger political or industrial liberty. It is insignificant in amount as compared with the aggregate wealth of America, or even of New York City. It lacks significance largely because its owners have only the income from their own wealth. The Astor wealth is static. The wealth of the Morgan associates is dynamic. The power and the growth of power of our financial oligarchs comes from wielding the savings and quick capital of others. In two of the three great life insurance companies the influence of J. P. Morgan & Co. and their associates is exerted without any individual investment by them whatsoever. Even in the Equitable, where Mr. Morgan bought an actual majority of all the outstanding stock, his investment amounts to little more than one-half of one per cent. of the assets of the company. The fetters which bind the people are forged from the people's own gold.

But the reservoir of other people's money, from which the investment bankers now draw their greatest power, is not the life insurance companies, but the banks and the trust companies. Bank deposits represent the really quick capital of the nation. They are the life blood of businesses. Their effective force is much greater than that of an equal amount of wealth permanently invested. The 34 banks and trust companies, which the Pujo Committee declared to be directly controlled by the Morgan associates, held $1,983,000,000 in deposits. Control of these institutions means the ability to lend a large part of these funds, directly and indirectly, to themselves; and what is often even more important, the power to prevent the funds being lent to any rival interests. These huge deposits can, in the discretion of those in control, be used to meet the temporary needs of their subject corporations. When bonds and stocks are issued to finance permanently these corporations, the bank deposits can in large part be loaned by the investment bankers in control to themselves and their associates; so that the securities may be carried by them until sold to investors. Or these bank deposits may be loaned to allied bankers, or jobbers in securities, or to speculators, to enable them to carry the bonds or stocks. Easy money tends to make securities rise in the market. Tight money nearly always makes them fall. The control by the leading investment bankers over the banks and trust companies is so great, that they can often determine for a time the market for money by lending or refusing to lend on the Stock Exchange. In this way, among others, they have power to affect the general trend of prices in bonds and stocks. Their power over a particular security is even greater. Its sale on the market may depend upon whether the security is favored or discriminated against when offered to the banks and trust companies, as collateral for loans.

Furthermore, it is the investment banker's access to other people's money in controlled banks and trust companies which alone enables any individual banking concern to take so large part of the annual output of bonds and stocks. The banker's own capital, however large, would soon be exhausted. And even the loanable funds of the banks would often be exhausted, but for the large deposits made in those banks by the life insurance, railroad, public service, and industrial corporations which the bankers also control. On December 31, 1912, the three leading life insurance companies had deposits in banks and trust companies aggregating $13,839,189.08. As the Pujo Committee finds:

"The men who through their control over the funds of our railroads and industrial companies are able to direct where such funds shall be kept and thus to create these great reservoirs of the people's money, are the ones who are in position to tap those reservoirs for the ventures in which they are interested and to prevent their being tapped for purposes of which they do not approve. The latter is quite as important a factor as the former. It is the controlling consideration in its effect on competition in the railroad and industrial world."

But the power of the investment banker over other people's money is often more direct and effective than that exerted through controlled banks and trust companies. J. P. Morgan & Co. achieve the supposedly impossible feat of having their cake and eating it too. They buy the bonds and stocks of controlled railroads and industrial concerns, and pay the purchase price; and still do not part with their money. This is accomplished by the simple device of becoming the bank of deposit of the controlled corporations, instead of having the company deposit in some merely controlled bank in whose operation others have at least some share. When J. P. Morgan & Co. buy an issue of securities the purchase money, instead of being paid over to the corporation, is retained by the banker for the corporation, to be drawn upon only as the funds are needed by the corporation. And as the securities are issued in large blocks, and the money raised is often not all spent until long thereafter, the aggregate of the balances remaining in the banker's hands are huge. Thus J. P. Morgan & Co. (including their Philadelphia house, called Drexel & Co.) held on November 1, 1912, deposits aggregating $162,491,819.65.

The operations of so comprehensive a system of concentration necessarily developed in the bankers overweening power. And the bankers' power grows by what it feeds on. Power begets wealth; and added wealth opens ever new opportunities for the acquisition of wealth and power. The operations of these bankers are so vast and numerous that even a very reasonable compensation for the service performed by the bankers, would, in the aggregate, produce for them incomes so large as to result in huge accumulations of capital. But the compensation taken by the bankers as commissions or profits is far from reasonable. Occupying, as they so frequently do, the inconsistent position of being at the same time seller and buyer, — the standard for so-called compensation actually applied, is not the "Rule of reason" but "All the traffic will bear." And this is true even where there is no sinister motive. The weakness of human nature prevents men from being good judges of their own deservings.

The syndicate formed by J. P. Morgan & Co. to underwrite the United States Steel Corporation took for their services securities which netted $62,500,000 in cash. Of this huge sum J. P. Morgan & Co. received, as syndicate managers, $12,500,000 in addition to the share which they were entitled to receive as syndicate members. This sum of $62,500,000 was only a part of the fees paid for the service of monopolizing the steel industry. In addition to the commissions taken specifically for organizing the United States Steel Corporation, large sums were paid for organizing the several companies of which it is composed. For instance, the National Tube Company was capitalized at $80,000,000 of stock; $40,000,000 of which was common stock. Half of this $40,000,000 was taken by J. P. Morgan & Co. and associates for promotion services; and the $20,000,000 stock so taken became later exchangeable into $25,000,000 of Steel Common. Commissioner of Corporations Herbert Knox Smith, found that:

"More than $150,000,000 of the stock of the Steel Corporation was issued directly or indirectly (through exchange) for mere promotion or underwriting services. In other words, nearly one-seventh of the total capital stock of the Steel Corporation appears to have been issued directly or indirectly to promoters' services." . . .

These large profits from promotions, underwritings and security purchases led to a revolutionary change in the conduct of our leading banking institutions. It was obvious that control by the investment bankers of the deposits in banks and trust companies was an essential element in their securing these huge profits. And the bank officers naturally asked, "Why then should not the banks and trust companies share in so profitable a field? Why should not they themselves become investment bankers too, with all the new functions incident to 'Big Business'?" To do so would involve a departure from the legitimate sphere of the banking business, — which is the making of temporary loans to other business concerns. But the temptation was irresistible. The invasion of the investment banker into the banks' field of operation was followed by a counter invasion by the banks into the realm of the investment banker. And most prominent among the banks were the National City and the First National of New York. But theirs was not a hostile invasion. The contending forces met as allies, joined forces to control the business of the country, and to "divide the spoils." The alliance was cemented by voting trusts, by interlocking directorates and by joint ownerships. There resulted the fullest "cooperation"; and more railroads, public service corporations, and great industrial concerns were brought into complete subjection.

VI. An Age of War and Prosperity

Woodrow Wilson

JUSTICE IN WAR AND IN PEACE

1917, 1918 DESPITE the fact that the powers of the President of the United States are carefully spelled out in the Constitution and therefore equally available to every man who holds the office, the way those powers are employed by the individual resident of the White House has a great deal to do with their practical force. "Weak" Presidents have used their authority only partially, they have employed their perquisites gingerly and unimaginatively. "Strong" ones have used their power to the full; indeed, they have often expanded the area of their authority and influence greatly simply by applying seemingly minor rights in novel and startling ways.

One of the most ingenious of our "strong" Presidents in this respect was Woodrow Wilson (1856-1924), who greatly broadened the scope of his office in a number of clever ways. One of the most important of these was also one of the simplest. Instead of following the precedent established in Jefferson's day of sending messages to the Hill by courier to be droned out by a mere clerk, he began to come in person to the Capitol where the magic of his oratory would inspire Congressmen to follow his leadership. In the process, he soon discovered, he was also able better to attract the attention of the public at large, adding greatly to the impact of his words.

Two of the most important of these personally delivered messages follow. The first, his call for a declaration of war against Germany (1917), would obviously have had a great impact in any case. But Wilson's presence at the Capitol, the depth of his feelings after his long struggle with his conscience to decide what course to follow in the crisis, clearly increased the force of his words. As he was leaving the chamber of the House of Representatives after the speech, even his bitter enemy, Henry Cabot Lodge (1850-1924), came forward to shake his hand. "Mr. President," Lodge said, "you have expressed in the loftiest manner possible the sentiments of the American people." Actually, Wilson had done more than this. By carefully distinguishing between the Kaiser's government and the German people, he made it possible to fight all-out against that government and still preserve the concept of a final peace based on fairness and magnanimity rather than on national aggrandizement and revenge.

The second message announced Wilson's famous Fourteen Points (1918) on which the postwar world was to be constructed. The impact of this speech on idealists all over the world was very great—too great, as time was to prove. For by raising their hopes for the future unrealistically high, it made their disillusionment monumental when the actual treaty ending the war had been hammered into shape. Nevertheless, the speech remains one of the most influential documents of the twentieth century. Its influence upon the settlement of both world wars was tremendous.

345

MESSAGE TO CONGRESS

(April 2, 1917)

Gentlemen of the Congress:

I have called the Congress into extraordinary session because there are serious, very serious, choices of policy to be made, and made immediately, which it was neither right nor constitutionally permissible that I should assume the responsibility of making.

On the third of February last I officially laid before you the extraordinary announcement of the Imperial German Government that on and after the first day of February it was its purpose to put aside all restraints of law or of humanity and use its submarines to sink every vessel that sought to approach either the ports of Great Britain and Ireland or the western coasts of Europe or any of the ports controlled by the enemies of Germany within the Mediterranean. That had seemed to be the object of the German submarine warfare earlier in the war, but since April of last year the Imperial Government had somewhat restrained the commanders of its undersea craft in conformity with its promise then given to us that passenger boats should not be sunk and that due warning would be given to all other vessels which its submarines might seek to destroy, when no resistance was offered or escape attempted, and care taken that their crews were given at least a fair chance to save their lives in their open boats. The precautions taken were meagre and haphazard enough, as was proved in distressing instance after instance in the progress of the cruel and unmanly business, but a certain degree of restraint was observed. The new policy has swept every restriction aside. Vessels of every kind, whatever their flag, their character, their cargo, their destination, their errand, have been ruthlessly sent to the bottom without warning and without thought of help or mercy for those on board, the vessels of friendly neutrals along with those of belligerents. Even hospital ships and ships carrying relief to the sorely bereaved and stricken people of Belgium, though the latter were provided with safe conduct through the proscribed areas by the German Government itself and were distinguished by unmistakable marks of identity, have been sunk with the same reckless lack of compassion or of principle.

I was for a little while unable to believe that such things would in fact be done by any government that had hitherto subscribed to the humane practices of civilized nations. International law had its origin in the attempt to set up some law which would be respected and observed upon the seas, where no nation had right of dominion and where lay the free highways of the world. By painful stage after stage has that law been built up, with meagre enough results, indeed, after all was accomplished that could be accomplished, but always with a clear view, at least, of what the heart and conscience of mankind demanded. This minimum of right the German Government has swept aside under the plea of retaliation and necessity and because it had no weapons which it could use at sea except these which it is impossible to employ as it is employing them without throwing to the winds all scruples of humanity or of respect for the understandings that were supposed to underlie the intercourse of the world. I am not now thinking of the loss of property involved, immense and serious as that is, but only of the wanton and wholesale destruction of the lives of non-combatants, men, women, and children, engaged in pursuits which have always, even in the darkest periods of modern history, been deemed innocent and legitimate. Property can be paid for; the lives of peaceful and innocent people cannot be. The present German submarine warfare against commerce is a warfare against mankind.

It is a war against all nations. American ships have been sunk, American lives taken, in ways which it has stirred us very deeply to learn of, but the ships and people of other neutral and friendly nations have been sunk and overwhelmed in the waters in the same way. There has been no discrimination. The challenge is to all mankind. Each nation must decide for itself how it will meet it. The choice we make for ourselves must be made with a moderation of counsel and a temperateness of judgment befitting our character and our motives as a nation. We must put excited feeling away. Our motive will not be revenge or the victorious assertion of the physical might of the nation, but only the vindication of right, of human right, of which we are only a single champion.

When I addressed the Congress on the twenty-sixth of February last I thought that it would suffice to assert our neutral rights with arms, our right to use the seas against unlawful interference, our right to keep our people safe against unlawful violence. But armed neutrality, it now appears, is impracticable. Because submarines are in effect outlaws when used as the German submarines have been used against merchant shipping, it is impossible to defend ships against their attacks as the law of nations has assumed that merchantmen would defend themselves against privateers or cruisers, visible craft giving chase upon the open sea. It is common prudence in such circumstances, grim necessity indeed, to endeavour to destroy them before they have shown their own intention. They must be dealt with upon sight, if dealt with at all. The German Government denies the right of neutrals to use arms at all within the areas of the sea which it has proscribed, even in the defense of rights which no modern publicist has ever before questioned their right to defend. The intimation is conveyed that the armed guards which we have placed on our merchant ships will be treated as beyond the pale of law and subject to be dealt with as pirates would be. Armed neutrality is ineffectual enough at best; in such circumstances and in the face of such pretensions it is worse than ineffectual; it is likely only to produce what it was meant to prevent; it is practically certain to draw us into the war without either the rights or the effectiveness of belligerents. There is one choice we cannot make, we are incapable of making: we will not choose the path of submission and suffer the most sacred rights of our nation and our people to be ignored or violated. The wrongs against which we now array ourselves are no common wrongs: they cut to the very roots of human life.

With a profound sense of the solemn and even tragical character of the step I am taking and of the grave responsibilities which it involves, but in unhesitating obedience to what I deem my constitutional duty, I advise that the Congress declare the recent course of the Imperial German Government to be in fact nothing less than war against the government and people of the United States; that it formally accept the status of belligerent which has thus been thrust upon it; and that it take immediate steps not only to put the country in a more thorough state of defense but also to exert all its power and employ all its resources to bring the Government of the German Empire to terms and end the war.

What this will involve is clear. It will involve the utmost practicable co-operation in counsel and action with the governments now at war with Germany, and, as incident to that, the extension to those governments of the most liberal financial credits, in order that our resources may so far as possible be added to theirs. It will involve the organization and mobilization of all the material resources of the country to supply the materials of war and serve the incidental needs of the nation in the most abundant and yet the most economical and efficient way possible. It will involve the immediate full equipment of the navy in all respects but particularly in supplying it with the best means of dealing with the enemy's submarines. It will involve the immediate addition to the armed forces of the United States already provided for by law in case of war at least five hundred thousand men, who should, in my opinion, be chosen upon the principle of universal liability to service, and also the authorization of subsequent additional increments of equal force so soon as they may be needed and can be handled in training. It will involve also, of course, the granting of adequate credits to the Government, sustained, I hope, so far as they can equitably be sustained by the present generation, by well conceived taxation.

I say sustained so far as may be equitable by taxation because it seems to me that it would be most unwise to base the credits which will now be necessary entirely on money borrowed. It is our duty, I most respectfully urge, to protect our people so far as we may against the very serious hardships and evils which would be likely to arise out of the inflation which would be produced by vast loans.

In carrying out the measures by which these things are to be accomplished we should keep constantly in mind the wisdom of interfering as little as possible in our own preparation and in the equipment of our own military forces with the duty, — for it will be a very practical duty, — of supplying the nations already at war with Germany with the materials which they can obtain only from us or by our assistance. They are in the field and we should help them in every way to be effective there.

I shall take the liberty of suggesting, through the several executive departments of the Government, for the consideration of your committees, measures for the accomplishment of the several objects I have mentioned. I hope that it will be your pleasure to deal with them as having been framed after very careful thought by the branch of the Government upon which the responsibility of conducting the war and safeguarding the nation will most directly fall.

While we do these things, these deeply momentous things, let us be very clear, and make very clear to all the world what our motives and our objects are. My own thought has not been driven from its habitual and normal course by the unhappy events of the last two months, and I do not believe that the thought of the nation has been altered or clouded by them. I have exactly the same things in mind now that I had in mind when I addressed the Senate on the twenty-second of January last; the same that I had in mind when I addressed the Congress on the third of February and on the twenty-sixth of February. Our object now, as then, is to vindicate the principles of peace and justice in the life of the world as against selfish and autocratic power and to set up amongst the really free and self-governed peoples of the world such a concert of purpose and of action as will henceforth ensure the observance of those principles. Neutrality is no longer feasible or desirable where the peace of the world is involved and the freedom of its peoples, and the menace to that peace and freedom lies in the existence of autocratic governments backed by organized force which is controlled wholly by their will, not by the will of their people. We have seen the last of neutrality in such circumstances. We are at the beginning of an age in which it will be insisted that the same standards of conduct and responsibility for wrong done shall be observed among nations and their governments that are observed among the individual citizens of civilized states.

We have no quarrel with the German people. We have no feeling toward them but one of sympathy and friendship. It was not upon their impulse that their government acted in entering this war. It was not with their previous knowledge or approval. It was a war determined upon as wars used to be determined upon in the old, unhappy days when peoples were nowhere consulted by their rulers and wars were provoked and waged in the interest of dynasties or of little groups of ambitious men who were accustomed to use their fellow men as pawns and tools. Self-governed nations do not fill their neighbour states with spies or set the course of intrigue to bring about some critical posture of affairs which will give them an opportunity to strike and make conquest. Such designs can be successfully worked out only under cover and where no one has the right to ask questions. Cunningly contrived plans of deception or aggression, carried, it may be, from generation to generation, can be worked out and kept from the light only within the privacy of courts or behind the carefully guarded confidences of a narrow and privileged class. They are happily impossible where public opinion commands and insists upon full information concerning all the nation's affairs.

A steadfast concert for peace can never be maintained except by a partnership of democratic nations. No autocratic government could be trusted to keep faith within it or observe its covenants. It must be a league of honour, a partnership of opinion. Intrigue would eat its vitals away; the plottings of inner circles who could plan what they would and render account to no one would be a corruption seated at its very heart. Only free peoples can hold their purpose and their honour steady to a common end and prefer the interests of mankind to any narrow interest of their own.

Does not every American feel that assurance has been added to our hope for the future peace of the world by the wonderful and heartening things that have been happening within the last few weeks in Russia? Russia was known by those who knew it best to have been always in fact democratic at heart, in all the vital habits of her thought, in all the intimate relationships of her people that spoke their natural instinct, their habitual attitude towards life. The autocracy that crowned the summit of her political structure, long as it had stood and terrible as was the reality of its power, was not in fact Russian in origin, character, or purpose; and now it has been shaken off and the great, generous Russian people have been

added in all their naive majesty and might to the forces that are fighting
for freedom in the world, for justice, and for peace. Here is a fit partner
for a League of Honour.

One of the things that has served to convince us that the Prussian
autocracy was not and could never be our friend is that from the very
outset of the present war it has filled our unsuspecting communities and
even our offices of government with spies and set criminal intrigues everywhere afoot against our national unity of counsel, our peace within and
without, our industries and our commerce. Indeed it is now evident that
its spies were here even before the war began; and it is unhappily not a
matter of conjecture but a fact proved in our courts of justice that the
intrigues which have more than once come perilously near to disturbing
the peace and dislocating the industries of the country have been carried
on at the instigation, with the support, and even under the personal direction of official agents of the Imperial Government accredited to the Government of the United States. Even in checking these things and trying
to extirpate them we have sought to put the most generous interpretation
possible upon them because we knew that their source lay, not in any hostile feeling or purpose of the German people towards us (who were, no
doubt, as ignorant of them as we ourselves were), but only in the selfish
designs of a Government that did what it pleased and told its people nothing. But they have played their part in serving to convince us at last that
that Government entertains no real friendship for us and means to act
against our peace and security at its convenience. That it means to stir up
enemies against us at our very doors the intercepted note to the German
Minister at Mexico City is eloquent evidence.

We are accepting this challenge of hostile purpose because we know that
in such a government, following such methods, we can never have a friend;
and that in the presence of its organized power, always lying in wait to
accomplish we know not what purpose, there can be no assured security
for the democratic governments of the world. We are now about to accept
gauge of battle with this natural foe to liberty and shall, if necessary,
spend the whole force of the nation to check and nullify its pretensions
and its power. We are glad, now that we see the facts with no veil of
false pretence about them, to fight thus for the ultimate peace of the world
and for the liberation of its peoples, the German peoples included: for the
rights of nations great and small and the privilege of men everywhere to
choose their way of life and of obedience. The world must be made safe
for democracy. Its peace must be planted upon the tested foundations of
political liberty. We have no selfish ends to serve. We desire no conquest,
no dominion. We seek no indemnities for ourselves, no material compensa-

tion for the sacrifices we shall freely make. We are but one of the champions of the rights of mankind. We shall be satisfied when those rights have been made as secure as the faith and the freedom of nations can make them.

Just because we fight without rancour and without selfish object, seeking nothing for ourselves but what we shall wish to share with all free peoples, we shall, I feel confident, conduct our operations as belligerents without passion and ourselves observe with proud punctilio the principles of right and of fair play we profess to be fighting for.

I have said nothing of the governments allied with the Imperial Government of Germany because they have not made war upon us or challenged us to defend our right and our honour. The Austro-Hungarian Government has, indeed, avowed its unqualified endorsement and acceptance of the reckless and lawless submarine warfare adopted now without disguise by the Imperial German Government, and it has therefore not been possible for this Government to receive Count Tarnowski, the Ambassador recently accredited to this Government by the Imperial and Royal Government of Austria-Hungary; but that Government has not actually engaged in warfare against citizens of the United States on the seas, and I take the liberty, for the present at least, of postponing a discussion of our relations with the authorities at Vienna. We enter this war only where we are clearly forced into it because there are no other means of defending our rights.

It will be all the easier for us to conduct ourselves as belligerents in a high spirit of right and fairness because we act without animus, not in enmity towards a people or with the desire to bring any injury or disadvantage upon them, but only in armed opposition to an irresponsible government which has thrown aside all considerations of humanity and of right and is running amuck. We are, let me say again, the sincere friends of the German people, and shall desire nothing so much as the early re-establishment of intimate relations of mutual advantage between us, — however hard it may be for them, for the time being, to believe that this is spoken from our hearts. We have borne with their present government through all these bitter months because of that friendship,—exercising a patience and forbearance which would otherwise have been impossible. We shall, happily, still have an opportunity to prove that friendship in our daily attitude and actions towards the millions of men and women of German birth and native sympathy who live amongst us and share our life, and we shall be proud to prove it towards all who are in fact loyal to their neighbours and to the Government in the hour of test. They are, most of them, as true and loyal Americans as if they had never known any other fealty or allegiance. They will be prompt to stand with us in rebuking and restraining the few who may be of a different mind and purpose. If there should be disloyalty, it will be dealt with with a firm hand of stern repression; but, if it lifts its head at all, it will lift it only here and there and without countenance except from a lawless and malignant few.

It is a distressing and oppressive duty, Gentlemen of the Congress, which I have performed in thus addressing you. There are, it may be, many months of fiery trial and sacrifice ahead of us. It is a fearful thing to lead this great peaceful people into war, into the most terrible and disastrous of all wars, civilization itself seeming to be in the balance. But the right is more precious than peace, and we shall fight for the things which we have always carried nearest our hearts, for democracy, for the right of those who submit to authority to have a voice in their own governments, for the rights and liberties of small nations, for a universal dominion of right by such a concert of free people as shall bring peace and safety to all nations and make the world itself at last free. To such a task we can dedicate our lives and our fortunes, everything that we are and everything that we have, with the pride of those who know that the day has come when America is privileged to spend her blood and her might for the principles that gave her birth and happiness and the peace which she has treasured. God helping her, she can do no other.

MESSAGE TO CONGRESS
(January 8, 1918)

Gentlemen of the Congress:

Once more, as repeatedly before, the spokesmen of the Central Empires have indicated their desire to discuss the objects of the war and the possible basis of a general peace. Parleys have been in progress at Brest-Litovsk between Russian representatives and representatives of the Central Powers to which the attention of all the belligerents has been invited for the purpose of ascertaining whether it may be possible to extend these parleys into a general conference with regard to terms of peace and settlement.

The Russian representatives presented not only a perfectly definite statement of the principles upon which they would be willing to conclude peace but also an equally definite program of the concrete application of those principles. The representatives of the Central Powers, on their part, presented an outline of settlement which, if much less definite, seemed susceptible of liberal interpretation until their specific program of practical terms was added. That program proposed no concessions at all either to the sovereignty of Russia or to the preferences of the populations with whose fortunes it dealt, but meant, in a word, that the Central Empires were to keep every foot of territory their armed forces had occupied — every province, every city, every point of vantage — as a permanent addition to their territories and their power.

It is a reasonable conjecture that the general principles of settlement which they at first suggested originated with the more liberal statesmen of Germany and Austria, the men who have begun to feel the force of their own people's thought and purpose, while the concrete terms of actual settlement came from the military leaders who have no thought but to keep what they have got. The negotiations have been broken off. The Russian representatives were sincere and in earnest. They cannot entertain such proposals of conquest and domination.

The whole incident is full of significance. It is also full of perplexity. With whom are the Russian representatives dealing? For whom are the representatives of the Central Empires speaking? Are they speaking for the majorities of their respective parliaments or for the minority parties, that military and imperialistic minority which has so far dominated their whole policy and controlled the affairs of Turkey and of the Balkan states which have felt obliged to become their associates in this war?

The Russian representatives have insisted, very justly, very wisely, and in the true spirit of modern democracy, that the conferences they have been holding with the Teutonic and Turkish statesmen should be held within open, not closed, doors, and all the world has been audience, as was desired. To whom have we been listening, then? To those who speak the spirit and intention of the resolutions of the German Reichstag of the 9th of July last, the spirit and intention of the Liberal leaders and parties of Germany, or to those who resist and defy that spirit and intention and insist upon conquest and subjugation? Or are we listening, in fact, to both, unreconciled and in open and hopeless contradiction? These are very serious and pregnant questions. Upon the answer to them depends the peace of the world.

But, whatever the results of the parleys at Brest-Litovsk, whatever the confusions of counsel and of purpose in the utterances of the spokesmen of the Central Empires, they have again attempted to acquaint the world with their objects in the war and have again challenged their adversaries to say what their objects are and what sort of settlement they would deem just and satisfactory. There is no good reason why that challenge should not be responded to, and responded to with the utmost candor. We did not wait for it. Not once, but again and again, we have laid our whole thought and purpose before the world, not in general terms only, but each time with sufficient definition to make it clear what sort of definite terms of settlement must necessarily spring out of them. Within the last week Mr. Lloyd George has spoken with admirable candor and in admirable spirit for the people and Government of Great Britain.

There is no confusion of counsel among the adversaries of the Central Powers, no uncertainty of principle, no vagueness of detail. The only secrecy of counsel, the only lack of fearless frankness, the only failure to make definite statement of the objects of the war, lies with Germany and her allies. The issues of life and death hang upon these definitions. No statesman who has the least conception of his responsibility ought for a moment to permit himself to continue this tragical and appalling outpouring of blood and treasure unless he is sure beyond a peradventure that the objects of the vital sacrifice are part and parcel of the very life of Society and that the people for whom he speaks think them right and imperative as he does.

There is, moreover, a voice calling for these definitions of principle and of purpose which is, it seems to me, more thrilling and more compelling than any of the many moving voices with which the troubled air of the world is filled. It is the voice of the Russian people. They are prostrate and all but helpless, it would seem, before the grim power of Germany, which has hitherto known no relenting and no pity. Their power, apparently, is shattered. And yet their soul is not subservient. They will not yield either in principle or in action. Their conception of what is right, of what is humane and honorable for them to accept, has been stated with a frankness, a largeness of view, a generosity of spirit, and a universal human sympathy which must challenge the admiration of every friend of mankind; and they have refused to compound their ideals or desert others that they themselves may be safe.

They call to us to say what it is that we desire, in what, if in anything, our purpose and our spirit differ from theirs; and I believe that the people of the United States would wish me to respond, with utter simplicity and frankness. Whether their present leaders believe it or not, it is our heartfelt desire and hope that some way may be opened whereby we may be privileged to assist the people of Russia to attain their utmost hope of liberty and ordered peace.

It will be our wish and purpose that the processes of peace, when they are begun, shall be absolutely open and that they shall involve and permit henceforth no secret understandings of any kind. The day of conquest and aggrandizement is gone by; so is also the day of secret covenants entered into in the interest of particular governments and likely at some unlooked-for moment to upset the peace of the world. It is this happy fact, now clear to the view of every public man whose thoughts do not still linger in an age that is dead and gone, which makes it possible for every nation whose purposes are consistent with justice and the peace of the world to avow now or at any other time the objects it has in view.

We entered this war because violations of right had occurred which touched us to the quick and made the life of our own people impossible unless they were corrected and the world secure once for all against their recurrence.

What we demand in this war, therefore, is nothing peculiar to ourselves. It is that the world be made fit and safe to live in; and particularly that it be made safe for every peace-loving nation which, like our own, wishes to live its own life, determine its own institutions, be assured of justice and fair dealing by the other peoples of the world as against force and selfish aggression.

All the peoples of the world are in effect partners in this interest, and for our own part we see very clearly that unless justice be done to others it will not be done to us. The program of the world's peace, therefore, is our program; and that program, the only possible program, as we see it, is this:

1. Open convenants of peace, openly arrived at, after which there shall be no private international understandings of any kind but diplomacy shall proceed always frankly and in the public view.

2. Absolute freedom of navigation upon the seas, outside territorial waters, alike in peace and in war, except as the seas may be closed in whole or in part by international action for the enforcement of international covenants.

3. The removal, so far as possible, of all economic barriers and the establishment of an equality of trade conditions among all the nations consenting to the peace and associating themselves for its maintenance.

4. Adequate guarantees given and taken that national armaments will be reduced to the lowest points consistent with domestic safety.

5. A free, open-minded, and absolutely impartial adjustment of all colonial claims, based upon a strict observance of the principle that in determining all such questions of sovereignty the interests of the populations concerned must have equal weight with the equitable claims of the government whose title is to be determined.

6. The evacuation of all Russian territory and such a settlement of all questions affecting Russia as will secure the best and freest cooperation of the other nations of the world in obtaining for her an unhampered and unembarrassed opportunity for the independent determination of her own political development and national policy and assure her of a sincere wel-

come into the society of free nations under institutions of her own choosing; and, more than a welcome, assistance also of every kind that she may need and may herself desire. The treatment accorded Russia by her sister nations in the months to come will be the acid test of their good will, of their comprehension of her needs as distinguished from their own interests, and of their intelligent and unselfish sympathy.

7. Belgium, the whole world will agree, must be evacuated and restored, without any attempt to limit the sovereignty which she enjoys in common with all other free nations. No other single act will serve as this will serve to restore confidence among the nations in the laws which they have themselves set and determined for the government of their relations with one another. Without this healing act the whole structure and validity of international law is forever impaired.

8. All French territory should be freed and the invaded portions restored, and the wrong done to France by Prussia in 1871 in the matter of Alsace-Lorraine, which has unsettled the peace of the world for nearly fifty years, should be righted, in order that peace may once more be made secure in the interest of all.

9. A readjustment of the frontiers of Italy should be affected along clearly recognizable lines of nationality.

10. The peoples of Austria-Hungary, whose place among the nations we wish to see safeguarded and assured, should be accorded the freest opportunity of autonomous development.

11. Rumania, Serbia, and Montenegro should be evacuated; occupied territories restored; Serbia accorded free and secure access to the sea; and the relations of the several Balkan states to one another determined by friendly counsel along historically established lines of allegiance and nationality; and international guarantees of the political and economic independence and territorial integrity of the several Balkan states should be entered into.

12. The Turkish portions of the present Ottoman Empire should be assured a secure sovereignty, but the other nationalities which are now under Turkish rule should be assured an undoubted security of life and an absolutely unmolested opportunity of autonomous development, and the Dardanelles should be permanently opened as a free passage to the ships and commerce of all nations under international guarantees.

13. An independent Polish state should be erected which should include the territories inhabited by indisputably Polish populations, which should be assured a free and secure access to the sea, and whose political and economic independence and territorial integrity should be guaranteed by international covenant.

14. A general association of nations must be formed under specific covenants for the purpose of affording mutual guarantees of political independence and territorial integrity to great and small states alike.

In regard to these essential rectifications of wrong and assertions of right we feel ourselves to be intimate partners of all the governments and peoples associated together against the imperialists. We cannot be separated in interest or divided in purpose. We stand together until the end.

For such arrangements and covenants we are willing to fight and to continue to fight until they are achieved; but only because we wish the right to prevail and desire a just and stable peace such as can be secured only by removing the chief provocations to war, which this program does remove.

We have no jealousy of German greatness, and there is nothing in this program that impairs it. We grudge her no achievement or distinction of learning or of pacific enterprise such as have made her record very bright and very enviable. We do not wish to injure her or to block in any way her legitimate influence or power. We do not wish to fight her either with arms or with hostile arrangements of trade if she is willing to associate herself with us and the other peace-loving nations of the world in covenants of justice and law and fair dealing.

We wish her only to accept a place of equality among the peoples of the world, — the new world on which we now live, — instead of a place of mastery.

Neither do we presume to suggest to her any alteration or modification of her institutions. But it is necessary, we must frankly say, and necessary as a preliminary to any intelligent dealings with her on our part, that we should know whom her spokesmen speak for when they speak to us, whether for the Reichstag majority or for the military party and the men whose creed is imperial domination.

We have spoken now, surely, in terms too concrete to admit of any further doubt or question. An evident principle runs through the whole program I have outlined. It is the principle of justice to all peoples and nationalities, and their right to live on equal terms of liberty and safety with one another, whether they be strong or weak.

Unless this principle be made its foundation no part of the structure of international justice can stand. The people of the United States could act upon no other principle; and to the vindication of this principle they are ready to devote their lives, their honor, and everything that they possess. The moral climax of this the culminating and final war for human liberty has come, and they are ready to put their own strength, their own highest purpose, their own integrity and devotion to the test.

Henry Cabot Lodge

AN EVIL THING WITH A HOLY NAME

◆{*1919*}◆ WOODROW Wilson (1856-1924) had taken the United States into the World War in order to make the world safe for democracy; quickly, as the conflict developed, he learned that victory on the battlefield would not alone accomplish this noble objective. A powerful international organization—he called it a League of Nations—would be necessary if the principles of justice were to triumph after the Central Powers had been defeated. First enunciated in his "Fourteen Points" speech of January 8, 1918, his proposal that such an organization guarantee the "political independence and territorial integrity of great and small nations alike" was developed in a series of British and American drafts and finally presented to the Versailles Peace Conference by Wilson himself in February, 1919.

Unquestionably the impact of the league idea on Americans was both heavy and favorable. As Senator Henry Cabot Lodge of Massachusetts (1850-1924), whose objections to the League of Nations proved so important in its defeat, himself confessed in a private letter: "I have no doubt that a large majority of the people of the country are very naturally fascinated by the idea of eternal preservation of the world's peace. . . . They are told that is what this league means." But the full significance of the proposed international organization was not clear to the average American in those happy days after the guns fell silent and before the difficulties of postwar readjustment had become apparent. Foes of the League soon began to point out the extent to which membership would involve surrendering America's cherished isolationism. Extremists (they were called "irreconcilables") made the most noise but it was probably the less obviously hostile, more reasonable critics who did most to swing public opinion away from the President on the League issue. And swing public opinion did, although the actual defeat of the proposal was a narrowly partisan political question settled in the Senate. The following selection from a speech delivered by Lodge in the Senate on February 28, 1919, typifies the kind of reasoning used by those opponents who objected to *Wilson's* league without rejecting offhand the whole concept of internationalism.

SPEECH IN THE SENATE

(February 28, 1919)

MR. PRESIDENT, all people, men and women alike, who are capable of connected thought abhor war and desire nothing so much as to make secure the future peace of the world. Everybody hates war. Everyone longs to make it impossible. We ought to lay aside once and for all the unfounded and really evil suggestion that because men may differ as to the best method of securing the world's peace in the future, anyone is against permanent peace, if it can be obtained, among all the nations of mankind.

Because one man goes to the Capitol in Washington by one street and another man by a different street it does not follow that they are not both going to the Capitol. We all earnestly desire to advance toward the preservation of the world's peace, and difference in method makes no distinction in purpose. It is almost needless to say that the question now before us is so momentous that it transcends all party lines. Party considerations and party interests disappear in dealing with such a question as this. I will follow any man and vote for any measure which in my honest opinion will make for the maintenance of the world's peace. I will follow no man and vote for no measure which, however well intended, seem in my best judgment to lead to discussions rather than to harmony among the nations or to injury, peril, or injustice to my country. No question has ever confronted the United States Senate which equals in importance that which is involved in the league of nations intended to secure the future peace of the world. There should be no undue haste in considering it. My one desire is that not only the Senate, which is charged with responsibility, but that the press and the people of the country should investigate every proposal with the utmost thoroughness and weigh them all carefully before they make up their minds. If there is any proposition or any plan which will not bear, which will not court the most thorough and most public discussion, that fact makes it an object of suspicion at the very outset. Beware of it; be on your guard against it. Demand that those who oppose the plan now offered present arguments and reasons, based on facts and history, and that those who favor it meet objections with something more relative than rhetoric, personal denunciation, and shrill shrieks that virtue is to be preferred to vice and that peace is better than war. Glittering and enticing generalities will not serve. We must have fact, details, and sharp, clear-cut definitions. The American people cannot give too much thought to this subject, and that they shall look into it with considerate eyes is all that I desire.

In the first place, the terms of the league — the agreements which we make, — must be so plain and so explicit that no man can misunderstand them. We must, so far as it can be done by human ingenuity, have every agreement which we make so stated that it will not give rise to different interpretations and to consequent argument. Misunderstandings as to terms are not a good foundation for a treaty to promote peace. . . .

In this draft prepared for a constitution of a league of nations, which is now before the world, there is hardly a clause about the interpretation of which men do not already differ. As it stands there is serious danger that the very nations which sign the constitution of the league will quarrel about the meaning of the various articles before a twelvemonth has passed.

It seems to have been very hastily drafted, and the result is crudeness and looseness of expression, unintentional, I hope. There are certainly many doubtful passages and open questions obvious in the articles which can not be settled by individual inference, but which must be made so clear and so distinct that we may all understand the exact meaning of the instrument to which we are asked to set our hands. The language of these articles does not appear to me to have the precision and unmistakable character which a constitution, a treaty, or a law ought to present. The language only too frequently is not the language of laws or statutes. The article concerning mandatories, for example, contains an argument and a statement of existing conditions. Arguments and historical facts have no place in a statute or a treaty. Statutory and legal language must assert and command, not argue and describe. I press this point because there is nothing so vital to the peace of the world as the sanctity of treaties. The suggestion that we can safely sign because we can always violate or abrogate is fatal not only to any league but to peace itself. You can not found world peace upon the cynical "scrap of paper" doctrine so dear to Germany. To whatever instrument the United States sets its hand it must carry out the provisions of that instrument to the last jot and tittle, and observe it absolutely both in letter and in spirit. If this is not done the instrument will become a source of controversy instead of agreement, of dissension instead of harmony. This is all the more essential because it is evident, although not expressly stated, that this league is intended to be indissoluble, for there is no provision for its termination or for the withdrawal of any signatory. We are left to infer that any nation withdrawing from the league exposes itself to penalties and probably to war. Therefore, before we ratify, the terms and language in which the terms are stated must be as exact and as precise, as free from any possibility of conflicting interpretations, as it is possible to make them. . . .

What I have just said indicates the vast importance of the form and the manner in which the agreements which we are to sign shall be stated. I now come to questions of substance, which seem to me to demand the most careful thought of the entire American people, and particularly of those charged with the responsibility of ratification. We abandon entirely by the proposed constitution the policy laid down by Washington in his Farewell Address and the Monroe doctrine. It is worse than idle, it is not honest, to evade, or deny this fact, and every fairminded supporter of this draft plan for a league admits it. I know that some of the ardent advocates of the plan submitted to us regard any suggestion of the importance of the Washington policy as foolish and irrelevant. Perhaps it is. Perhaps the time has come when the policies of Washington should be abandoned; but if we are to cast them aside I think that at least it should be done respectfully and with a sense of gratitude to the great man who formulated them. For nearly a century and a quarter the policies laid down in the Farewell Address have been followed and adhered to by the Government of the United States and by the American people. I doubt if any purely political declaration has even been observed by any people for so long a time. The principles of the Farewell Address in regard to our foreign relations have been sustained and acted upon by the American people down to the present moment. Washington declared against permanent alliances. He did not close the door on temporary alliances for particular purposes. Our entry in the great war just closed was entirely in accord with and violated in no respect the policy laid down by Washington. When we went to war with Germany we made no treaties with the nations engaged in the war against the German Government. The President was so careful in this direction that he did not permit himself ever to refer to the nations by whose side we fought as "allies," but always as "nations associated with us in the war." The attitude recommended by Washington was scrupulously maintained even under the pressure of the great conflict. Now, in the twinkling of an eye, while passion and emotion reign, the Washington policy is to be entirely laid aside and we are to enter upon a permanent and indissoluble alliance. That which we refuse to do in war we are to do in peace, deliberately, coolly, and with no war exigency. Let us not overlook the profound gravity of this step. . . .

But if we put aside forever the Washington policy in regard to our foreign relations we must always remember that it carries with it the corollary known as the Monroe doctrine. Under the terms of this league draft reported by the committee to the peace conference the Monroe doctrine disappears. It has been our cherished guide and guard for nearly a century. The Monroe doctrine is based on the principle of self-preservation. To say that it is a question of protecting the boundaries, the political integrity, of the American States, is not to see the Monroe doctrine. Boundaries have been changed among American States since the Monroe doctrine was enunciated. That is not the kernel of the doctrine. The real essence of that doctrine is that American questions shall be settled by Americans alone; that the Americans shall be separated from Europe and from the interference of Europe in purely American questions. That is the vital principle of the doctrine.

I have seen it said that the Monroe doctrine is preserved under article 10; that we do not abandon the Monroe doctrine, we merely extend it to all the world. How anyone can say this passes my comprehension. The Monroe doctrine exists solely for the protection of the American Hemisphere, and to that hemisphere it was limited. If you extend it to all the world, it ceases to exist, because it rests on nothing but the differentiation of the American Hemisphere from the rest of the world. Under this draft of the constitution of the league of nations, American questions and European questions and Asian and African questions are all alike put within the control and jurisdiction of the league. Europe will have the right to take part in the settlement of all American questions, and we, of course, shall have the right to share in the settlement of all questions in Europe and Asia and Africa. Europe and Asia are to take part in policing the American continent and the Panama Canal, and in return we are to have, by way of compensation, the right to police the Balkans and Asia Minor when we are asked to do so. Perhaps the time has come when it is necessary to do this, but it is a very grave step, and I wish now merely to point out that the American people ought never to abandon the Washington policy and the Monroe doctrine without being perfectly certain that they earnestly wish to do so. . . .

Two other general propositions, and I shall proceed to examine these league articles in detail. In article 10 we, in common, of course, with the other signatories and members of the projected league, guarantee the territorial integrity and the political independence of every member of the league. That means that we ultimately guarantee the independence and the boundaries, as now settled or as they may be settled by the treaty with Germany, of every nation on earth. If the United States agrees to guaranties of that sort we must maintain them. The word of the United States, her promise to guarantee the independence and the boundaries of any country, whether she does it alone or in company with other nations, whether she guarantees one country or all the countries of the world, is just as sacred as her honor — far more important than the maintenance of every financial pledge, which the people of this country would never consent to break.

I do not now say the time has not come when, in the interest of future peace, the American people may not decide that we ought to guarantee the territorial integrity of the far-flung British Empire, including her self-governing dominions and colonies, of the Balkan States, of China, or Japan, or of the French, Italian, and Portuguese colonies in Africa; but I do suggest that it is a very grave, a very perilous promise to make, because there is but one way by which such guaranties, if ever invoked, can be maintained, and that way is the way of force — whether military or economic force, it matters not. If we guarantee any country on the earth, no matter how small or how large, in its independence or its boundaries, that guarantee we must maintain at any cost when our word is once given, and we must be in constant possession of fleets and armies capable of enforcing these guarantees at a moment's notice. There is no need of arguing whether there is to be compulsive force behind this league. It is there in article 10 absolutely and entirely by the mere fact of these guaranties. The ranks of the armies and fleets of the navy made necessary by such pledges are to be filled and manned by the sons, husbands, and brothers of the people of America. I wish them carefully to consider, therefore, whether they are willing to have the youth of America ordered to war by other nations without regard to what they or their representatives desire. I would have them determine after much reflection whether they are willing to have the United States forced into war by other nations against her own will. They must bear in mind constantly that we have only one vote in the executive council, only one vote in the body of delegates, and a majority of the votes rules and is decisive.

I am not here to discuss the constitutional question of the sole right of Congress to declare war. That is a detail, as it relates only to the Constitution, which we may decide later. In my own opinion, we shall be obliged to modify the Constitution. I do not think, and I never can admit, that we can change or modify the Constitution by a treaty negotiated by the President and ratified by the Senate. I think that must be done, and can only be done, in the way prescribed by the Constitution itself, and to promise to amend our Constitution is a serious task and a doubtful undertaking.

I hope the American people will take time to consider this promise before they make it — because when it is once made it can not be broken — and ask themselves whether this is the best way of assuring perfect peace throughout the future years, which is what we are aiming at, for we all are aiming at the same object. A world's peace which requires at the outset preparations for war — for war either economic or military — in order to maintain that peace, presents questions and awakens thoughts which certainly ought to be soberly and discreetly considered.

The second general proposition to which I would call attention is this: We now in this draft bind ourselves to submit every possible international dispute or difference either to the league court or to the control of the executive council of the league. That includes immigration, a very live question, to take a single example. Are we ready to give to other nations the power to say who shall come into the United States and become citizens of the Republic? If we are ready to do this, we are prepared to part with the most precious of sovereign rights, that which guards our existence and our character as a Nation. Are we ready to leave it to other nations to determine whether we shall admit to the United States a flood of Japanese, Chinese, and Hindu labor? If we accept this plan for a league, this is precisely what we promise to do. I know that by following out all the windings of the provision for referring to the council or allowing the council to take charge of what has been called hitherto a conjusticiable question, we shall probably reach a point where it would not be possible to secure unanimous action by the league upon the question of immigration. But, Mr. President, I start with the proposition that there should be no jurisdiction in the league at all over that question; that it should be separated absolutely and entirely from any jurisdiction of the league. Are we prepared to have a league of nations — in which the United States has only one vote, which she could not cast on a dispute to which she was a party — open our doors, if they see fit, to any and all immigration from all parts of the world?

Mr. Taft has announced, in an article which appeared in the National Geographic Magazine, that the question of immigration will go before the international tribunal, and he says now that all organized labor is for the league. If American labor favors putting the restriction of immigration in the control of other nations they must have radically changed their minds and abandoned their most cherished policy. Certainly the gravity of such promises as are involved in the points I have suggested is sufficient to forbid haste. If such promises are to be given they must be given in cold blood with a full realization of what they mean and after the American people and those who represent them here have considered all that is involved with a serious care such as we have never been called upon to exercise before. We are asked to abandon the policies which we have adhered to during all our life as a Nation. We are asked to guarantee the political independence and the territorial integrity of every nation which chooses to join the league — and that means all nations as the President stated in his speech at Manchester. We are asked to leave to the decision of other nations, or to the jurisdiction of other nations, the question of what immigrants shall come to the United States. We are asked also to give up in part our sovereignty and our independence and subject our own will to the will of other nations, if there is a majority against our desires. We are asked, therefore, in a large and important degree to substitute internationalism for nationalism and an international state for pure Americanism. Certainly such things as these deserve reflection, discussion, and earnest thought.

I am not contending now that these things must not be done. I have no intention of opposing a blank negative to propositions which concern the peace of the world, which I am as anxious to see promoted as any living man can be; but I do say, in the strongest terms, that these things

I have pointed out are of vast importance not only to us but to the entire world, and a mistake now in making the league of nations might result in more war and trouble than the old system in its worst days. What I ask, and all I ask, is consideration, time, and thought. . . .

. . . When the United States enters into an indissoluble permanent alliance there ought to be, as I have said, no uncertainties in the terms of the agreement. I earnestly desire to do everything that can be done to secure the peace of the world, but these articles as they stand in this proposed constitution seem to give a rich promise of being fertile in producing controversies and misunderstandings. They also make some demands which I do not believe any nation would submit to in a time of stress. Therefore this machinery would not promote the peace of the world, but would have a directly opposite effect. It would tend to increase the subjects of misunderstanding and dispute among the nations. Is it not possible to draft a better, more explicit, less dangerous scheme than the one here and now presented? Surely we are not to be shut up to this as the last and only word to take or leave.

To those who object that the criticism of this tentative draft plan of the committee of the peace conference must be not only destructive but constructive it might be said that the burden of proof lies upon those who propose, in order to establish the future peace of the world, that the United States must curtail its independence, part with a portion of its sovereignty, and abandon all the international policies which have been so successful for more than a hundred years. Those who support the present draft of the constitution for the league must demonstrate that it is an improvement before they can expect its general acceptance. But the Senate can not at this time undertake to make plans for a league; because we are in the process of negotiation, and the Senate does not begin to act until the stage of ratification is reached. At the same time there are certain constructive propositions which it would be well, I think, for the peace conference to consider. If it is said that you can preserve the Monroe doctrine by extending it, which appears to me clearly to mean its destruction and to be a contradiction in terms, then let us put three lines into the draft for the league which will preserve the Monroe doctrine beyond any possibility of doubt or question. It is easily done. Let us also have, if we enter the league, a complete exclusion from the league's jurisdiction of such questions as are involved in immigration and the right of each country to say who shall come within its borders and become citizens. This and certain other questions vital to national existence ought to be exempted from any control or jurisdiction by the league or its officials by a very few words, such as can be found in the arbitration treaties of 1907. There should be some definite provision for peaceful withdrawal from the league if any nation desires to withdraw. Lastly, let us have a definite statement in the constitution of the league as to whether the league is to have an international force of its own or is to have the power to summon the armed forces of the different members of the league. Let it be stated in plain language whether the "measures," the "recommendations," or the suggestions of the executive council are to be binding upon the members of the league and are to compel them, technically or morally, to do what the league delegates and the executive council determine to be necessary. On the question of the use of force we should not proceed in the dark. If those who support the league decline to make such simple statements as these — I mean statements in the body of the instrument, not individual statements — it is impossible to avoid the conclusion that they are seeking to do by indirection and the use of nebulous phrases what they are not willing to do directly, and nothing could be more fatal to the preservation of the world's peace than this, for every exercise of power by the executive council which the signatories to the league might fairly consider to be doubtful would lead to very perilous controversies and to menacing quarrels.

Unless some better constitution for a league than this can be drawn, it seems to me, after such examination as I have been able to give, that the world's peace would be much better, much more surely prompted, by allowing the United States to go on under the Monroe doctrine, responsible for the peace of this hemisphere, without any danger of collision with Europe as to questions among the various American States, and if a league is desired it might be made up by the Euorpean nations whose interests are chiefly concerned, and with which the United States could coöperate fully and at any time, whenever coöperation was needed. I suppose I shall make myself the subject of derision for quoting from the Farewell Address, but it states a momentous truth so admirably that I can not refrain from giving it, for I think it ought to be borne in mind. Washington says:

> Europe has a set of primary interests which to us have none or a very remote relation. Hence she must be engaged in frequent controversies the causes of which are essentially foreign to our concerns. Hence, therefore, it must be unwise in us to implicate ourselves by artificial ties in the ordinary vicissitudes of her politics or the ordinary combinations and collisions of her friendships or enmities.

It must be remembered that if the United States enters any league of nations it does so for the benefit of the world at large, and not for its own benefit. The people of the United States are a peace-loving people. We have no boundaries to rectify, no schemes, and no desire for the acquisition or conquest of territory. We have in the main kept the peace in the American hemisphere. The States of South America have grown constantly more stable, and revolutions have well-nigh disappeared in the States south of those bordering on the Caribbean. No one questions that the United States is able to prevent any conflicts in the American hemisphere which would involve the world in any way or be more than passing difficulties, which in most cases could be settled by arbitration. If we join a league, therefore, it must be with a view to maintaining peace in Europe, where all the greatest wars have originated, and where there is always danger of war, and in Asia, where serious conflicts may arise at any moment. If we join a league, of course, we have in mind the danger of European conflicts springing up in such a way as to involve us in the defense of civilization, as has just happened in the war with Germany. But such wars as that are, fortunately, rare; so rare that one has never before occurred, and when the time came we took our part; but in the main our share in any league must be almost wholly for the benefit of others. We have the right, therefore, to demand that there shall be nothing in any agreement for the maintenance of the world's peace which is likely to produce new causes of difference and dissension, or which is calculated to injure the United States, or compel from us undue sacrifice, or put us in a position where we may be forced to serve the ambitions of others. There is no gain for peace in the Americas to be found by annexing the Americas to the European system. Whatever we do there we do from almost purely altruistic motives, and therefore we are entitled to consider every proposition with the utmost care in order to make sure that it does not do us injustice or render future conditions worse instead of better than they are at present.

To me the whole subject is one of enormous difficulties. We are all striving for a like result; but to make any real advances toward the future preservation of the world's peace will take time, care, and long consideration. We can not reach our objects by a world constitution hastily constructed in a few weeks in Paris in the midst of the excitement of a war not yet ended. The one thing to do, as I said in the Senate some time ago, and that which I now wish above all others, is to make the peace with Germany — to make a peace which by its terms will prevent her from breaking out again upon the world; to exclude Turkey from Europe, strengthen Greece, and give freedom and independence to the Armenians and to the Jewish and Christian populations of Asia Minor; to erect the barrier States for the Poles, Czecho-Slovaks, and Jugo-Slavs; to take possession of the Kiel Canal; to establish the Baltic States and free them from Russia and restore Danish Schleswig to Denmark. Provision must be made for indemnities or reparation, or by whatever name we choose to call the damages to be exacted from Germany. We ought, in my judgment, to receive indemnities which would enable us to provide for the *Lusitania* claims and for the destruction of our ships by submarines — to go no further. But the enormous losses of England and Italy in shipping should be made good, either in money or in kind. Belgium must be restored and fully compensated for her terrible injuries.

Finally there is France, and the indemnities to France ought to be ample and complete. . . . We ought then to make this peace with Germany and make it at once. Much time has been wasted. The delays have bred restlessness and confusion everywhere. Germany is lifting her head again. The whining after defeat is changing to threats. She is seeking to annex nine millions of Germans in German Austria. She is reaching out in Russia and reviving her financial and commercial penetration everywhere. Her fields have not been desolated nor her factories destroyed. Germany is again threatening, and the only source of a great war is to be found in the future as in the past in Germany. She should be chained and fettered now and this menace to the world's peace should be removed at once. Whatever else we fought for certainly our first and paramount purpose was to defeat Germany. The victory over Germany is not yet complete. Let it be made so without delay.

That which I desire above everything else, that which is nearest to my heart, is to bring our soldiers home. The making of a league of nations will not do that. We can only bring our soldiers home, entirely and completely, when the peace with Germany is made and proclaimed. Let that peace be made and I can assure the world that when the treaty of peace with Germany comes in this Chamber there will be no delay in the Senate of the United States. We must bring our men back from France — the men who fought the war, the men who made the personal sacrifice. Let us get them back at once, and to that end let us have the peace made with Germany, made now, and not delay it until the complicated questions of the league of nations can be settled with the care and consideration which they demand. What is it that delays the peace with Germany? Discussions over the league of nations; nothing else. Let us have peace now, in this year of grace 1919. That is the first step to the future peace of the world. The next step will be to make sure if we can that the world shall have peace in the year 1950 or 2000. Let us have the peace with Germany and bring our boys home. . . .

John Maynard Keynes
FAILURE AT VERSAILLES

❧{*1920*}❧ AT four o'clock on the morning of May 7, 1919, Herbert Hoover (1874-1964), a member of the American delegation to the Paris Peace Conference, was awakened by the arrival of a messenger with a copy of the just-released final draft of the Versailles Treaty. Despite the hour, Hoover began to read it at once, for as he well knew, the future of the whole world was tied to its clauses.

He was profoundly shocked by what he read. "Hate and revenge ran through the political and economic passages," he noted. Too disturbed to go back to bed, Hoover dressed and went out to pace the Paris streets. Soon he met General Jan Smuts (1870-1950) of South Africa and a young British delegate named John Maynard Keynes (1883-1946), an economist. They too were very distressed by the Treaty; the hopes raised by Wilson's Fourteen Points seemed utterly dashed. "We agreed that it was terrible and we would do what we could among our own nationals to make the dangers clear," Hoover later recalled.

Of the three Keynes was by far the least well-known and influential, but only he made any really effective move against the Treaty. Early in June he resigned as a delegate. Then, returning to England, he took up his pen to state "the grounds of his objection . . . to the whole policy of the Conference toward the economic problems of Europe." The result was *The Economic Consequences of the Peace.* After describing the economic organization of Europe before the war, Keynes went on to discuss the leaders and their ideas, which he then contrasted with the terms of the Versailles Treaty, stressing the extent to which "political considerations cut drastically across economic" in the drafting of various clauses. Finally, he painted a dark picture of the effects which the settlement was bound to have on Germany and on all Europe, and he suggested ways in which this bleak result might be avoided or modified.

Keynes's book was an instant sensation, and for two reasons. First of all, his arguments were both irrefutable and clearly presented. Germany could *not* pay what was demanded, and any unprejudiced person who read the *Economic Consequences* could understand why—neither jargon nor academic ponderosities cluttered its pages. Second, Keynes's acid portraits of the Big Four made his book a *succès de scandale.* Thus literary artistry, economic insight, and forthrightness combined to produce a *tour de force.*

Keynes, one of the most remarkable and important minds of the century, went on to develop a whole new school of economic thought, one which had a great impact on the financing of World War II and on our present concepts of how to avoid depressions.

THE ECONOMIC CONSEQUENCES OF THE PEACE

THE power to become habituated to his surroundings is a marked characteristic of mankind. Very few of us realize with conviction the intensely unusual, unstable, complicated, unreliable, temporary nature of the economic organization by which Western Europe has lived for the last half century. We assume some of the most peculiar and temporary of our late advantages as natural, permanent, and to be depended on, and we lay our plans accordingly. On this sandy and false foundation we scheme for social improvement and dress our political platforms, pursue our animosities and particular ambitions, and feel ourselves with enough margin in hand to foster, not assuage, civil conflict in the European family. Moved by insane delusion and reckless self-regard, the German people overturned the foundations on which we all lived and built. But the spokesmen of the French and British peoples have run the risk of completing the ruin, which Germany began, by a Peace which, if it is carried into effect, must impair yet further, when it might have restored, the delicate, complicated organization, already shaken and broken by war, through which alone the European peoples can employ themselves and live. . . .

. . . If the European Civil War is to end with France and Italy abusing their momentary victorious power to destroy Germany and Austria-Hungary now prostrate, they invite their own destruction also, being so deeply and inextricably intertwined with their victims by hidden psychic and economic bonds. . . .

. . . I shall study in some detail the economic and financial provisions of the Treaty of Peace with Germany. But it will be easier to appreciate the true origin of many of these terms if we examine here some of the personal factors which influenced their preparation . . .

Clemenceau was by far the most eminent member of the Council of Four, and he had taken the measure of his colleagues. He alone both had an idea and had considered it in all its consequences. His age, his character, his wit, and his appearance joined to give him objectivity and a defined outline in an environment of confusion. One could not despise Clemenceau or dislike him, but only take a different view as to the nature of civilized man, or indulge, at least, a different hope.

The figure and bearing of Clemenceau are universally familiar. At the Council of Four he wore a square-tailed coat of very good, thick black broadcloth, and on his hands, which were never uncovered, gray suède gloves; his boots were of thick black leather, very good, but of a country style, and sometimes fastened in front, curiously, by a buckle instead of laces. His seat in the room in the President's house, where the regular meetings of the Council of Four were held (as distinguished from their private and unattended conferences in a small chamber below), was on a square brocaded chair in the middle of the semicircle facing the fireplace, with Signor Orlando on his left, the President next by the fireplace, and the Prime Minister opposite on the other side of the fireplace on his right. He carried no papers and no portfolio, and was unattended by any personal secretary, though several French ministers and officials appropriate to the particular matter in hand would be present round him. His walk, his hand, and his voice were not lacking in vigor, but he bore nevertheless, especially after the attempt upon him, the aspect of a very old man conserving his strength for important occasions. He spoke seldom, leaving the initial statement of the French case to his ministers or officials; he closed his eyes often and sat back in his chair with an impassive face of parchment, his gray gloved hands clasped in front of him. A short sentence, decisive or cynical, was generally sufficient, a question, an unqualified abandonment of his ministers, whose face would not be saved, or a display of obstinacy reinforced by a few words in a piquantly delivered English. But speech and passion were not lacking when they were wanted, and the sudden outburst of words, often followed by a fit of deep coughing from the chest, produced their impression rather by force and surprise than by persuasion.

Not infrequently Mr. Lloyd George, after delivering a speech in English, would, during the period of its interpretation into French, cross the hearthrug to the President to reinforce his case by some *ad hominem* argument in private conversation, or to sound the ground for a compromise, — and this would sometimes be the signal for a general upheaval and disorder. The President's advisers would press round him, a moment later the British experts would dribble across to learn the result or see that all was well, and next the French would be there, a little suspicious lest the others were arranging something behind them, until all the room were on their feet and conversation was general in both languages. My last and most vivid impression is of such a scene — the President and the Prime Minister as the center of a surging mob and a babel of sound, a welter of eager, impromptu compromises and counter-compromises, all sound and fury signifying nothing, on what was an unreal question anyhow, the great issues of the morning's meeting forgotten and neglected; and Clemenceau silent and aloof on the outskirts — for nothing which touched the security of France was forward — throned, in his gray gloves, on the brocade chair, dry in soul and empty of hope, very old and tired, but surveying the scene with a cynical and almost impish air; and when at last silence was restored and the company had returned to their places, it was to discover that he had disappeared. . . .

When President Wilson left Washington he enjoyed a prestige and a moral influence throughout the world unequaled in history. His bold and measured words carried to the peoples of Europe above and beyond the voices of their own politicians. The enemy peoples trusted him to carry out the compact he had made with them; and the Allied peoples acknowledged him not as a victor only but almost as a prophet. In addition to this moral influence the realities of power were in his hands. The American armies were at the height of their numbers, disciplines, and equipment. Europe was in complete dependence on the food supplies of the United States; and financially she was even more absolutely at their mercy. Europe not only already owed the United States more than she could pay; but only a large measure of further assistance could save her from starvation and bankruptcy. Never had a philosopher held such weapons wherewith to bind the princes of this world. How the crowds of the European capitals pressed about the carriage of the President! With what curiosity, anxiety, and hope we sought a glimpse of the features and bearing of the man of destiny who, coming from the West, was to bring healing to the wounds of the ancient parent of his civilization and lay for us the foundations of the future.

The disillusion was so complete, that some of those who had trusted most hardly dared speak of it. Could it be true? they asked of those who returned from Paris. Was the Treaty really as bad as it seemed? What had happened to the President? What weakness or what misfortune had led to so extraordinary, so unlooked-for a betrayal?

Yet the causes were very ordinary and human. The President was not a hero or a prophet; he was not even a philosopher; but a generously intentioned man, with many of the weaknesses of other human beings, and lacking that dominating intellectual equipment which would have been necessary to cope with the subtle and dangerous spellbinders whom a tremendous clash of forces and personalities had brought to the top as triumphant masters in the swift game of give and take, face to face in Council, — a game of which he had no experience at all.

We had indeed quite a wrong idea of the President. We knew him to be solitary and aloof, and believed him very strong-willed and obstinate. We did not figure him as a man of detail, but the clearness with which he had taken hold of certain main ideas would, we thought, in combination with his tenacity, enable him to sweep through cobwebs. Besides these qualities he would have the objectivity, the cultivation, and the wide knowledge of the student. The great distinction of language which had marked his famous Notes seemed to indicate a man of lofty and powerful imagination. His portraits indicated a fine presence and a commanding delivery. With all this he had attained and held with increasing authority the first position in a country where the arts of the politician are not neglected. All of which, without expecting the impossible, seemed a fine combination of qualities for the matter in hand.

The first impression of Mr. Wilson at close quarters was to impair some but not all of these illusions. His head and features were finely cut and exactly like this photographs, and the muscles of his neck and the carriage of his head were distinguished. But, like Odysseus, the President looked wiser when he was seated; and his hands, though capable and fairly strong, were wanting in sensitiveness and finesse. The first glance at the President suggested not only that, whatever else he might be, his temperament was not primarily that of the student or the scholar, but that he had not much even of that culture of the world which marks M. Clemenceau and Mr. Balfour as exquisitely cultivated gentlemen of their class and generation. But more serious than this, he was not only insensitive to his surroundings in the external sense, he was not sensitive to his environment at all. What chance could such a man have against M. Lloyd George's unerring, almost medium-like, sensibility to every one immediately round him? To see the British Prime Minister watching the company, with six or seven senses not available to ordinary men, judging character, motive, and subconscious impulse, perceiving what each was thinking and even what each was going to say next, and compounding with telepathic instinct the argument or appeal best suited to the vanity, weakness, or self-interest of his immediate auditor, was to realize that the poor President would be playing blind man's buff in that party. Never could a man have stepped into the parlor a more perfect and predestined victim to the finished accomplishments of the Prime Minister. The Old World was tough in wickedness anyhow; the Old World's heart of stone might blunt the sharpest blade of the bravest knight-errant. But this blind and deaf Don Quixote was entering a cavern where the swift and glittering blade was in the hands of the adversary.

But if the President was not the philosopher-king, what was he? After all he was a man who had spent much of his life at a University. He was by no means a business man or an ordinary party politician, but a man of force, personality, and importance. What, then, was his temperament?

The clue once found was illuminating. The President was like a Nonconformist minister, perhaps a Presbyterian. His thought and his temperament were essentially theological not intellectual, with all the strength and the weakness of that manner of thought, feeling, and expression. . . .

. . . There can seldom have been a statesman of the first rank more incompetent than the President in the agilities of the council chamber. A moment often arrives when substantial victory is yours if by some slight appearance of a concession you can save the face of the opposition or conciliate them by a restatement of your proposal helpful to them and not injurious to anything essential to yourself. The President was not equipped with this simple and usual artfulness. His mind was too slow and unresourceful to be ready with *any* alternatives. The President was capable of digging his toes in and refusing to budge, as he did over Fiume. But he had no other mode of defense, and it needed as a rule but little manœuvering by his opponents to prevent matters from coming to such a head until it was too late. By pleasantness and an appearance of conciliation, the President would be manœuvered off his ground, would miss the moment for digging his toes in, and, before he knew where he had been got to, it was too late. Besides, it is impossible month after month in intimate and ostensibly friendly converse between close associates, to be digging the toes in all the time. Victory would only have been possible to one who had always a sufficiently lively apprehension of the position as a whole to reserve his fire and know for certain the rare exact moments for decisive action. And for that the President was far too slow-minded and bewildered.

He did not remedy these defects by seeking aid from the collective wisdom of his lieutenants. He had gathered round him for the economic chapters of the Treaty a very able group of business men; but they were inexperienced in public affairs, and knew (with one or two exceptions) as little of Europe as he did, and they were only called in irregularly as he might need them for a particular purpose. Thus the aloofness which had been found effective in Washington was maintained, and the abnormal reserve of his nature did not allow near him any one who aspired to moral equality or the continuous exercise of influence. His fellow-plenipotentiaries were dummies; and even the trusted Colonel House, with vastly more knowledge of men and of Europe than the President, from whose sensitiveness the President's dullness had gained so much, fell in to the background as time went on. All this was encouraged by his colleagues on the Council of Four, who, by the break-up of the Council of Ten, completed the isolation which the President's own temperament had initiated. Thus day after day and week after week, he allowed himself to be closeted, unsupported, unadvised, and alone, with men much sharper than himself, in situations of supreme difficulty, where he needed for success every description of resource, fertility, and knowledge. He allowed himself to be drugged by their atmosphere, to discuss on the basis of their plans and of their data, and to be led along their paths.

These and other various causes combined to produce the following situation. The reader must remember that the processes which are here compressed into a few pages took place slowly, gradually, insidiously, over a period of about five months.

As the President had thought nothing out, the Council was generally working on the basis of a French or British draft. He had to take up, therefore, a persistent attitude of obstruction, criticism, and negation, if the draft was to become at all in line with his own ideas and purpose. If he was met on some points with apparent generosity (for there was always a safe margin of quite preposterous suggestions which no one took seriously), it was difficult for him not to yield on others. Compromise was inevitable, and never to compromise on the essential, very difficult. Besides, he was soon made to appear to be taking the German part and laid himself open to the suggestion (to which he was foolishly and unfortunately sensitive) of being "pro-German." . . .

Now it was that what I have called his theological or Presbyterian temperament became dangerous. Having decided that some concessions were unavoidable, he might have sought by firmness and address and the use of the financial power of the United States to secure as much as he could of the substance, even at some sacrifice of the letter. But the President was not capable of so clear an understanding with himself as this implied. He was too conscientious. Although compromises were now necessary, he remained a man of principle and the Fourteen Points a contract absolutely binding upon him. He would do nothing that was not honorable; he would do nothing that was not just and right; he would do nothing that was contrary to his great profession of faith. Thus, without any abatement of the verbal inspiration of the Fourteen Points, they became a document for gloss and interpretation and for all the intellectual apparatus of self-deception, by which, I daresay, the President's forefathers had persuaded themselves that the course they thought it necessary to take was consistent with every syllable of the Pentateuch.

The President's attitude to his colleagues had now become: I want to meet you so far as I can; I see your difficulties and I should like to be able to agree to what you propose; but I can do nothing that is not just and right, and you must first of all show me that what you want does really fall within the words of the pronouncements which are binding on me. Then began the weaving of that web of sophistry and Jesuitical exegesis that was finally to clothe with insincerity the language and substance of the whole Treaty. The word was issued to the witches of all Paris:

> Fair is foul, and foul is fair.
> Hover through the fog and filthy air.

The subtlest sophisters and most hypocritical draftsmen were set to work, and produced many ingenious exercises which might have deceived for more than an hour a cleverer man than the President. . . .

. . . Perhaps the most decisive moment, in the disintegration of the President's moral position and the clouding of his mind, was when at last, to the dismay of his advisers, he allowed himself to be persuaded that the expenditure of the Allied Governments on pensions and separation allowances could be fairly regarded as "damage done to the civilian population of the Allied and Associated Powers by German aggression by land, by sea, and from the air," in a sense in which the other expenses of the war could not be so regarded. It was a long theological struggle in which, after the rejection of many different arguments, the President finally capitulated before a masterpiece of the sophist's art.

At last the work was finished; and the President's conscience was still intact. In spite of everything, I believe that his temperament allowed him to leave Paris a really sincere man; and it is probable that to this day he is genuinely convinced that the Treaty contains practically nothing inconsistent with his former professions.

But the work was too complete, and to this was due the last tragic episode of the drama. The reply of Brockdorff-Rantzau inevitably took the line that Germany had laid down her arms on the basis of certain assurances, and that the Treaty in many particulars was not consistent with these assurances. But this was exactly what the President could not admit; in the sweat of solitary contemplation and with prayers to God he had done *nothing* that was not just and right; for the President to admit that the German reply had force in it was to destroy his self-respect and to disrupt the inner equipoise of his soul; and every instinct of his stubborn nature rose in self-protection. In the language of medical psychology, to suggest to the President that the Treaty was an abandonment of his professions was to touch on the raw a Freudian complex. It was a subject intolerable to discuss, and every subconscious instinct plotted to defeat its further exploration.

Thus it was that Clemenceau brought to success, what had seemed to be a few months before, the extraordinary and impossible proposal that the Germans should not be heard. If only the President had not been so conscientious, if only he had not concealed from himself what he had been doing, even at the last moment he was in a position to have recovered lost ground and to have achieved some very considerable successes. But the President was set. His arms and legs had been spliced by the surgeons to a certain posture, and they must be broken again before they could be altered. To his horror, Mr. Lloyd George, desiring at the last moment all the moderation he dared, discovered that he could not in five days persuade the President of error in what it had taken five months to prove to him to be just and right. After all, it was harder to de-bamboozle this old Presbyterian than it had been to bamboozle him; for the former involved his belief in and respect for himself.

Thus in the last act the President stood for stubbornness and a refusal of conciliations. . . .

The categories of damage in respect of which the Allies were entitled to ask for Reparation are governed by the relevant passages in President Wilson's Fourteen Points of January 8, 1918, as modified by the Allied Governments in their qualifying Note, the text of which the President formally communicated to the German Government as the basis of peace on November 5, 1918. . . . That is to say, "compensation will be made by Germany for all damage done to the civilian population of the Allies and to their property by the aggression of Germany by land, by sea, and from the air." . . .

What damages, then, can be claimed from the enemy on a strict interpretation of our engagements? In the case of the United Kingdom the bid would cover the following items: —

(*a*) Damage to civilian life and property by the acts of an enemy Government including damage by air raids, naval bombardments, submarine warfare, and mines.

(*b*) Compensation for improper treatment of internal civilians.

It would not include the general costs of the war, or (*e.g.*) indirect damage due to loss of trade.

The French claim would include, as well as items corresponding to the above, —

(*c*) Damage done to the property and persons of civilians in the war area, and by aerial warfare behind the enemy lines.

(*d*) Compensation for loot of food, raw materials, live-stock, machinery, household effects, timber, and the like by the enemy Governments or their nationals in territory occupied by them.

(*e*) Repayment of fines and requisitions levied by the enemy Governments or their officers on French municipalities or nationals.

(*f*) Compensation to French nationals deported or compelled to do forced labor.

In addition to the above there is a further item of more doubtful character, namely —

(*g*) The expenses of the Relief Commission in providing necessary food and clothing to maintain the civilian French population in the enemy-occupied districts. . . .

The claims of the other Allies would be compiled on similar lines. . . .

Belgium	.$ 2,500,000,000
France	4,000,000,000
Great Britain	2,850,000,000
Other Allies	1,250,000,000
Total	.$10,600,000,000

I need not impress on the reader that there is much guesswork in the above, and the figure for France in particular is likely to be criticized. But I feel some confidence that the *general magnitude,* as distinct from the precise figures, is not hopelessly erroneous; and this may be expressed by the statement that a claim against Germany, based on the interpretation of the pre-Armistice engagements of the Allied Powers which is adopted above, would assuredly be found to exceed $8,000,000,000 and to fall short of $15,000,000,000.

This is the amount of the claim which we were entitled to present to the enemy. For reasons which will appear more fully later on, I believe that it would have been a wise and just act to have asked the German Government at the Peace Negotiations to agree to a sum of $10,000,000,-000 in final settlement, without further examination of particulars. This would have provided an immediate and certain solution, and would have required from Germany a sum which, if she were granted certain indulgences, it might not have proved entirely impossible for her to pay. This sum should have been divided up amongst the Allies themselves on a basis of need and general equity.

But the question was not settled on its merits. . . .

. . . I believe that the campaign for securing out of Germany the general costs of the war was one of the most serious acts of political unwisdom for which our statesmen have ever been responsible. To what a different future Europe might have looked forward if either Mr. Lloyd George or Mr. Wilson had apprehended that the most serious of the problems which claimed their attention were not political or territorial but financial and economic, and that the perils of the future lay not in frontiers or sovereignties but in food, coal, and transport. Neither of them paid adequate attention to these problems at any stage of the Conference. But in any event the atmosphere for the wise and reasonable consideration of them was hopelessly befogged by the commitments of the British delegation on the question of Indemnities. The hopes to which the Prime Minister had given rise not only compelled him to advocate an unjust and unworkable economic basis to the Treaty with Germany, but set him at variance with the President, and on the other hand with competing interests to those of France and Belgium. The clearer it became that but little could be expected from Germany, the more necessary it was to exercise patriotic greed and "sacred egotism" and snatch the bone from the juster claims and greater need of France or the well-founded expectations of Belgium. Yet the financial problems which were about to exercise Europe could not be solved by greed. The possibility of *their* cure lay in magnanimity.

Europe, if she is to survive her troubles, will need so much magnanimity from America, that she must herself practice it. It is useless for the Allies, hot from stripping Germany and one another, to turn for help to the United States to put the States of Europe, including Germany, on to their feet again. If the General Election of December, 1918, had been fought on lines of prudent generosity instead of imbecile greed, how much better the financial prospect of Europe might now be. I still believe that before the main Conference, or very early in its proceedings, the representatives of Great Britain should have entered deeply, with those of the United States, into the economic and financial situation as a whole, and that the former should have been authorized to make concrete proposals on the general lines (1) that all inter-allied indebtedness be canceled outright; (2) that the sum to be paid by Germany be fixed at $10,000,000,000; (3) that Great Britain renounce all claim to participation in this sum and that any share to which she proves entitled be placed at the disposal of the Conference for the purpose of aiding the finances of the New States about to be established; (4) that in order to make some basis of credit immediately available an appropriate proportion of the German obligations representing the sum to be paid by her should be guaranteed by all parties to the Treaty; and (5) that the ex-enemy Powers should also be allowed, with a view to their economic restoration, to issue a moderate amount of bonds carrying a similar guarantee. Such proposals involved an appeal to the generosity of the United States. But that was inevitable; and, in view of her far less financial sacrifices, it was an appeal which could fairly have been made to her. Such proposals would have been practicable. There is nothing in them quixotic or Utopian. And they would have opened up for Europe some prospect of financial stability and reconstruction. . . .

What had really happened was a compromise between the Prime Minister's pledge to the British electorate to claim the entire costs of the war and the pledge to the contrary which the Allies had given to Germany at the Armistice. The Prime Minister could claim that although he had not secured the entire costs of the war, he had nevertheless secured an important contribution towards them, that he had always qualified his promises by the limiting condition of Germany's capacity to pay, and that the bill as now presented more than exhausted this capacity as estimated by the more sober authorities. The President, on the other hand, had secured a formula, which was not too obvious a breach of faith, and had avoided a quarrel with his Associates on an issue where the appeals to sentiment and passion would all have been against him, in the event of its being made a matter of open popular controversy. In view of the Prime Minister's election pledges, the President could hardly hope to get him to abandon them in their entirety without a struggle in public; and the cry of pensions would have had an overwhelming popular appeal in all countries. Once more the Prime Minister had shown himself a political tactician of a high order.

A further point of great difficulty may be readily perceived between the lines of the Treaty. It fixes no definite sum as representing Germany's liability. This feature has been the subject of very general criticism, — that it is equally inconvenient to Germany and to the Allies themselves that she should not know what she has to pay or they what they are to receive. The method, apparently contemplated by the Treaty, of arriving at the final result over a period of many months by an addition of hundreds of thousands of individual claims for damage to land, farm buildings, and chickens, is evidently impracticable; and the reasonable course would have been for both parties to compound for a round sum without examination of details. If this round sum had been named in the Treaty, the settlement would have been placed on a more business-like basis.

But this was impossible for two reasons. Two different kinds of false statements had been widely promulgated, one as to Germany's capacity to pay, the other as to the amount of the Allies' just claims in respect of the devastated areas. The fixing of either of these figures presented a dilemma. A figure for Germany's prospective capacity to pay, not too much in excess of the estimates of most candid and well-informed authorities, would have fallen hopelessly far short of popular expectations both in England and in France. On the other hand, a definitive figure for damage done which would not disastrously disappoint the expectations which had been raised in France and Belgium might have been incapable of substantiation under challenge, and open to damaging criticism on the part of the Germans, who were believed to have been prudent enough to accumulate considerable evidence as to the extent of their own misdoings.

By far the safest course for the politicians was therefore, to mention no figure at all. . . .

. . . There is a great difference between fixing a definite sum, which though large is within Germany's capacity to pay and yet to retain a little for herself, and fixing a sum far beyond her capacity, which is then to be reduced at the discretion of a foreign Commission acting with the object of obtaining each year the maximum which the circumstances of that year permit. The first still leaves her with some slight incentive for enterprise, energy, and hope. The latter skins her alive year by year in perpetuity, and however skillfully and discreetly the operation is performed, with whatever regard for not killing the patient in the process, it would represent a policy which, if it were really entertained and deliberately practised, the judgment of men would soon pronounce to be one of the most outrageous acts of a cruel victor in civilized history. . . .

I cannot leave this subject as though its just treatment wholly depended either on our own pledges or on economic facts. The policy of reducing Germany to servitude for a generation, of degrading the lives of millions of human beings, and of depriving a whole nation of happiness should be abhorrent and detestable, — abhorrrent and detestable, even if it were possible, even if it enriched ourselves, even if it did not sow the decay of the whole civilized life of Europe. Some preach it in the name of Justice. In the great events of man's history, in the unwinding of the complex fates of nations Justice is not so simple. And if it were, nations are not authorized, by religion or by natural morals, to visit on the children of their enemies the misdoings of parents or of rulers. . . .

National Popular Government League

THE RED SCARE

◆{*1920*}◆   IN EARLY April 1917, when Woodrow Wilson was struggling to find some way of avoiding war with Germany, he warned the editor Frank I. Cobb, whose influential New York *World* had just come out for war, that such action might destroy the American system of government. "Once lead this people into war and they'll forget there ever was such a thing as tolerance," the President said. "The spirit of ruthless brutality will enter into the very fibre of our national life, infecting Congress, the courts, the policeman on the beat, the man in the street." Although democracy eventually survived, Wilson's prediction was correct — so much so that even he was affected by the hysteria of wartime, lending his approval to harsh restraints on civil liberties and foolish persecutions of all things German.

The most serious expression of war-born intolerance, however, came after the war was over. It developed out of the frustrations accompanying the making of peace and the reconversion of the economy to peacetime conditions, and also from a rising fear of alien radicals, triggered by the successful communist revolution in Russia. This was the "Red Scare" of 1919–20. Fearful that a handful of extremists might seize power and overturn the capitalist system, thousands of Americans were ready to justify any effort to root out subversive elements. Wilson's Attorney General, A. Mitchell Palmer, after resisting the hysteria for a time, succumber to it completely. His agents conducted a series of raids designed to round up alien radicals for deportation.

Few real subversives were captured in Palmer's net, but thousands of innocent men were deprived of their rights and otherwise mistreated. Eventually, the failure of Palmer's tactics to produce results led to a popular reaction and the Red Scare passed into history. In no small part the National Popular Government League's investigation of Department of Justice practices, conducted by a group of prominent liberal lawyers and jurists, including Felix Frankfurter, Ernest Freund, and Roscoe Pound, contributed to this salutary result. The following selection from the League's *Report* describes both Palmer's activities and the indignation they eventually aroused among friends of civil liberties.

ILLEGAL PRACTICES OF THE DEPARTMENT OF JUSTICE

To the american people:

For more than six months we, the undersigned lawyers, whose sworn duty it is to uphold the Constitution and Laws of the United States, have seen with growing apprehension the continued violation of that Constitution and breaking of those Laws by the Department of Justice of the United States government.

Under the guise of a campaign for the suppression of radical activities, the office of the Attorney General, acting by its local agents throughout the country, and giving express instructions from Washington, has committed continual illegal acts. Wholesale arrests both of aliens and citizens have been made without warrant or any process of law; men and women have been jailed and held *incommunicado* without access of friends or counsel; homes have been entered without search-warrant and property seized and removed; other property has been wantonly destroyed; workingmen and workingwomen suspected of radical views have been shamefully abused and maltreated. Agents of the Department of Justice have been introduced into radical organizations for the purpose of informing upon their members or inciting them to activities; these agents have even been instructed from Washington to arrange meetings upon certain dates for the express object of facilitating wholesale raids and arrests. In support of these illegal acts, and to create sentiment in its favor, the Department of Justice has also constituted itself a propaganda bureau, and has sent to newspapers and magazines of this country quantities of material designed to excite public opinion against radicals, all at the expense of the government and outside the scope of the Attorney General's duties.

We make no argument in favor of any radical doctrine as such, whether Socialist, Communist or Anarchist. No one of us belongs to any of these schools of thought. Nor do we now raise any question as to the Constitutional protection of free speech and a free press. We are concerned solely with bringing to the attention of the American people the utterly illegal acts which have been committed by those charged with the highest duty of enforcing the laws — acts which have caused widespread suffering and unrest, have struck at the foundation of American free institutions, and have brought the name of our country into disrepute.

These acts may be grouped under the following heads:

(1) Cruel and Unusual Punishments:

The Eighth Amendment to the United States Constitution provides:

> Excessive bail shall not be required nor excessive fines imposed, nor cruel and unusual punishments inflicted.

Punishments of the utmost cruelty, and heretofore unthinkable in America, have become usual. Great numbers of persons arrested, both aliens and citizens, have been threatened, beaten with blackjacks, struck with fists, jailed under abominable conditions, or actually tortured. . . .

(2) Arrests without Warrant:

The Fourth Amendment to the Constitution provides:

> The right of the people to be secure in their persons, houses, papers, and effects, against unreasonable searches and seizures, shall not be violated, and no Warrants shall issue, but upon probable cause, supported by Oath or affirmation, and particularly describing the place to be searched, and the persons or things to be seized.

Many hundreds of citizens and aliens alike have been arrested in wholesale raids, without warrants or pretense of warrants. They have then either been released, or have been detained in police stations or jails for indefinite lengths of time while warrants were being applied for. This practice of making mass raids and mass arrests without warrant has resulted directly from the instructions, both written and oral, issued by the Department of Justice at Washington. . . .

(3) Unreasonable Searches and Seizures:

The Fourth Amendment has been quoted above.

In countless cases agents of the Department of Justice have entered the homes, offices, or gathering places of persons suspected of radical affiliations, and, without pretense of any search warrant, have seized and removed property belonging to them for use by the Department of Justice. In many of these raids property which could not be removed or was not useful to the Department was intentionally smashed and destroyed. . . .

(4) Provocative Agents:

We do not question the right of the Department of Justice to use its agents in the Bureau of Investigation to ascertain when the law is being violated. But the American people has never tolerated the use of undercover provocative agents or "agents provocateurs," such as have been familiar in old Russia or Spain. Such agents have been introduced by the Department of Justice into the radical movements, have reached positions of influence therein, have occupied themselves with informing upon or instigating acts which might be declared criminal, and at the express direction of Washington have brought about meetings of radicals in order to make possible wholesale arrests at such meetings. . . .

(5) Compelling Persons to be Witnesses against Themselves:

The Fifth Amendment provides as follows:

> No person . . . shall be compelled in any criminal case to be a witness against himself, nor be deprived of life, liberty, or property, without due process of law.

It has been the practice of the Department of Justice and its agents, after making illegal arrests without warrant, to question the accused person and to force admissions from him by terrorism, which admissions were subsequently to be used against him in deportation proceedings. . . .

The Exhibits attached are only a small part of the evidence which may be presented to the continued violation of law by the Attorney General's Department. These Exhibits are, to the best of our knowledge and belief (based upon careful investigation), truthful both in substance and detail. Drawn mainly from the four centers of New York City, Boston, Mass., Detroit, Mich., and Hartford, Conn., we know them to be typical of conditions which have prevailed in many parts of the country.

Since these illegal acts have been committed by the highest legal powers in the United States, there is no final appeal from them except to the conscience and condemnation of the American people. American institutions have not in fact been protected by the Attorney General's ruthless suppression. On the contrary, those institutions have been seriously undermined, and revolutionary unrest has been vastly intensified. No organizations of radicals acting through propaganda over the last six months could have created as much revolutionary sentiment in America as has been created by the acts of the Department of Justice itself.

Even were one to admit that there existed any serious "Red manace" before the Attorney General started his "unflinching war" against it, his campaign has been singularly fruitless. Out of the many thousands suspected by the Attorney General (he had already listed 60,000 by name and history on November 14, 1919, aliens and citizens) what do the figures show of net results? Prior to January 1, 1920, there were actually deported 263 persons. Since January 1 there have been actually deported 18 persons. Since January 1 there have been ordered deported an additional 529 persons, and warrants for 1,547 have been cancelled (after full hearings and consideration of the evidence) by Assistant Secretary of Labor Louis F. Post, to whose courageous reestablishment of American Constitutional Law in deportation proceedings are due the attacks that have been made upon him. The Attorney General has consequently got rid of 810 alien suspects, which, on his own showing, leaves him at least 59,160 persons (aliens and citizens) still to cope with.

It has always been the proud boast of America that this is a government of laws and not of men. Our Constitution and laws have been based on the simple elements of human nature. Free men cannot be driven and repressed; they must be led. Free men respect justice and follow truth, but arbitrary power they will oppose until the end of time. There is no danger of revolution so great as that created by suppression, by ruthlessness, and by deliberate violation of the simple rules of American law and American decency.

It is a fallacy to suppose that, any more than in the past, any servant of the people can safely arrogate to himself unlimited authority. To proceed upon such a supposition is to deny the fundamental American theory of the consent of the governed. Here is no question of a vague and threatened menace, but a present assault upon the most sacred principles of our Constitutional liberty.

EXHIBIT I. HARTFORD JAIL SITUATION

In Bridgeport, Conn., on November 8, 1919, various workingmen had come together to discuss ways and means for buying an automobile to be employed for instruction purposes. The meeting was raided and 63 men arrested without warrants by agents of the Department of Justice and taken to the police station. A day or two later, 16 of these were released. The remaining 47, after being held three days in the police station, where they slept on iron bunks without cover or mattress, and where they were fed little or nothing, were transferred by the Department of Justice to the Hartford jail. Other persons who were arrested in this way or who had applied at the Hartford jail for permission to see their friends, were also taken up and confined in the jail. There were finally 97 men held for deportation. Most of them were questioned by Department of Justice agents; some were beaten or threatened with hanging or suffocation in order to obtain answers from them. Warrants of arrest for these men were requested and obtained from the Department of Labor by the Department of Justice. Most of the 97 prisoners remained in practically solitary confinement until the end of April—five months. When the facts finally came to the attention of Mr. Louis F. Post, Assistant Secretary of Labor, he ordered the men all transferred to the Immigrant Station at Deer Island, Boston.

During these five months the prisoners were allowed no reading matter; were kept alone in their cells except for occasional visits from Department of Justice agents or hearings before Department of Labor Inspectors; were refused, in some cases, knowledge of the charges against them; were refused, in some cases, knowledge of the amount of bail under which they were held; were allowed only 2 to 5 minutes a day to wash their face and hands at a sink outside their cells, and 5 minutes once a month to wash their bodies in a tub, were given practically no exercise, and were fed with foul and insufficient food.

In the Hartford jail there exist four punishment rooms, all alike, unventilated and utterly dark, size 4 feet 3 inches by 8 feet 10 inches, with solid concrete floors, no furniture of any kind, and placed over the pump room of the boiler so that the temperature in them becomes unbearably high. A number of the supposed anarchist or Communist prisoners, probably ten to fifteen, were confined in these rooms for periods of 36 to 60 hours. During their imprisonment in the suffocating heat without air, they were given one glass of water and one slice of bread every 12 hours. Some of them on being released had to be revived before they could be carried to their cells; one man who was in only 36 hours was able to get to his cell unaided.

These Hartford prisoners were practically buried alive for five months, being even denied the privilege of seeing their relatives or friends, who made constant attempts to communicate with them. Only after a lawyer had finally succeeded in gaining access to the jail, were the conditions at all ameliorated and the men ultimately moved to Deer Island. That there were no substantial charges against at least ten of them is shown by the fact that after being held in $10,000 bail for two months and a half, those ten were released without bail on January 24th. It seems probable that at least a majority had no political views of any special nature, but were simply workingmen of Russian nationality speaking little or no English. . . .

EXHIBIT 1a

STATE OF CONNECTICUT,
   City of Bridgeport, ss:

SEMEON NAKHWAT, being duly sworn, deposes and says:
I was born in Grodno, Russia, and am thirty-three years old and unmarried.

In the autumn of 1919 I was a member of the Union of Russian Workers. I am not an anarchist, Socialist or Bolshevik and do not take much interest in political theories. I joined the Russian Workers because I was a workman speaking Russian and wanted to associate with other Russians and have the benefit of the social intercourse and instruction in mechanics which the society gave. By trade I am a machinist.

On November 8, 1919, I was at a meeting of Russians in Bridgeport, who had come together to discuss ways and means for buying an automobile to be used for instruction purposes. At that time I was employed by the American Brass Co. in Ansonia as a machinist, working a ten-hour day at 46½ cents an hour. At the meeting I speak of, I was arrested with all the other men at the meeting, 63 in number. The arrest was made by Edward J. Hickey, a special agent of the Department of Justice, who had helping him about fourteen Bridgeport policemen in uniform and about nine Department of Justice agents in plain clothes. No warrant of arrest was shown me then or at any other time, nor did I see any warrant shown to anyone else who was arrested.

I was taken with the other men to the police station on Fairfield Avenue and held there three days, being in a cell with two other men. During these three days no one gave me any hearing or asked me any questions. I was then taken to Hartford, Conn., with about forty-eight of the men, being informed that the rest of those arrested had been released.

I was held in the Hartford Jail for six weeks without any hearing. In the seventh week I had one hearing before the Labor Department, which hearing was held in the Post Office Building, and was then returned to jail.

In the thirteenth week of my confinement Edward J. Hickey came into my cell and asked me to give him the address of a man called Boyko in Greenpoint, Brooklyn. I did not know this man and told Hickey that I did not. Hickey thereupon struck me twice with his fist, once in the forehead and once in the jaw, whereupon I fell. He then kicked me and I became unconscious. Hickey is a big man, weighing two hundred pounds. For three weeks after this I suffered severe pain where I was kicked in the back. . . .

EXHIBIT 1b

STATE OF CONNECTICUT,
> City of Bridgeport, ss:

PETER MUSEK, being duly sworn, says:

I reside at No. 437 Helen Street, Bridgeport, Conn. I am 33 years of age and am working as a tailor in Bridgeport. On the 24th day of December, 1919, I left Bridgeport for Hartford and applied for a pass to see a friend, Mike Lozuk, who was arrested on the 8th day of November, 1919, at a meeting place of Russians in Bridgeport. I heard that Lozuk was confined in the Hartford Jail and wanted to see me. As soon as I appeared in the U. S. Post Office Building at Hartford, Conn., where I asked for a pass to see Lozuk, I was searched and immediately put under arrest and questioned by an agent of the Department of Justice. Six men, I presume agents of the Department of Justice, questioned me and threatened to hang me if I do not tell them the truth. In one instance, an agent of the Department of Justice, whose name I do not know, brought a rope and tied it around my neck, stating that he will hang me immediately if I do not tell him who conducts the meetings and who are the main workers in an organization called the Union of Russian Workers. This inquisition lasted fully three hours, after which I was again threatened to be put into a gas-room and suffocated unless I gave more particulars about other men in the Union of Russian Workers. This was all done in the U. S. Post Office Building in the presence of six agents of the Department of Justice. . . .

On the 6th day of February, 1920, a few minutes after Anton Dimitroff was taken to the cellar, I was taken out from my cell and also brought to the basement of the jail and put into a cell high enough for me to stand up in and long enough for me to make about two and a half paces. When I was put in the cell, I heard the jailer say to somebody, "Give this man heat." When I came into the cell it was quite warm. Soon thereafter the floor became hot and I nearly roasted. I took my clothes off and remained absolutely naked but the heat was unbearable. About five o'clock a man brought a glass of cold water and one piece of bread. The cold water revived me a little and I heard the man say again, "Give him some more heat." After this the cell became even hotter. I could not stand on my feet any longer and I remained on the floor up to eight o'clock in the morning, when the door opened and a man handed me a glass of water and threw a piece of bread into the cell. I asked him to bring a doctor for I felt that I was going to die. But he laughted at me, stating that I was strong enough to hold out, and locked the door again. I could not eat the bread that was thrown into my cell that morning, for I felt terrible pain in my chest and half of my body was almost roasted from contact with the hot floor. I remained in the cell up to about eight o'clock of the night of February 8, 1920. . . .

EXHIBIT 2. RAID ON RUSSIAN PEOPLE'S HOUSE

On November 7, 1919, the most violent of six raids, by agents of the Department of Justice and the New York Bomb Squad, was made upon the Russian People's House, 133 East 15th Street, New York City, in search of supposed anarchists and anarchistic literature.

The executive committee of the Federated Unions of Russian Workers occupied an office in the building, which was confined to one room. The other rooms were used principally as educational classrooms, except a small restaurant or cafeteria.

At the time of the raid the Department agents had a few warrants for the arrest of supposed offenders. They went through the building and broke up and destroyed most of the furniture in the place, including desks and typewriting machines. They "beat up" the persons in the place, amounting to several hundred, with blackjacks and stair rails; broke up all the classes then in session and herded the students to the stairways, beating them as they went, shoving them from the landing on to the stairway so that many fell and rolled down the stairs and were trampled upon by those who were shoved after them.

After this raid several hundred prisoners were taken to the office of the Department of Justice at 13 Park Row and there put through the third degree of inquisition. Less than one-fifth of them were held for deportation charges and all the remainder were released to go about their business as being innocent of any wrongdoing.

Many of the persons assaulted suffered serious wounds, and one man who was taken to Ellis Island was in a terrible condition. The manner in which these acts were committed caused a mass meeting of protest to be held the following evening (November 8) at Madison Square Garden, presided over by Dudley Field Malone. . . .

EXHIBIT 2b

City of New York,
    County of New York,
        State of New York, ss:

MITCHEL LAVROWSKY, being duly sworn, deposes and says:
  . . . On the 7th day of November, 1919, I conducted a class in Russian at 133 East 15th Street, in the Borough of Manhattan, City of New York. At about 8:00 o'clock in the evening, while I was teaching algebra and Russian, an agent of the Department of Justice opened the door of the school, walked in with a revolver in his hands and ordered everybody in the school to step aside; then ordered me to step towards him. I wear eyeglasses and the agent of the Department of Justice ordered me to take them off. Then without any provocation, struck me on the head and simultaneously two others struck and beat me brutally. After I was beaten and without strength to stand on my feet, I was thrown down stairs and while I

rolled down, other men, I presume also agents of the Department of Justice, beat me with pieces of wood, which I later found out were obtained by breaking the banisters. I sustained a fracture of my head, left shoulder, left foot, and right side. Then I was ordered to wash myself and was taken, as I now understand, to 13 Park Row, Borough of Manhattan, City of New York, where I was examined by various people and released about 12:00 midnight.

(Signed)   M. LAVROWSKY.

EXHIBIT 9. IN THE MATTER OF GASPARE CANNONE

STATE OF NEW YORK,
   County of New York, ss:

WALTER NELLES, being duly sworn, says:

I am attorney for Gaspare Cannone. He was taken to Ellis Island on April 2, 1920, under a deportation warrant issued April 1 at the instance of Special Agents of the Department of Justice. Hearings were held at Ellis Island on April 14 and 15, and his case now awaits the decision of the Secretary of Labor.

The following is the substance of Cannone's sworn statements: He was seized at his home in Brooklyn by agents of the Department of Justice about noon on March 30, 1920, *without charge or warrant,* and taken to the office of the Department of Justice in the Park Row Building, New York City. There he was beaten and kicked by a handsome agent in a blue-striped silk shirt, in the presence of three other agents (one — Faulhaber — a stenographer, and one — Palmera — an Italian interpreter), who proceeded to interrogate him. They tried to get him to furnish evidence implicating persons named John Berry, Recchi, and Valdinoce (all entirely unknown to him) in the Washington bomb explosions of last year (of which he knew nothing). They continually beset him to "Tell the truth," "stop lying," "come across;" — and then, when he gave truthful answers to their questions, they called him a "damned liar," a "son of a bitch," and many other things of which the opprobrious meaning was clear, but which he knew too little English to understand exactly. He was told that they would be easy with him if he said what they wanted him to. Failing to get anything from him, they told him he would be deported.

He was held by the Department of Justice, and denied communication with anyone outside, from noon on March 30 to noon at April 2, when he was taken to Ellis Island. Each night he was taken to Police Headquarters and locked up in a bare cell without blankets or covering. He was given five meals in the four days.

On his last appearance in the Park Row office, Exhibit B (a photograph of which is hereto annexed) was put before him, and he was told to sign. He refused, because it was not a correct record of what he had said. Of the inherent likelihood that any free man in his senses would sign such a document, nothing need be said.

A forged signature of "Gaspare Cannone" was subscribed to Exhibit B. Agent Palmera swore, at the hearing at Ellis Island on April 14, 1920, that he had seen this "signature" *written by Cannone.* Comparison is invited between the photograph of this forgery and the photographs of Cannone's genuine signature; Cannone made the ten signatures (Exhibit F) at the hearing on April 15th; he had previously, on his arrival at Ellis Island two weeks earlier, made the other genuine signature (Exhibit G) in answer to the Inspector's question: "What is the correct spelling of your name?"

From his beating on March 30th Cannone retained for upwards of two weeks a conspicuous "black eye." Record of this was preserved in a photograph of him made for the Department of Justice at Police Headquarters on March 31, 1920. When I examined the Inspector's file relative to Cannone at Ellis Island on April 14th, I found in it four prints of this photograph, which I put in evidence at the hearing as Exhibit D. Annexed hereto is a photograph of this Exhibit.

The whole evidence against Cannone was Exhibit B. Advised at the outset of the hearing on April 14th that I would claim to have the deportation warrant vacated by reason of the criminal practices of the Department of Justice on March 30th and 31st in creating the alleged "evidence," Department of Justice Agents Faulhaber and Palmera, who testified on April 14th, determined to set up an alibi for themselves as to March 30th and 31st, and to deny, not that Cannone had been beaten at the Department of Justice, but that he had been beaten *in their presence.* They accordingly insisted that they had never seen Cannone until April 1, *after his arrest under the deportation warrant issued on that date,* and that it was on that date, and not before, that he made, *in their presence,* the statements attributed to him in Exhibit B. They overlooked, or perhaps were unaware of the existence of a written statement from their own office fixing the date of Exhibit B as *March 30th* — the day upon which Cannone says he was *beaten* in their presence. . . .

Bruce Barton

CHRIST AS A BUSINESSMAN

❧{ 1925 }❧ The early twenties was pre-eminently a time when businessmen and business values ruled the United States. "The policy of the Harding administration," historian John D. Hicks says, "was to do with alacrity whatever business wanted to have done." Harding's Secretary of the Treasury Andrew Mellon, called by his admirers the greatest head of that department since Alexander Hamilton, urged Congress to eliminate all taxes on corporate profits and reduce drastically those on upper-level incomes. President Calvin Coolidge outdid even Harding in conservatism and in sympathy to the business point of view. He cut government expenses sharply; he vetoed as "socialistic" bills regulating agricultural marketing and establishing public power projects; he appointed men favorable to private enterprise to the Federal Trade Commission and other supervisory boards. He was regarded by businessmen, in Professor Hicks' words, as "the ideal President."

The pervasiveness of the business viewpoint is well illustrated by the phenomenal success of *The Man Nobody Knows* (1925), a best-selling book written by Bruce Barton, an advertising executive. Barton attempted to prove, as the following selection shows, that Jesus Christ was the prototype of the modern businessman and that by adopting His precepts and techniques, modern Americans could achieve not merely virtue but also material success.

THE MAN NOBOODY KNOWS

THE little boy's body sat bolt upright in the rough wooden chair, but his mind was very busy.

This was his weekly hour of revolt.

The kindly lady who could never seem to find her glasses would have been terribly shocked if she had known what was going on inside the little boy's mind.

"You must love Jesus," she said every Sunday, "and God."

The little boy did not say anything. He was afraid to say anything; he was almost afraid that something would happen to him because of the things he thought.

Love God! Who was always picking on people for having a good time, and sending little boys to hell because they couldn't do better in a world which he had made so hard! Why didn't God take some one his own size?

Love Jesus! The little boy looked up at the picture which hung on the Sunday-school wall. It showed a pale young man with flabby forearms and a sad expression. The young man had red whiskers.

Then the little boy looked across to the other wall. There was Daniel, good old Daniel, standing off the lions. The little boy liked Daniel. He liked David, too, with the trusty sling that landed a stone square on the forehead of Goliath. And Moses, with his rod and his big brass snake. They were winners — those three. He wondered if David could whip Jeffries. Samson could! Say, that would have been a fight!

But Jesus! Jesus was the "lamb of God." The little boy did not know what that meant, but it sounded like Mary's little lamb. Something for girls — sissified. Jesus was also "meek and lowly," a "man of sorrows and acquainted with grief." He went around for three years telling people not to do things.

Sunday was Jesus' day; it was wrong to feel comfortable or laugh on Sunday.

The little boy was glad when the superintendent thumped the bell and announced: "We will now sing the closing hymn." One more bad hour was over. For one more week the little boy had got rid of Jesus.

Years went by and the boy grew up and became a business man. He began to wonder about Jesus.

He said to himself: "Only strong magnetic men inspire great enthusiasm and build great organizations. Yet Jesus built the greatest organization of all. It is extraordinary."

The more sermons the man heard and the more books he read the more mystified he became.

One day he decided to wipe his mind clean of books and sermons.

He said, "I will read what the men who knew Jesus personally said about him. I will read about him as though he were a new historical character, about whom I had never heard anything at all."

The man was amazed.

A physical weakling! Where did they get that idea? Jesus pushed a plane and swung an adze; he was a successful carpenter. He slept outdoors and spent his days walking around his favorite lake. His muscles were so strong that when he drove the money-changers out, nobody dared to oppose him!

A kill-joy! He was the most popular dinner guest in Jerusalem! The criticism which proper people made was that he spent too much time with publicans and sinners (very good fellows, on the whole, the man thought) and enjoyed society too much. They called him a "wine bibber and a gluttonous man."

A failure! He picked up twelve men from the bottom ranks of business and forged them into an organization that conquered the world.

When the man had finished his reading he exclaimed, "This is a man nobody knows.

"Some day," said he, "some one will write a book about Jesus. Every business man will read it and send it to his partners and his salesmen. For it will tell the story of the founder of modern business."

So the man waited for some one to write the book, but no one did. Instead, more books were published about the "lamb of God" who was weak and unhappy and glad to die.

The man became impatient. One day he said, "I believe I will try to write that book, myself."

And he did.

THE EXECUTIVE

It was very late in the afternoon.

If you would like to learn the measure of a man, that is the time of

day to watch him. We are all half an inch taller in the morning than
at night; it is fairly easy to take a large view of things when the mind
is rested and the nerves are calm. But the day is a steady drain of small
annoyances, and the difference in the size of men becomes hourly more
apparent. The little man loses his temper; the big man takes a firmer
hold.

It was very late in the afternoon in Galilee.

The dozen men who had walked all day over the dusty roads were
hot and tired, and the sight of a village was very cheering, as they looked
down on it from the top of a little hill. Their leader, deciding that they
had gone far enough, sent two members of the party ahead to arrange
for accommodations, while he and the others sat down by the roadside
to wait.

After a bit the messengers were seen returning, and even at a distance
it was apparent that something unpleasant had occurred. Their cheeks
were flushed, their voices angry, and as they came nearer they quickened
their pace, each wanting to be the first to explode the bad news. Breath-
lessly they told it — the people in the village had refused to receive them,
had given them blunt notice to seek shelter somewhere else.

The indignation of the messengers communicated itself to the others,
who at first could hardly believe their ears. This back-woods village
refuse to entertain their master — it was unthinkable. He was a famous
public character in that part of the world. He had healed sick people
and given freely to the poor. In the capital city crowds had followed
him enthusiastically, so that even his disciples had become men of importance, looked up to and talked about. And now to have this country
village deny them admittance as its guests —

"Lord, these people are insufferable," one of them cried. "Let us call
down fire from Heaven and consume them."

The others joined in with enthusiasm. Fire from Heaven — that was
the idea! Make them smart for their boorishness! Show them that they
can't affront *us* with impunity! Come, Lord, the fire —

There are times when nothing a man can say is nearly so powerful as
saying nothing. Every executive knows that instinctively. To argue
brings him down to the level of those with whom he argues; silence
convicts them of their folly; they wish they had not spoken so quickly;
they wonder what he thinks. The lips of Jesus tightened; his fine features showed the strain of the preceding weeks, and in his eyes there
was a foreshadowing of the more bitter weeks to come. He needed that
night's rest, but he said not a word. Quietly he gathered up his garments
and started on, his outraged companions following. It is easy to imagine

his keen disappointment. He had been working with them for three years . . . would they never catch a true vision of what he was about? He had so little time, and they were constantly wasting his time. . . . He had come to save mankind, and they wanted him to gratify his personal resentment by burning up a village!

Down the hot road they trailed after him, awed by his silence, vaguely conscious that they had failed again to measure up. "And they went to another village," says the narrative — nothing more. No debate; no bitterness; no futile conversation. In the mind of Jesus the thing was too small for comment. In a world where so much must be done, and done quickly, the memory could not afford to be burdened with a petty slight. "And they went to another village." . . .

HIS METHOD

Many leaders have dared to lay out ambitious programs, but this is the most daring of all:

"Go ye into all the world," Jesus said, "and preach the gospel *to the whole creation.*"

Consider the sublime audacity of that command. To carry Roman civilization across the then known world had cost millions of lives and billions in treasure. To create any sort of reception for a new idea or product to-day involves a vast machinery of propaganda and expense. Jesus had no funds and no machinery. His organization was a tiny group of uneducated men, one of whom had already abandoned the cause as hopeless, deserting to the enemy. He had come proclaiming a Kingdom and was to end upon a cross; yet he dared to talk of conquering all creation. What was the source of his faith in that handful of followers? By what methods had he trained them? What had they learned from him of the secrets of influencing men?

We speak of the law of "supply and demand," but the words have got turned around. With anything which is not a basic necessity the supply always precedes the demand. Elias Howe invented the sewing machine, but it nearly rusted away before American women could be persuaded to use it. With their sewing finished so quickly what would they ever do with their spare time? Howe had vision, and had made his vision come true; but he could not sell! So his biographer paints a tragic picture — the man who had done more than any other in his generation to lighten the labor of women is forced to attend the funeral of the woman he loved in a borrowed suit of clothes! . . .

What were his methods of training? How did he meet prospective believers? How did he deal with objections? By what sort of strategy did he interest and persuade?

He was making the journey back from Jerusalem after his spectacular triumph in cleansing the Temple, when he came to Jacob's Well, and being tired, sat down. His disciples had stopped behind at one of the villages to purchase food, so he was alone. The well furnished the water-supply for the neighboring city of the Samaritans, and after a little time a woman came out to it, carrying her pitcher on her shoulder. Between her people, the Samaritans, and his people, the Jews, there was a feud of centuries. To be touched by even the shadow of a Samaritan was defilement according to the strict code of the Pharisees; to speak to one was a crime. The woman made no concealment of her resentment at finding him there. Almost any remark from his lips would have kindled her anger. She would at least have turned away in scorn; she might have summoned her relatives and driven him off.

An impossible situation, you will admit. How could he meet it? How give his message to one who was forbidden by everything holy to listen? The incident is very revealing: there are times when any word is the wrong word; when only silence can prevail. Jesus knew well his precious secret. As the woman drew closer he made no move to indicate that he was conscious of her approach. His gaze was on the ground. When he spoke it was quietly, musingly, as if to himself:

"If you knew who I am," he said, "you would not need to come out here for water. I would give you living water."

The woman stopped short, her interest challenged in spite of herself; she set down the pitcher and looked at the stranger. It was a burning hot day; the well was far from the city; she was heated and tired. What did he mean by such a remark? She started to speak, checked herself and burst out impulsively, her curiosity overleaping her caution:

"What are you talking about? Do you mean to say you are greater than our father Jacob who gave us this well? Have you some magic that will save us this long walk in the sun?"

Dramatic, isn't it — a single sentence achieving triumph, arousing interest and creating desire. With sure instinct he followed up his initial advantage. He began to talk to her in terms of her own life, her ambitions, her hopes, knowing so well that each of us is interested first of all and most of all in himself. When the disciples came up a few minutes later they found an unbelievable sight — a Samaritan listening with rapt attention to the teaching of a Jew. . . .

Surely no one will consider us lacking in reverence if we say that every one of the "principles of modern salesmanship" on which business men so much pride themselves, are brilliantly exemplified in Jesus' talk and work. The first of these and perhaps the most important is the necessity for "putting yourself in step with your prospect." A great sales manager used to illustrate it in this way:

> "When you want to get aboard a street car which is already in motion, you don't run at it from right angles and try to make the platform in one wild leap," he would say. "If you do, you are likely to find yourself on the floor. No. You run along beside the car, increasing your pace until you are moving just as rapidly as it is moving and in the same direction. Then you step aboard easily, without danger or jolt.
>
> "The minds of busy men are in motion," he would continue. "They are engaged with something very different from the thought you have to present. You can't jump directly at them and expect to make an effective landing. You must put yourself in the other man's place; try to imagine what he is thinking; let your first remark be in line with his thoughts; follow it by another with which you know he will easily agree. Thus, gradually, your two minds reach a point where they can join without conflict. You encourage him to say 'yes' and 'yes' and 'that's right' and 'I've noticed that myself,' until he says the final 'yes' which is your favorable decision."

Jesus taught all this without ever teaching it. Every one of his conversations, every contact between his mind and others, is worthy of the attentive study of any sales manager. Passing along the shores of a lake one day, he saw two of the men whom he wanted as disciples. *Their* minds were in motion; their hands were busy with their nets; their conversation was about conditions in the fishing trade, and the prospects of a good market for the day's catch. To have broken in on such thinking with the offer of employment as preachers of a new religion would have been to confuse them and invite a certain rebuff. What was Jesus' approach?

"Come with me," he said, "and I will make you fishers of men."

Fishers . . . that was a word they could understand . . . fishers of men . . . that was a new idea . . . what was he driving at . . . fishers of men . . . it sounded interesting . . . well, what is it, anyway?

He sat on a hillside overlooking a fertile country. Many of the crowd who gathered around him were farmers, with their wives and sons and daughters. He wanted their interest and attention; it was important to make them understand, at the very outset, that what he had to say was nothing vague or theoretical but of direct and immediate application to their daily lives.

"A sower went forth to sow," he began, "and when he sowed some seeds fell by the wayside and the fowls came and devoured them up. . . ." Were they interested . . . *were* they? Every man of them had gone through that experience . . . the thievish crows . . . many a good day's work *they* had spoiled. . . . So this Teacher knew something about the troubles that farmers had to put up with, did he? Fair enough . . . let's hear what he has to say. . . .

. . . I propose in this chapter to speak of the advertisements of Jesus which have survived for twenty centuries and are still the most potent influence in the world.

Let us begin by asking why he was so successful in mastering public attention and why, in contrast, his churches are less so? The answer is twofold. In the first place he recognized the basic principle that all good advertising is news. He was never trite or commonplace; he had no routine. If there had been newspapers in those days, no city editor could have said, "No need to visit him to-day; he will be doing just what he did last Sunday." Reporters would have followed him every single hour, for it was impossible to predict what he would say or do; every action and word were news.

The activity begins at sunrise. Jesus was an early riser; he knew that the simplest way to live *more* than an average life is to add an hour to the fresh end of the day. At sunrise, therefore, we discover a little boat pushing out from the shore of the lake. It makes its steady way across and deposits Jesus and his disciples in Capernaum, his favorite city. He proceeds at once to the house of a friend, but not without being discovered. The report spreads instantly that he is in town, and before he can finish breakfast a crowd has collected outside the gate — a poor palsied chap among them.

The day's work is at hand.

Having slept soundly in the open air he meets the call with quiet nerves. The smile that carried confidence into even the most hopeless heart spreads over his features; he stoops down toward the sufferer.

"Be of good cheer, my son," he cries, "your sins are all forgiven."

Sins forgiven! Indeed! The respectable members of the audience draw back with sharp disapproval. "What a blasphemous phrase," they exclaim. "Who authorized him to exercise the functions of God? What right has he to decide whose sins shall be forgiven?"

Jesus sensed rather than heard their protest. He never courted controversy but he never dodged it; and much of his fame arose out of the reports of his verbal victories. Men have been elected to office — even such high office as the Presidency — by being so good-natured that they never made an enemy. But the leaders who are remembered are those who had plenty of critics and dealt with them vigorously.

"What's the objection?" he exclaimed, turning on the dissenters. "Why do you stand there and criticize? Is it easier to say, 'Thy sins be forgiven thee,' or to say, 'Arise, take up thy bed and walk?' The results are the same." Bending over the sick man again he said: "Arise, take up thy bed and go unto thine house."

The man stirred and was amazed to find that his muscles responded. Slowly, doubtingly he struggled to his feet, and with one great shout of happiness started off, surrounded by his jubilant friends. The critics had received their answer, but they refused to give up. For an hour or more they persisted in angry argument, until the meeting ended in a tumult.

Can you imagine the next day's issue of the *Capernaum News,* if there had been one?

PALSIED MAN HEALED

JESUS OF NAZARETH CLAIMS RIGHT TO

FORGIVE SINS

PROMINENT SCRIBES OBJECT

"BLASPHEMOUS," SAYS LEADING CITIZEN.

"BUT ANYWAY I CAN WALK," HEALED MAN

RETORTS.

Front page story number one and the day is still young.

One of those who had been attracted by the excitement was a tax-collector named Matthew. Being a man of business he could not stay through the argument, but slipped away early and was hard at work when Jesus passed by a few minutes before noon.

"Matthew, I want you," said Jesus.

That was all. No argument; no offer of inducements; no promise of rewards. Merely "I want you;" and the prosperous tax-collector closed his office, made a feast for the brilliant young teacher and forthwith announced himself a disciple.

* * *

PROMINENT TAX COLLECTOR JOINS

NAZARETH FORCES

MATTHEW ABANDONS BUSINESS TO PROMOTE

NEW CULT

* * *

GIVES LARGE LUNCHEON

Front page story number two.

The luncheon itself furnished the third sensation. It was not at all the kind of affair which a religious teacher would be expected to approve. Decidedly it was good-natured and noisy.

No theological test was applied in limiting the invitation. No one stood at the entrance to demand: "What is your belief regarding the birth of Jesus?" Or, "Have you or have you not been baptized?" The doors were flung wide, and, along with the disciples and the respectable folks, a swarm of publicans and sinners trooped in.

"Outrageous," grumbled the worthy folk. "Surely if this teacher had any moral standards he never would eat with such rabble."

They were shocked; but he was not. That he had condemned himself according to their formula worried him not a whit. His liking for folks overran all social boundaries; he just could not seem to remember that some people are nice people, proper people, and some are not.

"Come, come," he exclaimed to the Pharisees, "won't you ever get over nagging at me because I eat with these outsiders? Who needs the doctor most — they that are well or they that are sick?

"And here's another thing to think about," he added. "You lay so much stress on forms and creeds and occasions — do you suppose God cares about all that? What do you think he meant when he said: 'I will have mercy and not sacrifice?' Take that home and puzzle over it."

DEFENDS PUBLICANS AND SINNERS

* * *

JESUS OF NAZARETH WELCOMES THEM AT LUNCH

* * *

REBUKES PROMINENT PHARISEES

* * *

"CREEDS UNIMPORTANT," HE SAYS. "GOD WANTS

MERCY NOT SACRIFICE."

A fourth big story. You may be sure it was carried into hundreds of homes during the next few weeks, and formed the basis for many a long evening's discussion.

As the meal drew to its close there came a dramatic interruption — a ruler of the city made his way slowly to the head of the table and stood silent, bowed by the terrible weight of his grief. That morning he had sat at his daughter's bedside, clasping her frail white hand in his, watching the flutter of the pulse, trying by the force of his longing to hold that little life back from the precipice. And at last the doctors had told him that it was useless any more to hope. So he had come, this ruler, to the strange young man whose deeds of healing were the sensation of the day.

Was it too late? The ruler had thought so when he entered the door; but as he stood in that splendid presence a new thrilling conviction gripped him:

"Master, my daughter is even now dead," he exclaimed, "but come and lay your hand on her and she will live."

Jesus rose from his seat, drawn by that splendid outburst of faith and without hesitation or questioning he started for the door. All his life he seemed to feel that there was no limit at all to what he could do, if only those who beseeched him believed enough. Grasping the ruler's arm he led the way up the street, his disciples and the motley crowd hurrying along behind.

They had several blocks to travel, and before their journey was completed another interruption occurred.

A woman who had been sick for twelve years edged through the crowd, eluded the sharp eyes of the disciples and touched the hem of his garment. "For she said within herself, if I may but touch his garment, I shall be whole." . . . What an idea. . . . What a Personality his must have been to provoke such ideas. . . . "My daughter is dead, but lay your hands on her and she will live." . . . "I've been sick for twelve years; the doctors can do nothing, but if I only touch his coat I'll be all right." . . . How can the artists possibly have imagined that a sad-faced weakling could ever inspire such amazing ideas as these!

The woman won her victory. By that touch, by his smile, by the few words he spoke, her faith rose triumphant over disease. She "was made whole from that hour."

Again he moved forward, the crowd pressing hard. The ruler's residence was now in plain sight. The paid mourners, hired by the hour, were busy about the doorway; they increased their activities as their employer came in sight — hideous wails and the dull sounding of cymbals — a horrible pretense of grief. Quickening his stride Jesus was in the midst of them.

"Give place," he cried with a commanding gesture. "The maid is not dead but sleepeth."

They laughed him to scorn. Brushing them aside he strode into the house and took the little girl by the hand. The crowd looked on dumfounded, for at the magic of his touch she opened her eyes, and sat up.

Front page stories five and six. A woman sick twelve years, and healed! A child whom the doctors had abandoned for dead, sits up and smiles!

No wonder a thousand tongues were busy that night advertising his name and work. "The fame thereof went abroad into all that land," says the narrative. Nothing could keep it from going abroad. It was irresistible news!

He was advertised by his service, not by his sermons; this is the second noteworthy fact. Nowhere in the Gospels do you find it announced that:

Jesus of Nazareth Will Denounce
The Scribes and Pharisees in the
Central Synagogue
To-night at Eight O'Clock
Special Music

His preaching was almost incidental. On only one occasion did he deliver a long discourse, and that was probably interrupted often by questions and debates. He did not come to establish a theology but to lead a life. Living more healthfully than any of his contemporaries he spread health wherever he went. Thinking more daringly, more divinely, he expressed himself in thoughts of surpassing beauty, as naturally as a plant bursts into bloom. His sermons, if they may be called sermons, were chiefly explanatory of his service. He healed a lame man, gave sight to a blind man, fed the hungry, cheered the poor; and by these works he was advertised much more than by his words. . . .

These are Jesus' works, done in Jesus' name. If he were to live again, in these modern days, he would find a way to make them known — to be advertised by his service, not merely by his sermons. One thing is certain: he would not neglect the market-place. . . .

The present day market-place is the newspaper and the magazine. Printed columns are the modern thoroughfares; published advertisements are the cross-roads where the sellers and the buyers meet. Any issue of a national magazine is a world's fair, a bazaar filled with the products of the world's work. Clothes and clocks and candle-sticks; soup and soap and cigarettes; lingerie and limousines — the best of all of them are there, proclaimed by their makers in persuasive tones. That every other voice should be raised in such great market-places, and the voice of Jesus of Nazareth be still — this is a vital omission which he would find a way to correct. He would be a national advertiser today, I am sure, as he was the great advertiser of his own day. . . .

Take any one of the parables, no matter which — you will find that it exemplifies all the principles on which advertising text books are written. Always a picture in the very first sentence; crisp, graphic language and a message so clear that even the dullest can not escape it.

Ten Virgins Went Forth To Meet
A Bridegroom

A striking picture and a striking head-line. The story which follows has not a single wasted word:

> Five of the Virgins were wise, and five were foolish.
> They that were foolish took their lamps, and took no oil with them:
> But the wise took oil in their vessels with their lamps.
> While the bridegroom tarried, they all slumbered and slept.
> And at midnight there was a cry made, Behold the bridegroom cometh; go ye out to meet him.
> Then all those Virgins arose, and trimmed their lamps.
> And the foolish said unto the wise, "Give us of your oil for our lamps have gone out."
> But the wise answered, saying, "Not so; lest there be not enough for us and you; but go ye rather to them that sell, and buy for yourselves."
> And while they went to buy, the bridegroom came; and they that were ready went in with him to the marriage; and the door was shut.
> Afterward came also the other Virgins, saying, "Lord, Lord, open to me."
> But he answered and said, "Verily, I say unto you, I know you not . . ."
> Watch, therefore, for ye know neither the day nor the hour wherein the Son of man cometh.

Illustrate that with a drawing by a distinguished artist; set it up according to the best modern typography; bury it in a magazine with a hundred other pages — will it not stand out? Will it not grip the attention of even the most casual, and *make* itself read? . . .

THE FOUNDER OF MODERN BUSINESS

When Jesus was twelve years old his father and mother took him to the Feast at Jerusalem.

It was the big national vacation; even peasant families saved their pennies and looked forward to it through the year. Towns like Nazareth were emptied of their inhabitants except for the few old folks who were left behind to look after the very young ones. Crowds of cheerful pilgrims filled the highways, laughing their way across the hills and under the stars at night.

In such a mass of folk it was not surprising that a boy of twelve should be lost. When Mary and Joseph missed him on the homeward trip, they took it calmly and began a search among the relatives.

The inquiry produced no result. Some remembered having seen him in the Temple, but no one had seen him since. Mary grew frightened: where could he be? Back there in the city alone? Wandering hungry and tired through the friendless streets? Carried away by other travelers into a distant country? She pictured a hundred calamities. Nervously she and Joseph hurried back over the hot roads, through the suburbs, up through the narrow city streets, up to the courts of the Temple itself.

And there he was.

Not lost; not a bit worried. Apparently unconscious that the Feast was over, he sat in the midst of a group of old men, who were tossing questions at him and applauding the shrewd common sense of his replies. Involuntarily his parents halted — they were simple folk, uneasy among strangers and disheveled by their haste. But after all they *were* his parents, and a very human feeling of irritation quickly overcame their diffidence. Mary stepped forward and grasped his arm.

"Son, why hast thou thus dealt with us?" she demanded. "Behold thy father and I have sought thee sorrowing."

I wonder what answer she expected to receive. Did she ever know exactly what he was going to say: did any one in Nazareth quite understand this keen, eager lad, who had such curious moments of abstraction and was forever breaking out with remarks that seemed so far beyond his years?

He spoke to her now with deference, as always, but in words that did not dispel but rather added to her uncertainty.

"How is it that ye sought me?" he asked. "Wist ye not that I must be about my father's *business?*" . . .

What interests us most in this one recorded incident of his boyhood is the fact that for the first time he defined the purpose of his career. He did not say, "Wist ye not that I must practise preaching?" or "Wist ye not that I must get ready to meet the arguments of men like these?" The language was quite different, and well worth remembering. "Wist ye not that I must be about my father's *business?*" he said. He thought of his life as *business*. What did he mean by business? To what extent are the principles by which he conducted his business applicable to ours? And if he were among us again, in our highly competitive world, would his business philosophy work?

On one occasion, you recall, he stated his recipe for success. It was on the afternoon when James and John came to ask him what promotion they might expect. They were two of the most energetic of the lot, called "Sons of Thunder," by the rest, being noisy and always in the midst of some sort of a storm. They had joined the ranks because they liked him, but with no very definite idea of what it was all about; and now they wanted to know where the enterprise was heading, and just what there would be in it for them.

"Master," they said, "we want to ask what plans you have in mind for us. You're going to need big men around you when you establish your kingdom; our ambition is to sit on either side of you, one on your right hand and the other on your left."

Who can object to that attitude? If a man fails to look after himself, certainly no one will look after him. If you want a big place, go ask for it. That's the way to get ahead.

Jesus answered with a sentence which sounds poetically absurd.

"Whosoever will be great among you, shall be your minister," he said, "and whosoever of you will be the chiefest, shall be servant of all."

A fine piece of rhetoric, now isn't it? Be a good servant and you will be great; be the best possible servant and you will occupy the highest possible place. Nice idealistic talk but utterly impractical; nothing to take seriously in a common sense world. That is just what men thought for some hundreds of years; and then, quite suddenly, Business woke up to a great discovery. You will hear that discovery proclaimed in every sales convention as something distinctly modern and up to date. It is emblazoned in the advertising pages of every magazine.

Look through those pages.

Here is the advertisement of an automobile company, one of the greatest in the world. And why is it greatest? On what does it base its claim to leadership? On its huge factories and financial strength? They are never mentioned. On its army of workmen or its high salaried executives? You might read its advertisements for years without suspecting that it had either. No. "We are great because of our service," the advertisements cry. "We will crawl under your car oftener and get our backs dirtier than any of our competitors. Drive up to our service stations and ask for anything at all — it will be granted cheerfully. We serve; therefore we grow."

A manufacturer of shoes makes the same boast in other terms. "We put ourselves at your feet and give you everything that you can possibly demand." Manufacturers of building equipment, of clothes, of food; presidents of railroads and steamship companies; the heads of banks and investment houses — *all* of them tell the same story. "Service is what we are here for," they exclaim. They call it the "spirit of modern business"; they suppose, most of them, that it is something very new. But Jesus preached it more than nineteen hundred years ago. . . .

Herbert Hoover

RUGGED INDIVIDUALISM

✧{*1922*}✧ IN THE decade after the first World War, Herbert Hoover (1874-1964) was one of the most famous and highly regarded men in the entire world. Following a phenomenally successful career as a mining engineer, Hoover distinguished himself as an administrator and humanitarian through his work as head of the Committee for Relief in Belgium and then as United States Food Administrator. After service at the Versailles Peace Conference, he became Secretary of Commerce under Presidents Harding and Coolidge before winning the Presidency itself in 1928.

In the twenties Hoover's general view of government and society was dominant in America. The majority of the nation, tired out and disillusioned after two decades of reform and war, wanted no more of tight controls and personal sacrifices for some vaguely defined common good. Hoover, far too intelligent and too public spirited to advocate a program based on mere selfishness, developed in *American Individualism* (1922) a philosophy that suited the public's reactionary mood without completely neglecting the American tradition of progressivism and fair play. Hoover's practice as Secretary of Commerce and then as President did not measure up to the "progressive individualism" he describes in the following pages. His was a far more "rugged" and doctrinaire individualism than *American Individualism* would lead one to expect. The book, however, set the tone for the twenties. The philosophy seemed both forward looking and in the American tradition, both good for the country and good for the individual. Accepting this comfortable if somewhat glib interpretation of the American mission, the bulk of the population marched forward blithely and blindly under Hoover's leadership into the pit of the Great Depression.

AMERICAN INDIVIDUALISM

WE HAVE witnessed in this last eight years the spread of revolution over one-third of the world. The causes of these explosions lie at far greater depths than the failure of governments in war. The war itself in its last stages was a conflict of social philosophies—but beyond this the causes of social explosion lay in the great inequalities and injustices of centuries flogged beyond endurance by the conflict and freed from restraint by the destruction of war. The urgent forces which drive human society have been plunged into a terrible furnace. Great theories spun by dreamers to remedy the pressing human ills have come to the front of men's minds. Great formulas came into life that promised to dissolve all trouble. Great masses of people have flocked to their banners in hopes born of misery and suffering. Nor has this great social ferment been confined to those nations that have burned with revolutions.

Now, as the storm of war, of revolution and of emotion subsides there is left even with us of the United States much unrest, much discontent with the surer forces of human advancement. To all of us, out of this crucible of actual, poignant, individual experience has come a deal of new understanding, and it is for all of us to ponder these new currents if we are to shape our future with intelligence.

Even those parts of the world that suffered less from the war have been partly infected by these ideas. Beyond this, however, many have had high hopes of civilization suddenly purified and ennobled by the sacrifices and services of the war; they had thought the fine unity of purpose gained in war would be carried into great unity of action in remedy of the faults of civilization in peace. But from concentration of every spiritual and material energy upon the single purpose of war the scene changed to the immense complexity and the many purposes of peace.

Thus there loom up certain definite underlying forces in our national life that need to be stripped of the imaginary — the transitory — and a definition should be given to the actual permanent and persistent motivation of our civilization. In contemplation of these questions we must go far deeper than the superficials of our political and economic structure, for these are but the products of our social philosophy — the machinery of our social system.

Nor is it ever amiss to review the political, economic, and spiritual principles through which our country has steadily grown in usefulness and greatness, not only to preserve them from being fouled by false notions, but more importantly that we may guide ourselves in the road of progress.

Five or six great social philosophies are at struggle in the world for ascendency. There is the Individualism of America. There is the Individualism of the more democratic states of Europe with its careful reservations of castes and classes. There are Communism, Socialism, Syndicalism, Capitalism, and finally there is Autocracy — whether by birth, by possessions, militarism, or divine right of kings. Even the Divine Right still lingers on although our lifetime has seen fully two-thirds of the earth's population, including Germany, Austria, Russia, and China, arrive at a state of angry disgust with this type of social motive power anl throw it on the scrap heap.

All these thoughts are in ferment today in every country in the world. They fluctuate in ascendency with times and places. They compromise with each other in daily reaction on governments and peoples. Some of these ideas are perhaps more adapted to one race than another. Some

are false, some are true. What we are interested in is their challenge to
the physical and spiritual forces of America.

The partisans of some of these other brands of social schemes challenge us to comparison; and some of their partisans even among our
own people are increasing in their agitation that we adopt one or another or parts of their devices in place of our tried individualism. They
insist that our social foundations are exhausted, that like feudalism and
autocracy America's plan has served its purpose — that it must be abandoned.

There are those who have been left in sober doubt of our institutions
or are confounded by bewildering catchwords of vivid phrases. For in
this welter of discussions there is much attempt to glorify or defame
social and economic forces with phrases. Nor indeed should we disregard the potency of some of these phrases in their stir to action. — "The
dictatorship of the Proletariat," "Capitalistic nations," "Germany over
all," and a score of others. We need only to review those that have
jumped to horseback during the last ten years in order that we may be
properly awed by the great social and political havoc that can be worked
where the bestial instincts of hate, murder, and destruction are clothed
by the demagogue in the fine terms of political idealism.

For myself, let me say at the very outset that my faith in the essential
truth, strength, and vitality of the developing creed by which we have
hitherto lived in this country of ours has been confirmed and deepened
by the searching experiences of seven years of service in the backwash
and misery of war. Seven years of contending with economic degenera-
tion, with social disintegration, with incessant political dislocation, with
all of its seething and ferment of individual and class conflict, could but
impress me with the primary motivation of social forces, and the necessity for broader thought upon their great issues to humanity. And from
it all I emerge an individualist — an unashamed individualist. But let me
say also that I am an American individualist. For America has been
steadily developing the ideals that constitute progressive individualism.

No doubt, individualism run riot, with no tempering principle, would
provide a long category of inequalities, of tyrannies, dominations, and
injustices. America, however, has tempered the whole conception of individualism by the injection of a definite principle, and from this principle it follows that attempts at domination, whether in government or
in the processes of industry and commerce, are under an insistent curb.
If we would have the values of individualism, their stimulation to initiative, to the development of hand and intellect, to the high development
of thought and spirituality, they must be tempered with that firm and

fixed ideal of American individualism — *an equality of opportunity.* If we would have these values we must soften its hardness and stimulate progress through that sense of service that lies in our people.

Therefore, it is not the individualism of other countries for which I would speak, but the individualism of America. Our individualism differs from all others because it embraces these great ideals: *that while we build our society upon the attainment of the individual, we shall safeguard to every individual an equality of opportunity to take that position in the community to which his intelligence, character, ability, and ambition entitle him; that we keep the social solution free from frozen strata of classes; that we shall stimulate effort of each individual to achievement; that through an enlarging sense of responsibility and understanding we shall assist him to this attainment; while he in turn must stand up to the emery wheel of competition.*

Individualism cannot be maintained as the foundation of a society if it looks to only legalistic justice based upon contracts, property, and political equality. Such legalistic safeguards are themselves not enough. In our individualism we have long since abandoned the laissez faire of the 18th Century — the notion that it is "every man for himself and the devil take the hindmost." We abandoned that when we adopted the ideal of equality of opportunity — the fair chance of Abraham Lincoln. We have confirmed its abandonment in terms of legislation, of social and economic justice, — in part because we have learned that it is the hindmost who throws the bricks at our social edifice, in part because we have learned that the foremost are not always the best nor the hindmost the worst — and in part because we have learned that social injustice is the destruction of justice itself. We have learned that the impulse to production can only be maintained at a high pitch if there is a fair division of the product. We have also learned that fair division can only be obtained by certain restrictions on the strong and the dominant. . . .

The will-o'-the-wisp of all breeds of socialism is that they contemplate a motivation of human animals by altruism alone. It necessitates a bureaucracy of the entire population, in which, having obliterated the economic stimulation of each member, the fine gradations of character and ability are to be arranged in relative authority by ballot or more likely by a Tammany Hall or a Bolshevist party, or some other form of tyranny. The proof of the futility of these ideas as a stimulation to the development and activity of the individual does not lie alone in the ghastly failure of Russia, but it also lies in our own failure in attempts at nationalized industry.

Likewise the basic foundations of autocracy, whether it be class government or capitalism in the sense that a few men through unrestrained control of property determine the welfare of great numbers, is as far apart from the rightful expression of American individualism as the two poles. The will-o'-the-wisp of autocracy in any form is that it supposes that the good Lord endowed a special few with all the divine attributes. It contemplates one human animal dealing to the other human animals his just share of earth, of glory, and of immortality. The proof of the futility of these ideas in the development of the world does not lie alone in the grim failure of Germany, but it lies in the damage to our moral and social fabric from those who have sought economic domination in America, whether employer or employee.

We in America have had too much experience of life to fool ourselves into pretending that all men are equal in ability, in character, in intelligence, in ambition. That was part of the claptrap of the French Revolution. We have grown to understand that all we can hope to assure to the individual through government is liberty, justice, intellectual welfare, equality of opportunity, and stimulation to service.

It is in maintenance of a society fluid to these human qualities that our individualism departs from the individualism of Europe. There can be no rise for the individual through the frozen strata of classes, or of castes, and no stratification can take place in a mass livened by the free stir of its particles. This guarding of our individualism against stratification insists not only in preserving in the social solution an equal opportunity for the able and ambitious to rise from the bottom; it also insists that the sons of the successful shall not by any mere right of birth or favor continue to occupy their fathers' places of power against the rise of a new generation in process of coming up from the bottom. The pioneers of our American individualism had the good sense not to reward Washington and Jefferson and Hamilton with hereditary dukedoms and fixtures in landed estates, as Great Britain rewarded Marlborough and Nelson. Otherwise our American fields of opportunity would have been clogged with long generations inheriting their fathers' privileges without their fathers' capacity for service.

That our system has avoided the establishment and domination of class has a significant proof in the present Administration in Washington. Of the twelve men comprising the President, Vice-President, and Cabinet, nine have earned their own way in life without economic inheritance, and eight of them started with manual labor.

If we examine the impulses that carry us forward, none is so potent for progress as the yearning for individual self-expression, the desire for creation of something. Perhaps the greatest human happiness flows from personal achievement. Here lies the great urge of the constructive in-stinct of mankind. But it can only thrive in a society where the individ-ual has liberty and stimulation to achievement. Nor does the community progress except through its participation in these multitudes of achieve-ments.

Furthermore, the maintenance of productivity and the advancement of the things of the spirit depend upon the ever-renewed supply from the mass of those who can rise to leadership. Our social, economic, and in-tellectual progress is almost solely dependent upon the creative minds of those individuals with imaginative and administrative intelligence who create or who carry discoveries to widespread application. No race pos-sesses more than a small percentage of these minds in a single generation. But little thought has ever been given to our racial dependency upon them. Nor that our progress is in so large a measure due to the fact that with our increased means of communication these rare individuals are today able to spread their influence over so enlarged a number of lesser capable minds as to have increased their potency a million-fold. In truth, the vastly greater productivity of the world with actually less physical labor is due to the wider spread of their influence through the discovery of these facilities. And they can arise solely through the selec-tion that comes from the free-running mills of competition. They must be free to rise from the mass; they must be given the attraction of pre-miums to effort.

Leadership is a quality of the individual. It is the individual alone who can function in the world of intellect and in the field of leadership. If democracy is to secure its authorities in morals, religion, and states-manship, it must stimulate leadership from its own mass. Human lead-ership cannot be replenished by selection like queen bees, by divine right or bureaucracies, but by the free rise of ability, character, and intelligence.

Even so, leadership cannot, no matter how brilliant, carry progress far ahead of the average of the mass of individual units. Progress of the na-tion is the sum of progress in its individuals. Acts and ideas that lead to progress are born out of the womb of the individual mind, not out of the mind of the crowd. The crowd only feels: it has no mind of its own which can plan. The crowd is credulous, it destroys, it consumes, it hates, and it dreams — but it never builds. It is one of the most profound and important of exact psychological truths that man in the mass does not think but only feels. The mob functions only in a world of emo-tion. The demagogue feeds on mob emotions and his leadership is the leadership of emotion, not the leadership of intellect and progress. Popu-lar desires are no criteria to the real need; they can be determined only by deliberative consideration, by education, by constructive leadership. . . .

Economic Phases

That high and increasing standards of living and comfort should be the first of considerations in public mind and in government needs no apology. We have long since realized that the basis of an advancing civilization must be a high and growing standard of living for all the people, not for a single class; that education, food, clothing, housing, and the spreading use of what we so often term non-essentials, are the real fertilizers of the soil from which spring the finer flowers of life. The economic development of the past fifty years has lifted the general standard of comfort far beyond the dreams of our forefathers. The only road to further advance in the standard of living is by greater invention, greater elimination of waste, greater production and better distribution of commodities and services, for by increasing their ratio to our numbers and dividing them justly we each will have more of them.

The superlative value of individualism through its impulse to production, its stimulation to invention has, so far as I know, never been denied. Criticism of it has lain in its wastes but more importantly in its failures of equitable sharing of the product. In our country these contentions are mainly over the division to each of his share of the comforts and luxuries, for none of us is either hungry or cold or without a place to lay his head — and we have much besides. In less than four decades we have added electric lights, plumbing, telephones, gramophones, automobiles, and what not in wide diffusion to our standards of living. Each in turn began as a luxury, each in turn has become so commonplace that seventy or eighty per cent. of our people participate in them.

To all practical souls there is little use in quarreling over the share of each of us until we have something to divide. So long as we maintain our individualism we will have increasing quantities to share and we shall have time and leisure and taxes with which to fight out proper sharing of the "surplus." The income tax returns show that this surplus is a minor part of our total production after taxes are paid. Some of this "surplus" must be set aside for rewards to saving for stimulation of proper effort to skill, to leadership and invention — therefore the dispute is in reality over much less than the total of such "surplus." While there should be no minimizing of a certain fringe of injustices in sharing the results of production or in the wasteful use made by some of their share, yet there is vastly wider field for gains to all of us through cheapening the costs of production and distribution through the eliminating of their wastes, from increasing the volume of product by each and every one doing his utmost, than will ever come to us even if we can think out a method of abstract justice in sharing which did not stifle production of the total product. . . .

But those are utterly wrong who say that individualism has as its only end the acquisition and preservation of private property — the selfish snatching and boarding of the common product. Our American individualism, indeed, is only in part an economic creed. It aims to provide opportunity for self-expression, not merely economically, but spiritually as well. Private property is not a fetich in America. The crushing of the liquor trade without a cent of compensation, with scarcely even a discussion of it, does not bear out the notion that we give property rights any headway over human rights. Our development of individualism shows an increasing tendency to regard right of property not as an object in itself, but in the light of a useful and necessary instrument in stimulation of initiative to the individual; not only stimulation to him that he may gain personal comfort, security in life, protection to his family, but also because individual accumulation and ownership is a basis of selection to leadership in administration of the tools of industry and commerce. It is where dominant private property is assembled in the hands of the groups who control the state that the individual begins to feel capital as an oppressor. Our American demand for equality of opportunity is a constant militant check upon capital becoming a thing to be feared. Out of fear we sometimes even go too far and stifle the reproductive use of capital by crushing the initiative that makes for its creation. . . .

The domination by arbitrary individual ownership is disappearing because the works of today are steadily growing more and more beyond the resources of any one individual, and steadily taxation will reduce relatively excessive individual accumulations. The number of persons in partnership through division of ownership among stockholders is steadily increasing — thus 100,000 to 200,000 partners in a single concern are not uncommon. The overwhelmingly largest portion of our mobile capital is that of our banks, insurance companies, building and loan associations, and the vast majority of all this is the aggregated small savings of our people. Thus large capital is steadily becoming more and more a mobilization of the savings of the small holder — the actual people themselves — and its administration becomes at once more sensitive to the moral opinions of the people in order to attract their support. The directors and managers of large concerns, themselves employees of these great groups of individual stockholders, or policy holders, reflect a spirit of community responsibility.

Large masses of capital can only find their market for service or production to great numbers of the same kind of people that they employ and they must therefore maintain confidence in their public responsibilities in order to retain their customers. In times when the products of manufacture were mostly luxuries to the average of the people, the condition of their employees was of no such interest to their customers as when they cater to employees in general. Of this latter, no greater proofs need exist than the efforts of many large concerns directly dependent upon public good will to restrain prices in scarcity — and the very general desire to yield a measure of service with the goods sold. Another phase of this same development in administration of capital is the growth of a sort of institutional sense in many large business enterprises. The encouragement of solidarity in all grades of their employees in the common service and common success, the sense of mutuality with the prosperity of the community are both vital developments in individualism. . . .

A great test of the soundness of a social system must be its ability to evolve within itself those orderly shifts in its administration that enable it to apply the new tools of social, economic, and intellectual progress, and to eliminate the malign forces that may grow in the application of these tools. When we were almost wholly an agricultural people our form of organization and administration, both in the governmental and economic fields, could be simple. With the enormous shift in growth to industry and commerce we have erected organisms that each generation has denounced as Frankensteins, yet the succeeding generation proves them to be controllable and useful. The growth of corporate organizations, of our banking systems, of our railways, of our electrical power, of our farm coöperatives, of our trade unions, of our trade associations, and of a hundred others indeed develops both beneficent and malign forces. The timid become frightened. But our basic social ideas march through the new things in the end. Our demagogues, of both radical and standpat breed, thrive on demands for the destruction of one or another of these organizations as the only solution for their defects, yet progress requires only a guardianship of the vital principles of our individualism with its safeguard of true equality of opportunity in them.

Political Phases

It is not the primary purpose of this essay to discuss our political organization. Democracy is merely the mechanism which individualism invented as a device that would carry on the necessary political work of its social organization. Democracy arises out of individualism and prospers through it alone.

Without question, there exists, almost all over the world, unprecedented disquietude at the functioning of government itself. It is in part the dreamy social ferment of war emotion. It is in part the aftermath of a period when the Government was everything and the individual nothing, from which there is much stimulation to two schools of thought: one that all human ills can be cured by governmental regulation, and the other that all regulation is a sin.

During the war, the mobilization of every effort, the destruction of the normal demand and the normal avenues of distribution, required a vast excursion over the deadline of individualism in order that we might secure immediate results. Its continuation would have destroyed the initiative of our people and undermined all real progress. We are slowly getting back, but many still aspire to these supposed short cuts to the millennium.

Much of our discontent takes the form of resentment against the inequalities in the distribution of the sacrifices of war. Both silently and vocally there is complaint that while some died, others ran no risk, and yet others profited. For these complaints there is adequate justification. The facts are patent. However, no conceivable human intelligence would be able to manage the conduct of war so as to see that all sacrifices and burdens should be distributed equitably. War is destruction, and we should blame war for its injustices, not a social system whose object is construction. The submergence of the individual, however, in the struggle of the race could be but temporary — its continuance through the crushing of individual action and its equities would, if for no other reason, destroy the foundations of our civilization.

Looked at as the umpire in our social system, our Government has maintained an equality before the law and a development of legal justice and an authority in restraint of evil instincts that support this social system and its ideals so far as the imperfections of developing human institutions permit. It has gone the greatest distance of any government toward maintaining an equality of franchise; an equality of entrance to public office, and government by the majority. It has succeeded far beyond all others in those safeguards of equality of opportunity through education, public information, and the open channels of free speech and free press. It is, however, much easier to chart the course of progress to government in dealing with the abstract problems of order, political liberty, and stimulation to intellectual and moral advancement than it is to chart its relations to the economic seas. These seas are new and only partly discovered or explored.

Our Government's greatest troubles and failures are in the economic field. Forty years ago the contact of the individual with the Government had its largest expression in the sheriff or policeman, and in debates over political equality. In those happy days the Government offered but small interference with the economic life of the citizen. But with the vast development of industry and the train of regulating functions of the national and municipal government that followed from it; with the recent vast increase in taxation due to the war; — the Government has become through its relations to economic life the most potent force for maintenance or destruction of our American individualism.

The entrance of the Government began strongly three decades ago, when our industrial organization began to move powerfully in the direction of consolidation of enterprise. We found in the course of this development that equality of opportunity and its corollary, individual initiative, was being throttled by the concentration of control of industry and service, and thus an economic domination of groups builded over the nation. At this time, particularly, we were threatened with a form of autocracy of economic power. Our mass of regulation of public utilities and our legislation against restraint of trade is the monument to our intent to preserve an equality of opportunity. This regulation is itself proof that we have gone a long way toward the abandonment of the "capitalism" of Adam Smith.

Day by day we learn more as to the practical application of restrictions against economic and political domination. We sometimes lag behind in the correction of those forces that would override liberty, justice, and equality of opportunity, but the principle is so strong within us that domination of the few will not be tolerated. These restraints must keep pace with the growing complexity of our economic organization, but they need tuning to our social system if they would not take us into great dangers. As we build up our powers of production through the advancing application of science we create new forces with which men may dominate — railway, power, oil, and what not. They may produce temporary blockades upon equality of opportunity.

To curb the forces in business which would destroy equality of opportunity and yet to maintain the initiative and creative faculties of our people are the twin objects we must attain. To preserve the former we must regulate that type of activity that would dominate. To preserve the latter, the Government must keep out of production and distribution of commodities and services. This is the deadline between our system and socialism. Regulation to prevent domination and unfair practices, yet preserving rightful initiative, are in keeping with our social foundations. Nationalization of industry or business is their negation.

When we come to the practical problems of government in relation to these economic questions the test lies in two directions: Does this act safeguard an equality of opportunity? Does it maintain the initiative of our people? For in the first must lie the deadline against domination, and in the second the deadline in preservation of individualism against socialism. . . .

There are malign social forces other than our failures that would destroy our progress. There are the equal dangers both of reaction and radicalism. The perpetual howl of radicalism is that it is the sole voice of liberalism — that devotion to social progress is its field alone. These men would assume that all reform and human advance must come through government. They have forgotten that progress must come from the steady lift of the individual and that the measure of national idealism and progress is the quality of idealism in the individual. The most trying support of radicalism comes from the timid or dishonest minds that shrink from facing the result of radicalism itself but are devoted to defense of radicalism as proof of a liberal mind. . . .

The primary safeguard of American individualism is an understanding of it; of faith that it is the most precious possession of American civilization, and a willingness courageously to test every process of national life upon the touchstone of this basic social premise. Development of the human institutions and of science and of industry have been long chains of trial and error. Our public relations to them and to other phases of our national life can be advanced in no other way than by a willingness to experiment in the remedy of our social faults. The failures and unsolved problems of economic and social life can be corrected; they can be solved within our social theme and under no other system. The solution is a matter of will to find solution; of a sense of duty as well as of a sense of right and citizenship. No one who buys "bootleg" whiskey can complain of gunmen and hoodlumism.

H. L. Mencken
THE LAND OF THE BOOB

❧{*1926*}❧   THE BAD BOY of American letters in the 1920's was Henry Louis Mencken (1880-1956), Baltimore newspaperman, magazine editor, essayist, and lexicographer. One thing American he loved was the language, which he discussed with perception and scholarship in *The American Language,* first published in 1918 and republished with revisions and supplements several times thereafter. Most aspects of American life aroused his scorn. In the magazine *The American Mercury* and in books such as *Prejudices* (six series, 1919-1927) and *Notes on Democracy* (1926) he lambasted the low-brow middle-class public (a "booboisie" made up of *homo boobiens*), academic pomposity, the "bilge of idealism," Rotarians, Methodists, and reformers, the principles and practices of democracy, and practically all the tastes and traditions of the majority. Only for a few of the critical thinkers and writers of the time — such as Theodore Dreiser (1871-1945), Sherwood Anderson (1876-1941), and Sinclair Lewis (1885-1951) — did he ever have a good word.

His *American Mercury,* with its green cover, was seen on most American campuses in the hands of professors and students who thought of themselves as far advanced in their literary, political, and social views. In 1927 Walter Lippmann (1889-   ) referred to him as "the most powerful personal influence on this whole generation of educated people." Certainly Mencken contributed a great deal to the spirit and creed of contemporary intellectuals, who believed in social and sexual freedom, opposed the enforcement of propriety by legislation (such as the Volstead Act), smiled at conviction or commitments religious or political, enjoyed the debunking of heroes, and complained of the bad cultural consequences of mass production and the machine.

Mencken's manner, at once shocking and charming, is well illustrated by the concluding chapter from his *Notes on Democracy,* which follows.

THE FUTURE OF DEMOCRACY

WHETHER or not democrary is destined to survive in the world until the corruptible puts on incorruption and the immemorial Christian dead leap out of their graves, their faces shining and their yells resounding — this is something, I confess, that I don't know, nor is it necessary, for the purposes of the present inquiry, that I venture upon the hazard of a guess. My business is not prognosis, but diagnosis. I am not engaged in therapeutics, but in pathology. That simple statement of fact, I daresay, will be accepted as a confession, condemning me out of hand as unfit for my task, and even throwing a certain doubt upon my *bona fides.* For it is one of the peculiar intellectual accompaniments of democracy that the concept of the insoluble becomes unfashionable — nay, almost infamous. To lack a remedy is to lack the very license to discuss disease. The causes of this are to be sought, without question, in the nature of democracy itself. It came into the world as a cure-all, and it remains primarily a cure-all to this day. Any boil upon the body politic, however vast and raging, may be relieved by taking a vote; any flux of blood may be stopped by passing a law. The aim of government is to repeal the laws of nature, and re-enact them with moral amendments. War becomes simply a device to end war. The state, a mystical emanation from the mob, takes on a transcendental potency, and acquires the power to make over the father which begat it. Nothing remains inscrutable and beyond remedy, not even the way of a man with a maid. It was not so under the ancient and accursed systems of despotism, now happily purged out of the world. They, too, I grant you, had certain pretensions of an homeric gaudiness, but they at least refrained from attempts to abolish sin, poverty, stupidity, cowardice, and other such immutable realities. Mediaeval Christianity, which was a theological and philosophical *apologia* for those systems, actually erected belief in that immutability into a cardinal article of faith. The evils of the world were incurable: one put off the quest for a perfect moral order until one got to heaven, *post mortem*. There arose, in consequence, a scheme of checks and balances that was consummate and completely satisfactory, for it could not be put to a test, and the logical holes in it were chinked with miracles. But no more. To-day the Holy Saints are deposed. Now each and every human problem swings into the range of practical politics. The worst and oldest of them may be solved facilely by travelling bands of lady Ph.D.'s, each bearing the mandate of a Legislature of kept men, all unfaithful to their protectors.

Democracy becomes a substitute for the old religion, and the antithesis of it: the Ku Kluxers, though their reasoning may be faulty, are not far off the facts in their conclusion that Holy Church is its enemy. It shows all the magical potency of the great systems of faith. It has the power to enchant and disarm; it is not vulnerable to logical attack. I point for proof to the appalling gyrations and contortions of its chief exponents. Read, for example, the late James Bryce's "Modern Democracies." Observe how he amasses incontrovertible evidence that democracy doesn't work — and then concludes with a stout declaration that it does. Or, if his two fat volumes are too much for you, turn to some school reader and give a judicious perusal to Lincoln's Gettysburg Address, with its argument that the North fought the Civil War to save self-government to the world! — a thesis echoed in falsetto, and by feebler men, fifty years later. It is impossible, by any device known to philosophers, to meet doctrines of that sort; they obviously lie outside the range of logical ideas. There is, in the human mind, a natural taste for such hocus-pocus. It greatly simplifies the process of ratiocination, which is unbearably painful to the great majority of men. What dulls and baffles the teeth may be got down conveniently by an heroic gulp. No doubt there is an explanation here of the long-continued popularity of the dogma of the Trinity, which remains unstated in plain terms after two thousand years. And no doubt the dogma of Transubstantiation came under fire in the Reformation because it had grown too simple and comprehensible — because even the Scholastic philosophy had been unable to convert its plain propositions into something that could be believed without being understood. Democracy is shot through with this delight in the incredible, this banal mysticism. One cannot discuss it without colliding with preposterous postulates, all of them cherished like authentic hairs from the whiskers of Moses himself. I have alluded to its touching acceptance of the faith that progress is illimitable and ordained of God — that every human problem, in the very nature of things, may be solved. There are corollaries that are even more naïve. One, for example, is to the general effect that optimism is a virtue in itself — that there is a mysterious merit in being hopeful and of glad heart, even in the presence of adverse and immovable facts. This curious notion turns the glittering wheels of Rotary, and is the motive power of the political New Thoughters called Liberals. Certainly the attitude of the average American Liberal toward the so-called League of Nations offered superb clinical material to the student of democratic psychopathology. He began by arguing that the League would save the world. Confronted by proofs of its fraudulence, he switched to the doctrine that believing in it would save the world. So, later on, with the Washington Disarmament Conference. The man who hopes absurdly, it appears, is in some fantastic and gaseous manner a better citizen than the man who detects and exposes the truth. Bear this sweet democratic axiom clearly in mind. It is, fundamentally, what is the matter with the United States.

As I say, my present mandate does not oblige me to conjure up a system that will surpass and shame democracy as democracy surpasses and shames the polity of the Andaman Islanders or the Great Khan — a system full-blown and perfect, like Prohibition, and ready to be put into effect by the simple adoption of an amendment to the Constitution. Such a system, for all I know, may lie outside the farthest soarings of the human mind, though that mind can weigh the stars and know God. Until the end of the chapter the ants and bees may flutter their sardonic antennae at us in that department, as they do in others: the last joke upon man may be that he never learned how to govern himself in a rational and competent manner, as the last joke upon woman may be that she never had a baby without wishing that the Day of Judgment were a week past. I am not even undertaking to prove here that democracy is too full of evils to be further borne. On the contrary, I am convinced that it has some valuable merits, not often described, and I shall refer to a few of them presently. All I argue is that its manifest defects, if they are ever to be got rid of at all, must be got rid of by examining them realistically — that they will never cease to afflict all the more puissant and exemplary nations so long as discussing them is impeded by concepts borrowed from theology. As for me, I have never encountered any actual evidence, convincing to an ordinary jury, that *vox populi* is actually *vox Dei*. The proofs, indeed, run the other way. The life of the inferior man is one long protest against the obstacles that God interposes to the attainment of his dreams, and democracy, if it is anything at all, is simply one way of getting 'round those obstacles. Thus it represents, not a jingling echo of what seems to be the divine will, but a raucous defiance of it. To that extent, perhaps, it is truly civilized, for civilization, as I have argued elsewhere, is best described as an effort to remedy the blunders and check the cruel humours of the Cosmic Kaiser. But what is defiant is surely not official, and what is not official is open to examination.

For all I know, democracy may be a self-limiting disease, as civilization itself seems to be. There are obvious parodoxes in its philosophy, and some of them have a suicidal smack. It offers John Doe a means to rise above his place beside Richard Roe, and then, by making Roe his equal, it takes away the chief usufructs of the rising. I here attempt no pretty logical gymnastics: the history of democratic states is a history of disingenuous efforts to get rid of the second half of that dilemma. There is not only the natural yearning of Doe to use and enjoy the superiority that he has won; there is also the natural tendency of Roe, as an inferior man, to acknowledge it. Democracy, in fact, is always inventing class distinctions, despite its theoretical abhorrence of them. The baron has departed, but in his place stand the grand goblin, the supreme worthy archon, the sovereign grand commander. Democratic man, as I have remarked, is quite unable to think of himself as a free individual; he must belong to a group, or shake with fear and loneliness — and the group, of course, must have its leaders. It would be hard to find a country in which such brummagem serene highnesses are revered with more passionate devotion than they get in the United States. The distinction that goes with mere office runs far ahead of the distinction that goes with actual achievement. A Harding is regarded as genuinely superior to a Halsted, no doubt because his doings are better understood. But there is a form of human striving that is understood by democratic man even better than Harding's, and that is the striving for money. Thus the plutocracy in a democratic state, tends to take the place of the missing aristocracy, and even to be mistaken for it. It is, of course, something quite different. It lacks all the essential characters of a true aristocracy: a clean tradition, culture, public spirit, honesty, honour, courage — above all, courage. It stands under no bond of obligation to the state; it has no public duty; it is transient and lacks a goal. Its most puissant dignitaries of to-day came out of the mob only yesterday — and from the mob they bring all its peculiar ignobilities. As practically encountered, the plutocracy stands quite as far from the *honnête homme* as it stands from the Holy Saints. Its main character is its incurable timorousness; it is for ever grasping at the straws held out by demagogues. Half a dozen gabby Jewish youths, meeting in a back room to plan a revolution — in other words, half a dozen kittens preparing to upset the Matterhorn — are enough to scare it half to death. Its dreams are of banshees, hobgoblins, bugaboos. The honest, untroubled snores of a Percy or a Hohenstaufen are quite beyond it.

The plutocracy, as I say, is comprehensible to the mob because its aspirations are essentially those of inferior men: it is not by accident that Christianity, a mob religion, paves heaven with gold and precious stones, *i.e.,* with money. There are, of course, reactions against this ignoble ideal among men of more civilized tastes, even in democratic states, and sometimes they arouse the mob to a transient distrust of certain of the plutocratic pretensions. But that distrust seldom arises above mere envy, and the polemic which engenders it is seldom sound in logic or impeccable in motive. What it lacks is aristocratic disinterestedness, born of aristocratic security. There is no body of opinion behind it that is, in the strictest sense, a free opinion. Its chief exponents, by some divine irony, are pedagogues of one sort or another — which is to say, men chiefly marked by their haunting fear of losing their jobs. Living under such terrors, with the plutocracy policing them harshly on one side and the mob congenitally suspicious of them on the other, it is no wonder that their revolt usually peters out in metaphysics, and that they tend to abandon it as their families grow up, and the costs of heresy become prohibitive. The pedagogue, in the long run, shows the virtues of the Congressman, the newspaper editorial writer or the butler, not those of the aristocrat. When, by any chance, he persists in contumacy beyond thirty, it is only too commonly a sign, not that he is heroic, but simply that he is pathological. So with most of his brethren of the Utopian Fife and Drum Corps, whether they issue out of his own seminary or out of the wilderness. They are fanatics; not statesmen. Thus politics, under democracy, resolves itself into impossible alternatives. Whatever the label on the parties, or the war cries issuing from the demagogues who lead them, the practical choice is between the plutocracy on the one side and a rabble of preposterous impossibilists on the other. One must either follow the New York *Times,* or one must be prepared to swallow Bryan and the Bolsheviki. It is a pity that this is so. For what democracy needs most of all is a party that will separate the good that is in it theoretically from the evils that beset it practically, and then try to erect that good into a workable system. What it needs beyond everything is a party of liberty. It produces, true enough, occasional libertarians, just as despotism produces occasional regicides, but it tries them in the same drum-head way. It will never have a party of them until it invents and installs a genuine aristocracy, to breed them and secure them.

I have alluded somewhat vaguely to the merits of democracy. One of them is quite obvious: it is, perhaps, the most charming form of government ever devised by man. The reason is not far to seek. It is based upon propositions that are palpably not true — and what is not true, as everyone knows, is always immensely more fascinating and satisfying to the vast majority of men than what is true. Truth has a harshness that alarms them, and an air of finality that collides with their incurable romanticism. They turn, in all the great emergencies of life, to the ancient promises, transparently false but immensely comforting, and of all those ancient promises there is none more comforting than the one to the effect that the lowly shall inherit the earth. It is at the bottom of the dominant religious system of the modern world, and it is at the bottom of the dominant political system. The latter, which is democracy, gives it an even higher credit and authority than the former, which is Christianity. More, democracy gives it a certain appearance of objective and demonstrable truth. The mob man, functioning as citizen, gets a feeling that he is really important to the world — that he is genuinely running things. Out of his maudlin herding after rogues and mountebanks there comes to him a sense of vast and mysterious power — which is what makes archbishops, police sergeants, the grand goblins of the Ku Klux and other such magnificoes happy. And out of it there comes too, a conviction that he is somehow wise, that his views are taken seriously by his betters — which is what makes United States Senators, fortunetellers and Young Intellectuals happy. Finally, there comes out of it a glowing consciousness of a high duty triumphantly done — which is what makes hangmen and husbands happy.

All these forms of happiness, of course, are illusory. They don't last. The democrat, leaping into the air to flap his wings and praise God, is for ever coming down with a thump. The seeds of his disaster, as I have shown, lie in his own stupidity: he can never get rid of the naïve delusion — so beautifully Christian! — that happiness is something to be got by taking it away from the other fellow. But there are seeds, too, in the very nature of things: a promise, after all, is only a promise, even when it is supported by divine revelation, and the chances against its fulfilment may be put into a depressing mathematical formula. Here the irony that lies under all human aspiration shows itself: the quest for happiness, as always, brings only *un*happiness in the end. But saying that is merely saying that the true charm of democracy is not for the democrat but for the spectator. That spectator, it seems to me, is favoured with a show of the first cut and calibre. Try to imagine anything more heroically absurd! What grotesque false pretences! What a parade of obvious imbecilities! What a welter of fraud! But is fraud amusing? Then I retire forthwith as a psychologist. The fraud of democracy, I contend, is more amusing than any other — more amusing even, and by miles, then the fraud of religion. Go into your praying-chamber and give sober thought to any of the more characteristic democratic inventions: say, Law Enforcement. Or to any of the typical democratic prophets: say, the late Archangel Bryan. If you don't come out paled and palsied by mirth then you will not laugh on the Last Day itself, when Presbyterians step out of the grave like chicks from the egg, and wings blossom from their scapulae, and they leap into interstellar space with roars of joy.

I have spoken hitherto of the possibility that democracy may be a self-limiting disease, like measles. It is, perhaps, something more: it is self-devouring. One cannot observe it objectively without being impressed by its curious distrust of itself — its apparently ineradicable tendency to abandon its whole philosophy at the first sign of strain. I need not point to what happens invariably in democratic states when the national safety is menaced. All the great tribunes of democracy, on such occasions, convert themselves, by a process as simple as taking a deep breath, into despots of an almost fabulous ferocity. Lincoln, Roosevelt and Wilson come instantly to mind: Jackson and Cleveland are in the background, waiting to be recalled. Nor is this process confined to times of alarm and terror: it is going on day in and day out. Democracy always seems bent upon killing the thing it theoretically loves. I have rehearsed some of its operations against liberty, the very cornerstone of its political metaphysic. It not only wars upon the thing itself; it even wars upon mere academic advocacy of it. I offer the spectacle of Americans jailed for reading the Bill of Rights as perhaps the most gaudily humorous ever witnessed in the modern world. Try to imagine monarchy jailing subjects for maintaining the divine right of Kings! Or Christianity damning a believer for arguing that Jesus Christ was the Son of God! This last, perhaps, has been done: anything is possible in that direction. But under democracy the remotest and most fantastic possibility is a commonplace of every day. All the axioms resolve themselves into thundering paradoxes, many amounting to downright contradictions in terms. The mob is competent to rule the rest of us — but it must be rigorously policed itself. There is a government, not of men, but of laws — but men are set upon benches to decide finally what the law is and may be. The highest function of the citizen is to serve the state — but the first assumption that meets him, when he essays to discharge it, is an assumption of his disingenuousness and dishonour. Is that assumption commonly sound? Then the farce only grows the more glorious.

I confess, for my part, that it greatly delights me. I enjoy democracy immensely. It is incomparably idiotic, and hence incomparably amusing. Does it exalt dunderheads, cowards, trimmers, frauds, cads? Then the pain of seeing them go up is balanced and obliterated by the joy of seeing them come down. Is it inordinately wasteful, extravagant, dishonest? Then so is every other form of government: all alike are enemies to laborious and virtuous men. Is rascality at the very heart of it? Well, we have borne that rascality since 1776, and continue to survive. In the long run, it may turn out that rascality is necessary to human government, and even to civilization itself — that civilization, at bottom, is nothing but a colossal swindle. I do not know: I report only that when the suckers are running well the spectacle is infinitely exhilarating. But I am, it may be, a somewhat malicious man: my sympathies, when it comes to suckers, tend to be coy. What I can't make out is how any man can believe in democracy who feels for and with them, and is pained when they are debauched and made a show of. How can any man be a democrat who is sincerely a democrat?

Samuel Gompers

PURE AND SIMPLE UNIONISM

◆❧{*1920*}❧◆ MORE THAN any other one person, Samuel Gompers (1850-1924) can be considered the creator of "big labor" as a countervailing force to big business in the United States.

Born in London, the son of a Jewish couple who had gone there from Holland, Gompers voyaged with his family to New York in 1863. Here, as a cigar maker, he rose to leadership in the local union. He helped to found the American Federation of Labor, and from its organization in 1886 to his death in 1924 he served continuously (except for two years) as its president. The A. F. of L. grew slowly but steadily until the coming of the First World War, then more than doubled its membership in a few years. By 1920 there was an impressive total of more than five million union members in the country, and of these more than four million were affiliated with the A. F. of L. In the steel strike of 1919, the A. F. of L. had suffered a defeat, and during the next decade it was to fall off drastically in size and strength. In 1920, however, Gompers still stood near the peak of his career.

The success of his organization seemed to prove the wisdom of his principles. He advocated "pure and simple unionism": direct dealing with employers to obtain higher wages, shorter hours, and better working conditions; and the use of economic action, such as the strike and the boycott, to back up the worker's demands. He proposed no radical changes in the social or economic system (though perhaps the concept of collective bargaining itself implies a radical change in labor-management relations). In general he disliked political action. That is, he resisted proposals for government intervention to regulate wages and hours, and he advised against the formation of a labor party, though he counseled union members to vote for pro-labor candidates and (in 1924) endorsed Robert M. La Follette (1855-1925) for President.

On the one hand, Gompers fought those corporation leaders who refused to recognize and deal with unions. On the other hand, he fought the socialists, communists, and syndicalists (represented by the I. W. W. — the Industrial Workers of the World) who sought to make unionism a force for revolution. At times he was charged with neglecting unskilled laborers, and at times, when he cooperated with big businessmen, he was accused of "banqueting with the enemy." Despite opposition and criticism, he stuck to his object of getting "more and more" for his followers.

Gompers put his point of view, in simple terms, in the brief essays that follow. Both of these were circulated in pamphlets published by the A. F. of L. The first of the two pamphlets, "The Shorter Workday — Its Philosophy," bears no date but probably was issued at about the end of the First World War. The second, "Collective Bargaining," is dated 1920.

THE SHORTER WORKDAY — ITS PHILOSOPHY

DECREASING the hours of labor is a revolutionary force. Contrast the life of the toiler who works twelve hours with that of one who works eight hours. The difference in the workday affects personal habits, standards of living and social relations.

The man who works twelve hours spends perhaps one hour going to and from work, and surely sometime for meals — the rest of the day is for sleep and — shall we say — opportunity for self-improvement. Twelve long hours of work exhaust physical strength and fill the whole body with the poison of fatigue. The time for rest is sufficient only partially to counteract the fatigue and so the deadening effect of the poison is cumulative. There is neither energy, inclination, nor opportunity for the man or the woman who works twelve hours — the worker becomes only a work machine. The darkness under which he creeps to and from work hides his misery and his poverty from the world and often from himself.

Daylight and a chance to see, stir up discontent necessary to arouse action.

The individual who works eight hours or less does not each day exhaust his energy. He has time for recuperation and something more. His mind is more alert and active. He is capable of more vigorous and more effective work. He goes to and from work at a time when well-dressed people are on the streets. He really has time and opportunity for making comparisons and forming desires. He has longer time to stay at home, sees other homes better furnished, and consequently wants a better home for himself. He wants books, pictures, friends, entertainment. In short, he becomes a human being with intellectual desires and cravings. This change makes him a more valuable worker. Because his standard of living has changed he demands higher wages. Men and women will not continue indefinitely to work for wages that force them to live below their concepts of what constitutes standards of living.

This is why the shorter workday is one of the primary, fundamental demands of organized labor. The labor movement represents organized discontent with poorer conditions and definite purposeful effort to secure better. It represents ambition and ideals.

Before the labor movement of the United States was organized upon a permanent, national basis, the working day was from sun-up to sunset. During the thirties there were numerous efforts by trades to establish ten hours. By proclamation, in 1840, the ten-hour workday was established in the Navy Yard at Washington, D. C. During the latter sixties came a revival of the trade union movement, and the eight-hour day became the slogan. Eight Hour Leagues were formed. Local labor organizations and economic associations educated public opinion in the philosophy of eight hours and the benefits of the shorter workday. In 1868 a federal eight-hour law was enacted. The National Labor Union, organized in 1869, endorsed the eight-hour day. The Knights of Labor was formed the same year and added impetus to the eight-hour movement. During the seventies there were numerous trade strikes for the eight-hour day. There was conviction and desire, but the movement to obtain the results lacked direction and unity.

Three years after the American Federation of Labor was organized, based upon the principle of trade autonomy, the 1884 annual convention adopted a resolution that the trades should fix May 1, 1886, as a definite day and bend their efforts toward establishing an eight-hour day upon that date. The movement aroused enthusiasm and hope, and was stirring the working people all over the country. As the result of this united effort, trade unions increased greatly their numbers and powers. Lectures and talks were delivered, literature distributed and agitations held for the eight-hour cause. The opposition and the treatment of the leaders were of such a nature as to develop among them devotion and a spirit of consecration to the cause.

Eight hours was forcing its way with irresistible power into work-shops and factories. Many trade agreements were signed before May 1, but the dreadful Haymarket disaster in Chicago checked this unprec-edented progress. Nevertheless, three national unions established the eight-hour day during that campaign — the cigarmakers, the German typog-raphers, and the stonecutters.

The labor movement and the eight-hour cause were not permanently retarded. The A. F. of L. decided to select some one international each year, and to concentrate all efforts on securing the eight-hour day in that industry. As time went by this policy was no longer advisable, and secur-ing the shorter workday is now the concern of the organizations in each trade.

As the years have gone by, the eight-hour philosophy which originated in the misery and weary toil of workers has become an accepted prin-ciple of society and industry. Employers have learned that the short-hour worker is a better, more productive, more valuable worker than the one who drudges long hours for low wages. The short-hour worker has more vitality, more ability, more resources, to put into his work — he accomplishes more in a shorter period of time. As a natural result, de-creasing hours of daily work invariably results in increasing wages.

When employers have to pay higher wages to workers they place a higher estimate upon those services and increase managerial efficiency and secure improved machinery, tools, and methods in order to make labor power more effective. Thus the dignity of Labor, of which vote-seekers love to discourse, assumes reality through the economic collective power of workers who secure for themselves a shorter workday and higher wages.

Many apologists for long hours and low wages claim that the short workday and high wages necessarily result in higher costs of production and high selling prices and hence are contrary to the best interest of so-ciety. That theory is contradicted by facts — the individual production of the short hours, highly paid workers, is vastly greater than that of the long hours worker who always works under less advantageous con-ditions. Placing a high estimate upon human labor power stimulates the invention of machinery and the discovery of better methods. The cumu-lative effect of improvements is cheaper and increased production, hence lower selling prices and the benefits of all society.

The shorter workday movement originated in the need of overworked employes, and has been carried on through their unions assisted by other agencies that the workers have been able to convert to their cause. For workers under the government it is not possible to use the same methods of determining contractural relations as are used in dealing with private employers. For these workers legislation has been enacted to secure them less burdensome hours of work — but even in this case the initiative and the burden of work in securing the legislation have fallen upon organized labor. Legislation for shorter workdays in government employment is not only secured because of the economic power of the workers but it is enforced by the same power. Merely enacting a law does not guarantee the benefits of its enforcement — that depends upon the vigilance of those to be benefited. This is manifest in the continuous efforts of organized labor to prevail upon government officials to provide for the eight-hour day in government work and contracts. Meanwhile there are all the perils from the courts and Attorneys General that minimize and limit its application.

When an attempt is made to regulate by law relations between employers and employes in private industry, the difficulties are increased. Obviously the primary difficulty with securing results by legislation is its indirectness. Instead of dealing directly with the employer who has power to establish an eight-hour day in his industry, influence must be used with political representatives as well as the employers' lobbyists, and then upon government administrators and upon their deputies who are supposed to enforce the law. Violations of laws must be righted through the slow methods of litigation, which have regard for precedent and red tape rather than for justice and human rights.

Consider a few well-known examples of eight-hours by law: Colorado has an eight-hour day for miners, yet the whole country has been stirred by the courageous fight of the Colorado miners to secure, among other things, an eight-hour workday. Never will there be an eight-hour workday in the Colorado mines until there are miners' unions which force mine operators to operate their mines on an eight-hour basis and retain in their own power the enforcement of the regulation.

Consider what has happened in some shipyards which had government contracts requiring the eight-hour day. Workmen were employed upon the federal government work six or eight hours, and for two, three, or four hours more upon other work, not covered by such contracts.

Consider this statement of Secretary Iffland of the Journeymen Bakers'

International Union, one who has had experience with the law of New York to establish a ten-hour day in all bakeries:

> The local unions of the state of New York through agitation spent considerable money and time to be successful in passing the law, in which we succeeded in 1896. At that time we were of the opinion that by giving through our efforts the ten-hour day by law to the bakery workers of that state, they would realize what the organization could do to that effect, and by that would become members of our organization, but we had to find out very soon that we had made the mistake of our lives, as from that day on the members dropped from the organization, and the unorganized threw up to those who tried to organize them that they don't need an organization any more as they have the ten-hour workday by law.
>
> Not alone this, but members who used all their energy to pass the law have been insulted as corrupt politicians, etc., and the radical labor papers of course denounced at that time, such action taken by organized labor as nothing could be expected from the political organizations under the present system of society. We very soon had to find out that we were confronted to regain our strength and make good the loss of membership, as well as prestige in our organization in the state of New York, although the organization was weak, to institute agitation for a nine-hour workday, and it has proved that only through the effort of organized labor were we successful in gaining the shorter workday, and we welcomed the day when that law was declared unconstitutional.

Experience with legislation has taught that statutes are very much akin to repositories for exalted New Year resolutions unless there is some force that can and will give life and influence in the affairs of the people.

Another difficulty with the legislative method is the diffusion of effort. There are comparatively few people interested in the matter, and yet the whole body politic must be interested, educated and aroused to action.

Contrast this with the simple, direct methods of economic action. Those workers who want the shorter workday know why they want it, and they want it so intensely that they are ready to fight for it. Forceful independent men and women, they assume the responsibility of their own welfare and make sacrifices to secure their rights. By agreement or by strike, they secure what they need, and because they have won it themselves, they value it and maintain it. They are organized in such a way that they can give expression to their will and secure results in the most direct way possible.

Two influences have been operating to develop sentiment in favor of establishing in private industry, legislative regulation of contractual relations; one, an ardent enthusiasm to accomplish big results by one revolutionizing regulation, the other a sort of moral flabbiness that refuses to assume responsibility for its own life but endeavors to cast upon society not only all responsibility for the environment in which people live and work, but also responsibility for securing for them conditions that are desirable and helpful.

The latter is a repudiation of the characteristics that enabled Americans to get results. They never feared the hard places but dared to wrestle with a primeval country. They were red-blooded men and women with ruggedness in their wills. They were ready to fight for right and justice and equality, ready to defend what was rightfully theirs. This is the spirit that has made the American labor movement the most aggressive labor organization in the world, and has made its members the most efficient workers to be found anywhere. The American labor movement has done things for the workers despite hostility of employers and indifference of society.

Then as to the other influence — the desire to secure the big thing at one "fell swoop." That has appealed to the imagination of dreamers and those who are infected with intellectual phantasmagoria.

They forget that after all permanent changes and progress must come from within man. You can't "save" people — they must save themselves. Unless the working people are organized to express their desires and needs and organized to express their will, any other method tends to weaken initiative.

And this is not a narrow policy, unmindful of the difficulties and hardships that encompass overworked, exploited workers. The organized labor movement has done much for the unorganized; in incalculable ways the unorganized have been the beneficiaries of the fights and struggles of the organized.

Because of public opinion that has been formulated and roused by organized labor, the old workday of fourteen to sixteen hours has practically passed away. The twelve-hour workday obtains in but few industries, whereas ten, nine, and eight hour days have been secured by organizations. Then the benefit is necessarily bestowed upon allied trades, because of association in the same industry. The burden of the eight-hour fight has been borne by organized labor. Now there are few who deny Labor's claims, and there are many sympathetic scientists and publicists ready to substantiate them. This is a heritage the organized bestow upon the workers of today.

Organized labor created the sentiment for an eight-hour day — it has made possible and secured the eight-hour day for many trades. Without organized labor it would be impossible to maintain an eight-hour day in any trade or industry. The labor movement, which is the organized workers directing and controlling their own affairs and destinies, is the only dependable defense and protection of those who work for wages.

If the workers surrender control over working relations to legislative and adminstrative agents, they put their industrial liberty at the disposal of state agents. They strip themselves bare of means of defense — they can no longer defend themselves by the strike. To insure liberty and personal welfare, personal relations must be controlled only by those concerned.

But after all, even if it is the quicker way, is the quick way always the best way? Suppose you have a boy for whom you are fondly ambitious. You wish him to be a business or a professional success — do you start him in either at the age of ten, or do you wait upon the process of education? When he finally embarks in business or a profession, do you dictate and regulate each feature, or do you advise and leave the boy to solve his own problem and make his own decisions?

So with the eight-hour or shorter workday in private employment. It is as stated in the beginning, the fundamental objective for workers who are seeking better things. But when forced upon them by law, or given them without their appreciating its value, they frequently look upon it as injustice or hardship. They have not been able to make agreements for the adjustment of wages, hence they apprehend that decreasing the hours of work means to them decreased pay.

Often securing the eight-hour day by outside agencies means that organization is retarded or checked, which in time means that continued progress and future betterment will be practically impossible.

Doing for people what they can and ought to do for themselves is a dangerous experiment. In the last analysis the welfare of the workers depends upon their own initiative. Whatever is done under the guise of philanthropy or social morality which in any way lessens initiative is the greatest crime that can be committed against the toilers. Let social busy-bodies and professional "public morals experts" in their fads reflect upon the perils they rashly invite under this pretense of social welfare.

Some say that the state is an agency through which the people obtain results — that it exists for their service. But the state is not some impersonal thing. It has no existense outside the people that compose it. Its policies and movements can be directed only by those who are organized and therefore able to exercise power and exert influence. The working people who are unorganized have no part in determining the affairs of state — they may benefit or suffer from policies but they have no voice in them.

Organization in industry to be utilized in every field of beneficent activity is the only defense and protection of the workers. Those who would really benefit the workers through legislation or through economic action should lose no opportunity to further organization of the yet unorganized. If all the welfare workers, the social uplifters, the social legislative enthusiasts would apply the efforts and money they are now diverting to other causes to the work of promoting organization, they would greatly shorten the time necessary to put all workers in a position where they could solve their own problems, fight their own battles, and promote their own welfare as free, equal men and women.

Bear in mind that "Eternal vigilance is the price of liberty" is as essential today as when the warning was coined, or at any time in the world's history. It has its potent application to life and liberty in industry, as in the political life of our nation.

> Whether you work by the piece or work by the day,
> Decreasing the hours increases the pay.

Organize, Unite, Federate, to reduce the hours of labor.

COLLECTIVE BARGAINING

COLLECTIVE bargaining means that the organized employes of a trade or industry, through representatives of their own choosing, shall deal with the employer or employers in the making of wage scales and working conditions. Collective bargaining is the only practical proposal for adjusting relations between the management and the workers in a business way, assuring a fair deal to both sides.

Each individual joins with his fellow workman to ask collectively for better wages and conditions of employment that he could not secure through his own efforts alone. An employer of, say five hundred men, has an unfair advantage if he deals with them as individuals. To make the employes equal in power and influence to the employer they must be organized, and through regularly chosen representatives, meet the employer on a common footing. By conceding points on each side an agreement can be finally reached that will maintain better relations and therefore greater industrial peace.

In no other walk of life does the idea exist that a man must arbitrarily accept any offer that may be made by another. There are two sides always to an agreement. Each side ought to have equal chances to propose and insist upon what is considered a fair agreement.

Industrial peace can be secured only by the righting of wrongs suffered by the workers. If a body of workers has a grievance it can be adjusted only through conferences with the employer or his representative. As all can not meet the employer at one time it is necessary for them to select representatives to carry out their will as expressed collectively. This right is identical with that always held by the employer and never challenged by the law or the public.

In all spheres of activity in which employers, business men, public men and citizens generally have any matter in which their interests are involved, they not only avail themselves of appearing by their own representatives and counsel of their own choosing, whether in litigation before the courts or in business relations, but they are guaranteed even by the constitution of our country the right to be heard by counsel. The claim of the workers in this respect is founded upon the same fundamental beneficial principle — the right of the workers to be represented by counsel (not lawyers), representatives of their own number and of their own choice.

For instance, in great industries such as the iron and steel industry, the employes have nothing to say as to their wages and working conditions. They work twelve hours a day and every two weeks, in changing from day to night work, they are compelled to remain at their tasks for twenty-four hours straight. This has been the practice since the industry has been organized into corporations. There have been much opposition and grumbling from the employes, but these have never reached the heads of the corporation, or if they did, found no response.

The employes were unorganized. Collective bargaining, except for a short time years ago with a small number of highly skilled employes, was unknown. The great mass of workers had no voice in what they should receive. If a superintendent or foreman wished to change the conditions of employment, he could do so without question, as each department is expected to produce a certain amount in value. The straw bosses pinched and schemed to do it. The only way they ever tried was to take something away from the employes. They never considered that most efficient production could be secured only when agencies for assuring justice to employes and the best management and working conditions were established. It was this sort of industrial servitude that culminated many times in great strikes in the steel industry. It brought the strike of 1919. The head of the great corporation in that industry refused to meet representatives of the employes even to hear their grievances. If collective bargaining had been in force in that industry the twelve and twenty-four hour day would have disappeared years ago, and it would have been accomplished without a strike. Now the responsible head of that corporation knows so little of what the steel workers are thinking that he even asserts that they want the twelve-hour day.

As the employes were employed as individuals and kept apart by radical [racial?], creed, national prejudices and other means, they could not unite to submit their grievances until they became members of trades unions. They could not understand each other, nor could they succeed in eliminating the causes that had formerly kept them in isolated and hostile groups.

Collective bargaining in industry does not imply that wage earners shall assume control of industry, or responsibility for financial management. It proposes that the employes shall have the right to organize and to deal with the employer through selected representatives as to wages and working conditions.

Among the matters that properly come within the scope of collective bargaining are wages, hours of labor, conditions and relations of employment, the sanitary conditions of the plant, safety and comfort regulations and such other factors as would add to the health, safety and comfort of the employes, resulting in the mutual advantage of both employers and employes. But there is no belief held in the trades unions that its members shall control the plant or usurp the rights of the owners.

Collective bargaining takes into consideration not only mutually advantageous conditions and standards of life and work, but also the human equation, a desideratum too long neglected.

APPLICATION OF PRINCIPLES

Q. *What is collective bargaining?*

A. Simply a business proposition by which the organized employes in a trade or industry deal collectively with their employer or employers.

Q. *How is this accomplished?*

A. The employes in their union appoint a committee to draw up new wage scales and working conditions. These are reported to the union for consideration. Then in regular meeting each question is taken up and discussed from every angle. Finally the union agrees upon a wage-scale and working conditions to submit to the employer. A committee for this purpose is selected, as the entire number of employes can not meet in conference with the employer. This committee meets the employer or his representative and discusses the desires of the employes collectively through their union.

Q. *Does this committee have full power to act?*

A. No. It must report back to the union the result of its conference with the employer. If the report is satisfactory the union approves the settlement and an agreement for a stated period is signed by both parties. If unsatisfactory, further conferences with the employer or his representative are held until an agreement is reached.

Q. *What advantage has such a joint agreement?*

A. It removes friction that always exists where employes have no voice in the making of their wages and conditions of employment. It is democracy in industry as opposed to autocracy. The employes know what they are to receive for a certain period and therefore can plan ahead in buying a home or making improvements in their standard of living.

Q. *Does collective bargaining protect the employes?*

A. Yes. Employes can not be discharged at the will of a "straw boss." Charges against them must be made, and after a trial, if they are found true, then the offenders can be discharged. If untrue, they retain their positions.

Q. *What effect does this have on the "straw bosses"?*

A. It makes them more careful. They are not so arbitrary or do not seek trouble. It brings about mutually better feelings and relations.

Q. *Does the fact that an employe can not be discharged without cause make him more independent and likely to create friction?*

A. No. Men who are placed on their honor, which is the result of collective bargaining, feel they have an interest in the plant and make every effort to carry out the union agreement. They are not nagged, browbeaten or coerced. They take an interest in their work and the result is a better output and a lower turnover of labor. Their initiative powers are not curtailed and because of that they try to create new methods that will be of benefit to the business. They are men and not mere machines, and this results in better feeling between employers and employes.

Q. *Can unorganized employes bargain collectively?*

A. Not with a certainty that they will be treated fairly. Unorganized employes are subject to influences that will hamper their efforts for fair bargaining.

Q. *Why?*

A. Being unorganized they can not agree collectively to any proposition that will benefit them, as the influences referred to will divert them into accepting less than that to which they are entitled.

Q. *What are these influences?*

A. Men employed as individuals always retain the fear that they are to be discharged or have their wages lowered whenever the employer sees fit to do it. They are not in a position to enter objections to their working conditions because of these same fears. They are voiceless in their own affairs because they can not act collectively. Each is suspicious of the other. Some feel that they are overlooked by the employer while others are favorites who receive all the best work. Jealousies are created. Discontent is rife. Therefore when the unorganized employes all meet together to decide what they shall ask the employer they become cowardly for fear some other employe will report them to the employer. Those who take an active part always are the favorites of the employer and they advocate only those things to which the great majority of the employes would object if they were not afraid. The outcome of such a meeting is never satisfactory. Instead, discontent grows and in time the employes form a real trade union, and from that time on they do not fear to express their thoughts or openly object to the statements of those known as company men.

SUMMARY

Collective bargaining, it will be seen, makes for a better citizenship. It uplifts those who while unorganized were timid and servile. The industries accepting collective bargaining are stabilized and can face the future with certainty instead of doubt. Raising the standard of citizenship of the workers through collective bargaining affects the community in which they live. The standard of living is improved, the children are benefited through better chances for education and the home is made happier by the fact that the head of the family is able to earn a sufficient wage to support those dependent upon him. This is democracy in industry.

Autocracy in industry is where the employer fixes the wages and hours of employment arbitrarily. They must be accepted by the employes without question. Those who object are discharged. This creates a servile class that makes for an inferior citizenship.

The issue, then, is between collective bargaining and autocracy in industry. The good of the nation demands collective bargaining. There can be no defense for autocracy in industry.

VII. The Great Depression and the New Deal

Marriner S. Eccles

HOW TO END THE DEPRESSION

❧{*1933*}❧ IN THE bleak winter between the election of 1932 and Franklin D. Roosevelt's inauguration the following March, the Great Depression touched bottom. Declining production, rising unemployment, misery, and hopelessness seemed the dominant characteristics of American society. In this situation, in February 1933, a long procession of businessmen, labor leaders, and other prominent persons testified at hearings held in Washington by the Senate Finance Committee in an effort to find a way out of the depths. But no one seemed capable of offering a really new idea; the general tone is perhaps best epitomized in the words of Bernard Baruch (1870-   ), who urged: "Reject all plans which propose to postpone the working of natural processes."

Then, on February 24, a small, sharp-featured young Westerner named Marriner Eccles (1890-   ) took the stand. Eccles was a brilliantly successful banker and businessman, but little known outside his native Utah. Nevertheless, where others had mouthed disproved platitudes and vague generalities, he advanced a specific, practical, well-organized plan based on the idea that the government should spend money when times were bad and tighten its belt during periods of prosperity.

Eccles had been influenced by the writings of the American economist William T. Foster (1879-1950), who had said much the same thing some years earlier; his point of view had also been expounded with far more subtlety and refinement by the British economist, John Maynard Keynes (1883-1946). And his proposals did not produce any great stir at the time he made them. But many thoughtful observers were impressed by his concrete and clear-headed line of argument. Here was no impractical professor or theorist but a successful businessman speaking from experience; his words had weight. In any case, in November 1934 President Roosevelt appointed Eccles to a vacancy on the Federal Reserve Board and his public career was launched. Quickly he became one of the most influential molders of New Deal economic policy.

TESTIMONY BEFORE
THE SENATE FINANCE COMMITTEE

(February 24, 1933)

The CHAIRMAN. Mr. Eccles, give your name and your address for the record.

Mr. ECCLES. M. S. Eccles, Ogden, Utah.

The CHAIRMAN. You are interested in banking institutions in not only Utah, but Idaho?

Mr. Eccles. Yes.

The CHAIRMAN. You may proceed, Mr. Eccles.

Mr. ECCLES. Let me say at the outset that I am not appearing here as a representative of any one class or section. Nor am I suggesting measures designed to help my section of the country at the expense of any other section. The ideas I shall present have not been gained through contact with or interests in any one line of private or public occupation. . . .

The measures proposed by me, while more far-reaching than have been used to date, are predicated upon sound Government finance. Nor do they involve any measure of inflation of the popular brand. I believe the adoption of any or all of them would not in any degree weaken our gold standard or cheapen the gold content of our dollar. . . . The propositions I offer are all intended to bring about, by Government action, an increase of purchasing power on the part of all the people, resulting in an immediate and increasing volume in all lines of business with consequent diminution of unemployment and distress and gradual restoration of our national income. When this is accomplished, and not before, can the Government hope to balance its Budget and our people regain the standard of living to which the material wealth of this country entitles them.

Before effective action can be taken to stop the devastating effects of the depression, it must be recognized that the breakdown of our present economic system is due to the failure of our political and financial leadership to intelligently deal with the money problem. In the real world there is no cause nor reason for the unemployment with its resultant destitution and suffering of fully one-third of our entire population. We have all and more of the material wealth which we had at the peak of our prosperity in the year 1929. Our people need and want everything which our abundant facilities and resources are able to provide for them. The problem of production has been solved, and we need no further capital accumulation for the present, which could only be utilized in further increasing our productive facilities or extending further foreign credits. We have a complete economic plant able to supply a superabundance of not only all of the necessities of our people, but the comforts and luxuries as well. Our problem, then, becomes one purely of distribution. This can only be brought about by providing purchasing power sufficiently adequate to enable the people to obtain the consumption goods which we, as a nation, are able to produce. The economic system can serve no other purpose and expect to survive. . . .

. . . The nineteenth century economics will no longer serve our purpose — an economic age 150 years old has come to an end. The orthodox capitalistic system of uncontrolled individualism, with its free competition, will no longer serve our purpose. We must think in terms of the scientific, technological, interdependent machine age, which can only survive and function under a modified capitalistic system controlled and regulated from the top by government.

What I have said could no doubt be considered academic unless the discussion of it reveals some specific constructive propositions for solution of our immediate problems, which now call for first-aid measures due to the failure of those in authority to act sooner. Before offering and considering in detail what I will term a "five-point program," it is pertinent to consider the operation of our money world, how it has failed to be a servant in our real world and instead is our tyrant and master.

Money has no utility or economic value except to serve as a medium of exchange. Inflation and deflation are expressed in the increased and decreased purchasing power of money, which we speak of as a cheap dollar or a dear dollar according to what it will buy. At present our dollar is too valuable measured in terms of goods and services, or, conversely, goods and services are too cheap measured in dollars. Were it not for our debt structure the fluctuating and unstable dollar would not raise such havoc with our economic system. Our debt and credit structure is the very foundation of our capitalistic society and our unstable dollar results in a large measure from the uncontrolled operation of this system.

We could do business on the basis of any dollar value as long as we have a reasonable balance between the value of all goods and services if it were not for the debt structure. The debt structure has obtained its present astronomical proportions due to an unbalanced distribution of wealth production as measured in buying power during our years of prosperity. Too much of the product of labor was diverted into capital goods, and as a result what seemed to be our prosperity was maintained on a basis of abnormal credit both at home and abroad. The time came when we seemed to reach a point of saturation in the credit structure where, generally speaking, additional credit was no longer available, with the result that debtors were forced to curtail their consumption in an effort to create a margin to apply on the reduction of debts. This naturally reduced the demand for goods of all kinds, bringing about what appeared to be overproduction, but what in reality was underconsumption measured in terms of the real world and not the money world. This naturally brought about a failing in prices and unemployment. Unemployment further decreased the consumption of goods, which further increased unemployment, thus bringing about a continuing decline in prices. Earnings began to disappear, requiring economies of all kinds—decreases in wages, salaries, and time of those employed.

And thus the vicious cycle of deflation was continued until after nearly the four years we find one-third of our entire working population unemployed, with prices of everything greatly reduced, raw products of all kinds selling at an unprecedented low level; our national income reduced by 50 per cent with the aggregate debt burden greater than ever before, not in dollars but measured by present values which represents the ability to pay; fixed charges, such as taxes, railroad and utility rates, insurance and interest charges close to the 1929 level and requiring such a portion of the national income to meet them that the amount left for consumption goods is not sufficient to support the population.

Senator WALSH of Massachusetts. That is a good statement.

Mr. ECCLES. As a result of this pressure we hear demands for increased economics in every field, both public and private, which can only make for further distress and unemployment and less buying power. The debt structure, in spite of the great amount of liquidation during the past three years, is rapidly becoming unsupportable, with the result that foreclosures, receiverships and bankruptcies are increasing in every field; delinquent taxes are mounting and forcing the closing of schools, thus breaking down our educational system, and moratoriums of all kinds are being resorted to—all this resulting in a steady and gradual breaking down of our entire credit structure, which can only bring additional distress, fear, rebellion, and chaos. Individuals, corporations, cities, and States can not, of themselves, do anything except play according to the rules of the present money system and make their outgo balance their income, or ultimately "go broke." Most of them are unable, much as they may desire, to give consideration to helping the general situation except as they may influence the action of the Federal Government, which is in an entirely different category, it being able to make and change the rules of the game.

The Government controls the gold reserve, the power to issue money and credit, thus largely regulating the price structure. Through its power of taxation it can control the accumulation and distribution of wealth production. It can mobilize the resources of the Nation for the benefit of its people. . . .

We must correct the causes of the depression rather than deal with the effects of it, if we expect recovery with its attendant confidence and budget balancing. This can only be accomplished by government action tending to raise the price level of raw products and increasing employment, thus bringing about an increased demand for consumers' goods. . . .

Every effort has been used to bring this about by the Reconstruction Finance Corporation and the Federal reserve bank without result, demonstrating that extension of credit alone is not the solution. Credit is the secondary offensive when there is a basis of credit through the raising of the price level and an increase in the demand for goods requiring credit. Nor is the correction of our present difficulties to be found in a general scaling down of debts in an effort to bring them in relation to the present price levels. During the past three years there has been such tremendous liquidation and scaling down of debts that extraordinary measures have had to be taken to prevent a general collapse of the credit structure. If such a policy is continued what assurance is there that the influences radiating from a marking down of the claims of creditors will not result in a further decline of prices? In other words, after we have reduced all debts through a basis of scaling down 25 per cent to 50 per cent, what reason have we to expect that prices will not have a further decline by like amount? And then again, the practical difficulties of bringing about such an adjustment on a broad scale seem to be insurmountable.

The time element required would indefinitely prolong the depression; such a policy would necessitate the further liquidation of banks, insurance companies, and all credit institutions, for if the obligations of public bodies, corporations, and individuals were appreciably reduced the assets of such institutions would diminish correspondingly, forcing their liquidation on a large scale. Nothing would so hinder any possibility of recovery. Bank and insurance failures destroy confidence and spread disaster and fear throughout the economic world. The present volume of money would diminish with increased hoarding and decreased credit and velocity, making for further deflation and requiring increased Government support without beneficial results until we would be forced from the gold standard in spite of our 40 per cent of the world's gold, and, at that point, an undesirable and possibly uncontrolled inflation with all its attendant evils would likely result, and thus the very action designed to preserve the gold standard and reestablish confidence would destroy both.

In my opinion, we can bring about and support a price level which will reestablish employment and credit on a sound money basis if action is not too long delayed on the part of our Government. The last 10 days have changed the thing. I am not as certain as I was a week or two ago whether we can do it on the gold basis or not.

Senator SHORTRIDGE. You say the action of Government. You will come to it, I suppose?

Mr. ECCLES. Yes. I have got the five points here. . . .

I will cover those points.

Point No. 1. Unemployment relief. Without going into any detail or figures, it is recognized by everyone that our most urgent and acute problem to-day is to immediately provide adequate relief to the millions of our people who are destitute and unemployed in every corner of our Nation. It is national disgrace that such suffering should be permitted in this, the wealthiest country in the world. The present condition is not the fault of the unemployed, but that of our business, financial, and political leadership. It is incomprehensible that the people of this country should very much longer stupidly continue to suffer the wastes, the bread lines, the suicides, and the despair, and be forced to die, steal, or accept a miserable pittance in the form of charity which they resent, and properly resent. We shall either adopt a plan which will meet this situation under capitalism, or a plan will be adopted for us which will operate without capitalism.

Private charity is almost entirely exhausted. It is impossible for most of our political subdivisions to provide additional funds through borrowing or taxation. Many of them are in default at the present time in the meeting of their obligations and are unable to provide funds necessary to pay the expense of their schools and local government. I am on the Governor's Executive Unemployment Relief Committee of my State and although I am sure the unemployed receive as much or more than in many sections of the country, available funds are entirely inadequate to meet the situation, which is daily becoming more difficult to control.

I advocate that the Government make available, as the most urgent of all emergency measures, at least $500,000,000 to be distributed to the States as required, as a gift and not as a loan, on a per capita basis in such amounts as will enable the relief organizations of each State to take care of the needs of the unemployed in a more adequate manner than has heretofore been possible. For this reason, that when it is made as a loan there is resistance to borrowing. There is a cutting down to a point of starvation. When a State has to borrow the money that is the attitude of the public officials of the State as a result of the demands of business leaders and taxpayers generally for economy.

Senator WALSH of Massachusetts. When it is a gift the lid is off?

Senator GORE. Where does the Federal Government get this money to give to the States?

Mr. ECCLES. Where did it get $27,000,000,000 during the war to waste? . . .

Senator WALSH of Massachusetts. How can you justify giving money out of the Federal Treasury to the State of New York, whose per capita indebtedness is insignificant compared to the Federal Government, who is the great treasure house for the Federal Government to go to for its money, on the theory that it is so bankrupt, it is so helpless that it can not take care of its poor and starving people? We might as well confess bankruptcy if we ever reach that situation.

Mr. ECCLES. Well, there is this difference. A state, of course, is in the same financial category as corporations and individuals in that they do not have the power of issuing money or credit. The Federal Government is entirely in a different category because it controls the money system. It is true that the State of New York and the State of Pennsylvania and these other States are creditor sections, not debtor States. In other words, the wealth of the State is less than the wealth of the people living in the State. . . .

2. Financing of self-liquidation projects and public works.

I quote from Dr. W. T. Foster:

> This much, in fairness, we must say for the Russian plan. If anywhere in Russia they had as many available trained carpenters and masons and brick-layers and engineers and architects and all the rest, and as much available steel and lumber and brick and all the other building materials as we have here, they would not sit around and stupidly hand out charity to the unemployed. They would use the surplus men and the surplus materials, and they would clean out these festering sores, and make decent dwelling places for the people. Incidentally, there would be no unemployment. Now, what can be done under communism or socialism, can be done under capitalism in the United States, if we have sense enough to set up an adequate flow of currency and credit in the right channels.

Senator WALSH of Massachusetts. What public works are there in Utah that can be undertaken?

Mr. ECCLES. Ogden needs a new water system and a high school.

Senator WALSH of Massachusetts. Are there any more highways you need, considering now the conditions in this country, considering that there is no man to-day can predict they will be any better 10 years from now? It is all in the hands of the gods. Considering the conditions in this country, considering that the money borrowed has to be paid for in taxation, what more public works are needed in your State than are there now?

Mr. Eccles. Of course, the way I look at this matter is that we have the power to produce, just as the period of prosperity after the war demonstrated when we had a standard of living for a period from 1921 to 1929 which, of course, was far in excess of what it is now. Yet in spite of that standard of living we saved too much as I have previously tried to show.

Senator Gore. You have got Foster in the back of your head?

Mr. Eccles. I only wish there were more who had. We saved too much in this regard, that we added too much to our capital equipment, creating overproduction in one case and underconsumption in the other because of uneconomical distribution of wealth production. . . .

We now see, after nearly four years of depression, that private capital will not go into public works or self-liquidating projects except through government and that if we leave our "rugged individual" to follow his own interest under these conditions he does precisely the wrong thing. Each corporation for its own protection discharges men, reduces pay rolls, curtails its orders for raw materials, postpones construction of new plants and pays off bank loans, adding to the surplus of unusable funds. Every single thing it does to reduce the flow of money makes the situation worse for business as a whole. The production of wealth and the consumer's ability to buy starts with the pay roll and the individual producers of raw material, the agriculturist. To-day we are losing close to two billions per month of national income due to unemployment, resulting in the inability of our people to purchase the goods necessary to sustain our production. Is there any program of economy and Budget balancing on the part of our Government as important as to stop this great loss and all the attendant human suffering, devastation, and destruction?

I believe that an essential part of the program to end the cycle of deflation is by the Government supplying the credit for self-liquidating projects and loans to the State for public works. I have the following program to propose:

Senator Shortridge. That is under your No. 2?

Mr. Eccles. Yes.

That the Government make available $1,000,000,000 to be added to the $1,500,000,000 already made available through the Reconstruction Finance Corporation for self-liquidating projects, making a total of $2,500,000,000. A separate agency should be set up to take over this division from the Reconstruction Finance Corporation and administer these funds. Emergency speed, such as was resorted to during the time of war, is necessary for the success of this plan. The self-liquidating plan to date has been utterly ineffective due to the failure to get the funds out; this is largely due to limitations of the law and red tape administration. And, I might say, the high interest rates.

Senator SHORTRIDGE. What is the rate?

Mr. ECCLES. It is 5½ and 6 per cent on self-liquidating projects. Those are the rates that I have been familiar with or heard.

In order to obtain speed, I would recommend the appointment of a civilian nonpolitical commission of not to exceed five representative leaders in each State, to serve without compensation, whose duty it would be to encourage development of public works and liquidating projects in their respective States as rapidly as possible. Loans should be made on a very liberal basis as to terms of payment and security. . . .

. . . No. 3 is the allotment plan.

The allotment plan, at least for the present, should be confined to our three major crops — wheat, cotton, and hogs. Now, I would like to eliminate hogs. I am not clear in my mind of the practicability of it. I think it involves complications in carrying it out that may defeat the whole plan. So I would suggest the wheat and the cotton as being far more practicable. Its purpose would be to raise the prices of these products by the amount of the tariff, which at present is ineffective due to the exportable surplus, the domestic price being, therefore, determined by the world price. To accomplish this, Government control, regulation, and sponsorship is necessary. However, the operation of the plan should be decentralized as much as possible, working through the State farm organizations which in turn would work through the country farm organizations, thus placing the responsibility of the success of the plan as much as possible on the local units, which are better able to control the determined reduction in acreage and production. This plan in no way would put a financial burden on the Government except the comparatively small cost required for a proper central regulation and control. And I believe that there is already plenty being spent by the Government through its Department of Agriculture and other agencies to take care of the necessary supervision by some sort of a reorganization.

The increase in prices brought about by this plan would, of course, be paid for by the consumers, but in this respect it would be no different than the effect of the tariff on the prices of those manufactured and agricultural products where the tariff is now effective in maintaining a domestic price higher than the world price. In other words, the domestic allotment plan, in its operation, might be termed an inverted tariff. If the domestic price level is going to be maintained by a tariff on some of our agricultural products and most of our manufactured products, then the prices of our major agricultural products must be raised to a domestic level by making a tariff effective through an allotment or similar plan; otherwise, the balance and equilibrium necessary to the operation of our economic system and, I might say, the velocity of our money can not be maintained, and the whole price structure will be kept out of adjustment as a result.

Objection is raised to the allotment plan on the ground that it will increase the cost of those products covered by it to the consumer, whose purchasing power is already close to the vanishing point. It will not only do that, but it will tend to increase the price structure generally, if it accomplishes the results desired.

An increase in the price of cotton will cause some increase in the price of wool, silk and rayon; an increase in the price of hogs — and of course I am eliminating hogs here — will tend to increase the price of all other meat products; and likewise, an increase in the price of wheat will tend to increase the price of other grain products, as all competitive products are influenced by the price of the product which is the cheapest. . . .

Senator Gore. It is estimated this domestic plan will take a billion dollars out of the pockets of the consumer and turn them over to the farmer. You have already proposed to give a half a billion dollars to the cities to buy that with. I can follow you if you raise the price of cotton cloth and food and then tax the people and give money to the people to buy it with; I can see how you get things going that way.

Mr. Eccles. That is right. . . .

. . . The allotment plan may be a long way from the perfect solution of the farm problem, but something must be tried. Our progress up to date in every field is the result of experimentation, trial, and error. The allotment plan may need to be changed or modified from time to time, but that can be done as experience determines. I believe that some form of the allotment plan is necessary as a permanent measure as long as a tariff policy is in effect in this country. The allotment plan is no more artificial than the tariff, the money system and all the regulatory operations of the Government. Our whole economic system, in the same sense, is artificial and must of necessity continue so unless we revert to a primitive society.

Refinancing Farm Mortgages

The allotment plan, to be effective, should be followed immediately by a refunding of farm mortgages on an immense scale and on a long-term basis at a low rate of interest. The seriousness of the farm-mortgage problem is evidenced by the farm strike in all parts of the country, the moratoriums being forcibly granted and the legislation designed to relieve debtors being proposed in every agricultural State. As a means of meeting this problem, I have the following to suggest:

Enlarge the scope and size of the Federal land banks so as to enable them to take over mortgages up to an amount of, say, $5,000,000,000; this amount can be increased if conditions warrant. . . .

Farm mortgages at present are possibly the most undesirable and frozen of all loans, and frozen loans are preventing, to some extent, the necessary expansion of credit. The plan I have proposed will very effectively and immediately make liquid billions of dollars of assets for which there is no market today, while at the same time it will bring about a reduction of at least one-third of the average annual payments on the farm debt now required to be made by farm mortgage debtors without requiring any financing or loss by the Federal Government, thus bringing about the necessary relief in the farm-mortgage field. This plan has the advantage, as a result of the Government guarantee of the Federal land bank bonds, of diverting surplus funds carried in the great creditor sections into the direct financing of farm mortgages where it is impossible even at a high rate of interest, which farmers can not pay, to attract those funds directly.

The combination of the allotment plan and the farm mortgage refinancing plan will provide, in an effective manner, a sound farm relief program, thus saving our entire agricultural industry from what otherwise would likely be a general collapse, and at the same time greatly expanding the purchasing power of our entire agricultural population, thus helping to bring about a revival of industry.

Interallied Debts

No program designed to bring this country out of the depression can be considered apart from the relations of this country to the rest of the world unless a policy of complete isolation is adopted and an embargo put on gold exports and our domestic economy adjusted to meet such a condition.

Our international problems are far more difficult and will be slower to work out because of our inability to control the action of other nations. These problems can be met only through international conferences over a period of time. The most important of these problems and the one which must be settled before any progress can be made in the meeting of our domestic or other foreign problems is the problem of interallied debts.

There is a great demand on the part of the public and most of the press of this country that these debts be paid. It seems to me that our political leaders have lacked the courage to face this problem in a realistic manner. This has greatly contributed to prolonging the depression. The public, generally speaking, is not fully informed as to the impossibility of our foreign debtors complying with these demands, which can only be complied with at the expense of our own people.

Senator SHORTRIDGE. Right there. I know of one country that defaulted in a certain payment and the very day, almost, that it defaulted it loaned an equal amount to another country.

Mr. ECCLES. That is true. . . . It is elementary that debts between nations can ultimately be paid only in goods, gold, or services, or a combination of the three. We already have over 40 per cent of the gold supply of the world — that is not true; it is between 35 and 40 per cent — and as a result most of the former gold standard countries have been forced to leave that standard and currency inflation has been the result. This has greatly reduced the cost of producing foreign goods in terms of our dollars and has made it almost impossible for foreign countries to buy American goods because of the high price of our dollar measured in the depreciated value of their money. This naturally has resulted in debtors trying to meet their obligations by producing and selling more than they buy, thus enabling them to have a favorable balance of trade necessary to meet their obligations to us. If this country is to receive payment of foreign debts, it must buy and consume more than it produces, thus creating a trade balance favorable to our debtors.

In order to prevent this and reduce the pressure of foreign goods on the American market a high tariff wall has been built and we now hear demands on all sides for a further increase in this tariff due to the effects of depreciated currencies on our price structure. It is, therefore, evident that this pressure on our markets by goods from foreign countries would be greatly reduced if the burden of the debt were lifted from our foreign debtors, thus allowing our prices, as well as their own, to rise.

We must either choose between accepting sufficient foreign goods to pay the foreign debts owing to this country, or cancel the debts. This is not a moral problem, but a mathematical one. Foreign debtors, no doubt, would be delighted to pay their debts to this country if we would make it possible for them to do so by reducing our tariff and accepting the goods which they have to offer.

No one would be as greatly benefited by the cancellation of these foreign debts owing to our Government as American agriculture and American labor. A comparatively small portion of our population would make up this loss to the Treasury through the payment of income and inheritance tax which would be made productive by the revival of business. . . . The program which I have proposed is largely of an emergency nature designed to bring rapid economic recovery. However, when recovery is restored, I believe that in order to avoid future diastrous depressions and sustain a balanced prosperity, it will be necessary during the next few years for the Government to assume a greater control and regulation of our entire economic system. There must be a more equitable distribution of wealth production in order to keep purchasing power in a more even balance with production.

If this is to be accomplished there should be a unification of our banking system under the supervision of the Federal reserve bank in order to more effectively control our entire money and credit system; a high income and inheritance tax is essential in order to control capital accumulations (this division of taxes should be left solely to the central government — the real property and sales tax left to the States); there should be national child labor, minimum wage, unemployment insurance and old age pension laws (such laws left up to the States only create confusion and can not meet the situation nationally unless similar and uniform laws are passed by all States at the same time, which is improbable); all new capital issues offered to the public and all foreign financing should receive the approval of an agency of the Federal Government; this control should also extend to all means of transportation and communication so as to insure their operation in the public interest. A national planning board, similar to the industries board during the war, is necessary to the proper coordination of public and private activities of the economic world. . . . I feel that one of two things is inevitable: That either we have got to take a chance on meeting this unemployment problem and this low-price problem or we are going to get a collapse of our credit structure, which means a collapse of our capitalistic system, and we will then start over. And I therefore would like to see us attempt to regulate and operate our economy which to-day requires more action from the top due to our entire interdependency than it did in our earlier days. We have drifted in this country into a form of collectivism in many lines of business, when you consider our great corporations and farm organizations.

Senator GORE. Let me ask you this. I do not mean for you to dilate on it. But you say our credit structure is in danger. And I think it is. I think our mischief results largely from overstraining of credit. Your proposal seems to be that for the excessive use of credit we use more credit. Is that not true?

Mr. Eccles. No; that is not true.

Senator Gore. It seems like every scheme you suggested was for the Government to advance money to somebody.

Mr. Eccles. You have got to take care of the unemployed or you are going to have revolution in this country. . . .

When you get enough unemployed they will control the Government and change our present political, social, and economic system.

Senator Gore. There is the trouble. And that is the danger here. They brought pressure to bear in the House to get tobacco, butter-fat, and goobers included in this domestic allotment. You get enough unemployed in this country organized and there are no brakes you can put on your scheme. That is the history of Rome. The dole destroyed Rome. It is going to destroy England and France and Germany and this country.

The Chairman. We thank you for your statement, Mr. Eccles.

Franklin D. Roosevelt

FREEDOM FROM FEAR

❧*1933*❧ The Great Depression of the 1930's was a worldwide phenomenon and there is a great deal to be said for the argument of Herbert Hoover (1874-1964) that nothing he could have done as President would have prevented it. It is also true that Hoover was to a large extent a "victim" of the depression; no doubt any President elected in 1928 would have been blamed for the troubles of the following years and therefore defeated in 1932.

Furthermore, it is clear that Franklin Delano Roosevelt's (1882-1945) New Deal did not provide a completely satisfactory solution for the problems of the depression. Despite all the agencies and activities, real economic recovery did not come until the economy was stimulated by the outbreak of World War II. Nevertheless, Roosevelt's election marked an important change in American history. His administration accomplished a break-through in the area of federal responsibility for the national welfare. It opened an era in which practical objectives tended to predominate over philosophical conceptions of the proper role of government in the social and economic affairs of the people.

In a very important sense the chief contribution of Roosevelt to this development was psychological. From his first hour in office his air of cheerfulness and his willingness to experiment caught the public's imagination, thus restoring confidence. Nothing demonstrates this so well as his first inaugural address, which in a moment changed the mood of the whole nation. Equally important in changing the national point of view toward the depression was his first "fireside chat." In this radio address, delivered not to a formal audience but to the people in their homes, the President (as much by his warm, confident, and confidential manner as by his ideas) convinced the public that his administration would act intelligently, fairly, imaginatively, and vigorously to solve the pressing problems of the day.

INAUGURAL ADDRESS

(March 4, 1933)

I AM CERTAIN that my fellow Americans expect that on my induction into the Presidency I will address them with a candor and a decision which the present situation of our Nation impels. This is preeminently the time to speak the truth, the whole truth, frankly and boldly. Nor need we shrink from honestly facing conditions in our country today. This great Nation will endure as it has endured, will revive and will prosper. So, first of all, let me assert my firm belief that the only thing we have to fear is fear itself — nameless, unreasoning, unjustified terror which paralyzes needed efforts to convert retreat into advance. In every dark hour of our national life a leadership of frankness and vigor has met with that understanding and support of the people themselves which is essential to victory. I am convinced that you will again give that support to leadership in these critical days.

In such a spirit on my part and on yours we face our common difficulties. They concern, thank God, only material things. Values have shrunken to fantastic levels; taxes have risen; our ability to pay has fallen; government of all kinds is faced by serious curtailment of income; the means of exchange are frozen in the currents of trade; the withered leaves of industrial enterprise lie on every side; farmers find no markets for their produce; the savings of many years in thousands of families are gone.

More important, a host of unemployed citizens face the grim problem of existence, and an equally great number toil with little return. Only a foolish optimist can deny the dark realities of the moment.

Yet our distress comes from no failure or substance. We are stricken by no plague of locusts. Compared with the perils which our forefathers conquered because they believed and were not afraid, we have still much to be thankful for. Nature still offers her bounty and human efforts have multiplied it. Plenty is at our doorstep, but a generous use of it languishes in the very sight of the supply. Primarily this is because rulers of the exchange of mankind's goods have failed through their own stubbornness and their own incompetence, have admitted their failure, and have abdicated. Practices of the unscrupulous money changers stand indicted in the court of public opinion, rejected by the hearts and minds of men.

True they have tried, but their efforts have been cast in the pattern of an outworn tradition. Faced by failure of credit they have proposed only the lending of more money. Stripped of the lure of profit by which to induce our people to follow their leadership, they have resorted to exhortations, pleading tearfully for restored confidence. They know only the rules of a generation of self-seekers. They have no vision, and when there is no vision the people perish.

The money changers have fled from their high seats in the temple of our civilization. We may now restore that temple to the ancient truths. The measure of the restoration lies in the extent to which we apply social values more noble than mere monetary profit.

Happiness lies not in the mere possession of money; it lies in the joy of achievement, in the thrill of creative effort. The joy and moral stimulation of work no longer must be forgotten in the mad chase of evanescent profits. These dark days will be worth all they cost us if they teach us that our true destiny is not to be ministered unto but to minister to ourselves and to our fellow men.

Recognition of the falsity of material wealth as the standard of success goes hand in hand with the abandonment of the false belief that public office and high political position are to be valued only by the standards of pride of place and personal profit; and there must be an end to a conduct in banking and in business which too often has given to a sacred trust the likeness of callous and selfish wrongdoing. Small wonder that confidence lanquishes, for it thrives only on honesty, on honor, on the sacredness of obligations, on faithful protection, on unselfish performance; without them it cannot live.

Restoration calls, however, not for changes in ethics alone. This Nation asks for action, and action now.

Our greatest primary task is to put people to work. This is no unsolvable problem if we face it wisely and courageously. It can be accomplished in part by direct recruiting by the Government itself, treating the task as we would treat the emergency of a war, but at the same time, through this employment, accomplishing greatly needed projects to stimulate and reorganize the use of our natural resources.

Hand in hand with this we must frankly recognize the overbalance of population in our industrial centers and, by engaging on a national scale in a redistribution, endeavor to provide a better use of the land for those best fitted for the land. The task can be helped by definite efforts to raise the values of agricultural products and with this the power to purchase the output of our cities. It can be helped by preventing realistically the tragedy of the growing loss through foreclosure of our small homes and our farms. It can be helped by insistence that the Federal,

State, and local governments act forthwith on the demand that their cost be drastically reduced. It can be helped by the unifying of relief activities which today are often scattered, uneconomical, and unequal. It can be helped by national planning for and supervision of all forms of transportation and of communications and other utilities which have a definitely public character. There are many ways in which it can be helped, but it can never be helped merely by talking about it. We must act and act quickly.

Finally, in our progress toward a resumption of work we require two safeguards against a return of the evils of the old order: there must be a strict supervision of all banking and credits and investments, so that there will be an end to speculation with other people's money; and there must be provision for an adequate but sound currency.

These are the lines of attack. I shall presently urge upon a new Congress, in special session, detailed measures for their fulfillment, and I shall seek the immediate assistance of the several States.

Through this program of action we address ourselves to putting our own national house in order and making income balance outgo. Our international trade relations, though vastly important, are in point of time and necessity secondary to the establishment of a sound national economy. I favor as a practical policy the putting of first things first. I shall spare no effort to restore world trade by international economic readjustment, but the emergency at home cannot wait on that accomplishment.

The basic thought that guides these specific means of national recovery is not narrowly nationalistic. It is the insistence, as a first consideration, upon the interdependence of the various elements in and parts of the United States — a recognition of the old and permanently important manifestation of the American spirit of the pioneer. It is the way to recovery. It is the immediate way. It is the strongest assurance that the recovery will endure.

In the field of world policy I would dedicate this Nation to the policy of the good neighbor — the neighbor who resolutely respects himself and, because he does so, respects the rights of others — the neighbor who respects his obligations and respects the sanctity of his agreements in and with a world of neighbors.

If I read the temper of our people correctly, we now realize as we have never realized before our interdependence on each other; that we cannot merely take but we must give as well; that if we are to go forward, we must move as a trained and loyal army willing to sacrifice for the good of a common discipline, because without such discipline no progress is made, no leadership becomes effective. We are, I know, ready and willing to submit our lives and property to such discipline, because it makes possible a leadership which aims at a larger good. This I propose to offer, pledging that the larger purpose will bind upon us all as a sacred obligation with a unity of duty hitherto evoked only in time of armed strife.

With this pledge taken, I assume unhesitatingly the leadership of this great army of our people dedicated to a disciplined attack upon our common problems.

Action in this image and to this end is feasible under the form of government which we have inherited from our ancestors. Our Constitution is so simple and practical that it is possible always to meet extraordinary needs by changes in emphasis and arrangement without loss of essential form. That is why our constitutional system has proved itself the most superbly enduring political mechanism the modern world has produced. It has met every stress of vast expansion of territory, of foreign wars, of bitter internal strife, of world relations.

It is to be hoped that the normal balance of Executive and legislative authority may be wholly adequate to meet the unprecedented task before us. But it may be that an unprecedented demand and need for undelayed action may call for temporary departure from that normal balance of public procedure.

I am prepared under my constitutional duty to recommend the measures that a stricken Nation in the midst of a stricken world may require. These measures, or such other measures as the Congress may build out of its experience and wisdom, I shall seek, within my constitutional authority, to bring to speedy adoption.

But in the event that the Congress shall fail to take one of these two courses, and in the event that the national emergency is still critical, I shall not evade the clear course of duty that will then confront me. I shall ask the Congress for the one remaining instrument to meet the crisis — broad Executive power to wage a war against the emergency, as great as the power that would be given to me if we were in fact invaded by a foreign foe.

For the trust reposed in me I will return the courage and the devotion that befit the time. I can do no less.

We face the arduous days that lie before us in the warm courage of national unity; with the clear consciousness of seeking old and precious moral values; with the clean satisfaction that comes from the stern performance of duty by old and young alike. We aim at the assurance of a rounded and permanent national life.

We do not distrust the future of essential democracy. The people of the United States have not failed. In their need they have registered a mandate that they want direct, vigorous action. They have asked for discipline and direction under leadership. They have made me the present instrument of their wishes. In the spirit of the gift I take it.

In this dedication of a Nation we humbly ask the blessing of God. May He protect each and every one of us. May He guide me in the days to come.

THE FIRST "FIRESIDE CHAT"

AN INTIMATE TALK WITH THE PEOPLE OF THE UNITED STATES
ON BANKING, MARCH 12, 1933

I WANT to talk for a few minutes with the people of the United States about banking — with the comparatively few who understand the mechanics of banking but more particularly with the overwhelming majority who use banks for the making of deposits and the drawing of checks. I want to tell you what has been done in the last few days, why it was done, and what the next steps are going to be. I recognize that the many proclamations from state capitols and from Washington, the legislation, the Treasury regulations, etc., couched for the most part in banking and legal terms, should be explained for the benefit of the average citizen. I owe this in particular because of the fortitude and good temper with which everybody has accepted the inconvenience and hardships of the banking holiday. I know that when you understand what we in Washington have been about I shall continue to have your cooperation as fully as I have had your sympathy and help during the past week.

First of all, let me state the simple fact that when you deposit money in a bank the bank does not put the money into a safe deposit vault. It invests your money in many different forms of credit — bonds, commercial paper, mortgages and many other kinds of loans. In other words, the bank puts your money to work to keep the wheels of industry and of agriculture turning around. A comparatively small part of the money you put into the bank is kept in currency — an amount which in normal times is wholly sufficient to cover the cash needs for the average citizen. In other words, the total amount of all the currency in the country is only a small fraction of the total deposits in all of the banks.

What, then, happened during the last few days of February and the first few days of March? Because of undermined confidence on the part of the public, there was a general rush by a large portion of our population to turn bank deposits into currency or gold — a rush so great that the soundest banks could not get enough currency to meet the demand. The reason for this was that on the spur of the moment it was, of course, impossible to sell perfectly sound assets of a bank and convert them into cash except at panic prices far below their real value.

By the afternoon of March 3d scarcely a bank in the country was open to do business. Proclamations temporarily closing them in whole or in part had been issued by the Governors in almost all the States.

It was then that I issued the proclamation providing for the nationwide bank holiday, and this was the first step in the Government's reconstruction of our financial and economic fabric.

The second step was the legislation promptly and patriotically passed by the Congress confirming my proclamation and broadening my powers so that it became possible in view of the requirement of time to extend the holiday and lift the ban of that holiday gradually. This law also gave authority to develop a program of rehabilitation of our banking facilities. I want to tell our citizens in every part of the Nation that the national Congress — Republicans and Democrats alike — showed by this action a devotion to public welfare and a realization of the emergency and the necessity for speed that it is difficult to match in our history.

The third stage has been the series of regulations permitting the banks to continue their functions to take care of the distribution of food and household necessities and the payment of payrolls.

This bank holiday, while resulting in many cases in great inconvenience, is affording us the opportunity to supply the currency necessary to meet the situation. No sound bank is a dollar worse off than it was when it closed its doors last Monday. Neither is any bank which may turn out not to be in a position for immediate opening. The new law allows the twelve Federal Reserve Banks to issue additional currency on good assets and thus the banks which reopen will be able to meet every legitimate call. The new currency is being sent out by the Bureau of Engraving and Printing in large volume to every part of the country. It is sound currency because it is backed by actual, good assets.

A question you will ask is this: why are all the banks not to be reopened at the same time? The answer is simple. Your Government does not intend that history of the past few years shall be repeated. We do not want and will not have another epidemic of bank failures.

As a result, we start tomorrow, Monday, with the opening of banks in the twelve Federal Reserve Banks cities — those banks which on first examination by the Treasury have already been found to be all right. This will be followed on Tuesday by the resumption of all their functions by banks already found to be sound in cities where there are recognized clearing houses. That means about 250 cities of the United States.

On Wednesday and succeeding days banks in smaller places all through the country will resume business, subject, of course, to the Government's physical ability to complete its survey. It is necessary that the reopening of banks be extended over a period in order to permit the banks to make applications for necessary loans, to obtain currency needed to meet their requirements and to enable the Government to make common sense checkups.

Let me make it clear to you that if your bank does not open the first day you are by no means justified in believing that it will not open. A bank that opens on one of the subsequent days is in exactly the same status as the bank that opens tomorrow.

I know that many people are worrying about State banks not members of the Federal Reserve System. These banks can and will receive assistance from member banks and from the Reconstruction Finance Corporation. These State banks are following the same course as the National banks except that they get their licenses to resume business from the State authorities, and these authorities have been asked by the Secretary of the Treasury to permit their good banks to open up on the same schedule as the national banks. I am confident that the State Banking Departments will be as careful as the national Government in the policy relating to the opening of banks and will follow the same broad policy.

It is possible that when the banks resume a very few people who have not recovered from their fear may again begin withdrawals. Let me make it clear that the banks will take care of all needs — and it is my belief that hoarding during the past week has become an exceedingly unfashionable pastime. It needs no prophet to tell you that when the people find that they can get their money — that they can get it when they want it for all legitimate purposes — the phantom of fear will soon be laid. People will again be glad to have their money where it will be safely taken care of and where they can use it conveniently at any time. I can assure you that it is safer to keep your money in a reopened bank than under the mattress.

The success of our whole great national program depends, of course, upon the cooperation of the public — on its intelligent support and use of a reliable system.

Remember that the essential accomplishment of the new legislation is that it makes it possible for banks more readily to convert their assets into cash than was the case before. More liberal provision has been made for banks to borrow on these assets at the Reserve Banks and more liberal provision has also been made for issuing currency on the security of these good assets. This currency is not fiat currency. It is issued only on adequate security, and every good bank has an abundance of such security.

One more point before I close. There will be, of course, some banks unable to open without being reorganized. The new law allows the Government to assist in making these reorganizations quickly and effectively and even allows the Government to subscribe to at least a part of new capital which may be required.

I hope you can see from this elemental recital of what your Government is doing that there is nothing complex, or radical, in the process.

We had a bad banking situation. Some of our bankers had shown themselves either incompetent or dishonest in their handling of the people's funds. They had used the money entrusted to them in speculations and unwise loans. This was, of course, not true in the vast majority of our banks, but it was true in enough of them to shock the people for a time into a sense of insecurity and to put them into a frame of mind where they did not differentiate, but seemed to assume that the acts of a comparative few had tainted them all. It was the Government's job to straighten out this situation and do it as quickly as possible. And the job is being performed.

I do not promise you that every bank will be reopened or that individual losses will not be suffered, but there will be no losses that possibly could be avoided; and there would have been more and greater losses had we continued to drift. I can even promise you salvation for some at least of the sorely pressed banks. We shall be engaged not merely in reopening sound banks but in the creation of sound banks through reorganization.

It has been wonderful to me to catch the note of confidence from all over the country. I can never be sufficiently grateful to the people for the loyal support they have given me in their acceptance of the judgment that has dictated our course, even though all our processes may not have seemed clear to them.

After all, there is an element in the readjustment of our financial system more important than currency, more important than gold, and that is the confidence of the people. Confidence and courage are the essentials of success in carrying out our plan. You people must have faith; you must not be stampeded by rumors or guesses. Let us unite in banishing fear. We have provided the machinery to restore our financial system; it is up to you to support and make it work.

It is your problem no less than it is mine. Together we cannot fail.

Henry Wallace

THE FARM PROBLEM IN WORLD PERSPECTIVE

❧*1934*❧ OF ALL the men close to Franklin D. Roosevelt (1882-1945) during the early days of the New Deal, none seemed better suited for his job than Henry A. Wallace (1888-   ), the Secretary of Agriculture. Only forty-five years of age and looking ten years younger, he possessed all the characteristics of a typical New Dealer. A third generation farm leader (his father had been Harding's Secretary of Agriculture and his grandfather the founder of an important farm journal), Wallace's technical mastery of agricultural matters was outstanding. He was an expert plant geneticist and a first-rate dirt farmer. He also possessed in full the vigor, pragmatic approach, and idealistic zeal so often found in the men around Roosevelt.

Under Wallace the New Deal agricultural program got off to a good start. The Agricultural Adjustment Act of 1933 provided a means of raising farm income by paying farmers to limit production, and by 1934 a sharp rise in the prices of basic commodities was under way. The Secretary, however, was far from satisfied. He knew that other factors had had much to do with the "success" of the AAA, and he realized that a really satisfactory solution of the farm problem involved international questions concerning industrial tariffs, world trade, and other matters in addition to farm products themselves. Thus, when the Foreign Policy Association and the World Peace Foundation asked him to prepare an essay on world affairs, he produced, in the spring of 1934, a stirring pamphlet, *America Must Choose.*

This brief study was an immediate success. In a few months there were 100,000 copies in print; soon it was being widely reprinted in the United States and also abroad. This was the result, no doubt, of the forcefulness of Wallace's language, his clear presentation of the alternatives, and the almost complete absence of partisanship in his discussion of an extremely controversial issue. Although he ended by suggesting what was essentially a rather weak compromise (which was thoroughly in the New Deal tradition), the boldness of his title and the vigor of his presentation raised his stature immensely in the public eye. Soon, according to some who knew him well at the time, he began to show signs of aspiring to succeed Roosevelt in the White House. In any case, after the publication of *America Must Choose* he was to remain a major figure on the national scene for a decade and a half.

AMERICA MUST CHOOSE

YOUTH IS greedy and not much given to reflection. When hurt, the child bawls; then, smiling through tears, reaches hopefully for the first offered toy or cooky. Young persons or nations display characteristically a gusty temper, passing quickly into an ignorant hopefulness, an expansive optimism, which at its proper time of life is charming. But for a nation come of age to persist in infantile attitudes and habits of mind is unsuitable and perilous.

During the recent war period certain things happened which made it certain that the United States would never go back completely to the old happy individual sort of thing which had marked our expansion as a nation. If during the postwar year of "normalcy" we had made certain adjustments, we might possibly have regained some measure of that happy individualism. But we did not do so, and now we are fated for grave adjustments, with no chance to turn back.

Much as we all dislike them, the new types of social control that we have now in operation are here to stay, and to grow on a world or national scale. We shall have to go on doing all these things we do not want to do. The farmer dislikes production control instinctively. He does not like to see land idle and people hungry. The carriers dislike production control because it cuts down loadings. The processors dislike it because of the processing tax. The consumer dislikes it because it adds to the price of food. Practically the entire population dislikes our basic program of controlling farm production; and they will do away with it unless we can reach the common intelligence and show the need of continuing to plan. We must show that need of continuing if we are to save in some part the institutions which we prize.

Enormously difficult adjustments confront us, whatever path we take. There are at least three paths: internationalism, nationalism and a planned middle course. We cannot take the path of internationalism unless we stand ready to import nearly a billion dollars more goods than we did in 1929. What tariffs should we lower? What goods shall we import? Which goods? Tariff adjustments involve planning just as certainly as internal adjustments do. Even foreign loans might involve a certain amount of planning. When we embarked on our terrific postwar expansion of foreign loans, we did not plan. We plunged in blindly, and soon any reasonable observer could predict that the whole thing was bound to blow up. . . .

The middle path between economic internationalism and nationalism is the path we shall probably take in the end. We need not go the whole way on a program involving an increase of a billion dollars a year in imports. There are intermediate points between internationalism and nationalism, and I do not think we can say just where we are headed yet. We shall be under increasing difficulties, no matter which way we tend, as our people become more and more familiar with the discomforts of the procedure.

My own bias is international. It is an inborn attitude with me. I have very deeply the feeling that nations should be naturally friendly to each other and express that friendship in international trade. At the same time we must recognize as realities that the world at the moment is ablaze with nationalist feeling, and that with our own tariff impediments it is highly unlikely that we shall move in an international direction very fast in the next few years. Therefore, we must push with the greatest vigor possible our retreat from surplus acres, and seek to arouse the intellectual stamina necessary to meet and triumph over unpopular facts. . . .

As a foundation and framework of the new American design, we have undertaken to put our farmland into better order. We are out to subdue competitive overproduction. In consequence we are forced to think of what we ought to do with the 43 million marginal acres of plowland we are going to take out of cultivation in 1934 because the world no longer will pay us for the extra wheat, cotton and corn we have been growing there. We are not going to have a random expansion and exploitation conducted without regard to human values, as we have in the past.

Theoretically, we recognize that this bringing of order out of chaos should extend as rapidly as possible into world agreements. But until such agreements can be made we must work to set our own land in order. To do so is not incompatible with plans for world cooperation. It might even be argued that we must learn to cooperate at home before we are fit to practice world cooperation in agriculture, trade and the arts of peace.

As things are now, our millions of surplus acres breed nothing but confusion, poverty and waste. As long as we remain a creditor nation with high tariff policies, refusing to accept foreign goods in payment, those acres should not be tilled. Until our people have the vision to adopt a long-time world trading policy which is in keeping with our position as creditors, we must engage in the delicate processes of adjusting basic production downward. . . .

From 1926 on it became increasingly plain that modern technique applied to agriculture and to the production of other raw materials was heaping up a world-wide oversupply. World overproduction played an important part in the ever-descending spiral which began in 1930.

When the present administration came into power on March 4, 1933, it had been for several years apparent that there is no longer an effective foreign purchasing power for our customary exportable surplus of cotton, wheat, lard and tobacco at prices high enough to assure social stability in the United States. It was apparent that more than 40 million acres of American soil were producing material which could not be consumed within the country, and which could probably not be consumed even were all our industrial payrolls again to blossom magically to the pumped-up boom-time levels of 1929. It was apparent that, with things as they are and with our inherited attitude to tariffs, it would be impossible to re-establish a large American trade abroad at once, or in the next few years.

Accordingly, the present administration is conducting an orderly retreat from surplus acreage. In essence, it is a program of governmental adjustment payments to cooperating farmers, rewarding a cooperative adjustment of acreage pro-rata, farm by farm. In the administration of this and of auxiliary or fortifying measures, the Farm Act of May 12, 1933 give us wide permissive powers. Of the present Congress (1934), we shall probably ask amendments permitting an even wider, and far more selective, retirement of acreage on a more permanent basis.

At present none of our production schedules for export crops will be adjusted to a strictly domestic basis. Our foreign trade in these crops has very seriously dwindled, but we still have foreign customers for cotton, tobacco and certain foodstuffs. We want to keep that trade if possible and get more foreign trade if we can. Our immediate effort is to organize American agriculture to reduce its output to domestic need, plus that amount which we can export with profit. . . .

We do not claim that the action taken under the Agricultural Adjustment Act or the National Recovery Act, or any other of the emergency acts, helpful as they may have been temporarily, constitute a fundamental plan for American agriculture. What we have done has been frankly experimental and emergency in nature, but we are working on something that is going to be permanent. We are well aware that our present machinery for production adjustment may not be at all like the machinery we shall have to design and operate for the longer future.

Using government money derived from processing taxes, we have asked the voluntary cooperation of the American farmer in making emergency adjustments to present world conditions. Thus we are sparring with the situation until the American people are ready to face facts. The bare, distasteful facts, I mean, on such matters of policy as exports, imports, tariffs, international currency exchange, export quotas, import quotas and international debts. These are the weapons of economic warfare which are more deadly than artillery. These economic weapons are so subtle that they have a nasty way of bouncing back on you with redoubled force when you think you are using them against the enemy. Fundamentally these weapons are spiritual in nature, although this is not recognized by businessmen and by very few statesmen.

The problem of statesmanship is to mold a policy leading toward a higher state for humanity, and to stick by that policy and make it seem desirable to the people in spite of short-time pressure to the contrary. True statesmanship and true religion have much in common. Both are beset by those who, professing to be able politicians and hardheaded men of affairs, are actually so exclusively interested in the events of the immediate future or the welfare of a small class that from the broader, long-time point of view they are thoroughly impractical and theoretical.

Ever since the war we have blundered along refusing to reconcile our professions with the realities. Under cover of enormous foreign loans, we seemed to be acting on some international plan; but in reality there was no plan.

The failure to adopt any nationally approved plan during the postwar years has of course been disastrous for all of our major producing groups, but it has been most disastrous in its effect on agriculture. The loss of billions of dollars of agricultural income can be charged directly to this cause. The foreign loans we made to sustain our expanded productive capacity after the war, merely concealed the true nature of our situation. When the loans ended — as they were sure to, since we refused to accept sufficient goods in payment — our artificial market for the surplus disappeared overnight.

In hurriedly making adjustments to a changed, chaotic world, we have been forced rapidly in the same nationalist direction which other nations have been taking more gradually and deliberately since the war.

Of course, there are a few of our manufacturing industries which would require readjustment if we continue to follow the national plan exclusively, but for the most part the burden of the adjustments will fall on agriculture.

International planning, on the other hand, would throw the greater burden of adjustment on factories rather than on farms.

American agriculture has not benefited by tariffs, except spottily and for short periods of time. Despite that fact, both Republican and Democratic representatives of our agricultural regions have done their best to put up agricultural tariffs every time industrial tariffs were put up. Unfortunately for agriculture, most of the tariffs given to it are either immediately or in the long run worthless paper tariffs. In tariff matters agriculture has played Esau to the industrial Jacob. Cotton, wheat and lard obviously can never benefit from a tariff as long as we export half our cotton, one-fifth of our wheat, and one-third of our lard. Such products as butter, beef cattle, wool and flaxseed may be helped by the tariff for a number of years but, as the cotton, wheat and hog men shift their attention to the protected products, it is rapidly discovered that the tariff benefits, even on these products of which we do not have any exportable surplus, is a temporary thing. . . .

In well-developed countries like the United States and England, the maximum of consumers' wealth can best be attained with a low tariff. This is an economic truism, which so far as I know is not disputed except by politicians who have an axe to grind or those who, like the farmers of my native Iowa, have been made the intellectual, emotional and habitual victims of the class just mentioned.

So deepseated, however, is our national inclination for the hair of the dog which bit us that when the dairy and beef cattle situations came to a head this winter a few politically minded farm leaders, steeped in the towering tariff tradition of the northern states, proposed to cure the trouble by putting on still higher tariffs. You cannot cure an organic disease with larger doses of the quack poison that caused the distress. At the present time we import only 1.2 per cent of all our dairy products and less than 87/100 of one per cent of all our beef and veal.

Since coming to Washington I have been called upon by many with similar proposals. It has astonished me to find that there is perhaps as much high tariff sentiment in the Democratic, and presumably more agrarian party today, as there is in the Republican party. As a matter of fact, the party line on this tariff question seems erased. Tariffs have become very largely a question of local interests and prejudices. I am especially interested to note certain rather enthusiastic responses to low tariff and world trade suggestions in our great eastern seaports. I think this is because certain people are beginning to see that free trade would tend in the future to develop the Eastern seaports, whereas a strictly isolationist policy would tend in general to develop the interior of the country.

That, however, is problematical; and the fact remains that the pain and distress of nationalist readjustment, and a retreat from world markets would bear down far more heavily on agriculture than on industry. The explosions as to milk which I have recorded are advance signs of the pain of just such adjustments as will be required with increasing insistence if we proceed resolutely along the path of a restricted, regimented, nationalist development.

Under nationalism we must be prepared to make permanent the retirement of from 40 to 100 million acres of crop land. Forty million, if we take out good land; 100 million if we take out the worst. Furthermore, if we continue year after year with only 25 or 30 million acres of cotton in the South instead of 40 or 45 million acres, it may be necessary after a time to shift part of the southern population, and there is a question as to just what kind of activity these southern farm laborers should engage in. We will find exactly the same dilemma, although not on quite such a great scale, in the corn and wheat belts.

In ordinary times which have not been upset by the terrific impact of a great war, matters of this sort could be worked out gradually. But this is not the case now and the point I am making is that if the path of utter nationalism is followed, there must be a definite, conscious planning effort put forth, even greater in its complexity than the effort of the great war itself. The thing can be done, but it requires the understanding allegiance of the people. To attain that requires time and literally hundreds of millions of personal contacts as the educational or propaganda process is carried out.

If we finally go all the way toward nationalism, it may be necessary to have compulsory control of marketing, licensing of plowed land, and base and surplus quotas for every farmer for every product for each month in the year. We may have to have government control of all surpluses, and a far greater degree of public ownership than we have now. It may be necessary to make a public utility out of agriculture and apply to it a combination of an Esch-Cummins Act and an Adamson Act. Every plowed field would have its permit sticking up on its post. . . .

International trade is not necessarily complicated. If we allow ourselves again to approach world trading as if it were a sacred and impenetrable mystery, then we are likely again to get into another jam. The considerations which make international business desirable are plain. Recently I heard for the first time a saying popular in Arkansas. It was that Arkansas could build a wall a mile high around its borders and go right on living and doing business. That may be true; but I doubt if even the noisiest orator in Arkansas would claim that the people there could live as well or as spaciously as they do even now, exchanging goods and services with the people of other states. It is equally obvious that we take only meager advantage of this opportunity to exchange special products or special capacities if we coop up the process within national boundaries.

I say, then, that in respect to raw materials and handicraft products, world exchangeability is as desirable now as it ever was; and I deny that mechanization wipes out national differences in skill and ingenuity.

Where it seems to do so, I think the result is impermanent. Chinese to whom we send machine-tools may turn out a good Ford car, but the next improvement in the car and in the machinery which makes it, would be likely to occur on this side of the water. On the contrary, we could train American workmen for years on end and equip them with the best Chinese devices, yet the best Chinese embroidery would still come from China. Granting then a certain tendency of modern equipment to standardize and level the product, there remains for the long pull a great variety of inherent national advantages which, in a sane and neighborly world, would allow plenty of room for trade. . . .

Our own maneuvers of social discipline to date have been mildly persuasive and democratic. We have paid cash to farmers to cooperate in necessary reductions of acreage, pro-rata. We have appealed to the patriotism of corporate and individual manufacturers, transporters and storekeepers, with a passing part-way appeal to consumer sentiment for a necessary reduction in working hours and raises of pay. We have called for criticism and have heard it, so far as the pressure of events allowed, receptively. Following since March 4, last, a new design for American life, we have been letting people out of jail for the crime of expressing disagreement, instead of putting them in.

I want to see things go on that way. I would hate to live in a country where individual thought is punished and stifled, and where speech is no longer free. Even if the strictest nationalist discipline reared for us here at home, exclusively, a towering physical standard of living, I would consider the spiritual price too high. I think, too, that this would be pretty much the temper of the rest of the country; but there is no telling. A rampant nationalist feeling grows by what it feeds on, and it swells to unpredictable proportions with marvelous speed. Once it gets going headlong it puts down objection brutally; and the speed of the march is thus accelerated.

That might prove just as true in this country as elsewhere. Regimentation without stint might indeed, I sometimes think, go farther and faster here than anywhere else, if we once took the bit in our teeth and set up for a 100 per cent American conformity in everything. We are a people given to excess. I recall particularly the pressure toward conformity brought to bear during our wartime Liberty Loan drives; and we all have seen the same thing more or less repeated on a smaller scale whenever a town had a Y.M.C.A. or something of the sort to build. These outbursts of local high-pressure are not necessarily plotted and pushed from above. During the first year's cotton plow-up campaign in the South, for example, time did not permit sending out anything from national headquarters at Washington very much more than the contract itself. We had no slogans or banners, and very few set speeches. We had no insignia for the farmer who signed up to put on his mailbox. We knew what pressure would fall on the man who had no mark on his mail-box; and we purposely wished to avoid things like that. We wanted the thing put as a plain take-it-or-leave-it inducement to voluntary cooperation; and all our national plans and directions were drawn with that in mind.

Immediately, however, many local communities formed drives in the old 100 per cent "come along or be accounted a traitor" spirit; and before the thing was over there was even, I am told, a little night-riding, with the neighbors coming in to take out the cotton of the man who refused to sign. The American spirit as yet knows little of moderation, whichever way it turns.

There are certain satisfactions to be derived, no doubt, from a strict overhead discipline. Troops and officers in the late war seem, for all their complaining, to have recognized that. I hear veterans now recalling with a certain yearning how simple everything seemed in those days. In the Army, everything was arranged for them: the question of sustenance, of choosing clothing, of mapping journeys, of deciding who was important and who was not. Everything right down to dental work, medical attention, and bedtime was arranged for them, as for a child. Beyond all that, though the work was murderous, the citizen in arms was illumined with a glowing purpose; he had a mission without the dollar sign marked visibly upon it; and the nation accorded him signs of awe and admiration which, generally speaking, he has not enjoyed since. Mad as it sounds, I think that thousands of men were happier in the Army than they have ever been since; and the same thing extended in a measure to the civilian population. All felt themselves part of something greater than themselves.

The ruthless development of nationalist peacetime programs permits much of that same exalted frenzy, and generally requires more and more of the same as it goes along. I am aware of the higher possibilities of such a ferment. William James wrote most persuasively of the need of "a moral equivalent for war." Cautiously and tentatively, the New Deal in America has already evoked a little of this spirit. If we go on trying to keep things whirling within nationalist limits, it seems certain that we shall count less on social discipline voluntarily aroused and more on direct compulsion. Under such conditions the traditional American spirit would soon be, it seems to me, as a spring, tightly coiled, and ready to burst out dangerously in any direction. I wonder if we could stand the strain.

A surprising number of farmers after a year of voluntary production control are writing me letters insisting that hereafter the cooperation of all farmers be compelled absolutely; and that every field, cotton-gin, cow, and chicken be licensed; and that the strictest sort of controls be applied to transportation and marketing. I believe they mean it, but I wonder very seriously whether they are ready for such measures, and if they really know what they are asking for. . . .

Great prosperity is possible for the United States if we follow the strictly nationalist course, but in such case we must be prepared for a fundamental planning and regimentation of agriculture and industry far beyond that which anyone has yet suggested. To carry out such a program effectively, with our public psychology as it is, may require a unanimity of opinion and disciplined action even greater than that which we experienced in the years 1917-1919.

Nevertheless, the national path remains wide open to us. We can travel it if we want to. We can get along completely on sugar raised at home, even though the cost may be twice what it otherwise would be. We can completely substitute the use of rayon for silk. We can raise our own tea and get along without coffee. We can even raise our own rubber for perhaps 30 cents a pound. If the national will is completely bent in this direction we can arrive together at a self-contained life, but the process of transition to this self-contained Utopia is certain to be extremely difficult. It may require a great amount of governmental aid to take care of people formerly engaged in import and export businesses. It will mean the shifting of millions of people from the farms of the South. But these are minor considerations, in comparison with the extraordinarily complete control of all the agencies of public opinion which is generally necessary to keep the national will at a tensity necessary to carry through a program of isolated prosperity.

Traditionally, the Democratic party is the party of low tariffs. Actually, Democratic administrations have never made changes in the tariff structure great enough to increase foreign purchasing power to the extent demanded by the present world dilemma. If we are going to increase foreign purchasing power enough to sell abroad our normal surpluses of cotton, wheat and tobacco at a decent price, we shall have to accept nearly a billion dollars more goods from abroad than we did in

1929. We shall have to get that much more in order to service the debts that are coming to us from abroad and have enough left over to pay us a fair price for what we send abroad.

This will involve a radical reduction in tariffs. That might seriously hurt certain industries, and a few kinds of agricultural businesses, such as sugar-beet-growing and flax-growing. It might also cause pain for a while to wool-gatherers and to farmers who supply material for various edible oils. I think we ought to face that fact. If we are going to lower tariffs radically, there may have to be some definite planning whereby certain industries or businesses will have to be retired. The government might have to help furnish means for the orderly retirement of such businesses, and even select those which are thus to be retired.

Closing down some of the factories would be of grave national concern, not only because of the resulting unemployment, but also because some types of factories are needed in time of war. It would seem, therefore, that international planning must include a complete survey, item by item, of all the products that enter into our annual output, and a conscious decision as to which kind of products we might receive in large quantities from abroad, in time of peace, without jeopardizing those industries which we absolutely require in time of war.

We begin here to touch on one of the most potent arguments invoked in this country against international trading and world-wide dealings of any sort. We are instinctively suspicious of "entangling alliances" in matters of trade and of world government alike. We are afraid of the struggle which international trade in the past has very often been. We picture international trade as even more cut-throat, remorseless and unscrupulous than the most piratical performances of our home barons of commerce and finance in New York and Chicago.

I doubt if international trade, at its worst, is any worse than that. I see the seeds of war alike in *laissez-faire* accumulating pressing surpluses at home, and in seeking by hook or crook to thrust such surpluses abroad. Whether such a system is permitted freely to secrete and discharge its own poison within national borders or about the world at large, the pressure of ungoverned surpluses seems to me an equal stimulant to ruination and slaughter, before and during wars.

Some say that world trade leads to world-mindedness, world sympathies, world peace. Others say that world trade just gets you out among strangers who trim you, and step on your feet, and have you fighting before you know it. All such talk seems to me, if weighed in the balance, to come to nothing either way. The real question is how the trading is done. If it is done blindly in response to expansive greed, without planning or governance, it is likely to get you into serious trouble, whether you are trading at home or abroad.

A clean-cut program of planned international trade or barter would be far less likely to get us into war, I think, than the attempts to function internationally as sellers, yet nationalistically as buyers, inaugurated under Presidents Harding and Coolidge, and followed by President Hoover. Such tactics pursued in the past by older nations led to bloody foreclosure proceedings, at the point of guns. Not dissimilar current programs in other countries have created a dangerous degree of tension throughout the civilized world, and there are many who think that sooner or later the pressure will be bound to blow itself off in another orgy of human killing. We have blown off pressure that way very often in the past.

No sane and conscientious man will count lightly the risk of another great war, nor fail to do all in his power by every means possible to lessen that tragic risk. Straight, cool-headed thinking about the sort of economic warfare which is followed by actual warfare was never more needed than now. This time, it would seem, it is nationalist pressure that is heading us toward the abyss. The last time, it was supposed to be international pressures, expressed in dreams and deeds of imperialism, intricately bound up with foreign loans.

It comes to this: If we insist upon selling without buying, we have to lend our surplus to foreign countries, and never take it back. It stays abroad. But we think we still own it, and that makes us figure out ways and means of keeping the investment safe. We must have some security that transcends the good faith of the borrower. There is no surer path to war.

The method of reciprocal trade, on the other hand, leads to peace. It makes no sales without providing opportunities for the buyers to pay the bill. Since the bill does not remain outstanding indefinitely, and does not have to be collected at the point of a gun, it makes new business easy to get and profitable. . . .

We are approaching in the world today one of the most dramatic moments in history. Will we allow catastrophe to overtake us and, as a result, force us to retire to a more simple, peasant-like form of existence, or will we meet the challenge and expand our hearts, so that we are fitted to wield with safety the power which is ours almost for the asking? From the point of view of transportation and communication, the world is more nearly one world than ever before. From the point of view of tariff walls, nationalist strivings, and the like, the nations of the world are more separated today than ever before. Week by week tension is increasing to an unbelievable degree. Here resides both danger and opportunity.

The religious keynote, the economic keynote, the scientific keynote of the new age must be the overwhelming realization that mankind now has such mental and spiritual powers and such control over nature that the doctrine of the struggle for existence is definitely outmoded and replaced by the higher law of cooperation. When cooperation becomes a living reality in the spiritual sense of the term, when we have defined certain broad objectives which we all want to attain, when we can feel the significance of the forces at work not merely in our own lives, not merely in our own class, not merely in our own nation, but in the world as a whole — then the vision of Isaiah and the insight of Christ will be on their way toward realization.

This cooperation to which I refer depends for its strength on a revival of a deep recognition on the part of the individual that the world is in very truth one world, that human nature is such that all men can look on each other as brothers, that the potentialities of nature and science are so far-reaching as to remove many of the ancient limitations. This concept which now seems cloudy and vague to practical people must be more than the religious experience of the mystic. It must grow side by side with a new social discipline which leaves free the soul of man. Never has there been such a glorious chance to develop this feeling as in this country today. . . .

No matter how fervently nationalist or free-trade in principle our planned future policy may be, the jostle of world circumstances will be almost certain to take us across middle ground. With the modern world as it is, absolutely free trade is a dream probably never to be realized; and so is a completely independent national economy. Somewhere between these improbable extremes lies the proper course; and that is the course we are following now. But the trouble is that we have at present no markers set up to guide on. With great spirit, but with no commonly understood destination, we are veering off this way and that as obstacles arise. We are temporizing until we have established a definite marker which most of our people will be willing to accept as our destination for generations to come. . . .

The widest range of alternatives between nationalism and internationism I have roughly stated thus: If we continue toward nationalism we must be prepared to make permanent the withdrawal from cultivation of over 50 million acres of fairly good farmland, and face the consequences of all the social and economic dislocations which are bound to ensue. If, on the other hand, we choose not to put our agriculture under so high a degree of interior tension and discipline, we must drastically lower tariffs and reorganize industry, so that we can receive from abroad another billion dollars worth of goods each year.

The planned middle course I propose as a basis for present discussion is one precisely halfway between these two extremes: a line of march along which we would lower tariffs enough to bring in another half-billion dollars worth of goods annually, and permanently retract of our good agricultural land some 35 million acres.

To depict the pain this course would cause industry on the one hand, and agriculture on the other, would be but to restate in less demanding terms, facts and speculations developed in previous sections of this pamphlet, in respect to the price of unmodified isolation, on the one hand, and of an unmodified drive for world markets, on the other. The fact that agriculture would suffer far the more under isolation, and that industry would bear the brunt of changes necessary to widespread renewal of world trade, may here, however, be briefly reiterated; for here is a fact suggesting that a planned middle course is the fairest and wisest for all concerned.

Whatever course we choose, I should like here to emphasize that — agriculture, finance, labor — every man and every woman in this country have a common stake in seeing that we go back to simple horse-trading common sense in our dealings with other countries, and lay off all such intricate paper deals and debts as put us where we were on March 4, last. It would pay us all to become more import-minded. Let us get it straight in our heads that we should not make loans abroad until we have first achieved a lowering of tariffs that will permit the repayment of our loans.

This, in essence, should be our New Deal method of dealing abroad. Again and again, we shall be tempted under stress to postpone the New Deal method — goods for goods — and take another flyer on the Old Deal loan method, a contortion based on the oldtime mercantile dream of selling limitless quantities of goods indefinitely, and buying hardly anything. . . .

There is world trade to be had. By paying the price the United States can get its share. What is that price? It must buy abroad as well as sell abroad. It must import as well as export. In its general form, this proposition excites no opposition; but its particular applications do. Arrangements to bring in more goods, so that more may be sent out, involve pains as well as profits, and neither the pains nor the profits affect all citizens equally. It does not appeal strongly to an American manufacturer to be told that if he will sacrifice a part of his domestic market to his foreign competitors, our farmers will have a better foreign market. He wants to know at once if there is not a way to do the trick without hurting anyone. There is none.

There will be actual pain, from dislocations in the business structure, and psychological pain from dislocations of traditional attitudes, and from denials of the traditional American opportunity to rule or misrule one's own business in one's own way, regardless of general consequences; whatever course we choose.

It should be recognized that our surplus problems here in the United States, and the resulting necessity of keeping parts of our factories idle and withdrawing acreage, or of widening foreign markets, or of doing these things in combination, is really part of a world surplus problem. This country has more industrial as well as more agricultural capacity than it needs for home consumption. Surplus capacity in industry shows up mainly in unemployment, rather than in a persistent accumulation of commodities; but in all branches of our economic life there is an identical tendency for production to overrun consumption. Other nations have just the same trouble, as we know from the prevalance of unemployment and dole systems throughout the world.

It happens that in this nation the surplus problem is most acute because most of our customers already owe us more money than they can pay.

Now, it is this discrepancy between production-power and domestic consumption which makes all nations wish to sell more abroad than they buy abroad, and gives rise to economic nationalism in its most determined forms. There can be little doubt that the trouble traces, in whole or in part, to a maldistribution of income. That doctrine is implicit in our New Deal, which seeks to compensate for falling markets by building up purchasing power at home.

On a national and on a world scale alike, the tendency of old-time opportunist capitalism to pile up surpluses and to polarize wealth leads to disaster. Planned production and plans for a better distribution of income are essential to safe and decent business within nations, and among nations. Whether you are an extreme free trader, in principle, or an extreme isolationist, maldistribution will kill any attempt toward plenty, security and release.

Throughout the world, the Old Deal balanced production with consumption by a steady increase in the number of consumers beyond the nation's borders, by means of loans. This system minus the usual component of force worked for us, or seemed to work, for some years after the war. It broke down when our loans went bad; and our loans went bad because we refused to become import-minded.

Now we are trying a new method, a New Deal, which seems to me to rest on irresistible logic. We are trying to build up consumption per capita at home, as a substitute for the continual search for new consumers abroad. Our new method involves a planned redistribution of the national income, in contrast with the unplanned redistribution that takes place regularly, and usually unhappily, in every major economic crisis the civilized world over.

In the typical business breakdown, wealth tends to become more concentrated than ever. Creditors get more of the national income; debtors and wage-earners get less. Consumption of commodities declines, since buying power gravitates away from need and toward satiety. Those who need goods cannot buy. Those who can buy have no need. To force exports, with no provision for payment in kind, seems to be the only way out.

Our New Deal seeks to promote consumption more soundly. It directs purchasing power to those in need, by wage advances and alleviations of debt. It lessens the need to force exports. It looks toward balancing production with consumption at home.

Increased consumption so promoted does not absorb every surplus. Boom wages would not melt our total cotton or wheat supply. Even at the 1929 levels, we would still be in a jam. Better distributed purchasing power does tend, however, to create a larger demand. If we cannot eat all our wheat or wear all our cotton, we can swap what we have left over for something that we want. A wage-earner with purchasing power left over after his family has all the necessaries, may want some luxuries from abroad. With the money he sends away in payment, a foreign customer may pay for some of our wheat or cotton.

There is no more effective way to melt surpluses in any country than to put buying power in the hands of the people there. Our New Deal method has great advantages in that it tends to simplify not only the domestic but the foreign trade problem. It does so first by diminishing the quantities that must perforce be sold abroad, and secondly by blunting the objection to accepting imports in payment. Well-distributed purchasing power permits the country to buy more foreign as well as more home products.

It is evident that the chief factors in our problem are linked, and cannot be separated. First there is the retreat from excessive farm production for export. How far the retreat should go depends, of course, on the state of the demand abroad and at home. The foreign demand will vary with the facilities we afford other nations to send us goods in exchange — that is to say, how much we dare lower tariffs. Plainly, the farm retreat ties up with our tariff policy, which in turn hangs upon the success of the New Deal.

Revision of our tariff downward will have far better prospects if our New Deal succeeds than if it fails. Success in the New Deal will mean an increase in and a better distribution of purchasing power. Manufacturers and wage-earners will be no longer in terror for their businesses or their jobs, and will be quicker to acknowledge the necessity for the country to buy where it expects to sell. If we can set our own chaotic system into better order, there will be not only more willingness, there will be more power to buy abroad. With a margin over necessities, the average citizen will be able to pay for useful and desirable foreign goods. And at the same time he will be able to continue supporting home industry. He will buy more farm goods too. Thus the farm surpluses will come under an attack from three quarters simultaneously — from the farm retreat, from a more enlightened tariff policy, and from an improved purchasing power, which will aid agriculture by increasing domestic consumption directly and also by increasing the ability of our foreign customers to sell goods here. . . .

What I have tried to show is that there are sound arguments on both sides of this question. The nationalist rests his case on the idea that we cannot expect any longer to trade with the world as we used to. He does not expect an adequate natural revival of foreign demand, and believes it would be folly for us to stimulate the demand artificially by loans.

The internationalist position, on the other hand, is less pessimistic about natural foreign trade prospects. The internationalist does not regard loans as the only means of brightening those prospects and enlarging them. He holds that there is no possible way of making loans eventually secure unless we become import-minded. He would rather trust to tariff concessions and other means of developing trade reciprocally. He considers the pains of this course to be less than those of a nationalist program.

I lean to the international solution. But it is no open and shut question. It needs study, and above all dispassionate discussion. Unfortunately, those arguments which appeal to fear, to suspicion of neighbor nations, to narrow self-interest, and to ingrained hatred of change are the arguments which will be most loudly invoked. I want to see the whole question examined by our people in a new spirit.

John Maynard Keynes

HOW TO CURE THE RECESSION

❈{*1938*}❈ BEYOND question the most influential economist of the present century has been John Maynard Keynes (1883-1946). First projected into the world spotlight by his acid *Economic Consequences of the Peace,* he went on to a brilliant career as a Cambridge professor, a highly successful speculator, and a leader of England's Bloomsbury set. However, his most important work was his book, *The General Theory of Employment, Interest, and Money,* which advanced a revolutionary concept of how to cope with cyclical depressions. Instead of tightening the public belt in bad times by reducing expenditures and balancing the budget, Keynes argued that governments should reduce taxes and increase their expenditures, thus putting money into the hands of consumers.

Keynes visited the United States in 1934 and explained some of his ideas to President Roosevelt, but the latter did not fully understand them. While the New Deal did adopt policies advocated by Keynes, it did not formally accept his doctrine. Then, after an upswing in the economy that carried into 1937, the country was hit hard by the so-called "recession" of 1937-1938. Following developments closely from the vantage point of the British Isles, Keynes thought he saw both the cause of the slump and a way of ending it. So he wrote the following remarkable letter to Roosevelt.

Despite the persuasiveness and charm of Keynes argument, his letter did not convince Roosevelt; he sent the economist a polite routine reply, drafted by Secretary of the Treasury Morgenthau (1891-   ). But eventually the logic of events demonstrated the soundness of Keynes' line of reasoning, if not to Roosevelt at least to the majority of American economists and to many important New Dealers.

LETTER TO PRESIDENT ROOSEVELT

KING'S COLLEGE, CAMBRIDGE

Private and personal

February 1, 1938

Dear Mr. President,

You received me so kindly when I visited you some three years ago that I make bold to send you some bird's eye impressions which I have formed as to the business position in the United States. You will appreciate that I write from a distance, that I have not re-visited the United States since you saw me, and that I have access to few more sources of information than those publicly available. But sometimes in some respects there may be advantages in these limitations! At any rate, those things which I think I see, I see very clearly.

1. I should agree that the present recession is partly due to an "error

of optimism" which led to an over-estimation of future demand, when orders were being placed in the first half of this year. If this were all, there would not be too much to worry about. It would only need time to effect a readjustment; — though, even so, the recovery would only be up to the point required to take care of the *revised* estimate of current demand, which might fall appreciably short of the prosperity reached last spring.

2. But I am quite sure that this is not all. There is a much more troublesome underlying influence. The recovery was mainly due to the following factors: —

(i) the solution of the credit and insolvency problems, and the establishment of easy short-term money;

(ii) the creation of an adequate system of relief for the unemployed;

(iii) public works and other investments aided by Government funds or guarantees;

(iv) investment in the instrumental goods required to supply the increased demand for consumption goods;

(v) the momentum of the recovery thus initiated.

Now of these (i) was a prior condition of recovery, since it is no use creating a demand for credit, if there is no supply. But an increased supply will not by itself generate an adequate demand. The influence of (ii) evaporates as employment improves, so that there is a dead point beyond which this factor cannot carry the economic system. Recourse to (iii) has been greatly curtailed in the past year. (iv) and (v) are functions of the forward movement and cease — indeed (v) is reversed — as soon as the position fails to improve further. The benefit from the momentum of recovery as such is at the same time the most important and the most dangerous factor in the upward movement. It requires for its continuance, not merely the maintenance of recovery, but always *further* recovery. Thus it always flatters the early stages and steps from under just when support is most needed. It was largely, I think, a failure to allow for this which caused the "error of optimism" last year.

Unless, therefore, the above factors were supplemented by others in due course, the present slump could have been predicted with absolute certainty. It is true that the existing policies will prevent the slump from proceeding to such a disastrous degree as last time. But they will not by themselves — at any rate, not without a large scale recourse to (iii) — maintain prosperity at a reasonable level.

3. Now one had hoped that the needed supplementary factors would be organised in time. It was obvious what these were — namely increased investment in durable goods such as housing, public utilities and trans-

port. One was optimistic about this because in the United States at the present time the opportunities, indeed the necessity, for such developments were unexampled. Can your Administration escape criticism for the failure of these factors to mature?

Take housing. When I was with you three and a half years ago the necessity for effective new measures was evident. I remember vividly my conversations with Riefler at that time. But what happened? Next to nothing. The handling of the housing problem has been really wicked. I hope that the new measures recently taken will be more successful. I have not the knowledge to say. But they will take time, and I would urge the great importance of expediting and yet further aiding them. Housing is by far the best aid to recovery because of the large and continuing scale of potential demand; because of the wide geographical distribution of this demand; and because the sources of its finance are largely independent of the Stock Exchanges. I should advise putting most of your eggs in this basket, *caring* about this more than about anything, and making absolutely sure that they are being hatched without delay. In this country we partly depended for many years on direct subsidies. There are few more proper objects for such than working class houses. If a direct subsidy is required to get a move on (we gave our subsidies *through* the local authorities), it should be given without delay or hesitation.

Next utilities. There seems to be a deadlock. Neither your policy nor anyone else's is able to take effect. I think that the litigation by the utilities is senseless and ill-advised. But a great deal of what is alleged against the wickedness of holding companies as such is surely wide of the mark. It does not draw the right line of division between what should be kept and what discarded. It arises too much out of what is dead and gone. The real criminals have cleared out long ago. I should doubt if the controls existing to-day are of much *personal* value to any-one. No-one has suggested a procedure by which the eggs can be unscrambled. Why not tackle the problem by insisting that the *voting power* should belong to the real owners of the equity, and leave the existing *organisations* undisturbed, so long as the voting power is so rearranged (e.g. by bringing in preferred stockholders) that it cannot be controlled by the holders of a minority of the equity?

Is it not for you to decide either to make real peace or to be much more drastic the other way? Personally I think there is a great deal to be said for the ownership of all the utilities by publicly owned boards. But if public opinion is not yet ripe for this, what is the object of chasing the utilities round the lot every other week? If I was in your place, I should buy out the utilities at fair prices in every district where the situation was ripe for doing so, and announce that the ultimate ideal was to make this policy nation-wide. But elsewhere I would make peace on liberal terms, guaranteeing fair earnings on new investments and a fair basis of valuation in the event of the public taking them over hereafter. The process of evolution will take at least a generation. Meanwhile a policy of *competing* plants with losses all round is a ramshackle notion.

Finally the railroads. The position there seems to be exactly what it was three or four years ago. They remain, as they were then, potential sources of substantial demand for new capital expenditure. Whether hereafter they are publicly owned or remain in private hands, it is a matter of national importance that they should be made solvent. Nationalise them if the time is ripe. If not, take pity on the overwhelming problems of the present managements. And here too let the dead bury their dead. (To an Englishman, you Americans, like the Irish, are so terribly historically minded!)

I am afraid I am going beyond my province. But the upshot is this. A convincing policy, whatever its details may be, for promoting large-scale investment under the above heads is an urgent necessity. These things take time. Far too much precious time has passed.

4. I must not encumber this letter with technical suggestions for re-revival of sources of demand. If demand and confidence re-appear, the problems of the capital market will not seem so difficult as they do to-day. Moreover it is a highly technical problem.

5. Businessmen have a different set of delusions from politicians; and need, therefore, different handling. They are, however, much milder than politicians, at the same time allured and terrified by the glare of publicity, easily persuaded to be 'patriots', perplexed, bemused, indeed terrified, yet only too anxious to take a cheerful view, vain perhaps but very unsure of themselves, pathetically responsive to a kind word. You could do anything you like with them, if you would treat them (even the big ones), not as wolves and tigers, but as domestic animals by nature, even though they have been badly brought up and not trained as you would wish. It is a mistake to think that they are more *immoral* than politicians. If you work them into the surly, obstinate, terrified mood, of which domestic animals, wrongly handled, are so capable, the nation's burdens will not get carried to market; and in the end public opinion will veer their way. Perhaps you will rejoin that I have got quite a wrong idea of what all the back-chat amounts to. Nevertheless I record accurately how it strikes observers here.

6. Forgive the candour of these remarks. They come from an enthu-

siastic well-wisher of you and your policies. I accept the view that durable investment must come increasingly under state direction. I sympathise with Mr. Wallace's agricultural policies. I believe that the S.E.C. is doing splendid work. I regard the growth of collective bargaining as essential. I approve minimum wage and hours regulation. I was altogether on your side the other day, when you deprecated a policy of general wage reductions as useless in present circumstances. But I am terrified lest progressive causes in all the democratic countries should suffer injury, because you have taken too lightly the risk to their prestige which would result from a failure measured in terms of immediate prosperity. There *need* be no failure. But the maintenance of prosperity in the modern world is extremely *difficult*; and it is so easy to lose precious time.

> I am
> Mr. President
> Yours with great respect and faithfulness,
> [*Signed*] JM KEYNES

John Steinbeck
MIGRANT LABOR

❦1939❦ ALTHOUGH meteorologists had long warned that the high plains west of the 98th meridian were unsuited for ordinary agriculture because of the periodic droughts that plagued the region, American farmers repeatedly pushed out beyond that line during the "wet" phases of the weather cycle. Thus, in areas like Oklahoma and western Kansas during the "wet" 1920's, millions of acres formerly given over to natural grasses were plowed up and put to the cultivation of wheat and other grains.

Then, in the early thirties, came the inevitable arid phase, and with it high winds and blazing sun. The plow-pulverized soils, no longer held in place in dry weather by the interlaced roots of the hardy grasses, were now swept up and away in vast black clouds of dust. The region became known as the "dust bowl," and when the winds subsided and the rains came it was a barren desert, its rich humus gone, its hardpan subsoil soon gashed by ugly, rain-formed gullies.

To the horrors of the dust bowl were added, for the Western farmer, the miseries of the Great Depression, worse perhaps for him than for the industrial worker. The result was a mass migration from the plains states, some driven away by drought and erosion, others, like the protagonists in John Steinbeck's novel, by the collapse of the farm economy.

In *The Grapes of Wrath,* which was published in 1939, Steinbeck (1902-   ) captured perfectly the mood of these migrants and their pitiful plight. In the space available here it is not possible to tell even in outline the whole story of the Joad family and the other "Okies" in this novel, but the following selection fairly portrays the nature of the work and offers a few typical scenes from the Joad saga. *The Grapes of Wrath* was an immense literary and popular success, but it is also the book which best captures the spirit of the depression and the indignation and frustration of the liberals of the thirties who searched for ways and means of ending it.

THE GRAPES OF WRATH

To the red country and part of the gray country of Oklahoma, the last rains came gently, and they did not cut the scarred earth. The plows crossed and recrossed and scattered weed colonies and grass along the sides of the roads so that the gray country and the dark red country began to disappear under a green cover. In the last part of May the sky grew pale and the clouds that had hung in high puffs for so long in the spring were dissipated. The sun flared down on the growing corn day after day until a line of brown spread along the edge of each green bayonet. The clouds appeared, and went away, and in a while they did not try any more. The weeds grew darker green to protect themselves, and they did not spread any more. The surface of the earth crusted, a thin hard crust, and as the sky became pale, so the earth became pale, pink in the red country and white in the gray country.

In the water-cut gullies the earth dusted down in dry little streams. Gophers and ant lions started small avalanches. And as the sharp sun struck day after day, the leaves of the young corn became less stiff and erect; they bent in a curve at first, and then, as the central ribs of strength grew weak, each leaf tilted downward. Then it was June, and the sun shone more fiercely. The brown lines on the corn leaves widened and moved in on the central ribs. The weeds frayed and edged back toward their roots. The air was thin and the sky more pale; and every day the earth paled.

In the roads where the teams moved, where the wheels milled the ground and the hooves of the horses beat the ground, the dirt crust broke and the dust formed. Every moving thing lifted the dust into the air: a walking man lifted a thin layer as high as his waist, and a wagon lifted the dust as high as the fence tops, and an automobile boiled a cloud behind it. The dust was long in settling back again.

When June was half gone, the big clouds moved up out of Texas and the Gulf, high heavy clouds, rain-heads. The men in the fields looked up at the clouds and sniffed at them and held wet fingers up to sense the wind. And the horses were nervous while the clouds were up. The rain-heads dropped a little spattering and hurried on to some other country.

Behind them the sky was pale again and the sun flared. In the dust there were drop craters where the rain had fallen, and there were clean splashes on the corn, and that was all.

A gentle wind followed the rain clouds, driving them on northward, a wind that softly clashed the drying corn. A day went by and the wind increased, steady, unbroken by gusts. The dust from the roads fluffed up and spread out and fell on the weeds beside the fields, and fell into the fields a little way. Now the wind grew strong and hard and it worked at the rain crust in the corn fields. Little by little the sky was darkened by the mixing dust, and the wind felt over the earth, loosened the dust, and carried it away. The wind grew stronger. The rain crust broke and the dust lifted up out of the fields and drove gray plumes into the air like sluggish smoke. The corn threshed the wind and made a dry, rushing sound. The finest dust did not settle back to earth now, but disappeared into the darkening sky.

The wind grew stronger, whisked under stones, carried up straws and old leaves, and even little clods, marking its course as it sailed across the fields. The air and the sky darkened and through them the sun shone redly, and there was a raw sting in the air. During a night the wind raced faster over the land, dug cunningly among the rootlets of the corn, and the corn fought the wind with its weakened leaves until the roots were freed by the prying wind and then each stalk settled wearily sideways toward the earth and pointed the direction of the wind.

The dawn came, but no day. In the gray sky a red sun appeared, a dim red circle that gave a little light, like dusk; and as that day advanced, the dusk slipped back toward darkness, and the wind cried and whimpered over the fallen corn.

Men and women huddled in their houses, and they tied handkerchiefs over their noses when they went out, and wore goggles to protect their eyes.

When the night came again it was black night, for the stars could not pierce the dust to get down, and the window lights could not even spread beyond their own yards. Now the dust was evenly mixed with the air, an emulsion of dust and air. Houses were shut tight, and cloth wedged around doors and windows, but the dust came in so thinly that it could not be seen in the air, and it settled like pollen on the chairs and tables, on the dishes. The people brushed it from their shoulders. Little lines of dust lay at the door sills.

In the middle of that night the wind passed on and left the land quiet. The dust-filled air muffled sound more completely than fog does. The people, lying in their beds, heard the wind stop. They awakened when the rushing wind was gone. They lay quietly and listened deep into the stillness. Then the roosters crowed, and their voices were muffled, and the people stirred restlessly in their beds and wanted the morning. They knew it would take a long time for the dust to settle out of the air. In the morning the dust hung like fog, and the sun was as red as ripe new blood. All day the dust sifted down from the sky, and the next day it sifted down. An even blanket covered the earth. It settled on the corn, piled up on the tops of the fence posts, piled up on the wires; it settled on roofs, blanketed the weeds and trees.

The people came out of their houses and smelled the hot stinging air and covered their noses from it. And the children came out of the houses, but they did not run or shout as they would have done after a rain. Men stood by their fences and looked at the ruined corn, drying fast now, only a little green showing through the film of dust. The men were silent and they did not move often. And the women came out of the houses to stand beside their men — to feel whether this time the men would break. The women studied the men's faces secretly, for the corn could go, as long as something else remained. The children stood near by, drawing figures in the dust with bare toes, and the children sent exploring senses out to see whether men and women would break. The children peeked at the faces of the men and women, and then drew careful lines in the dust with their toes. Horses came to the watering troughs and nuzzled the water to clear the surface dust. After a while the faces of the watching men lost their bemused perplexity and became hard and angry and resistant. Then the women knew that they were safe and that there was no break. Then they asked, What'll we do? And the men replied, I don't know. But it was all right. The women knew it was all right, and the watching children knew it was all right. Women and children knew deep in themselves that no misfortune was too great to bear if their men were whole. The women went into the houses to their work, and the children began to play, but cautiously at first. As the day went forward the sun became less red. It flared down on the dust-blanketed land. The men sat in the doorways of their houses; their hands were busy with sticks and little rocks. The men sat still — thinking — figuring . . .

THE OWNERS of the land came onto the land, or more often a spokesman for the owners came. They came in closed cars, and they felt the dry earth with their fingers, and sometimes they drove big earth augers into the ground for soil tests. The tenants, from their sun-beaten dooryards, watched uneasily when the closed cars drove along the fields. And at last the owner men drove into the dooryards and sat in their cars to talk out of the windows. The tenant men stood beside the cars for a while, and then squatted on their hams and found sticks with which to mark the dust.

In the open doors the women stood looking out, and behind them the children — corn-headed children, with wide eyes, one bare foot on top of the other bare foot, and the toes working. The women and the children watched their men talking to the owner men. They were silent.

Some of the owner men were kind because they hated what they had to do, and some of them were angry because they hated to be cruel, and some of them were cold because they had long ago found that one could not be an owner unless one were cold. And all of them were caught in something larger than themselves. Some of them hated the mathematics that drove them, and some were afraid, and some worshiped the mathematics because it provided a refuge from thought and from feeling. If a bank or a finance company owned the land, the owner man said, The Bank — or the Company — needs — wants — insists — must have — as though the Bank or the Company were a monster, with thought and feeling, which had ensnared them. These last would take no responsibility for the banks or the companies because they were men and slaves, while the banks were machines and masters all at the same time. Some of the owner men were a little proud to be slaves to such cold and powerful masters. The owner men sat in the cars and explained. You know the land is poor. You've scrabbled at it long enough, God knows.

The squatting tenant men nodded and wondered and drew figures in the dust, and yes, they knew, God knows. If the dust only wouldn't fly. If the top would only stay on the soil, it might not be so bad.

The owner men went on leading to their point: You know the land's getting poorer. You know what cotton does to the land; robs it, sucks all the blood out of it.

The squatters nodded they knew, God knew. If they could only rotate the crops they might pump blood back into the land.

Well, it's too late. And the owner men explained the workings and the thinkings of the monster that was stronger than they were. A man can hold land if he can just eat and pay taxes; he can do that.

Yes, he can do that until his crops fail one day and he has to borrow money from the bank.

But — you see, a bank or a company can't do that, because those creatures don't breathe air, don't eat side-meat. They breathe profits; they eat the interest on money. If they don't get it, they die the way you die without air, without sidemeat. It is a sad thing, but it is so. It is just so.

The squatting men raised their eyes to understand. Can't we just hang on? Maybe the next year will be a good year. God knows how much cotton next year. And with all the wars — God knows what price cotton will bring. Don't they make explosives out of cotton? And uniforms? Get enough wars and cotton'll hit the ceiling. Next year, maybe. They looked up questioningly.

We can't depend on it. The bank — the monster has to have profits all the time. It can't wait. It'll die. No, taxes go on. When the monster stops growing, it dies. It can't stay one size.

Soft fingers began to tap the sill of the car window, and hard fingers tightened on the restless drawing sticks. In the doorways of the sunbeaten tenant houses, women sighed and then shifted feet so that the one that had been down was now on top, and the toes working. Dogs came sniffing near the owner cars and wetted on all four tires one after another. And chickens lay in the sunny dust and fluffed their feathers to get the cleansing dust down to the skin. In the little sties the pigs grunted inquiringly over the muddy remnants of the slops.

The squatting men looked down again. What do you want us to do? We can't take less share of the crop — we're half starved now. The kids are hungry all the time. We got no clothes, torn an' ragged. If all the neighbors weren't the same, we'd be ashamed to go to meeting.

And at last the owner men came to the point. The tenant system won't work any more. One man on a tractor can take the place of twelve or fourteen families. Pay him a wage and take all the crop. We have to do it. We don't like to do it. But the monster's sick. Something's happened to the monster.

But you'll kill the land with cotton.

We know. We've got to take cotton quick before the land dies. Then we'll sell the land. Lots of families in the East would like to own a piece of land.

The tenant men looked up alarmed. But what'll happen to us? How'll we eat?

You'll have to get off the land. The plows'll go through the dooryard.

And now the squatting men stood up angrily. Grampa took up the land, and he had to kill the Indians and drive them away. And Pa was born here, and he killed weeds and snakes. Then a bad year came and he had to borrow a little money. An' we was born here. There in the door — our children born here. And Pa had to borrow money. The bank owned the land then, but we stayed and we got a little bit of what we raised.

We know that — all that. It's not us, it's the bank. A bank isn't like a man. Or an owner with fifty thousand acres, he isn't like a man either. That's the monster.

Sure, cried the tenant men, but it's our land. We measured it and broke it up. We were born on it, and we got killed on it, died on it. Even if it's no good, it's still ours. That's what makes it ours — being born on it, working it, dying on it. That makes ownership, not a paper with numbers on it.

We're sorry. It's not us. It's the monster. The bank isn't like a man.

Yes, but the bank is only made of men.

No, you're wrong there — quite wrong there. The bank is something else than men. It happens that every man in a bank hates what the bank does, and yet the bank does it. The bank is something more than men, I tell you. It's the monster. Men made it, but they can't control it.

The tenants cried, Grandpa killed Indians, Pa killed snakes for the land. Maybe we can kill banks — they're worse than Indians and snakes. Maybe we got to fight to keep our land, like Pa and Grandpa did.

And now the owner men grew angry. You'll have to go.

But it's ours, the tenant men cried. We ——

No. The bank, the monster owns it. You'll have to go.

We'll get our guns, like Grandpa when the Indians came. What then?

Well — first the sheriff, and then the troops. You'll be stealing if you try to stay, you'll be murderers if you kill to stay. The monster isn't men, but it can make men do what it wants.

But if we go, where'll we go? How'll we go? We got no money.

We're sorry, said the owner men. The bank, the fifty-thousand-acre owner can't be responsible. You're on land that isn't yours. Once over the line maybe you can pick cotton in the fall. Maybe you can go on relief. Why don't you go on west to California? There's work there, and it never gets cold. Why, you can reach out anywhere and pick an orange. Why, there's always some kind of crop to work in. Why don't you go there? And the owner men started their cars and rolled away.

The tenant men squatted down on their hams again to mark the dust with a stick, to figure, to wonder. Their sunburned faces were dark, and their sun-whipped eyes were light. The women moved cautiously out of the doorways toward their men, and the children crept behind the women, cautiously, ready to run. The bigger boys squatted beside their fathers, because that made them men. After a time the women asked, What did he want?

And the men looked up for a second, and the smolder of pain was in their eyes. We got to get off. A tractor and a superintendent. Like factories.

Where'll we go? the women asked.

We don't know. We don't know.

And the women went quickly, quietly back into the houses and herded the children ahead of them. They knew that a man so hurt and so perplexed may turn in anger, even on people he loves. They left the men alone to figure and to wonder in the dust.

After a time perhaps the tenant man looked about — at the pump put in ten years ago, with a goose-neck handle and iron flowers on the spout, at the chopping block where a thousand chickens had been killed, at the hand plow lying in the shed, and the patent crib hanging in the rafters over it.

The children crowded about the women in the houses. What we going to do, Ma? Where we going to go?

The women said, We don't know, yet. Go out and play. But don't go near your father. He might whale you if you go near him. And the women went on with the work, but all the time they watched the men squatting in the dust — perplexed and figuring.

The tractors came over the roads and into the fields, great crawlers moving like insects, having the incredible strength of insects. They crawled over the ground, laying the track and rolling on it and picking it up. Diesel tractors, puttering while they stood idle; they thundered when they moved, and then settled down to a droning roar. Snub-nosed monsters, raising the dust and sticking their snouts into it, straight down the country, across the country, through fences, through dooryards, in and out of gullies in straight lines. They did not run on the ground, but on their own roadbeds. They ignored hills and gulches, water courses, fences, houses.

The man sitting in the iron seat did not look like a man; gloved, goggled, rubber dust mask over nose and mouth, he was a part of the monster, a robot in the seat. The thunder of the cylinders sounded through the country, became one with the air and the earth, so that earth and air muttered in sympathetic vibration. The driver could not control it — straight across country it went, cutting through a dozen farms and straight back. A twitch at the controls could swerve the cat', but the driver's hands could not twitch because the monster that built the tractor, the monster that sent the tractor out, had somehow got into the driver's hands, into his brain and muscle, had goggled him and muzzled him — goggled his mind, muzzled his speech, goggled his perception, muzzled his protest. He could not see the land as it was, he could not smell the land as it smelled; his feet did not stamp the clods or feel the warmth and power of the earth. He sat in an iron seat and stepped on iron pedals. He could not cheer or beat or curse or encourage the extension of his power, and because of this he could not cheer or whip or curse or encourage himself. He did not know or own or trust or beseech the land. If a seed dropped did not germinate, it was nothing. If the young thrusting plant withered in drought or drowned in a flood of rain, it was no more to the driver than to the tractor.

He loved the land no more than the bank loved the land. He could admire the tractor — its machined surfaces, its surge of power, the roar of its detonating cylinders; but it was not his tractor. Behind the tractor rolled the shining disks, cutting the earth with blades — not plowing but surgery, pushing the cut earth to the right where the second row of disks cut it and pushed it to the left; slicing blades shining, polished by the cut earth. And pulled behind the disks, the harrows combing with iron teeth so that the little clods broke up and the earth lay smooth. Behind the harrows, the long seeders — twelve curved iron penes erected in the foundry, orgasms set by gears, raping methodically, raping without passion. The driver sat in his iron set and he was proud of the straight lines he did not will, proud of the tractor he did not own or love, proud of the power he could not control. And when that crop grew, and was harvested, no man had crumbled a hot clod in his fingers and let the earth sift past his fingertips. No man had touched the seed, or lusted for the growth. Men ate what they had not raised, had no connection with the bread. The land bore under iron, and under iron gradually died; for it was not loved or hated, it had no prayers or curses.

At noon the tractor driver stopped sometimes near a tenant house and opened his lunch: sandwiches wrapped in waxed paper, white bread, pickle, cheese, Spam, a piece of pie branded like an engine part. He ate without relish. And tenants not yet moved away came out to see him, looked curiously while the goggles were taken off, and the rubber dust mask, leaving white circles around the eyes and a large white circle around nose and mouth. The exhaust of the tractor puttered on, for fuel is so cheap it is more efficient to leave the engine running than to heat the Diesel nose for a new start. Curious children crowded close, ragged children who ate their fried dough as they watched. They watched hungrily the unwrapping of the sandwiches, and their hunger-sharpened noses smelled the pickle, cheese, and Spam. They didn't speak to the driver. They watched his hand as it carried food to his mouth. They did not watch him chewing; their eyes followed the hand that held the sandwich. After a while the tenant who could not leave the place came out and squatted in the shade beside the tractor.

"Why, you're Joe Davis's boy!"

"Sure," the driver said.

"Well, what you doing this kind of work for — against your own people?"

"Three dollars a day. I got damn sick of creeping for my dinners — and not getting it. I got a wife and kids. We got to eat. Three dollars a day, and it comes every day."

"That's right," the tenant said. "But for your three dollars a day fifteen or twenty families can't eat at all. Nearly a hundred people have to go out and wander on the roads for your three dollars a day. Is that right?"

And the driver said, "Can't think of that. Got to think of my own kids. Three dollars a day, and it comes every day. Times are changing, mister, don't you know? Can't make a living on the land unless you've got two, five, ten thousand acres and a tractor. Crop land isn't for little guys like us any more. You don't kick up a howl because you can't make Fords, because you're not the telephone company. Well, crops are like that now. Nothing to do about it. You try to get three dollars a day someplace. That's the only way."

The tenant pondered. "Funny thing how it is. If a man owns a little property, that property is him, it's part of him, and it's like him. If he owns property only so he can walk on it and handle it and be sad when it isn't doing well, and feel fine when the rain falls on it, that property is him, and some ways he's bigger because he owns it. Even if he isn't successful he's big with his property. That is so."

And the tenant pondered more. "But let a man get property he doesn't see, or can't take time to get his fingers in, or can't be there to walk on it — why, then the property is the man. He can't do what he wants, he can't think what he wants. The property is the man, stronger than he is. And he is small, not big. Only his possessions are big — and he's the servant of his property. That is so, too."

The driver munched the branded pie and threw the crust away. "Times are changed, don't you know? Thinking about stuff like that don't feed the kids. Get your three dollars a day, feed your kids. You got no call to worry about anybody's kids but your own. You get a reputation for talking like that, and you'll never get three dollars a day. Big shots won't give you three dollars a day if you worry about anything but your three dollars a day."

"Nearly a hundred people on the road for your three dollars. Where will we go?"

"And that reminds me," the driver said, "you better get out soon. I'm going through the dooryard after dinner."

"You filled in the well this morning."

"I know. Had to keep the line straight. But I'm going through the dooryard after dinner. Got to keep the lines straight. And — well, you know Joe Davis, my old man, so I'll tell you this. I got orders where there's a family not moved out — if I have an accident — you know, get too close and cave the house in a little well, I might get a couple of dollars. And my youngest kid never had no shoes yet."

"I built it with my hands. Straightened old nails to put the sheathing on. Rafters are wired to the stringers with baling wire. It's mine. I built it. You bump it down—I'll be in the window with a rifle. You even come too close and I'll pot you like a rabbit."

"It's not me. There's nothing I can do. I'll lose my job if I don't do it. And look — suppose you kill me? They'll just hang you, but long before you're hung there'll be another guy on the tractor, and he'll bump the house down. You're not killing the right guy."

"That's so," the tenant said. "Who gave you orders? I'll go after him. He's the one to kill."

"You're wrong. He got his orders from the bank. The bank told him, 'clear those people out or it's your job.'"

"Well there's a president of the bank. There's a board of directors. I'll fill up the magazine of the rifle and go into the bank."

The driver said, "Fellow was telling me the bank gets orders from the East. The orders were, 'Make the land show profit or we'll close you up.'"

"But where does it stop? Who can we shoot? I don't aim to starve to death before I kill the man that's starving me."

"I don't know. Maybe there's nobody to shoot. Maybe the thing isn't men at all. Maybe, like you said, the property's doing it. Anyway I told you my orders."

"I got to figure," the tenant said. "We all got to figure. There's some way to stop this. It's not like lightning or earthquakes. We've got a bad thing made by men, and by God that's something we can change." The tenant sat in his doorway, and the driver thundered his engine and started off, tracks falling and curving, harrows combing, and the phalli of the seeder slipping into the ground. Across the dooryard the tractor cut, and the hard, foot-beaten ground was seeded field, and the tractor cut through again; the uncut space was ten feet wide. And back he came. The iron guard bit into the house-corner, crumbled the wall, and wrenched the little house from its foundation so that it fell sideways, crushed like a bug. And the driver was goggled and a rubber mask covered his nose and mouth. The tractor cut a straight line on, and the air and the ground vibrated with its thunder. The tenant man stared after it, his rifle in his hand. His wife was beside him, and the quiet children behind. And all of them stared after the tractor. . . .

HIGHWAY 66 is the main migrant road. 66 — the long concrete path across the country, waving gently up and down on the map, from the Mississippi to Bakersfield — over the red lands and the gray lands, twisting up into the mountains, crossing the Divide and down into the bright and terrible desert, and across the desert to the mountains again, and into the rich California valleys.

66 is the path of a people in flight, refugees from dust and shrinking land, from the thunder of tractors and shrinking ownership, from the desert's slow northward invasion, from the twisting winds that howl up out of Texas, from the floods that bring no richness to the land and steal what little richness is there. From all of these the people are in flight, and they come into 66 from the tributary side roads, from the wagon tracks and the rutted country roads. 66 is the mother road, the road of flight. . . .

THE ancient overloaded Hudson creaked and grunted to the highway at Sallisaw and turned west and the sun was blinding. But on the concrete road Al built up his speed because the flattened springs were not in danger any more. From Sallisaw to Gore is twenty-one miles and the Hudson was doing thirty-five miles an hour. From Gore to Warner thirteen miles; Warner to Checotah fourteen miles; Checotah a long jump to Henrietta — thirty-four miles, but a real town at the end of it. Henrietta to Castle nineteen miles, and the sun was overhead, and the red fields, heated by the high sun, vibrated the air.

Al, at the wheel, his face purposeful, his whole body listening to the car, his restless eyes jumping from the road to the instrument panel. Al was one with his engine, every nerve listening for weakness, for the thumps or squeals, hums and chattering that indicate a change that may cause a breakdown. He had become the soul of the car.

Granma, beside him on the seat, half slept, and whimpered in her sleep, opened her eyes to peer ahead, and then dozed again. And Ma sat beside Granma, one elbow out the window and the skin reddening under the fierce sun. Ma looked ahead too, but her eyes were flat and did not see the road or the fields, the gas stations, the little eating sheds. She did not glance at them as the Hudson went by.

Al shifted himself on the broken seat and changed his grip on the steering wheel. And he sighed, "Makes a racket, but I think she's awright. God knows what she'll do if we got to climb a hill with the load we got. Got any hills 'tween here an' California, Ma?"

Ma turned her head slowly and her eyes came to life. "Seems to me they's hills," she said. " 'Course I dunno. But seems to me I heard they's hills an' even mountains. Big ones."

Granma drew a long whining sigh in her sleep.

Al said, "We'll burn right up if we got climbin' to do. Have to throw out some a' this stuff. Maybe we shouldn' a brang that preacher."

"You'll be glad a that preacher 'fore we're through," said Ma. "That preacher'll help us." She looked ahead at the gleaming road again.

Al steered with one hand and put the other on the vibrating gearshift lever. He had difficulty in speaking. His mouth formed the words silently before he said them aloud. "Ma — " She looked slowly around at him, her head swaying a little with the car's motion. "Ma, you scared a goin'? You scared a goin' to a new place?"

Her eyes grew thoughtful and soft. "A little," she said. "Only it ain't like scared so much. I'm jus' a settin' here waitin'. When somepin happens that I got to do somepin — I'll do it."

"Ain't you thinkin' what's it gonna be like when we get there? Ain't you scared it won't be nice like we thought?"

"No," she said quickly. "No, I ain't. You can't do that. I can't do that. It's too much — livin' too many lives. Up ahead they's a thousan' lives we might live, but when it comes, it'll on'y be one. If I go ahead on all of 'em, it's too much. You got to live ahead 'cause you're so young, but — it's jus' the road goin' by for me. An' it's jus' how soon they gonna wanta eat some more pork bones." Her face tightened. "That's all I can do. I can't do no more. All the rest'd get upset if I done any more'n that. They all depen' on me jus' thinkin' about that." . . .

Castle to Paden twenty-five miles and the sun passed the zenith and started down. And the radiator cap began to jiggle up and down and steam started to whish out. Near Paden there was a shack beside the road and two gas pumps in front of it; and beside a fence, a water faucet and a hose. Al drove in and nosed the Hudson up to the hose. As they pulled in, a stout man, red of face and arms, got up from a chair behind the gas pumps and moved toward them. He wore brown corduroys, and suspenders and a polo shirt; and he had a cardboard sun helmet, painted silver, on his head. The sweat beaded on his nose and under his eyes and formed streams in the wrinkles of his neck. He strolled toward the truck, looking truculent and stern.

"You folks aim to buy anything? Gasoline or stuff?" he asked.

Al was out already, unscrewing the steaming radiator cap with the tips of his fingers, jerking his hand away to escape the spurt when the cap should come loose. "Need some gas, mister."

"Got any money?"

"Sure. Think we're beggin'?"

The truculence left the fat man's face. "Well, that's all right, folks. He'p yourself to water." And he hastened to explain. "Road is full a people, come in, use water, dirty up the toilet, an' then, by God, they'll steal stuff an' don't buy nothin'. Got no money to buy with. Come beggin' a gallon gas to move on."

Tom dropped angrily to the ground and moved toward the fat man. "We're payin' our way," he said fiercely. "You got no call to give us a goin'-over. We ain't asked you for nothin' ."

"I ain't," the fat man said quickly. The sweat began to soak through his short-sleeved polo shirt. "Jus' he'p yourself to water, and go use the toilet if you want."

Winfield had got the hose. He drank from the end and then turned the stream over his head and face, and emerged dripping. "It ain't cool," he said.

"I don' know what the country's comin' to," the fat man continued. His complaint had shifted now and he was no longer talking to or about the Joads. "Fifty-sixty cars a folks go by ever' day, folks all movin' west with kids an' househol' stuff. Where they goin'? What they gonna do?"

"Doin' the same as us," said Tom. "Goin' someplace to live. Tryin' to get along. That's all."

"Well, I don' know what the country's comin' to. I jus' don' know. Here's me tryin' to get along, too. Think any them big new cars stops here? No, sir! They go on to them yella-painted company stations in town. They don't stop no place like this. Most folks stops here ain't got nothin'."

Al flipped the radiator cap and it jumped into the air with a head of steam behind it, and a hollow bubbling sound came out of the radiator. On top of the truck, the suffering hound dog crawled timidly to the edge of the load and looked over, whimpering, toward the water. Uncle John climbed up and lifted him down by the scruff of the neck. For a moment the dog staggered on stiff legs and then he went to lap the mud under the faucet. In the highway the cars whizzed by, glistening in the heat, and the hot wind of their going fanned into the service-station yard. Al filled the radiator with the hose.

"It ain't that I'm tryin' to git trade outa rich folks," the fat man went on. "I'm jus' tryin' to git trade. Why, the folks that stops here begs gasoline an' they trades for gasoline. I could show you in my back room the stuff they'll trade for gas an' oil: beds an' baby buggies an' pots an' pans. One family traded a doll their kid had for a gallon. An' what'm I gonna do with the stuff, open a junk shop? Why, one fella wanted to gimme his shoes for a gallon. An' if I was that kinda fella I bet I could git — " He glanced at Ma and stopped.

Jim Casy had wet his head, and the drops still coursed down his high forehead, and his muscled neck was wet, and his shirt was wet. He moved over beside Tom. "It ain't the people's fault," he said. "How'd you like to sell the bed you sleep on for a tankful a gas?"

"I know it ain't their fault. Ever' person I talked to is on the move for a damn good reason. But what's the country comin' to? That's what I wanta know. What's it comin' to? Fella can't make a livin' no more. Folks can't make a livin' farmin'. I ask you, what's it comin' to? I can't figure her out. Ever'body I ask, they can't figure her out. Fella wants to trade his shoes so he can git a hundred miles on. I can't figure her out." He took off his silver hat and wiped his forehead with his palm. And Tom took off his cap and wiped his forehead with it. He went to the hose and wet the cap through and squeezed it and put it on again. Ma worked a tin cup out through the side bars of the truck, and she took water to Granma and to Grampa on top of the load. She stood on the bars and handed the cup to Grampa, and he wet his lips, and then shook his head and refused more. The old eyes looked up at Ma in pain and bewilderment for a moment before the awareness receded again.

Al started the motor and backed the truck to the gas pump. "Fill her up. She'll take about seven," said Al. "We'll give her six so she don't spill none."

The fat man put the hose in the tank. "No, sir," he said. "I jus' don't know what the country's comin' to. Relief an' all."

Casy said, "I been walkin' aroun' in the country. Ever'body's askin' that. What we comin' to? Seems to me we don't never come to nothin'. Always on the way. Always goin' and goin'. Why don't folks think about that? They's movement now. People moving. We know why, an' we know how. Movin' 'cause they got to. That's why folks always move. Movin' 'cause they want somepin better'n what they got. An' that's the on'y way they'll ever get it. Wantin' it an' needin' it, they'll go out an' git it.

It's bein' hurt that makes folks mad to fightin'. I been walkin' aroun' the country, an' hearin' folks talk like you."

The fat man pumped the gasoline and the needle turned on the pump dial, recording the amount. "Yeah, but what's it comin' to? That's what I want ta know." . . .

ONCE California belonged to Mexico and its land to Mexicans; and a horde of tattered feverish Americans poured in. And such was their hunger for land that they took the land — stole Sutter's land, Guerrero's land, took the grants and broke them up and growled and quarreled over them, those frantic hungry men; and they guarded with guns the land they had stolen. They put up houses and barns, they turned the earth and planted crops. And these things were possession, and possession was ownership.

The Mexicans were weak and fed. They could not resist, because they wanted nothing in the world as frantically as the Americans wanted land.

Then, with time, the squatters were no longer squatters, but owners; and their children grew up and had children on the land. And the hunger was gone from them, the feral hunger, the gnawing, tearing hunger for land, for water and earth and the good sky over it, for the green thrusting grass, for the swelling roots. They had these things so completely that they did not know about them any more. . . .

And it came about that owners no longer worked on their farms. They farmed on paper; and they forgot the land, the smell, the feel it it, and remembered only that they owned it, remembered only that they gained and lost by it. And some of the farms grew so large that one man could not even conceive of them any more, so large that it took batteries of bookkeepers to keep track of interest and gain and loss; chemists to test the soil, to replenish; straw bosses to see that the stooping men were moving along the rows as swiftly as the material of their bodies could stand. Then such a farmer really became a storekeeper, and kept a store. He paid the men, and sold them food, and took the money back. And after a while he did not pay the men at all, and saved bookkeeping. These farms gave food on credit. A man might work and feed himself; and when the work was done, he might find that he owed money to the company. And the owners not only did not work the farms any more, many of them had never seen the farms they owned.

And then the dispossessed were drawn west—from Kansas, Oklahoma, Texas, New Mexico; from Nevada and Arkansas families, tribes, dusted out, tractored out. Carloads, caravans, homeless and hungry; twenty thousand and fifty thousand and a hundred thousand and two hundred thousand. They streamed over the mountains, hungry and restless — restless as ants, scurrying to find work to do — to lift, to push, to pull, to pick, to cut anything, any burden to bear, for food. The kids are hungry. We got no place to live. Like ants scurrying for work, for food and most of all for land.

We ain't foreign. Seven generations back Americans, and beyond that Irish, Scotch, English, German. One of our folks in the Revolution, an' they was lots of our folk in the Civil War — both sides. Americans.

They were hungry, and they were fierce. And they had hoped to find a home, and they found only hatred. Okies — the owners hated them because the owners knew they were soft and the Okies strong, that they were fed and the Okies hungry; and perhaps the owners had heard from their grandfathers how easy it is to steal land from a soft man if you are fierce and hungry and armed. The owners hated them. And in the towns, the storekeepers hated them because they had no money to spend. There is no shorter path to a storekeeper's contempt, and all his admirations are exactly opposite. The town men, little bankers, hated Okies because there was nothing to gain from them. They had nothing. And the laboring people hated Okies because a hungry man must work, and if he must work, if he has to work, the wage payer automatically gives him less for his work; and then no one can get more.

"We ain't no bums," Tom insisted. "We're lookin' for work. We'll take any kind a work."

The young man paused in fitting the brace to the valve slot. He looked in amazement at Tom. "Lookin' for work?" he said. "So you're lookin' for work. What ya think ever'body else is lookin' for? Di'monds? What you think I wore my ass down to a nub lookin' for?" He twisted the brace back and forth.

Tom looked about at the grimy tents, the junk equipment, at the old cars, the lumpy mattresses out in the sun, at the blackened cans on fire-blackened holes where the people cooked. He asked quietly, "Ain't they no work?"

"I don' know. Mus' be. Ain't no crop right here now. Grapes to pick later, an' cotton to pick later. We're a-movin' on, soon's I get these here valves groun'. Me an' my wife an' my kids. We heard they was work up north. We're shovin' north, up aroun' Salinas." . . . Tom said, "Back home some fellas come through with han'bills — orange ones. Says they need lots a people out here to work the crops."

The young man laughed. "They say they's three hundred thousan' us folks here, an' I bet ever' dam' fam'ly seen them han'bills."

"Yeah, but if they don' need folks, what'd they go to the trouble puttin' them things out for?"

"Use your head, why don'cha?"

"Yeah, but I wanta know."

"Look," the young man said. "S'pose you got a job a work, an' there's jus' one fella wants the job. You got to pay 'im what he asts. But s'pose they's a hunderd men." He put down his tool. His eyes hardened and his voice sharpened. "S'pose they's a hunderd men wants that job. S'pose them men got kids, an' them kids is hungry. S'pose a lousy dime'll buy a box a mush for them kids. S'pose a nickel'll buy at leas' somepin for them kids. An' you got a hunderd men. Jus' offer 'em a nickel — why, they'll kill each other fightin' for that nickel. Know what they was payin', las' job I had? Fifteen cents an hour. Ten hours for a dollar an' a half, an' ya can't stay on the place. Got to burn gasoline gettin' there." He was panting with anger, and his eyes blazed with hate. "That's why them han'bills was out. You can print a hell of a lot of han'bills with what ya save payin' fifteen cents an hour for fiel' work." . . .

The young man squatted on his heels. "I'll tell ya," he said quietly. "They's a big son-of-a-bitch of a peach orchard I worked in. Takes nine men all the year roun'." He paused impressively. "Takes three thousan' men for two weeks when them peaches is ripe. Got to have 'em or them peaches'll rot. So what do they do? They send out han'bills all over hell. They need three thousan', an' they get six thousan'. They get them men for what they wanta pay. If ya don' wanta take what they pay, goddamn it, they's a thousan' men waitin' for your job. So ya pick, an' ya pick, an' then she's done. Whole part a the country's peaches. All ripe together. When ya get 'em picked, ever'goddamn one is picked. There ain't another damn thing in that part a the country to do. An' then them owners don' want you there no more. Three thousan' of you. The work's done. You might steal, you might get drunk, you might jus' raise hell. An' besides, you don' look nice, livin' in ol' tents; an' it's a pretty country, but you stink it up. They don' want you aroun'. So they kick you out, they move you along. That's how it is." . . .

Tom said angrily, "Them peaches got to be picked right now, don't they? Jus' when they're ripe?"

"'Course they do."

"Well, s'pose them people got together an' says, 'Let 'em rot.' Wouldn' be long 'fore the price went up, by God!"

The young man looked up from the valves, looked sardonically at Tom. "Well, you figgered out somepin, didn' you. Come right outa your own head."

"I'm tar'd," said Tom. "Drove all night. I don't wanta start no argument. An' I'm so goddam tar'd I'd argue easy. Don' be smart with me. I'm askin' you."

The young man grinned. "I didn' mean it. You ain't been here. Folks figgered that out. An' the folks with the peach orchard figgered her out too. Look, if the folks gets together, they's a leader — got to be — fella that does the talkin'. Well, first time this fella opens his mouth they grab 'im an' stick 'im in jail. An' if they's another leader pops up, why, they stick '*im* in jail."

Tom said, "Well, a fella eats in jail anyways."

"His kids don't. How'd you like to be in an' your kids starvin' to death?"

"Yeah," said Tom slowly. "Yeah."

"An' here's another thing. Ever hear a' the blacklist?"

"What's that?"

"Well, you jus' open your trap about us folks gettin' together, an' you'll see. They take your pitcher an' send it all over. Then you can't get work nowhere. An' if you got kids ———"

Tom took off his cap and twisted it in his hands. "So we take what we can get, huh, or we starve; an' if we yelp we starve."

The young man made a sweeping circle with his hand, and his hand took in the ragged tents and the rusty cars.

Tom looked down at his mother again, where she sat scraping potatoes. And the children had drawn closer. He said, "I ain't gonna take it. Goddamn it, I an' my folks ain't no sheep. I'll kick the hell outa somebody."

"Like a cop?"

"Like anybody."

"You're nuts," said the young man. "They'll pick you right off. You got no name, no property. They'll find you in a ditch, with the blood dried on your mouth an' your nose. Be one little line in the paper — know what it'll say? 'Vagrant foun' dead.' An' that's all. You'll see a lot of them little lines, 'Vagrant foun' dead.' " . . .

THE spring is beautiful in California. Valleys in which the fruit blossoms are fragrant pink and white waters in a shallow sea. Then the first tendrils of the grapes, swelling from the old gnarled vines, cascade down to cover the trunks. The full green hills are round and soft as breasts. And on the level vegetable lands are the mile-long rows of pale green lettuce And then the leaves break out on the trees, and the petals drop from the fruit trees and carpet the earth with pink and white. The centers of the blossoms swell and grow and color: cherries and apples, peaches and pears, figs which close the flower in the fruit. All California quickens with produce, and the fruit grows heavy, and the limbs bend gradually under the fruit so that little crutches must be placed under them to support the weight. . . .

And first the cherries ripen. Cent and a half a pound. Hell, we can't pick 'em for that. Black cherries and red cherries, full and sweet, and the birds eat half of each cherry and the yellowjackets buzz into the holes the birds made. And on the ground the seeds drop and dry with black shreds hanging from them.

The purple prunes soften and sweeten. My God, we can't pick them and dry and sulphur them. We can't pay wages, no matter what wages. And the purple prunes carpet the ground. And first the skins wrinkle a little and swarms of flies come to feast, and the valley is filled with the odor of sweet decay. The meat turns dark and the crop shrivels on the ground.

And the pears grow yellow and soft. Five dollars a ton. Five dollars for forty fifty-pound boxes; trees pruned and sprayed, orchards cultivated — pick the fruit, put it in boxes, load the trucks, deliver the fruit to the cannery — forty boxes for five dollars. We can't do it. And the yellow fruit falls heavily to the ground and splashes on the ground. The yellowjackets dig into the soft meat, and there is a smell of ferment and rot.

Then the grapes — we can't make good wine. People can't buy good wine. Rip the grapes from the vines good grapes, rotten grapes, wasp-stung grapes. Press stems, press dirt and rot.

But there's mildew and formic acid in the vats.

Add sulphur and tannic acid.

The smell from the ferment is not the rich odor of wine, but the smell of decay and chemicals. . . .

The decay spreads over the State, and the sweet smell is a great sorrow on the land. Men who can graft the trees and make the seed fertile and big can find no way to let the hungry people eat their produce. Men who have created new fruits in the world cannot create a system whereby their fruits may be eaten. And the failure hangs over the State like a great sorrow.

The works of the roots of the vines, of the trees, must be destroyed to keep up the price, and this is the saddest, bitterest thing of all. Carloads of oranges dumped on the ground. The people came for miles to take the fruit, but this could not be. How would they buy oranges at twenty cents a dozen if they could drive out and pick them up? And men with hoses squirt kerosene on the oranges, and they are angry at the crime, angry at the people who have come to take the fruit. A million people hungry, needing the fruit—and kerosene sprayed over the golden mountains.

And the smell of rot fills the country.

Burn coffee for fuel in the ships. Burn corn to keep warm, it makes a hot fire. Dump potatoes in the rivers and place guards along the banks to keep the hungry people from fishing them out. Slaughter the pigs and bury them, and let the putrescence drip down into the earth.

There is a crime here that goes beyond denunciation. There is a sorrow here that weeping cannot symbolize. There is a failure here that topples all our success. The fertile earth, the straight tree rows, the sturdy trunks, and the ripe fruit. And children dying of pellagra must die because a profit cannot be taken from an orange. And coroners must fill in the certificates —died of malnutrition—because the food must rot, must be forced to rot.

The people come with nets to fish for potatoes in the river, and the guards hold them back; they come in rattling cars to get the dumped oranges, but the kerosene is sprayed. And they stand still and watch the potatoes float by, listen to the screaming pigs being killed in a ditch and covered with quicklime, watch the mountains of oranges slop down to a putrefying ooze; and in the eyes of the people there is the failure; and in the eyes of the hungry there is a growing wrath. In the souls of the people the grapes of wrath are filling and growing heavy, growing heavy for the vintage. . . .

VIII. The Decline and Fall of Isolationism

Henry L. Stimson

WAR AN ILLEGAL THING

⟨*1932*⟩ WE "condemn recourse to war" and we "renounce it as an instrument of national policy." We "agree that the settlement or solution of all disputes or conflicts . . . shall never be sought except by pacific means." These were the essential phrases of the Kellogg-Briand Pact, which fifteen nations, including the United States, signed at Paris on August 25, 1928, and which almost every other nation in the world joined later.

Some critics dismissed this pact of peace as meaningless. An "international kiss," one sarcastic Senator called it. Others believed, however, that the pact had, or could be made to have, great significance for the future of international relations. The most influential advocate of this view was Henry L. Stimson (1867-1950).

Stimson had a remarkable career. He held one important office or another under no fewer than six Presidents — Theodore Roosevelt, William Howard Taft, Calvin Coolidge, Herbert Hoover, Franklin D. Roosevelt, and Harry S. Truman. It might be said that he also served under one other President, Woodrow Wilson, for he was a colonel of artillery in the First World War.

As Hoover's Secretary of State, Stimson faced difficult tasks at a time when the prosperity and peace of the 1920's were giving way to the depression and disorder of the 1930's. The most serious violence occurred in Manchuria, which was overrun by Japanese troops (1931-1932). In an effort to arouse world opinion against the Japanese action, Stimson invoked the Kellogg-Briand Pact (as well as the Nine-Power Pact of 1922) and announced that the United States would refuse to recognize territorial or other changes made in violation of its treaty rights. His nonrecognition policy became known as the Stimson Doctrine. On August 8, 1932, he elaborated upon the significance of the pact, as he viewed the matter, in an address he delivered before the Council on Foreign Relations in New York. In this speech he would have gone even farther in committing the United States to resistance against aggression if President Hoover, more devoted than he to old-fashioned neutrality, had not censored three pages of the manuscript.

By his interpretation of the Kellogg-Briand Pact, Stimson provided an authoritative basis for the concept of "collective security" — the idea that the United States should combine with other "peace-loving" nations to prevent or punish aggressive war. He also provided a basis for much of the legal thinking behind the trials of Nazi leaders at Nuremberg after the Second World War (1946). These men were charged, among other crimes, with conspiracy to wage aggressive war in violation of the pact, which Germany too had signed. At Nuremberg the chief American prosecutor, Robert H. Jackson (1892-1954), declared that unless the pact altered the legal status of wars of aggression, it had no meaning at all. Then Jackson quoted Stimson to show that the pact had, indeed, made a change. The speech of 1932, from which Jackson quoted, follows.

THE PACT OF PARIS:
THREE YEARS OF DEVELOPMENT

FOUR YEARS AGO the United States joined with France in the initiation of the Pact of Paris—the so-called Briand-Kellogg Pact for the Renunciation of War. A year later, in 1929, the Pact became formally effective, and it has now been adhered to by sixty-two nations. Scarcely had its ratification been announced on July 24, 1929, when it became subjected to the first of a series of difficult challenges which are still going on. In the defense of the Pact in these tests the American Government has been a leader. I believe it would be appropriate, in the light of this three years' history, to take stock now of what the Pact is, the direction in which it is developing, and the part which we may hope that it eventually will play in the affairs of the world.

Events have been moving so rapidly since the World War, and we have been so close to them, that it is difficult to obtain an adequate perspective. I think, therefore, that it would be well to summarize briefly the background out of which this great treaty came and against which it must be judged.

Prior to the World War many men had had visions of a warless world and had made efforts to accomplish the abolition of war, but these efforts had never resulted in any very general or effective combinations of nations directed towards that end. During the centuries which had elapsed since the beginnings of international law, a large part of that law had been a development of principles based upon the existence of war. The existence and legality of war were to a large extent the central facts out of which these legal principles grew and on which they rested. Thus the development of the doctrine of neutrality was predicated upon the duty of a neutral to maintain impartiality between two belligerents. This further implies that each belligerent has equal rights and is owed equal duties by the neutral. It implies that the war between them is a legal situation out of which these rights and obligations grow. Therefore, it is contrary to this aspect of international law for the neutral to take sides between belligerents or to pass a moral judgment upon the rightfulness or wrongfulness of the cause of either—at least to the extent of translating such a judgement into action. So long as a neutral exercised this strict impartiality, international law afforded to him, his commerce, and his property, certain rights of protection. And during the generations which preceded the World War much of the growth of international humanitarianism was associated with attempts, not to abolish war but to narrow and confine its destructive effects by the development of these doctrines of neutrality. Their chief purpose was to produce oases of safety for life and property in a world which still recognized and legalized the destruction of human life and property as one of the regular methods for the settlement of international controversies and the maintenance of international policy.

The mechanical inventions of the century preceding the World War, and the revolutionary changes in industrial and social organization by which they were accompanied, have, however, produced inevitable effects upon the concept of war which I have described. Communities and nations became less self-contained and more interdependent; the populations of industrialized states became much larger and more dependent for their food supplies upon far distant sources; the civilized world thus became very much vulnerable to war. On the other hand, with these mechanical advances modern armies became more easily transportable and therefore larger and were armed with far more destructive weapons. By these changes on either side the inconsistency of war with normal life became sharper and more acute; the destructiveness of war to civilization became more emphatic; the abnormality of war became more apparent. The laws of neutrality became increasingly ineffective to prevent even strangers to the original quarrel from being drawn into the general conflict.

Finally there came the World War, dragging into its maelstrom almost the entire civilized world; tangible proof was given of the impossibility of confining modern war within any narrow limits; and it became evident to the most casual observer that if this evolution were permitted to continue, war, perhaps the next war, would drag down and utterly destroy our civilization.

Before this war was over it began to be called "a war to end war," and at the Peace Conference at Versailles the victorious nations entered into a covenant which sought to reduce the possibility of war to its lowest terms. The League of Nations Covenant did not undertake entirely to proscribe wars between nations. It left unrestricted a zone in which such wars might occur without reprobation. Furthermore, it provided under certain circumstances for the use of force by the community of nations against a wrongdoer as a sanction. It created a community group of nations pledged to restrict war and equipped with machinery for that purpose. Some of this machinery, notably article II, which provides, on a threat of war, for the calling of a conference for purposes of conciliation, has on several occasions proved a valuable influence in the prevention of war. Another important and beneficent result of the League organization has been the regular conferences which are held between the representatives of the different nations. These discussions have often proved to be effective agencies for the settlement of controversies and thus for war prevention. By them there also has been developed, particularly among the nations of Europe, a community spirit which can be evoked to prevent war. In all of these ways there has been produced the beginning of a group sentiment which is wholly at variance with some of the old doctrines in respect to war.

Nine years later, in 1928, came the still more sweeping step of the Pact of Paris, the Briand-Kellogg Treaty. In this treaty substantially all the nations of the world have united in a covenant in which they renounce war altogether as an instrument of national policy in their relations with one another and have agreed that the settlement of all disputes or conflicts of whatever nature among them should never be sought except by pacific means.

The change of attitude on the part of world public opinion toward former customs and doctrines, which is evidenced by these two treaties, is so revolutionary that it is not surprising that the progress has outstripped the landmarks and orientation of many observers. The treaties signalize a revolution in human thought, but they are not the result of impulse or thoughtless sentiment. At bottom they are the growth of necessity, the product of a consciousness that unless some such step were taken modern civilization might be doomed. Under its present organization the world simply could not go on recognizing war, with its constantly growing destructiveness, as one of the normal instrumentalities of human life. Human organization has become too complex, too fragile, to be subjected to the hazards of the new agencies of destruction turned loose under the sanction of international law. So the entire central point from which the problem was viewed was changed. War between nations was renounced by the signatories of the Briand-Kellogg Pact. This means that it has become illegal throughout practically the entire world. It is no longer to be the source and subject of rights. It is no longer to be the principle around which the duties, the conduct, and the rights of nations revolve. It is an illegal thing. Hereafter when two nations engage in armed conflict either one or both of them must be wrongdoers—violators of the general treaty. We no longer draw a circle about them and treat them with the punctilios of the duelist's code. Instead we denounce them as lawbreakers.

By that very act we have made obsolete many legal precedents and have given the legal profession the task of reëxamining many of its codes and treatises.

The language of the Briand-Kellogg Treaty and the contemporaneous statements of its founders make its purpose clear. Some of its critics have asserted that the Pact was really not a treaty at all; that it was not intended to confer rights and impose liabilities; that it was a mere group of unilateral statements made by the signatories, declaring a pious purpose on the part of each, of which purpose that signatory was to be the sole judge and executor, and for a violation of which no other signatory could call him to account.

If such an interpretation were correct, it would reduce the Pact to a mere gesture. If its promises conferred no rights as between the members of the community of signatories, it would be a sham. It would be worse than a nullity, for its failure would carry down the faith of the world in other efforts for peace.

But such critics are wrong. There is nothing in the language of the Pact nor in its contemporaneous history to justify any such an interpretation. On its face it is a treaty containing definite promises. In its preamble it expressly refers to the "benefits furnished by this treaty," and states that any signatory power violating its promise shall be denied those benefits. The correspondence of the framers of the treaty shows that they intended it to be a treaty which would confer benefits, which might be lost by a violation thereof. During the period when the treaty was under negotiation, Mr. Kellogg declared in a public address, made before this very body on March 15, 1928: "If war is to be abolished it must be through the conclusion of a specific treaty solemnly binding the parties not to resort to war with one another. It cannot be abolished by a mere declaration in the preamble of a treaty." In drafting the treaty Mr. Kellogg rightly and tenaciously fought for a clear, terse prohibition free from any detailed definitions or reservations. In his own words, he sought "a treaty so simple and unconditional that the people of all nations could understand it, a declaration which could be a rallying point for world sentiment, a foundation on which to build a world peace." Any other course would have opened the door to technicalities and destructive limitations.

As it stands, the only limitation to the broad convenant against war is the right of self-defense. This right is so inherent and universal that it was not deemed necessary even to insert it expressly in the treaty. It is also so well understood that it does not weaken the treaty. It exists in the case of the individual under domestic law, as well as in the case of the nation and its citizens under the law of nations. Its limits have been clearly defined by countless precedents. A nation which sought to mask imperialistic policy under the guise of the defense of its nationals would soon be unmasked.

It could not long hope to confuse or mislead public opinion on a subject so well understood or in a world in which facts can be so easily ascertained as they can be under the journalistic conditions of today.

Again, the Briand-Kellogg Pact provides for no sanctions of force. It does not require any signatory to intervene with measures of force in case the Pact is violated. Instead it rests upon the sanction of public opinion, which can be made one of the most potent sanctions in the world. Any other course, through the possibility of entangling the signatories in international politics, would have confused the broad and simple aim of the treaty and prevented the development of that public opinion upon which it most surely relies. Its efficacy depends upon the will of the people of the world to make it effective. If they desire to make it effective, it will be irresistible. Those critics who scoff at it have not accurately appraised the evolution in world opinion since the World War.

From the day of its ratification on July 24, 1929, it has been the determined aim of the American Government to make this sanction of public opinion effective and to insure that the Pact of Paris should become a living force in the world. We have recognized the hopes which it represented. We have resolved that they should not be disappointed. We have recognized that its effectiveness depends upon the cultivation of the mutual fidelity and good faith of the group of nations which has become its signatories, and which comprise virtually all of the nations of the world. We have been determined that the new order represented by this great treaty shall not fail.

In October 1929 President Hoover joined with Mr. Ramsay MacDonald, the Prime Minister of Great Britain, in a joint statement at the Rapidan in which they declared: "Both our Governments resolve to accept the Peace Pact not only as a declaration of good intentions, but as a positive obligation to direct national policy in accordance with its pledge." That declaration marked an epoch.

In the summer of 1929 hostilities threatened between Russia and China in northern Manchuria. Both nations were signatories of the Pact. It was the most difficult portion of the world in which such a challenge to this treaty could have occurred. Yet we at once took steps to organize public opinion in favor of peace. We communicated with the Governments of Great Britain, Japan, France, Italy and Germany, and the attention of the Governments of Russia and China was formally called to their obligations under the Treaty. Later during the same autumn, when hostilities actually broke out and military forces of Russia had crossed the Manchurian boundary and attacked the forces of China, our Government communicated with all the signatories of the Pact, suggesting that they urge upon Russia and China a peaceful solution of the controversy between them. Thirty-seven of these nations associated themselves with our action or signified their approval of our attitude. Although the aspect of the controversy had been extremely threatening and the forces of Russia had penetrated nearly a hundred miles within the boundaries of China, the restoration of the *status quo ante* was accepted by both parties and the invading forces were promptly withdrawn.

Two years later, in September 1931, hostilities broke out between the armed forces of Japan and China in the same quarter of the world, Manchuria, and the situation was brought to the attention of the Council of the League of Nations, which happened to be then in session at Geneva. Our Government was invited to confer as to the bearing of the Pact of Paris upon the controversy. We promptly accepted the invitation, designating a representative to meet with the Council for that purpose; and the attention of the two disputants was called to their obligaions under the Pact by France, Great Britain, Germany, Italy, Spain, Norway and the United States — those nations, other than the United States, being members of the Council then in session.

The hostilities between Japanese and Chinese armed forces continued and protracted efforts towards conciliation were made by the Council of the League, which had taken jurisdiction of the matter. The American Government maintained its attitude of sympathetic coöperation with the efforts of the Council and acting independently through the diplomatic channels endeavored to reënforce the Council's efforts at conciliation. Finally, when in spite of these efforts Japan had occupied all of Manchuria, the American Government formally notified both that country and China, on January 7, 1932, that it would not recognize any situation, treaty, or agreement which might be brought about by means contrary to the covenant and obligations of the Pact of Paris. Subsequently, on March 11, this action of the American Government was endorsed by the Assembly of the League of Nations, at a meeting in which fifty nations were represented. On that occasion, under circumstances of the utmost formality and solemnity, a resolution was adopted, unanimously, Japan alone refraining from voting, in which the Assembly declared that, "it is incumbent upon the members of the League of Nations not to recognize any situation, treaty or agreement which may be brought about by means contrary to the Covenant of the League of Nations or to the Pact of Paris."

These successive steps cannot be adequately appraised unless they are measured in the light of the vital change of point of view which I have described in the opening of this address. They were the acts of nations which were bound together by a new viewpoint towards war, as well as by covenants which made that viewpoint a reality. Except for this new viewpoint and these new covenants, these transactions in far-off Manchuria, under the rules of international law theretofore obtaining, might not have been deemed the concern of the United States and these fifty other nations. Under the former concepts of international law when a conflict occurred, it was usually deemed the concern only of the parties to the conflict. The others could only exercise and express a strict neutrality alike towards the injured and the aggressor. If they took any action or even expressed an opinion, it was likely to be deemed a hostile act towards the nation against which it was directed. The direct individual interest which every nation has in preventing a war had not yet been fully realized, nor had that interest been given legal recognition. But now under the covenants of the Briand-Kellogg Pact such a conflict becomes of legal concern to everybody connected with the Treaty. All of the steps taken to enforce the treaty must be judged by this new situation. As was said by M. Briand, quoting the words of President Coolidge: "An act of war in any part of the world is an act that injures the interests of my country." The world has learned that great lesson and the execution of the Briand-Kellogg Treaty codified it.

Thus the power of the Briand-Kellogg Treaty cannot be adequately appraised unless it is assumed that behind it rests the combined weight of the opinion of the entire world united by a deliberate covenant which gives to each nation the right to express its moral judgment. When the American Government took the responsibility of sending its note of January 7 last, it was a pioneer. It was appealing to a new common sentiment and to the provisions of a Treaty as yet untested. Its own refusal to recognize the fruits of aggression might be of comparatively little moment to an aggressor. But when the entire group of civilized nations took their stand beside the position of the American Government, the situation was revealed in its true sense. Moral disapproval, when it becomes the disapproval of the whole world, takes on a significance hitherto unknown in international law. For never before has international opinion been so organized and mobilized.

Another consequence which follows this development of the Briand-Kellogg Treaty, which I have been describing, is that consultation between the signatories of the Pact when faced with the threat of its violation becomes inevitable. Any effective invocation of the power of world opinion involves discussion and consulation. As long as the signatories of the Pact of Paris support the policy which the American Government has endeavored to establish during the past three years of arousing a united and living spirit of public opinion as a sanction to the Pact, as long as this course is adopted and endorsed by the great nations of the world who are signatories of that Treaty, consultations will take place as an incident to the unification of that opinion. The course which was followed in the Sino-Japanese controversy last winter conclusively proves that fact. The moment a situation arose which threatened the effectiveness of this Treaty, which the peoples of the world have come to regard as so vital to the protection of their interests, practically all the nations consulted in an effort to make effective the great peaceful purposes of that Treaty.

That the Pact thus necessarily carries with it the implication of consultation has perhaps not yet been fully appreciated by its well-wishers who have been so anxious that it be implemented by a formal provision for consultation. But with the clarification which has been given to its significance by the developments of the last three years, and the vitality with which it has been imbued by the positive construction put upon it, the misgivings of these well-wishers should be put at rest. That the American people subscribe to this view is made clear by the fact that each of the platforms recently adopted by the two great party conventions at Chicago contains a plank endorsing the principle of consultation.

I believe that this view of the Briand-Kellogg Treaty which I have been discussing will become one of the great and permanent policies of our nation. It is founded upon conceptions of law and ideals of peace which are among our most cherished faiths. It is a policy which combines the readiness to coöperate for peace and justice in the world, which Americans have always manifested, while at the same time it preserves the independence of judgment and the flexibility of action upon which we have always insisted. I believe that this policy must strike a chord of sympathy in the conscience of other nations. We all feel that the dreadful lessons taught by the World War must not be forgotten. The determination to abolish war which emerged from that calamity must not be relaxed. These aspirations of the world are expressed in this great Treaty. It is only by continued vigilance that it can be built into an effective living reality. The American people are serious in their support and evaluation of the Treaty. They will not fail to do their share in this endeavor.

Albert Einstein

A CRUCIAL DECISION

✦{*1939*}✦ THE tremendous significance of atomic weapons in the modern world makes obvious the importance of the following document, a simple letter written to Franklin D. Roosevelt on the eve of World War II by a great scientist. The actions suggested by Albert Einstein (1879-1955) were not immediately taken. Despite his great prestige and his obvious competence in a field the development of which his genius had made possible, the great cost and the almost inconceivable immensity of the forces involved made it difficult for the President to grasp what had to be done. However, some two months later, another scientist named Alexander Sachs managed to convince him that atomic weapons of hitherto undreamt of power could be constructed, and that the Germans — now fully launched upon World War II — were actively working to develop them. Roosevelt then moved with vigor and decisiveness. Soon the Manhattan Project was under way. "Because Roosevelt," writes his biographer, James M. Burns, "[was] willing to gamble hundreds of millions of dollars against the unknown, the project went forward to the awful climax of Hiroshima."

LETTER TO PRESIDENT ROOSEVELT

Albert Einstein
Old Grove Rd.
Nassau Point
Peconic, Long Island

August 2nd, 1939

F. D. Roosevelt,
President of the United States,
White House
Washington, D. C.

Sir:

Some recent work by E. Fermi and L. Szilard, which has been communicated to me in manuscript, leads me to expect that the element uranium may be turned into a new and important source of energy in the immediate future. Certain aspects of the situation which has arisen seem to call for watchfulness and, if necessary, quick action on the part of the Administration. I believe therefore that it is my duty to bring to your attention the following facts and recommendations:

In the course of the last four months it has been made probable — through the work of Joliot in France as well as Fermi and Szilard in America — that it may become possible to set up a nuclear chain reaction in a large mass of uranium, by which vast amounts of power and large quantities of new radium-like elements would be generated. Now it appears almost certain that this could be achieved in the immediate future.

This new phenomenon would also lead to the construction of bombs, and it is conceivable — though much less certain —that extremely powerful bombs of a new type may thus be constructed. A single bomb of this type, carried by boat and exploded in a port, might very well destroy the whole port together with some of the surrounding territory. However, such bombs might very well prove to be too heavy for transportation by air.

The United States has only very poor ores of uranium in moderate quantities. There is some good ore in Canada and the former Czechoslovakia, while the most important source of uranium is Belgian Congo.

In view of this situation you may think it desirable to have some permanent contact maintained between the Administration and the group of physicists working on chain reactions in America. One possible way of achieving this might be for you to entrust with this task a person who has your confidence and who could perhaps serve in an inofficial capacity. His task might comprise the following:

a) to approach Government Departments, keep them informed of the further development, and put forward recommendations for Government action, giving particular attention to the problem of securing a supply of uranium ore for the United States;

b) to speed up the experimental work, which is at present being carried on within the limits of the budgets of University laboratories, by providing funds, if such funds be required, through his contacts with private persons who are willing to make contributions for this cause, and perhaps also by obtaining the co-operation of industrial laboratories which have the necessary equipment.

I understand that Germany has actually stopped the sale of uranium from the Czechoslovakian mines which she has taken over. That she should have taken such early action might perhaps be understood on the ground that the son of the German Under-Secretary of State, von Weizsäcker, is attached to the Kaiser-Wilhelm-Institut in Berlin where some of the American work on uranium is now being repeated.

Your very truly,
[*signed*] ALBERT EINSTEIN

Franklin D. Roosevelt
AID TO BRITAIN

1940, 1941 IN THE period between the two World Wars it was official American policy to steer clear of all foreign conflicts. The Neutrality Act of 1937, for example, forbade the shipment of arms or even the lending of money to either side in any international or civil war. However, after the outbreak of World War II and particularly after the fall of France, it became obvious to President Roosevelt (1882-1945) that the national interest called for active aid to the foes of Nazism. Nevertheless, public opinion, while divided, seemed more concerned with keeping out of the conflict than with helping the British and their allies. So strong was the anti-war feeling that in the closing days of his 1940 election campaign against Wendell Willkie (1892-1944), Roosevelt felt compelled to assure the voters: "I have said this before, but I shall say it again and again and again: Your boys are not going to be sent into any foreign wars."

But after the election, responding to a frank letter from Prime Minister Winston Churchill (1871-1965) pointing out that England had nearly exhausted her supply of dollars for the purchase of arms and was in danger of being strangled by German sub-warfare, Roosevelt decided upon the bold expedient of the "lend-lease" program. His fireside chat of December 29, 1940, one of the most important of his career, was his way of explaining the need for such a program to the American people. The talk shows Roosevelt at his best: clear, calm, frank, and sensible, but also inspiring.

Then, encouraged by the immediate and strongly favorable public reaction to the fireside chat, Roosevelt presented his "lend-lease" plan to Congress, in his annual message on January 6, 1941. That document, which included the so-called "Four Freedoms," completed the conversion of public opinion. Although the Lend-Lease Bill was debated hotly for some two months it finally passed both Houses of Congress with handsome majorities. Thereafter it could be assumed that the United States was committed to all-out aid to England. While American soldiers had not yet been committed to the battle, it is fair to say that active United States participation in World War II began with the passage of the Lend-Lease Act.

FIRESIDE CHAT ON NATIONAL SECURITY

(December 29, 1940)

My friends:

THIS IS not a fireside chat on war. It is a talk on national security; because the nub of the whole purpose of your President is to keep you now, and your children later, and your grandchildren much later, out of a last-ditch war for the preservation of American independence and all the things that American independence means to you and to me and to ours.

Tonight, in the presence of a world crisis, my mind goes back eight years to a night in the midst of a domestic crisis. It was a time when the wheels of American industry were grinding to a full stop, when the whole banking system of our country had ceased to function.

I well remember that while I sat in my study in the White House, preparing to talk with the people of the United States, I had before my eyes the picture of all those Americans with whom I was talking. I saw the workmen in the mills, the mines, the factories; the girl behind the counter; the small shopkeeper; the farmer doing his spring plowing; the widows and the old men wondering about their life's savings.

I tried to convey to the great mass of American people what the banking crisis meant to them in their daily lives.

Tonight, I want to do the same thing, with the same people, in this new crisis which faces America.

We met the issues of 1933 with courage and realism.

We face this new crisis — this new threat to the security of our nation — with the same courage and realism.

Never before since Jamestown and Plymouth Rock has our American civilization been in such danger as now.

For, on September 27, 1940, by an agreement signed in Berlin, three powerful nations, two in Europe and one in Asia, joined themselves together in the threat that if the United States of America interfered with or blocked the expansion program of these three nations — a program aimed at world control — they would unite in ultimate action against the United States.

The Nazi masters of Germany have made it clear that they intend not only to dominate all life and thought in their own country, but also to enslave the whole of Europe, and then to use the resources of Europe to dominate the rest of the world.

It was only three weeks ago their leader stated this: "There are two worlds that stand opposed to each other." And then in defiant reply to his opponents, he said this: "Others are correct when they say: With this world we cannot ever reconcile ourselves. . . . I can beat any other power in the world." So said the leader of the Nazis.

In other words, the Axis not merely admits but *proclaims* that there can be no ultimate peace between their philosophy of government and our philosophy of government.

In view of the nature of this undeniable threat, it can be asserted, properly and categorically, that the United States has no right or reason to encourage talk of peace, until the day shall come when there is a clear intention on the part of the aggressor nations to abandon all thought of dominating or conquering the world.

At this moment, the forces of the states that are leagued against all peoples who live in freedom, are being held away from our shores. The Germans and the Italians are being blocked on the other side of the Atlantic by the British, and by the Greeks, and by thousands of soldiers and sailors who were able to escape from subjugated countries. In Asia, the Japanese are being engaged by the Chinese nation in another great defense.

In the Pacific Ocean is our fleet.

Some of our people like to believe that wars in Europe and in Asia are of no concern to us. But it is a matter of most vital concern to us that European and Asiatic war-makers should not gain control of the oceans which lead to this hemisphere.

One hundred and seventeen years ago the Monroe Doctrine was conceived by our Government as a measure of defense in the face of a threat against this hemisphere by an alliance in Continental Europe. Thereafter, we stood on guard in the Atlantic, with the British as neighbors. There was no treaty. There was no "unwritten agreement."

And yet, there was the feeling, proven correct by history, that we as neighbors could settle any disputes in peaceful fashion. The fact is that during the whole of this time the Western Hemisphere has remained free from aggression from Europe or from Asia.

Does anyone seriously believe that we need to fear attack anywhere in the Americas while a free Britain remains our most powerful naval neighbor in the Atlantic? Does anyone seriously believe, on the other hand, that we could rest easy if the Axis powers were our neighbors there?

If Great Britain goes down, the Axis powers will control the continents of Europe, Asia, Africa, Australia, and the high seas — and they will be in a position to bring enormous military and naval resources against this hemisphere. It is no exaggeration to say that all of us, in all the Americas, would be living at the point of a gun — a gun loaded with explosive bullets, economic as well as military.

We should enter upon a new and terrible era in which the whole world, our hemisphere included, would be run by threats of brute force. To survive in such a world, we would have to convert ourselves permanently into a militaristic power on the basis of war economy.

Some of us like to believe that even if Great Britain falls, we are still safe, because of the broad expanse of the Atlantic and of the Pacific.

But the width of those oceans is not what it was in the days of clipper ships. At one point between Africa and Brazil the distance is less than from Washington to Denver, Colorado — five hours for the latest type of bomber. And at the North end of the Pacific Ocean America and Asia almost touch each other.

Even today we have planes that could fly from the British Isles to New England and back again without refueling. And remember that the range of the modern bomber is ever being increased.

During the past week many people in all parts of the nation have told me what they wanted me to say tonight. Almost all of them expressed a courageous desire to hear the plain truth about the gravity of the situation. One telegram, however, expressed the attitude of the small minority who want to see no evil and hear no evil, even though they know in their hearts that evil exists. That telegram begged me not to tell again of the ease with which our American cities could be bombed by any hostile power which had gained bases in this Western Hemisphere. The gist of that telegram was: "Please, Mr. President, don't frighten us by telling us the facts."

Frankly and definitely there is danger ahead — danger against which we must prepare. But we well know that we cannot escape danger, or the fear of danger, by crawling into a bed and pulling the covers over our heads.

Some nations of Europe were bound by solemn non-intervention pacts with Germany. Other nations were assured by Germany that they need *never* fear invasion. Non-intervention pact or not, the fact remains that they *were* attacked, overrun and thrown into the modern form of slavery at an hour's notice, or even without any notice at all. As an exiled leader of one of these nations said to me the other day — "The notice was a minus quantity. It was given to my Government two hours after German troops had poured into my country in a hundred places."

The fate of these nations tells us what it means to live at the point of a Nazi gun.

The Nazis have justified such actions by various pious frauds. One of these frauds is the claim that they are occupying a nation for the purpose of "restoring order." Another is that they are occupying or controlling a nation on the excuse that they are "protecting it" against the aggression of somebody else.

For example, Germany has said that she was occupying Belgium to save the Belgians from the British. Would she then hesitate to say to any South American country, "We are occupying you to protect you from aggression by the United States"?

Belgium today is being used as an invasion base against Britain, now fighting for its life. Any South American country, in Nazi hands, would always constitute a jumping-off place for German attack on any of the other Republics of this hemisphere.

Analyze for yourselves the future of two other places nearer to Germany if the Nazis won. Could Ireland hold out? Would Irish freedom be permitted as an amazing pet exception in an unfree world? Or the Islands of the Azores which still fly the flag of Portugal after five centuries? You and I think of Hawaii as an outpost of defense in the Pacific. And yet, the Azores are closer to our shores in the Atlantic than Hawaii is on the other side.

There are those who say that the Axis powers would never have any desire to attack the Western Hemisphere. That is the same dangerous form of wishful thinking which has destroyed the powers of resistance of so many conquered peoples. The plain facts are that the Nazis have proclaimed, time and again, that all other races are their inferiors and therefore subject to their orders. And most important of all, the vast resources and wealth of this American Hemisphere constitute the most tempting loot in all the round world.

Let us no longer blind ourselves to the undeniable fact that the evil forces which have crushed and undermined and corrupted so many others are already within our own gates. Your Government knows much about them and every day is ferreting them out.

Their secret emissaries are active in our own and in neighboring countries. They seek to stir up suspicion and dissension to cause internal strife. They try to turn capital against labor, and vice versa. They try to reawaken long slumbering racial and religious enmities which should have no place in this country. They are active in every group that promotes intolerance. They exploit for their own ends our natural abhorrence of war. These trouble-breeders have but one purpose. It is to divide our people into hostile groups and to destroy our unity and shatter our will to defend ourselves.

There are also American citizens, many of them in high places, who, unwittingly in most cases, are aiding and abetting the work of these agents. I do not charge these American citizens with being foreign agents. But I do charge them with doing exactly the kind of work that the dictators want done in the United States.

These people not only believe that we can save our skins by shutting our eyes to the fate of other nations. Some of them go much further than that. They say that we can and should become the friends and even the partners of the Axis powers. Some of them even suggest that we should imitate the methods of the dictatorships. Americans never can and never will do that.

The experience of the past two years has proven beyond doubt that no nation can appease the Nazis. No man can tame a tiger into a kitten by stroking it. There can be no appeasement with ruthlessness. There can be no reasoning with an incendiary bomb. We know now that a nation can have peace with the Nazis only at the price of total surrender.

Even the people of Italy have been forced to become accomplices of the Nazis; but at this moment they do not know how soon they will be embraced to death by their allies.

The American appeasers ignore the warning to be found in the fate of Austria, Czechoslovakia, Poland, Norway, Belgium, the Netherlands,

Denmark, and France. They tell you that the Axis powers are going to win anyway; that all this bloodshed in the world could be saved; that the United States might just as well throw its influence into the scale of a dictated peace, and get the best out of it that we can.

They called it a "negotiated peace." Nonsense! Is it a negotiated peace if a gang of outlaws surrounds your community and on threat of extermination makes you pay tribute to save your own skins?

Such a dictated peace would be no peace at all. It would be only another armistice, lending to the most gigantic armament race and the most devastating trade wars in all history. And in these contests the Americas would offer the only real resistance to the Axis powers.

With all their vaunted efficiency, with all their parade of pious purpose in this war, there are still in their background the concentration camp and the servants of God in chains.

The history of recent years proves that shootings and chains and concentration camps are not simply the transient tools but the very altars of modern dictatorships. They may talk of a "new order" in the world, but what they have in mind is only a revival of the oldest and the worst tyranny. In that there is no liberty, no religion, no hope.

The proposed "new order" is the very opposite of a United States of Europe or a United States of Asia. It is not a Government based upon the consent of the governed. It is not a union of ordinary, self-respecting men and women to protect themselves and their freedom and their dignity from oppression. It is an unholy alliance of power and pelf to dominate and enslave the human race.

The British people and their allies today are conducting an active war against this unholy alliance. Our own future security is greatly dependent on the outcome of that fight. Our ability to "keep out of war" is going to be affected by that outcome.

Thinking in terms of today and tomorrow, I make the direct statement to the American people that there is far less chance of the United States getting into war, if we do all we can now to support the nations defending themselves against attack by the Axis than if we acquiesce in their defeat, submit tamely to an Axis victory, and wait our turn to be the object of attack in another war later on.

If we are to be completely honest with ourselves, we must admit that there is risk in any course we may take. But I deeply believe that the great majority of our people agree that the course I advocate involves the least risk now and the greatest hope for world peace in the future.

The people of Europe who are defending themselves do not ask us to do their fighting. They ask us for the implements of war, the planes, the tanks, the guns, the freighters which will enable them to fight for their liberty and for our security. Emphatically we must get these weapons to them in sufficient volume and quickly enough, so that we and our children will be saved the agony and suffering of war which others have had to endure.

Let not the defeatists tell us that it is too late. It will never be earlier. To-morrow will be later than today.

Certain facts are self-evident.

In a military sense Great Britain and the British Empire are today the spearhead of resistance to world conquest. They are putting up a fight which will live forever in the story of human gallantry.

There is no demand for sending an American Expeditionary Force outside our own borders. There is no intention by any member of your Government to send such a force. You can, therefore, nail any talk about sending armies to Europe as deliberate untruth.

Our national policy is not directed toward war. Its sole purpose is to keep war away from our country and our people.

Democracy's fight against world conquest is being greatly aided, and must be more greatly aided, by the rearmament of the United States and by sending every ounce and every ton of munitions and supplies that we can possibly spare to help the defenders who are in the front lines. It is no more unneutral for us to do that than it is for Sweden, Russia and other nations near Germany, to send steel and ore and oil and other war materials into Germany every day in the week.

We are planning our own defense with the utmost urgency; and in its vast scale we must integrate the war needs of Britain and the other free nations which are resisting aggression.

This is not a matter of sentiment or of controversial personal opinion. It is a matter of realistic, practical military policy, based on the advice of our military experts who are in close touch with existing warfare. These military and naval experts and the members of the Congress and the Ad-ministration have a single-minded purpose — the defense of the United States.

This nation is making a great effort to produce everything that is necessary in this emergency — and with all possible speed. This great effort requires great sacrifice.

I would ask no one to defend a democracy which in turn would not defend everyone in the nation against want and privation. The strength of this nation shall not be diluted by the failure of the Government to protect the economic well-being of its citizens.

If our capacity to produce is limited by machines, it must ever be remembered that these machines are operated by the skill and the stamina of the workers. As the Government is determined to protect the rights of the workers, so the nation has a right to expect the men who man the machines will discharge their full responsibilities to the urgent needs of defense.

The worker possesses the same human dignity and is entitled to the same security of position as the engineer or the manager or the owner. For the workers provide the human power that turns out the destroyers, the airplanes and the tanks.

The nation expects our defense industries to continue operation without interruption by strikes or lock-outs. It expects and insists that management and workers will reconcile their differences by voluntary or legal means, to continue to produce the supplies that are so sorely needed.

And on the economic side of our great defense program, we are, as you know, bending every effort to maintain stability of prices and with that the stability of the cost of living.

Nine days ago I announced the setting up of a more effective organization to direct our gigantic efforts to increase the production of munitions. The appropriation of vast sums of money and a well coordinated executive direction of our defense efforts are not in themselves enough. Guns, planes, ships and many other things have to be built in the factories and arsenals of America. They have to be produced by workers and managers and engineers with the aid of machines which in turn have to be built by hundreds of thousands of workers throughout the land.

In this great work there has been splendid cooperation between the Government and industry and labor; and I am very thankful.

American industrial genius, unmatched throughout the world in the solution of production problems, has been called upon to bring its resources and its talents into action. Manufacturers of watches, farm implements, linotypes, cash registers, automobiles, sewing machines, lawn mowers and locomotives are now making fuses, bomb packing crates, telescope mounts, shells, pistols and tanks.

But all our present efforts are not enough. We must have more ships, more guns, more planes — more of everything. This can only be accomplished if we discard the notion of "business as usual." This job cannot be done merely by superimposing on the existing productive facilities the added requirements of the nation for defense.

Our defense efforts must not be blocked by those who fear the future consequences of surplus plant capacity. The possible consequences of failure of our defense efforts now are much more to be feared.

After the present needs of our defense are past, a proper handling of the country's peace-time needs will require all the new productive capacity — if not more.

No pessimistic policy about the future of America shall delay the immediate expansion of those industries essential to defense. We need them.

I want to make it clear that it is the purpose of the nation to build now with all possible speed every machine, every arsenal, every factory that we need to manufacture our defense material. We have the men — the skill — the wealth — and above all, the will.

I am confident that if and when production of consumer or luxury goods in certain industries requires the use of machines and raw materials that are essential for defense purposes, then such production must yield, and will gladly yield, to our primary and compelling purpose.

I appeal to the owners of plants — to the managers — to the workers — to our own Government employees — to put every ounce of effort into producing these munitions swiftly and without stint. With this appeal I give you the pledge that all of us who are officers of your Government will devote ourselves to the same whole-hearted extent to the great task that lies ahead.

As planes and ships and guns and shells are produced, your Government, with its defense experts, can then determine how best to use them to defend this hemisphere. The decision as to how much shall be sent abroad and how much shall remain at home must be made on the basis of our over-all military necessities.

We must be the great arsenal of democracy. For us this is an emergency as serious as war itself. We must apply ourselves to our task with the same resolution, the same sense of urgency, the same spirit of patriotism and sacrifice as we would show were we at war.

We have furnished the British great material support and we will furnish far more in the future.

There will be no "bottlenecks" in our determination to aid Great Britain. No dictator, no combination of dictators, will weaken that determination by threats of how they will construe that determination.

The British have received invaluable military support from the heroic Greek army, and from the forces of all the governments in exile. Their strength is growing. It is the strength of men and women who value their freedom more highly than they value their lives.

I believe that the Axis powers are not going to win this war. I base that belief on the latest and best information.

We have no excuse for defeatism. We have every good reason for hope

— hope for peace, hope for the defense of our civilization and for the building of a better civilization in the future.

I have the profound conviction that the American people are now determined to put forth a mightier effort than they have ever yet made to increase our production of all the implements of defense, to meet the threat to our democratic faith.

As President of the United States, I call for that national effort. I call for it in the name of this nation which we love and honor and which we are privileged and proud to serve. I call upon our people with absolute confidence that our common cause will greatly succeed.

ANNUAL MESSAGE TO CONGRESS

(January 6, 1941)

Mr. President, Mr. Speaker, Members of the Seventy-seventh Congress:

I address you, the Members of the Seventy-seventh Congress, at a moment unprecedented in the history of the Union. I use the word "unprecedented," because at no previous time has American security been as seriously threatened from without as it is today.

Since the permanent formation of our Government under the Constitution, in 1789, most of the periods of crisis in our history have related to our domestic affairs. Fortunately, only one of these — the four-year War Between the States — ever threatened our national unity. Today, thank God, one hundred and thirty million Americans, in forty-eight States, have forgotten points of the compass in our national unity. . . .

As long as the aggressor nations maintain the offensive, they — not we — will choose the time and the place and the method of their attack.

That is why the future of all the American Republics is today in serious danger.

That is why this Annual Message to the Congress is unique in our history.

That is why every member of the Executive Branch of the Government and every member of the Congress faces great responsibility and great accountability.

The need of the moment is that our actions and our policy should be devoted primarily — almost exclusively — to meeting this foreign peril. For all our domestic problems are now a part of the great emergency.

Just as our national policy in internal affairs has been based upon a decent respect for the rights and the dignity of all our fellow men within our gates, so our national policy in foreign affairs has been based on a decent respect for the rights and dignity of all nations, large and small. And the justice of morality must and will win in the end.

Our national policy is this:

First, by an impressive expression of the public will and without regard to partisanship, we are committed to all-inclusive national defense.

Second, by an impressive expression of the public will and without regard to partisanship, we are committed to full support of all those resolute peoples, everywhere, who are resisting aggression and are thereby keeping war away from our Hemisphere. By this support, we express our determination that the democratic cause shall prevail; and we strengthen the defense and the security of our own nation.

Third, by an impressive expression of the public will and without regard to partisanship, we are committed to the proposition that principles of morality and considerations for our own security will never permit us to acquiesce in a peace dictated by aggressors and sponsored by appeasers. We know that enduring peace cannot be bought at the cost of other people's freedom. . . .

New circumstances are constantly begetting new needs for our safety. I shall ask this Congress for greatly increased new appropriations and authorizations to carry on what we have begun.

I also ask this Congress for authority and for funds sufficient to manufacture additional munitions and war supplies of many kinds to be turned over to those nations which are now in actual war with aggressor nations.

Our most useful and immediate role is to act as an arsenal for them as well as for ourselves. They do not need man power, but they do need billions of dollars worth of the weapons of defense.

The time is near when they will not be able to pay for them all in ready cash. We cannot, and we will not, tell them that they must surrender, merely because of present inability to pay for the weapons which we know they must have.

I do not recommend that we make them a loan of dollars with which to pay for these weapons — a loan to be repaid in dollars.

I recommend that we make it possible for those nations to continue to obtain war materials in the United States, fitting their orders into our own program. Nearly all their matériel would, if the time ever came, be useful for our own defense.

Taking counsel of expert military and naval authorities, considering what is best for our own security, we are free to decide how much should be kept here and how much should be sent abroad to our friends who by their determined and heroic resistance are giving us time in which to make ready our own defense.

For what we send abroad, we shall be repaid within a reasonable time following the close of hostilities, in similar materials, or, at our option, in other goods of many kinds, which they can produce and which we need.

Let us say to the democracies: "We Americans are vitally concerned in your defense of freedom. We are putting forth our energies, our resources and our organizing powers to give you the strength to regain and maintain a free world. We shall send you, in ever-increasing numbers, ships, planes, tanks, guns. This is our purpose and our pledge."

In fulfillment of this purpose we will not be intimidated by the threats of dictators that they will regard as a breach of international law or as an act of war our aid to the democracies which dare to resist their aggression. Such aid is not an act of war, even if a dictator should unilaterally proclaim it so to be.

When the dictators, if the dictators, are ready to make war upon us, they will not wait for an act of war on our part. They did not wait for Norway or Belgium or the Netherlands to commit an act of war.

Their only interest is in a new one-way international law, which lacks mutuality in its observance, and, therefore, becomes an instrument of oppression.

The happiness of future generations of Americans may well depend upon how effective and how immediate we can make our aid felt. No one can tell the exact character of the emergency situations that we may be called upon to meet. The Nation's hands must not be tied when the Nation's life is in danger.

We must all prepare to make the sacrifices that the emergency — almost as serious as war itself — demands. Whatever stands in the way of speed and efficiency in defense preparations must give way to the national need.

A free nation has the right to expect full cooperation from all groups. A free nation has the right to look to the leaders of business, of labor, and of agriculture to take the lead in stimulating effort, not among other groups but within their own groups.

The best way of dealing with the few slackers or trouble makers in our midst is, first, to shame them by patriotic example, and, if that fails, to use the sovereignty of Government to save Government.

As men do not live by bread alone, they do not fight by armaments alone. Those who man our defenses, and those behind them who build our defenses, must have the stamina and the courage which come from unshakable belief in the manner of life which they are defending. The mighty action that we are calling for cannot be based on a disregard of all things worth fighting for.

The Nation takes great satisfaction and much strength from the things which have been done to make its people conscious of their individual stake in the preservation of democratic life in America. Those things have toughened the fiber of our people, have renewed their faith and strengthened their devotion to the institutions we make ready to protect.

Certainly this is no time for any of us to stop thinking about the social and economic problems which are the root cause of the social revolution which is today a supreme factor in the world.

For there is nothing mysterious about the foundations of a healthy and strong democracy. The basic things expected by our people of their political and economic systems are simple. They are:

Equality of opportunity for youth and for others.

Jobs for those who can work.

Security for those who need it.

The ending of special privilege for the few.

The preservation of civil liberties for all.

The enjoyment of the fruits of scientific progress in a wider and constantly rising standard of living.

These are the simple, basic things that must never be lost sight of in the turmoil and unbelievable complexity of our modern world. The inner and abiding strength of our economic and political systems is dependent upon the degree to which they fulfill these expectations.

Many subjects connected with our social economy call for immediate improvement.

As examples:

We should bring more citizens under the coverage of old-age pensions and unemployment insurance.

We should widen the opportunities for adequate medical care.

We should plan a better system by which persons deserving or needing gainful employment may obtain it.

I have called for personal sacrifice. I am assured of the willingness of almost all Americans to respond to that call.

A part of the sacrifice means the payment of more money in taxes. In my Budget Message I shall recommend that a greater portion of this great defense program be paid for from taxation than we are paying today. No person should try, or be allowed, to get rich out of this program;

and the principle of tax payments in accordance with ability to pay should be constantly before our eyes to guide our legislation.

If the Congress maintains these principles, the voters, putting patriotism ahead of pocketbooks, will give you their applause.

In the future days, which we seek to make secure, we look forward to a world founded upon four essential human freedoms.

The first is freedom of speech and expression — everywhere in the world.

The second is freedom of every person to worship God in his own way — everywhere in the world.

The third is freedom from want — which, translated into world terms, means economic understandings which will secure to every nation a healthy peacetime life for it inhabitants — everywhere in the world.

The fourth is freedom from fear — which, translated into world terms, means a world-wide reduction of armaments to such a point and in such a thorough fashion that no nation will be in a position to commit an act of physical aggression against any neighbor — anywhere in the world.

That is no vision of a distant millennium. It is a definite basis for a kind of world attainable in our own time and generation. That kind of world is the very antithesis of the so-called new order of tyranny which the dictators seek to create with the crash of a bomb.

To that new order we oppose the greater conception — the moral order. A good society is able to face schemes of world domination and foreign revolutions alike without fear.

Since the beginning of our American history, we have been engaged in change — in a perpetual peaceful revolution — a revolution which goes on steadily, quietly adjusting itself to changing conditions — without the concentration camp or the quick-lime in the ditch. The world order which we seek is the cooperation of free countries, working together in a friendly, civilized society.

This nation has placed its destiny in the hands and heads and hearts of its millions of free men and women; and its faith in freedom under the guidance of God. Freedom means the supremacy of human rights everywhere. Our support goes to those who struggle to gain those rights or keep them. Our strength is our unity of purpose.

To that high concept there can be no end save victory.

Wendell Willkie

INTERNATIONAL COOPERATION

◆{*1943*}◆ THE COLLAPSE of isolationism as an effective political force in the United States after World War II was probably inevitable. Revolutionary advances in transportation and communication and the development of the atomic bomb made it impossible for all but the most obtuse Americans to ignore the rest of the world, or to live in the splendid insularity of the 1880's or even in the fool's paradise variety of isolation that had been popular in the 1920's.

Inevitable or not, however, two individuals had a great deal to do with the completeness and smoothness of the massive shift in opinion that took place during and after the War. One was Senator Arthur Vandenberg (1884-1951) of Michigan, a lifelong isolationist and the most influential Republican member of Congress in matters concerning foreign relations. When President Roosevelt was able to convert him to the internationalist position, isolationism in Congress was dealt a death blow.

The second key figure was another Republican, Wendell L. Willkie (1892-1944). Franklin Delano Roosevelt (1882-1945) defeated Willkie for the Presidency in 1940, but as titular head of the Republican party during most of the War, the former utility magnate and "barefoot Wall Street lawyer" was extremely influential. Although never an isolationist, it was only after his government-sponsored trip around the world in 1942 that he launched an all out campaign for "One World." His book of that name, describing his trip, sold more than two million copies and reigned over the best-seller lists for many weeks. The impact of Vandenberg's conversion struck only the politicians; the enthusiasm and obvious sincerity of Willkie's *One World* affected the masses. Thus the way was prepared for the easy acceptance of American membership in the United Nations and for an era of active, constructive American participation in world affairs.

ONE WORLD

IN A four-engined Consolidated bomber, converted for transport service and operated by United States Army officers, I left Mitchel Field, New York, on August 26, to see what I could of the world and the war, its battle fronts, its leaders, and its people. Exactly forty-nine days later, on October 14, I landed in Minneapolis, Minnesota. I had encircled the world, not in the northern latitudes where the circumference is small, but on a route which crossed the equator twice.

I had traveled a total of 31,000 miles, which — looked at as a figure — still impresses and almost bewilders me. For the net impression of my trip was not one of distance from other peoples, but of closeness to them. If I had ever had any doubts that the world has become small and completely interdependent, this trip would have dispelled them altogether.

The extraordinary fact is that to cover this enormous distance we were in the air a total of only 160 hours. We usually flew from eight to ten hours a day when we were on the move, which means that out of the forty-nine days given to the trip, I had about thirty days on the ground for the accomplishment of the purposes in hand. The physical business of moving from one country to another, or from one continent to another, was no more arduous than the trips an American businessman may make any day of his life to carry on his business. In fact, moving about the world came to seem so easy that I promised the president of a great central Siberian republic to fly back some week end in 1945 for a day's hunting. And I expect to keep the engagement.

There are no distant points in the world any longer. I learned by this trip that the myriad millions of human beings of the Far East are as close to us as Los Angeles is to New York by the fastest trains. I cannot escape the conviction that in the future what concerns them must concern us, almost as much as the problems of the people of California concern the people of New York.

Our thinking in the future must be world-wide. . . .

In the air, between stops, an airplane gives a modern traveler a chance to map in his mind the land he is flying over. From Beirut to Lydda, to Bagdad, to Teheran, we had fairly long flights on which to compare notes and to sort out impressions. Before we left Iran for the Soviet Union, I had made up my own mind about the answers to some of the most immediate and pressing questions I had asked myself about the Middle East.

In the first place, I was convinced that all these peoples were more on our side than against us. Partly, this was simply because America was far away and not exercising any control over them. These are important reasons, by the way, for such popularity as the Germans still enjoy — in Iran, for example. In addition, America's entry into the war had convinced large numbers that whatever might be the temporary setbacks, the United Nations would eventually win. In other words, these peoples of the Middle East who have been overrun by successive conquerors since before the days of Alexander the Great have a large element of the purely practical in their thinking and an instinct for survival that leads them to pick the winning side before the conclusion becomes obvious.

In the second place, I was convinced that some sort of yeast was at work in nearly all the places I visited. Even the strictest kind of neutrality cannot keep the war from working its profound and violent changes on all the peoples who live in this region. Their lives will change more in the next ten years than they have in the last ten centuries.

In the third place, I found no automatic guarantee that these changes will be in our favor. The magic of our Western political ideas has been sharply challenged in the minds of many Moslems, many Arabs, many Jews, many Iranians. They have watched us now at close range, for almost a generation, while we have been fighting each other and ourselves and questioning the central structure of our own beliefs. Everywhere I found polite but skeptical people, who met my questions about their problems and difficulties with polite but ironic questions about our own. The maladjustments of races in America came up frequently, and I believe every government official I talked to wondered about our relations to Vichy. Arab and Jew were curious to know if our expressions of freedom meant only new and enlarged mandated areas which in the Lebanon and Syria and Palestine, rightly or wrongly, had come to mean to them a form of foreign tyranny.

Finally, everywhere I went in the Middle East I found a kind of technological backwardness along with poverty and squalor. Any American who makes this comment lays himself open, I realize, to the charge of being overconscious of bathtubs. But I understood in Jerusalem for the first time how so many other Americans have gone there with a real feeling of returning to Biblical times. The reason was that they were in truth returning to Biblical times, where little has changed in two thousand years. Modern airlines, oil pipe lines, macadam streets, or even plumbing constitute a thin veneer on the surface of a life which in essence is as simple and as hard as it was before there was any West. The only major exceptions to this one finds in the developments, industrial, agricultural, and cultural, which have been made under the supervision of the world Zionist movement or where the Arabs have, as in Bagdad, achieved a measure of self-government.

Four things, it seemed to me, these peoples need, in varying degree and in different ways. They need more education. They need more public-health work. They need more modern industry. And they need more of the social dignity and self-confidence which come from freedom and self-rule. . . .

A visitor for the first time to Russia inevitably reflects now and then upon the past. One late afternoon in Kuibyshev I found myself thinking of pre-revolutionary times. I walked alone to the edge of the steep bank on the western side of the Volga and sat on a park bench looking down at the river. The government had given us a Red Army rest home right at the river's edge. There was a biting cold already in the air, but the leaves were still on the trees. Along the bank stretched small, un-painted *dachas* — the country bungalows of which Russians are so fond — and pine trees, and there was an air of deep quiet and strength, like the great river below. Beyond the pine trees was wheat land rolling down the river to Stalingrad, where Russian soldiers were holding a mass of rubble against Nazi tanks and planes.

At the river's edge, below me, a boat had finished unloading its cargo of birch logs. The logs were stacked in a pile that must have covered several acres. With the Don Basin lost, with war industries getting every lump of coal available, this was the only fuel Russian cities would have to burn in the cold winter to come. A shepherd led a flock of sheep along the shore. In the middle of the river a tanker, loaded full, was moving slowly upstream. A young Russian soldier walked along the path behind the sheep, kicking pebbles into the river with his foot. When he took off his hat, the wind ruffled his hair to make him look even younger, and it was only then that I noticed his hat had the insignia of the NKVD, or secret police.

I thought of the pre-1917 shipbuilder who had built the resthouse behind me as a summer home. I had been told that he had been a power in the land, a tight-fisted shipowner and grain merchant who had prospered in the commerce of the Volga when the town had been called Sambara and been liquidated when it was called Kuibishev, for the Samaran revolutionist who devised the first Five-Year Plan. The house had stayed, a little less shabby than its neighbors, because the Red Army had found it useful.

I could see, it seemed to me, the entire generation of men and women except for those who escaped to other lands, and they were relatively few, who had been destroyed, the families that had been scattered, the loyalties that had been broken, the thousands who had died from war and assassination and starvation, in the name of the revolution.

The true story of that period will probably never be told in detail. For practically the whole upper and middle classes of Russia have been completely exterminated. And Russians today find the story a heroic achievement.

I had not realized before coming to Russia to what extent that is true. For I had not sufficiently taken into account, in appraising modern Russia, that it is ruled by and composed almost entirely of people whose parents had no property, no education, and only a folk heritage. That there is hardly a resident of Russia today whose lot is not as good as or better than his parents' lot was prior to the revolution. The Russian individual, like all individuals, naturally finds some good in a system that has improved his own lot, and has a tendency to forget the ruthless means by which it has been brought about. This may be difficult for an American to believe or like. But it was plainly the explanation among all sorts of people, everywhere, and it was clearly expressed during a stimulating evening I spent in Moscow when I was trying to put a group of intelligent modern Russians on the spot to defend their system.

But I had not gone to Russia to remember the past. Besides my concrete assignments for the President, I had gone determined to find an answer for myself to the actual problems posed for our generation of Americans by the simple fact that the Soviet Union, whether we like it or not, exists.

Some of these answers I believe I found, at least to my own satisfaction. I can sum up the three most important in a few sentences.

First, Russia is an effective society. It works. It has survival value. The record of Soviet resistance to Hitler has been proof enough of this to most of us, but I must admit in all frankness that I was not prepared to believe before I went to Russia what I now know about its strength as a going organization of men and women.

Second, Russia is our ally in this war. The Russians, more sorely tested by Hitler's might even than the British, have met the test magnificently. Their hatred of Fascism and the Nazi system is real and deep and bitter. And this hatred makes them determined to eliminate Hitler and exterminate the Nazi blight from Europe and the world.

Third, we must work with Russia after the war. At least it seems to me and there can be no continued peace unless we learn to do so.

Those conclusions were reinforced by what I saw and heard in various parts of the Soviet Union. I saw one portion of the Russian front, close enough to know something at first hand of what the Red Army has done. I saw a good many of the factories behind the front, where the Soviet workers have fooled too many of our experts by keeping up a steady flow of supplies to the fighting men. And I saw collective farms. Behind the factories and the farms, I saw and talked with the Soviet newspapermen and writers who have given all Russians the strangely exalted feeling of being in a crusade. Behind the journalists, I saw the Kremlin, having talked twice at great length with Mr. Stalin, and observed something of how power is really exercised under the dictatorship of the proletariat. Finally, behind all these, I saw the Russian people from one end of Russia to the other, and if my sampling of the 200,000,000 was absurdly small, it had the advantage of being chosen entirely by chance. . . .

On the personal side Stalin is a simple man, with no affectations or poses. He does not seek to impress by any artificial mannerisms. His sense of humor is a robust one, and he laughs readily at unsubtle jokes and repartee. Once I was telling him of the Soviet schools and libraries I had seen — how good they seemed to me. And I added, "But if you continue to educate the Russian people, Mr. Stalin, the first thing you know you'll educate yourself out of a job."

He threw his head back and laughed and laughed. Nothing I said to him, or heard anyone else say to him, through two long evenings, seemed to amuse him as much.

Strange as it may seem, Stalin dresses in light pastel shades. His well-known tunic is of finely woven material and is apt to be a soft green or a delicate pink; his trousers a light-tannish yellow or blue. His boots are black and highly polished. Ordinary social pleasantries bother him a little. As I was leaving him after my first talk, I expressed appreciation of the time he had given me, the honor he conferred in talking so candidly. A little embarrassed, he said:

"Mr. Willkie, you know I grew up a Georgian peasant. I am unschooled in pretty talk. All I can say is I like you very much."

Inevitably, Stalin's simple ways have set a fashion of a kind for other soviet leaders. Especially in Moscow and in Kuibishev, there is an absence of flamboyance about Russian leaders that is remarkable. They all dress simply. They talk little and listen well. A surprising number of them are young, in their thirties. It would be my guess, which I could not prove or document, that Stalin likes a pretty heavy turnover of young people in his immediate entourage in the Kremlin. It is his way, I think, of keeping his ear to the ground . . .

Since I have returned to the United States, Mr. Stalin has defined the program, as he sees it, of the Anglo-American-Soviet coalition in the European war. These are the goals he calls for:

"Abolition of racial exclusiveness, equality of nations and integrity of their territories, liberation of enslaved nations and restoration of their sovereign rights, the right of every nation to arrange its affairs as it wishes, economic aid to nations that have suffered and assistance to them in attaining their material welfare, restoration of democratic liberties, the destruction of the Hitlerite regime."

We may ask: does Stalin mean what he says? Some will point out that only two years ago Russia was in an alliance of expediency with Germany. I make no defense of expediency, military, political, temporary, or otherwise. For I believe the moral losses of expediency always far outweigh the temporary gains. And I believe that every drop of blood saved through expediency will be paid for by twenty drawn by the sword. But a Russian, feeling that by the German alliance his country was buying time might well remind the democracies of Munich, and of the seven million tons of the best grade of scrap iron the United States shipped to Japan between 1937 and 1940.

Perhaps we can better measure the good faith of Stalin's statement in the light of the millions of Russians who have already died defending their fatherland and of the sixty million who have become slaves of the Nazis; in those other millions of Russian men and women who are working feverishly sixty-six hours a week in factories and mines to forge and produce instruments of war for the fighters at the front; and in the effort that went into the almost miraculous movement of great factories, hundreds of miles, that they might operate, uninterrupted, beyond Nazi reach. For it is in the attitude of the people that we may find the best interpretation of Stalin's purpose.

Many among the democracies fear and mistrust Soviet Russia. They dread the inroads of an economic order that would be destructive of their own. Such fear is weakness. Russia is nether going to eat us nor seduce us. That is — and this is something for us to think about — that is, unless our democratic institutions and our free economy become so frail through abuse and failure in practice as to make us soft and vulnerable. The best answer to Communism is a living, vibrant, fearless democracy — economic, social, and political. All we need to do is to stand up and perform according to our professed ideals. Then those ideals will be safe. . . .

When you fly around the world in forty-nine days, you learn that the world has become small not only on the map, but also in the minds of men. All around the world, there are some ideas which millions and millions of men hold in common, almost as much as if they lived in the same town. One of these ideas and one which I can report without hesitation, has tremendous significance for us in America; it is the mixture of respect and hope with which the world looks to this country.

Whether I was talking to a resident of Belem or Natal in Brazil, or one toting his burden on his head in Nigeria, or a prime minister or a king in Egypt, or a veiled woman in ancient Bagdad, or a shah or a weaver of carpets in legendary Persia, now known as Iran, or a follower of Ataturk in those streets of Ankara which look so like the streets of our Middle Western cities, or to a strong-limbed, resolute factory worker in Russia, or to Stalin himself, or the enchanting wife of the great Generalissimo of China, or a Chinese soldier at the front, or a fur-capped hunter on the edge of the trackless forests of Siberia — whether I was talking to any of these people, or to any others, I found that they all have one common bond, and that is their deep friendship for the United States.

They, each and every one, turn to the United States with a friendliness that is often akin to genuine affection. I came home certain of one clear and significant fact; that there exists in the world today a gigantic reservoir of good will toward us, the American people.

Many things have created this enormous reservoir. At the top of the list go the hospitals, schools, and colleges which Americans — missionaries, teachers, and doctors — have founded in the far corners of the world. Many of the new leaders of old countries — men who are today running Iraq or Turkey or China — have studied under American teachers whose only interest has been to spread knowledge. Now, in our time of crisis, we owe a great debt to these men and women who have made friends for us.

Good will has also been stored up for us, like credit in a bank account, by those Americans who have pioneered in the opening of new roads, new airways, new shipping lines. Because of them, the peoples of the world think of us as a people who move goods, and ideas, and move them fast. They like us for this, and they respect us.

Our motion pictures have played an important role in building up this reservoir of friendliness. They are shown all over the world. People of every country can see with their own eyes what we look like, can hear our voices. From Natal to Chungking I was plied with questions about American motion-picture stars — questions asked eagerly by shopgirls and those who served me coffee, and just as eagerly by the wives of prime ministers and kings.

There are still other reasons for our reserve of good will abroad. The people of every land, whether industrialized or not, admire the aspirations and accomplishments of American labor, which they have heard about, and which they long to emulate. Also they are impressed by American methods of agriculture, business, and industry. In nearly every country I went to, there is some great dam or irrigation project, some harbor or factory, which has been built by Americans. People like our works, I found, not only because they help to make life easier and richer, but also because we have shown that American business enterprise does not necessarily lead to attempts at political control.

I found this dread of foreign control everywhere. The fact that we are not associated with it in men's minds has caused people to go much farther in their approval of us than I had dared to imagine. I was amazed to discover how keenly the world is aware of the fact that we do not seek

— anywhere, in any region — to impose our rule upon others or to exact special privileges.

All the people of the earth know that we have no sinister designs upon them, that even when we have in the past withdrawn from international affairs into a false self-sufficiency, it was without sinister purpose. And they know that, now we are in this war, we are not fighting for profit, or loot, or territory, or mandatory power over the lives or the governments of other people. That, I think, is the single most important reason for the existence of our reservoir of good will around the world.

Everywhere I went around the world, and I mean literally everywhere, I found officers and men of the United States Army. Sometimes they were in very small units; in other places they filled enormous army camps which covered acres of some foreign country. In every situation in which I found them, they were adding to the good will foreign peoples hold toward America.

A striking example of this was the crew of our C-87 Army plane. None of its officers or enlisted men had ever been abroad before except on a fighting assignment. They were not trained diplomats. Most of them spoke no foreign language. But everywhere we landed, they made friends for America. I shall remember for a long time the sight of the Shah of Iran, just after we had given him the first airplane ride of his life, shaking hands with Major Richard Kight, our pilot, and looking at him with what I can only describe as a mixture of admiration and envy.

I was proud of American soldiers everywhere I saw them. I felt a confidence that our citizens' army, uninterested in entrenching themselves as professional army men, would automatically help to preserve the reservoir of good will which our generation inherits, and would at the same time find out, through firsthand experience, why this is America's war.

For, as I see it, the existence of this reservoir is the biggest political fact of our time. No other Western nation has such a reservoir. Ours must be used to unify the peoples of the earth in the human quest for freedom and justice. It must be maintained so that, with confidence, they may fight and work with us against the gigantic evil forces that are seeking to destroy all that we stand for, all that they hope for. The preservation of this reservoir of good will is a sacred responsibility, not alone toward the aspiring peoples of the earth, but toward our own sons who are fighting this battle on every continent. For the water in this reservoir is the clean, invigorating water of freedom. . . .

People in the United States are apt to conclude that there is no such thing as public opinion or the operation of its power in countries under absolute forms of government. As a matter of fact, in every absolutely governed country I visited, the government had elaborate methods of determining what the people were thinking. Even Stalin has his form of "Gallup poll," and it is recorded that Napoleon at the height of his power, as he sat astride his white horse amid the smoldering ruins of Moscow, anxiously waited for his daily courier's report of what the mobs in Paris were thinking.

In every country I saw around the world, I found some kind of public opinion operating powerfully both on the course of the war and on the slowly emerging ideas of peace. In Bagdad I found it in the conversation in every coffeehouse, and there are a multitude of them. In Russia, it was expressed in great factory meetings and in the talk of Russians everywhere, who, however contrary it may seem to our notion of Soviet Russia, exchange ideas in private conversation almost as freely as we do. In China, newspapers though not as unrestricted as ours, nevertheless with a surprising freedom reflect and lead public opinion. No man I talked to in China, whether he was the leader of the Communist party, a factory worker, a college professor, or a soldier seemed to have any hesitancy about expressing his views, and many of the views were in conflict with some of the policies of the government.

This was plain in the questions they asked about America after the war, about Great Britain, and, when I was in China, about Russia. The whole world seemed to me in an eager, demanding, hungry, ambitious mood ready for incredible sacrifices if only they could see some hope that those sacrifices would prove worth while.

Europe in 1917 was probably in much the same mood. It is an inevitable corollary of blood and war weariness. Then, in 1917, Lenin gave the world one set of answers. A little later Wilson gave it another. Neither set of answers ever became blood-and-bone part of the war, but were superimposed on it, in the various treaties of peace. So neither set of answers redeemed the war or made it anything more than a costly fight for power. It ended with an armistice, not a real peace.

I do not believe this war need be the same. There are now, during the war, common purposes in the minds of men living as far apart as the citizens of Great Britain and the Free Commonwealth of Nations, the Americans, the Russians, and the Chinese. But we shall have to make articulate and real our common purposes.

The people must define their purposes during the war. I have quite deliberately tried to provoke discussion of those purposes among the peoples of the various countries of the world. For I live in a constant dread that this war may end before the people of the world have come to a common understanding of what they fight for and what they hope for after the war is over. I was a soldier in the last war and after that war was over, I saw our bright dreams disappear, our stirring slogans become the jests of the cynical, and all because the fighting peoples did not arrive at any common postwar purposes while they fought. It must be our resolve to see that that does not happen again. . . .

If our withdrawal from world affairs after the last war was a contributing factor to the present war and to the economic instability of the past twenty years — and it seems plain that it was — a withdrawal from the problems and responsibilities of the world after this war would be sheer disaster. Even our relative geographical isolation no longer exists.

At the end of the last war, not a single plane had flown across the Atlantic. Today that ocean is a mere ribbon, with airplanes making regular scheduled flights. The Pacific is only a slightly wider ribbon in the ocean of the air, and Europe and Asia are at our very doorstep.

America must choose one of three courses after this war: narrow nationalism, which inevitably means the ultimate loss of our own liberty; international imperialism, which means the sacrifice of some other nation's liberty; or the creation of a world in which there shall be an equality of opportunity for every race and every nation. I am convinced the American people will choose, by overwhelming majority, the last of these courses. To make this choice effective, we must win not only the war, but also the peace, and we must start winning it now.

To win this peace three things seem to me necessary — first, we must plan now for peace on a world basis; second, the world must be free, politically and economically, for nations and for men, that peace may exist in it; third, America must play an active, constructive part in freeing it and keeping its peace.

When I say that peace must be planned on a world basis, I mean quite literally that it must embrace the earth. Continents and oceans are plainly only parts of a whole, seen, as I have seen them, from the air. England and America are parts. Russia and China, Egypt, Syria and Turkey, Iraq and Iran are also parts. And it is inescapable that there can be no peace for any part of the world unless the foundations of peace are made secure throughout all parts of the world.

This cannot be accomplished by mere declarations of our leaders, as in an Atlantic Charter. Its accomplishment depends primarily upon acceptance by the peoples of the world. For if the failure to reach international understanding after the last war taught us anything it taught us this: even if war leaders apparently agree upon generalized principles and slogans while the war is being fought, when they come to the peace table they make their own interpretations of their previous declarations. So unless today, while the war is being fought, the people of the United States and of Great Britain, of Russia and of China, and of all the other United Nations, fundamentally agree on their purposes, fine and idealistic expressions of hope such as those of the Atlantic Charter will live merely to mock us as have Mr. Wilson's Fourteen Points. The Four Freedoms will not be accomplished by the declarations of those momentarily in power. They will become real only if the people of the world forge them into actuality.

When I say that in order to have peace this world must be free, I am only reporting that a great process has started which no man — certainly not Hitler — can stop. Men and women all over the world are on the march, physically, intellectually, and spiritually. After centuries of ignorant and dull compliance, hundreds of millions of people in eastern Europe and Asia have opened the books. Old fears no longer frighten them. They are no longer willing to be Eastern slaves for Western profits. They are beginning to know that men's welfare throughout the world is interdependent. They are resolved, as we must be, that there is no more place for imperialism within their own society than in the society of nations. The big house on the hill surrounded by mud huts has lost its awesome charm.

Our Western world and our presumed supremacy are now on trial. Our boasting and our big talk leave Asia cold. Men and women in Russia and China and in the Middle East are conscious now of their own potential strength. They are coming to know that many of the decisions about the future of the world lie in their hands. And they intend that these decisions shall leave the peoples of each nation free from foreign domination, free for economic, social, and spiritual growth.

Economic freedom is as important as political freedom. Not only must people have access to what other peoples produce, but their own products must in turn have some chance of reaching men all over the world. There will be no peace, there will be no real development, there will be no economic stability, unless we find the method by which we can begin to break down the unnecessary trade barriers hampering the flow of goods. Obviously, the sudden and uncompromising abolition of tariffs after the war could only result in disaster. But obviously, also, one of the freedoms we are fighting for is freedom to trade. I know there are many men, particularly in America, where our standard of living exceeds the standard of living in the rest of the world, who are genuinely alarmed at such a prospect, who believe that any such process will only lessen our own standard of living. The reverse of this is true.

Many reasons may be assigned for the amazing economic development of the United States. The abundance of our national resources, the freedom of our political institutions, and the character of our population have all undoubtedly contributed. But in my judgment the greatest factor has been the fact that by the happenstance of good fortune there was created here in America the largest area in the world in which there were no barriers to the exchange of goods and ideas.

And I should like to point out to those who are fearful one inescapable fact. In view of the astronomical figures our national debt will assume by the end of this war, and in a world reduced in size by industrial and transportation developments, even our present standard of living in America cannot be maintained unless the exchange of goods flows more freely over the whole world. It is also inescapably true that to raise the standard of living of any man anywhere in the world is to raise the standard of living by some slight degree of every man everywhere in the world.

Finally, when I say that this world demands the full participation of a self-confident America, I am only passing on an invitation which the peoples of the East have given us. They would like the United States and the other United Nations to be partners with them in this grand adventure. They want us to join them in creating a new society of independent nations, free alike of the economic injustices of the West and the political malpractices of the East. But as partners in that great new combination they want us neither hesitant, incompetent, nor afraid. They want partners who will not hesitate to speak out for the correction of injustice anywhere in the world.

Our allies in the East know that we intend to pour out our resources in this war. But they expect us now — not after the war — to use the enormous power of our giving to promote liberty and justice. Other peoples, not yet fighting, are waiting no less eagerly for us to accept the most challenging opportunity of all history — the chance to help create a new society in which men and women the world around can live and grow invigorated by independence and freedom.

IX. Contemporary Problems, Domestic and Foreign

Earl Warren

DESEGREGATION OF PUBLIC SCHOOLS

❖{*1954*}❖ Soon after the ending of the Civil War and the passage of the thirteenth, fourteenth, and fifteenth amendments, it became painfully clear to believers in equal rights for the Negro that mere constitutional pronunciamentoes were insufficient to achieve the objective they sought. For a time, through the use of armed force and through new legislation, Northern friends of the Negro continued the battle, but with the passage of years interest slackened and enthusiasm declined. The Supreme Court speeded this process along in two important late-nineteenth century decisions, the Civil Rights cases (see pp. 106 ff.) and Plessy *v*. Ferguson (1896), which held, in effect, that the owners of restaurants, theaters, trolley cars, and other business which catered to the general public could arbitrarily exclude Negroes or segregate them from white patrons, and that in interstate transportation and in education, segregation of the races was legal so long as the Negroes were provided with "separate but equal" accommodations.

Two World Wars, the concentrated force of world public opinion, increasing Negro discontent, and a variety of other causes gradually made this condition more and more intolerable. Increasingly it was apparent that "separate" facilities in the South were seldom "equal"; indeed, that the mere fact of separation, being itself degrading, made equality impossible. A series of Supreme Court decisions in the 1950's indicated a growing awareness of these truths, and then, in 1954, Chief Justice Earl Warren (1891-   ) dealt a death blow to segregation in the case of *Brown* v. *Board of Education of Topeka*.

The Brown case dealt only with segregation in the public schools and of course it is obvious that many men's minds were not changed by the Chief Justice's decision. The "death" of segregation has been anything but instantaneous. Nevertheless, since 1954 the movement for real equality has been gathering force year by year. One by one the bastions of segregation have crumbled. *Brown* v. *Topeka* marks a great turning point in our history, the full significance of which no one can yet appreciate.

BROWN v. BOARD OF EDUCATION OF TOPEKA

Mr. Chief Justice Warren: These cases come to us from the States of Kansas, South Carolina, Virginia, and Delaware. They are premised on different facts and different local conditions, but a common legal question justifies their consideration together in this consolidated opinion.

In each of the cases, minors of the Negro race, through their legal representatives, seek the aid of the courts in obtaining admission to the public schools of their community on a nonsegregated basis. In each instance, they had been denied admission to schools attended by white children under laws requiring or permitting segregation according to race. This segregation was alleged to deprive the plaintiffs of the equal protection of the laws under the Fourteenth Amendment. In each of the cases other than the Delaware case, a three-judge federal district court denied relief to the plaintiffs on the so-called "separate but equal" doctrine announced by this Court in *Plessy vs. Ferguson,* 163 U.S. 537. Under that doctrine, equality of treatment is accorded when the races are provided substantially equal facilities, even though these facilities be separate. In the Delaware case, the Supreme Court of Delaware adhered to that doctrine, but ordered that the plaintiffs be admitted to the white schools because of their superiority to the Negro schools.

The plaintiffs contend that segregated public schools are not "equal" and cannot be made "equal," and that hence they are deprived of the equal protection of the laws. Because of the obvious importance of the question presented, the Court took jurisdiction. Argument was heard in the 1952 Term, and reargument was heard this Term on certain questions propounded by the Court.

Reargument was largely devoted to the circumstances surrounding the adoption of the Fourteenth Amendment in 1868. It covered exhaustively consideration of the Amendment in Congress, ratification by the states, then existing practices in racial segregation, and the views of proponents and opponents of the Amendment. This discussion and our own investigation convince us that, although these sources cast some light, it is not enough to resolve the problem with which we are faced. At best, they are inconclusive. The most avid proponents of the post-War Amendments undoubtedly intended them to remove all legal distinctions among "all persons born or naturalized in the United States." Their opponents, just as certainly, were antagonistic to both the letter and the spirit of the Amendments and wished them to have the most limited effect. What others in Congress and the state legislatures had in mind cannot be determined with any degree of certainty.

An additional reason for the inconclusive nature of the Amendment's history, with respect to segregated schools, is the status of public education at that time. In the South, the movement toward free common schools, supported by general taxation, had not yet taken hold. Education of white children was largely in the hands of private groups. Education of Negroes was almost nonexistent, and practically all of the race were illiterate. In fact, any education of Negroes was forbidden by law in some states. Today, in contrast, many Negroes have achieved outstanding success in the arts and sciences as well as in the business and professional world. It is true that public school education at the time of the Amendment had advanced further in the North, but the effect of the Amendment on Northern States was generally ignored in the congressional debates. Even in the North, the conditions of public education did not approximate those existing today. The curriculum was usually rudimentary; ungraded schools were common in rural areas; the school term was but three months a year in many states; and compulsory school attendance was virtually unknown. As a consequence, it is not surprising that there should be so little in the history of the Fourteenth Amendment relating to its intended effect on public education.

In the first cases in this Court construing the Fourteenth Amendment, decided shortly after its adoption, the Court interpreted it as proscribing all state-imposed discriminations against the Negro race. The doctrine of "separate but equal" did not make its appearance in this Court until 1896 in the case of *Plessy v. Ferguson, supra,* involving not education but transportation. American courts have since labored with the doctrine for over half a century. In this Court, there have been six cases involving the "separate but equal" doctrine in the field of public education. In *Cunning v. County Board of Education,* 175 U.S. 528, and *Gong Lum v. Rice,* 275 U.S. 78, the validity of the doctrine itself was not challenged. In more recent cases, all on the graduate school level, inequality was found in that specific benefits enjoyed by white students were denied to Negro students of the same educational qualifications. *Missouri ex rel. Gaines v. Canada,* 305 U.S. 337; *Sipuel v. Oklahoma,* 332 U.S. 631; *Sweatt v. Painter,* 339 U.S. 629; *McLaurin v. Oklahoma State Regents,* 339 U.S. 637. In none of these cases was it necessary to re-examine the doctrine to grant relief to the Negro plaintiff. And in *Sweatt v. Painter, supra,* the Court expressly reserved decision on the question whether *Plessy v. Ferguson* should be held inapplicable to the public education.

In the instant cases, that question is directly presented. Here, unlike *Sweatt v. Painter,* there are findings below that the Negro and white schools involved have been equalized, or are being equalized, with respect to buildings, curricula, qualifications and salaries of teachers, and other "tangible" factors. Our decision, therefore, cannot turn on merely a comparison of these tangible factors in the Negro and white schools involved in each of the cases. We must look instead to the effect of segregation itself on public education.

In approaching this problem, we cannot turn the clock back to 1868 when the Amendment was adopted, or even to 1896 when *Plessy v. Ferguson* was written. We must consider public education in the light of its full development and its present place in American life throughout the

Nation. Only in this way can it be determined if segregation in public schools deprives these plaintiffs of the equal protection of the laws.

Today, education is perhaps the most important function of state and local governments. Compulsory school attendance laws and the great expenditures for education both demonstrate our recognition of the importance of education to our democratic society. It is required in the performance of our most basic public responsibilities, even service in the armed forces. It is the very foundation of good citizenship. Today it is a principal instrument in awakening the child to cultural values, in preparing him for later professional training, and in helping him to adjust normally to his environment. In these days, it is doubtful that any child may reasonably be expected to succeed in life if he is denied the opportunity of an education. Such an opportunity, where the state has undertaken to provide it, is a right which must be made available to all on equal terms.

We come then to the question presented: Does segregation of children in public schools solely on the basis of race, even though the physical facilities and other "tangible" factors may be equal, deprive the children of the minority group of equal educational opportunities? We believe that it does.

In *Sweatt v. Painter, supra,* in finding that a segregated law school for Negroes could not provide them equal educational opportunities, this Court relied in large part on "those qualities which are incapable of objective measurement but which makes for greatness in a law school." In *McLaurin v. Oklahoma State Regents, supra,* the Court, in requiring that a Negro admitted to a white graduate school be treated like all other students, again resorted to intangible considerations: ". . . his ability to study, to engage in discussions and exchange views with other students, and, in general, to learn his profession." Such considerations apply with added force to children in grade and high schools. To separate them from others of similar age and qualifications solely because of their race generates a feeling of inferiority as to their status in the community that may affect their hearts and minds in a way unlikely ever to be undone. The effect of this separation on their educational opportunities was well stated by a finding in the Kansas case by a court which nevertheless felt compelled to rule against the Negro plaintiffs:

> Segregation of white and colored children in public schools has a detrimental effect upon the colored children. The impact is greater when it has the sanction of the law; for the policy of separating the races is usually interpreted as denoting the inferiority of the negro group. A sense of inferiority affects the motivation of a child to learn. Segregation with the

sanction of law, therefore, has a tendency to [retard] the education and mental development of negro children and to deprive them of some of the benefits they would receive in a racial[ly] integrated school system.

Whatever may have been the extent of psychological knowledge at the time of *Plessy v. Ferguson,* this finding is amply supported by modern authority. Any language in *Plessy v. Ferguson* contrary to this finding is rejected.

We conclude that in the field of public education the doctrine of "separate but equal" has no place. Separate educational facilities are inherently unequal. Therefore, we hold that the plaintiffs and others similarly situated for whom the actions have been brought are, by reasons of the segregation complained of, deprived of the equal protection of the laws guaranteed by the Fourteenth Amendment. This disposition makes unnecessary any discussion whether such segregation also violates the Due Process Clause of the Fourteenth Amendment.

Because these are class actions, because of the wide applicability of this decision, and because of the great variety of local conditions, the formulation of decrees in these cases presents problems of considerable complexity. On reargument, the consideration of appropriate relief was necessarily subordinated to the primary question — the constitutionality of segregation on public education. We have now announced that such segregation is a denial of the equal protection of the laws. . . .

Martin Luther King

A WAY OUT FOR THE NEGRO

⊰{1958}⊱ ON THE evening of December 1, 1955, Mrs. Rosa Parks of Montgomery, Alabama, left the downtown department store where she was employed as a seamstress and boarded a Cleveland Avenue bus. Being a Negro, she dutifully took a seat toward the rear, immediately behind the section reserved for white passengers. Soon, however, as homeward-bound workers and shoppeds crowded aboard, the white section of the bus became filled, and then, following long-established regulations, the driver ordered Mrs. Parks and three other Negroes to give up their places. The others complied but Mrs. Parks refused to move. As a result, upon the driver's complaint, she was arrested.

Previously other Negroes had rebelled against the Montgomery ordinance segregating city buses, but the case of Mrs. Parks was different. She was a woman of impeccable reputation, widely known in the community for her work in the National Association for the Advancement of Colored People. So, too, the times were different. The local Negroes' long-smothered hopes for improving their lot had been revived by the then-recent Supreme Court decision in the case of *Brown* v. *Topeka,* pointing toward the desegregation of public schools. In any case, a handful of leading Negroes hurriedly organized a boycott of the buses to protest against segregation and Mrs. Parks's arrest. The response was immediate and enthusiastic; when the buses rolled on Monday morning, December 5, scarcely a Negro in the community was aboard. Soon newspapers all over the land were headlining the Montgomery "bus strike." With amazing self-discipline and orderliness, the Negroes of Montgomery held to their refusal to ride on segregated buses for over a year. Finally, after a Supreme Court decision outlawing the segregation ordinance, their fight was won.

Among the leaders in this long struggle was a young Baptist minister named Martin Luther King (1929-   ). It was King who turned the movement from a militant boycott into a crusade, and he did so by stressing passive resistance as a general device for protesting the mistreatment of the Negro race. His book describing the struggle, *Stride Toward Freedom,* attracted wide notice and played a major role in the development of the "sit in" technique that has been used so effectively in the drive to desegregate lunch counters and other public facilities in the South. In the following selection from that book, the Reverend Mr. King explains how he came to espouse the philosophy of passive resistance.

PILGRIMAGE TO NONVIOLENCE

OFTEN the question has arisen concerning my own intellectual pilgrimage to nonviolence. In order to get at this question it is necessary to go back to my early teens in Atlanta. I had grown up abhorring not only segregation but also the oppressive and barbarous acts that grew out of it. I had passed spots where Negroes had been savagely lynched, and had watched the Ku Klux Klan on its rides at night. I had seen police brutality with my own eyes, and watched Negroes receive the most tragic injustice in the courts. All of these things had done something to my growing personality. I had come perilously close to resenting all white people.

I had also learned that the inseparable twin of racial injustice was economic injustice. Although I came from a home of economic security and relative comfort, I could never get out of my mind the economic insecurity of many of my playmates and the tragic poverty of those living around me. During my late teens I worked two summers, against my father's wishes — he never wanted my brother and me to work around white people because of the oppressive conditions — in a plant that hired both Negroes and whites. Here I saw economic injustice firsthand, and realized that the poor white was exploited just as much as the Negro. Through these early experiences I grew up deeply conscious of the varieties of injustice in our society.

So when I went to Atlanta's Morehouse College as a freshman in 1944 my concern for racial and economic justice was already substantial. During my student days at Morehouse I read Thoreau's *Essay on Civil Dis-*

obedience for the first time. Fascinated by the idea of refusing to coöperate with an evil system, I was so deeply moved that I reread the work several times. This was my first intellectual contact with the theory of nonviolent resistance.

Not until I entered Crozer Theological Seminary in 1948, however, did I begin a serious intellectual quest for a method to eliminate social evil. Although my major interest was in the fields of theology and philosophy, I spent a great deal of time reading the works of the great social philosophers. I came early to Walter Rauschenbusch's *Christianity and the Social Crisis,* which left an indelible imprint on my thinking by giving me a theological basis for the social concern which had already grown up in me as a result of my early experiences. Of course there were points at which I differed with Rauschenbusch. I felt that he had fallen victim to the nineteenth-century "cult of inevitable progress" which led him to a superficial optimism concerning man's nature. Moreover, he came perilously close to identifying the Kingdom of God with a particular social and economic system — a tendency which should never befall the Church. But in spite of these shortcomings Rauschenbusch had done a great service for the Christian Church by insisting that the gospel deals with the whole man, not only his soul but his body; not only his spiritual well-being but his material well-being. It has been my conviction ever since reading Rauschenbusch that any religion which professes to be concerned about the souls of men and is not concerned about the social and economic conditions that scar the soul, is a spiritually moribund religion only waiting for the day to be buried. It well has been said: "A religion that ends with the individual, ends."

After reading Rauschenbusch, I turned to a serious study of the social and ethical theories of the great philosophers, from Plato and Aristotle down to Rousseau, Hobbes, Bentham, Mill, and Locke. All of these masters stimulated my thinking — such as it was — and, while finding things to question in each of them, I nevertheless learned a great deal from their study.

During the Christmas holidays of 1949 I decided to spend my spare time reading Karl Marx to try to understand the appeal of communism for many people. For the first time I carefully scrutinized *Das Kapital* and *The Communist Manifesto.* I also read some interpretive works on the thinking of Marx and Lenin. In reading such Communist writings I drew certain conclusions that have remained with me as convictions to this day. First I rejected their materialistic interpretation of history. Communism, avowedly secularistic and materialistic, has no place for God.

This I could never accept, for as a Christian I believe that there is a creative personal power in this universe who is the ground and essence of all reality — a power that cannot be explained in materialistic terms. History is ultimately guided by spirit, not matter. Second, I strongly disagreed with communism's ethical relativism. Since for the Communist there is no divine government, no absolute moral order, there are no fixed, immutable principles; consequently almost anything — force, violence, murder, lying — is a justifiable means to the "millennial" end. This type of relativism was abhorrent to me. Constructive ends can never give absolute moral justification to destructive means, because in the final analysis the end is preëxistent in the mean. Third, I opposed communism's political totalitarianism. In communism the individual ends up in subjection to the state. True, the Marxist would argue that the state is an "interim" reality which is to be eliminated when the classless society emerges; but the state is the end while it lasts, and man only a means to that end. And if any man's so-called rights or liberties stand in the way of that end, they are simply swept aside. His liberties of expression, his freedom to vote, his freedom to listen to what news he likes or to choose his books are all restricted. Man becomes hardly more, in communism, than a depersonalized cog in the turning wheel of the state.

This deprecation of individual freedom was objectionable to me. I am convinced now, as I was then, that man is an end because he is a child of God. Man is not made for the state; the state is made for man. To deprive man of freedom is to relegate him to the status of a thing, rather than elevate him to the status of a person. Man must never be treated as a means to the end of the state, but always as an end within himself.

Yet, in spite of the fact that my response to communism was and is negative, and I considered it basically evil, there were points at which I found it challenging. The late Archbishop of Canterbury, William Temple, referred to communism as a Christian heresy. By this he meant that communism had laid hold of certain truths which are essential parts of the Christian view of things, but that it had bound up with them concepts and practices which no Christian could ever accept or profess. Communism challenged the late Archbishop and it should challenge every Christian — as it challenged me — to a growing concern about social justice. With all of its false assumptions and evil methods, communism grew as a protest against the hardships of the underprivileged. Communism in theory emphasized a classless society, and a concern for social justice, though the world knows from sad experience that in practice it created new classes and a new lexicon of injustice. The Christian ought always to be challenged by any protest against unfair treatment of the poor, for Christianity is itself such a protest, nowhere expressed more eloquently than in Jesus' words: "The Spirit of the Lord is upon me, because he hath anointed me to preach the gospel to the poor; he hath sent me to heal the brokenhearted, to preach deliverance to the captives, and recovering of sight to the blind, to set at liberty them that are bruised, to preach the acceptable year of the Lord."

I also sought systematic answers to Marx's critique of modern bourgeois culture. He presented capitalism as essentially a struggle between the owners of the productive resources and the workers, whom Marx regarded as the real producers. Marx interpreted economic forces as the dialectical process by which society moved from feudalism through capitalism to socialism, with the primary mechanism of this historical movement being the struggle between economic classes whose interests were irreconcilable. Obviously this theory left out of account the numerous and significant complexities — political, economic, moral, religious, and psychological — which played a vital role in shaping the constellation of institutions and ideas known today as Western civilization. Moreover, it was dated in the sense that the capitalism Marx wrote about bore only a partial resemblance to the capitalism we know in this country today.

But in spite of the shortcomings of his analysis, Marx had raised some basic questions. I was deeply concerned from my early teen days about the gulf between superfluous wealth and abject poverty, and my reading of Marx made me ever more conscious of this gulf. Although modern American capitalism had greatly reduced the gap through social reforms, there was still need for a better distribution of wealth. Moreover, Marx had revealed the danger of the profit motive as the sole basis of an economic system: capitalism is always in danger of inspiring men to be more concerned about making a living than making a life. We are prone to judge success by the index of our salaries or the size of our automobiles, rather than by the quality of our service and relationship to humanity — thus capitalism can lead to a practical materialism that is as pernicious as the materialism taught by communism.

In short, I read Marx as I read all of the influential historical thinkers — from a dialectical point of view, combining a partial yes and a partial no. In so far as Marx posited a metaphysical materialism, an ethical relativism, and a strangulating totalitarianism, I responded with an unambiguous "no"; but in so far as he pointed to weaknesses of traditional capitalism, contributed to the growth of a definite self-consciousness in the masses, and challenged the social conscience of the Christian churches. I responded with a definite "yes."

My reading of Marx also convinced me that truth is found neither in Marxism nor in traditional capitalism. Each represents a partial truth. Historically capitalism failed to see the truth in collective enterprise and Marxism failed to see the truth in individual enterprise. Nineteenth-century capitalism failed to see that life is social and Marxism failed and still fails to see that life is individual and personal. The Kingdom of God is neither the thesis of individual enterprise nor the antithesis of collective enterprise, but a synthesis which reconciles the truths of both.

During my stay at Crozer, I was also exposed for the first time to the pacifist position in a lecture by Dr. A. J. Muste. I was deeply moved by Dr. Muste's talk, but far from convinced of the practicability of his position. Like most of the students of Crozer, I felt that while war could never be a positive or absolute good, it could serve as a negative good in the sense of preventing the spread and growth of an evil force. War, horrible as it is, might be preferable to surrender to a totalitarian system — Nazi, Fascist, or Communist.

During this period I had about despaired of the power of love in solving social problems. Perhaps my faith in love was temporarily shaken by the philosophy of Nietzsche. I had been reading parts of *The Genealogy of Morals* and the whole of *The Will to Power*. Nietzsche's glorification of power — in his theory all life expressed the will to power — was an outgrowth of his contempt for ordinary morals. He attacked the whole of the Hebraic-Christian morality — with its virtues of piety and humility, its otherworldliness and its attitude toward suffering — as the glorification of weakness, as making virtues out of necessity and impotence. He looked to the development of a superman who would surpass man as man surpassed the ape.

Then one Sunday afternoon I traveled to Philadelphia to hear a sermon by Dr. Mordecai Johnson, president of Howard University. He was there to preach for the Fellowship House of Philadelphia. Dr. Johnson had just returned from a trip to India, and, to my great interest, he spoke of the life and teachings of Mahatma Gandhi. His message was so profound and electrifying that I left the meeting and bought a half-dozen books on Gandhi's life and works.

Like most people, I had heard of Gandhi, but I had never studied him seriously. As I read I became deeply fascinated by his campaigns of non-violent resistance. I was particularly moved by the Salt March to the Sea and his numerous fasts. The whole concept of "Satyagraha" (*Satya* is truth which equals love, and *agraha* is force; "Satyagraha," therefore, means truth-force or love force) was profoundly significant to me. As I delved deeper into the philosophy of Gandhi my skepticism concerning the power of love gradually diminished, and I came to see for the first time its potency in the area of social reform. Prior to reading Gandhi, I had about concluded that the ethics of Jesus were only effective in individual relationship. The "turn the other cheek" philosophy and the "love your enemies" philosophy were only valid, I felt, when individuals were in conflict with other individuals; when racial groups and nations were in conflict a more realistic approach seemed necessary. But after reading Gandhi, I saw how utterly mistaken I was.

Gandhi was probably the first person in history to lift the love ethic of Jesus above mere interaction between individuals to a powerful and effective social force on a large scale. Love for Gandhi was a potent instrument for social and collective transformation. It was in this Gandhian emphasis on love and nonviolence that I discovered the method for social reform that I had been seeking for so many months. The intellectual and moral satisfaction that I failed to gain from the utilitarianism of Bentham and Mill, the revolutionary methods of Marx and Lenin, the social-contracts theory of Hobbes, the "back to nature" optimism of Rousseau, and the superman philosophy of Nietzsche, I found in the nonviolent resistance philosophy of Gandhi. I came to feel that this was the only morally and practically sound method open to oppressed people in their struggle for freedom.

But my intellectual odyssey to nonviolence did not end here. During my last year in theological school, I began to read the works of Reinhold Niebuhr. The prophetic and realistic elements in Niebuhr's passionate style and profound thought were appealing to me, and I became so enamored of his social ethics that I almost fell into the trap of accepting uncritically everything he wrote.

About this time I read Niebuhr's critique of the pacifist position. Niebuhr had himself once been a member of the pacifist ranks. For several years, he had been national chairman of the Fellowship of Reconciliation. His break with pacifism came in the early thirties, and the first full statement of his criticism of pacifism was in *Moral Man and Immoral Society*. Here he argued that there was no intrinsic moral difference between violent and nonviolent resistance. The social consequences of the two methods were different, he contended, but the differences were in degree rather than kind. Later Niebuhr began emphasizing the irresponsibility of relying on nonviolent resistance when there was no ground for believing that it would be successful in preventing the spread of totalitarian tyranny. It could only be successful, he argued, if the groups against whom the resistance was taking place had some degree of moral conscience, as was the case in Gandhi's struggle against the British. Niebuhr's ultimate rejection of pacifism was based primarily on the doctrine of man. He argued that pacifism failed to do justice to the reformation doctrine of justification by faith, substituting for it a sectarian perfectionism which believes "that divine grace actually lifts men out of the sinful contradictions of history and establishes him above the sins of the world."

At first, Niebuhr's critique of pacifism left me in a state of confusion. As I continued to read, however, I came to see more and more the shortcomings of his position. For instance, many of his statements revealed that he interpreted pacifism as a sort of passive nonresistance to evil expressing naïve trust in the power of love. But this was a serious distortion. My study of Gandhi convinced me that true pacifism is not nonresistance to evil, but nonviolent resistance to evil. Between the two positions, there is a world of difference. Gandhi resisted evil with as much vigor and power as the violent resister, but he resisted with love instead of hate. True pacifism is not unrealistic submission to evil power, as Niebuhr contends. It is rather a courageous confrontation of evil by the power of love, in the faith that it is better to be the recipient of violence than the inflicter of it, since the latter only multiplies the existence of violence and bitterness in the universe, while the former may develop a sense of shame in the opponent, and thereby bring about a transformation and change of heart.

In spite of the fact that I found many things to be desired in Niebuhr's philosophy, there were several points at which he constructively influenced my thinking. Niebuhr's great contribution to contemporary theology is that he has refuted the false optimism characteristic of a great segment of Protestant liberalism, without falling into the anti-rationalism of the continental theologian Karl Barth, or the semi-fundamentalism of other dialectical theologians. Moreover, Niebuhr has extraordinary insight into human nature, especially the behavior of nations and social groups. He is keenly aware of the complexity of human motives and of the relation between morality and power. His theology is a persistent reminder of the reality of sin on every level of man's existence. These elements in Niebuhr's thinking helped me to recognize the illusions of a superficial optimism concerning human nature and the dangers of a false idealism. While I still believed in man's potential for good, Niebuhr made me realize his potential for evil as well. Moreover, Niebuhr helped me to recognize the complexity of man's social involvement and the glaring reality of collective evil.

Many pacifists, I felt, failed to see this. All too many had an unwarranted optimism concerning man and leaned unconsciously toward self-righteousness. It was my revolt against these attitudes under the influence of Niebuhr that accounts for the fact that in spite of my strong leaning toward pacifism, I never joined a pacifist organization. After reading Niebuhr, I tried to arrive at a realistic pacifism. In other words, I came to see the pacifist position not as sinless but as the lesser evil in the circumstances. I felt then, and I feel now, that the pacifist would have a greater appeal if he did not claim to be free from the moral dilemmas that the Christian nonpacifist confronts.

The next stage of my intellectual pilgrimage to nonviolence came during my doctoral studies at Boston University. Here I had the opportunity to talk to many exponents of nonviolence, both students and visitors to the campus. Boston University School of Theology, under the influence of Dean Walter Muelder and Professor Allen Knight Chalmers, had a deep sympathy for pacifism. Both Dean Muelder and Dr. Chalmers had a passion for social justice that stemmed, not from a superficial optimism, but from a deep faith in the possibilities of human beings when they allowed themselves to become co-workers with God. It was at Boston University that I came to see that Niebuhr had overemphasized the corruption of human nature. His pessimism concerning human nature was not balanced by an optimism concerning divine nature. He was so involved in diagnosing man's sickness of sin that he overlooked the cure of grace.

I studied philosophy and theology at Boston University under Edgar S. Brightman and L. Harold DeWolf. Both men greatly stimulated my thinking. It was mainly under these teachers that I studied personalistic philosophy — the theory that the clue to the meaning of ultimate reality is found in personality. This personal idealism remains today my basic philosophical position. Personalism's insistence that only personality — finite and infinite — is ultimately real strengthened me in two convictions: it gave me metaphysical and philosophical grounding for the idea of a personal God, and it gave me a metaphysical basis for the dignity and worth of all human personality.

Just before Dr. Brightman's death, I began studying the philosophy of Hegel with him. Although the course was mainly a study of Hegel's monumental work, *Phenomenology of Mind,* I spent my spare time reading his *Philosophy of History* and *Philosophy of Right.* There were points in Hegel's philosophy that I strongly disagreed with. For instance, his absolute idealism was rationally unsound to me because it tended to swallow up the many in the one. But there were other aspects of his thinking that I found stimulating. His contention that "truth is the whole" led me to a philosophical method of rational coherence. His analysis of the dialectical process, in spite of its shortcomings, helped me to see that growth comes through struggle.

In 1954 I ended my formal training with all of these relatively divergent intellectual forces converging into a positive social philosophy. One of the main tenets of this philosophy was the conviction that nonviolent resistance was one of the most potent weapons available to oppressed people in their quest for social justice. At this time, however, I had merely an intellectual understanding and appreciation of the position, with no firm determination to organize it in a socially effective situation.

When I went to Montgomery as a pastor, I had not the slightest idea that I would later become involved in a crisis in which nonviolent resistance would be applicable. I neither started the protest nor suggested it. I simply responded to the call of the people for a spokesman. When the protest began, my mind, consciously or unconsciously, was driven back to the Sermon on the Mount, with its sublime teachings on love, and the Gandhian method of nonviolent resistance. As the days unfolded, I came to see the power of nonviolence more and more. Living through the actual experience of the protest, nonviolence became more than a method to which I gave intellectual assent; it became a commitment to a way of life. Many of the things that I had not cleared up intellectually concerning nonviolence were now solved in the sphere of practical action.

Since the philosophy of nonviolence played such a positive role in the Montgomery Movement, it may be wise to turn to a brief discussion of some basic aspects of this philosophy.

First, it must be emphasized that nonviolent resistance is not a method for cowards; it does resist. If one uses this method because he is afraid or merely because he lacks the instruments of violence, he is not truly nonviolent. This is why Gandhi often said that if cowardice is the only alternative to violence, it is better to fight. He made this statement conscious of the fact that there is always another alternative; no individual or group need submit to any wrong, nor need they use violence to right the wrong; there is the way of nonviolence resistance. This is ultimately the way of the strong man. It is not a method of stagnant passivity. The phrase "passive resistance" often gives the false impression that this is a sort of "do-nothing method" in which the resister quietly and passively accepts evil. But nothing is further from the truth. For while the nonviolent resister is passive in the sense that he is not physically aggressive toward his opponent, his mind and emotions are always active, constantly seeking to persuade his opponent that he is wrong. The method is passive physically, but strongly active spiritually. It is not passive nonresistance to evil, it is active nonviolent resistance to evil.

A second basic fact that characterizes nonviolence is that it does not seek to defeat or humiliate the opponent, but to win his friendship and understanding. The nonviolent resister must often express his protest through noncoöperation or boycotts, but he realizes that these are not ends themselves; they are merely means to awaken a sense of moral shame in the opponent. The end is redemption and reconciliation. The aftermath of nonviolence is the creation of the beloved community, while the aftermath of violence is tragic bitterness.

A third characteristic of this method is that the attack is directed against forces of evil rather than against persons who happen to be doing the evil. It is evil that the nonviolent resister seeks to defeat, not the persons victimized by evil. If he is opposing racial injustice, the nonviolent resister has the vision to see that the basic tension is not between races. As I like to say to the people in Montgomery: "The tension in this city is not between white people and Negro people. The tension is, at bottom, between justice and injustice, between the forces of light and the forces of darkness. And if there is a victory, it will be victory not merely for fifty thousand Negroes, but a victory for justice and the forces of light. We are out to defeat injustice and not white persons who may be unjust."

A fourth point that characterizes nonviolent resistance is a willingness to accept suffering without retaliation, to accept blows from the opponent without striking back. "Rivers of blood may have to flow before we gain our freedom, but it must be our blood," Gandhi said to his countrymen. The nonviolent resister is willing to accept violence if necessary, but never to inflict it. He does not seek to dodge jail. If going to jail is necessary, he enters it "as a bridegroom enters the bride's chamber."

One may well ask: "What is the nonviolent resister's justification for this ordeal to which he invites men, for this mass political application of the ancient doctrine of turning the other cheek?" The answer is found in the realization that unearned suffering is redemptive. Suffering, the nonviolent resister realizes, has tremendous educational and transforming possibilities. "Things of fundamental importance to people are not secured by reason alone, but have to be purchased with their suffering," said Gandhi. He continues: "Suffering is infinitely more powerful than the law of the jungle for converting the opponent and opening his ears which are otherwise shut to the voice of reason."

A fifth point concerning nonviolent resistance is that it avoids not only external physical violence but also internal violence of spirit. The nonviolent resister not only refuses to shoot his opponent but he also refuses to hate him. At the center of nonviolence stands the principle of love. The nonviolent resister would contend that in the struggle for human dignity, the oppressed people of the world must not succumb to the temptation of becoming bitter or indulging in hate campaigns. To retaliate in kind would do nothing but intensify the existence of hate in the universe. Along the way of life, someone must have sense enough and morality enough to cut off the chain of hate. This can only be done by projecting the ethic of love to the center of our lives.

In speaking of love at this point, we are not referring to some sentimental or affectionate emotion. It would be nonsense to urge men to love their oppressors in an affectionate sense. Love in this connection means understanding, redemptive good will. Here the Greek language comes to our aid. There are three words for love in the Greek New Testament. First, there is *eros*. In Platonic philosophy *eros* meant the yearning of the soul for the realm of the divine. It has now come to a sort of aesthetic or romantic love. Second, there is *philia* which means intimate affection between personal friends. *Philia* denotes a sort of reciprocal love; the person loves because he is loved. When we speak of loving those who oppose us, we refer to neither *eros* nor *philia;* we speak of a love which is expressed in the Greek word *agape*. *Agape* means understanding, redeeming good will for all men. It is an overflowing love which is purely spontaneous, unmotivated, groundless, and creative. It is not set in motion by any quality or function of its object. It is the love of God operating in the human heart.

Agape is disinterested love. It is a love in which the individual seeks not his own good, but the good of his neighbor (1 Cor. 10:24). *Agape* does not begin by discriminating between worthy and unworthy people, or any qualities people possess. It begins by loving others *for their sakes*. It is an entirely "neighbor-regarding concern for others," which discovers the neighbor in every man it meets. Therefore, *agape* makes no distinction between friend and enemy; it is directed toward both. If one loves an individual merely on account of his friendliness, he loves him for the sake of the benefits to be gained from the friendship, rather than for the friend's own sake. Consequently, the best way to assure oneself that Love is disinterested is to have love for the enemy-neighbor from whom you can expect no good in return, but only hostility and persecution.

Another basic point about *agape* is that it springs from the *need* of the other person — his need for belonging to the best in the human family. The Samaritan who helped the Jew on the Jericho Road was "good" because he responded to the human need that he was presented with. God's love is eternal and fails not because man needs his love. St. Paul assures us that the loving act of redemption was done "while we were yet sinners" — that is, at the point of our greatest need for love. Since the white man's personality is greatly distorted by segregation, and his soul is greatly scarred, he needs the love of the Negro. The Negro must love the white man, because the white man needs his love to remove his tensions, insecurities, and fears.

Agape is not a weak, passive love. It is love in action. *Agape* is love seeking to preserve and create community. It is insistence on community even when one seeks to break it. *Agape* is a willingness to sacrifice in the interest of mutuality. *Agape* is a willingness to go to any length to restore community. It doesn't stop at the first mile, but it goes the second mile to restore community. It is a willingness to forgive, not seven times, but seventy times seven to restore community. The cross is the eternal expression of the length to which God will go in order to restore broken community. The resurrection is a symbol of God's triumph over all the forces that seek to block community. The Holy Spirit is the continuing community creating reality that moves through history. He who works against community is working against the whole of creation. Therefore, if I respond to hate with a reciprocal hate I do nothing but intensify the cleavage in broken community. I can only close the gap in broken community by meeting hate with love. If I meet hate with hate, I become depersonalized, because creation is so designed that my personality can only be fulfilled in the context of community. Booker T. Washington was right: "Let no man pull you so low as to make you hate him." When he pulls you that low he brings you to the point of working against community; he drags you to the point of defying creation, and thereby becoming depersonalized.

In the final analysis, *agape* means a recognition of the fact that all life is interrelated. All humanity is involved in a single process, and all men are brothers. To the degree that I harm my brother, no matter what he is doing to me, to that extent I am harming myself. For example, white men often refuse federal aid to education in order to avoid giving the Negro his rights; but because all men are brothers they cannot deny Negro children without harming their own. They end, all efforts to the contrary, by hurting themselves. Why is this? Because men are brothers. If you harm me, you harm yourself.

Love, *agape,* is the only cement that can hold this broken community together. When I am commanded to love, I am commanded to restore community, to resist injustice, and to meet the needs of my brothers.

A sixth basic fact about nonviolent resistance is that it is based on the conviction that the universe is on the side of justice. Consequently, the believer in nonviolence has deep faith in the future. This faith is another reason why the nonviolent resister can accept suffering without retaliation. For he knows that in his struggle for justice he has cosmic companionship. It is true that there are devout believers in nonviolence who find it difficult to believe in a personal God. But even these persons believe in the existence of some creative force that works for universal wholeness. Whether we call it an unconscious process, an impersonal Brahman, or a Personal Being of matchless power and infinite love, there is a creative force in this universe that works to bring the disconnected aspects of reality into a harmonious whole.

John F. Kennedy

THE NEW FRONTIER

{1961} It is impossible, so shortly after the event, to say with any assurance that John F. Kennedy's Inaugural Address had an impact on the country and on history comparable to that of most of the other selections here presented. As Kennedy (1917-1963) himself said in this speech, history will be the final judge of his deeds and those of the American people, and history requires more time than has passed since January 20, 1961 to arrive at its judgments. Nevertheless, whatever its ultimate importance, it was a brilliant statement of American ideals and objectives, recognized at once as such, both at home and abroad, and without regard for party.

Some compared it to Lincoln's First Inaugural, and aside from the general mood and the cadence of President Kennedy's prose, there are passages in the speech strikingly similar to Lincoln's. Kennedy's "In your hands, my fellow citizens, more than in mine, will rest the final success or failure of our course" could not have been penned without thought of Lincoln's "In *your* hands, my dissatisfied fellow-countrymen, and not in *mine,* is the momentous issue of civil war." Some have also found lines reminiscent of Franklin Roosevelt's First Inaugural. But the speech must stand on its own to win its place, and as a speech, it certainly does.

INAUGURAL ADDRESS

(January 20, 1961)

My fellow citizens:

We observe today not a victory of party but a celebration of freedom — symbolizing an end as well as a beginning — signifying renewal as well as change. For I have sworn before you and Almighty God the same solemn oath our forebears prescribed nearly a century and three quarters ago.

The world is very different now. For man holds in his mortal hands the power to abolish all form of human poverty and to abolish all form of human life. And, yet, the same revolutionary beliefs for which our forebears fought are still at issue around the globe — the belief that the rights of man come not from the generosity of the state but from the hand of God.

We dare not forget today that we are the heirs of that first revolution. Let the word go forth from this time and place, to friend and foe alike, that the torch has been passed to a new generation of Americans — born in this century, tempered by war, disciplined by a cold and bitter peace, proud of our ancient heritage — and unwilling to witness or permit the slow undoing of those human rights to which this nation has always been committed, and to which we are committed today.

Let every nation know, whether it wish us well or ill, that we shall pay any price, bear any burden, meet any hardship, support any friend or oppose any foe in order to assure the survival and success of liberty.

This much we pledge — and more.

To those old Allies whose cultural and spiritual origins we share, we pledge the loyalty of faithful friends. United, there is little we cannot do in a host of new co-operative ventures. Divided, there is little we can do — for we dare not meet a powerful challenge at odds and split asunder.

To those new states whom we now welcome to the ranks of the free, we pledge our word that one form of colonial control shall not have passed merely to be replaced by a far more iron tyranny. We shall not always expect to find them supporting our every view. But we shall always hope to find them strongly supporting their own freedom — and to remember that, in the past, those who foolishly sought to find power by riding on the tiger's back inevitably ended up inside.

To those peoples in the huts and villages of half the globe struggling to break the bonds of mass misery, we pledge our best efforts to help them help themselves, for whatever period is required — not because the

Communists are doing it, not because we seek their votes, but because it is right. If the free society cannot help the many who are poor, it can never save the few who are rich.

To our sister republics south of our border, we offer a special pledge — to convert our good words into good deeds — in a new alliance for progress — to assist free men and free Governments in casting off the chains of poverty. But this peaceful revolution of hope cannot become the prey of hostile powers. Let all our neighbors know that we shall join with them to oppose aggression or subversion anywhere in the Americas. And let every other power know that this Hemisphere intends to remain the master of its own house.

To that world assembly of sovereign states, the United Nations, our last best hope in an age where the instruments of war have far outpaced the instruments of peace, we renew our pledge of support — to prevent its becoming merely a forum for invective — to strengthen its shield of the new and the weak — and to enlarge the area to which its writ may run.

Finally, to those nations who would make themselves our adversary, we offer not a pledge but a request: that both sides begin anew the quest for peace, before the dark powers of destruction unleashed by science engulf all humanity in planned or accidental self-destruction.

We dare not tempt them with weakness. For only when our arms are sufficient beyond doubt can we be certain beyond doubt that they will never be employed.

But neither can two great and powerful groups of nations take comfort from their present course — both sides overburdened by the cost of modern weapons, both rightly alarmed by the steady spread of the deadly atom, yet both racing to alter that uncertain balance of terror that stays the hand of mankind's final war.

So let us begin anew — remembering on both sides that civility is not a sign of weakness and sincerity is always subject to proof. Let us never negotiate out of fear. But let us never fear to negotiate.

Let both sides explore what problems unite us instead of belaboring the problems that divide us.

Let both sides, for the first time, formulate serious and precise proposals for the inspection and control of arms — and bring the absolute power to destroy other nations under the absolute control of all nations.

Let both sides join to invoke the wonders of science instead of its terrors. Together let us explore the stars, conquer the deserts, eradicate disease, tap the ocean depths and encourage the arts and commerce.

Let both sides unite to heed in all corners of the earth the command of Isaiah — to "undo the heavy burdens . . . (and) let the oppressed go free."

And if a beachhead of co-operation can be made in the jungles of suspicion, let both sides join in the next task: creating, not a new balance of power, but a new world of law, where the strong are just and the weak secure and the peace preserved forever.

All this will not be finished in the first 100 days. Nor will it be finished in the first 1,000 days, nor in the life of this Administration, nor even perhaps in our lifetime on this planet. But let us begin.

In your hands, my fellow citizens, more than in mine, will rest the final success or failure of our course. Since this country was founded, each generation has been summoned to give testimony to its national loyalty. The graves of young Americans who answered that call encircle the globe.

Now the trumpet summons us again — not as a call to bear arms, though arms we need — not as a call to battle, through embattled we are — but a call to bear the burden of a long twilight struggle, year in and year out, "rejoicing in hope, patient in tribulation" — a struggle against the common enemies of man: tyranny, poverty, disease and war itself.

Can we forge against these enemies a grand and global alliance, north and south, east and west, that can assure a more fruitful life for all mankind? Will you join in that historic effort?

In the long history of the world, only a few generations have been granted the role of defending freedom in its hour of maximum danger. I do not shrink from this responsibility — I welcome it. I do not believe that any of us would exchange places with any other people or any other generation. The energy, the faith and the devotion which we bring to this endeavor will light our country and all who serve it — and the glow from that fire can truly light the world.

And so, my fellow Americans: Ask not what your country will do for you — ask what you can do for your country.

My fellow citizens of the world: Ask not what America will do for you, but what together we can do for the freedom of man.

Finally, whether you are citizens of America or of the world, ask of us the same high standards of strength and sacrifice that we shall ask of you. With a good conscience our only sure reward, with history the final judge of our deeds, let us go forth to lead the land we love, asking His blessing and His help, but knowing that here on earth God's work must truly be our own.

Lyndon B. Johnson
POVERTY AND CIVIL RIGHTS

⊰{1964}⊱ WHEN the assassination of John F. Kennedy placed Lyndon B. Johnson in the White House, the new President's position was both difficult and full of opportunity. His reputation was more that of a political manipulator than a statesman and his knowledge of foreign affairs was thought to be somewhat less than extensive. He also lacked Kennedy's wry humor, youthful charm, and stylistic gifts, and intellectuals distrusted his energetic but somewhat imprecise tendency to substitute action and emotion for logic. At the same time most citizens, drawn together by the shock of the senseless murder of his predecessor, were ready to subordinate partisanship, at least for a season, and respond warmly to the President's plea for "the help of all Americans" in his effort to carry out the Kennedy program. Johnson also had the advantage of an intimate knowledge of Congress: its methods, its spirit, its men. His service in the national legislature dated back to New Deal days, and he had long been recognized by Congressmen of both parties as one of their "natural" leaders. Kennery had been a senator too, but he had never really been a major figure on Capitol Hill.

In any case, the new President astounded the country by winning Congressional approval for a series of measures, designed by his predecessor, whose future before the assassination had seemed dark indeed. Taxes were reduced, foreign aid appropriations passed without drastic cuts, and finally, in July 1964, the Kennedy civil rights bill became law. In addition, Johnson's own "war on poverty" bill was passed. In November 1963, men had wondered if Johnson could fill Kennedy's shoes; within a matter of months they were calling him one of the great political geniuses of the 20th century.

The following selections reveal something of Johnson's style and point of view. The first is his special message placing the anti-poverty bill before Congress; the second his radio address after signing the Civil Rights Act.

MESSAGE TO CONGRESS, 1964

To the Congress of the United States:

WE ARE citizens of the richest and most fortunate nation in the history of the world.

One hundred and eighty years ago we were a small country struggling for survival on the margin of a hostile land.

Today we have established a civilization of freemen which spans an entire continent.

With the growth of our country has come opportunity for our people — opportunity to educate our children, to use our energies in productive work, to increase our leisure — opportunity for almost every American to hope that through work and talent he could create a better life for himself and his family.

The path forward has not been an easy one.

But we have never lost sight of our goal: an America in which every citizen shares all the opportunities of his society, in which every man has a chance to advance his welfare to the limit of his capacities.

We have come a long way toward this goal.

We still have a long way to go.

The distance which remains is the measure of the great unfinished work of our society.

To finish that work I have called for a national war on poverty. Our objective: total victory.

There are millions of Americans — one-fifth of our people — who have not shared in the abundance which has been granted to most of us, and on whom the gates of opportunity have been closed.

What does this poverty mean to those who endure it?

It means a daily struggle to secure the necessities for even a meager existence. It means that the abundance, the comforts, the opportunities they see all around them are beyond their grasp.

Worst of all, it means hopelessness for the young.

The young man or woman who grows up without a decent education, in a broken home, in a hostile and squalid environment, in ill health or in the face of racial injustice — that young man or woman is often trapped in a life of poverty.

He does not have the skills demanded by a complex society. He does not know how to acquire those skills. He faces a mounting sense of despair which drains initiative and ambition and energy.

Our tax cut will create millions of new jobs — new exits from poverty.

But we must also strike down all the barriers which keep many from using those exits.

The war on poverty is not a struggle simply to support people, to make them dependent on the generosity of others.

It is a struggle to give people a chance.

It is an effort to allow them to develop and use their capacities, as we have been allowed to develop and use ours, so that they can share, as others share, in the promise of this Nation.

We do this, first of all, because it is right that we should.

From the establishment of public education and land-grant colleges through agricultural extension and encouragement to industry, we have pursued the goal of a nation with full and increasing opportunities for all its citizens.

The war on poverty is a further step in that pursuit.

We do it also because helping some will increase the prosperity of all.

Our fight against poverty will be an investment in the most valuable of our resources — the skills and strength of our people.

And in the future, as in the past, this investment will return its cost manifold to our entire economy.

If we can raise the annual earnings of 10 million among the poor by only $1,000, we will have added $14 billion a year to our national output. In addition, we can make important reductions in public assistance payments which now cost us $4 billion a year, and in the large costs of fighting crime and delinquency, disease and hunger.

This is only part of the story.

Our history has proved that each time we broaden the base of abundance, giving more people the chance to produce and consume, we create new industry, higher production, increased earnings, and better income for all.

Giving new opportunity to those who have little will enrich the lives of all the rest.

Because it is right, because it is wise, and because, for the first time in our history, it is possible to conquer poverty, I submit, for the consideration of the Congress and the country, the Economic Opportunity Act of 1964.

The act does not merely expand old programs or improve what is already being done.

It charts a new course.

It strikes at the causes, not just the consequences of poverty.

It can be a milestone in our 180-year search for a better life for our people.

This act provides five basic opportunities.

It will give almost half a million underprivileged young Americans the opportunity to develop skills, continue education, and find useful work.

It will give every American community the opportunity to develop a comprehensive plan to fight its own poverty — and help them to carry out their plans.

It will give dedicated Americans the opportunity to enlist as volunteers in the war against poverty.

It will give many workers and farmers the opportunity to break through particular barriers which bar their escape from poverty.

It will give the entire Nation the opportunity for a concerted attack on poverty through the establishment, under my direction, of the Office of Economic Opportunity, a national headquarters for the war against poverty.

This is how we propose to create these opportunities.

First. We will give high priority to helping young Americans who lack skills, who have not completed their education, or who cannot complete it because they are too poor.

The years of high school and college age are the most critical stage of a young person's life. If they are not helped then, many will be condemned to a life of poverty which they, in turn, will pass on to their children.

I therefore recommend the creation of a Job Corps, a work-training program, and a work study program.

A new National Job Corps will build toward an enlistment of 100,000 young men. They will be drawn from those whose background, health, and education make them least fit for useful work.

Those who volunteer will enter more than 100 camps and centers around the country.

Half of these young men will work, in the first year, on special conservation projects to give them education, useful work experience, and to enrich the natural resources of the country.

Half of these young men will receive, in the first year, a blend of training, basic education, and work experience in job training centers.

These are not simply camps for the underprivileged. They are new educational institutions, comparable in innovation to the land-grant colleges. Those who enter them will emerge better qualified to play a productive role in American society.

A new national work-training program operated by the Department of Labor will provide work and training for 200,000 American men and women between the ages of 16 and 21. This will be developed through State and local governments and nonprofit agencies.

Hundreds of thousands of young Americans badly need the experience, the income, and the sense of purpose which useful full- or part-time work can bring. For them such work may mean the difference between finishing school or dropping out. Vital community activities from hospitals and playgrounds to libraries and settlement houses are suffering because there are not enough people to staff them.

We are simply bringing these needs together.

A new national work-study program operated by the Department of Health, Education, and Welfare will provide Federal funds for part-time jobs for 140,000 young Americans who do not go to college because they cannot afford it.

There is no more senseless waste than the waste of the brainpower and skill of those who are kept from college by economic circumstance. Under this program they will, in a great American tradition, be able to work their way through school.

They and the country will be richer for it.

Second. Through a new community-action program we intend to strike at poverty at its source — in the streets of our cities and on the farms of our countryside among the very young and the impoverished old.

This program asks men and women throughout the country to prepare long-range plans for the attack on poverty in their own local communities.

These are not plans prepared in Washington and imposed upon hundreds of different situations.

They are based on the fact that local citizens best understand their own problems, and know best how to deal with those problems.

These plans will be local plans striking at the many unfilled needs which underlie poverty in each community, not just one or two. Their components and emphasis will differ as needs differ.

These plans will be local plans calling upon all the resources available to the community — Federal and State, local and private, human and material.

And when these plans are approved by the Office of Economic Opportunity, the Federal Government will finance up to 90 percent of the additional cost for the first 2 years.

The most enduring strength of our Nation is the huge reservoir of talent, initiative and leadership which exists at every level of our society.

Through the community action program we call upon this, our greatest strength, to overcome our greatest weakness.

Third. I ask for the authority to recruit and train skilled volunteers for the war against poverty.

Thousands of Americans have volunteered to serve the needs of other lands. Thousands more want the chance to serve the needs of their own land. They should have that chance.

Among older people who have retired, as well as among the young, among women as well as men, there are many Americans who are ready to enlist in our war against poverty.

They have skills and dedication. They are badly needed.

If the State requests them, if the community needs and will use them, we will recruit and train them and give them the chance to serve.

Fourth. We intend to create new opportunities for certain hard-hit groups to break out of the pattern of poverty.

Through a new program of loans and guarantees we can provide incentives to those who will employ the unemployed.

Through programs of work and retraining for unemployed fathers and mothers we can help them support their families in dignity while preparing themselves for new work.

Through funds to purchase needed land, organize cooperatives, and create new and adequate family farms we can help those whose life on the land has been a struggle without hope.

Fifth. I do not intend that the war against poverty become a series of uncoordinated and unrelated efforts — that it perish for lack of leadership and direction.

Therefore this bill creates, in the Executive Office of the President, a new Office of Economic Opportunity. Its Director will be my personal chief of staff for the war against poverty. I intend to appoint Sargent Shriver to this post.

He will be directly responsible for these new programs. He will work with and through existing agencies of the Government.

This program — the Economic Opportunity Act — is the foundation of our war against poverty. But it does not stand alone.

For the past 3 years this Government has advanced a number of new proposals which strike at important areas of need and distress.

I ask the Congress to extend those which are already in action, and to establish those which have already been proposed.

There are programs to help badly distressed areas such as the Area Redevelopment Act, and the legislation now being prepared to help Appalachia.

There are programs to help those without training find a place in today's complex society — such as the Manpower Development Training Act and the Vocational Education Act for youth.

There are programs to protect those who are specially vulnerable to the ravages of poverty — hospital insurance for the elderly, protection for migrant farm-workers, a food stamp program for the needy, coverage for millions not now protected by a minimum wage, new and expanded unemployment benefits for men out of work, a housing and community development bill for those seeking decent homes.

Finally there are programs which help the entire country, such as aid to education which, by raising the quality of schooling available to every American child, will give a new chance for knowledge to the children of the poor.

I ask immediate action on all these programs.

What you are being asked to consider is not a simple or an easy program. But poverty is not a simple or an easy enemy.

It cannot be driven from the land by a single attack on a single front. Were this so we would have conquered poverty long ago.

Nor can it be conquered by government alone.

For decades American labor and American business, private institutions and private individuals have been engaged in strengthening our economy and offering new opportunity to those in need.

We need their help, their support, and their full participation.

Through this program we offer new incentives and new opportunities for cooperation, so that all the energy of our Nation, can be brought to bear on our common enemy.

Today, for the first time in our history, we have the power to strike away the barriers to full participation in our society. Having the power, we have the duty.

The Congress is charged by the Constitution to "provide * * * for the general welfare of the United States." Our present abundance is a measure of its success in fulfilling that duty. Now Congress is being asked to extend that welfare to all our people.

The President of the United States is President of all the people in every section of the country. But this office also holds a special responsibility to the distressed and disinherited, the hungry and the hopeless of this abundant Nation.

It is in pursuit of that special responsibility that I submit this message to you today.

The new program I propose is within our means. Its cost of $970 million is 1 percent of our national budget — and every dollar I am requesting for this program is already included in the budget I sent to Congress in January.

But we cannot measure its importance by its cost.

For it charts an entirely new course of hope for our people.

We are fully aware that this program will not eliminate all the poverty in America in a few months or a few years. Poverty is deeply rooted and its causes are many.

But this program will show the way to new opportunities for millions of our fellow citizens.

It will provide a lever with which we can begin to open the door to our prosperity for those who have been kept outside.

It will also give us the chance to test our weapons, to try our energy and ideas and imagination for the many battles yet to come. As conditions change, and as experience illuminates our difficulties, we will be prepared to modify our strategy.

And this program is much more than a beginning.

Rather it is a commitment. It is a total commitment by this President, and this Congress, and this Nation, to pursue victory over the most ancient of mankind's enemies.

On many historic occasions the President has requested from Congress the authority to move against forces which were endangering the well-being of our country.

This is such an occasion.

On similar occasions in the past we have often been called upon to wage war against foreign enemies which threatened our freedom. Today we are asked to declare war on a domestic enemy which threatens the strength of our Nation and the welfare of our people.

If we now move forward against this enemy — if we can bring to the challenges of peace the same determination and strength which has brought us victory in war — then this day and this Congress will have won a secure and honorable place in the history of the Nation, and the enduring gratitude of generations of Americans yet to come.

LYNDON B. JOHNSON.
THE WHITE HOUSE, *March 16, 1964.*

RADIO ADDRESS, 1964

My fellow Americans:

I am about to sign into law the Civil Rights Act of 1964. I want to take this occasion to talk to you about what that law means to every American.

One hundred and eighty-eight years ago this week a small band of valiant men began a long struggle for freedom.

They pledged their lives, their fortunes, and their sacred honor not only to found a nation but to forge an ideal of freedom, not only for political independence but for personal liberty, not only to eliminate foreign rule but to establish the rule of justice in the affairs of men.

That struggle was a turning point in our history.

Today in far corners of distant continents the ideals of those American patriots still shape the struggles of men who hunger for freedom.

This is a proud triumph. Yet those who founded our country knew that freedom would be secure only if each generation thought to renew and enlarge its meaning.

From the Minutemen at Concord to the soldiers in Vietnam, each generation has been equal to that trust.

Americans of every race and color have worked to build a nation of widening opportunities.

Now, our generation of Americans has been called on to continue the unending search for justice within our own borders.

We believe that all men are created equal—yet many are denied equal treatment.

We believe that all men have certain unalienable rights—yet many Americans do not enjoy those rights.

We believe that all men are entitled to the blessings of liberty—yet millions are being deprived of those blessings, not because of their own failures but because of the color of their skin.

The reasons are deeply imbedded in history and tradition and the nature of man. We can understand without rancor or hatred how all this happened. But it cannot continue.

Our Constitution, the foundation of our Republic forbids it. The principles of our freedom forbid it. And the law I will sign tonight forbids it. That law is the product of months of the most careful debate and discussion. It was proposed more than one year ago by our late and beloved President, John F. Kennedy. It received the bipartisan support of more than two-thirds of the members of both the House and the Senate. An overwhelming majority of Republicans as well as Democrats voted for it.

It has received the thoughtful support of tens of thousands of civic and religious leaders in all parts of this nation, and it is supported by the great majority of the American people.

The purpose of this law is simple. It does not restrict the freedom of any American as long as he respects the rights of others. It does not give special treatment to any citizen. It does say that those who are equal before God shall now also be equal in the polling booths, in the classrooms, in the factories, and in hotels, and restaurants, and movie theatres, and other places that provide service to the public.

I'm taking steps to implement the law under my constitutional obligation to take care that the laws are faithfully executed.

First, I will send to the Senate my nomination of LeRoy Collins to be Director of the Community Relations Service.

Governor Collins will bring the experience of a long career of distinguished public service to the task of helping communities solve problems of human relations through reason and common sense.

Second, I shall appoint an advisory committee of distinguished Americans to assist Governor Collins in his assignment.

Third, I am sending Congress a request for supplemental appropriations to pay for necessary costs of implementing the law and asking for immediate action.

Fourth, already today in a meeting of my Cabinet this afternoon I directed the agencies of this government to fully discharge the new responsibilities imposed upon them by the law and to do it without delay and to keep me personally informed of their progress.

Fifth, I am asking appropriate officials to meet with representative groups to promote greater understanding of the law and to achieve a spirit of compliance.

We must not approach the observance and enforcement of this law in a vengeful spirit. Its purpose is not to punish. Its purpose is not to divide but to end divisions which have lasted all too long.

Its purpose is national not regional. Its purpose is to promote a more abiding commitment to freedom, a more constant pursuit of justice and a deeper respect for human dignity.

We will achieve these goals because most Americans are law-abiding citizens who want to do what is right. This is why the Civil Rights Act relies first on voluntary compliance, then on the efforts of local communities and states to secure the rights of citizens.

It provides for the national authority to step in only when others cannot or will not do the job.

This Civil Rights Act is a challenge to all of us to go to work in our communities and our states, in our homes and in our hearts to eliminate the last vestiges of injustice in our beloved country.

So, tonight I urge every public official, every religious leader, every business and professional man, every working man, every housewife—I urge every American to join in this effort to bring justice and hope to all people and to bring peace to our land.

My fellow citizens, we have come now to a time of testing. We must not fail.

Let us hasten that day when our unmeasured strength and our unbounded spirit will be free to do the great works ordained to this nation by the just and wise God who is the Father of us all.

Thank you and good night.

Earl Warren

REDISTRICTING OF STATE LEGISLATURES

❧{*1964*}❧ A CONVINCING argument can be made for the proposition that in the years since World War II the Supreme Court has been the most powerful and effective branch of the federal government. Under the leadership of Chief Justice Earl Warren, whom President Eisenhower appointed to the Court in 1953, the judges have repeatedly handed down decisions that have basically altered the very structure of American society. The school desegregation case (*Brown* v. *Board of Education,* see above, pp. 547-551) is the best known and most dramatic of these decisions, but it is possible that a series of cases settled on June 15, 1964 will have an even more fundamental influence on the future course of American history.

These cases involved the question of the apportionment of seats in both houses of state legislatures. Ever since colonial times, legislatures have used their power to define the districts from which their members are chosen to influence their own make up and favor the interests of a special class or political party. Sometimes they have done so by controlling the *shape* of districts, those in control adjusting district lines to maximize their own strength and limit that of their opponents. This is known as "gerrymandering," the name being derived from that of Elbridge Gerry, an early 19th-century Governor of Massachusetts who was adept at this type of manipulation. More common and far more effective has been the practice of varying the *size* of legislative districts, the dominant party carving its own areas of strength into many districts of relatively small population and lumping large numbers of people in regions where the other party is strong into few districts. Generally speaking, since 1900 the practice has been to under-represent cities to the advantage of rural areas, and since the era of the New Deal, that has usually meant favoring the Republicans at the expense of the Democrats.

The Court's decisions in the series of cases here under consideration promise to force the redistricting of nearly all the state legislatures in the nation. The effect of this on state and national history is certain to be very great. Particularly controversial is Justice Warren's handling of the so-called "federal analogy," the argument that since the United States Senate represents geographical units rather than population, it is proper for one house of a state legislature to do the same thing.

REYNOLDS *v.* SIMS

Mr. Chief Justice Warren delivered the opinion of the Court.

Involved in these cases are an appeal and two cross-appeals from a decision of the Federal District Court for the Middle District of Alabama holding invalid, under the Equal Protection Clause of the Federal Constitution, the existing and two legislatively proposed plans for the apportionment of seats in the two houses of the Alabama Legislature, and ordering into effect a temporary reapportionment plan comprised of parts of the proposed but judicially disapproved measures. . . .

Plaintiffs below alleged that the last apportionment of the Alabama Legislature was based on the 1900 federal census, despite the requirement of the State Constitution that the legislature be reapportioned decennially. They asserted that, since the population growth in the State from 1900 to 1960 had been uneven, Jefferson and other counties were now victims of serious discrimination with respect to the allocation of legislative representation. As a result of the failure of the legislature to reapportion itself, plaintiffs asserted, they were denied "equal suffrage in free and equal elections . . . and the equal protection of the laws" in violation of the Alabama Constitution and the Fourteenth Amendment to the Federal Constitution.

Undeniably the Constitution of the United States protects the right of all qualified citizens to vote, in state as well as in federal elections. A consistent line of decisions by this Court in cases involving attempts to deny or restrict the right of suffrage has made this indelibly clear. It has been repeatedly recognized that all qualified voters have a constitutionally protected right to vote, *Ex parte Yarbrough,* 110 U. S. 651, and to have their votes counted, *United States* v. *Mosley,* 238 U. S. 383. . . .

The right to vote freely for the candidate of one's choice is of the essence of a democratic society, and any restrictions on that right strike at the heart of representative government. And the right of suffrage can be denied by a debasement or dilution of the weight of a citizen's vote just as effectively as by wholly prohibiting the free exercise of the franchise. . . .

Legislators represent people, not trees or acres. Legislators are elected by voters, not farms or cities or economic interests. As long as ours is a representative form of government, and our legislatures are those instruments of government elected directly by and directly representative of the people, the right to elect legislators in a free and unimpaired fashion is a bedrock of our political system. It could hardly be gainsaid that a constitutional claim had been asserted by an allegation that certain otherwise qualified voters had been entirely prohibited from voting for members of their state legislature. And, if a State should provide that the votes of citizens in one part of the State should be given two times or five times or 10 times the weight of votes of citizens in another part of the State, it could hardly be contended that the right to vote of those residing in the disfavored areas had not been effectively diluted. It would appear extraordinary to suggest that a state could be constitutionally permitted to enact a law providing that certain of the state's voters could vote two, five, or 10 times for their legislative representatives, while voters living elsewhere could vote only once. And it is inconceivable that a state law to the effect that, in counting votes for legislators, the votes of citizens in one part of the State would be multiplied by two, five, or 10, while the votes of persons in another area would be counted only at face value, could be constitutionally sustainable. Of course, the effect of state legislative districting schemes which give the same number of representatives to unequal numbers of constituents is identical. . . .

Logically, in a society ostensibly grounded on representative government, it would seem reasonable that a majority of the people of a State could elect a majority of that State's legislators. To conclude differently, and to sanction minority control of state legislative bodies, would appear to deny majority rights in a way that far surpasses any possible denial of minority rights that might otherwise be thought to result. Since legislatures are responsible for enacting laws by which all citizens are to be governed, they should be bodies which are collectively responsive to the popular will.

And the concept of equal protection has been traditionally viewed as re-quiring the uniform treatment of persons standing in the same relation to the governmental action questioned or challenged. With respect to the allocation of legislative representation, all voters, as citizens of a State, stand in the same relation regardless of where they live. Any suggested criteria for the differentiation of citizens are insufficient to justify any discrimination, as to the weight of their votes, unless relevant to the permissible purposes of legislative apportionment. Since the achieving of fair and effective representation for all citizens is concededly the basic aim of legislative apportionment, we conclude that the Equal Protection Clause guarantees the opportunity for equal participation by all voters in the election of state legislators. Diluting the weight of votes because of place of residence impairs basic constitutional rights under the Fourteenth Amendment just as much as invidious discriminations based upon factors such as race, *Brown* v. *Board of Education,* 347 U. S. 483, or economic status, *Griffin* v. *Illinois,* 351 U. S. 12, *Douglas v. California,* 372 U. S. 353. Our constitutional system amply provides for the protection of minorities by means other than giving them majority control of state legislatures. And the democratic ideals of equality and majority rule, which have served this Nation so well in the past, are hardly of any less significance for the present and the future.

We are told that the matter of apportioning representation in a state legislature is a complex and many-faceted one. We are advised that States can rationally consider factors other than population in apportioning legislative representation. We are admonished not to restrict the power of the States to impose differing views as to political philosophy on their citizens. We are cautioned about the dangers of entering into political thickets and mathematical quagmires. Our answer is this: a denial of constitutionally protected rights demands judicial protection; our oath and our office require no less of us. . . .

We hold that, as a basic constitutional standard, the Equal Protection Clause requires that the seats in both houses of a bicameral state legislature must be apportioned on a population basis. Simply stated, an individual's right to vote for state legislators is unconstitutionally impaired when its weight is in a substantial fashion diluted when compared with votes of citizens living in other parts of the State. Since, under neither the existing apportionment provisions nor under either of the proposed plans was either of the houses of the Alabama Legislature apportioned on a population basis, the District Court correctly held that all three of these schemes were constitutionally invalid. . . .

Legislative apportionment in Alabama is signally illustrative and symptomatic of the seriousness of this problem in a number of the States. At the time this litigation was commenced, there had been no reapportionment of seats in the Alabama Legislature for over 60 years. Legislative inaction, coupled with the unavailability of any political or judicial remedy, had resulted, with the passage of years, in the perpetuated scheme becoming little more than an irrational anachronism. Consistent failure by the Alabama Legislature to comply with state constitutional requirements as to the frequency of reapportionment and the bases of legislative representation resulted in a minority strangle hold on the State Legislature. Inequality of representation in one house added to the inequality in the other. With the crazy-quilt existing apportionment virtually conceded to be invalid, the Alabama Legislature offered two proposed plans for consideration by the District Court, neither of which was to be effective until 1966 and neither of which provided for the apportionment of even one of the two houses on a population basis. We find that the court below did not err in holding that neither of these proposed reapportionment schemes, considered as a whole, "meets the necessary constitutional requirements." . . .

LUCAS *v*. COLORADO

MR. CHIEF JUSTICE WARREN delivered the opinion of the Court.

Involved in this case is an appeal from a decision of the Federal District Court for the District of Colorado upholding the validity, under the Equal Protection Clause of the Fourteenth Amendment to the Federal Constitution, of the apportionment of seats in the Colorado Legislature pursuant to the provisions of a constitutional amendment approved by the Colorado electorate in 1962. . . .

At the November 1962 general election, the Colorado electorate adopted proposed Amendment No. 7 by a vote of 305,700 to 172,725, and defeated proposed Amendment No. 8 by a vote of 311,749 to 149,822. Amendment No. 8, rejected by a majority of the voters, prescribed an apportionment plan pursuant to which seats in both houses of the Colorado Legislature would purportedly be apportioned on a population basis. Amendment No. 7, on the other hand provided for the apportionment of the House of Representatives on the basis of population, but essentially maintained the existing apportionment in the Senate, which was based on a combination of population and various other factors. . . .

In *Reynolds* v. *Sims,* decided also this date, we held that the Equal Protection Clause requires that both houses of a bicameral state legislature must be apportioned substantially on a population basis. Of course, the court below assumed, and the parties apparently conceded, that the Colorado House of Representatives, under the statutory provisions enacted by the Colorado Legislature in early 1963 pursuant to Amendment No. 7's dictate that the legislature should create 65 House districts "as nearly equal in population as may be," is now apportioned sufficiently on a population basis to comport with federal constitutional requisites. We need not pass on this question, since the apportionment of Senate seats, under Amendment No. 7, clearly involves departures from population-based representation too extreme to be constitutionally permissible, and there is no indication that the apportionment of the two houses of the Colorado General Assembly, pursuant to the 1962 constitutional amendment, is severable. We therefore conclude that the District Court erred in holding the legislative apportionment plan embodied in Amendment No. 7 to be constitutionally valid. Under neither Amendment No. 7's plan, nor, of course, the previous statutory scheme, is the overall legislative representation in the two houses of the Colorado Legislature sufficiently grounded on population to be constitutionally sustainable under the Equal Protection Clause.

Except as an interim remedial procedure justifying a court in staying its hand temporarily, we find no significance in the fact that a nonjudicial, political remedy may be available for the effectuation of asserted rights to equal representation in a state legislature. Courts sit to adjudicate controversies involving alleged denials of constitutional rights. While a court sitting as a court of equity might be justified in temporarily refraining from the issuance of injunctive relief in an apportionment case in order to allow for resort to an available political remedy, such as initiative and referendum, individual constitutional rights cannot be deprived, or denied judicial effectuation, because of the existence of a nonjudicial remedy through which relief against the alleged malapportionment, which the individual voters seek, might be achieved. An individual's constitutionally protected right to cast an equally weighted vote cannot be denied even by a vote of a majority of a State's electorate, if the apportionment scheme adopted by the voters fails to measure up to the requirements of the Equal Protection Clause. Manifestly, the fact that an apportionment plan is adopted in a popular referendum is insufficient to sustain its constitutionality or to induce a court of equity to refuse to act. As stated by this Court in *West Virginia State Bd. of Educ.* v. *Barnette,* 319 U. S. 624, 638, "One's right to life, liberty, and property . . . and other fundamental rights may not be submitted to vote; they depend on the outcome of no elections." A citizen's constitutional rights can hardly be infringed simply because a majority of the people choose to do so. We hold that the fact that a challenged legislative apportionment plan was approved by the electorate is without federal constitutional significance, if the scheme adopted fails to satisfy the basic requirements of the Equal Protection Clause, as delineated in our opinion in *Reynolds* v. *Sims*. And we conclude that the fact that a practicably available political remedy, such as initiative and referendum, exists under state law provides justification only for a court of equity to stay its hand temporarily while recourse to such a remedial device is attempted or while proposed initiated measures relating to legislative apportionment are pending and will be submitted to the State's voters at the next election.

Because of the imminence of the November 1962 election, and the fact that two initiated proposals relating to legislative apportionment would be voted on by the State's electorate at that election, the District Court properly stayed its hand and permitted the 1962 election of legislators to be conducted pursuant to the existing statutory scheme. But appellees' argument, accepted by the court below, that the apportionment of the Colorado Senate, under Amendment No. 7, is rational because it takes into account a variety of geographical, historical, topographic and economic considerations fails to provide an adequate justification for the substantial disparities from population-based representation in the allocation of Senate seats to the disfavored populous areas. And any attempted reliance on the so-called federal analogy is factually as well as constitutionally without merit.

Since the apportionment of seats in the Colorado Legislature, under the provisions of Amendment No. 7, fails to comport with the requirements of the Equal Protection Clause, the decision below must be reversed. . . .

George F. Kennan

CONTAINMENT OF COMMUNISM

❧{1947}❧ BY THE Truman Doctrine and the Marshall Plan the United States had already begun a policy of "containing" Soviet expansion when, in July, 1947, an article rationalizing this policy appeared in the magazine *Foreign Affairs*. The title of the article was "The Sources of Soviet Conduct," and the author's name was given only as "X." Later the mysterious Mr. X was revealed as George F. Kennan (1904-   ), the head of the State Department's new policy planning staff, which was charged with the making of long-range plans for the conduct of American diplomacy. Thus the article was an authoritative exposition of official thinking. It was, indeed, an expression of the point of view behind American strategy in the "cold war." Despite differences in emphasis, this basic view continued to guide policy makers throughout the Truman and Eisenhower administrations and into the Kennedy-Johnson administration.

Kennan, a career diplomat of wide experience in Washington and abroad, was appointed ambassador to the Soviet Union in 1952. Later he devoted himself to lecturing and writing on current American policy (with which he has not always agreed) and to producing an exhaustive study of the history of the Russian Revolution.

THE SOURCES OF SOVIET CONDUCT

I

The political personality of Soviet power as we know it today is the product of ideology and circumstances: ideology inherited by the present Soviet leaders from the movement in which they had their political origin, and circumstances of the power which they now have exercised for nearly three decades in Russia. There can be few tasks of psychological analysis more difficult than to try to trace the interaction of these two forces and the relative role of each in the determination of official Soviet conduct. Yet the attempt must be made if that conduct is to be understood and effectively countered.

It is difficult to summarize the set of ideological concepts with which the Soviet leaders came into power. Marxian ideology, in its Russian-Communist projection, has always been in process of subtle evolution. The materials on which it bases itself are extensive and complex. But the outstanding features of Communist thought as it existed in 1916 may perhaps be summarized as follows: (*a*) that the central factor in the life of man, the fact which determines the character of public life and the "physiognomy of society," is the system by which material goods are produced and exchanged; (*b*) that the capitalist system of production is a nefarious one which inevitably leads to the exploitation of the working class by the capital-owning class and is incapable of developing adequately the economic resources of society or of distributing fairly the material goods produced by human labor; (*c*) that capitalism contains the seeds of its own destruction and must, in view of the inability of the capital-owning class to adjust itself to economic change, result eventually and inescapably in a revolutionary transfer of power to the working class; and (*d*) that imperialism, the final phase of capitalism, leads directly to war and revolution.

The rest may be outlined in Lenin's own words: "Unevenness of economic and political development is the inflexible law of capitalism. It follows from this that the victory of Socialism may come originally in a few capitalist countries or even in a single capitalist country. The victorious proletariat of that country, having expropriated the capitalists and having organized Socialist production at home, would rise against the remaining capitalist world, drawing to itself in the process the oppressed classes of other countries." [1] It must be noted that there was no assumption that capitalism would perish without proletarian revolution. A final push was needed from a revolutionary proletariat movement in order to tip over the tottering structure. But it was regarded as inevitable that sooner or later that push be given.

For fifty years prior to the outbreak of the Revolution, this pattern of thought had exercised great fascination for the members of the Russian revolutionary movement. Frustrated, discontented, hopeless of finding self-expression — or too impatient to seek it — in the confining limits of the Tsarist political system, yet lacking wide popular support for their choice of bloody revolution as a means of social betterment, these revolutionists found in Marxist theory a highly convenient rationalization for their own instinctive desires. It afforded pseudo-scientific justification for their impatience, for their categoric denial of all value in the Tsarist system, for their yearning for power and revenge and for their inclination to cut corners in the pursuit of it. It is therefore no wonder that they had come to believe implicitly in the truth and soundness of the Marxian-Leninist teachings, so congenial to their own impulses and emotions. Their sincerity need not be impugned. This is a phenomenon as old as human nature itself. It has never been more aptly described than by Edward Gibbon, who wrote in *The Decline and Fall of the Roman Empire:* "From enthusiasm to imposture the step is perilous and slippery; the demon of Socrates affords a memorable instance how a wise man may deceive himself; how a good man may deceive others, how the conscience may slumber in a mixed and middle state between self-illusion and voluntary fraud." And it was with this set of conceptions that the members of the Bolshevik Party entered into power.

Now it must be noted that through all the years of preparation for revolution, the attention of these men, as indeed of Marx himself, had been centered less on the future form which Socialism[2] would take than on the necessary overthrow of rival power which, in their view, had to precede the introduction of Socialism. Their views, therefore, on the positive program to be put into effect, once power was attained, were for the most part nebulous, visionary and impractical. Beyond the nationalization of industry

[1] *Concerning the Slogans of the United States of Europe, August* 1915 (Official Soviet edition of Lenin's works).
[2] Here and elsewhere in this paper "Socialism" refers to Marxist or Leninist Communism, not to liberal Socialism of the Second International variety.

and the expropriation of large private capital holdings there was no agreed program. The treatment of the peasantry, which according to the Marxist formulation was not of the proletariat, had always been a vague spot in the pattern of Communist thought; and it remained an object of controversy and vacillation for the first ten years of Communist power.

The circumstances of the immediate post-Revolution period — the existence in Russia of civil war and foreign intervention, together with the obvious fact that the Communists represented only a tiny minority of the Russian people — made the establishment of dictatorial power a necessity. The experiment with "war Communism" and the abrupt attempt to eliminate private production and trade had unfortunate economic consequences and caused further bitterness against the new revolutionary regime. While the temporary relaxation of the effort to communize Russia, represented by the New Economic Policy, alleviated some of this economic distress and thereby served its purpose, it also made it evident that the "capitalistic sector of society" was still prepared to profit at once from any relaxation of governmental pressure, and would, if permitted to continue to exist, always constitute a powerful opposing element to the Soviet regime and a serious rival for influence in the country. Somewhat the same situation prevailed with respect to the individual peasant who, in his own small way, was also a private producer.

Lenin, had he lived, might have proved a great enough man to reconcile these conflicting forces to the ultimate benefit of Russian society, though this is questionable. But be that as it may, Stalin, and those whom he led in the struggle for succession to Lenin's position of leadership, were not the men to tolerate rival political forces in the sphere of power which they coveted. Their sense of insecurity was too great. Their particular band of fanaticism, unmodified by any of the Anglo-Saxon traditions of compromise, was too fierce and too jealous to envisage any permanent sharing of power. From the Russian-Asiatic world out of which they had emerged they carried with them a skepticism as to the possibilities of permanent and peaceful coexistence of rival forces. Easily persuaded of their own doctrinaire "rightness," they insisted on the submission or destruction of all competing power. Outside of the Communist Party, Russian society was to have no rigidity. There were to be no forms of collective human activity or association which would not be dominated by the Party. No other force in Russian society was to be permitted to achieve vitality or integrity. Only the Party was to have structure. All else was to be an amorphous mass.

And within the Party the same principle was to apply. The mass of Party members might go through the motions of election, deliberation, decision and action; but in these motions they were to be animated not by their own individual wills but by the awesome breath of the Party leadership and the overbrooding presence of "the world."

Let it be stressed again that subjectively these men probably did not seek absolutism for its own sake. They doubtless believed — and found it easy to believe — that they alone knew what was good for society and that they would accomplish that good once their power was secure and unchallengeable. But in seeking that security of their own rule they were prepared to recognize no restrictions, either of God or man, on the character of their methods. And until such a time as that security might be achieved, they placed far down on their scale of operational priorities the comforts and happiness of the peoples entrusted to their care.

Now the outstanding circumstance concerning the Soviet regime is that down to the present day this process of political consolidation has never been completed and the men in the Kremlin have continued to be predominantly absorbed with the struggle to secure and make absolute the power which they seized in November 1917. They have endeavored to secure it primarily against forces at home, within Soviet society itself. But they have also endeavored to secure it against the outside world. For ideology, as we have seen, taught them that the outside world was hostile and that it was their duty eventually to overthrow the political forces beyond their borders. The powerful hands of Russian history and tradition reached up to sustain them in this feeling. Finally, their own aggressive intransigence with respect to the outside world began to find its own reaction; and they were soon forced, to use another Gibbonesque phrase, "to chastise the contumacy" which they themselves had provoked. It is an undeniable privilege of every man to prove himself right in the thesis that the world is his enemy; for if he reiterates it frequently enough and makes it the background of his conduct he is bound eventually to be right.

Now it lies in the nature of the mental world of the Soviet leaders, as well as in the character of their ideology, that no opposition to them can be officially recognized as having any merit or justification whatsoever. Such opposition can flow, in theory, only from the hostile and incorrigible forces of dying capitalism. As long as remnants of capitalism were officially recognized as existing in Russia, it was possible to place on them, as an internal element, part of the blame for the maintenance of a dictatorial form of society. But as these remnants were liquidated, little by little, this justification fell away; and when it was indicated officially that they had been finally destroyed, it disappeared altogether. And this fact created one of the most basic of the compulsions which came to act upon the Soviet regime: since capitalism no longer existed in Russia and since it could not be admitted that there could be serious or widespread opposition to the

Kremlin springing spontaneously from the liberated masses under its authority, it became necessary to justify the retention of the dictatorship by stressing the menace of capitalism abroad.

This began at an early date. In 1924, Stalin specifically defended the retention of the "organs of suppression," meaning, among others, the army and the secret police, on the ground that "as long as there is a capitalist encirclement there will be danger of intervention with all the consequences that flow from that danger." In accordance with that theory, and from that time on, all internal opposition forces in Russia have consistently been portrayed as the agents of foreign forces of reaction antagonistic to Soviet power.

By the same token, tremendous emphasis has been placed on the original Communist thesis of a basic antagonism between the capitalist and Socialist worlds. It is clear, from many indications, that this emphasis is not founded in reality. The real facts concerning it have been confused by the existence abroad of genuine resentment provoked by Soviet philosophy and tactics and occasionally by the existence of great centers of military power, notably the Nazi regime in Germany and the Japanese Government of the late 1930's, which did indeed have aggressive designs against the Soviet Union. But there is ample evidence that the stress laid in Moscow on the menace confronting Soviet society from the world outside its borders is founded not in the realities of foreign antagonism but in the necessity of explaining away the maintenance of dictatorial authority at home.

Now the maintenance of this pattern of Soviet power, namely, the pursuit of unlimited authority domestically, accompanied by the cultivation of the semi-myth of implacable foreign hostility, has gone far to shape the actual machinery of Soviet power as we know it today. Internal organs of administration which did not serve this purpose withered on the vine. Organs which did serve this purpose became vastly swollen. The security of Soviet power came to rest on the iron discipline of the Party, on the severity and ubiquity of the secret police, and on the uncompromising economic monopolism of the state. The "organs of suppression," in which the Soviet leaders had sought security from rival forces, became in large measure the masters of those whom they were designed to serve. Today the major part of the structure of Soviet power is committed to the perfection of the dictatorship and to the maintenance of the concept of Russia as in a state of seige, with the enemy lowering beyond the walls. And the millions of human beings who form that part of the structure of power must defend at all costs this concept of Russia's position, for without it they are themselves superfluous.

As things stand today, the rulers can no longer dream of parting with these organs and suppression. The quest for absolute power, pursued now for nearly three decades with a ruthlessness unparalleled (in scope at least) in modern times, has again produced internally, as it did externally, its own reaction. The excesses of the police apparatus have fanned the potential opposition to the regime into something far greater and more dangerous than it could have been before those excesses began.

But least of all can the rulers dispense with the fiction by which the maintenance of dictatorial power has been defended. For this fiction has been canonized in Soviet philosophy by the excesses already committed in its name; and it is now anchored in the Soviet structure of thought by bonds far greater than those of mere ideology.

II

So much for the historical background. What does it spell in terms of the political personality of Soviet power as we know it today?

Of the original ideology, nothing has been officially junked. Belief is maintained in the basic badness of capitalism, in the inevitability of its destruction, in the obligation of the proletariat to assist in that destruction and to take power into its own hands. But stress has come to be laid primarily on those concepts which relate most specifically to the Soviet regime itself: to its position as the sole truly Socialist regime in a dark and misguided world, and to the relationships of power within it.

The first of these concepts is that of the innate antagonism between capitalism and Socialism. We have seen how deeply that concept has become imbedded in foundations of Soviet power. It has profound implications for Russia's conduct as a member of international society. It means that there can never be on Moscow's side any sincere assumption of a community of aims between the Soviet Union and powers which are regarded as capitalism. It must invariably be assumed in Moscow that the aims of the capitalist world are antagonistic to the Soviet regime and, therefore, to the interests of the peoples it controls. If the Soviet Government occasionally sets its signature to documents which would indicate the contrary, this is to be regarded as a tactical maneuver permissible in dealing with the enemy (who is without honor) and should be taken in the spirit of *caveat emptor*. Basically, the antagonism remains. It is postulated. And from it flow many of the phenomena which we find disturbing in the Kremlin's conduct of foreign policy: the secretiveness, the lack of frankness, the duplicity, the war suspiciousness, and the basic unfriendliness of purpose. These phenomena are there to stay, for the foreseeable future. There can be variations of degree and of emphasis. When there is something the Russians want from us, one or the other of these features of their policy may be thrust temporarily into the background; and when that happens there will always be Americans who will leap forward with gleeful announcements that "the Russians have changed," and some who will even try to take credit for having brought about such "changes." But we should not be misled by tactical maneuvers. These characteristics of Soviet policy, like the postulate from which they flow, are basic to the internal nature of Soviet power, and will be with us, whether in the foreground or the background, until the internal nature of Soviet power is changed.

This means that we are going to continue for a long time to find the Russians difficult to deal with. It does not mean that they should be considered as embarked upon a do-or-die program to overthrow our society by a given date. The theory of the inevitability of the eventual fall of capitalism has the fortunate connotation that there is no hurry about it. The forces of progress can take their time in preparing the final *coup de grâce*. Meanwhile, what is vital is that the "Socialist fatherland" — that oasis of power which has been already won for Socialism in the person of the Soviet Union — should be cherished and defended by all good Communists at home and abroad, its fortunes promoted, its enemies badgered and confounded. The promotion of premature, "adventuristic" revolutionary projects abroad which might embarrass Soviet power in any way would be an inexcusable, even a counter-revolutionary act. The cause of Socialism is the support and promotion of Soviet power, as defined in Moscow.

This brings us to the second of the concepts important to contemporary Soviet outlook. This is the infallibility of the Kremlin. The Soviet concept of power, which permits no focal points of organization outside the Party itself, requires that the Party leadership remain in theory the sole repository of truth. For if truth were to be found elsewhere, there would be justification for its expression in organized activity. But it is precisely that which the Kremlin cannot and will not permit.

The leadership of the Communist Party is therefore always right, and has been always right ever since in 1929 Stalin formalized his personal power by announcing that decisions of the Politburo were being taken unanimously.

On the principle of infallibility there rests the iron discipline of the Communist Party. In fact, the two concepts are mutually self-supporting. Perfect discipline requires recognition of infallibility. Infallibility requires the observance of discipline. And the two together go far to determine the behaviorism of the entire Soviet apparatus of power. But their effect cannot be understood unless a third factor be taken into account: namely, the fact that the leadership is at liberty to put forward for tactical purposes any particular thesis which it finds useful to the cause at any particular moment and to require the faithful and unquestioning acceptance of that thesis by the members of the movement as a whole. This means that truth is not a constant but is actually created, for all intents and purposes, by the Soviet leaders themselves. It may vary from week to week, from month to month. It is nothing absolute and immutable — nothing which flows from objective reality. It is only the most recent manifestation of the wisdom of those in whom the ultimate wisdom is supposed to reside, because they represent the logic of history. The accumulative effect of these factors is to give to the whole subordinate apparatus of Soviet power an unshakeable stubbornness and steadfastness in its orientation. This orientation can be changed at will by the Kremlin but by no other power. Once a given party line has been laid down on a given issue of current policy, the whole Soviet governmental machine, including the mechanism of diplomacy, moves inexorably along the prescribed path, like a persistent toy automobile wound up and headed in a given direction, stopping only when it meets with some unanswerable force. The individuals who are the components of this machine are unamenable to argument or reason which comes to them from outside sources. Their whole training has taught them to mistrust and discount the glib persuasiveness of the outside world. Like the white dog before the phonograph, they hear only the "master's voice." And if they are to be called off from the purposes last dictated to them, it is the master who must call them off. Thus the foreign representative cannot hope that his words will make any impression on them. The most that he can hope is that they will be transmitted to those at the top, who are capable of changing the party line. But even those are not likely to be swayed by any normal logic in the words of the bourgeois representative. Since there can be no appeal to common purposes, there can be no appeal to common mental approaches. For this reason, facts speak louder than words to the ears of the Kremlin; and words carry the greatest weight when they have the ring of reflecting, or being backed up by, facts of unchallengeable validity.

But we have seen that the Kremlin is under no ideological compulsion to accomplish its purposes in a hurry. Like the Church, it is dealing in ideological concepts which are of long-term validity, and it can afford to be patient. It has no right to risk the existing achievements of the revolution for the sake of vain baubles of the future. The very teachings of Lenin himself require great caution and flexibility in the pursuit of Communist purposes. Again, these precepts are fortified by the lessons of Russian history: of centuries of obscure battles between nomadic forces over the stretches of a vast unfortified plain. Here caution, circumspection, flexibility and deception are the valuable qualities; and their value finds natural appreciation in the Russian or the oriental mind. Thus the Kremlin has no compunction about retreating in the face of superior force. And being under the compulsion of no timetable, it does not get panicky under the necessity for such retreat. Its political action is a fluid stream which moves constantly, wherever it is permitted to move, toward a given goal. Its main concern is to make sure that it has filled every nook and cranny available to it in the basin of world power. But if it finds unassailable barriers in its path, it accepts these philosophically and accommodates itself to them. The main thing is that there should always be pressure, increasing constant pressure, toward the desired goal. There is no trace of any feeling in Soviet psychology that that goal must be reached at any given time.

These considerations make Soviet diplomacy at once easier and more difficult to deal with than the diplomacy of individual aggressive leaders like Napoleon and Hitler. On the one hand it is more sensitive to contrary force, more ready to yield on individual sectors of the diplomatic front when that force is felt to be too strong, and thus more rational in the logic and rhetoric of power. On the other hand it cannot be easily defeated or discouraged by a single victory on the part of its opponents. And the patient persistence by which it is animated means that it can be effectively countered not by sporadic acts which represent the momentary whims of democratic opinion but only by intelligent long-range policies on the part of Russia's adversaries — policies no less steady in their purpose, and no less variegated and resourceful in their application, than those of the Soviet Union itself.

In these circumstances it is clear that the main element of any United States policy toward the Soviet Union must be that of a long-term, patient but firm and vigilant containment of Russian expansive tendencies. It is important to note, however, that such a policy has nothing to do with outward histrionics: with threats or blustering or superfluous gestures of outward "toughness." While the Kremlin is basically flexible in its reaction to political realities, it is by no means unamenable to considerations of prestige. Like almost any other government, it can be placed by tactless and threatening gestures in a position where it cannot afford to yield even though this might be dictated by its sense of realism. The Russian leaders are keen judges of human psychology, and as such they are highly conscious that loss of temper and of self-control is never a source of strength in political affairs. They are quick to exploit such evidences of weakness. For these reasons, it is a *sine qua non* of successful dealing with Russia that the foreign government in question should remain at all times cool and collected and that its demands on Russian policy should be put forward in such a manner as to leave the way open for a compliance not too detrimental to Russian prestige.

III

In the light of the above, it will be clearly seen that the Soviet pressure against the free institutions of the Western world is something that can be contained by the adroit and vigilant application of counter-force at a series of constantly shifting geographical and political points, corresponding to the shifts and maneuvers of Soviet policy, but which cannot be charmed or talked out of existence. The Russians look forward to a duel of infinite duration, and they see that already they have scored great successes. It must be borne in mind that there was a time when the Communist Party represented far more of a minority in the sphere of Russian national life than Soviet power today represents in the world community.

But if ideology convinces the rulers of Russia that truth is on their side and that they can therefore afford to wait, those of us on whom that ideology has no claim are free to examine objectively the validity of that premise. The Soviet thesis not only implies complete lack of control by the West over its own economic destiny, it likewise assumes Russian unity, discipline and patience over an infinite period. Let us bring this apocalyptic vision down to earth, and suppose that the Western world finds the strength and resourcefulness to contain Soviet power over a period of ten to fifteen years. What does that spell for Russia itself?

The Soviet leaders, taking advantage of the contributions of modern technique to the arts of despotism, have solved the question of obedience within the confines of their power. Few challenge their authority; and even those who do are unable to make that challenge valid as against the organs of suppression of the state.

The Kremlin has also proved able to accomplish its purpose of building up in Russia, regardless of the interests of the inhabitants, an industrial foundation of heavy metallurgy, which is, to be sure, not yet complete but which is nevertheless continuing to grow and is approaching those of the other major industrial countries. All of this, however, both the maintenance of internal political security and the building of heavy industry, has been carried out at a terrible cost in human life and in human hopes and energies. It has necessitated the use of forced labor on a scale unprecedented in modern times under conditions of peace. It has involved the neglect or abuse of other phases of Soviet economic life, particularly agriculture, consumers' goods production, housing and transportation.

To all that, the war has added its tremendous toll of destruction, death and human exhaustion. In consequence of this, we have in Russia today a population which is physically and spiritually tired. The mass of the people are disillusioned, skeptical and no longer as accessible as they once were to the magical attraction which Soviet power still radiates to its followers abroad. The avidity with which people seized upon the slight respite accorded to the Church for tactical reasons during the war was eloquent testimony to the fact that their capacity for faith and devotion found little expression in the purposes of the regime.

In these circumstances, there are limits to the physical and nervous strength of people themselves. These limits are absolute ones, and are binding even for the cruelest dictatorship, because beyond them people cannot be driven. The forced labor camps and the other agencies of constraint provide temporary means of compelling people to work longer hours than their own volition or mere economic pressure would dictate; but if people survive them at all they become old before their time and must be considered as human casualties to the demands of dictatorship. In either case their best powers are no longer available to society and can no longer be enlisted in the service of the state.

Here only the younger generation can help. The younger generation, despite all vicissitudes and sufferings, is numerous and vigorous; and the Russians are a talented people. But it still remains to be seen what will be the effects of mature performance of the abnormal emotional strains of childhood which Soviet dictatorship created and which were enormously increased by the war. Such things as normal security and placidity of home environment have practically ceased to exist in the Soviet Union outside of the most remote farms and villages. And observers are not yet sure whether that is not going to leave its mark on the over-all capacity of the generation now coming into maturity.

In addition to this, we have the fact that Soviet economic development, while it can list certain formidable achievements, has been precariously spotty and uneven. Russian Communists who speak of the "uneven development of capitalism" should blush at the contemplation of their own national economy. Here certain branches of economic life, such as the metallurgical and machine industries, have been pushed out of all proportion to other sectors of economy. Here is a nation striving to become in a short period one of the great industrial nations of the world while it still has no highway network worthy of the name and only a relatively primitive network of railways. Much has been done to increase efficiency of labor and to teach primitive peasants something about the operation of machines. But maintenance is still a crying deficiency of all Soviet economy. Construction is hasty and poor in quality. Depreciation must be enormous. And in vast sectors of economic life it has not yet been possible to instill into labor anything like the general culture of production and technical self-respect which characterizes the skilled worker of the West.

It is difficult to see how these deficiencies can be corrected at an early date by a tired and dispirited population working largely under the shadow of fear and compulsion. And as long as they are not overcome, Russia will remain economically a vulnerable, and in a certain sense an impotent nation, capable of exporting its enthusiasms and of radiating the strange charm of its primitive political vitality but unable to back up those articles of export by the real evidences of material power and prosperity.

Meanwhile, a great uncertainty hangs over the political life of the Soviet Union. That is the uncertainty involved in the transfer of power from one individual or group of individuals to others.

This is, of course, outstandingly the problem of the personal position of Stalin. We must remember that his succession to Lenin's pinnacle of preeminence in the Communist movement was the only such transfer of individual authority which the Soviet Union has experienced. That transfer took twelve years to consolidate. It cost the lives of millions of people and shook the state to its foundations, the attendant tremors were felt all through the international revolutionary movement, to the disadvantage of the Kremlin itself.

It is always possible that another transfer of preeminent power may take place quietly and inconspicuously, with no repercussions anywhere. But again, it is possible that the questions involved may unleash, to use some of Lenin's words, one of those "incredibly swift transitions" from "delicate deceit" to "wild violence" which characterize Russian history, and may shake Soviet power to its foundations.

But this is not only a question of Stalin himself. There has been, since 1938, a dangerous congealment of political life in the higher circles of Soviet power. The All-Union Party Congress, in theory the supreme body of the Party, is supposed to meet not less often than once in three years. It will soon be eight full years since its last meeting. During this period membership in the Party has numerically doubled. Party mortality during the war was enormous, and today well over half of the Party members are persons who have entered since the last Party congress was held. Meanwhile, the same small group of men has carried on at the top through an amazing series of national vicissitudes. Surely there is some reason why the experiences of the war brought basic political changes to every one of the great governments of the West. Surely the causes of that phenomenon are basic enough to be present somewhere in the obscurity of Soviet political life, as well. And yet no recognition has been given to these causes in Russia.

It must be surmised from this that even within so highly disciplined an organization as the Communist Party there must be a growing divergence in age, outlook and interest between the great mass of Party members, only so recently recruited into the movement, and the little self-perpetuating clique of men at the top, whom most of these Party members have never met, with whom they have never conversed, and with whom they can have no political intimacy.

Who can say whether, in these circumstances, the eventual rejuvenation of the higher spheres of authority (which can only be a matter of time) can take place smoothly and peacefully, or whether rivals in the quest for higher power will not eventually reach down into these politically immature and inexperienced masses in order to find support for their respective claims. If this were ever to happen, strange consequences could flow for the Communist Party: for the membership at large has been exercised only in the practices of iron discipline and obedience and not in the arts of compromise and accommodation. And if disunity were ever to seize and paralyze the Party, the chaos and weakness of Russian society would be revealed in forms beyond description. For we have seen that Soviet power is only a crust concealing an amorphous mass of human beings among whom no independent organizational structure is tolerated. In Russia there is not even such a thing as local government. The present generation of Russians have never known spontaneity of collective action. If, consequently, anything were ever to occur to disrupt the unity and efficacy of the Party as a political instrument, Soviet Russia might be changed overnight from one of the strongest to one of the weakest and most pitiable of national societies.

Thus the future of Soviet power may not be by any means as secure as Russian capacity for self-delusion would make it appear to the men in the Kremlin. That they can keep power themselves, they have demonstrated. That they can quietly and easily turn it over to others remains to be proved. Meanwhile, the hardships of their rule and the vicissitudes of international life have taken a heavy toll of the strength and hopes of the great people on whom their power rests. It is curious to note that the ideological power of Soviet authority is strongest today in areas beyond the frontiers of Russia, beyond the reach of its police power. This phenomenon brings to mind a comparison used by Thomas Mann in his great novel *Buddenbrooks*. Observing that human institutions often show the greatest outward brilliance at a moment when inner decay is in reality farthest advanced, he compared the Buddenbrook family, in the days of its greatest glamour to one of those stars whose light shines most brightly on this world when in reality it has long since ceased to exist. And who can say with assurance that the strong light still cast by the Kremlin on the dissatisfied peoples of the Western world is not the powerful afterglow of a constellation which is in actuality on the wane? This cannot be proved. And it cannot be disproved. But the possibility remains (and in the opinion of this writer it is a strong one) that Soviet power, like the capitalist world of its conception, bears within it the seeds of its own decay, and that the sprouting of these seeds is well advanced.

IV

It is clear that the United States cannot expect in the foreseeable future to enjoy political intimacy with the Soviet regime. It must continue to regard the Soviet Union as a rival, not a partner, in the political arena. It must continue to expect that Soviet policies will reflect no abstract love of peace and stability, no real faith in the possibility of a permanent happy coexistence of the Socialist and capitalist worlds, but rather a cautious, persistent pressure toward the disruption and weakening of all rival influence and rival power.

Balanced against this are the fact that Russia, as opposed to the Western world in general, is still by far the weaker party, that Soviet policy is highly flexible, and that Soviet society may well contain deficiencies which will eventually weaken its own total potential. This would of itself warrant the United States entering with reasonable confidence upon a policy of firm containment, designed to confront the Russians with unalterable counterforce at every point where they show signs of encroaching upon the interests of a peaceful and stable world.

But in actuality the possibilities for American policy are by no means limited to holding the line and hoping for the best. It is entirely possible for the United States to influence by its actions the internal developments, both within Russia and throughout the international Communist movement, by which Russian policy is largely determined. This is not only a question of the modest measure of informational activity which this government can conduct in the Soviet Union and elsewhere, although that, too, is important. It is rather a question of the degree to which the United States can create among the peoples of the world generally the impression of a country which knows what it wants, which is coping successfully with the problems of its internal life and with the responsibilities of a World Power, and which has a spiritual vitality capable of holding its own among the major ideological currents of the time. To the extent that such an impression can be created and maintained, the aims of Russian Communism must appear sterile and quixotic, the hopes and enthusiasm of Moscow's supporters must wane, and added strain must be imposed on the Kremlin's foreign policies. For the palsied decrepitude of the capitalist world is the keystone of Communist philosophy. Even the failure of the United States to experience the early economic depression which the ravens of the Red Square have been predicting with such complacent confidence since hostilities ceased would have deep and important repercussions throughout the Communist world.

By the same token, exhibitions of indecision, disunity and internal disintegration within this country have an exhilarating effect on the whole Communist movement. At each evidence of these tendencies, a thrill of hope and excitement goes through the Communist world; a new jauntiness can be noted in the Moscow tread; now groups of foreign supporters climb on to what they can only view as the band wagon of international politics; and Russian pressure increases all along the line in international affairs.

It would be an exaggeration to say that American behavior unassisted and alone could exercise a power of life and death over the Communist movement and bring about the early fall of Soviet power in Russia. But the United States has it in its power to increase enormously the strains under which Soviet policy must operate, to force upon the Kremlin a far greater degree of moderation and circumspection than it has had to observe in recent years, and in this way to promote tendencies which must eventually find their outlet in either the break-up or the gradual mellowing of Soviet power. For no mystical, Messianic movement — and particularly not that of the Kremlin — can face frustration indefinitely without eventually adjusting itself in one way or another to the logic of that state of affairs.

Thus the decision will really fall in large measure in this country itself. The issue of Soviet-American relations is in essence a test of the over-all worth of the United States as a nation among nations. To avoid destruction the United States need only measure up to its own best traditions and prove itself worthy of preservation as a great nation.

Surely, there was never a fairer test of national quality than this. In the light of these circumstances, the thoughtful observer of Russian-American relations will find no cause for complaint in the Kremlin's challenge to American society. He will rather experience a certain gratitude to a Providence which, by providing the American people with this implacable challenge, has made their entire security as a nation dependent on their pulling themselves together and accepting the responsibilities of moral and political leadership that history plainly intended them to bear.

John F. Kennedy

RUSSIAN MISSILES IN CUBA

⊰{ *1962* }⊱ PRESIDENT KENNEDY's pledge to conduct the affairs of state imaginatively and vigorously yet on a high moral plane was put to a severe test within a few months of his inauguration by the affair of the Bay of Pigs. On April 17, 1961, a force of some 1,600 Cubans, exiles hostile to the pro-communist regime of Fidel Castro, launched an invasion of their homeland from a Central American base. The assault, badly organized and inadequately supplied, was utterly crushed by the Castro forces. Over 1,200 of the invaders were captured.

It quickly became apparent that the United States Central Intelligence Agency (C.I.A.) had "masterminded" the attack and though it was also obvious that the plan had been developed while Eisenhower was still in office, Kennedy had rightly to bear most of the criticism that followed the fiasco. This criticism ranged from moral condemnation of his interference in the internal affairs of an independent nation to denunciation of his failure, once having undertaken the operation, to carry it through successfully.

It was against this background that Kennedy faced, in October 1962, one of the most difficult problems ever dealt with by an American President. For some time it had been known that the Russians were supplying the Castro government with "defensive" arms. But in October United States reconaissance planes discovered that Russian missile bases capable of launching an attack on the United States had been set up on Cuban soil. To accept this situation would have been intolerable, but how to force the Russians out without precipitating a nuclear war? How Kennedy answered this question is dramatically revealed in his radio address explaining the situation to the American people on October 22, 1962. No single event of his administration did so much to restore the damage to his reputation that had resulted from the Bay of Pigs tragedy. It is also possible that the President's actions produced a basic turning point in the long cold war between the Communist world and the Western Powers.

RADIO ADDRESS, 1962

THIS Government as promised has maintained the closest surveillance of the Soviet military build-up on the island of Cuba.

Within the past week unmistakable evidence has established the fact that a series of offensive missile sites is now in preparation on that imprisoned island.

The purpose of these bases can be none other than to provide a nuclear strike capability against the Western Hemisphere.

Upon receiving the first preliminary hard information of this nature last Tuesday morning at 9 A.M., I directed that our surveillance be stepped up. And having now confirmed and completed our evaluation of the evidence and our decision on a course of action, this Government feels obliged to report this new crisis to you in fullest detail.

The characteristics of these new missile sites indicate two distinct types of installations. Several of them include medium-range ballistic missiles capable of carrying a nuclear warhead for a distance of more than 1,000 nautical miles.

Each of these missiles, in short, is capable of striking Washington, D.C., the Panama Canal, Cape Canaveral, Mexico City or any other city in the southeastern part of the United States, in Central America or in the Caribbean area.

Additional sites not yet completed appear to be designed for intermediate-range ballistic missiles capable of traveling more than twice as far, and thus capable of striking most of the major cities in the Western Hemisphere ranging as far north as Hudson's Bay, Canada, and as far south as Lima, Peru.

In addition, jet bombers, capable of carrying nuclear weapons, are now being uncrated and assembled in Cuba while the necessary air bases are being prepared.

This urgent transformation of Cuba into an important strategic base by the presence of these large long-range and clearly offensive weapons of sudden mass destruction constitutes an explicit threat to the peace and security of all the Americas in flagrant and deliberate defiance of the Rio Pact of 1947, the traditions of this nation and hemisphere, the joint resolution of the 87th Congress, the Charter of the United Nations and my own public warnings to the Soviets on Sept. 4 and 13.

This action also contradicts the repeated assurances of Soviet spokesmen both publicly and privately delivered that the arms build-up in Cuba would retain its original defensive character and that the Soviet Union had no need or desire to station strategic missiles on the territory of any other nation.

The size of this undertaking makes clear that it had been planned for some months.

Yet only last month after I had made clear the distinction between any introduction of ground-to-ground missiles and the existence of defensive antiaircraft missiles, the Soviet Government publicly stated on Sept. 11 that, and I quote, the armaments and military equipment sent to Cuba are designed exclusively for defensive purposes, unquote, that there is—and I quote the Soviet Government—there is no need for the Soviet Government to shift its weapons for a retaliatory blow to any other country, for instance, Cuba, unquote, and that—and I quote the Government—the Soviet Union has so powerful rockets to carry these nuclear warheads that there is no need to search for sites for them beyond the boundaries of the Soviet Union, unquote.

That statement was false.

Only last Thursday, as evidence of this rapid offensive build-up was already in my hand, Soviet Foreign Minister Gromyko told me in my office that he was instructed to make it clear once again, as he said his Government had already done, that Soviet assistance to Cuba, and I quote, pursued solely the purpose of contributing to the defense capabilities of Cuba, unquote.

That, and I quote him, "training by Soviet specialists of Cuba nationals in handling defensive armaments was by no means offensive," and that if it were otherwise, Mr. Gromyko went on, "the Soviet Government would never become involved in rendering such assistance."

That statement also was false.

Neither the United States of America nor the world community of nations can tolerate deliberate deception and offensive threats on the part of any nation, large or small. We no longer live in a world where only the actual firing of weapons represents a sufficient challenge to a nation's security to constitute maximum peril.

Nuclear weapons are so destructive and ballistic missiles are so swift that any substantially increased possibility of their use or any sudden change in their deployment may well be regarded as a definite threat to peace.

For many years both the Soviet Union and the United States, recognizing this fact, have deployed strategic nuclear weapons with great care, never upsetting the precarious status quo which insured that these weapons would not be used in the absence of some vital challenge.

Our own strategic missiles have never been transferred to the territory of any other nation under a cloak of secrecy and deception and our history, unlike that of the Soviets since the end of World War II, demonstrated that we have no desire to dominate or conquer any other nation or impose our system upon its people.

Nevertheless, American citizens have become adjusted to living daily on the bull's-eye of Soviet missiles located inside the U.S.S.R. or in submarines.

In that sense missiles in Cuba add to an already clear and present danger—although it should be noted the nations of Latin America have never previously been subjected to a potential nuclear threat.

But this secret, swift, extraordinary build-up of Communist missiles in an area well-known to have a special and historical relationship to the United States and the nations of the Western Hemisphere, in violation of

Soviet assurances and in defiance of American and hemispheric policy—this sudden, clandestine decision to station strategic weapons for the first time outside of Soviet soil—is a deliberately provocative and unjustified change in the status quo which cannot be accepted by this country if our courage and our commitments are ever to be trusted again, by either friend or foe.

The nineteen thirties taught us a clear lesson. Aggressive conduct, if allowed to go unchecked and unchallenged, ultimately leads to war.

This nation is opposed to war. We are also true to our word.

Our unswerving objective, therefore, must be to prevent the use of these missiles against this or any other country; and to secure their withdrawal or elimination from the Western Hemisphere.

Our policy has been one of patience and restraint, as befits a peaceful and powerful nation which leads a world-wide alliance.

We have been determined not to be diverted from our central concerns by mere irritants, and fanatics. But now further action is required. And it is underway. And these actions may only be the beginning.

We will not prematurely or unnecessarily risk the course of worldwide nuclear war in which even the fruits of victory would be ashes in our mouth, but neither will we shrink from that risk at any time it must be faced.

Acting, therefore, in the defense of our own security and of the entire Western Hemisphere and under the authority entrusted to me by the Constitution as endorsed by the resolution of the Congress, I have directed that the following initial steps be taken immediately:

First, to halt this offensive build-up, a strict quarantine of all offensive military equipment under shipment to Cuba is being initiated. All ships of any kind bound for Cuba from whatever nation or port will, where they are found to contain cargoes of offensive weapons, be turned back. This quarantine will be extended if needed to other types of cargo and carriers.

We are not at this time, however, denying the necessities of life as the Soviets attempted to do in their Berlin blockade of 1948.

Second, I have directed the continued and increased close surveillance of Cuba and its military build-up.

The foreign ministers of the O.A.S. in their communique of Oct. 6 rejected secrecy on such matters in this hemisphere. Should these offensive military preparations continue, thus increasing the threat to the hemisphere, further action will be justified.

I have directed the armed forces to prepare for any eventualities, and I trust that in the interests of both the Cuban people and the Soviet technicians at the sites, the hazards to all concerned of continuing this threat will be recognized.

Third, it shall be the policy of this nation to regard any nuclear missile launched from Cuba against any nation in the Western Hemisphere as an attack by the Soviet Union on the United States requiring a full retaliatory response upon the Soviet Union.

Fourth, as a necessary military precaution, I have reinforced our base at Guantanamo, evacuated today the dependents of our personnel there and ordered additional military units to be on a stand-by alert basis.

Fifth, we are calling tonight for an immediate meeting of the organization of consultation under the Organization of American States to consider this threat to hemispheric security and to invoke Articles 6 and 8 of the Rio Treaty in support of all necessary action.

The United Nations Charter allows for regional security arrangements and the nations of this hemisphere decided long ago against the military presence of outside powers.

Our other allies around the world have also been alerted.

Sixth, under the Charter of the United Nations we are asking tonight that an emergency meeting of the Security Council be convoked without delay to take action against this latest Soviet threat to world peace.

Our resolution will call for the prompt dismantling and withdrawal of all offensive weapons in Cuba under the supervision of U. N. observers before the quarantine can be lifted.

Seventh, and finally, I call upon Chairman Khrushchev to halt and eliminate this clandestine, reckless and provocative threat to world peace and to stable relations between our two nations.

I call upon him further to abandon this course of world domination and to join in an historic effort to end the perilous arms race and to transform the history of man.

He has an opportunity now to move the world back from the abyss of destruction by returning to his Government's own words that it had no need to station missiles outside its own territory, and withdrawing these weapons from Cuba; by refraining fom any action which will widen or deepen the present crisis, and then by participating in a search for peaceful and permanent solutions.

This nation is prepared to present its case against the Soviet threat to peace and our own proposals for a peaceful world at any time and in any forum—in the O.A.S., in the United Nations, or in any other meeting that could be useful without limiting our freedom of action.

We have, in the past, made strenuous efforts to limit the spread of nuclear weapons. We have proposed the elimination of all arms and military bases in a fair and effective disarmament treaty. We are prepared to discuss new proposals for the removal of tensions on both sides including the possibilities of a genuinely independent Cuba free to determine its own destiny.

We have no wish to war with the Soviet Union, for we are a peaceful people who desire to live in peace with all other peoples.

But it is difficult to settle or even discuss these problems in an atmosphere of intimidation.

That is why this latest Soviet threat or any other threat which is made either independently or in response to our actions this week must and will be met with determination.

Any hostile move anywhere in the world against the safety and freedom of peoples to whom we are committed including in particular the brave people of West Berlin will be met by whatever action is needed.

Finally, I want to say a few words to the captive people of Cuba to whom this speech is being directly carried by special radio facilities.

I speak to you as a friend, as one who knows of your deep attachment to your fatherland, as one who shares your aspirations for liberty and justice for all.

And I have watched and the American people have watched with deep sorrow how your nationalist revolution was betrayed and how your fatherland fell under foreign domination.

Now your leaders are no longer Cuban leaders inspired by Cuban ideals. They are puppets and agents of an international conspiracy which has turned Cuba against your friends and neighbors in the Americas and turned it into the first Latin-American country to become a target for nuclear war, the first Latin-American country to have these weapons on its soil.

These new weapons are not in your interests. They contribute nothing to your peace and well being; they can only undermine it.

But this country has no wish to cause you to suffer or to impose any system upon you. We know that your lives and land are being used as pawns by those who deny your freedom. Many times in the past the Cuban people have risen to throw out tyrants who destroyed their liberty.

And I have no doubt that most Cubans today look forward to the time when they will be truly free, free from foreign domination, free to choose their own leaders, free to select their own system, free to own their own land, free to speak and write and worship without fear of degradation.

And then shall Cuba be welcomed back to the society of free nations and to the associations of this hemisphere.

My fellow citizens, let no one doubt that this is a difficult and dangerous effort on which we have set out. No one can foresee precisely what course it will take, or what course or casualties will be incurred.

Many months of sacrifice and self-discipline lie ahead, months in which both our patience and our will will be tested. Months in which many threats and denunciations will keep us aware of our dangers. But the greatest danger of all would be to do nothing.

The path we have chosen for the present is full of hazards, as all paths are. But it is the one most consistent with our character and courage as a nation and our commitments around the world.

The cost of freedom is always high, but Americans have always paid it.

And one path we shall never choose, and that is the path of surrender, or submission.

Our goal is not the victory of might, but the vindication of right; not peace at the expense of freedom, but both peace and freedom here in this hemisphere, and, we hope, around the world.

God willing, that goal will be achieved.

J. William Fulbright

MYTHS OF FOREIGN POLICY

⚜{*1964*}⚜ THE SHOCK of the Cuban crisis passed swiftly after Khrushchev withdrew his missiles from that island and the public commenced hopefully to consider the possibility that Russia was as eager as the United States to avoid a nuclear holocaust. Fear nevertheless remained, and the country showed little indication of relaxing its guard or reducing its gigantic expenditures for defense. At the same time, some Americans, increasingly concerned about social problems at home, began to suggest that a reallotment of energy and money could safely be made by the government. For example, they subjected the all-out national effort to beat the Russians to the moon to considerable criticism, arguing that part of the billions consigned to the moon program should be spent instead on education, slum clearance, and similar much-needed public works.

This was the situation when Senator J. William Fulbright of Arkansas delivered a speech on foreign policy at the University of North Carolina, on April 5, 1964. Fulbright, a former president of the University of Arkansas, had long been one of the leading architects of American foreign policy. His commitment to internationalism and to resisting Russian aggression was complete. He had given his name to the Fulbright educational exchange program, which had sent thousands of American students and professors to foreign countries and brought other thousands of foreign scholars to American shores. Since 1959, he had been chairman of the powerful Senate Foreign Relations Committee. His speech, recommending important changes of focus and emphasis in United States policy, attracted wide attention and criticism. Liberals generally favored it, whereas most of the leading politicians of both parties attacked it sharply.

SPEECH AT CHAPEL HILL, N.C., 1964

DURING the past 20 years the emphasis of our public policy has been heavily weighted on measures for the common defense to the considerable neglect of the program to promote the liberty and welfare of our people. The reason for this, of course, has been the exacting demands of two world wars and an intractable cold war, which have wrought vast changes in the character of American life.

Of all the changes in American life brought by the cold war, the most important by far, in my opinion, has been the vast diversion of energy and resources from the creative pursuits of a civilized society to the conduct of a costly and interminable struggle for world power.

Or, to put it more precisely in our case, to negate the efforts of others to acquire world dominion. We have been compelled, or at least we have felt ourselves to be compelled, to reverse the traditional order of our national priority, relegating individual and community life to places on the scale below the enormously expensive military and state activities that constitute our program of national security.

This is, of course, not the only change in American life brought about by the cold war. There have been many others, some most welcome and constructive. Directly or indirectly the world struggle with Communism has stimulated the economic and industrial expansion. It has accelerated the pace of intellectual inquiry and scientific discovery, it has broken the shell of American isolationism and greatly increased public knowledge and awareness of the world outside the United States.

At the same time, the continuing world conflict has cast its shadow on the tone of American life by introducing a strand of apprehension and tension into a national style which has traditionally been one of buoyant optimism. The continuing and inconclusive struggle, new in American experience, has in Dr. Walt Rostow's words imposed a sense of limitation on the nation's own image of itself, a limitation which has been accepted with greater or less maturity and which has touched the nation's domestic life at many points with elements of escapism, with a tendency to search for scapegoats, beset with simple worry and with much thoughtful disconsolate effort as well.

Overriding all these changes, however, good or bad as they may be, has been the massive diversion of wealth and talent from individual and community life to the increasingly complex and costly effort to maintain a minimum level of national security in a world in which no nation can be immune from the threat of sudden catastrophe.

We have had to turn away our hopes in order to concentrate our fears, and the result has been a cumulative neglect of these things which bring happiness and beauty and fulfillment into our lives. The public happiness, in August Heckscher's terms, has become a luxury to be postponed to some distant day when the dangers which now beset us will have disappeared.

This, I think, is the real meaning of the cold war in American life. It has consumed money, time and, above all, talent that could otherwise be used to build schools and homes and hospitals, to remove the blight of ugliness that is spreading over the cities and highways of America, and to overcome poverty and hopelessness that afflicts the lives of one-fifth of the people in an otherwise affluent society.

It has put a high premium on avoiding innovation at home, because new programs involve controversy as well as expense, and it is felt that we cannot afford domestic divisions at a time when external challenges require us to maintain the highest possible degree of national unity.

Far more pervasively than the United Nations or the Atlantic community could ever do, the cold war has encroached upon our sovereignty. It has given the Russians a major voice in determining what proportion of our Federal budget must be allocated to the military and what proportion therefore cannot be made available for domestic, social and economic projects.

At least as striking as the inversion of priorities which the cold war has enforced upon American life is the readiness with which the American people have consented to defer programs for their welfare and happiness in favor of costly military and extravagant space programs.

Indeed, if the Congress accurately reflects the temper of the country, then the American people are not only willing, they are eager to sacrifice education and urban renewal and public health programs, to say nothing of foreign aid, to the requirements of the armed forces and the space agency.

There is indeed a most striking paradox in the fact that military budgets of over $50 billion are adopted by the Congress after only perfunctory debate while domestic education and welfare programs involving sums which are mere fractions of the military budget are painstakingly examined and then either considerably reduced or rejected outright.

The cold war, it seems clear, is an excuse as well as a genuine cause for the diversion of our energies from domestic well-being to external security.

We have been preoccupied with foreign affairs for 25 years and, while striking progress has been made in certain areas of our national life, the agenda of neglect has grown steadily longer.

We can no longer afford to defer problems of slums and crime and poverty and inadequate education until some more tranquil time in the future. These problems have become urgent if not intolerable in an affluent society.

It is entirely reasonable to defer domestic programs in time of an all-out national effort such as World War II, but in the present cold war it is not reasonable to defer our domestic needs until more tranquil times, for the simple reason that there may be no more tranquil times in this generation or in this century.

In the long run the solution of our domestic problems has as vital a bearing on the success of our foreign policy as on the public happiness at home. We must therefore reassess the priorities of our public policy with a view to redressing the disproportion between our military and space efforts on the one hand and our education and human-welfare programs on the other.

We must distinguish between necessity and preference in our preoccupation with national security, judging our military needs by a standard which takes new account of the fact that armaments are only one aspect of national security.

The single-minded dedication with which we Americans have committed ourselves to the struggle with Communism is a manifestation of a national tendency to interpret problems in moral and absolutist terms.

We have therefore been greatly shocked since our emergence as a world power to find ourselves confronted with revolutionary ideologies which reject the faith in individual liberty and limited government that has served our own society so well.

Because of these predilections the cold war has seemed to represent a profound challenge to our moral principles as well as to our security and other national interests.

We have responded by treating Communist ideology itself as distinct from the physical power and the expansionist policies of Communist states as a grave threat to the free world. The cold war, as a result, has been a more dangerous, costly and irreconcilable conflict than it would be if we and the Communist states confined it to those issues which involve the security and vital interests of the rival power blocs.

The ideological element in the cold war, reinforced by the moralist tendencies of the American people, has also the effect of making the world conflict a much more disruptive element in American life than it would be if it were regarded primarily in terms of its effect on our national security.

To an extent the issue between the Communists and the free world is moral and ideological, but ideas and principles in themselves threaten no nation's vital interests except insofar as they are implemented as national policies. It is the latter, therefore, that are our proper concern.

To the extent that we are able to remove the crusading spirit and the passions of ideology from the cold war, we can reduce its danger and intensity and relax its powerful hold on the minds and hearts of our people.

The fears and the passions of ideological conflict had diverted the minds and energies of our people from the constructive task of a free society to a morbid preoccupation with the dangers of Communist aggression abroad and subversion and disloyalty at home.

This problem did not end with the McCarthy era of a decade ago, nor is it confined to the neurotic fantasies of today's fanatic extremists. The cold-war malady affects a much broader spectrum of the American society. It affects millions of sensible and intelligent citizens whose genuine concern with national security has persuaded them that the prosecution of the cold war is our only truly essential national responsibility — that missiles and nuclear armament and space flights are so vital to the safety of the nation that it is almost unpatriotic to question their cost and their proliferation.

This particular aspect takes the form often of always insisting that we must be first — first in everything, and especially first on the moon.

Without becoming militarists in the sense of committing themselves to the military virtue as standards of personal behavior, the American people have nonetheless come to place great and, in my opinion, excessive faith in military solutions to political problems.

Many Americans have come to regard our defense establishments as the heart and soul of our foreign policy, rather than as one of a number of instruments of foreign policy whose effectiveness depends not only on its size and variety but also on the skill and the restraint with which it is used.

Our easy reliance on the military establishment as the foundation of our foreign policy is not unlike the reliance which we place on automobiles, upon televisions and refrigerators. They work in a predictable and controllable manner, and on the rare occasions when they break down, any good mechanic can put them back in working order.

Like any other piece of machinery, our military establishment can be no better than the judgment of those who control it. In a democracy control is intended to be exercised by the people and their elected representatives. To a very considerable extent, the American people are not now exercising effective control over the armed forces.

To the extent that the American people and the Congress shrink from questioning the size and cost of our defense establishment, they are permitting military men, with their highly specialized viewpoint, to make political judgments of the greatest importance regarding the priorities of public policy and the allocation of public funds.

The abnegation of responsibilities by the Congress in this field is strikingly illustrated by debate or more actually by its non-debate on the defense budget.

In today's world there is no question that the United States must spend billions to keep up its defenses. But record-breaking budgets year after year do not necessarily mean a stronger nation. The bigger any government program gets, the greater are the dangers the funds will be wasted and the goals of the program will become entangled in a morass of vested interests, venal political considerations and the rivalries that inevitably evolve from them.

The ease with which the defense budgets are enacted by Congress is in no small degree viewed through the enormous importance of defense spending for the economy. Defense contracts and great numbers of workers, who are also voters, all over the country have a vested interest in the high level of defense spending.

The truly astonishing thing about the uncritical importance which the American people and their representatives give the military establishment is the apparent enthusiasm with which the sacrifice of personal and community interests is made.

While the cold war and our enormously costly national security programs pre-empt so much of our time and attention and national wealth, the most important resource of our country — its human resources — are being extravagantly wasted and neglected.

The cold war has diverted us from problems both quantitative and qualitative. The quantitative problem is essentially to devise ways of elevating one-fifth of our people who live in poverty to the level of the four-fifths who live in greater material abundance than any other society in history.

The qualitative problem is to find ways of bringing meaning and purpose and standards of excellence into the lives of a people who, because of their material affluence, are free as no people have ever been before to shape a spiritual and intellectual environment of their own choice.

While the attention and industry of our public policy have been focused through these postwar years on crises in Berlin, in Cuba and the Far East, America almost behind our backs has been more and more taking on the physical appearance and the cultural atmosphere of a honky-tonk of continental proportions.

This is not to suggest that intellectual, artistic and scientific excellence has been abandoned in our country. On the contrary, it is being pursued by more people with more energy and more striking results than at any time in our history.

But the pursuit of excellence and creativity remain the occupation of an elite segment of our society.

I do not think we can avoid the conclusion that, despite a broadening interest in the arts, the level of popular taste in America remains far below what it can be, and ought to be.

It is difficult to judge what is the most depressing sight in New York City — the jungle of antiseptic mass towers that have taken order and humanity out of the midtown area, the sprawling slums that are never far away, or the dreary acres of identical brick housing devoid of any charm or individuality that constitute urban renewal.

The first thing we must do toward raising the quality of American life is to turn some part of our thought and our creative energy away from the cold war which has engaged them for so long, back in on America itself. If we do this we may find that the most vital resources of our nation for its public happiness and its security remain locked within our own frontiers, in our cities, in our countryside, in our work and in our leisure, in the hearts and the minds of our people.